CW00959252

A GARDENER'S GUIDE TO ANNUALS & PERENNIALS

A GARDENER'S GUIDE TO
ANNUALS & PERENNIALS

AN ILLUSTRATED DIRECTORY OF VARIETIES AND A PRACTICAL GUIDE TO GROWING THEM SUCCESSFULLY

RICHARD BIRD

LORENZ BOOKS

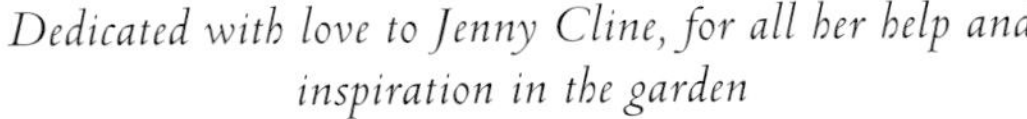
Dedicated with love to Jenny Cline, for all her help and inspiration in the garden

This edition is published by Lorenz Books

Lorenz Books is an imprint of Anness Publishing Ltd
Hermes House, 88-89 Blackfriars Road, London SE1 8HA
tel. 020 7401 2077; fax 020 7633 9499
www.lorenzbooks.com; info@anness.com

UK agent: The Manning Partnership Ltd, 6 The Old Dairy, Melcombe Road, Bath BA2 3LR; tel. 01225 478444; fax 01225 478440; sales@manning-partnership.co.uk

UK distributor: Grantham Book Services Ltd, Isaac Newton Way, Alma Park Industrial Estate, Grantham, Lincs NG31 9SD; tel. 01476 541080; fax 01476 541061; orders@gbs.tbs-ltd.co.uk

North American agent/distributor: National Book Network, 4501 Forbes Boulevard, Suite 200, Lanham, MD 20706; tel. 301 459 3366; fax 301 429 5746; www.nbnbooks.com

Australian agent/distributor: Pan Macmillan Australia, Level 18, St Martins Tower, 31 Market St, Sydney, NSW 2000;
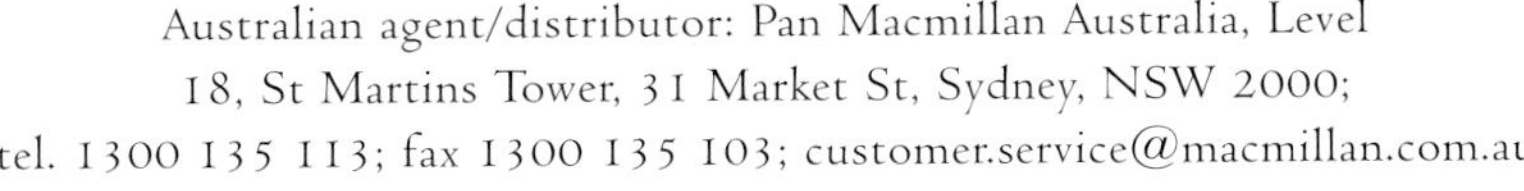
tel. 1300 135 113; fax 1300 135 103; customer.service@macmillan.com.au

New Zealand agent/distributor: David Bateman Ltd, 30 Tarndale Grove, Off Bush Road, Albany, Auckland; tel. (09) 415 7664; fax (09) 415 8892

A CIP catalogue record for this book is available from the British Library.

Publisher: Joanna Lorenz
Editorial Director: Helen Sudell
Editor: Ann Kay
Designer: Michael Morey
Editorial Reader: Jay Thundercliffe
Production Controller: Wanda Burrows

1 2 3 4 5 6 7 8 9 10

Note: Bracketed terms are intended for American readers

Contents

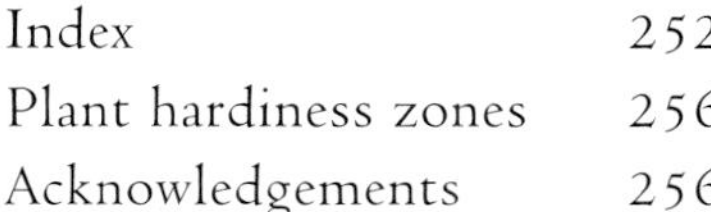

Introduction

In spite of a modern tendency for television personalities to create gardens with few or no plants, there is no doubt in most people's minds that without plants a garden is simply not a garden. There is something about the presence of plants – their colour, shape and fragrance – that lifts the spirits in a very special way. Annuals and perennials are the two most popular types of flowering plants, offering a vast selection of ways to add that vital colour and stimulus to every kind of garden.

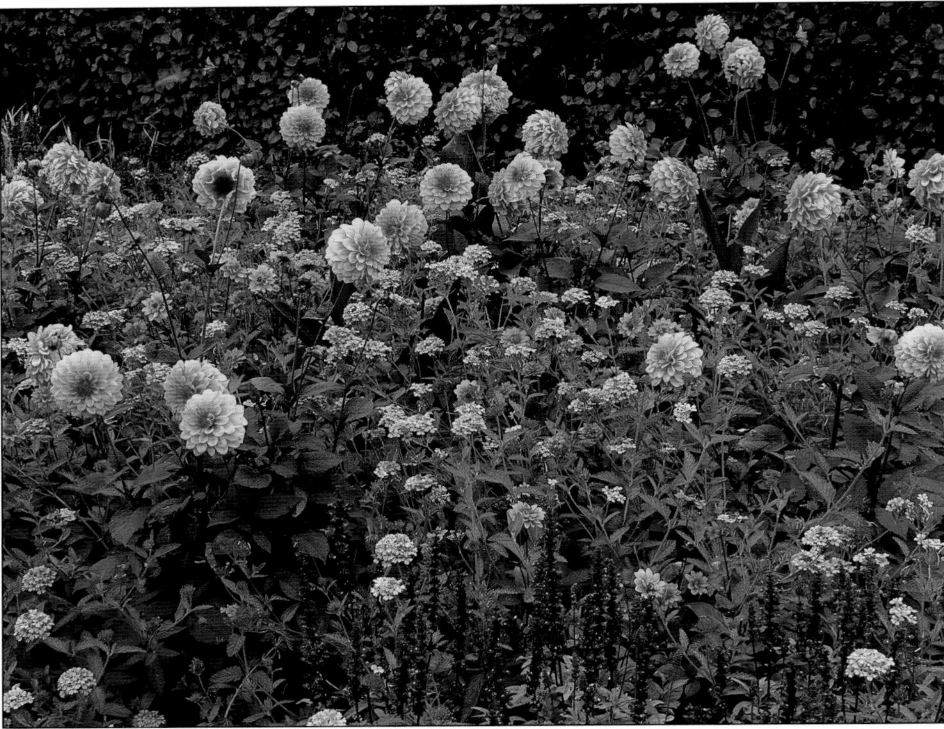

Anyone can produce this magnificent array of dahlias, verbenas and salvias. It remains colourful for a long period – from midsummer well into autumn.

Enjoying plants

Plants give pleasure to people in many different ways. The majority of gardeners enjoy filling space with colour, shape and texture as well as planning a garden to make the most of their chosen plants' strong points. There are others for whom it is the plant itself that is of principal interest. They are less interested in how the plant fits into the overall picture of the garden, or indeed how the garden looks as a whole, and are more absorbed by growing a particular type of plant to absolute perfection. These gardeners may only grow plants in order to show them, or simply because they enjoy the challenge of growing rare and difficult types.

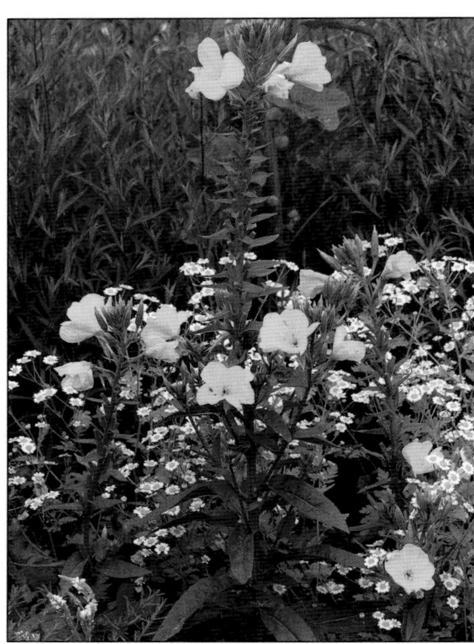

Oenothera biennis and *Tanacetum parthenium* produce a fine yellow and white scheme.

There are others still who garden simply because they enjoy working in the open air and get a real joy from cultivation. For them it is the process as well as the results that matter. The huge variety of annuals and perennials that are available, and the many ways in which they can be grown, can easily cater to all these different approaches.

Starting out

Tackling a large bare patch may seem a rather daunting task to somebody who has not done any gardening before, but it is nothing like as difficult as some experts would have you believe.

Gardening is rather like decorating a room: naturally a certain amount of time and effort is involved, but if you are not satisfied with the result you can always change it. This is particularly true

This border mixes annuals, hardy perennials and tender perennials treated as annuals.

This selection of perennials, growing beside water, shows the vast range of shapes and textures that can be used as well as the value of foliage.

with annual plants as they give you the opportunity to start from scratch each year.

Working with colour

Many beginners are worried about combining colours, but the key is simply to go for plants and effects that you like without worrying about what other people do.

Remember that we all have some ability where colour is concerned: we choose what goes with what when we get dressed each day and we choose colours for decorating and furnishing our homes. Planning a garden is really no different. In the same way that there are fashion magazines to help you choose your style, so there is no shortage of different kinds of gardening magazine to browse through for inspiration, and there is nothing more enjoyable than wandering around other people's gardens in search of good ideas.

Learning the ropes

There is also no need to worry about gardening techniques. Most gardening is common sense and if you do make a mistake, just remember that you can always put it right next year, or even the year after. Having said that, there are, of course, basic sensible and effective practices that have developed over many generations, and all of these are clearly outlined in this book.

Choosing your plants

Plants form the basis of all good gardens and we have produced two detailed directories which will introduce you to the very best annuals and perennials.

There are far more annuals and perennials available than we could hope to include in this book, but the directories have been specially devised to act as a comprehensive basis. As you develop your garden you will become more interested in certain plants rather than others. You will then be able to create your own database of information from nursery catalogues, magazines, books and the internet. Soon you may even find that you have turned into one of those gardeners for whom studying plants is as fascinating as actually growing them.

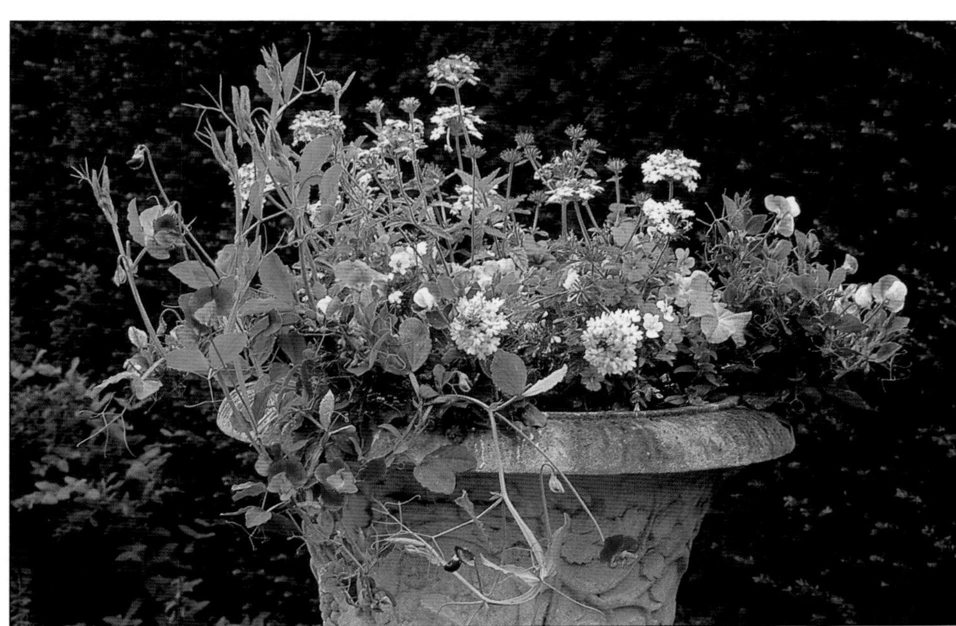

An informal container – featuring annual sweet peas, tender verbenas and perennial violas – demonstrates just how effectively annuals and perennials can be mixed.

How plants are named

All living things are classified according to a system based on principles that were devised by the 18th-century Swedish botanist, Carl Linnaeus. This system states that a particular plant genus (plural: genera) is a group of plants containing similar species. Beyond that there may be plants that are simply a slight variation of a species, or are a hybrid (cross) of different species or variations.

Scientific names

Under this system, plants have botanical names – often Latin but also derived from other languages – that consist of the genus name (for example, *Verbena*), followed by the name that denotes the particular species (for example, *hastata*). Some genera contain a huge number of species that may include annuals, perennials, shrubs and trees, while others contain just one species. Although all members of a genus are assumed to be related to each other, this is not always visually obvious. It is useful to keep in mind that a species is defined scientifically as individuals that are alike and tend naturally to breed with each other.

Despite this system, botanists and taxonomists (the experts who classify living things) often disagree about the basis on which a plant has been named. This is why it is useful for a plant to retain its synonym (abbreviated to syn. in the text), or alternative name. Incorrect names often gain widespread usage, and in some cases, two plants thought to have separate identities, and with two different names, are found to be the same plant.

A well-known example of naming confusion is the genus *Pelargonium*. Until the 19th century, pelargonium plants were included in the genus *Geranium*, and despite being classified separately for over a century, they are still popularly known as geraniums.

Variations on a theme

Genetically, many plants are able to change over time to adapt to a changing environment. In the wild, individuals within a species that are not well adapted will not survive, so all survivors will look the same. The average garden is a more controlled environment, so gardeners can choose to encourage and grow on variations within a species that have small but pleasing differences such as variegated leaves and double flowers. The terms for these variations are subspecies (abbreviated to subsp.), variety (var.), form (f., similar to variety and often used interchangeably) and cultivar. A cultivar is a variation that would not occur in the wild but has been produced and maintained solely by cultivation. Variations are given names in single quotes, for example *Papaver orientale* 'Allegro'.

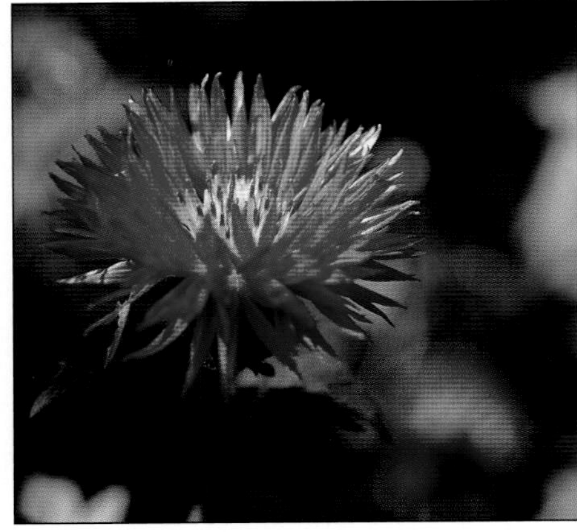

This is *Centaurea hypoleuca* 'John Coutts'. John Coutts is the name that has been given to a dark pink form of the pink knapweed species, *Centaurea hypoleuca*.

Hybrids

When plant species breed with each other, the result is a hybrid. Rare in the wild, crossing is very common among plant-breeders, done specially in order to produce plants with desirable qualities such as larger or double blooms, variegated foliage and greater frost resistance. A multiplication sign (x) is used to indicate a hybrid, and the name often gives a clear idea of the hybrid's origins.

Plant Groups

A Group of plants is a group of very similar variations. Their names do not have quotation marks around them – for example *Tradescantia* Andersoniana Group.

The geranium is a well-known case of naming confusion, as many plants that actually belong to the genus *Pelargonium* are very commonly referred to as geraniums.

How to use the directories

There are two directory sections: one features annual plants, and the other perennials. Within each directory, plants are arranged alphabetically, by genus. Each main entry features a general introduction to that genus, plus specific useful information such as tips on propagation and which hardiness zone the genus belongs to. This is followed by a selection of plants from that genus, also arranged alphabetically according to their most widely accepted names. One of these entries might be a species, a hybrid (or group of hybrids), a variety, form or cultivar. Each is given a useful description that may include height and spread.

Caption
The full botanical name of the plant in question is given with each photograph.

Genus name
This is the internationally accepted botanical name for a group of related plant species.

Common name
This popular, non-scientific name applies to the whole of the plant genus.

Cultivation
This section gives the level of sun or shade that the plants described in the selection either require or tolerate, advice on the best type of soil in which they should be grown, and any other helpful tips that might be appropriate.

Propagation
This section gives essential information on how and when to increase the plant – from seed, by dividing plants or by taking various types of cutting. Many annuals entries also give the best temperature at which to propagate a plant, often with specific centigrade (and Fahrenheit) figures given.

Individual plant entry
This starts with the current botanical name of the plant in bold, and this can refer to a species, subspecies, hybrid, variant or cultivar. If a synonym (syn.) is given, this provides the synonym, or synonyms (alternative names) for a plant. A common name may be given after the botanical name.

Plant description
This gives a description of the plant, along with any other information that may be helpful and relevant.

Paeonia lactiflora 'Bowl of Beauty'

PAEONIA
Peony
One of the most popular of all perennial species, these beautiful plants suit almost any type of garden, from old-fashioned cottage gardens to modern formal ones. There are only about 30 species of peony, most of which are in cultivation, but hundreds of cultivars have been bred from them. The typical peony has a bowl-shaped flower in varying shades of red, pink or white. There are also some rather fine yellows. The foliage of peonies is also very attractive.
Cultivation Peonies need a deep rich soil, so add plenty of well-rotted organic material. They will grow in either sun or a light shade. They often take a while to settle down after being disturbed so try not to move them once established. Z3–5.
Propagation They can be divided in spring but this is not easy and they will take a while to settle down. Root cuttings taken in early winter is the easiest method.

***Paeonia lactiflora* 'Bowl of Beauty'**
Deep rose-red petals and a large central boss of yellow make this a superb peony. H 75cm (30in) S 1m (3ft).

Photograph
Each entry features a full-colour photograph that makes identification easy.

Genus introduction
This provides a general introduction to the genus and may state the number of species within that genus. Other information featured here may include general advice on usage, preferred conditions, and plant-care, as well as subspecies, hybrids (indicated by an x symbol in the name), varieties and cultivars (featuring names in single quotes) that are available.

Additional information

This page shows a basic entry from the perennials directory. Other information supplied in the directories includes:

How to obtain (Annuals directory): this gives advice on getting hold of plants as seeds, plants or trays of plants.
Uses (Annuals directory): if given, this section advises on how to get the best from a plant – using in borders or containers or to brighten up dark corners, for example.
Other plants (both directories): if given, these sections provide brief information about common types that are available and other recommended (often rarer) plants to look out for.

Plant hardiness zone
A plant hardiness zone is given at the end of this section. Zones give a general indication of the average annual minimum temperature for a particular geographical area. The smaller number indicates the northernmost zone it can survive in and the higher number the southernmost zone that the plant will tolerate. In most cases, only one zone is given. (See page 256 for details of zones and a zone map.)

Size information
The average expected height and spread of a genus or individual plant is frequently given, although growth rates may vary depending on location and conditions. Metric measurements always precede imperial ones. Average heights and spreads are given (as H and S) wherever possible and appropriate, and more consistently for perennials, although it must be noted that dimensions can vary a great deal.

Styling with annuals and perennials

Theoretically, there is no need to differentiate between annuals and perennials as they are both flowering or foliage plants. However, gardeners do tend to use them in slightly different ways. This is partly because of the annual's brief life and partly because annuals tend to be more brightly coloured than perennials, lending themselves to vivid displays. Perennials are more permanent and, although some do have bright colours, they are usually more muted.

In this section we look at the differing roles that the two types of plants can play. We also look at the different ways in which they can be combined to create a range of gardening styles, varying from the informality of the traditional cottage garden to the more clinical lines of a formal garden, where symmetry is all.

Generally, the style of a garden reflects its owner's lifestyle and personality. Gardens should always have a positive and uplifting atmosphere, so there is no point in creating a place where you feel uncomfortable. Use the following advice as guidance, but never be afraid to follow your own instinct.

A lovely cottage garden effect is created along this informal path using both annuals and perennials. The lush foliage helps to provide bulk.

Annuals and their role

Annuals are ephemeral plants: they flower for one season only and then they are gone. This may seem to be a disadvantage in a garden context, but in fact it can be a great benefit, especially for those gardeners who like to have something different in their beds each year.

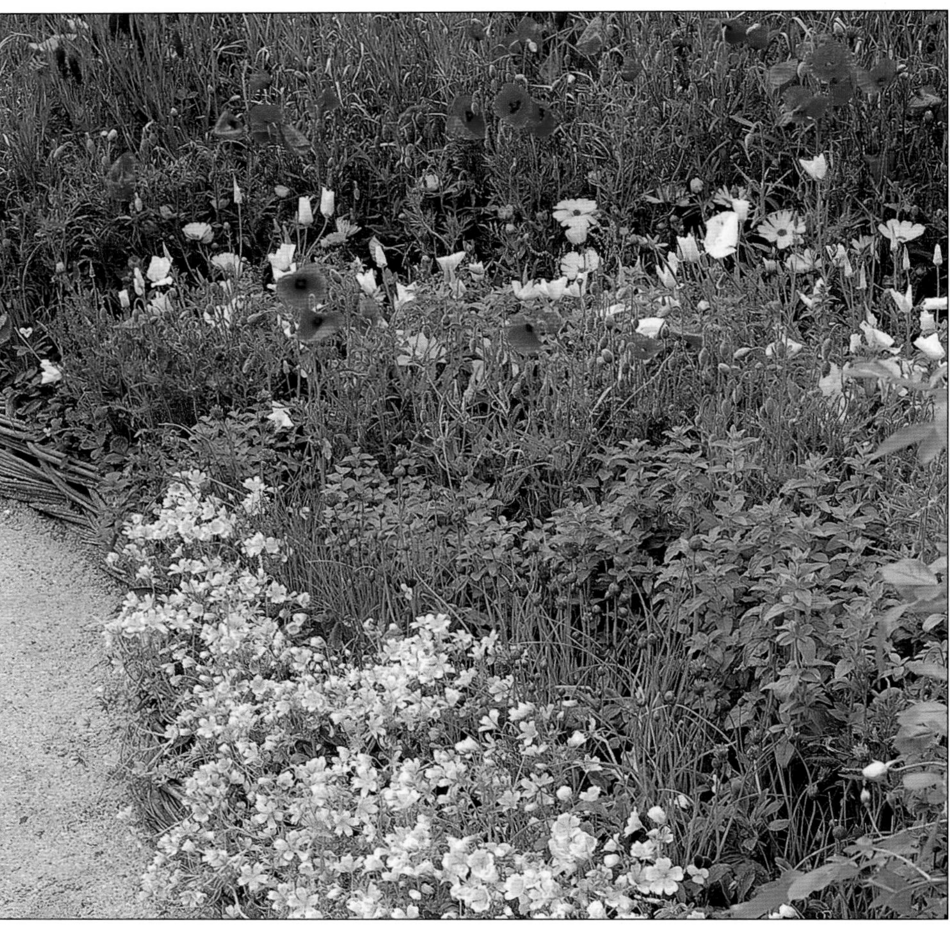

Limnanthes douglasii, the poached egg plant, creates a perfect border to this wildflower garden, which is dominated by annuals.

What is an annual?

There are basically four different types of plant that are considered annuals from the garden point of view. The most common are the true annuals, which grow from seed, flower and produce their own seed within a year. There are many examples of these, but poppies and nasturtiums are popular ones. Closely allied to these are the biennials. These grow from seed one year and then flower during the next. Foxgloves and evening primroses are familiar examples.

Then there are those perennials that are tender, and so are treated as annuals and started afresh each year. Pelargoniums and busy Lizzies are good examples. Finally, there is another group of perennials that are used as annuals. These are simply short-lived perennials that are better grown from scratch each year. Frequently planted examples of these are wallflowers and sweet Williams.

Hardiness

Since most annuals grow and flower within the year, hardiness may not seem to be an important factor to take into consideration, but it can be if you plan to grow your own annuals from seed. Hardy annuals can be sown outside and will withstand late frosts, but half-hardy or tender annuals must be raised under glass and not planted out until after the risk of frost has passed. Alternatively, half-hardy or tender annuals can be sown directly where they are to flower, but again only after the threat of frost is over.

Great diversity

One of the great advantages of using annuals is that the design of a garden need not be fixed: you can change the colour, texture and shape of the plantings each year if you wish. At the end of the flowering season you simply rip out the plants, then decide which annuals you want to plant for the next season. They come in all shapes, sizes and colours, so the gardener has a virtually limitless palette from which to create planting schemes. This versatility means that annuals can be used as massed bedding or mixed with other plants, such as perennials, or they can be used in containers such as hanging baskets, large pots or window boxes. They also provide a wide range of flowers that can be cut for the house.

Annuals can be ideal for the smallest of spaces. Here, bright red pelargoniums are used very effectively in simple pots on a wall.

Long-flowering annuals

Ageratum
Antirrhinum majus
Argyranthemum
Begonia x semperflorens
Brachycome iberidifolia
Calendula officinalis
Impatiens
Lobelia erinus
Nicotiana
Pelargonium
Petunia
Salvia
Tagetes
Tropaeolum majus
Verbena x hybrida
Viola x wittrockiana
Zinnia elegans

Using annual plants is not all about making the most of showcasing the flowers. In this container, for example, silver foliage has been used to great effect.

Mixing it

Annuals can be used to great advantage mixed with perennials and shrubs. One big advantage that annuals have over perennials is that they tend to flower over long periods, often throughout the whole summer. So, in a mixed border, annuals can provide a permanent thread of colour.

Their temporary nature can also be put to good use. Often it will take several years before shrubs or perennials reach their final spread, and during this time there will be areas of bare earth around these plants. Annuals can readily be used here as attractive temporary fillers until the other plants eventually use up all of the space.

Annuals can also add a touch of lightness and almost frivolity to an otherwise staid border. For example, a border predominantly full of shrubs, perhaps planted for their interesting leaves, can be enlivened by massed plantings of bold summer annuals in front of and in between the shrubs. Each type of plant will complement the other.

Hanging displays

Annuals make wonderful container plants, whether in tubs, window boxes or hanging baskets. They usually last the whole season, providing constant attractive colour, though regular watering is a must for continuous flowering. Once the season is over, you can completely change your scheme for the following year simply by changing the plants. You might perhaps try hot oranges and reds one year, followed by softer, cooler blues and whites the next.

Pathways can provide a wonderful opportunity to display annuals to their full advantage. Change the colour and pattern each year to create a slightly different mood as you approach your front door.

Planning a bedding scheme and then watching it come to life can be a great deal of fun. Although not as popular currently as they once were, these schemes provide a stimulating challenge for the inventive mind.

Perennials and their role

When a dream garden springs into our minds, the linchpins of the borders will usually be the perennials, with their great wealth of colours, textures and forms. They provide an enormous selection of plants that will fit in with any style of gardening and will satisfy both the keen and lazy gardener.

What is a perennial?

Perennials are just what they say – perennial – though the description must be modified slightly, as it could apply to any plant that lasts more than a year. In fact, it generally applies to herbaceous material that is grown in general borders. In other words, it excludes trees, shrubs and plants that are grown in rock gardens or in greenhouses, even though these all might be long-lived. Most perennials die back in winter and then regenerate the following year, though some remain green right through the winter. From the gardening point of view, perennials are generally considered hardy – that is, they are able to withstand at least a certain amount of frost.

Changing scene

Most perennials have a relatively short flowering season. This may be seen as a disadvantage, but in fact it can be a great asset because it means that the garden is never static, it never becomes boring. It allows the borders to be planned in such a way that they present an ever-changing scene. It is possible, for example, to have a spring border of blue and yellow that transforms itself over the months into a pink and mauve border in the summer and then perhaps to hot colours for the autumn. Such coordination needs careful planning, of course, but that is half the fun of gardening.

Use vivid, exciting colours to create a "hot" border. Just like beds of annual plants, herbaceous borders of perennials can be colour themed in all kinds of creative ways.

Foliage effect

Perennials are not only about flower colour. Many have interesting foliage in a wide range of colours, from greens, silvers and purples to yellows and creams. All these help to create a backdrop against which the flowers can be seen to advantage. Longer lasting than flowers, foliage forms the main structure of the borders throughout the growing season.

Herbaceous borders

Perennials can be used in many ways. One of the most effective is creating a herbaceous border entirely from perennials. These are usually planted in drifts, creating a sumptuous tapestry of colours through summer and autumn. Traditionally, herbaceous borders were found in large gardens, but smaller versions can easily be created to great effect.

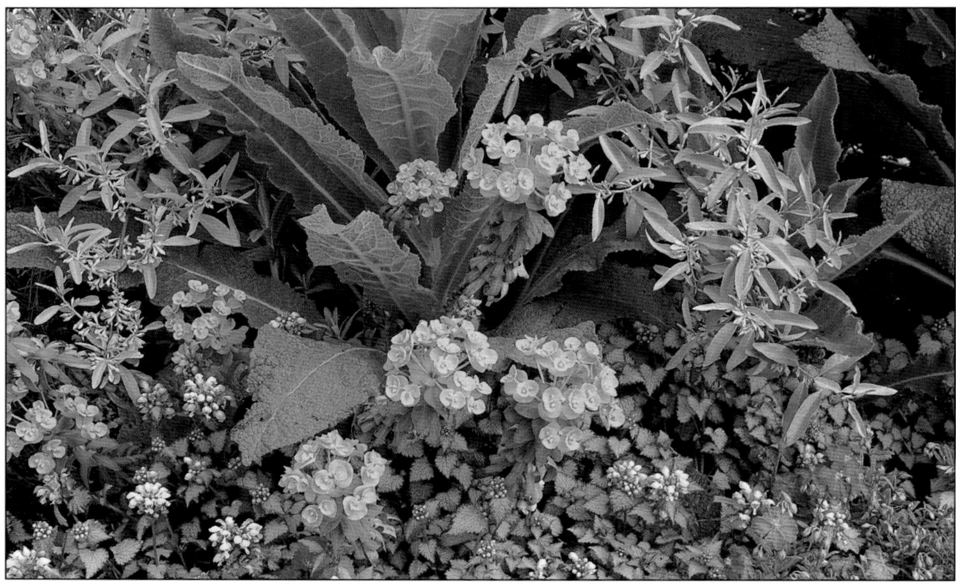

This mixed border of perennials, annuals and shrubs shows the effects that can be achieved by combining a variety of different shapes, colours and textures.

Mixed borders

Many gardeners prefer to use a mixture of plants, perhaps using shrubs as the backbone and main structure of the garden and mixing in other plants to give differing colours throughout the year. Perennials are perfect for this role, particularly as there are a large number that like to grow in the light shade that is provided by being planted under or close to shrubs. Although shrubs form the structure, the perennials usually provide the majority of the plants. In some cases these may be a single large clump, but drifts of the bigger plants and carpets of the lower growing ones look better than scattering the plants around at random.

Potted perennials

It is often thought that the only place for perennials is in a large garden, but perennials are suited to all sizes of garden. They can be grown in a patio garden or even on a balcony or roof garden. As long as you are prepared to water them, they may be grown in containers, which can then be placed anywhere, including in gardens that are paved over and have no native soil at all.

Hardy perennials

Hardy perennials, as their name implies, are those that will tolerate frost and will reappear every year. Some tender perennials may be killed by frosts, although sometimes the frost will just kill off the exposed foliage, and the plant will regenerate from the roots. Although it is mainly temperature related, hardiness can be affected by soil conditions, and often a borderline plant will be more hardy in a free-draining soil than in a heavy damp one.

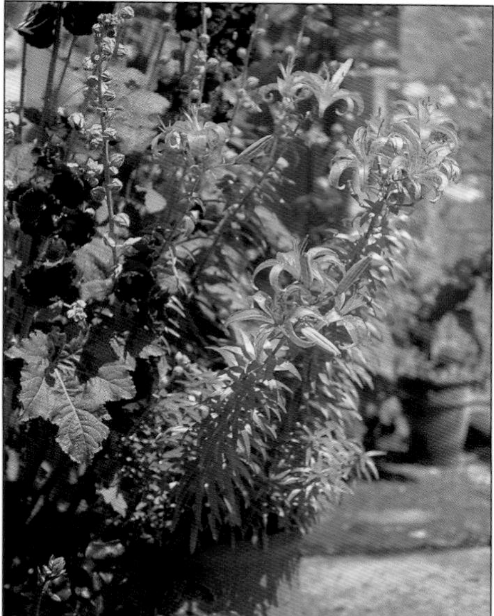

Many perennials, such as this lily, are ideal for tubs. Just move into position when in flower.

Plant-lovers

There are more varieties of perennial plants than any other type of plant available to the gardener. Some gardeners make a virtue of this and indulge their love of plants by creating special collections. Others collect a particular species, pinks (*Dianthus*) or hostas, for example, or favour broader groups – variegated plants are a very popular subject. There are also gardeners who seek out rare and difficult-to-grow plants, just to test their skills, and others who might make a collection of plants mentioned in, for example, the works of Shakespeare. The possibilities are almost endless.

Perennials are not dependent on their flowers for their attraction. Many earn their keep as foliage plants, with the shapes and colour providing plenty of interest, as seen here.

Different styles of flower garden

There are various styles of garden to choose from, although there are no definitive rules and there is no reason why gardeners should not choose a mixture of designs. Having said that, there are a number of styles that have a proven track record, and it is perhaps worthwhile considering the pursuit of just one of them until you are confident enough to mix different styles.

In this cottage garden, the planting has seemingly been done at random and a wonderful mix of different types of plants creates a lively, natural atmosphere.

Lifestyle considerations

The basic advice is simple: choose a style of garden that you like. There are, however, various other factors that may be worth taking into consideration. Your lifestyle is one of the most important of these. However much you may like formal gardens, there is no point in designing a neat garden that needs to be kept in pristine condition in order to look its best if you are not naturally a tidy person or never have the time to keep it neat.

Likewise, a precise garden will be an uphill struggle if you have young children playing football or riding bicycles around and over the borders. The family dog is also likely to have a say in this matter. A more informal style, which would be in keeping with your life, would be a more sensible and realistic choice. At a later stage in your life, a family garden may no longer be required, at which point, with possibly considerably more time on your hands, you could perhaps reconsider and think of other options.

A family garden needs to take into account the interests and activities of all family members (including pets) and the gardener may have to make certain compromises.

Looking at the options

If you are new to gardening, you may have a vague idea of what you want but no firm idea about the reality. In this case, it will pay to spend a summer wandering around other gardens. Try to look at the best. The big gardens that are open to the public will have teams of gardeners at their beck and call, but there are still lessons and ideas to be learnt from them. A bit more realistic are the private gardens that open just once or twice a year. Most of these are designed and tended by their owners with little or no help. Look, make notes and, if you get the chance, talk to the owner and find out the problems and benefits of such a garden.

Another simple idea is to peer over fences (without being a nuisance) as you walk the dog and make critical appraisals of neighbouring gardens. What is right and what is wrong with them? What would you do to improve them? You can also watch television for inspiration, and look through gardening magazines and books.

This predominantly herbaceous border also features a few roses. A keen gardener who loves to design with colour has been at work here.

Making notes

Some gardeners are able to keep detailed notes of what they see and ideas that they may adopt. Others are hopeless at this, and while they start out with good intentions, they soon run out of steam. One way around this is to take photographs as reminders. Another effective and low-effort method is to tear out pages from magazines that inspire you or leave markers tucked into books. Books and magazines can provide a really broad wealth of information, especially during the winter months when there is relatively little to look at in the gardens themselves.

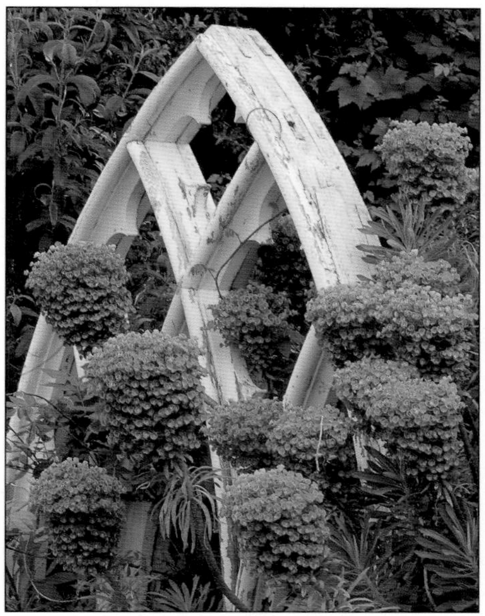

Look for simple but effective ideas such as this creative use of an old window frame.

Keep it simple

One of the biggest problems that new gardeners have is that they get carried away with their plans. They have grand ideas and can visualize just how their dream garden will look when finished, but they fail to consider the reality of the situation and to ask themselves some key questions. Is the garden big enough for all these ideas? Have they got enough money to pay for all the plants or hard landscaping that is required? And, above all, will they have the time not only to do the original work but also to maintain the garden once the initial enthusiasm has worn off?

Cottage gardens

Many people dream of a cottage in the country, with roses growing around the door and a feast of colour in the garden in front. Well, the good news is that you don't need to move to the country or even have a cottage to create such an attractive garden.

What is a cottage garden?

It is very difficult to define a cottage garden. We all know one when we see one, but describing them is not the easiest thing to do. Generally, they have an old-fashioned look. The real skill in creating a successful cottage garden is to design the borders to look as if they have not been designed at all. There is not much in the way of hard landscaping, just flowerbeds, and these are full to the brim with colourful plants.

Traditionally, the plants would be tough, hardy ones that needed little care. Most would be plants that had been grown for generations, such as primulas, hollyhocks, foxgloves and aquilegias. Today many new hybrids are considered suitable, especially if they are bright and brash.

Even containers can be given a cottage garden feel, simply by keeping them informal.

Cottage plants

Plants for a cottage garden tend, as has already been noted, to be old-fashioned plants that have been around for years. Many are annuals and biennials that self-sow, so the gardener does not have to think about new plants: they just appear.

One reason for using these old favourites, apart from their appearance, is that they are usually less prone to pests and diseases and hardier than many modern cultivars (which is why they have been around for a long time). In other words, they need little looking after. Unfortunately, some of these traditional plants, such as lupins and

Plants for a cottage garden

Alcea rosea
Anemone x *hybrida*
Aquilegia vulgaris
Aster novae-angliae
Aster novi-belgii
Astrantia major
Bellis perennis
Campanula portenschlagiana
Campanula persicifolia
Chrysanthemum
Dianthus (pinks)
Dicentra spectabilis
Doronicum
Geranium ibericum
Geum rivale
Lathyrus odoratus
Lilium candidum
Lupinus
Lysimachia nummularia
Meconopsis cambrica
Myrrhis odorata
Paeonia officinalis
Polemonium caeruleum
Primula
Pulmonaria
Saponaria officinalis
Sedum spectabile
Sempervivum
Stachys byzantina
Viola

Old-fashioned plants such as these polyanthus, forget-me-nots and aquilegias are perfect for spring in the cottage garden.

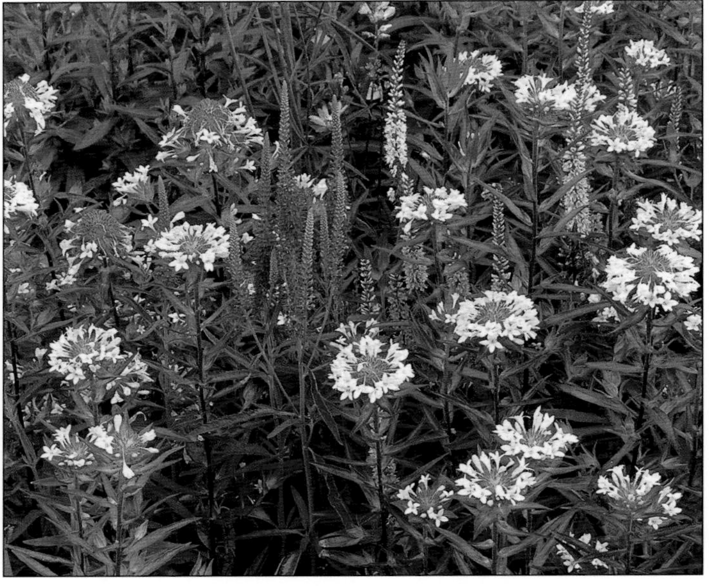

Some old-fashioned annuals, such as this *Collomia grandiflora* (the white flowers), have almost disappeared but are well worth searching out.

hollyhocks, have now developed diseases and pests, which makes them less reliable than they once were, though they can still be grown to great effect as short-lived plants.

The layout

If there is any characteristic to a cottage garden it is the hazy effect that all the intermingled colours create. The traditional image is one of a garden in which the plants seem to have been planted at random without any thought of planning. Gaps would be filled as they became available, and self-sowing plants would dot themselves around at will. Whether cottage gardens of the past really were this accidental or were just designed to look so, we may never actually know, but these days there is a tendency to exert at least a little control over the design in order to create the most pleasing picture that you can.

Getting it right

The backdrop to a cottage-garden style is important. For example, it will look better against an older house than a modern one. This certainly doesn't mean that you have to live in a cottage in order to have a cottage garden. It just means that you must modify the situation somehow: for example, perhaps soften a modern house with roses, or create a cottage garden in the rear garden away from the house, dividing it off by using shrubs or trellising covered with climbers.

Although often claimed to be low-maintenance, cottage gardens do need a great deal of work. In summer, plenty of deadheading and tidying is required to prevent the garden looking a mess. Tight planting helps to reduce the amount of weeding and staking that is needed, but this can make access difficult when deadheading plants towards the back of the border.

A path leading up to a cottage's front door is definitely at its most welcoming when it is lined with an abundance of interesting colours.

A selection of vegetables

Most cottage gardens had a vegetable garden that had to supply produce for the family all year round. This often ran straight into the flower garden, with flowers and vegetables mixing where they met. Many vegetables have ornamental qualities and can happily be grown among flowers. A wigwam of runner beans, for example, is wonderful visually. Many vegetable gardens were also arranged in a decorative manner known as the potager. One big disadvantage of growing vegetables among the flowers or in a decorative manner is that gaps are left when you pick the produce.

This wonderful haze of colour typifies a cottage garden. It may look totally random and unplanned but a certain degree of clever control has been exercised.

Formal gardens

Gardens usually reflect their owners in one way or another. An untidy, relaxed person will often have an untidy and relaxed garden, whereas an elegant person who likes everything to be in its place may well opt for a formal garden. Such a garden is usually a positive feature of the home rather than just an outdoor space.

What is a formal garden?

Generally, a formal garden is one that has some formal qualities about it. This usually means that the shapes within the garden are geometric. Thus lines tend to be straight or in precise curves, such as a circle, rather than sinuous and informal. Beds are frequently square, rectangular or circular. Sometimes they might even be triangular, but this is an awkward shape in the garden because the corners are difficult to plant as well as being tricky to mow around.

Another aspect of formality is that there is often regular repetition, in other words certain plants or even whole beds may be repeated at regular intervals. This creates symmetry, which is an important part of such gardens. Calmness and tranquillity are the qualities that usually sum up the formal garden.

Sparseness

Formal gardens can contain as much planting as you like, but many rely on relatively few plants set in key positions. Often a round pond set in a gravelled area with just a couple of clumps of marginal plants – irises, perhaps, and a few water lilies – can look quite stunning in its simplicity. Long vistas down paths also create a feeling of calmness.

Formal plants

Any plants may be used in formal gardens, but there are many that are preferred because they have a formality about them either in their natural overall shape or the quality of the leaves. Others, mainly shrubs but also some ground-cover plants, lend themselves to being trimmed into formal shapes. Clumps of hostas and irises are valuable because of their regular leaf shapes, while grasses such as miscanthus or plants such as yucca or cordyline all have their fountains of leaves. Many ferns also produce this graceful fountain shape. Other plants that work very well in formal gardens are the

Straight lines and geometric patterns make this garden look very formal. Even the container has a symmetrical appearance.

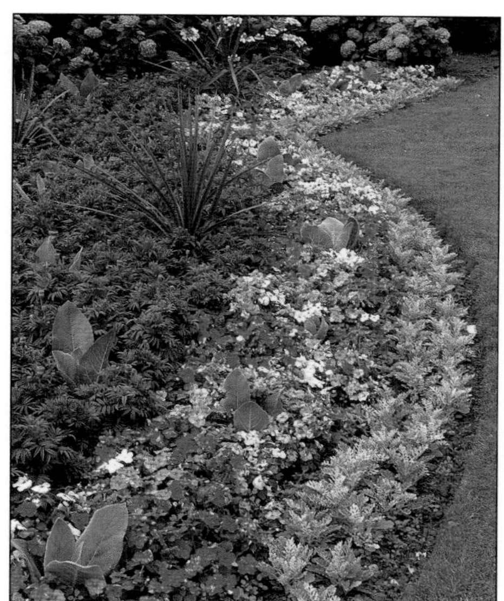

Bedding laid out in lines with a regular repeat of certain plants or colours is one way to add formality to a bed or a whole garden.

statuesque ones, such as verbascum. Annuals all of the same height, such as salvias, or in rounded clumps, such as busy Lizzies in a large container, can also contribute to a very formal look.

The role of containers

Containers can often play an extremely important part in a formal garden scheme, especially large ones filled with a single plant. A classic example is agapanthus placed at the entrance to a patio or at the bottom of some steps. Again, plants with a fountain shape, such as yucca or grasses, are ideal subjects for positions such as these. A series of pots set at regular intervals down a path is also a useful device. The pots can contain perennials, annuals or shrubs, but they should have a neat overall appearance.

Plants for a formal garden

Good leaves or shape
Agapanthus
Asplenium
Athyrium
Bergenia
Cardiocrinum
Cortaderia
Crambe
Dierama
Digitalis
Euphorbia
Foeniculum
Hosta
Lilium
Matteuccia struthiopteris
Miscanthus
Pennisetum
Sisyrinchium
Stipa
Veratrum
Verbascum
Yucca
Zantedeschia

Good in-fill plants
Ageratum
Alchemilla
Antirrhinum
Bellis perennis
Callistephus chinensis
Diascia
Lobelia erinus
Myosotis sylvatica
Nicotiana alata (N. affinis)
Petunia
Tagetes erecta
Tagetes patula

Sculpture and dramatic containers, even if they do not contain plants, help to give the garden an air of formality.

Maintenance

Compared with many other types of garden, formal gardens are relatively easy to maintain, although at times it is more like housework than gardening. The general design rarely needs changing, so there is little planting unless you are using areas of bedding plants. With good mulching there should be little weeding, so it is mainly down to trimming and keeping the hard surfaces in good order.

Boxed in

Many formal gardens use box hedges to line paths or even to surround beds completely. In really extravagant gardens a series of box hedges are used to create a knot garden. The beds within these hedges may be restricted to one or two plant types, with annual bedding plants often used to paint blocks of colour within the green outlines of the box. This type of formal garden is often constructed on a grand scale, but it can be successfully emulated in smaller gardens.

Straight lines – whether they consist of low hedging or bedding plants (the latter is seen here) – and geometric shapes can create great clarity of design in a formal scheme.

Informal gardens

Most of us do not have the time to commit ourselves regularly to our garden, however much we wish we could. We also have conflicting demands on the garden: it is not just something beautiful or something to contemplate but also a place to live in and enjoy. So we end up creating an informal garden that suits our lifestyle. It is none the worse for that.

This spot in the garden is a wonderful place to relax, as it is surrounded by a comfortable, unstructured mixture of different types of plants.

What is an informal garden?

An informal garden is everything a formal garden isn't. It is a garden designed around our tastes and lifestyle. The borders are full of plants that we like but not necessarily planted with military precision. The lines are not regular but comfortable and enjoyable, a bit like a favourite chair. There are lots of different things to see, but they are not necessarily connected in such a rigid way as in a formal garden. There is plenty of room for children to play, and no one gets too hysterical if a ball gets into the beds or the shape of a shrub is spoilt by being turned into a camp. The gardener still takes a lot of trouble over how it is planted and how it looks, but the garden carries with it an air of comfortable informality.

Informal plants

Virtually any plant is suitable for an informal garden – that is the joy of this garden type (this is why no box containing a listing of recommended plants has been given here). It is the way in which plants are used, not the plants themselves, that is key.

What you could do if you wish is to create different areas for different plants. For example, if you are particularly fond of plants that favour damp conditions, you could make one area into a bog garden. Similarly, a rock garden or a gravel bed could be introduced for plants that tend to favour drier conditions. You can also create a more mixed garden, with annuals, perennials, climbers, shrubs and even trees, combined and arranged as you please. You could also experiment with using colours and textures in various creative ways.

There is certainly no formality here, and the gardener is free to remove or add plants without upsetting the balance of the scheme.

Here, the delightful edging to the path has all the colour but none of the rigid formality of a bedding scheme.

The importance of grass

Grass and hard surfaces have an important role to play in informal gardens. In many cases, such a garden will be a family one and grass has the obvious importance as a play area. But grass and surfaces also have a visual importance. If the whole garden is filled with flowering plants, the eye becomes restless: there is too much to see. An expanse of grass gives the eye a chance to rest and acts as a foil to the liveliness of the borders.

The edge of the grass, paving or path also acts as a defining limit to the border by creating an edge, which, again, is very important visually. Such an area of grass does not have to be kept pristine, mown with perfect stripes. It can be a hard-wearing, everyday sort of lawn, which copes with bicycles and ball games, and still has just the same visual effect.

Maintenance

Informal gardens can become rather high in maintenance, particularly if irregular attention is given to them. It is an inescapable fact that garden jobs don't just go away if they are ignored, they just get bigger. So if you leave the weeding for a few weeks, the effort to rid the borders of weeds can become a daunting task that takes a long time to do. Similarly, if herbaceous perennials and shrubs are left growing, with no attention paid to them, they will merrily go on growing until the garden becomes almost over-run and a major operation is needed to get everything back to the original plan. It is therefore important to do a little bit of work often rather than a lot in sudden bursts. With a little bit of attention, informal gardens are easy to maintain.

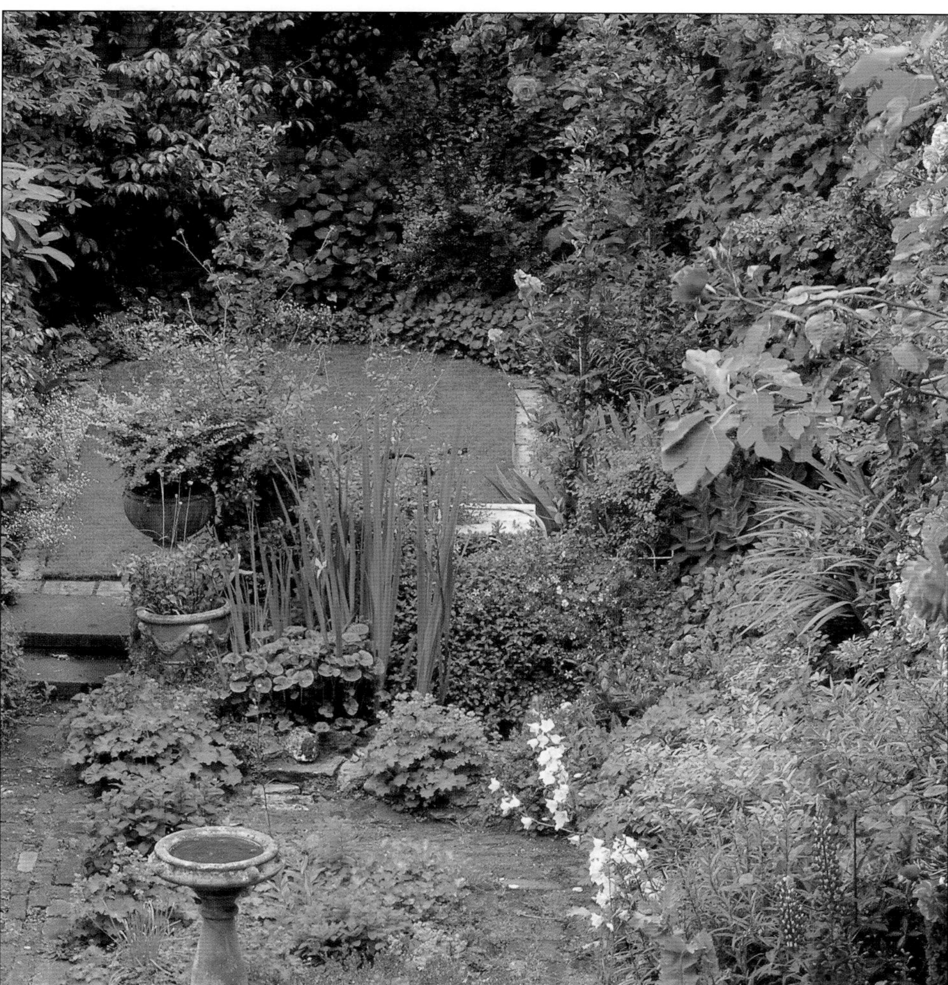

The seemingly random but not untidy nature of this garden is really charming. It has a delightfully informal, but still cared for, appearance.

Containers can be used just as much in informal arrangements as they are in formal gardens. They are especially useful for providing temporary fills.

Wildflower gardens

With the increasing reduction of wild habits for many plants, many people have begun to look afresh at what they are losing and have gained an appreciation of their native flora. This has encouraged them to create areas within their own garden in which wild flowers can flourish, partly to help to preserve these flowers and partly because they simply enjoy them.

What is a wildflower garden?

A wildflower garden is one in which native flowers are grown in as near wild conditions as possible. The idea of wild conditions is not so much to create a picturesque landscape but more to create conditions in which the flowers will grow.

There are several types of garden all based on habitats in the wild. The most common is a wildflower meadow. Next are those based on plants of the cornfield and arable land, which like the disturbed soil of the open border. Then there are the woodland plants that need a shady garden. Finally, there are the wetland plants, which need a pond, stream or boggy area. Once established, wildflower gardens or borders are wonderful for attracting native birds and insects. They are, after all, their natural food.

The pretty *Anemone nemorosa* is an easy, non-invasive plant to grow. Plant it under shrubs or under a hedgerow.

When planning a wildflower garden, do not source your plants from those growing in the wild. Although they seem to be there for the gathering, always resist the temptation and buy seed from a respectable seed merchant instead. Leave the plants in the wild for others to enjoy.

Wildflower meadows

These are best created by first sowing grass or using an existing lawn. Once the "meadow" has become established, mow it regularly to eliminate the coarser grasses. Now is the time to plant the wildflowers. They are more likely to become established if you grow the plants from seed in pots and then transplant them into the grass than if you simply scatter the seed. Prevent rank grass from taking over by mowing in high summer after the plants have seeded and then at least a couple more times before winter sets in. Do not leave the grass lying after cutting.

Cornfield plants

Many wildflowers will not grow in grass, needing disturbed soil to flourish. Poppies, cornflowers and corn marigolds are examples of these. They are mainly annuals and can be grown from seed in pots and then transplanted or sown directly from seed. Once established, they will self-sow and then reappear every year. A border can be devoted to them or they can be mixed into a general border.

Here it is early spring in the meadow garden, with *Fritilaria meleagris*, the snake's head fritillary, making a welcome appearance.

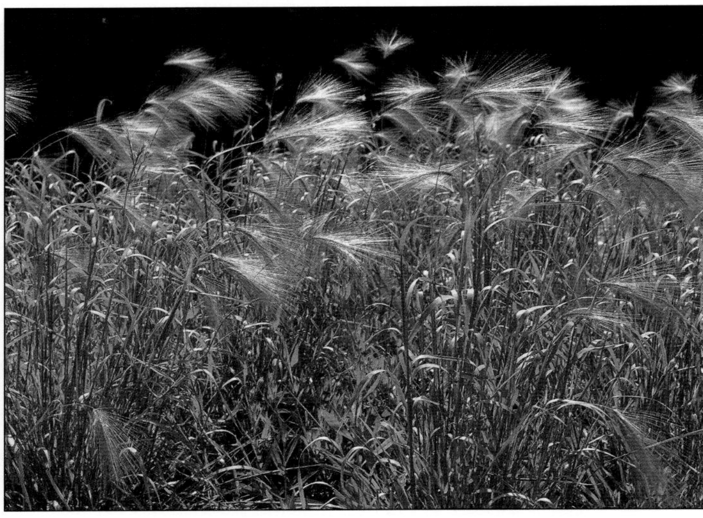

Non-invasive grasses are ideal for wildflower gardens. This is the annual *Hordeum jubatum*, sparkling in the sun.

Chrysanthemum segetum is one of many cornfield flowers that are ideal for wildflower beds.

Woodland plants

There are a number of woodland species that make very attractive planting in shady areas, perhaps under shrubs or trees or perhaps on the sunless side of a house or fence. Most woodland flowers tend to grow in deciduous woods and put in an appearance in the early spring before the trees come into leaf. This is so that they get enough sun and rain to grow and develop. Primroses, wood anemones and bluebells are good examples of these. It is not necessary to have a wood in order to grow them – they will be quite happy growing under deciduous shrubs and a good use of space.

Water plants

These can be a bit more problematic in that many native water or bog plants can be rather rampant and tend to take over. They need good management to keep them under control. The conditions that these plants enjoy are also very conducive to weeds, so be prepared for regular weeding. They can be grown in the same way as any other water- or bog-loving plants.

Plants for a wildflower garden

Wildflower meadows
Achillea millefolium
Campanula rotundifolia
Cardamine pratensis
Centaurea scabiosa
Geranium pratense
Hypericum perforatum
Leontodon hispidus
Malva moschata
Narcissus pseudonarcissus
Primula veris
Ranunculus acris
Succisa pratensis

Cornfield plants
Centaurea cyanus
Chrysanthemum segetum
Papaver rhoeas

Woodland plants
Anemone nemorosa
Convallaria majalis
Digitalis purpurea
Hyacinthoides non-scripta
Primula vulgaris

Water gardens
Butomus umbellatus
Caltha palustris
Eupatorium cannabinum
Filipendula ulmaria
Iris pseudacorus
Mentha aquatica

Although normally considered a border plant, *Camassia* makes an excellent plant for the wild meadow garden.

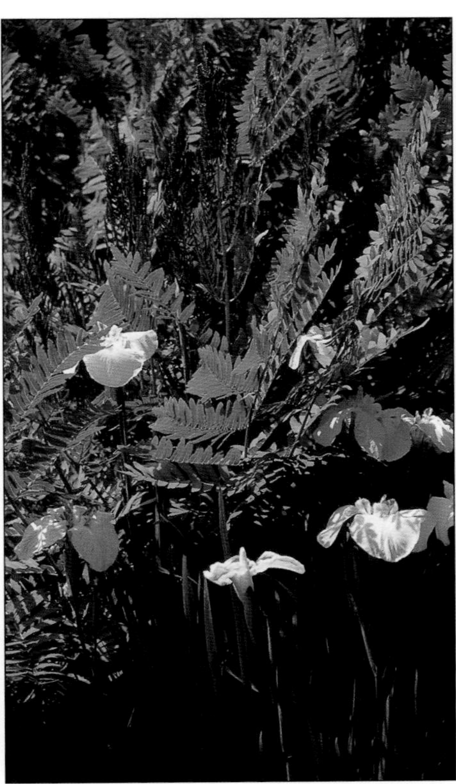

Ferns make good plants for shady areas of wildflower gardens. In wetter areas the royal fern, *Osmunda regalis*, is ideal.

Coping with different conditions

Sometimes we are lucky enough when buying a house to get one with a garden that offers us pretty much what we wanted, or at least offering excellent growing conditions. If we are very lucky, we may even be able to choose the house specifically for the garden. However, for most of us, we select the house and then simply have to accept the garden along with it. This can present the keen gardener with a variety of situations, both in terms of weather and soil conditions. Although the weather cannot be altered, quite a bit can be done to improve the soil and make it suitable for our chosen plants. Alternatively, we can just decide to accept what the garden offers, and select those plants that like a wide range of conditions. Similarly, the size of the garden is usually predetermined, with little chance of increasing it. Again, it is perfectly possible to create a delightful garden within the constraints that this puts upon you.

Over the next few pages we look at the most important conditions under which you may have to create a garden. Very few gardeners start from scratch, as there is usually some form of garden already in existence, giving some indication of the conditions you might expect there.

Making the most of the slope, this gravel garden is ideal for growing dry-loving and sun-loving plants.

Dry gardens

Once upon a time there was only one type of dry garden – one that was naturally so. Nowadays, with the increasing desire to create a number of habitats in which to grow the widest range of plants, many gardeners set out actually to create these conditions. In either case, there are a large number of varied annuals and perennials that suit a dry environment.

Dry conditions

Just because a garden is dry does not necessarily mean that it receives very little rain. There are many gardens that receive a lot of rain and yet are still dry under foot. The reason for this is that the soil is very free-draining and any moisture that falls, either from clouds or from a watering can, passes quickly through it. These are mainly sandy or gravelly soil, but chalky soils can also be very free-draining. As well as losing water quickly, many dry soils are also poor in terms of nutrients. The water passing through leeches out the nutrients, taking the food that plants require well below the level of their roots. Many seaside gardens are of this nature.

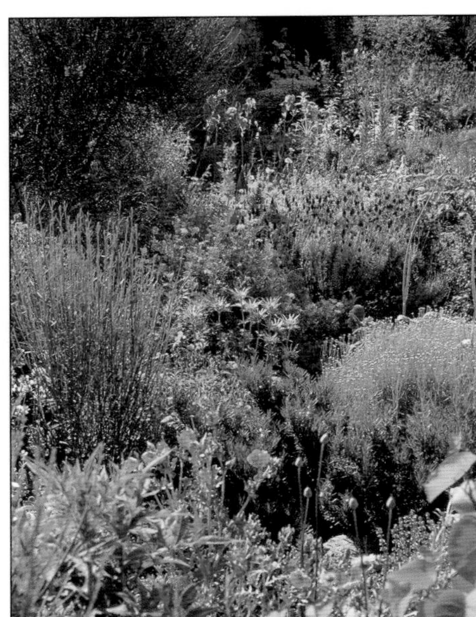

A surprisingly large number of plants like dry conditions and a very attractive garden can be built around them.

Plants for dry gardens

Allium hollandicum
Argemone
Artemisia
Atriplex hortensis
Bergenia
Canna
Centranthus
Cerinthe major
Cortaderia
Crambe
Elymus
Eryngium
Eschscholzia
Euphorbia
Foeniculum
Glaucium flavum
Lavatera
Onopordon acanthium
Ophiopogon planiscapus 'Nigrescens'
Papaver somniferum
Pennisetum
Salvia
Sedum
Stachys byzantinus
Verbascum
Yucca

Altering the conditions

It is possible to increase the water-retentiveness of dry soil so that you can grow a much wider range of plants in it. This is done by adding well-rotted organic material to the soil when you dig it. Garden compost (soil mix) or farmyard

Grasses are excellent for dry gardens. The larger ones create imposing clumps against which the other plants are set.

This mixed border features plants from regions with a Mediterranean climate. Dry gardens increase the number of plants we can grow.

Annuals, such as this marigold (*Calendula*) and vipers bugloss (*Echium vulgare*), will self-sow to provide next year's plants.

This is the ultimate dry garden: houseleeks (*Sempervivum*) growing on a house porch. Stonecrops (*Sedum*) also like such a position.

manure are good additives and will improve soil conditions appreciably, especially as they are rich in nutrients. Mulching with organic materials also helps a great deal. A covering of composted bark, for example, will considerably cut down water loss into the atmosphere. It will also gradually become incorporated into the soil, improving the condition. Unfortunately, most dry soils are "hungry", and gardeners need to add material both into the soil and on to its surface on a regular basis.

Living with dry soils

While it is in general terms a good thing to try to improve soil conditions, it is possible to live with them by choosing your plants carefully. Many plants have adapted their demands so that they are able to live with drought or partial drought, particularly plants that come originally from Mediterranean climates. It is very important to choose plants that will tolerate such dry soils. If you try to get ordinary plants to grow in them, you will be disappointed because they will not be able get enough moisture or food from the soil. If, however, you choose plants that have adapted to these conditions, you should have few problems in creating an interesting garden.

Plants for dry conditions

Few gardens have desert conditions, so you don't have to go to extremes and grow only succulents, such as cacti, that tolerate such places. However, there are a lot of plants that come from parts of the world where, for example, dry summers are followed by wet autumns and winters. Many annuals come from these areas, as do bulbs and many silver-leaved plants – try combining these to create an unusual but beautiful garden where their subtle colours are well set off by a gravel background. Weed these areas well, or the effect will be ruined.

Creating a gravel garden

Many gardeners specifically set out to create dry conditions by adding great quantities of gravel to the ordinary soil. This increases its drainage ability and makes it suitable for plants that you may not have been able to grow before.

Damp gardens

The idea of damp gardens conjures up a rather unpleasant image of a garden in which no one would want to linger, but, depending on how the situation is handled, they can be rather beautiful. Apart from anything else, many colours, especially the yellows, stand out so well in gloomy conditions.

Aruncus dioicus does best in a moist situation, either in a bed that is moisture-retentive or on the edge of a bog garden.

Many plants like a situation where the air never dries out and the soil remains slightly damp, such as along the banks of a stream.

What is a damp garden?

A garden can be considered damp in two ways. The first is where the soil is heavy and constantly damp, even though the weather is sunny and bright. The second way can occur near certain coasts. The coastal climate in question is one where the weather is frequently overcast, with rain, drizzle or mist being common, and where, even when it is sunny, the air is still "buoyant" (moving and life-sustaining as opposed to stagnant) and slightly moist, especially under trees. Both are conditions that most gardeners dread, but both can be turned to advantage. Visits to other gardens with similar conditions will soon stimulate you, showing what can be achieved with a bit of determination and a good waterproof jacket.

Wet soil

There are two solutions to the problem of wet soils: one is to deal with it and the other is to live with it. In the first case, improving the condition of the soil, especially by adding grit and organic material to it, will help greatly by improving the soil's ability to let the water pass through. Allied to this should be improved drainage. If you simply dig and improve the soil, the bed will fill up with water, held in place by the surrounding poor soil like a sump. You must make certain that the water can drain out of the bed by laying drains either to a soakaway or a nearby ditch. Another possibility is to lead the water to a lower part of the garden, where you can create a pond. Any garden that stays persistently damp should have a proper drainage system installed to get the water away.

This colourful damp meadow and ditch is full of moisture-loving plants such as candelabra primulas, astilbes and water irises.

A mass of colourful primulas – plants for which a damp position is absolutely ideal. They will self-sow to make this an even better display.

Bog gardens

Living with damp soils is another interesting prospect. The gardener simply has to accept the fact that the soil is always wet and create a bed that is based on plants that like boggy conditions. Fortunately, there are a large number of colourful plants that do like such conditions. If the soil is too heavy, it will help if plenty of well-rotted organic matter is incorporated into it. If there is water actually lying on or just below the surface, this should be removed by laying drains.

Here a small, damp garden has been built into the edge of a pond. This type of situation really broadens out the range of plants that can be grown.

Creating boggy conditions

While some gardeners go to great expense to get rid of boggy areas, others do the reverse and deliberately create such conditions. One way to do this would be to dig a pond-shaped hole, about 45cm/18in, deep and line it with an old pond liner. Puncturing a few holes in the lowest places will allow excess water to drain away. The hole can then be filled with good soil laced with plenty of well-rotted organic material. The soil should not be allowed to dry out.

Grasses that grow on the damp banks of streams or ponds, hanging their leaves over the water, can look extremely effective.

Damp climate

A damp climate can be a boon if you want to grow plants such as the blue meconopsis, which likes the moist air that reminds it of its Himalayan home. Many other plants do best in a moist, buoyant atmosphere. Primulas and hostas, for example, relish it. In Britain, the maritime climate of Scotland produces some wonderful gardens, growing plants such as primulas, hostas and meconopsis. In many such areas, the soil is surprisingly free-draining. In mountain and hilly areas, for example, the underlying rocks often allow the frequent rain to filter away remarkably quickly, leaving the soil dry. So if there is a prolonged hot spell it is important to water.

Plants for a bog garden

Aconitum napellus
Ajuga reptans
Aruncus dioicus
Astilbe x *arendsii*
Astilboides tabularis
Astrantia major
Caltha palustris
Cardamine pratensis
Cimifuga simplex
Darmera peltata
Dierama pulcherimum
Dodecatheon meadia
Eupatorium
Euphorbia griffithii
Euphorbia palustris
Filipendula ulmaria
Gentiana asclepiadea
Geum rivale
Gunnera manicata
Hemerocallis fulva
Hosta
Iris ensata
Iris orientalis
Iris sibirica
Ligularia
Lobelia cardinalis
Lobelia 'Queen Victoria'
Lobelia siphilitica
Lychnis flos-cuculi
Lysichiton
Lysimachia nummularia
Lysimachia punctata
Lythrum virgatum
Meconopsis betonicifolia
Mimulus cardinalis
Mimulus lewisii
Parnassia palustris
Persicaria bistorta
Petasites japonicus var. *giganteus*
Primula bulleyana
Primula denticulata
Primula florindae
Primula japonica
Primula pulverulenta
Primula vialii
Ranunculus aconitifolius
Rheum palmatum
Rodgersia
Sarracenia purpurea
Schizostylis coccinea
Symphytum ibericum
Telekia speciosum
Trollius

Shady gardens

Like so many other problems in gardening, this one will go away if you make a slight adjustment of attitude and decide to embrace the shade rather than be daunted by it. A visit to any of the big gardens will show shady areas that have been successfully planted, and there is no reason why you should not do the same on a smaller scale.

Coping with shade

For some reason, many people simply ignore the fact that an area is shady and attempt to grow annuals and other sun-loving plants in it. These inevitably languish and frequently die, and the gardeners get very despondent.

There is really no excuse for this problem as a large number of plants are available that actually like shady conditions. Perhaps the colours of these plants might not be so dazzling as the sun-lovers – there are not many bright reds, for example – but they are still colourful enough to put on a good display. Many plants that like shade are yellow, and so stand out well in the gloomy light.

As well as plants with bright flowers, there are many foliage plants that can be used very effectively in such areas. Some have light, variegated or silver-splashed foliage, such as yellow archangel (*Lamium galeobdolon*), which tend to illuminate the darker corners. Others, such as hostas, have shiny leaves, and these catch and reflect the light, once again helping to brighten up the relative darkness.

Miniature woodlands

Many shade-loving plants grow in woodlands, and they appear, flower, seed and die back all before the trees come into leaf. The absence of leaves above them means that the plants have access to both the sun and the rain. Once the leaves on the trees emerge, the plants die back and remain dormant until the following winter or spring.

These plants, including wood anemones and bluebells, can be planted in a garden in odd pockets

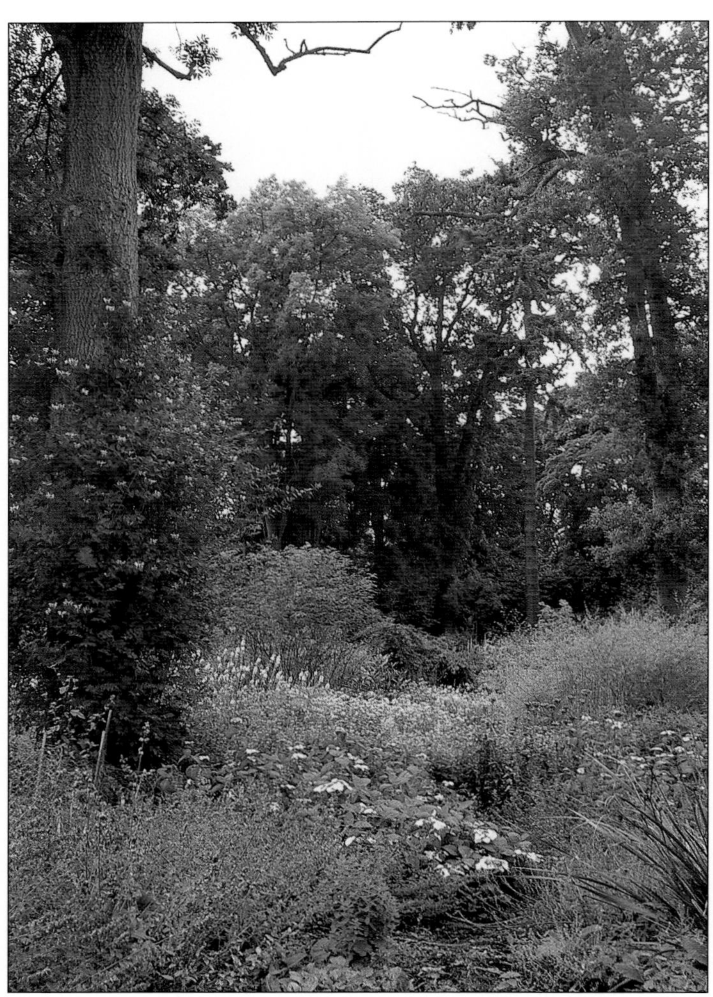

A shady border has been carved out of this mature wood. Here there is sufficient light to grow a wide range of plants.

Anemones, here the double *Anemone ranunculoides*, are perfect woodland plants to grow under the shade of shrubs.

Even a single tree, such as this quince, is sufficient to create a small woodland garden with a range of plants.

Spring-flowering bulbs, such as these blue scillas, make natural carpets for shady areas. Hellebores are also a very good subject.

of shade, such as under deciduous shrubs. Here, the plants can be seen in spring, but later in the year nothing will grow here because the soil will be covered by the shrub's leaves. This makes good use of space. Several such shrubs, perhaps of varying height and with this type of under-planting, can be used to create a miniature woodland, even in the heart of a town.

Lack of sunlight

The north side of a house (south in the southern hemisphere) is often considered a problem area because of its lack of direct sunlight. Again, it is quite possible to create an effective border there simply by choosing plants that like the shade. Most woodland plants, for example, will grow there.

Dry shade

An area that is both dry and shady is one of the worst problems to cope with because most shade-loving plants are woodland plants, which thrive in a moist, fibre-rich soil. Soils can be improved by adding plenty of well-rotted organic material to them – leaf mould is a natural material to use.

Creating shade

Sometimes it can be a problem if you have no shade in the garden when you want to grow plants such as hellebores, which do not like too much sun. Try building a wooden or metal framework over which you stretch shade-netting, creating nice dappled shade. These structures may not look elegant but they are ideal for their intended purpose. They are also useful for temporarily housing shade-loving plants while bushes or trees become large enough to provide natural shade.

Reducing shade

You can increase the amount of light reaching the plants under trees by removing some of the branches, especially the lower ones. Alternatively, you can thin the branches so that more dappled light reaches the ground. If the trees are listed, then you may have to seek permission before removing any limbs. In basement and other dark patios, the amount of light can be increased by painting walls white to reflect what light there is.

Winter aconites thrive in shade. Give them a moist woodland-type soil with plenty of leaf mould and they will colonize.

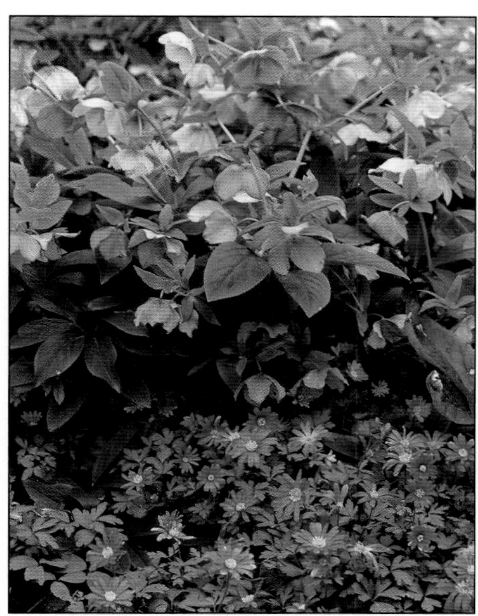
Anemone blanda and hellebores are two good choices to brighten up a patch of light shade.

Some plants for the shade

Alchemilla mollis
Anemone nemorosa
Arum italicum
Aruncus dioicus
Bergenia
Brunnera macrophylla
Caltha palustris
Campanula latifolia
Cardamine
Cardiocrinum giganteum
Carex pendula
Clintonia
Convallaria majalis
Corydalis flexuosa
Dicentra
Digitalis purpurea
Dryopteris filix-mas
Epimedium
Eranthis hyemalis
Euphorbia amygdaloides robbiae
Geranium
Helleborus
Hosta
Houttuynia cordata
Iris foetidissima
Kirengshoma
Lamium galeobdolon
Lathyrus vernus
Lilium martagon
Liriope muscari
Meconopsis
Milium effusum 'Aureum'
Myosotis sylvatica
Persicaria affinis
Phlox divaricata
Phlox stolonifera
Podophyllum peltatum
Polygonatum
Polystichum setiferum
Primula
Pulmonaria
Sanguinaria canadensis
Smilacina
Smyrnium perfoliatum
Stylophorum
Symphytum grandiflorum
Tellima grandiflora
Trillium
Uvularia
Vancouveria

Small gardens

More and more people are living in houses or apartments that only have small gardens; some, indeed are minute. The keen gardener's heart may sink at such limitations, but it is surprising what you can pack into a small space. As always, it just needs some imagination and determination to create a garden to be proud of.

Packing them in

If you more interested in growing plants than having space in which to sit around or have barbecues, then the amount of hard surfaces or lawn should be reduced to a minimum and as much space as possible devoted to borders. Avoid grass unless you have somewhere to store a lawnmower, because mowers need sheds and sheds take up valuable space.

Although there are recommended planting distances for plants, these, like many rules in gardening, can be ignored and the plants set close together for maximum impact. Some will object and crowd other plants out, but these can be culled totally and replaced by something not so vigorous or kept in place by trimming. Tightly packed plants need to be watered and fed regularly because they are taking a lot of water and nutrients out of the soil.

A curved path gives the impression that more garden exists just around the corner. Such illusions make a garden seem much bigger.

One of a kind

Rather than having a drift of one particular plant, as you might in a bigger garden, you should restrict yourself to one plant of each species, otherwise the whole garden could end up with just one or two different types of plant in it. This can make the borders look rather spotty, so drifts can be created using different plants of a similar colour.

The best single plants are those that produce several stems, creating a small clump. Those that produce just a single stem can look rather lost, although there are many such plants, verbascums for example, that make a wonderful accent as they emerge from the surrounding plants. Similarly, a single red poppy can look stunning and will definitely draw the eye.

Foliage plants

A small garden benefits from foliage plants in the same way that large gardens do from grasses. Foliage plants will help to calm down the liveliness of the border and produce somewhere for the eye to rest. This is important in a small garden packed with plants, as the overall appearance can become overly busy. Another use of foliage in any garden, but particularly in a small garden, is to surround a single flowering plant with green or silver leaves so that it makes the flowers stand out, accenting them with a posy effect.

Vertical space

Every bit of space in a small garden is at a premium to a plant-lover, so it is important to remember that a garden is three-dimensional. Climbing plants can be used against walls or fences. It may also be possible to use one or two posts or tripods, if there is space, to add to

Every inch of space needs to be used to maximum effect in a small garden, including, as here, window sills.

Use containers planted up with annuals and perennials, such as this hosta, to fill out any odd corners.

Plants to cut back

Achillea	*Eupatorium*
Aconitum	*Foeniculum*
Aruncus	*Helenium*
Aster	*Rudbeckia*
Campanula	*Sanguisorba*

this vertical accent. As well as climbers, annuals can be used in hanging baskets and window boxes to add colour at or above eye level.

Easy ways to cheat

It is possible to use a few optical tricks to make the garden look bigger. Cover the fences with plants so that the margins of the garden cannot be seen. This trick works particularly well if there is a neighbouring garden with shrubs and other plants peering over the fence, as it will look as if your garden continues. Use a winding path that disappears around a corner at the bottom of the garden so that it seems as if your garden continues out of sight. Paler-coloured plants set towards the end of a short garden will deceive the eye and appear farther away than they are.

Large mirrors covering a wall can give the impression that the wall does not exist and the garden carries on, though the mirrors must be angled so that anyone approaching cannot see their own reflection. Another idea is to erect an arch, which can be covered with climbing plants, just in front of a wall, and then back the arch with a mirror to give the impression that the garden continues under the arch. Similarly, using a *trompe l'oeil* painting on a wall, perhaps a picture of a gate opening into another garden, will deceive viewers into believing that more lies beyond.

Well-planned use of plenty of foliage – so that you cannot see the boundary edges of the garden – is a simple way to make the space feel a great deal larger.

Miniaturizing plants

Many taller perennial plants can be made to grow shorter simply by cutting them back to the ground when they have made about 45cm/18in of growth. The plants re-grow but will usually flower when they have obtained only about half their normal height and size.

With imagination and determination, an amazing number of plants can be crammed into a small space.

Even a modest water feature has been fitted into this extremely small garden. Annual and perennial foliage plants help to fill space without making the garden feel cramped.

Large gardens

Most gardeners with large gardens manage to fill them in one way or another, even if involves putting much of the space down to lawns. Large lawns can be elegant, but without children to play on them they can seem a bit excessive, and there are many more interesting things you could do with the space.

Having a large garden not only allows you to create lavish bedding displays but also gives plenty of scope for walkways and features such as arches.

Large-scale plantings

Plenty of space means that you can create large-scale plantings, including sweeping herbaceous borders. These are large borders that were traditionally filled only with perennial plants, although these days a number of annuals and even shrubs are often included. The plants are planted in drifts, often with five or more plants in each area, so that the border is "painted" with broad strokes of colour.

It is important that any such borders should be deep as well as long; tall plants in a narrow border rarely work. Try and make the depth of the border twice that of the tallest plants. Two borders often work better than one, and two parallel ones with a grass path between them is ideal. The path should preferably be as wide as the borders are deep. Such borders are displayed best if they are grown against a green hedge. Yew is ideal and it is not as slow growing as many people think. A fairly respectable hedge can be achieved in about five years and it will begin to mature at eight.

It is equally possible to use large areas of bedding material, especially if you like to create intricate patterns in colour and texture. There are a number of plants that can be used for these, some growing to a very even height, while others can be used to vary this or to create accents or focal points. These beds can be laid out directly on the ground, surrounded by lawns, or they can form part of a more complicated plan in which a knot garden of box hedges is created, with the bedding plants used as in-fills. Great fun can be had by creating a low-level maze in this kind of way, using a mixture of paths and beds.

Plenty of space to play with means that passionate gardeners can be creative on a grand scale, as these enormous herbaceous borders show.

As well as straight borders, spacious gardens allow huge, swirling areas of plants that show off their colour and shape to maximum effect.

Large plants

Aruncus	*Helianthus*
Cephalaria	*Heliopsis*
Cimifuga	*Inula magnifica*
Cortaderia	*Lavatera cachemiriana*
Cosmos	*Ligularia*
Cynara cardunculus	*Macleaya*
Delphinium	*Miscanthus*
Eremurus	*Rheum*
Eupatorium purpureum	*Rudbeckia laciniata*
Gunnera manicata	*Sanguisorba*
	Verbascum

If you have a large space, you can indulge in some of the most impressive plants available. This *Gunnera manicata* is one of the largest perennials used in gardens.

Gardens within gardens

Another good idea for a large garden is to divide it up into a series of smaller gardens. Dividing in this way creates spaces that are more intimate – more like individual rooms than one vast space. This can be effective in country gardens, where the landscape is already expansive and open. Each "room" should be given its own individual character, some formal, some informal, with varied planting. Perhaps one could be a white garden while another could contain only fragrant flowers (a seat would be invaluable in this one).

Large plants

It sounds obvious, but many people forget that a large garden needs large plants, especially if you keep it fairly open. If you have a large pond, then a huge clump of *Gunnera manicata* will look impressive. Great fountains of leaves erupting from large clumps of grasses, such as pampas (*Cortaderia*) or miscanthus, can create focal points at the end of paths or at the bottom of long lawns. They look even better if planted where the evening light shines through them.

Working with a large space

Large gardens that are intensively cultivated can use up a lot of time and a great deal of money, so a large-scale development should be embarked on only if you feel confident that you will have sufficient time. Fortunately, time can often offset costs, because you can propagate all your own material rather than buying it, but a large garden almost always needs a lot of plants to work really successfully.

Finally, the wind is a factor that cannot be forgotten in large gardens, especially where tall plants are likely to be grown in clumps, with nothing behind or in front to protect them from being blown over. A windbreak could be created around the garden, and plants staked if necessary.

Although shrubs are another topic altogether, it is worth saying here that they can be very useful in large gardens, as providers of valuable wind protection.

Family gardens

Keen gardeners who start a family quickly discover that neat gardens and active children do not often mix. Since there is no point trying to stop the children using the garden, or constantly telling them to get off this area and not touch that plant, a compromise is needed whereby everyone can live happily. Remember that a garden should be a fun place for everyone.

Children in the garden

Whatever you do, children will always be children, and quite rightly so. They will want to play ball and racket games in the garden, and will want to career around on bikes and in go-karts. These things present problems for the gardener – balls will crash through the borders, bringing down plants; cyclists or go-karters will veer off the lawn or path and end up lying in a nest of tangled plants.

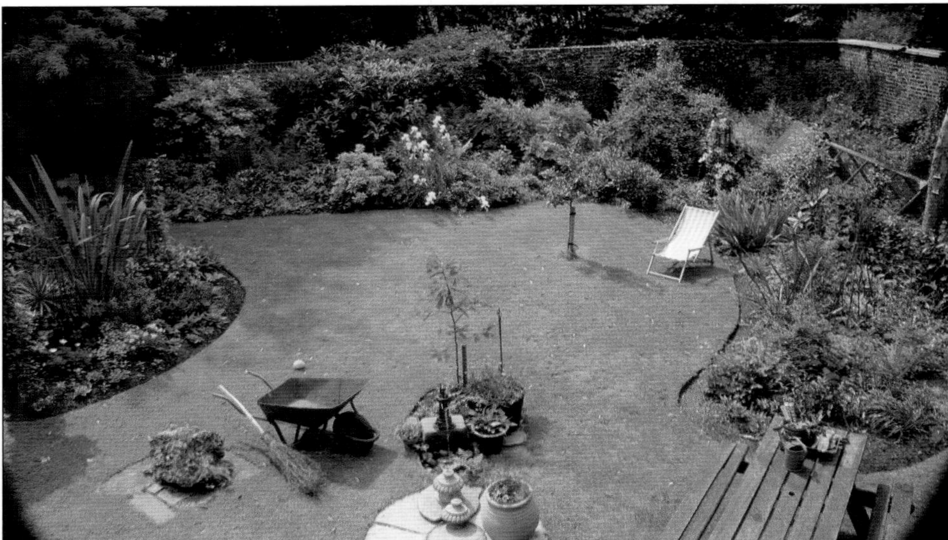

In the ideal family garden there should be plenty of space and a range of provisions, so everybody is able to relax and play in their own way.

Play space

To some extent, trouble can be avoided by creating a family garden where there is room for all activities. Plenty of lawn or hard surface should be provided on which children can play. There could also be special areas for them, perhaps with swings, sandpits, "camps" or "houses". The very best gardens are those with a variety of nooks and crannies in which children can hide, so, if possible, you could try creating some of these.

If you can, provide as much lawn area as possible – for children to play without falling on hard surfaces or wreaking havoc in the borders.

Some features can be built with the future in mind. This sand pit, for example, can eventually be turned into a water feature.

Easy plants for children to grow

Antirrhinum	*Lobelia*
Calendula	*Tagetes*
Helianthus annuus	*Thunbergia alata*
Lathyrus odoratus	*Tropaeolum majus*

Separate rooms

Your garden may be large enough for you to divide it up into a number of areas, each for a particular activity. This may, for example, include an area for playthings as well as a place for growing precious plants.

Children's gardens

Many young children are very keen on gardening – they love to see things growing. Although eager to help you with your gardening, most children are happiest of all with a small plot of their own. Encourage them to grow annuals, which are quick to germinate and produce colourful results of which they can be justifiably proud. A small selection of quick-growing vegetables will also delight. Children's interests can wane as rapidly as they began, so be prepared to absorb the plot back into the garden. Alternatively, provide them with long-flowering plants, such as *Tagetes*, which will fill the space over a long period.

Tough lawns

The family lawn can take quite a beating and it will be impossible to keep it perfectly pristine. Instead of using the soft grasses that would be needed for a high-quality lawn, use some of the tougher species, which will stand the considerable wear and tear of family life. These can be used singly or as mixtures of one or more species. Once the family has grown up, you can then switch to a better-quality grass.

Tough grass seed for lawns

Axonopus (carpet grass)
Eremochloa ophiuroides (centipede grass)
Lolium perenne (perennial ryegrass)
Paspalum notatum (bahia grass)
Poa pratensis (Kentucky blue grass)

Pets

Cats, dogs and other pets are also part of the family, and friction can often erupt when they flatten plants or dig up borders. Low fences can deter them from running into borders, but with some dogs it will be necessary to fence off your flower garden completely. Wild birds that you feed in winter also need to be taken into account, as they will often strip plants of flowers or berries that you want to keep. There is little you can do about this except grow plants that they do not touch (skimmia berries, for example, are rarely eaten) or cover plants with a network of dark cotton.

Dining out

It is not only children who indulge in non-gardening pursuits. Most of the family want to do other things at some time or other, and space for relaxing is very important. This may just involve a spot for sitting or for lounging in the sun, or more likely will also include some provision for eating, possibly with a barbecue area.

It is a good idea to surround places where you relax with fragrant plants. These will be most welcome if you sit outside in the evening once the sun has gone down. Remember that certain blues and whites show up especially well in the fading light, so try to use plants with flowers of these colours. In a barbecue area, grow a few herbs so that they can be easily picked and used.

Always provide plenty of space and facilities for relaxation. After all, that is one of the prime functions of a garden.

Special ways with annuals and perennials

If you have a big garden, and plenty of free time at your disposal, then you can indulge in just about every aspect of gardening. However, if you do not have these luxuries, you may well find that you have the space to do only one thing properly, and so you specialize. Alternatively, you may want to garden for just one particular purpose, such as providing cut flowers for your home or local community centre.

There are many ways in which you can specialize, and a few are suggested here. It is possible, for example, to have a border or even a whole small garden devoted to plants that include your name. There are over 100 plants that contain the name Helen, for example, including *Aster novi-belgii* 'Helen' and *Dianthus* 'Helen'. You could create a garden filled with plants mentioned in the works of Shakespeare, or in books by your favourite novelist. Research is involved here, of course, but this kind is usually very enjoyable. In any case, rather than devote a whole garden to any of these themes, you could restrict yourself to just a single border or an area within the main garden. The possibilities are endless and the result is likely to be a unique garden that no one else will have.

Borders can be restricted to one colour or a group of colours. In this scheme, yellows are predominant, but a sprinkling of hot reds has been added to provide some interest.

Fragrant gardens

When thinking of flowers, one's first thoughts normally concern their colour. One of their most important qualities as far as many gardeners are concerned, however, is their smell. Most people have evocative childhood memories of particular flower fragrances, usually associated with a specific garden – often a grandparent's.

Scents

There is nothing quite like the scent of a garden on a summer's day, particularly if associated with the drowsy hum of bees and the fluttering of butterflies. Generally, a warm, sunny day brings out the scents, but there are some that are much more noticeable during or after rain. Scent in a flower is a bonus as far as we are concerned, but nature imbued flowers with it for a reason: to attract pollinators. For this reason, many winter flowers are sweet-smelling. There are not many pollinators around at that time of year and so the flowers have to work particularly hard to attract them.

Some plants throw out their scent with gay abandon and can be smelt at large distances. Others are much more discreet, and you have to put your nose almost into them before the fragrance is detectable. Many of the latter are more apparent once they have been picked and placed in a warm room. Some are only noticeable during the evening as the light fades. Presumably these attract night-flying moths.

The fragrant garden

Not all the plants should be fragrant, or they will become too overpowering and you will be unable to differentiate between the conflicting scents. Place scented plants at key points around the

Sweet Williams, *Dianthus barbatus*, have a very distinctive smell – the kind of smell that often triggers memories such as a garden from your childhood.

Placing fragrant flowers near to a window will often flood the rooms beyond with a wonderful scent, especially on warm, balmy summer evenings.

Plants with scented foliage

Agastache
Anthemis punctata cupaniana
Artemisia
Melittis melissophylum
Mentha
Meum athamanticum
Morina longifolia
Nepeta
Pelargonium graveolens
Perovskia atriplicifolia
Salvia

garden so that there is the impression that the whole garden is perfumed. Also, try if possible to get a spread of plants so that there are scents throughout the seasons, including winter.

Scent-testing

Try to smell your plants before you acquire them, as some may not be as scented as you wish. Breeders of flowers went through a long period when smell was low down on their list of priorities when creating new plants. Thus many modern sweet peas are not sweet at all: they are scentless. Similarly, many modern pinks are without scent.

Another reason for trying out scents, either in other gardens or at the point of sale, is that you may not like the fragrance of some plants: they may be too sweet and sickly or they may bring back certain unpleasant memories.

Siting fragrant flowers

Fragrant flowers can be placed anywhere you like in the garden, but there are some situations where they are a must. One of the best positions is near places where you sit and relax, as soothing scents will help to recharge your batteries.

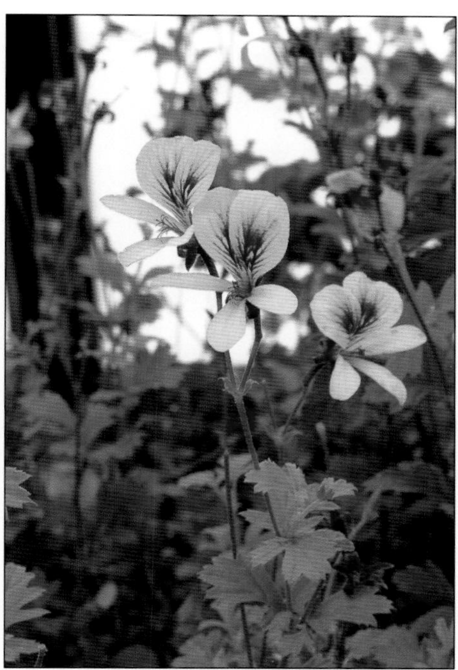

Many pelargoniums have scented foliage, with the fragrances offered by different varieties ranging from citrus fruits and rose to nutmeg.

Another good place is near windows or doors, so that the scent wafts into the house when the flowers open during a warm day or evening.

Placing fragrant plants next to the driveway, so that you notice them as you get out of the car, is a wonderful way of indicating to the senses that you have arrived home after work, and certainly helps you to relax.

Scents to avoid

Not all plants emit a pleasant scent, and some, such as those that attract flies as pollinators, are downright putrid. However attractive the flowers, *Dracunculus vulgaris*, for example, is not a plant to place near the house. Other cases are not quite so clear cut. Examples such as *Phuopsis stylosa* or *Lilium pyrenaicum* smell of foxes, which some people find repulsive, while others find it mildly attractive.

Fragrant foliage

It is not only flowers that can be scented: a lot of plant foliage is too. In some cases, as with flowers, warmth brings out the fragrance, but in most cases the leaves or stems have to be crushed in order to release it. In extreme cases, such as lawn chamomile, *Chamaemelum nobile* 'Treneague', or thyme, the plants are best placed under foot, so that as you walk on them you send up clouds of scent. With most fragrantly foliaged plants, however, it is best to site them near to a path, so that you can run your fingers through them as you walk by.

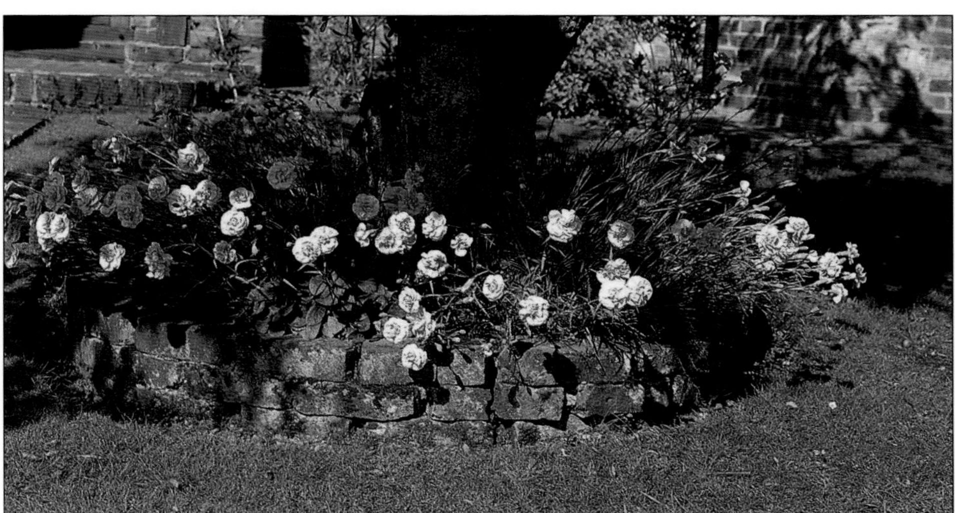

Pinks (*Dianthus*), both the annual and perennial types, provide a distinctively old-fashioned fragrance to borders. Here, the plant used is *D.* 'Doris'.

Colour gardens

All plants are coloured, so what is a "colour" garden? Well, some gardeners like to use particular colour schemes, choosing either all pastel or all bright colours, for example, rather than just dotting colour around the garden at random. A favourite idea is to create a border or even a whole garden of a single colour – a particularly popular choice being white.

Here an exciting, vibrant border has been created, composed entirely of a well-selected range of hot colours such as golds, oranges and reds. These sorts of colours make us feel energetic and dynamic, so they may not be the best choice for a corner where you go to unwind.

Choosing colours

We all know what colours are, although we may see them slightly differently. What we don't all agree on is which colours are pleasing and which are not. Inevitably, because we are all different, our feelings about certain colours or combinations vary dramatically. Therefore, although there may seem to be codes or formulas for colour use, it is important to do what pleases you; after all, the garden is for you. For a long time, mixing oranges and purples would have been deemed one of the worst sins in gardening, but now influential gardeners are much more adventurous and many will readily combine these colours.

Arranging colours

Using colours in drifts can make a big impact in a garden, and if the drifts are planted so that they merge harmoniously rather than jump suddenly from one extreme to another, then so much the better. In this way mauves might merge into blues, and yellows into oranges, creating a soft, fluid design that leads the eye around the garden.

If you want to create something more eye-catching, then try planting contrasting colours such as orange and mauve together. If you are not brave enough to put them right next to each other, use a foliage plant between them to soften the impact. As with so many other aspects of designing gardens, it is best to see how other people use colour and then follow those ideas that you like.

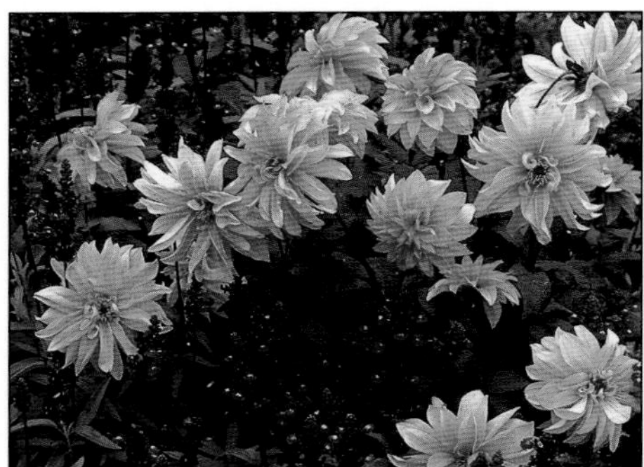

Contrasting colours can make a bold visual statement. These pinkish-orange dahlias stand out vividly against the deep blue salvias.

Creating different moods

Colours can have a significant effect on our mood. Hot colours such as oranges and flame reds are lively and exciting, whereas the lighter pastel colours are cool and soothing. Dark purples are sombre and heavy and, if overdone in a garden, can produce a leaden appearance.

Single-colour gardens

Experimental gardeners can have great fun by devoting a border or even a whole garden to a single bloom colour – white is an especially popular choice. Such gardens are not truly just one colour anyway, because you have to take the foliage into account. So, a "white" garden is usually made up of white, green and perhaps silver and grey. Even the white may vary from a creamy or a yellowish white to bluish-white, and it takes a fair amount of skill to balance these different variations.

Soft, pastel colours can create a tranquil, peaceful feeling. Here, pink alliums mix with white geraniums and blue salvias.

A border devoted to white flowers creates a very peaceful atmosphere. Surprisingly, using just one colour need never be boring.

White flowers

Achillea ptarmica
Anaphalis margaritacea
Anemone x *hybrida* 'Honorine Jobert'
Anemone nemorosa
Antirrhinum majus
Argyranthemum frutescens
Bellis
Campanula latiloba alba
Convallaria majalis
Crambe cordifolia
Dianthus
Dicentra spectabile 'Alba'
Digitalis purpurea 'Alba'
Epilobium angustifolium 'Album'
Geranium sanguineum 'Album'
Gypsophila paniculata
Iberis sempervirens
Lamium maculatum 'White Nancy'
Lathyrus
Leucanthemum 'Everest'
Lilium
Lysimachia clethroides
Nicotiana sylvestris
Omphalodes linifolia
Osteospermum 'Whirligig'
Paeonia
Penstemon 'White Bedder'
Petunia
Phlox paniculata 'Fujiama'
Polygonatum x *hybridum*
Ranunculus aconitifolius
Romneya coulteri
Smilacina
Viola
Zantedeschia aethiopica

Two-colour gardens

This variation on the single-colour planting idea involves a border, or whole garden, being planted with two different colours. White and gold or yellow and blue are two popular and pleasing combinations. The two colours can be equal in quantity or mainly one with a touch of the other as a contrast.

Hot colours

Vibrant and exciting bright orange, flame red and orange-yellow can be great fun to play with. They attract the eye and can create a focal point in the garden. But, like parties, they are great fun once in a while but can lose their appeal if done to excess. Certainly, a whole garden planted in these colours would become tiring after a short while, so it is better to create just one border or a part of a border, placing them in key positions. They can also look effective on the far side of a pond.

Contrasting colours

Using colours that contrast particularly boldly with each other can add drama to a border and will draw the eye. Many people find that some contrasting colours are more acceptable than others. Most would agree that bright red looks fabulous with green, for example, but they may be more reserved about other combinations, such as orange with purple. As with hot colours, gardeners should always bear in mind that dramatic contrasts can begin to jar if used too much.

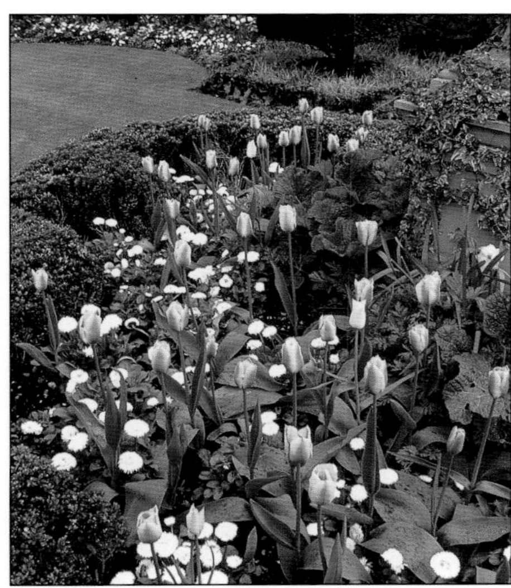
You can create a white garden in spring, as seen here, and then change the plants to have a "hot" red garden in the summer.

The hotter colours may be dramatic and thrilling, but remember that even excitement can become boring if it is overdone, and you certainly don't want to produce something that amounts to a visual assault. Restricting bold colours to one border is often much more pleasing.

Water gardens

Water has been one of the basic building blocks of decorative gardens since gardens first began. Whether it is still or moving, it has a calming tranquillity about it that sums up the essence of a garden. Water can be used in a wide variety of ways, including features that are suitable for the smaller garden.

What are water features?

There is a wide range of possibilities for using water in the garden, ranging from lakes in big ones to just a dustbin lid full of water in a small one. Water can be used in the form of a static pond or pool, or it can be used as a stream, with all the movement that implies. Streams can involve cascades, waterfalls and pools, and can become a striking feature of the garden. It is also possible to use water in such a way that there is no standing water at all, just water seeping between fixed pebbles.

All these possibilities can involve plants in one way or another, allowing you to use plants and to create effects that a garden without water cannot achieve.

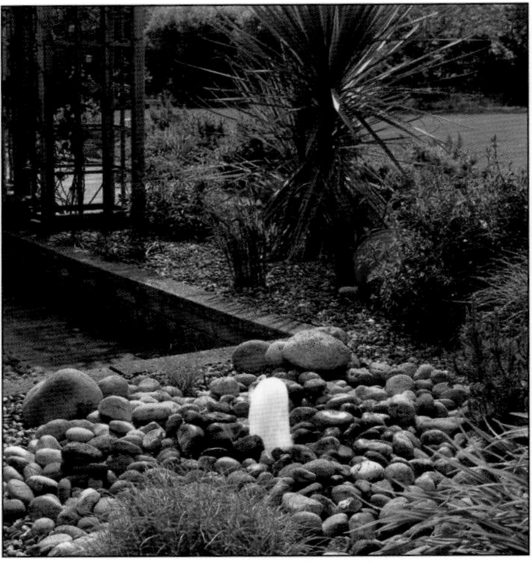

Water features do not need to contain any standing water. Here, bubble fountains give sound and image without the dangers.

Areas of contrast

Water complements the plants in a garden beautifully. It can create tranquil, reflective areas as a contrast to some lively planting, or it can bustle along in a stream, in contrast to the static plants, creating a sparkling streak of silver. Water can also produce noise, such as the tinkling of a fountain or the more regular pouring of a waterspout. The movement of water in a stream can also be very soothing to watch.

Wildlife

One of the many reasons why gardeners like ponds and other water features in their gardens is that they attract wildlife. They produce a source of drinking and bathing water for a large number of birds and insects, and ponds can also attract toads. Other animals, especially nocturnal ones, may drink from a pond at night. Such wildlife is attracted not only to the water but also to the plants that surround it, which furnish them with valuable cover and food.

Plants and water

One of the advantages of having a water feature is that it lets you extend the range of plants featured in your garden to include those that enjoy growing in or around water.

Some plants, such as water lilies, thrive in the deep water itself, while others prefer the shallow water margins, where they can get their roots down into the mud. Other plants like the muddy edges of a pond, where they are generally out of

Different types of garden can always be combined. This is a water garden where colour effects have also been created – using flowers in gold and white.

You can create water gardens on a modest scale, as this stream and pool demonstrate.

Water allows the gardener to use plants that cannot be grown in any other way. These water lilies are a prime example.

the water but where their roots are occasionally submerged. Another group, such as hostas and rodgersias, like the area next to the pond, which is out of water but still damp, while mimulus and many primulas relish being planted beside a stream, where they are occasionally splashed and where the air is nice and buoyant. The range of plants within all these different groups is enormous.

Waterside plants

Aruncus	*Lysichiton*
Astilbe	*Lysimachia*
Caltha	*Lythrum*
Cardamine	*Mimulus*
Cimifuga	*Onoclea sensibilis*
Darmera peltata	*Osmunda regalis*
Eupatorum	*Peltiphyllum peltatum*
Filipendula	*Persicaria bistorta*
Gunnera	*Phragmites*
Hosta	*Primula*
Iris ensata	*Rheum*
Iris sibirica	*Rodgersia*
Ligularia	*Trollius*
Lobelia cardinallis	

Bog gardens

Many of the plants that like growing on the margins of ponds can be grown to really great effect in a bog garden. This is commonly defined as an area that has a great deal of moisture-retaining humus in the soil, so that it never dries out, though this does not mean that it has to be squelchy. If, for any reason, you want to get rid of a pond, rather than filling it in you can simply puncture the lining so that the water drains away, and then fill it up with some fibrous material to make your perfect bog garden.

Safety

Water can be dangerous, especially to young children, so very careful thought must be given before you start to dig deep holes in your garden for ponds of any kind. There are various attractive compromises. It is possible to create relatively safe features in which water bubbles out of, say, a rock and then disappears between fixed stones into a safe underground reservoir. This idea leaves no surface water, which can prove to be dangerous.

A pond can be especially appealing if it is designed so that it blends in with the rest of the garden, adding to the overall scene rather than being a totally separate feature. Placing water features where they are "discovered" as something of a surprise also adds a delightful touch.

Specialist flower gardens

The majority of people grow plants in order to create an attractive garden in which they can relax and enjoy themselves. Others, however, do so because they simply enjoy the process of growing plants or even need to grow plants. In the latter cases, the actual appearance of the garden will be of less importance than the plants it produces.

Cut flowers

These are an important part of many people's lives. Most gardeners cut a few flowers for the house, but some grow plants especially for that very purpose, devoting part or even all of the garden to producing them. Rows of flowering sweet peas or plants with attractive foliage such as hostas are their common fare. Most people don't need to have their whole garden turned over to the production of flowers for cutting, but some gardeners enjoy providing displays for churches or hospitals or even selling them at local markets.

For them it is important to know which plants can be used as cut stems and which last longest in water. There are many old favourites, but it is often exciting to discover new ones from the vast range of plants that gardeners have at their beck and call, so it is always worth experimenting. Buy one plant of something that might be suitable. Try it and, if it works, propagate it so that you have a row of unusual material.

The average gardener does not want to devote the whole garden to cut flowers and probably doesn't have room for even a border of such things. It is, however, easy to incorporate a number of plants for cutting among the other plants in the borders. Wigwams of sweet peas, for example, look good as well as providing cut material.

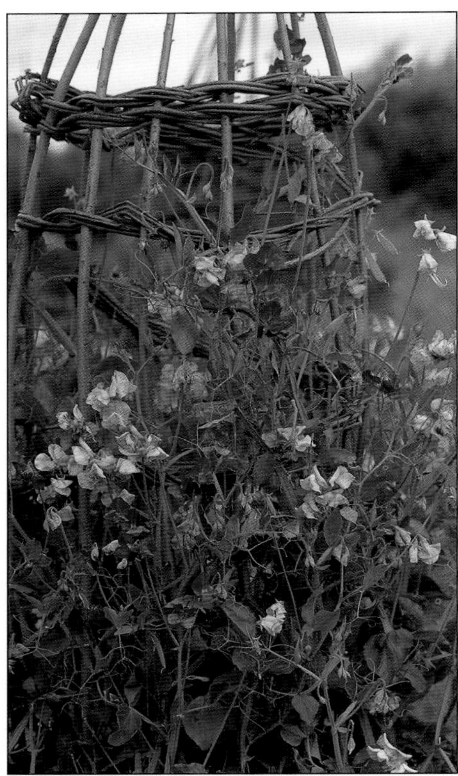

Sweet peas are typically grown for exhibition and cut flower purposes and need not be grown in the main decorative beds.

Phlox makes an excellent cut flower. As well as being grown in special beds for cutting, phlox is a good choice for borders.

Flower shows

There is a long tradition, especially among cottage gardeners, of growing plants for exhibition. Most tend these days to be local affairs, where there are mixed shows, but there are still a number of local and national shows that are devoted in whole or in part to one type of flower. Thus sweet peas, chrysanthemums and dahlias are still popular with exhibitors. Pinks (*Dianthus*), auriculas, and irises are also still shown fairly extensively.

These plants can be grown in the general borders, but growing them in separate beds, albeit more practical than attractive, means that the gardener can tend them easily and bring them on to their very best.

Specialist growers

Some gardeners are interested in particular plants, often to the exclusion of others. They may grow them as part of a decorative garden or they may grow them in special beds designed to suit their particular plants. Examples of some of the more popular groups of plants for growing in general beds are hellebores, geraniums and hostas.

Some collectors with large collections, however, grow them in beds devoted to their specialization. These plants will often need special growing conditions, and so lovers of alpine plants will construct special raised beds where the soil is very free-draining, while those interested in hellebores may well construct shade beds made with wooden frames covered with shade netting. These may not be the most elegant of gardens, but they serve the purpose for which the gardener requires them and certainly suit the needs of the plants, as the conditions are tailor made for them.

There are many flowers in the garden that can be cut for drying. This perennial, *Anaphalis nepalenis*, is just one good example.

Small nurseries

There are certain gardeners who get so passionate about plants that they are not content with the confines of their own garden and may want to start growing them for everybody else as well. What might have started out as a conventional garden soon turns into a small nursery. Frequently, such a garden will contain plants planted randomly in stock beds, so that they are readily available for propagation. It will also contain lots of plants grown in pots, ready for sale.

Flowers for cutting

Acanthus	*Delphiniums*
Achillea	*Eryngium*
Alstroemeria	*Gypsophila*
Aster	*Heliopsis*
Callistephus chinensis	*Lathyrus odoratus*
	Liatris
Chrysanthemum	*Molucella*
Convallaria majalis	*Physalis*
Dahlia	*Rudbeckia*
Dianthus	*Solidago*

Other ways of gardening

None of these types of gardens may be conventional but they are certainly all perfectly worthwhile ways of gardening. There are undoubtedly many people who gain a great deal of enjoyment from these kinds of specialist approaches.

Most specialist gardeners are likely to have started out simply by devoting a relatively small plot to their purpose until enthusiasm has really taken over. Such specialization can be exciting and if you succumb you will come to know a great deal about plants.

Growing rare plants

As mentioned before, there are other gardeners who are not especially interested in gardens as such; they are really only interested in growing plants. While they may not specialize in any particular genus or family, they get their enjoyment from growing unusual and rare plants.

One of the reasons that some plants are rare in gardens is straightforward – they are very difficult to grow. This presents a challenge to certain gardeners, who will spend a lot of time making certain that the conditions are just right and giving nurturing attention to individual plants, much more than would be given to normal ones. Many people find this a particularly exciting form of gardening.

Bear in mind that if you want to produce larger flowers, such as the delphiniums shown here, primarily for cutting purposes, then it may be best to grow them in separate beds, as cutting from a decorative bed will leave big gaps.

Container gardens

While most traditional gardens consist of beds, with possibly areas of lawn or hard surface, it is possible to have a garden without these. It is even possible to have a garden on a balcony or rooftop without any access to a conventional garden. The secret? Containers.

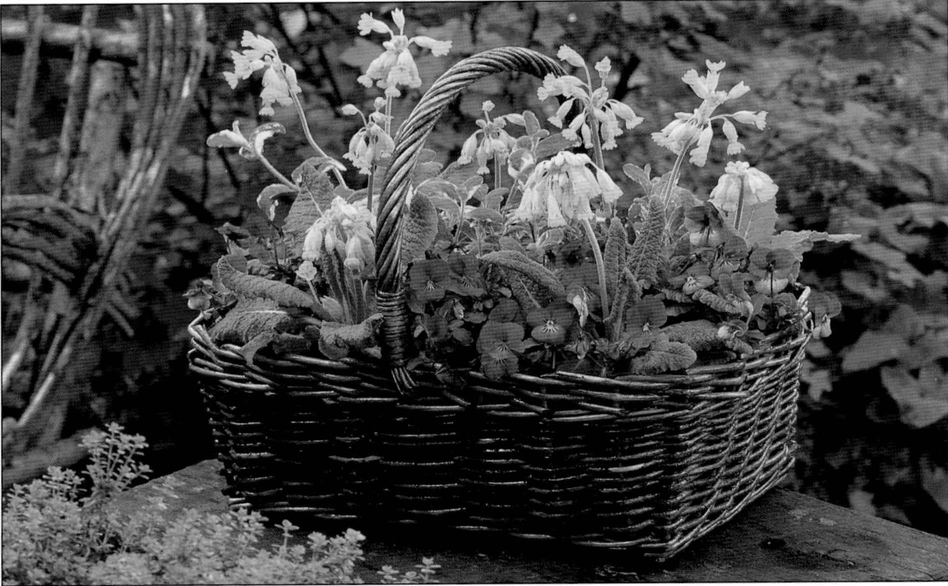

An unusual container of perennial plants. These cowslips (*Primula veris*) and violas provide the perfect colourful and informal combination for this basket.

What are containers?

Plants can be grown in any form of container, from a small yogurt carton to a large terracotta pot. Pots made of plastic or ceramic, as well as wooden barrels and tubs, are frequently used, and there has been an increase in the popularity of metal containers. Although virtually any container can be used to contain plants, it is important to remember the dignity of the plant and avoid planting it in something completely unsuitable. A plastic tub with the name of the product it once contained still on the side, for example, does the plant no favours.

Containers come in a number of forms. The obvious one is a round pot, varying in size from a small terracotta pot to a large ceramic one. Wood is frequently used to construct boxes of various types, including large square Versailles tubs and rectangular window boxes. Containers can also come in the form of baskets. Ordinary willow baskets can be stood on the ground, hiding a lesser container within them, but more usually they are made of metal or plastic and are used as hanging containers.

Where to use containers

Containers can be used anywhere in the garden and are particularly useful for people who have no proper beds or borders. They can be placed on the ground, stood on plinths or walls, hung from poles or walls or stood on balconies and roof gardens.

Pots can be used singly as focal points placed at the end of paths or on the top of steps. A large,

Containers can be seasonal, such as this lovely spring bouquet of primroses and violets. Plants from these containers can be planted out in the garden after flowering.

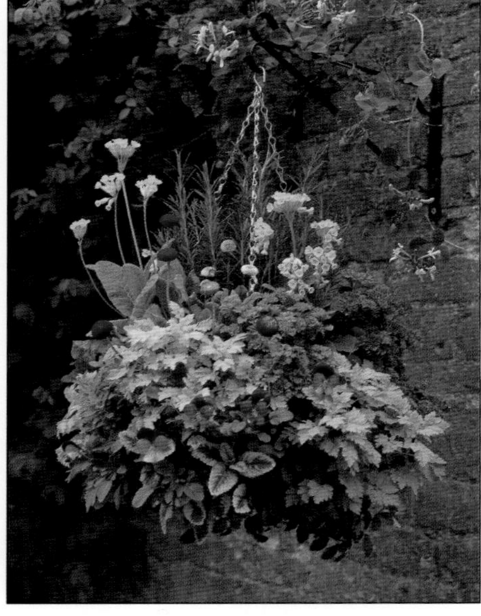

Perennials can even be used in hanging baskets. Violas, cowslips, and feverfew feature here.

Containers need not be filled with flowering colour, as these foliage plants show. Grasses are particularly successful container choices.

A collection of pots can be used as a substitute for a border in a small garden. To change the design, all you need do is move the pots around.

stunning pot containing a plant with good architectural qualities will certainly draw the eye.

Used in pairs, pots make good punctuation points when placed on either side of gateways, archways or other entrances. A pair of terracotta pots containing standard box trees on either side of a front door can transform the entrance into something very stylish. Similarly, a pair of pots on either side of the bottom or top of a flight of stairs is very effective.

When arranged in groups, pots tend to look best if they are different sizes, especially if the plants at the back are taller than those at the front. In formal gardens, a series of containers with similar content can be placed at intervals down a path or around a pool.

Plants for containers

Agapanthus	*Hosta*
Ageratum	*Impatiens*
Alonsoa	*Lobelia*
Argyranthemum	*Nemisia*
Begonia	*Pelargonium*
Bellis	*Petunia*
Bidens ferulifolia	*Phormium*
Brachycome iberidifolia	*Primula*
Cordyline australis	*Senecio cinerea*
Diascia	*Tagetes*
Felicia amelloides	*Tropaeolum*
Helichrysum petiolare	*Verbena* x *hybrida*
	Viola x *wittrockiana*

Mobility

Pots can be moved around the garden, giving you the opportunity to change the scene throughout the seasons. Plants that are out of flower can be tucked away and brought out when the blooms break open. They can also be moved into areas of a border or bed that happen to be rather dull at the time. Large pots are very heavy once full of soil, so it is important to get help when moving them.

Container plants

A wide range of plants can be used in containers. In fact, virtually any plant is suitable, although those with long taproots tend to be unhappy unless the pot is really deep.

Some plants are used almost exclusively in containers. Trailing plants, for example, have been bred especially for hanging baskets and window boxes. Although annuals are the most popular for temporary baskets, which last for only one season, perennials can be useful for more permanent settings. Many, such as agapanthus, are flowering, but some, such as hostas and ferns, are used as foliage plants to add substance to any grouping of pots.

Colour in a pot

Containers can be used to add gaiety to a scene, and these are usually bursting with bright colours. There is no reason, however, why the colours should not be more subdued and subtle. A container with a single colour can frequently be more effective than one with many colours, and the colours can be combined by grouping the pots.

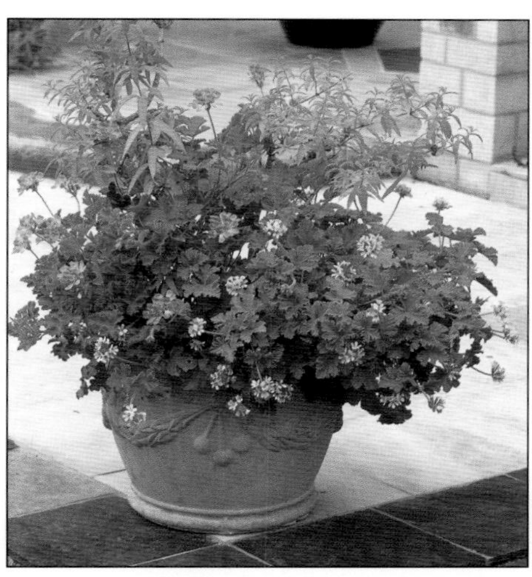

Containers do not have to be complicated creations. Here, a couple of pelargoniums give plenty of foliage and flower interest.

Pulmonarias are grown as flowering plants for spring, but if they are cut back after flowering, the new foliage will remain fresh throughout the summer.

Prickly foliage may make a plant difficult to weed around, but it does provide a contrast to the surrounding leaves.

The texture can be velvety, rough or smooth. A velvety texture gives the plant interest, and the tiny hairs that give the feeling of velvet can add a greyish-white bloom to the leaves. Rough leaves may often be dull, whereas smooth leaves are frequently shiny and bright.

The shape is very important. Some plants have long, spiky leaves, while others can be almost round, with or without lobes and/or serrations, with lots of variations in between these two extremes. A mixture of shapes makes a border more interesting, especially when contrasting shapes are used. On the other hand, using plants with leaves of the same shape can make the border more calming and tranquil, though there is inevitably an inherent danger of also making it more boring.

Foliage as a background

While an eye-catching garden can be created entirely out of interesting foliage, it is more common to use a combination of foliage and flowers to create your composition. Most borders consist of a mixture of plants grown specifically for their foliage and other foliage plants that provide an especially effective backdrop for the flowers.

Green will act as the perfect background to most colours, but works particularly well with its complementary colour, red. Silver works well with softer colours, although a bright red or magenta will stand out beautifully against it. Purple is a difficult colour as a background, as it can become very leaden if used in excess, but it works well with contrasting orange and flame colours.

Foliage as foliage

Leaves are quite capable of being a feature on their own. There may not be such a wide variety of foliage colours as there are for flowers, but there are still enough to paint a picture solely made up of leaves, especially when taking shape and texture into account too.

One advantage of a purely foliage garden is that it has a much longer season than one devoted to flowers. In fact, if you take evergreen plants into account, the foliage garden is always in season. However, most plants flower at some point, so few gardens are devoted entirely to foliage, though some foliage purists cut off flower stems as they appear.

Foliage works particularly well in shady or woodland-type areas, and the addition of some variegated foliage here and there will add welcome touches of lightness.

A border devoted to silver foliage works well, but most silver-leaved plants grow only in sunny situations, so you will need to plan your borders accordingly.

Ferns are superb foliage plants to use in shady positions. They act as a brilliant foil for flowering plants.

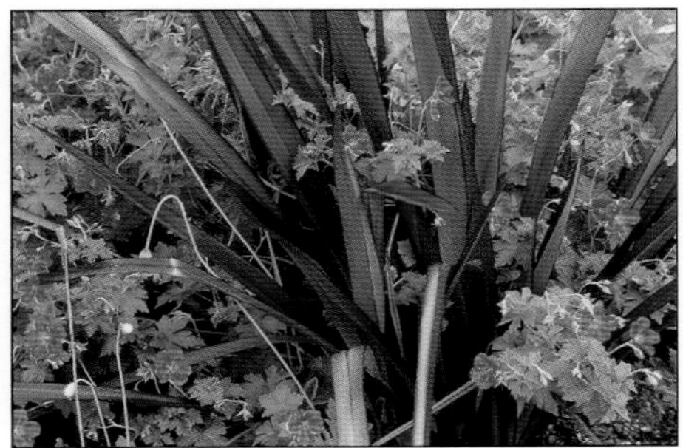

Dramatic effects can often be created if interesting or bold shapes are used, as in these sword-like leaves.

Differently shaped plants

Some plants have such a dominant shape that they are always bound to catch the eye. A great fountain of pampas grass (*Cortaderia*) is a good example, or the jagged candelabra of the giant biennial Scotch thistle (*Onopordum*), which towers above the viewer. These spectacular plants are invaluable in the garden as focal points, since they catch the eye.

Architectural plants – those with usefully sculptural shapes – can be placed in a border to heighten its interest or in places such as at the end of a path or the end of the garden, often in splendid isolation. They can be planted in the ground or in pots. Either way, they act as living sculptures and provide features that immediately attract the eye.

Such plants work well in a formal garden, used singly as centrepieces or planted at intervals along either a path or border to give a sense of rhythm. Sometimes large plants are necessary to complete the scene. For example, the giant leaves of *Gunnera manicata* look perfect beside a large pond, while not many garden sights can better a stand of *Stipa gigantea* set by itself where the evening sun can shine through its leaves.

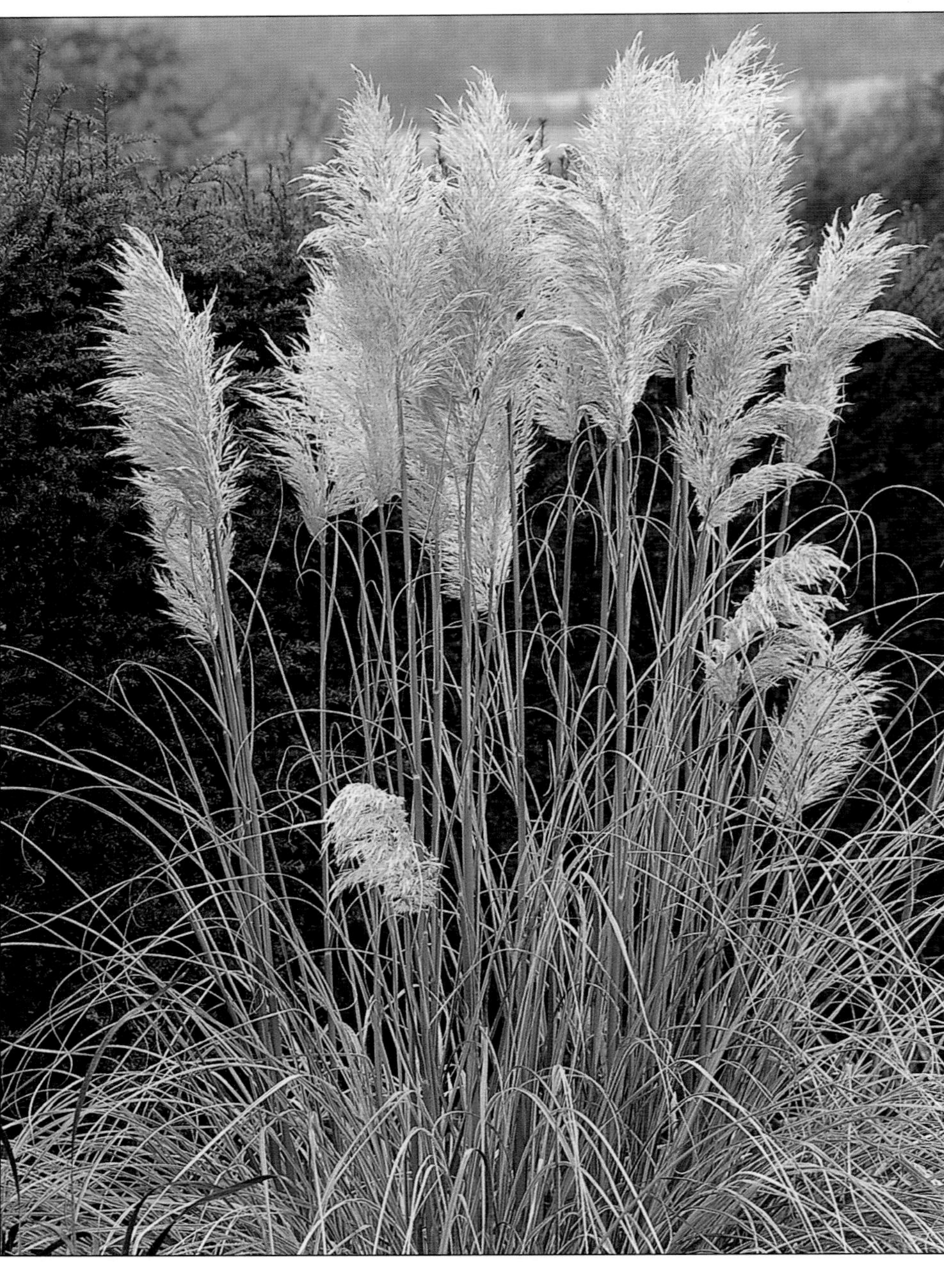

The ever-popular pampas grass, *Cortaderia*, is a particularly stately plant and is extremely eye-catching, whether grown by itself or as part of a border.

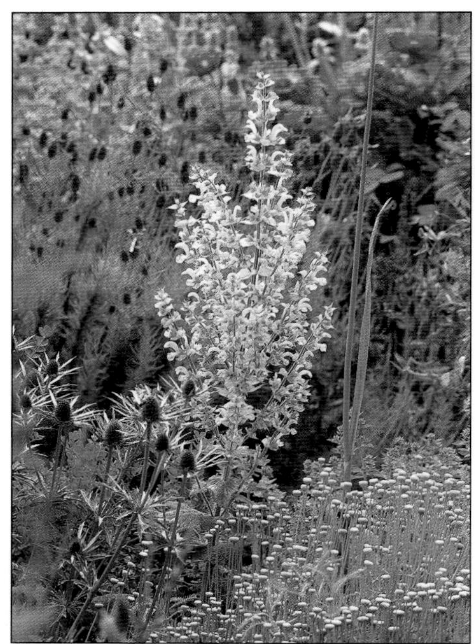

Salvia sclarea's upright nature makes it, quite literally, stand out in the crowd, creating a focal point in this border.

A vast choice of shapes

Next time you visit a large garden, take a look at the wide variety of shapes there are among the plants. Some are tall and thin, others are flat and mat-like. In some the leaves erupt like a fountain, while in others the foliage forms a tight clump, frequently in rounded hummocks, perhaps even a ball. All these different shapes can be used to great advantage to give variation within the bed or border.

Close-up shots of flowers on packets of seeds or on pot labels usually show the flower in detail but rarely the whole plant. You need to check the plant out, either in a book

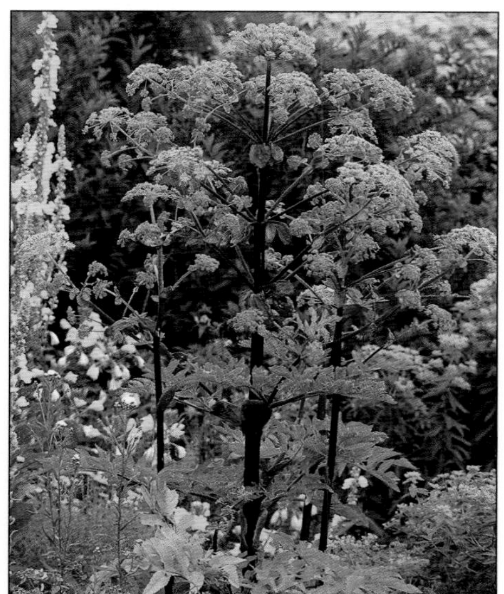

The tall stems and rounded flower heads of this angelica create a distinctive, cloud-like image in the border that sets it apart.

or by looking at it in another garden, to see what shape it will have. The shape of the flowers, and their colour, can also add to a plant's architectural quality. *Liatris*, for example, erupts like fireworks, while *Limnanthes* forms a carpet.

Working with plant height

The general rule of thumb with regard to heights is perfectly sensible – plant the shorter plants at the front and the taller ones at the back. This can, however, produce a very regimented picture, rather like a school choir, so try to vary this slightly by bringing some taller plants forwards. This will break the formality and also obscure some plants, so that they are revealed only as you walk along the length of the border, making it more interesting.

There are some plants, such as *Verbena bonariensis*, that, while tall, are also very sparse and wiry. Such plants can be planted towards the front of the border, where they will create a misty effect as you look through them to the plants behind.

Working with different shapes

Finding good ways to work with plant shapes is more complex than working with height. Learn by looking at other gardens and deciding what you think works well. Contrasting shapes certainly make a border more interesting. So, the sword-like leaves of an iris contrast well when planted in front of the giant leaves of a *Rheum* (ornamental rhubarb) or the filigree foliage of *Myrrhis* (sweet cicely). Likewise, frothy grasses or the sword-like spikes of an iris work well with the more substantially leaved hostas.

Plants with useful sculptural shapes

Acanthus spinosus
Alcea rosea
Angelica archangelica
Cortaderia selloana
Crambe cordifolia
Cynara cardunculus
Delphinium
Gunnera manicata
Inula magnifica
Ligularia
Macleaya cordata
Miscanthus sinensis
Onopordum
Phormium tenax
Rheum
Ricinus
Stipa gigantea
Telekia speciosa
Verbascum

Here, sword-like, spiky leaves draw the eye up and away, and in doing so create a sudden burst of energy in the middle of the border.

Ground-cover plants

Very few gardeners have as much time to spend in their gardens as they would wish, and so anything that helps to save them some time in the garden is well worth considering. Ground cover is one such valuable aid: it cuts down the amount of weeding needed, and covers large areas with just one plant, so saving on planting.

What are ground-cover plants?

They are exactly what the name suggests: plants that cover the ground. Some are creeping plants that spread out to form a dense mat, others are a large planting of individual plants, each one merging into the next to provide a close mass. Most tend to be low-growing, though this is not essential, and any dense-growing plant will suffice. Some gardeners consider any plants grown closely together as ground cover, but the term is usually reserved for those plants that have a proven record for dense growth.

Most ground-cover plants flower at some point, but they are mainly used as foliage plants, which ensures that they cover the ground for the maximum length of time. Many can simply be left until they die back naturally, but others, such as pulmonarias, are best sheared over at the end of flowering so that they acquire a set of fresh and more attractive leaves.

A perfect bank of *Geranium macrorrhizum*, one of the most useful of ground cover plants for creating an effectively impenetrable layer.

Purposes of ground cover

There are several reasons for using ground cover. The first and most obvious one is that a dense covering of plants inhibits the germination and growth of weeds from beneath them. In other words, it cuts down the amount of weeding that is required for the area they cover.

Another use is to cover large areas with attractive plants. This is particularly important in large gardens, where there are often areas that need planting but are not suitable for borders, such as under trees, where a carpet of plants can be very attractive.

A third use of ground cover is to deal with areas that are difficult to cultivate. Banks, for example, may be awkward to cope with, as are those barren strips of earth in the middle of some driveways, which are the perfect place for thymes or similar low-growing plants.

Limitations of ground cover

Ground cover is not all good news, however. There are some downsides, particularly if you have only a small garden, where space is a premium

Geranium macrorrhizum will grow in dry conditions in fairly dark shade, and yet it not only gives good leaf cover, but also provides attractive flowers.

Use plants such as *Pratia* to carpet and soften paving that is not walked on.

(though for larger gardens the advantages certainly outweigh the disadvantages).

The first is that a large spread of the same plant can be rather boring. This may not trouble you if you are not over-interested in plants as such but just want to keep your garden tidy. However, many gardeners feel that they would rather use their space for different plants, creating a more interesting scene.

The second disadvantage is that ground cover is not quite as efficient as it is often portrayed to be. Any perennial weeds left in the ground when it was prepared will certainly penetrate the cover, and any thinning of the cover will allow in light and aid the germination of weed seed. So it is essential to prepare the soil thoroughly in the first place, removing all traces of weeds, and then to make certain that the plants are in the best of health and maintain their tight cover. Shearing them over from time to time helps to keep them dense.

The third problem is rubbish. So often ground-cover areas are left to themselves, and they have a habit of catching any pieces of paper or other bits of rubbish that blow past. You just need to remember to check the plants every so often and remove any rubbish that has accumulated.

Ground-cover plants

Acaena
Alchemilla mollis
Anemone x *hybrida*
Bergenia
Brunnera macrophylla
Convallaria majalis
Crambe cordifolia
Epimedium
Euphorbia amygdaloides robbiae
Geranium x *cantabrigiense*
Geranium endressii
Geranium macrorrhizum
Geranium nodusum
Geranium x *oxonianum*
Gunnera
Hosta
Houtuynia cordata
Lysimachia nummularia
Maianthemum
Persicaria affinis
Petasites
Pulmonaria
Rheum
Rodgersia
Symphytum
Tiarella cordifolia
Tolmiea menziesii
Vancouveria

Hostas always provide good ground cover, as long as the soil is not too dry. Use a mix of the different varieties to inject more visual interest.

Climbing plants

Most climbing plants are shrubby, but there are a number of herbaceous perennials and annuals that can be used to great effect as climbers in the garden. They have the advantage over shrubby climbers in that there is no complicated pruning regime: they are simply cut back or removed at the end of the season.

Climbing and scrambling

Most of the herbaceous and annual climbers are really scramblers rather than true climbers. Ivy, for example, will stick to any surface, and honeysuckle will twine its way up anything. In other words, they can scramble up through other plants, using them for support, rather than twining their way up a pole. Nasturtiums, for example, will not climb up a simple tripod or post but will happily scramble up through a bush, to a surprising height.

The few true climbers include the golden hop (*Humulus lupulus* 'Aureus'), which will climb up poles or even a thin string or wire. Sweet peas are another good example: they have tendrils and can cling to their support, but are often helped by being tied in at regular intervals.

Vertical planting

A three-dimensional garden is much more interesting than one on a single level: by adding height you break the monotony of a flat appearance. Height can be achieved by tall plants but further height can be obtained by using climbers held on a variety of poles, trellises or other supports.

Supports

A wide variety of supports can be used. Being mainly scramblers, most herbaceous and annual climbers are best grown through some form of twiggy framework. This could be pea sticks (branches of trees or shrubs such as hazel cut in winter) stuck in the ground. Alternatively, the climbers can be allowed to scramble up through a low-growing shrub, often providing colour after the shrub has finished flowering. Another option is a tripod of poles with string or netting wrapped round it to give the plant support.

For true climbers, such as hops or *Cobaea*, poles, strings, trellises or frameworks can be used. These can also be used by scrambling plants, as long as they are tied to the supports.

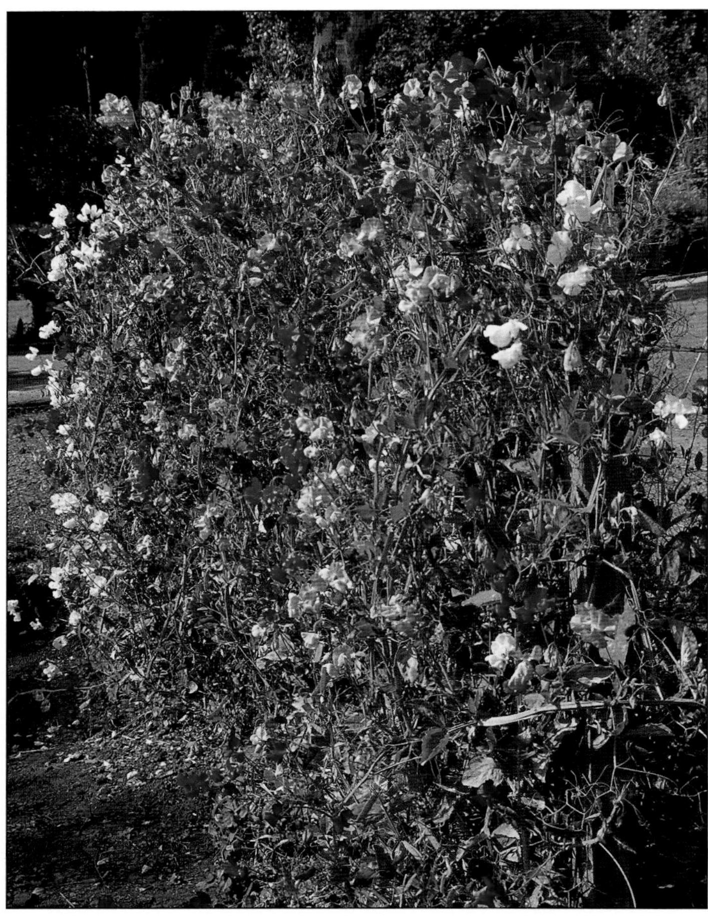

Sweet peas are probably the most widely grown of all annual climbers. They work in so many different types and styles of gardening.

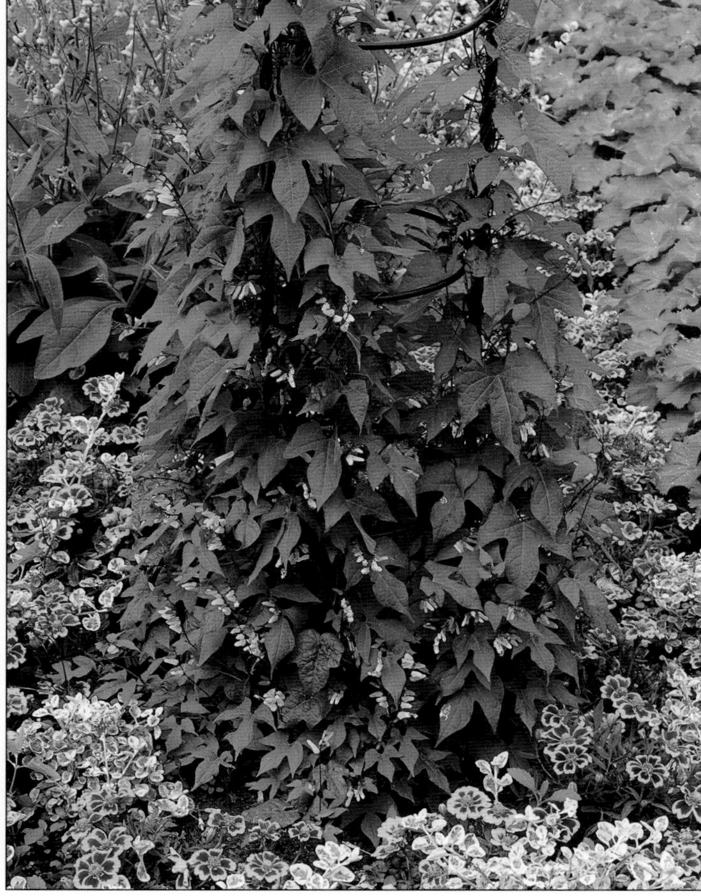

Ipomoea lobata is a valuable annual climber and is one of the few that works well in colourful or exotic bedding schemes.

Lablab purpureus has become a very popular annual climber, partly because of its pea-like flowers and seed pods and partly due to its attractive purple foliage.

Marginal planting

While height can be used anywhere you like in the garden, one of the more favoured areas is around the margins. This is partly because this will form a backdrop to the rest of the garden and partly because it can be used to screen out neighbouring gardens or buildings. Trellising provides a good support for this kind of position.

Another way of using climbers around the margins is to use them on walls. Here they may cover an ugly wall or simply be used to break up its expanse. The most likely reason for keen gardeners, however, is that it is simply an available space on which yet another plant can be grown.

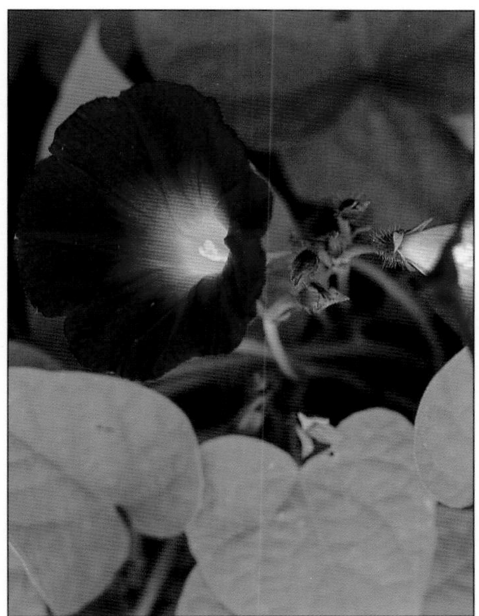
Convolvulus tricolor 'Royal Ensign' has long been a popular favourite and is widely grown for its lovely flowers.

Different heights

With the exception of hops, the annual *Caiophera* and one or two others, herbaceous and annual climbers are not very vigorous and will not climb to great heights.

Those that can reach greater heights, however, can be used to climb over a frame to form an arbour or a pergola. Hops, for example, create a wonderfully dappled shade that is perfect for sitting under.

Less energetic climbers can also be used in conjunction with more vigorous shrubby climbers. For example, *Eccremocarpus* will grow to advantage through the bare base of clematis, which often shed their lower leaves.

Extending the season

Growing climbers through shrubs or other plants can add to the length of the flowering season. Most annual and perennial climbers flower from midsummer onwards, as the plants have to put on quite a large amount of growth before they bloom. Many shrubs flower in spring, after which they can be considered a foliage plant, but growing a late-flowering climber through them gives them another lease of life. Virtually all perennial and annual climbers can be used in this way.

Climbing plants

Caiophera
Clematis erecta
Clematis x *durandii*
Clematis heracleifolia
Clematis jouiana
Cobaea scandens
Convolvulus tricolor
Eccremocarpus scaber
Humulus lupulus 'Aureus'
Ipomoea
Lablab purpureus (syn. *Dolichos lablab*)
Lagenaria
Lathyrus
Mikania scandens
Rhodochiton atrosanguineum
Solanum dulcamara 'Variegatum'
Thunbergia alata
Tropaeolum

The golden hop, *Humulus lupulus* 'Aureus', is a fast-growing perennial climber that will densely cover a pergola, arbour or framework.

Gardening techniques

Gardening is one of those imprecise sciences in which there are often several ways of achieving the same results – and equally enthusiastic proponents for each different method. For example, one of the most successful commercial propagators achieves incredible results simply by pushing cuttings straight into the compost (soil mix), leaves and all, yet most other gardeners would throw up their hands in horror at this.

Having said that, there are many basic routines and techniques that are universally accepted as working well and which have been proved by constant use over many centuries. Many of these are included in this section. The best approach is to start by following the advice given here, but if you find that certain things work better for you when you use another method, then by all means stick with that. All our garden environments – soils, climates and plantings – are different, as is the temperament of each gardener, so it is not surprising that techniques will vary from garden to garden.

What follows are reliable, widely accepted routines recommended to achieve and maintain an attractive garden – in particular, one filled with annuals and perennials. However, since the techniques are basic ones that apply generally to all kinds of gardening, any beginner following them will get a thorough grounding that will be useful in any garden.

The excellent supports for these delphiniums will soon become invisible, hidden by the plants' foliage.

Soil preparation

Preparing the soil properly is one of the most important tasks that a gardener performs. No matter how well you design your garden, you will not get any decent results unless you have taken some trouble in preparation. This is particularly important where perennial plants are concerned, as these will remain in situ for many years without any chance of having their soil revitalized, except at surface level.

Ideal soils

Short of excavating the whole site and replacing it with perfect soil, you will have to manage with the soil that exists in your garden. However, it is possible, and usually desirable, to modify the soil to make it as near perfect as possible.

The perfect soil is a loamy one, which is open to allow free drainage of excess moisture but contains sufficient organic material to retain enough moisture for the plants. But even this ideal soil may need modifying in certain circumstances.

If you grow woodland plants, for example, then more organic material should be added to keep the soil moist, like the leaf mould that naturally forms under the trees. In addition to improving the condition of the soil, this organic material will also provide a great deal of nutrition for the plants. If, on the other hand, you grow Mediterranean-type plants, then they are likely to need sharper drainage, so more grit should be added to the soil.

Improving the soil

The best way to improve soil is to add well-rotted organic material as you dig it over. Make sure that you maintain the soil's levels of nutrition by top-dressing it with more material over the years.

Well-rotted farmyard manure is still one of the best soil conditioners.

Nowadays there is a really wide range of organic material readily available. Some of this will be sold by your local garden centre, but the very best kind is homemade garden compost (soil mix).

Farmyard manure is another excellent organic choice, but this needs to be well rotted before it can be put on the soil, and you may not always have the space – in a place where you don't mind strong smells lingering – to leave it to rot. Stables are a good source of manure, and it can often be had for free as long as you collect it yourself.

As much garden material as possible, such as these spent annuals, should be composted and returned to the soil.

Leaf mould can be made by collecting fallen leaves and allowing them to rot down. The leaves should be collected from your own garden or road, then either placed in a mesh enclosure or put in bags, punctured at intervals to allow air in. Do not go down to the woods and remove leaves from under the trees, as this will upset the natural balance. Bags of composted bark or other material mixed with farmyard manure are sold by garden centres and nurseries.

Avoid using peat, as this breaks down rapidly in the soil, has little nutritive value and is unsound environmentally, as the peat bogs are fast becoming depleted.

Heavy soils also benefit from having grit added to them. The best size is horticultural grit, which is about 4mm/⅛in in diameter.

Composting

Buy or make a compost (soil mix) bin and fill it with any material you cut from the garden: spent plant stems, leaves and flowers, grass cuttings, shredded hedge and shrub trimmings. Also add any non-cooked vegetable waste from the kitchen, such as peelings.

Avoid adding thick layers of just one material, such as grass cuttings, which can go very slimy. It is better to add thinner layers of different materials in order to keep the compost well balanced, and to fork the heap over now and then. Adding more material is a constant process – continue until the box is full.

Ideally, you should have three boxes: one that you are adding to, one that is rotting down and almost ready to use, and one from which you are using the ready compost. Water the material if it is too dry, and keep each box covered. Leave until it has rotted down into a crumbly, sweet-smelling compost.

MAKING A NEW BED

1 Mark out the bed with a garden line or, as here, with canes. It is very important to remove all perennial weeds. Try to do this by hand if possible. If you do use weedkiller, always apply it according to the maker's instructions on the packet, and make sure you leave the bed until all the weeds have died.

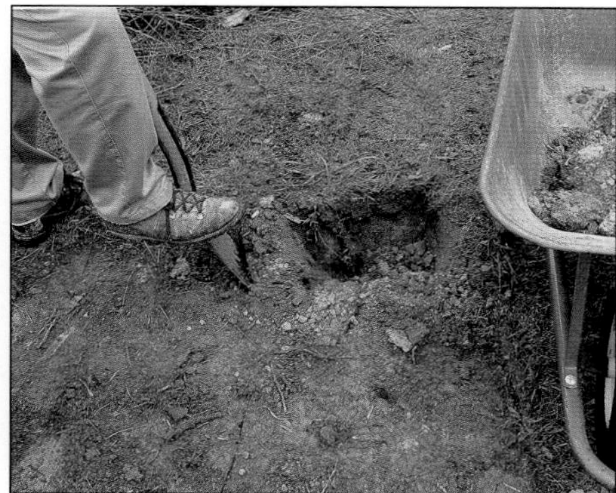

2 Start digging a new bed by making a trench one spade's depth deep across one end. Place the excavated soil into a wheelbarrow and take it to the other end of the plot, where it will be used to fill in the final trench.

3 Now place a layer of well-rotted organic material – such as garden compost (soil mix) or farmyard manure – along the bottom of the trench, breaking it up and spreading it over the soil. Be generous and use as much material as possible.

4 Dig the next row, tipping the soil on top of the compost, filling in the first trench and creating a new one. Add compost to the bottom of this and repeat until the whole plot is dug, leaving the final trench empty.

5 Add a layer of compost to the final trench and then fill it in using the soil excavated from the first trench. The digging is now complete and if time allows, you can leave the bed over the winter so the weather will break the soil down.

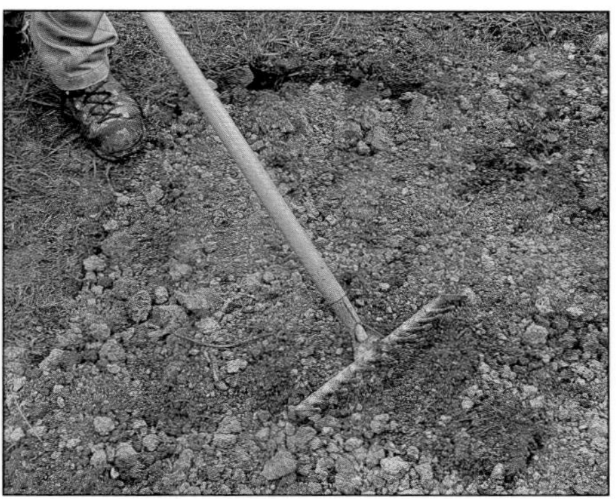

6 If prepared in the autumn, by the spring the weather will have broken down the soil to a fine tilth (consistency). Remove any weeds that have reappeared and then rake over the bed, using the back of the rake to break up any larger lumps if necessary.

Clearing the weeds

It is vital to remove any perennial weeds from the planned borders or beds before you start any planting, as you will never be able to clear them once the plants are growing. With lighter soils, this can be done by digging the beds over and removing the weeds by hand. With heavier soils, it may be necessary to use herbicides. If this is done properly, it should be a one-off operation and there will be no need to reapply chemicals, so no damage will be done to the environment.

You can cover the area to be cleared with black plastic or an old carpet to stop weed growth, but this must be left in place for up to two years to be certain that the tougher weeds have died off. Unless the bed is out of sight, you may not want to have this unattractive covering on view for such a long time.

Organic materials

Garden compost (soil mix)
Farmyard manure
Leaf mould
Spent mushroom compost
Seaweed
Spent hops
Composted bark

Digging the soil

Always aim to dig soil over several months before the bed is to be planted, adding in organic material as you go and removing any weeds. Leave it for three or four months and then remove any weeds that have returned or resprouted. Fork or rake the soil over, and then the bed should be ready for planting.

Acquiring plants

There are various different ways of obtaining plants to stock your garden. The most obvious one is to buy them from some source or another, although this can turn out to be an expensive option. If you are lucky, friends and family may give them to you. You could also grow some plants yourself – from seed, cuttings or divisions.

Plant quality

If you buy your plants, you must always try to obtain the very best. Poor-quality plants may be cheaper, but they will rarely develop in the way you hope they might and so can be a disappointment. The best plants are not necessarily the largest ones, as they often take a while to settle down, allowing more modest plants to overtake them. Those of a medium size are usually best.

The plant should be in character (in other words, growing in the way that nature intended, whether bushy, slender or hummock-forming), and not be drawn or stunted. The new growth should be strong and bushy. Below the soil, the roots should not be pot-bound (wound around and around the pot in a tight mass). This can be checked by simply removing the plant carefully from its pot and having a look.

An interesting garden has a large number of different plants, which can be acquired from a variety of sources.

Another very important thing to check for when obtaining plants is whether the plant is diseased or harbouring any pests. If it looks sick or is covered in greenfly (aphids), you should reject it out of hand. Finally, don't choose a plant in full flower unless you want to be certain of the flower colour; it is better to choose one that is still in bud.

Buying plants

A large number of different outlets sell plants these days, from nurseries and garden centres to your local grocery store or neighbour's yard sale. There are no fixed rules about which is best but there are some useful points to bear in mind.

Many specialist nurseries are extremely good places to stock up, as the owners will grow their own plants, which are frequently of high quality. As well as being knowledgeable, the owners are often sole operators with small overheads, so the plants may be cheaper than those in larger garden centres.

Plants in your local grocery store are often left over from other sales points and may be pot-bound. They are less likely to be looked after properly and may be unlabelled or labelled incorrectly (as can be the case with plants sold at local fairs).

Plants as gifts

This is one of the best ways of obtaining plants. Not only are they free, but, if you have admired a plant, and a cutting is then taken for you or the plant divided, you know exactly what you are getting. It is wise to make a note of a plant's name straightaway, especially if you have been given several different cuttings or divisions.

If you think that a dug-up plant may be infected with root pests, wash off all the soil and pot it up in fresh compost (soil mix). Put any cuttings you are offered straight into a plastic bag and seal it. Pot them up as soon as possible.

Plants can be obtained as "plugs", which contain only a small amount of compost and need transplanting as soon as possible.

Bigger plants can be obtained in modules or in pots. These also need to be potted on to larger containers or planted out.

Do not buy pot-bound plants (left). The roots should be evenly spread through the compost (soil mix) and not tightly wound (right).

Whole trays of modules can be purchased from garden centres, saving the trouble of raising your own plants.

It is quite easy (and cheaper) to obtain plants by increasing your own stock. Here, cuttings are being taken from home-grown dahlias.

Growing your own

In many ways, growing your own plants is the most satisfying way of stocking your garden, as you have the satisfaction of feeling that you have created something from nothing. Seed is still fairly cheap and is widely available in a wonderful range of perennials and annuals. You do not need much equipment to germinate them and grow them on; most can be grown in open soil.

Seeds can be bought from seed companies, garden centres and some general-purpose stores. There are also specialist societies that run seed exchanges, where you can get unusual seeds not carried by other sources. Certain botanical gardens also offer seed that can be difficult to obtain elsewhere, so giving you the chance to grow some unusual and unique plants. You can, of course, collect your own seed and propagate from this. This is not difficult and can be very rewarding, as you are actively involved with every stage of the plant's life.

There are other methods of propagating plants – dividing and taking cutting from your own plants, for example. This does mean that you won't be introducing new plants to your garden, but it is the perfect way of increasing your stock of favourite plants and ideal if you need large numbers of the same plants for creating drifts of colour.

Low-maintenance plants

Acaena
Alchemilla mollis
Antirrhinum
Bergenia
Epimedium
Geranium macrorrhizum
Hosta
Impatiens
Pelargonium
Penstemon
Persicaria affinis
Pulmonaria
Tagetes
Vancouveria

Choosing plants for a low-maintenance garden

The ideal low-maintenance garden uses hard surfaces rather than grass, to reduce or eliminate the need for mowing. If you take this route, choose plants that you think will look good in this kind of situation – you might want more colourful or luxuriant plants to make up for the lack of green lawn, for example. Remember that using ground cover reduces the need for weeding.

Concentrate on plants that are self-supporting, so that you do not need to do any staking. Also, try to use plants that do not need deadheading and only require cutting back once a year. Foliage plants such as hostas are ideal in these kinds of situations. Long-flowering annuals are also a boon, as they will perform for the whole summer with only the occasional bit of attention – just some deadheading and the cutting back of straggling stems.

Containers and hanging baskets need daily watering and deadheading to look at their best, so you may want to stick to plants in beds, which need far less watering. Reduce the need for watering further by using plenty of mulches, which help to prevent water evaporation from the soil and cut down on weeding.

Signs of a healthy plant

General healthy appearance
Strong growth
Not drawn or too big
Not too small or stunted
No pests or diseases
No roots wound around inside the pot or container

Border plants can be lifted and divided in spring to provide more plants. *Sisyrinchium striatum* (seen here) are easy to divide.

Planting

Take your time when planting new acquisitions. The more attention they are given, the better they will establish themselves and the better they will continue growing. After all, there is no point in buying or raising plants from seed only to kill them later on. The techniques are simple and mainly common sense, but they are worth emphasizing.

This attractive border, featuring yellow and gold perennials, has benefited greatly from thorough soil preparation before any planting was done.

Vital preliminaries

The importance of good soil preparation has already been explained, but it is worth restating that soil must be properly prepared prior to any planting. Even if you are just filling a gap in a bed or border, it is still worth digging over the spot, removing any weeds and adding well-rotted garden compost (soil mix) to rejuvenate it. An hour or so before planting, give the plants, still in their pots, a thorough watering.

If the weather is wet or the soil very wet, avoid planting until it has dried out or you will compact the soil. If it is necessary to get on with the planting, use a plank of wood to walk on to spread your weight.

Finding the right place

There are two considerations to make when deciding where to plant: one visual and the other physical. Whether you are planting up a whole border or just filling a small gap, it is important to try to visualize what the small plant you have in your hand will look like when it is fully grown.

You will have to consider how big your plant will eventually become and how it will relate to its neighbours. Is it far enough away from them to avoid swamping them? Is it short enough not to hide the plants behind it or tall enough to be seen over the plants in front? Is it the right colour and shape for this spot? All these things must be considered before you start to plant. It is especially important to get it right the first time with perennials, if you can, as you may not want to move them for several years.

Plenty of space has been left around the various plants in this gravel bed. This allows them to develop healthily without swamping each other.

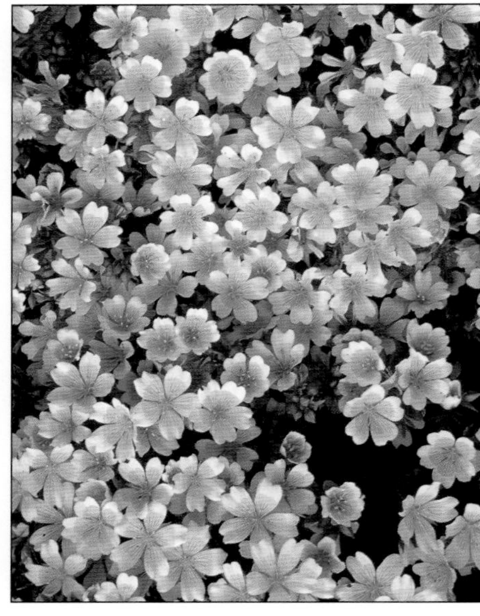

Limnanthes douglasii is an excellent annual for filling in temporary gaps in a perennial border.

PLANTING A BED

1 If the bed was dug in the autumn, winter weather should have broken down the soil. In spring, rake over the soil and remove weeds. Sprinkle bonemeal over the top of the soil to give plants a good start (wear rubber or latex gloves when handling bonemeal preparations).

2 Draw a grid on a planting plan and then mark out a scaled-up version on the bed, using sand or compost (soil mix). Alternatively, you can use string stretched between canes to mark out the planting plan.

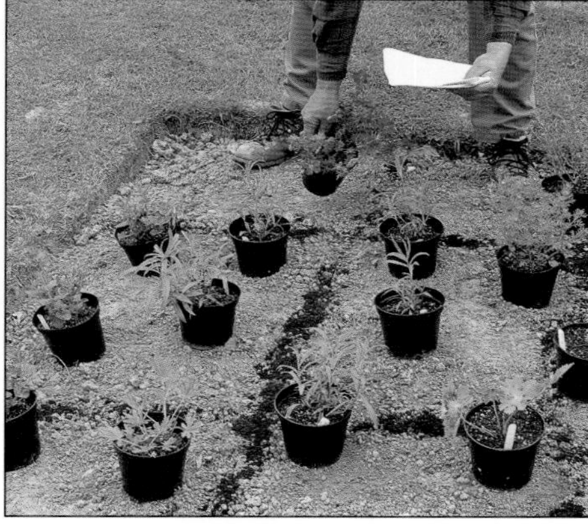

3 Using your planting plan and grid as a guide, lay out the plants, still in their pots, on the ground. Now stand back, and try to envisage the border as it will be, and make any necessary adjustments.

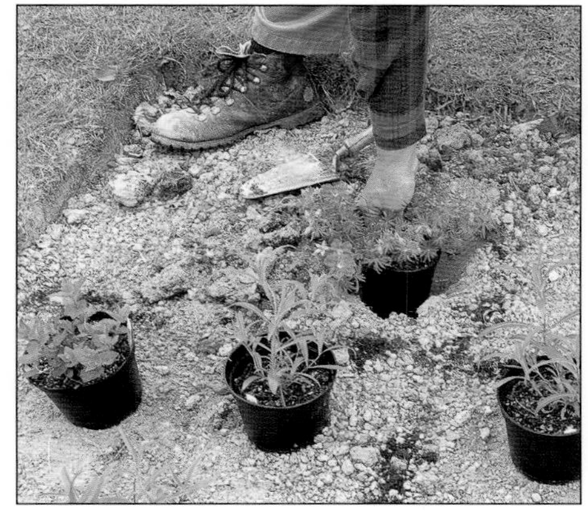

4 Dig a hole with a trowel or spade and, with the plant still in its pot, check that the depth and width is right. Adjust if necessary.

5 Remove the plant from the pot and place in the planting hole. Fill in the hole with soil and then firm the plant in.

6 When the bed is completely planted, water in all the plants. They should be kept watered until they have become established.

Temporary fillings

Perennial plants will usually take a while, sometimes up to several years, to fill out their allotted space properly. Rather than have bare earth showing while you are waiting, it is an excellent idea to fill the space with annuals. Temporary gaps in a border can also be filled with annuals. It's not a good idea to choose young annuals for this job, as they will take time to develop. Instead, keep back a few annuals growing in pots, so that they can be used as mature plants, ready to fill any space immediately.

7 Cover the soil between the plants with a layer of mulch, such as composted bark, to keep weeds down and preserve moisture.

8 If you are concerned that you will not remember what the plants are, mark each one with a plastic label. If you always put these labels in the same place – say, to the right of the plant – you can hide them from view and yet still locate them if necessary at any time.

Staking

Supporting plants is one of those tasks that many of us never seem to get around to until it is too late and the plants have collapsed in a messy heap. At this stage, trying to give them some form of support always spells disaster, as the plants look as though they have been forced into a straitjacket. The answer is to get the stakes into place before they are actually needed.

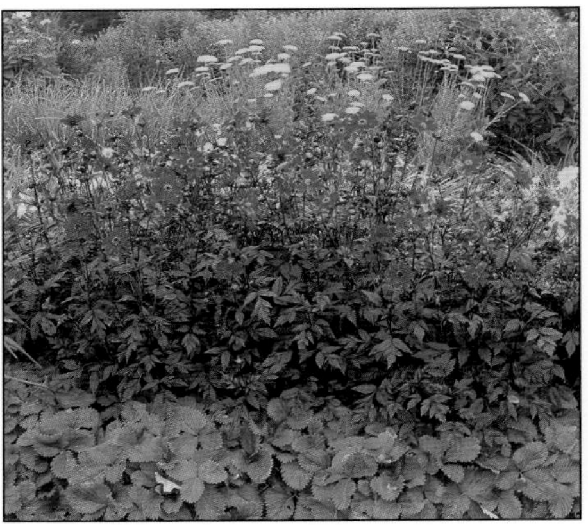

One way to avoid staking is to choose short cultivars such as this dahlia, 'Bishop of Llandaff', which needs no support.

Proprietary stakes can be used to form a linked hoop around and through the plant. They are available in different heights.

Why stake?

Some plants are used to growing in isolation and have strong stems that need no support, while others are more used to growing closely with other plants, giving each other mutual support. In the garden, an artificial situation is created and plants are often grown in discrete clumps, often with bare earth between them, which leaves them vulnerable to winds.

Plants with especially large or double flower heads are good candidates for staking. The heavy heads often make the plant droop over, particularly after rain, when the sheer number of petals means that the flower holds a lot of rainwater.

To keep your garden looking at its best, always support the heavier and taller plants. Even low-growers may flop and need support, especially those next to a path or lawn.

Alternatives to staking

One way to keep everything upright without stakes is to emulate nature and place your plants close together, so that they support one another. This does, however, inevitably affect the appearance of the border, and so is perhaps best suited to informal and cottage-style gardens. Another natural way of offering support is to allow sprawling plants, such as geraniums, to clamber up through the lower branches of shrubs.

Timing

The most important thing about staking is not to wait until the plant is fully grown but to apply supports when the plant is about a third to half grown. In this way the stems of the plant will grow up through the support, and a few will emerge outside the framework, therefore hiding it in a very natural way. The hidden stakes will then make a good job of supporting the plant.

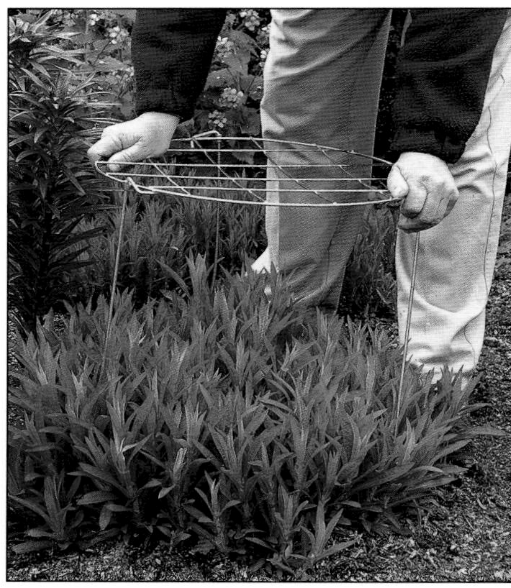

Hoops with cross wires make excellent supports but are rather inflexible as their width cannot be adjusted.

A hoop on a single pole can have its height adjusted as an individual plant grows, so giving it continual support.

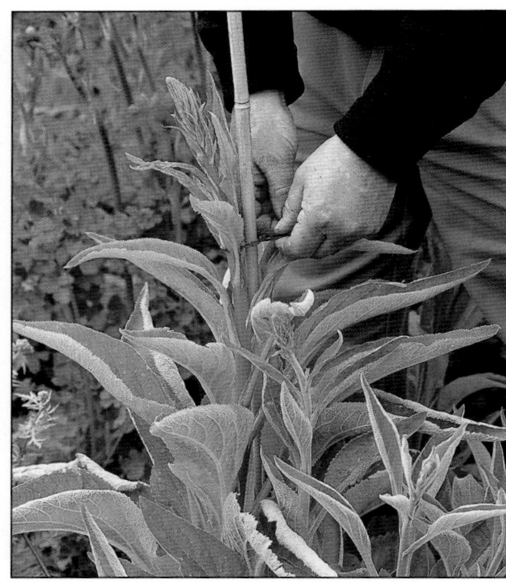

A tall, single-stemmed plant can be supported with a cane (stake). Place it at the back of the plant, where it cannot be seen.

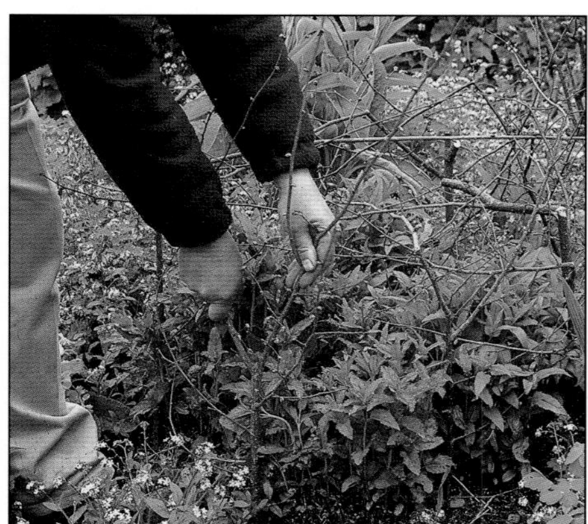

A network of pea sticks (branches or twigs from a shrub) can be erected over or around a plant clump to support plants as they grow.

Individual stems

Some plants, such as foxgloves, have one main flowering stem, and if these are weak or in a particularly exposed position, then they may need support. In this type of situation, a single cane (stake) – preferably painted green – can be inserted into the soil immediately behind the plant, so that it is hidden from view as much as possible. Tie the plant stem to the cane with soft string. Another alternative here is to use the widely available proprietary supports that feature an upright rod and a holding ring.

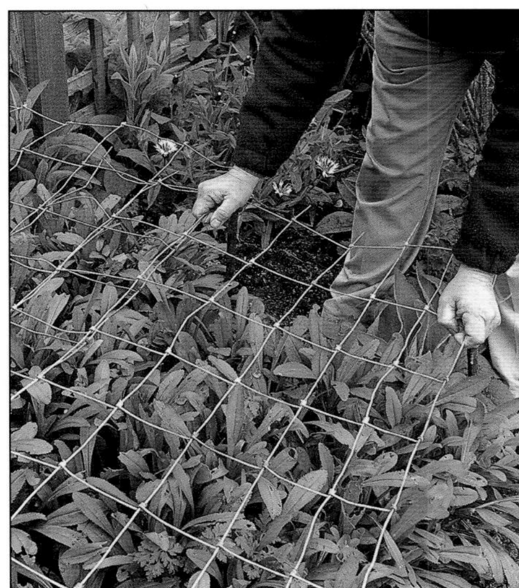

A sheet of stock fencing held horizontally on posts will give secure support to a plant covering a large area.

STAKING LILIES

1 First position the metal stake, about 15cm (6in) away from the emerging stem. Now release one side of the ring and carefully trap the lily stem within.

2 Clip the second end of the ring into the hole that is provided on the metal support. The lily now has freedom to move but is not able to stray too far.

Home-made supports

Pea sticks (usually branches of shrubs such as hazel, cut in the winter) make good supports. Push them into the ground around the clump, then bend the tops over and intertwine them to form a horizontal mesh just above the growing plant. Tie the twigs together for extra support. If twigs are not available, stick in a number of canes around the plant and weave a web of strings between them, again forming a mesh through which the plant will grow.

For a large clump of plants, place several stout sticks around and in the clump, and tie a piece of large-mesh wire netting to them so that it is supported horizontally just above the growing plant. The stems will then pass through this as they grow.

Proprietary supports

All kinds of ready-made supports are currently available, from a range of outlets. Some of these are hoops supported horizontally above the plant, while others consist of individual stakes linked together around and across the plant. Although these are relatively expensive, they do a good job, are easily assembled and taken down, and will last for a very long time.

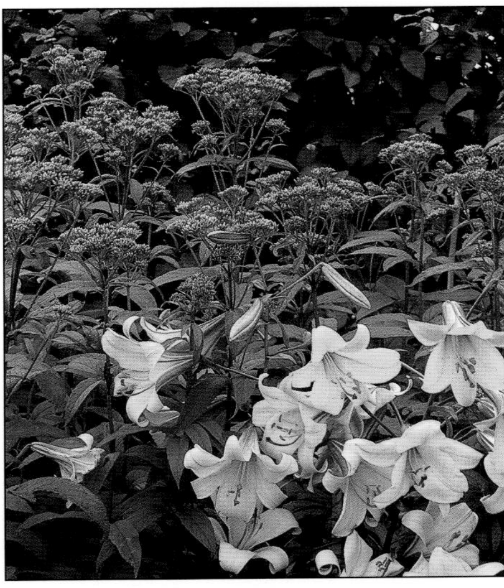

Staking should give plants the support they need, but must be well hidden so that the plants' beauty is not spoiled.

Watering and feeding

Plants, like animals, will not grow without water and food. To a certain extent, these are naturally provided for by way of rainfall and nutrients available from the atmosphere and from decaying vegetation. The competition for water and nutrients in a crowded border, however, frequently means that there is not enough natural supply in a full garden. These supplies can also partially or completely fail. This is why it is important keep a garden well watered and fed.

A well-watered and fed border will keep the plants looking fresh and lasting longer.

A good soaking

The principal thing about watering is that you should always make certain that adequate water is applied. Watering so that only the surface of the soil is damp will make the plant's roots grow towards the surface rather than deep down, which leaves the plant vulnerable during hot periods or times when you do not water. As a rule of thumb, try to give the equivalent of 2.5cm/1in of rain each time, which should ensure that the ground around the plant or the compost (soil mix) in the container is soaked.

Methods of watering

Watering cans are easy and versatile to use, and enable you to put the water exactly where you want it. However, they do make the job quite arduous if you have a lot to do. Special pump-action watering cans can be used to water containers that are above head height, such as hanging baskets.

You can fill your watering cans from water butts placed under any drainpipes from roofs to collect rainwater. This means that not only are you "recycling" rainwater in the same way that nature would do, but also that you are watering your garden with water that is not full of chemicals and is also, for those on water meters, free.

For larger areas, garden hoses are useful. These can be connected to sprinklers, which deliver water in droplet form, like rain. To give you a rough idea of how long it takes to deliver the necessary 2.5cm/1in, place a jam jar or similar container somewhere under the sprinkler. Hand-held sprays can also be attached to hoses, but again you must be sure to apply enough water before moving on to the next plant.

Another way is to use a dribble system, whereby a special hose with small holes in it is laid throughout the border, so that water slowly

Plants can be watered individually by using a lance spray attached to a hose. This is time-consuming but worth the effort.

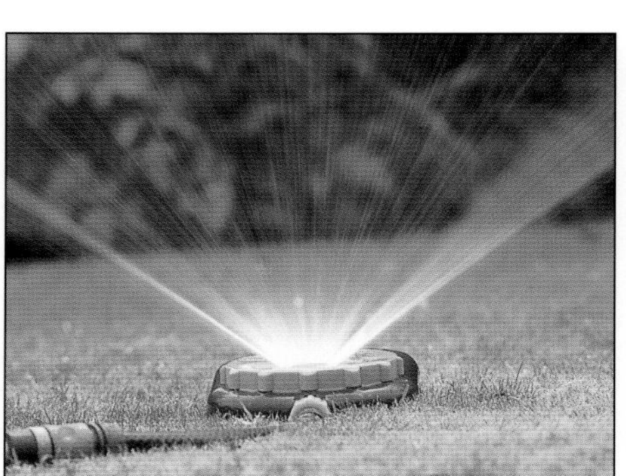

A large area can be covered with a sprinkler. Place jam jars or other containers around the area to judge the amount of water delivered.

A dribble hose (a hose with holes in it) can be hidden among plants in a border to allow gentle, controlled watering.

Mulching will help to preserve the moisture in a border by cutting down the amount of water that evaporates.

It is possible to feed as you water, using special attachments that add a controlled amount of fertilizer to the water.

Granular or pelleted fertilizer can be scattered around the plant, ensuring that it is only used where it is needed.

dribbles out over a long period of time. These pipes can be buried below the mulch, thus reducing wastage through evaporation.

Watering with hoses or sprinklers may be subject to local water authority controls, especially during drought conditions, when you will need them most. There may also be regulations regarding connections to the water mains. Check that you are not infringing any regulations.

Preserving moisture

In addition to watering, it is important to preserve as much of the moisture in the soil as you can for plant use. The best way to do this is to cover the soil with a mulch, such as leaf mould, grass cuttings or composted or chipped bark. A layer of about 10cm/4in is ideal. Apply the mulch either after rain or after watering the bed thoroughly.

Feeding

In the garden, we tend to clear the beds of all dying and dead vegetation, so there is little chance of it rotting down where it lies and returning to the soil as nutrients, as would happen in the wild. However, the prudent gardener does not throw away all these leftovers but composts them and then returns them to the soil, which considerably increases the nutritional value of the soil.

Preparing the soil thoroughly with garden compost will pay great dividends, but the added nutrients will not last forever. In the case of annuals, the soil can be prepared afresh each year, but for perennials, which are left in situ for several years, it is impossible to do this. It is, however, possible to top-dress the soil each autumn or spring by covering the soil with a mulch of well-rotted garden compost, farmyard manure or composted bark. This can be worked into the top layer of the soil with a fork, while being careful not to disturb the plants' roots. Alternatively, it can be left on the top as a mulch, which the worms will gradually take down below the surface. The nutrients it contains will in any event be washed down towards the roots by the rain.

If a mulch is not available, a balanced fertilizer can be used instead to add nutrients, spread at the manufacturer's recommended levels, but this is second-best to organic material.

Collecting your own water

Place a water butt underneath the gutter of a greenhouse, shed or garage to catch the water as it runs off the roof. Rainwater is slightly acidic and so is ideal for watering acid-loving plants, especially if you live in a hard-water area. It will also save water and money spent on metered water.

You can easily collect sufficient water in a water butt to keep a collection of acid-loving plants perfectly happy right through the summer. If you are more ambitious, you can now obtain kits that link water butts together, so creating a really effective water storage system for your garden.

The butt should be easy to use, so make sure there is room to get a water can under the tap. Keep the butt covered at all times so that the water remains sweet and clean.

You can also recycle water that has been used for washing or bathing in the house. Known as "grey-water", it is suitable for applying to established plants in borders and on lawns, but is best used immediately and not stored.

Weeding

This is the aspect of gardening that the majority of people dislike the most. However, this is usually because they leave it much too late and by the time they do make the time for it, the beds are infested with weeds and it becomes an uphill battle to clear them. When weeding is done on a regular basis, it can be very quick and even pleasurable, and the resulting weed-free beds are always a joy to see.

Timing

As a general rule, the best time to weed is as soon as you see one. If you keep on top of the weeds, weeding rarely becomes a problem and certainly never a chore.

Ideally, you should go over all the beds during the winter or early spring to clear out any weeds. Once cleared of weeds, they should be mulched. If these two processes are done at the beginning of the growing season, then there is a very good chance that you will have little to do later on except pull out the odd rogue that appears. If, however, you wait until the weather warms up before tackling the weeds, you will find that they are ahead of you.

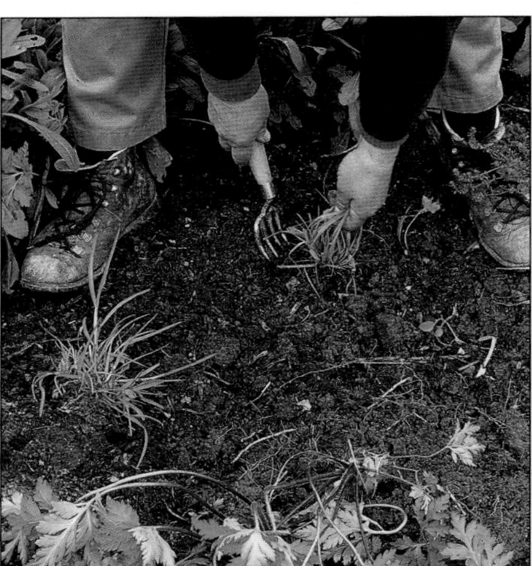

The safest way of controlling weeds in a border is to remove them by hand, rather than with chemicals.

Closely packed planting in a garden border acts as a kind of natural ground cover, usefully suppressing the growth of any weed seedlings.

Weed killers

Using chemicals in a planted border is not a good idea. They can be used to make an initial clearance, but once the plants are in place it can be a disastrous procedure. However careful you are, there is bound to be some drift, with odd drops falling on actual plants. Chemicals can also translocate from roots to roots. If a border is prepared properly in the first place and then weeded regularly by hand, there should be no need to use chemicals anyway.

Hand-weeding

The best way to tackle weeds in a border is to hand-weed. If the soil is loose or there is a good depth of mulch on it, this may simply mean pulling the weed gently out. If, however, there is a possibility of the weed breaking off and leaving its roots in the soil, use a hand fork or trowel to loosen the soil first.

In the late winter, as the plants are just appearing through the soil, it is a good idea to fork the soil over lightly, working in well-rotted organic material as you go. As you do this, you can easily pull out any weeds that are present.

If a plant becomes infested with a persistent perennial weed, such as couch grass, then it is best to dig the whole plant out, wash the soil off the roots, remove the weed and replant the plant. If you try to remove the couch grass while the plant is still in the ground, then the pieces of weed that grow through it will only regenerate and you will have to start again.

Hoeing

Some gardeners like to use a hoe to weed their beds, but this can be as dangerous as chemicals. So often, fragile new shoots or even whole plants get hoed off a fraction of a second before you realize that they are not a weed, leading to many lost plants and a considerable amount of bad temper. The other problem is that, although hoeing can be effective for annual weeds, it is no

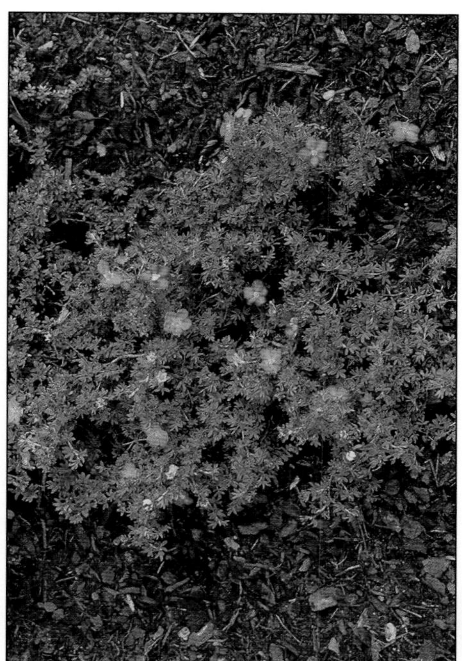

A composted bark mulch will suppress weed growth, but clean the ground well beforehand.

good just cutting off the top of perennial weeds – you need to get the roots out as well.

Mulching

One of the greatest aids to weeding is mulching, since it prevents the weeds from forming in the first place. A layer of some material that will keep the light from the soil will inhibit the germination of weed seeds, so keeping the border free of weeds. If, however, there are already perennial weeds in the border, then the mulch will not help. This is because the weeds will simply grow through the material in the same way as the plants.

Organic mulches, such as leaf mould and composted or chipped bark, are best, as they will eventually rot down and improve the soil. Most will also look more sympathetic in the borders, creating a good background against which to see the plants, though this is not the case with straw or grass cuttings.

Black plastic mulches are efficient but ugly. Some gardeners try to avoid the plastic showing by covering it with a shallow layer of earth or another mulch, such as bark, but this inevitably washes off in places or is revealed by birds pecking among the covering layer, and the ugly plastic makes a reappearance.

Mulches

Cardboard: effective but ugly
Chipped/composted bark: very good
Farmyard manure: good if weed-free
Garden compost (soil mix): good
Geotextiles and black plastic: good but very ugly
Grass cuttings: good but ugly
Gravel: good in certain areas
Leaf mould: very good
Newspaper: good but very ugly
Peat: poor
Sawdust: good but ugly
Shredded prunings: very good
Spent hops: good
Spent mushroom compost: good
Straw: good but ugly
Woodchips: good but some people find them ugly

EFFECTIVE WEEDING

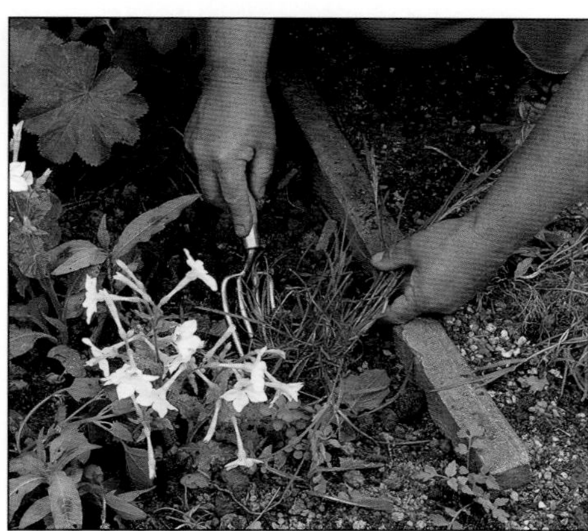

1 Where plants are growing close together, the best way of removing weeds is to either pull them out by hand or dig them out using a hand fork. Perennial weeds must be dug out whole and not simply chopped off, or they will soon return.

2 Where there is more room, hoes can be used in a border, but take care not to damage your precious plants in the process. In hot weather, hoed-up weeds can be left to shrivel, but it looks much less messy if they are all removed to the compost heap.

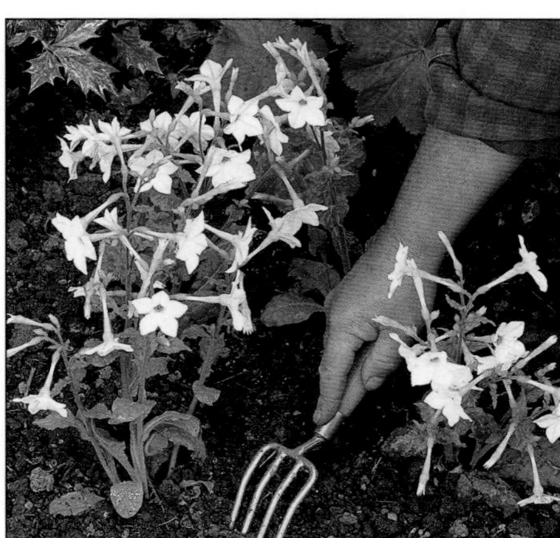

3 After weeding, rake through the border with a fork, or if the plants are far enough apart, with a rake. This will tidy up the bed and level off the surface, removing any footprints and any weed remnants.

4 It is a good idea to apply or renew a mulch after weeding. As well as helping to prevent weeds from reappearing, this will also preserve moisture. Composted or chipped bark will set the plants off well.

Routine plant maintenance

One of the easiest ways of making a garden unattractive is to leave old flower heads and dying stalks on the plants. Trimming them off not only makes the garden look tidier and more appealing but also allows the remaining flowers to shine out and be seen, as well as encouraging new blooms. The three main techniques that will keep your plants both beautiful and healthy are pinching out, deadheading and cutting back.

Getting into the routine

The difference between a garden that is regularly attended and one that is only occasionally looked after is quite amazing, especially towards the end of summer or in the autumn. The dead or dying material not only looks untidy but also obscures those plants that are still fresh. At the start of the season, some judicious pinching out will benefit some annuals from the very beginning.

As with weeding, if you leave deadheading and cutting back for too long, they can become onerous tasks. If you do a little each week, then they become much easier as well as benefiting the appearance of the garden. This applies not only to beds and borders but also to hanging baskets and containers.

Removing fading flowers and seed pods from annuals will preserve energy and help to keep them flowering for longer.

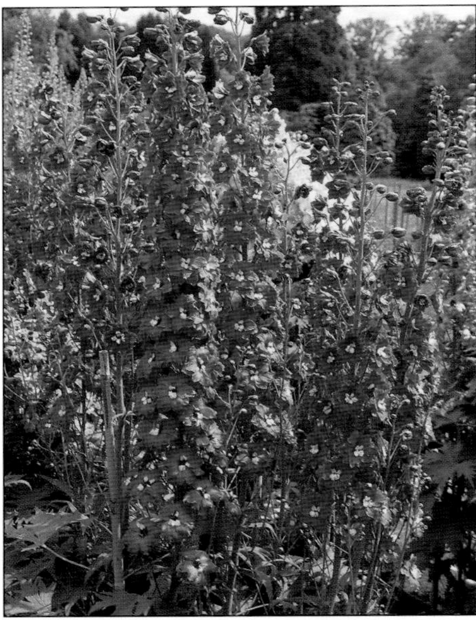

A second flush of delphinium flowers can often be obtained by removing the initial flower spikes as they fade.

Pinching out

If left to their own devices, many plants will grow only one main stem. In a bedding scheme, for example, this would result in a forest of tall spindly spikes with large gaps in between them rather than a desirable carpet of flowers and foliage. To avoid this effect, pinch out the growing tip of each main spike. This will cause the stem to produce side shoots. These will make the plants much more bushy, and further pinching out will increase the effect.

Pinching out the main stems from certain annuals and perennials will help them to bush out and develop into a fuller plant.

Deadheading

Once a flower starts to fade, you should cut it off. The actual point of the cut varies depending on the plant. If the flower is the only one on the stem, then the whole stem should be cut back to its base. If it is a multi-flowered stem, then the cut should be where the individual flower's stem joins the other stems. If it is a flower spike, then the whole spike should be removed. Try not to leave odd bits of stem sticking up, which looks untidy.

If the foliage is still attractive and the stem is covered with leaves, remove the flower head at some point towards the top of the stem, making the cut close to or behind a leaf so that it does not show. If this is done with, for example, spikes of lupins or delphiniums, you are likely to encourage side shoots, which will produce new spikes of flowers.

Some plants, particularly those with smaller blooms, have masses of flowers, making it almost impossible to deadhead the flowers singly. Geraniums are a good example of this, and the finished flowers are best dealt with as a whole. This means waiting until the majority of the flowers are finished, then cutting over the whole plant or cutting it down completely.

Advantages of deadheading

The improved appearance of plants after deadheading has already been stressed, but there is another benefit to this task too.

If you remove a dying flower, then instead of putting an extraordinary amount of its energy into producing a seed-head, the plant will divert its energy into producing more flowers. So the more you deadhead, the more flowers you are likely to get and the longer the plant will go on flowering.

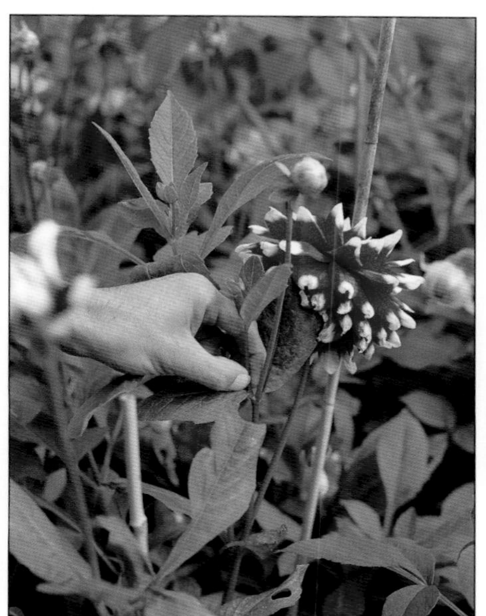

Pinching out the subsidiary shoots of plants such as these dahlias concentrates the growth in the main blooms.

DEADHEADING

1 Using scissors, a sharp knife or secateurs (pruners), snip off the flowers neatly and cleanly where they join the stem. Sometimes the whole head of flowers needs to be removed – cut these back to the first set of leaves. Dead flower heads and other clippings can be added to the compost heap.

2 Regular – and carefully executed – deadheading produces a considerably cleaner and healthier looking arrangement. Dead flowers ruin the best of plants, as well as using up vital energy in seed production. It takes only a short time and the effort is always worthwhile.

Cutting back

Once early-flowering plants are cut down to the ground, they will re-shoot. In most cases, this means that they will produce a fresh set of leaves, giving the plant a second life as a foliage plant for the rest of the season. Pulmonaria, for example, finish flowering in spring and, if left to their own devices, the leaves will soon become rather tatty and tired-looking. If, however, they are sheared over immediately after flowering, they produce new foliage that remains fresh-looking throughout the rest of the summer. A similar thing happens with *Alchemilla mollis* and many other plants. Some cut-back plants will also have a second flowering.

Once plants are dead or obviously dying, they should be cut back right down to the ground. If plants are cut back so that stumps are left, it becomes difficult to cut next year's stems close to the ground, and so with each year that passes, the plant becomes increasingly surrounded by more, and higher, stumps.

On some plants, it is only the taller flowering stems that wilt, while the base of the plant remains green. In such cases, cut off the wilting stems only, as low as possible.

Sometimes, as mentioned above, a plant may still be green but will look rather bedraggled. Here the benefit of being cut down is that it will grow afresh. Such plants should be cut close to the ground, removing all the old growth but leaving any new foliage that might already be appearing among the old stems. In this scenario, cutting back is mainly considered worth the effort for the new growth that appears, as this rejuvenates the plant. Sometimes, however, such new growth is required for propagation purposes. For example, there is not much suitable cutting growth when violas are in full flower or once they have finished flowering, but if they are cut to the ground the new shoots are just perfect for such a purpose.

CUTTING BACK GREEN PLANTS

1 Some herbaceous plants remain green throughout winter. Cut back to sound growth, removing dead and leggy material.

2 Here, the old stems have been cut off so that they are level with the emerging growth, so as not to damage it.

Autumn and winter tasks

Many non-gardeners think of the cooler months as the dead season, when little is happening. In fact, there is plenty to do: lifting certain plants, removing any remaining dead material, forking over beds to weed them and open the soil, and then top-dressing them. Your garden machinery should also be thoroughly checked over and oiled. Finally, there is the excitement of sitting down with seed catalogues and planning how your garden will look in the coming seasons.

Winter is a good time for catching up on tool and machinery maintenance. It will save a lot of time when you are busy in spring.

Borders and beds

One thing to make sure you get done before the frosts set in is to lift more vulnerable plants. Tender plants such as pelargoniums should be potted up and overwintered in a greenhouse (or take cuttings if you don't have much storage space). Tender bulbs such as gladioli should be lifted if you live in a cold area, especially if your soil is heavy. Dry them, then store them somewhere frost-free and check every few weeks.

Another major job is to remove all the dead stems and foliage from the previous year. Some gardeners like to leave these as long as possible to provide the birds with a source of food in the form of seeds and any insects that hide in the dead foliage. Others leave it because it gives structure and something to look at during the winter months.

Other gardeners are eager to clear the ground as soon as possible. In addition to giving you a much tidier-looking garden, the main benefit of this is that you avoid leaving the clearing up to the last minute in early spring, when there are suddenly lots of other jobs to do. If work is then delayed due to bad weather, it can have a knock-on effect for the rest of the year.

You can have the best of both worlds if you cut the dead material and then hang it up so that the birds can still get at it. All the material removed from the beds should eventually be composted so that its goodness can be returned to the soil. Hardened stems are best shredded first, if possible.

Once the borders have been cleared, lightly fork them over to open up the soil and to remove all weeds, before top-dressing them with well-rotted organic material up to 10cm/4in thick. The beds are now well prepared for the next season. Any new planting should be done in either the early autumn or spring.

Avoid working on the beds if the soil is too wet. If it becomes a necessity, then use a wooden plank to stand on, as this will spread your weight and limit damage to the soil.

Winter plant care

Remember that not all plants die back in winter and that there are a surprising number that still produce flowers and foliage. There is generally not much to do to these except enjoy them.

One thing that is generally not required is watering. If, however, you have containers that are in the lee of the house or a wall, so that they get little rain, they should be watered occasionally if the soil gets dry. This should be sparingly done so that the soil is left just moist and not wringing wet.

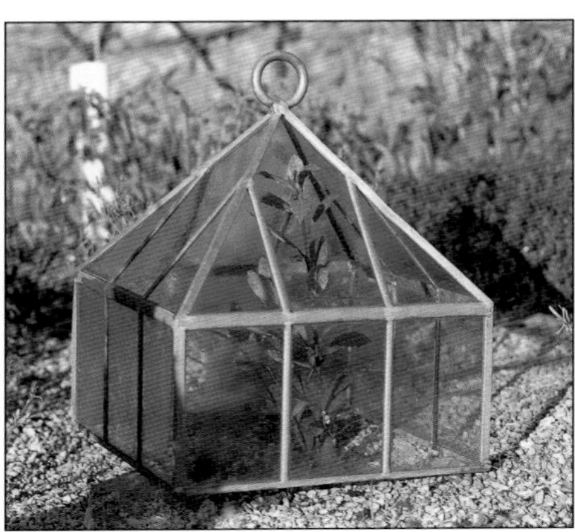

Here is a decorative way of giving slightly tender plants winter protection. Remove the container during warmer, damp weather.

Tender plants such as these pelargoniums need protection in a frost-free glass house during the winter months.

Winter-flowering perennials

Anemone nemorosa
Eranthis hyemalis
Euphorbia rigida
Helleborus:
- *H. niger*
- *H. orientalis*
- *H. purpurascens*

Iris unguicularis
Primula vulgaris
Pulmonaria rubra
Viola odorata

Garden machinery

Once autumn draws in and winter begins, the lawnmowers, strimmers and hedge cutters tend to be put away and forgotten about until they are next needed. This is, however, the ideal time to have them checked over properly and maintained, ready to use next season. Even if you are not doing this straight away, all your machines should be thoroughly cleaned and oiled.

Catalogue joys

One of the most enjoyable aspects of gardening is the planning. The weather may be unsuitable for gardening itself, but there is nothing more pleasurable than sitting down with a pile of catalogues, dreaming of what you could do if only your garden was twenty times larger.

On a more practical note, this is the time to look seriously at the catalogues to choose the seeds and plants you will be using next year in your hanging baskets and borders. The perennial plants may be constant factors, but you have much greater freedom with annuals, and if you are bold enough you can try something completely different. You might be seduced by the novelties in the catalogue or you might decide to change the colour scheme from, say, reds and yellows to blues and yellows, or even to all white.

LIFTING AND REPLANTING DAHLIAS

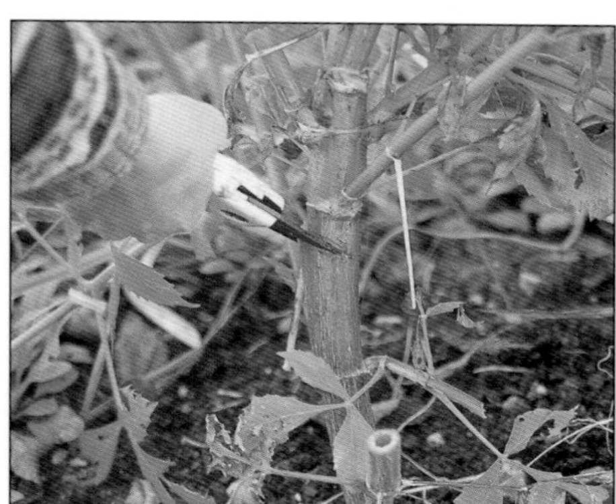

1 The time to lift the dahlias for winter storage is just as the first frosts blacken the foliage or when it naturally begins to die back. Remove the foliage and cut back the stems, leaving about 20cm (8in) of each one attached to the tuber.

2 Fork gently around the plant, leaving a radius of 25–40cm (10–16in) from the main stem, depending on the amount of growth it has made. Gently lift the root, taking great care not to damage the tubers. Now carefully remove the soil from around the tubers. Heavy soils may need to be washed off with water from a hose or tap.

3 Place the plant upside down in a box so that any moisture can drain from the hollow stems. Store in a dry, frost-free place and remove the soil from the tubers once it has dried off. Dust any damaged tubers with a fungicide such as yellow or green sulphate of ammonia and then place in boxes of barely moist peat. Overwinter in a dry, well-ventilated, cool, frost-free place.

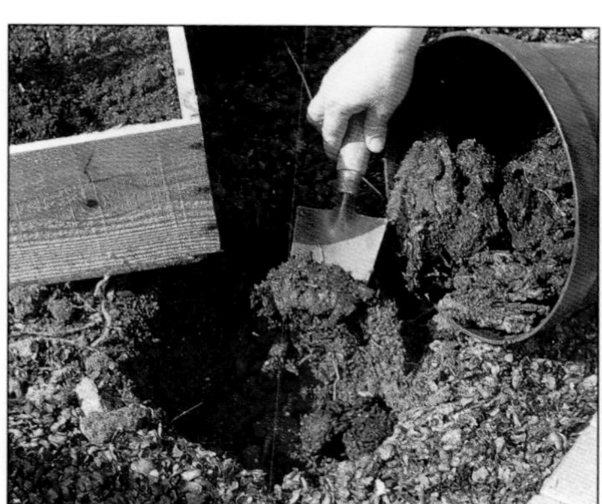

4 When green shoots emerge in spring, water sparingly to keep the compost (soil mix) moist. In late spring or early summer, after all risk of frost has passed, choose a sunny, sheltered spot and prepare a deep planting hole. Add a generous quantity of well-rotted manure or a long-term granular feed, and mix well into the soil at the bottom of the hole.

5 Carefully lower the dahlia into the prepared hole. Add more soil or compost around the plant as necessary to bring up to soil level. The hole should be bigger than the dahlia so that there is room to spread out the tubers. Adjust the hole depth if necessary so that the soil level is the same as the previous year (this level can be seen on the plant).

6 Gently firm the soil surrounding the plant, making sure as you do so that there are no gaps or air-pockets – either around the plant or between the tubers. Firm the soil down first with your hands, gently and carefully, and then more decisively with your foot. Water the plant and the area around it and then add a layer of mulch.

Sowing seeds in pots

There is something immensely satisfying about putting a seed, which is often no larger than a speck of dust, in the ground, knowing that it will eventually grow into a gorgeous plant. This is the basic miracle of nature, and yet although you may plant hundreds of seeds each year, every tiny seedling still seems just as wonderful as the last.

Getting the quantity right

One of the main mistakes made by beginners is to sow too much seed. Unless you are creating a large bedding scheme, you rarely need more than a dozen plants and often, in the case of perennials, only three or five (odd numbers always look better than even ones in the garden).

Of course, you should grow a few more than you need in case some die, and you may want extras for giving away. If you grow many more than you need, however, you will waste a lot of time pricking the plants out as well as the expense of extra pots and potting compost (soil mix), most of which will end up on the compost heap. For most purposes, you need sow no more than what a 9cm (3½in) pot will contain, and very rarely indeed will you need a half tray, let alone a whole tray.

Sowing your own seed gives you plenty of plants with which you can plan magnificent container or border displays.

SOWING IN POTS

1 Fill the pot to the rim with compost (soil mix) and then gently firm it down. (Don't ram it down, or it will compact.)

2 Sow the seeds thinly across the surface. In the case of large seeds, such as sunflowers, each seed can be placed individually so that they are equidistantly spaced.

3 Cover the seeds, preferably with a layer of horticultural grit, but alternatively with a thin layer of fine compost if grit isn't available. At this stage, remember to label the pot, as one pot of seeds looks very much like another, and you will soon forget which is which.

4 Water the pot either from below, by standing it in a tray of water until the surface of the compost changes colour, or from above, by using a fine-rosed watering can. Place the pot in a propagator or in a shady place in a greenhouse.

A good start

Apart from ending up with too many plants, there are other good reasons for sowing a few seeds at a time in small pots and then pricking out to other pots or trays – and avoiding the temptation to simply sow in trays and then weed the seedlings out. Starting a few seeds at a time gives them the best conditions at the fragile start of their life. You do not want hundreds of germinating seeds vying for goodness from the growing medium, nor do you want intertwined roots. A few good seedlings is preferable to lots of sickly ones, so it is best to transfer to other pots or trays when selecting your strongest seedlings. Also, if space is at a premium, large trays can be a problem.

Composts

For sowing, use a proprietary seed compost (growing medium). This has only a limited amount of fertilizer in it because, at this stage, most of the nutrients will come from the seeds themselves. Once you prick the seedlings out, they will need extra food, and so a potting compost should be used.

There are arguments for and against using either a soil-based compost or a soilless compost as a growing medium, but in the end it comes down to personal preference and what is available locally.

Pricking out

When your seedlings do start to grow, they should be pricked out as soon as their first true leaves make an appearance (this is the second pair of leaves; the first pair are the seed leaves). To prick out your seedlings, place each one very carefully in its own individual pot. Bedding plants, which are often needed in much larger numbers than other plants, are often pricked into trays or cellular trays. The tray is filled with compost and a hole is made for each seedling. Remember that you should never leave plants in trays for too long as they are shallow and the roots will soon become terribly intertwined.

Hardening off

This is a vital part of the process. It is important that you not take plants directly from the greenhouse or cold frame and put them in the garden. The shock of sudden exposure to colder, dryer air could set back their growth significantly or even kill them off completely. Instead, harden the plants off gradually.

A couple of weeks before the plants are needed, place the pots outside for an hour or so each day and then return them to the greenhouse or cold frame. Repeat this process every day, leaving them outside for longer and longer periods of time on each occasion, until eventually they are left out over night. They are now safe to plant out in your garden. If they are tender plants, do not start hardening them off until the threat of frost has passed.

PRICKING OUT INTO POTS

1 If the seedlings have been in a heated propagator, harden them off to the greenhouse temperature before pricking out, by gradually opening the propagator vents over a couple of days. Gently knock out the pot of seedlings on to the bench.

2 Now, proceeding very gently and carefully so that you don't damage the fragile seedlings, break open the ball of compost so that individual seedlings can be removed. The compost should be relatively soft and so this should be fairly easy.

3 Separate the seedlings one at a time as each is required. Always lift and carry a seedling by its leaves, and never by its roots or stem. Use a label or pencil to ease the seedling from the compost without risk of tearing the roots.

4 Hold the seedling over the centre of the pot, keeping your hand steady by resting it against the side of the pot, and pour good quality potting compost around it until the pot is full to the brim.

5 Tap the pot on the bench to settle the compost and then gently firm down with your thumbs or fingers so that the final level is below the rim of the pot.

6 Water the pots with a watering can fitted with a fine rose. Keep the seedlings in the greenhouse or somewhere warm until they have started growing away, then harden them off over a week or more by allowing them increasing amounts of time in the open air, or with a cold frame, by gradually opening it.

Sowing seeds in open ground

Many new gardeners think that all flowers start as seeds grown in pots, but in fact a large number of flowering plants can be sown directly into the soil. This is, of course, what happens in nature anyway. The advantage of pots is that they reduce the competition for food and water, giving the seedlings a flying start. However, if weeds are kept at bay, then the same is true of seeds sown in open ground.

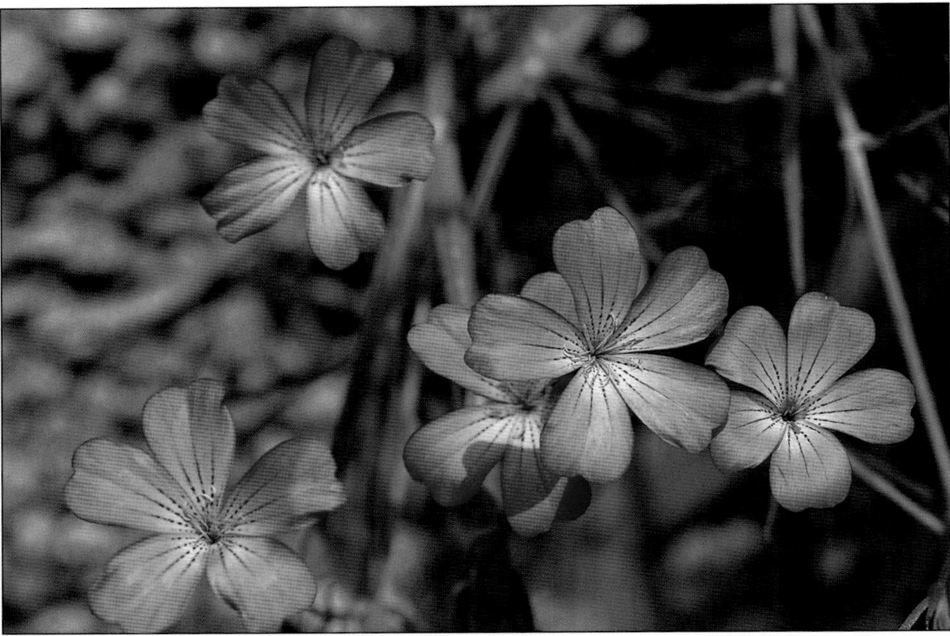

The corncockle, *Agrostemma*, is a plant of disturbed ground that flourishes naturally in cornfields, so it is perfect for sowing in the flower border.

Which seeds to sow outside

You can try sowing virtually any seeds directly into the soil, but there are normally some types that will grow better if they are sown in pots. For example, many annuals, particularly the tender ones, are better started off in pots or trays. This is because you can steal a march on nature by getting them into growth in a greenhouse ready to be planted out as mature plants once the frosts have definitely finished. If you choose to sow them in open ground instead, you would have to wait until the end of the harsh weather, which would then mean that the resulting plants would flower four to six weeks later. In other words, they would not be coming into flower until the summer is almost over.

By contrast, hardy annuals, which will withstand the frosts, can be sown outside in either the autumn or spring, so that the plants are already mature by the beginning of summer. Sowing these plants outside in the first place saves a great deal of time and trouble.

Most perennials can be sown outside, either where they are to flower ultimately or in special beds, but because small numbers are usually involved it is often easier to sow them in pots.

Where to sow

Most directly sown annuals are sown where they are to flower. The exception to this are the biennials, such as wallflowers or sweet Williams, which are usually grown in rows in a seedbed or the vegetable garden and then transplanted into their flowering place in the autumn.

Perennials are normally sown in rows. They can be sown where they are to grow, but because only one, three or five plants are needed at the most, the seedlings can easily get swamped and lost in the hurly-burly of the border. Draw out some shallow drills in the fine soil and sow the seeds thinly along them. Draw some of the soil back over the seeds, then water them. Label each row as you sow it so that you don't forget which is which.

Aftercare

Once your sowing is done, the soil should be kept moist, which may mean watering if the weather is dry. As the seedlings appear, thin them out, making sure that you remove any that are too close together; each plant should have enough room to develop properly. The best rule of thumb here is simple: the larger the final plant, the more space it will

The seeds of different kinds of plants can be scattered over the bare earth to create colourful mixed displays.

SOWING IN OPEN GROUND

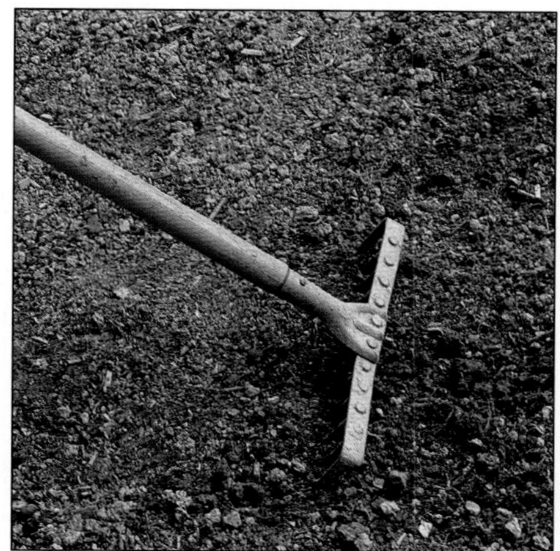

1 Thoroughly prepare the ground by digging the soil and breaking it down into a fine tilth (consistency) using a rake. You should not work the soil when it is too wet or it will become compacted.

2 If you plan to use several different blocks of plants, mark out the design on the soil using contrasting coloured sand or compost (soil mix). Broadcast the seed by hand so that it is thinly spread right across the appropriate area. It will probably be necessary to thin out the seedlings when they appear.

3 Gently rake the seed in so that it is covered by a thin layer of soil. Some gardeners prefer to sow their seed in short rows rather than by broadcasting. This makes it easier to weed when the seed first comes up. To sow in rows, first draw out shallow drills with a hoe.

4 Now sow the seed thinly along each row and rake the soil back over them. By carefully thinning the seedlings, the resulting overall pattern of the plants will appear to be random and not in rows.

5 Finally, gently water the whole bed, using a watering can fitted with a fine rose.

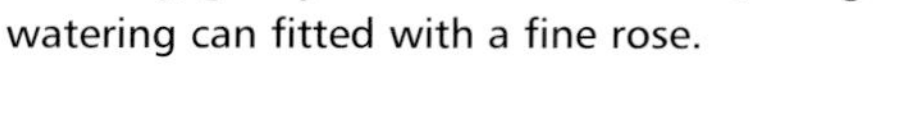

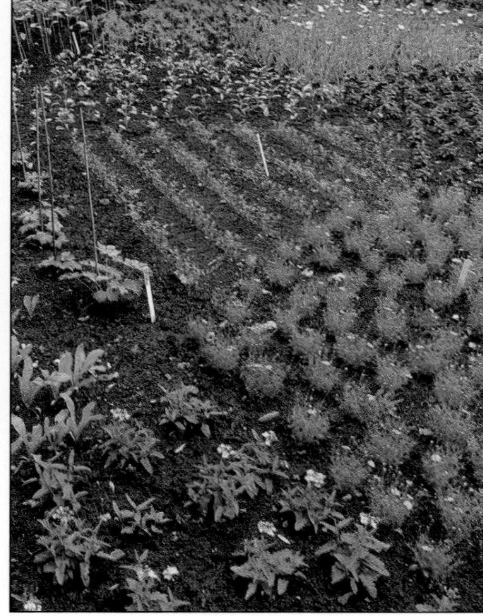

6 *(right)* A bed planted with annuals begins to fill out soon after sowing and planting.

require around it. This is not quite so important in row-sown plants as these will be planted into their final positions later. Keep the young plants weeded and healthy.

Transplanting

Plants that are grown in rows elsewhere can be transplanted into their final flowering position as soon as they are large enough to be handled without risk of damaging them. With biennials such as wallflowers, there is no need to do this until the ground has been cleared in the autumn.

With "broadcast" seed (handfuls of seed thrown out over the soil's surface, as opposed to being put into rows of channels), too many plants often develop. Some of these can be dug up carefully and transplanted elsewhere. Water the plants before moving them, and then dig them up, retaining as much soil as you possibly can around the roots. Dig a larger hole than the roots, place the plant in it and then refill with soil, gently but firmly pressing it down, then water again.

Dividing plants

One of the quickest ways of obtaining a new plant is to divide an existing plant into two (or more) pieces and replant both bits. This is not only a method of obtaining new plants but also a way of ensuring that old plants stay young and productive. It is not a difficult technique to learn and soon becomes second nature.

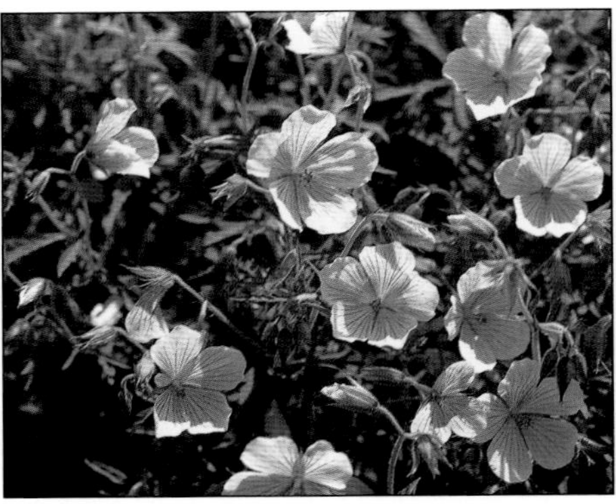

Many hardy geraniums are typical of the type of plant that can be divided to increase their numbers and to keep them healthy.

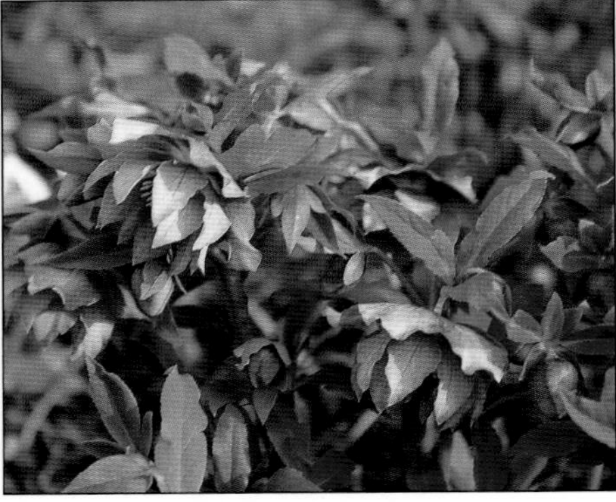

Double hellebores will only come true if they are increased by division, as seed will often produce inferior plants.

Advantages of dividing plants

Growing new plants from seed is fun and often essential if you want to grow plants to which you would otherwise have no ready access. However, seed can be a bit of a hit and miss method, because you cannot guarantee exactly what you are going to get. A plant is likely to differ from its parent: it may be shorter or taller, the foliage may be slightly different and the colour of the flower can vary considerably.

With annuals, this may not matter or there may be a sufficient degree of conformity, but with perennials it can be more of a problem. It is no good, for example, sowing seed from many of the cultivars of geraniums, as they will not come true. The plants are likely to be inferior (although there is always a chance than one might be better).

Division (and cuttings, which are dealt with elsewhere), by contrast, involves taking a bit of the original plant and reproducing it exactly. This is very important for most named perennial cultivars.

Brute force

There are several ways of dividing a plant. One popular and very easy method is by brute force: simply dig up the plant, cut a chunk off it with a sharp spade and then replant both pieces separately. This is very effective for some of the larger clump-forming plants. It does leave a lot of severed material, which can rot and, in theory, cause problems, but rarely seems to.

A refinement of this is to insert two forks into the dug-up clump, back to back, and then lever them apart, forcing the plant into two pieces, continuing until the pieces are small enough. With the exception of the older, centre pieces of the plant, which should be discarded, the pieces of plant can be replanted immediately. It is, however, always a good idea to use the opportunity to rejuvenate the soil by digging it and adding some well-rotted organic material. The best time to divide plants in this way is the spring.

Manipulation

A more sophisticated approach is to use your hands. Many plants, if shaken so the soil falls off and gently manipulated with the fingers, will fall apart into separate crowns, each of which can be either replanted in the soil or put into pots until they are needed. This is only possible with plants grown in lighter soils, although it is still possible on heavier soils if the plant is manipulated in a bucket of water. More stubborn plants, such as hellebores, can have the water washed off first with a garden hose.

It is difficult to visualize what actually happens until you try it, and then you will be surprised how easily

Using two forks back-to-back is a crude but effective method of division. It is best used with fibrous-rooted plants.

Dividing plants by manipulating them with your hands in a bucket of water produces divisions whose roots are not torn or broken.

the plant comes apart in your hands. Some plants, such as hostas for example, may need a sharp knife to separate the crowns, but generally they just fall apart.

Normally, divisions are made in spring, but if the plants are transferred to pots they can be divided at any point during the growing season.

Replanting

Larger divisions can be treated as normal plants and replanted immediately into the soil. Make certain that the plants are kept moist until they have re-established themselves, and protect them from strong winds. Smaller divisions recover more quickly if they are first grown on in pots and then planted out the following spring. Pot-grown divisions may need hardening off.

Splitting for health

Many perennials get old and woody after a few years. They die off towards the centre of the plant and the flowering becomes less profuse. If these plants are dug up, the old centres thrown away and some of the younger, outside growth replanted, the plant will be totally rejuvenated.

Larger divisions can be planted directly back into the soil – as long as you make sure that they are well watered and mulched.

DIVIDING BY HAND

1 Dig up a section of the plant, making sure that it is large enough to provide the quantity of material that you require.

2 Hold the plant firmly at the base and shake it vigorously so that the soil falls off and the roots are exposed.

3 Gently pull the plant into individual pieces, simply by manipulating it with your hands. Many plants, such as this sisyrinchium, will come apart very easily.

4 The pieces should now be potted up individually using a good compost (soil mix). Place in a shaded cold frame for a few days and then harden off.

Plants suitable for division

Acanthus
Achillea
Aconitum
Agapanthus
Anaphalis
Anemone
Anthemis
Artemisia
Aster
Astilbe
Astrantia
Bergenia
Campanula (some)
Convallaria
Coreopsis
Crambe
Delphinium
Epilobium
Epimedium
Euphorbia (some)
Galega
Geranium (some)
Helenium
Helianthus
Helleborus
Hemerocallis
Heuchera
Hosta
Inula
Iris
Kniphofia
Lamium
Liatris
Ligularia
Lobelia
Lychnis
Lysimachia
Lythrum
Meconopsis
Mentha
Monarda
Nepeta
Ophiopogon
Persicaria
Phlomis
Phormium
Physostegia
Polemonium
Polygonatum
Potentilla
Primula
Pulmonaria
Ranunculus
Rheum
Rudbeckia
Salvia (some)
Scabiosa
Schizostlis
Sedum
Sidalcea
Sisyrinchium
Smilacina
Solidago
Stachys
Symphytum
Tanacetum
Thalictrum
Tradescantia
Trollius
Uvularia
Vancouveria
Veronica

Cuttings

Taking cuttings requires slightly more dexterity than dividing plants, but is still surprisingly easy. This is certainly an important technique for a gardener to master, as some plants cannot be reproduced any other way. It is also the ideal method to use when the owner of an admired plant may not want to dig it up and divide it, but is more than willing to snip a little bit off for you.

Why take cuttings?

Like making divisions, taking cuttings is a vegetative way of propagation. In other words, it is taking part of the original plant and reproducing it, and therefore it will have all the same qualities as its parent. It takes a bit more time and trouble than making divisions but is an essential technique as not all plants are easily divided. This is particularly true for those plants that do not spread, but are restricted to a central rosette, as well as many taprooted plants (which have just one long, main root).

Useful equipment

Unlike other propagation methods, you can grow cuttings with various levels of sophistication: equipment varies from costly mist propagators (for the serious gardener who wants

Plants for basal cuttings

Achillea	*Lythrum*
Anthemis	*Macleaya*
Artemisia	*Mentha*
Aster	*Monarda*
Campanula	*Nepeta*
Chrysanthemum	*Perovskia*
Crambe	*Phlox*
Dahlia	*Physostegia*
Delphinium	*Platycodon*
Diascia	*Salvia*
Epilobium	*Scabiosa*
Gaillardia	*Sedum*
Helenium	*Senecio* (some)
Knautia	*Solidago*
Lupinus	*Verbena*
Lychnis	*Viola*

STRIKING CUTTINGS

1 Take short cuttings from the new growth at the base of the plant. These cuttings are usually to be found naturally in the spring, but they can be created by cutting the plant hard back so that new growth is formed. Place your cuttings in a plastic bag and then seal the bag.

2 To pot up your cuttings, first trim their base. Cut through the stem just below a leaf joint and then remove all the leaves, except for a few at the top. Make certain that all the cuts are clean and not jagged. A scalpel or sharp scissors are the best tools to use for this purpose, although some gardeners simply use sharp fingernails.

3 Place the cuttings in a pot of cutting compost (planting mix) made up of 50:50 sharp sand and peat or peat substitute. You can grow up to 12 in a pot. If you prefer, dip the bottom 1cm/½in of the cutting in a rooting powder before putting it in the hole. This helps some of the more difficult species to root and also prevents rotting. However, many gardeners find this quite unnecessary for most perennials.

4 Label and date the pot. Thoroughly water and place the pot in a propagator. You can use a plastic bag, but do make sure that no leaves are touching the plastic. Seal with an elastic band.

5 When the roots of the cuttings start to appear at the drainage holes of the pot, gently remove the contents.

6 Pot up the rooted cuttings once again, this time in individual pots, using a good quality potting compost (soil mix). Keep covered for a few days and then harden off.

TAKING ROOT CUTTINGS

1 Very carefully dig the plant out from the ground. You must try to make sure that the thicker roots are not damaged in the process.

2 Now wash away any soil that is clinging to the roots and then remove one or more of the thicker roots.

3 Cut the roots into lengths of about 5–8cm (2–3in). Now make a horizontal cut at the top of the cutting and a slanting cut at the bottom.

4 Fill the pot with a cutting compost (planting mix) and insert the cuttings vertically with the horizontal cut at the top, so that the latter cuts are just level with the soil surface.

5 Cover with fine grit, water and put in a frame. In spring, shoots should emerge and new roots should form. Once you are sure that there are roots, pot them up individually. Treat as any young plant.

quantity or those dealing with plants that are tricky to propagate) through medium-priced propagators to simple plastic bags (fine for the average gardener). The purpose of any type of apparatus is the same: to create a close, moist atmosphere around the cuttings so that they do not dry out.

Composts

A special compost (soil mix) called cutting compost is usually used. This will vary in composition, but is basically 50 per cent sand (for drainage) and 50 per cent a moisture-retaining medium (traditionally peat but now more likely to be a peat substitute).

Taking cuttings

Cuttings should be fresh growth that is not too soft and not too old. The shoot chosen should not have flower buds, or be in flower or seed. The best cuttings for most plants are basal ones – the young growth found at the base of a plant either in spring or after the plant has been cut to the ground later in the season. With a few plants, such as penstemons, you can take cuttings from any part of a shoot, but normally you would just take them from the tip. Cuttings vary in length depending on the plant, but try to make them at least several pairs of leaves long – say, 3–7cm (1¼–3in) – or longer than this and then trim them off when potting them up. As soon as you have taken a cutting, put it in a plastic bag and seal it.

Striking cuttings

Now "strike" (pot up) your cuttings, as shown on the opposite page. Place cuttings in a hole made by a dibber or pencil, and firm the compost down, making sure that your cuttings' bottom leaves are above the level of the compost and that the leaves of different cuttings do not touch.

Aftercare

If your potted-on cuttings are in plastic bags, turn the bag inside out once a day to remove condensation. Keep the compost moist and make sure that the pot or propagator is in a light place, but out of the sun. Once roots have formed on the cuttings, pot them up in other pots.

Root cuttings

Some plants can be grown from a small piece of root. There aren't vast numbers of plants that suit this, but for some, such as pulsatilla or oriental poppies, it is the only effective reproductive method. The best time to take root cuttings is when a plant is dormant – usually winter. Because new growth often starts below ground well before the end of winter, the usual time for taking such cuttings is early winter.

Plants for root cuttings

Acanthus
Anchusa
Anemone x *hybrida*
Campanula
Catananche
Echcinops
Eryngium
Gaillardia
Geranium
Gypsophila
Limonium
Macleaya
Mertensia
Morisia monanthos
Ostrowski magnifica
Papaver orientale
Phlox
Primula denticulata
Pulsatilla
Romneya
Stokesia laevis
Symphytum
Trollius
Verbascum

Container gardening

All kinds of garden can benefit from the use of containers. In small patios or balconies, this may be the only form of gardening possible. In larger gardens, containers are used to add another dimension to the overall design – one of their great virtues is that they add a three-dimensional quality.

Types of container

A wide variety of containers are suitable for gardens and they are generally chosen for their visual suitability. The most crucial factor is that they must have a drainage hole, so that excess water can find its way out – waterlogged plants soon die.

Another issue is that they must be frost-proof if they are to stand outside in winter without the risk of cracking or shattering. Containers should also be secure. Those that are on windowsills or are hanging must obviously be very tightly attached so that they do not fall on anyone. Perhaps less obvious, but still very important, is that pots standing on the ground must be firmly planted so that they do not topple over if knocked. A large pot filled with damp compost (soil mix) can be extremely heavy and could potentially cause a severe injury.

Which compost?

There are various composts on the market suitable for containers. Some are just called potting composts, while others claim to be specially formulated for containers. There is not much difference between them, and the final choice is personal and depends on what works best for you.

Some of the "container composts" differ from potting compost in that they contain special water-retaining granules. These hold an amazing amount of water and release it slowly for the plants' use without the compost becoming waterlogged. These granules are readily available to buy, in several forms, and can be added to any compost, so you are not restricted to composts that already contain them. The other thing that all composts contain is a slow-release fertilizer. This comes in the form of granules, which release their nutrients over a long period.

Suitable perennials for containers

Acanthus
Agapanthus
Bergenia
Cordyline
Dianthus
Diascia
Euphorbia
Geranium
Geum
Hemerocallis
Heiuchera
Hosta
Iris
Nepeta
Oenothera fruiticosa glauca
Phormium tenax
Primula
Sedum
Stachys byzantina
Verbena

Getting the best results

As mentioned, all containers must have good drainage in the form of one or more holes at their lowest part. Cover these with broken bits of pot, tiles or irregularly shaped stones, so that water can pass out but the compost is retained.

If you are using plain compost, pour it straight from the bag into the container. If you want to add water-retaining granules, pour some compost into a bucket, mix in the granules at the suggested rate, and pour the mixture into the container.

PLANTING UP A CONTAINER

1 Cover the bottom of the container with small stones or some pieces of tile or pottery, so that water can drain freely from the pot.

2 Partly fill the pot with a good quality potting compost (soil mix). Loose slow-release fertilizer and water-retaining granules can also be mixed with the compost before the pot is filled.

3 Scoop a hole in the compost and insert the plant, positioning it so that the top of the root-ball (roots) will be level with the surface of the compost.

4 Place any extra plants you wish to include around the edge of the main plant. Add more compost to fill any gaps, and firm down.

5 Insert a fertilizer pellet if you have decided to use one, rather than the loose fertilizer granules. Water thoroughly.

PLANTING UP A HANGING BASKET

1 Stand the basket on a large pot or bucket, in order to make it easier to work with. Carefully place the basket liner in position so that it fills the basket. Half-fill the liner with compost, then mix in some water-retaining crystals, following the manufacturer's instructions, to help prevent the basket from drying out. Also add some slow-release fertilizer; this will remove the necessity to feed throughout the summer.

2 Cut holes about 4cm (1½in) across in the side of the liner. Shake some of the earth off the root-ball (roots) of one of the side plants and wrap it in a strip of plastic. Poke it through the hole, remove the plastic and spread the roots out. When all the side plants are in place, fill up your basket with compost, adding more water-retaining crystals and slow-release fertilizer.

3 Plant up the rest of the basket, packing the plants much more tightly together than you would in the open ground. Smooth out the surface of the compost, removing any excess or adding a little more as necessary. Water, then hang the basket indoors until all danger of frost has passed.

Firm down the compost and top up with more so that the surface is about 2–5cm (1–2in) below the container's rim (depending on its size).

A container full of compost can be very heavy, so place it in its final position before planting it up, or you may not be able to move it there. You could put it on a wheeled trolley sold especially for containers, ready to move into position.

Hanging baskets

Ever increasing in popularity, hanging baskets can provide a riot of colour all summer long. Most hanging baskets include tender annuals so they cannot be placed outside until after the last frosts, but they can be made up in advance and left indoors until the danger of frosts has passed, by which time the basket will have filled out and with luck be in full flower.

The most successful baskets are those in which the framework cannot be seen, as it is entirely masked by plants. In many cases, the hanging basket will look like a ball of plants.

Any combination of plants can be used to create different schemes. A wonderful pot-pourri of colours can be achieved with a mixed planting, although a more sophisticated effect can be created if you use plants in the same colour or even plants of just one variety.

Watering

Containers need watering every day, sometimes more in hot, sunny conditions. Water-retaining granules help to provide some moisture, but you will still have to water on most days when it doesn't rain. Smaller containers dry out quicker than large ones because of their higher ratio of surface area to volume.

Containers sheltered from the rain, and those that contain large plants whose leaves may prevent the rain reaching the compost, may need watering even after rain.

In winter it is important not to overwater; the compost should be just moist. Automatic watering systems can be installed if you have a lot of pots or if you are often away.

Feeding

Most composts use a slow-release fertilizer, which will often last long enough to see you through the season – check the manufacturer's instructions. If necessary, top-dress with more fertilizer, which is readily available. If you make your own garden compost, you can add a slow-release fertilizer either in granules or in the tablets, which are just pressed into the soil.

Popular annuals for hanging baskets

Anagallis	*Lathyrus*
Antirrhinum	*Lurential*
Asarina	*Lobelia*
Begonia	*Myosotis*
Bidens	*Nicotiana*
Brachycome	*Pelargonium*
Camissonia	*Petunia*
Cerinthe	*Sanvitalia*
Chrysanthemum	*Schizanthus*
Diascia	*Senecio*
Echium	*Tagetes*
Felicia	*Tropaeolum*
Fuchsia	*Viola* × *wittrockiana*
Helichrysum	

Pests and diseases

Most gardeners fear pests and diseases more than anything else, and these fears are only exacerbated by the vast array of bottles, packets and sprays now found in garden centres and nurseries. In fact, serious garden problems are fairly rare and there is little reason for most gardeners to worry. The good news is that common sense is often preferable to a chemical armoury.

What causes trouble?

It is surprising how few pests and diseases actually affect perennials and annuals. Those pests that are a nuisance, such as slugs and rabbits, are big enough to be dealt with manually without recourse to chemicals. The other major pest is greenfly (aphids), but even they attack only a few plants and should not present a real threat.

Viral diseases can suddenly appear, with leaves and plants becoming distorted or discoloured, and you may need to resort to chemicals to halt their spread.

Mixed planting

Many of these problems can be overcome by having a mixed community of plants. Pests and diseases are less likely to catch hold in a mixed cottage garden than in one that specializes in just one type of plant. In the latter case, a disease is likely to affect all the plants, while in the former it will affect just a few plants, and therefore not become a serious threat. Any holes that are caused by losses from pest or disease damage will also not be so visible.

A mixed garden contains a large number of beneficial insects, which prey on the pest insects, and this results in a balanced community in which the pests will rarely get the upper hand.

Rabbits can cause a lot of damage to plants, as they have done here. Placing netting round the garden is the only solution.

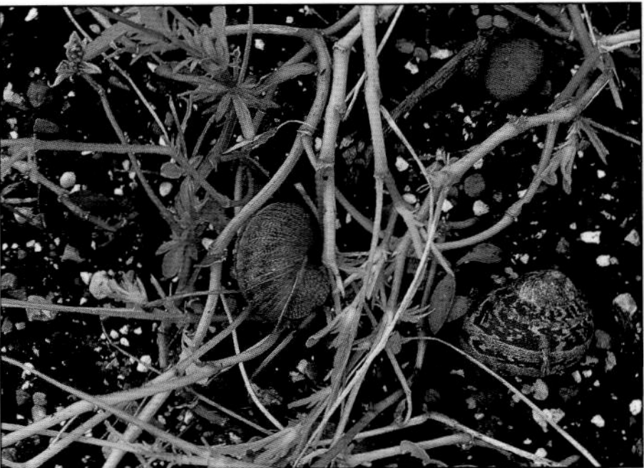

Slugs and snails are two of the gardener's worst enemies. A night-time patrol with a torch will capture a lot of them at work.

Good hygiene

Another way of ensuring that diseases rarely get a hold is to practise good hygiene. Remove all dead and dying material from the beds and borders, and be alert for any signs of diseased material so that you can deal with the problem promptly. If viruses attack, remove and burn the affected plants.

Attacking the problem by hand

With the best will in the world, problems do occur. There can be few gardens, for example, where slugs are not a nuisance, especially in early spring when the succulent shoots are first appearing. You can, of course, try to use only "slug-proof" plants, but when slugs are hungry they will eat most plants, so if you remove their favourite food, their tastes are likely to change. You can use slug bait if you are careful to ensure that pets and other animals cannot get at either the bait or the slugs once they have eaten it.

One of the best methods for getting rid of slugs is to go out in the evening as it gets dark with a torch and collect the emerging slugs in a bucket and dispose of them at some distance. (Don't throw them over your neighbour's fence: they will just crawl back and your neighbour will not be best pleased.) After a few nights, you will have reduced the population sufficiently

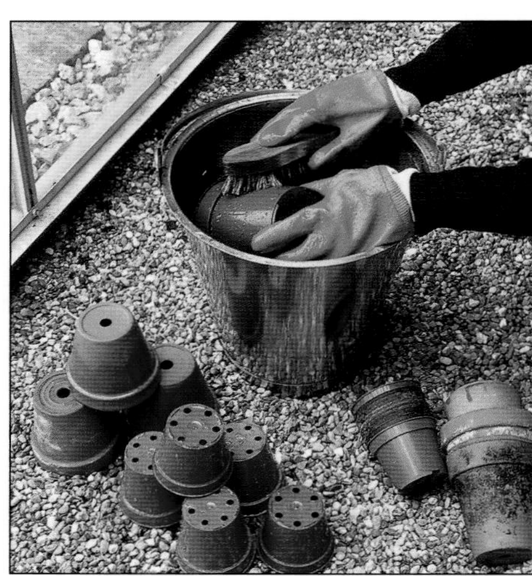

Cleaning pots by washing and scrubbing them is a good basic hygiene practice that will help prevent problems with young plants.

With some severe outbreaks of pests or diseases it may be necessary to resort, with great care, to the use of chemicals.

Damage by the caterpillars of moths and butterflies can ruin flowers. Picking them off by hand is the most effective treatment.

Greenfly and blackfly (aphids) are common pests. A mixed garden will usually provide sufficient predator insects to combat them.

Fungal diseases, such as this case of mildew, are a constant problem. Good hygiene and avoidance of overcrowding help.

so that they are no longer a problem, at least for a while. Caterpillars can also be removed by hand.

Rabbits are another big problem in some gardens. Here the only real solution is to place a rabbit-proof fence around the whole garden. You could just fence off individual borders, but the fencing does look ugly and is less obtrusive if placed around the whole boundary.

Natural predators

Introducing or encouraging beneficial insects can have a surprisingly dramatic impact on the number of pests in your garden. Check out which pests your plants are likely to fall prey to, and then simply encourage their natural predators into your garden.

Ladybirds (ladybugs) and larvae: eat aphids, scale insects, mealy bugs and caterpillars

Hoverflies and larvae: eat up to 50 aphids a day

Lacewings: eat aphids, woolly aphids, spider mites, scale insects and caterpillars

Ground beetles: eat slugs, flat worms, cabbage and carrot rootfly (eggs and larvae), vine weevils and spider mites

Anthocorid bugs: eat vine weevil larvae, caterpillars, midge larvae and spider mites

Centipedes: eat slugs and snails

Small outbreaks of aphids can be left to other predators to deal with, but if they begin to accumulate you can remove them either by running your fingers up the stems and squashing them or by simply removing the stem.

Chemical means

There are chemicals available for dealing for most pests and diseases, and if your garden suffers a serious outbreak then you may need to resort to them. Do not, however, spray widely as a precautionary measure, and spray only the parts of the plant that are affected. It is very important to follow the instructions on the bottle, packet or spray. At all costs avoid spraying the whole garden "just in case".

Regulations with regard to horticultural chemicals are in a state of flux and many traditional ones have been banned. Even some new ones leave the market only a few years after going on the shelves. Similarly, some chemicals are banned in some countries and not in others. So, if you need to treat a particular problem, consult your garden centre and make certain that you obtain something that is appropriate for your problem.

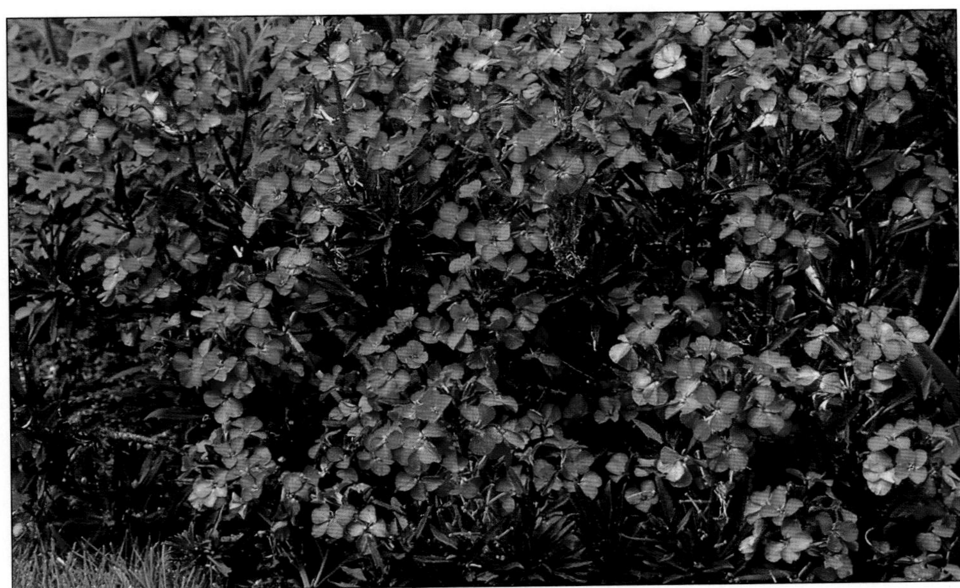

Thorough soil preparation and good general hygiene routines will help to keep plants, such as this lovely wallflower, looking fresh and healthy.

Organic gardening

In recent years, organic gardening has moved to the forefront. Like so many other aspects of gardening, however, organic practice often involves little more than plain common sense: in this case, using only natural organic materials and not using inorganic (synthetically manufactured) substances unless absolutely essential. In other words, generally working with nature rather than against it. If you follow these rules in your garden, then you are pretty well organic already.

The chemicals issue

So, in essence, organic gardening amounts simply to gardening without the use of chemicals (although some naturally occurring chemicals are allowed).

Chemicals are often used by gardeners as a form of shortcut: it is so much easier to spray a border full of weeds than it is remove all of the weeds by hand. A slight change of mindset is all that is needed here. Gardeners need to try and accept that gardening is inherently a time-consuming occupation, and that it is far better to spend a bit more time on a chore rather than waste your money on all kinds of unnecessary chemicals.

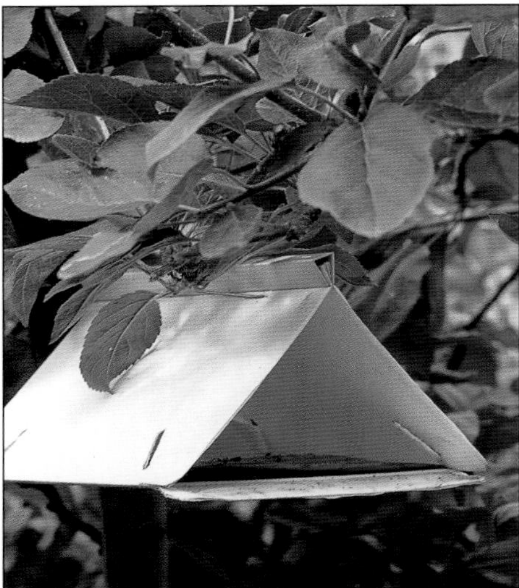

Sticky traps such as this use pheromones to attract insects, which then get trapped by the sticky substance inside.

Advantages of organic gardening

In terms of flower gardening specifically with annuals and perennials, the visual results of following organic principles are pretty minimal, but over time there are great advantages to the garden as a whole. If, for example, you treat the soil with well-rotted organic materials, such as garden compost (soil mix) or farmyard manure, then the structure of the soil will be improved and the plants fed at the same time. If, on the other hand, you just add chemical feeds to the soil, you will have well-grown plants, but, over the years, the structure of the soil will break down and in the long term plants will suffer.

A build-up of residues within the soil and run-off into watercourses is another problem that can develop if you use chemical fertilizers. They do not break down in the same way that organic fertilizers, such as bonemeal, do. The same is true of using

Try to provide places for lacewings and other beneficial insects to overwinter. This raised box, which has been stuffed with straw, is an ideal winter home for them.

Pests may be confused and so deterred from attacking certain plants if the latter are surrounded by another very different type of plant, such as the marigolds seen here.

Surrounding prized plants with slug traps, such as this piece of guttering filled with water, may deter attacks.

chemicals to kill weeds or attack pests and diseases. Also, these chemicals often have unwanted side-effects. Pesticides aimed at killing greenfly (aphids) often also destroy beneficial insects such as bees, which are essential to gardening.

How can you be organic?

Starting with the soil, always try to use well-rotted organic material when preparing or top-dressing beds. You will find that this will improve the structure of the soil as well as providing nutrients.

If you need to feed plants, then choose organic fertilizers, such as bonemeal, made from naturally occurring materials. (Note that you will need to wear rubber/latex gloves when you are handling bonemeal preparations.) You can also make your own very effective foliar feeds for a quick pick-up by steeping nettles or comfrey in water and then watering or spraying the plants with the resulting liquid.

Always remove any weeds by hand, when you are digging over a bed, rather than resorting to chemicals. When you are preparing a new bed or border, rather than spray the whole thing with weedkiller, simply cover it with some black plastic sheeting or an old carpet – to deprive weeds of the light that they need to grow. When weeding existing borders, once again work by hand for the very best results.

Rid your borders of any slugs and caterpillars by manually removing them rather than killing them by bait, and keep a well-balanced border of mixed plantings, so that severe bouts of particular infestations are less likely to occur.

Friendly insects

- Anthocorid bugs
- Bees
- Centipedes
- Earwigs*
- Ground beetles
- Harvestmen
- Lacewings
- Ladybirds (ladybugs)
- Parasitic wasps and flies
- Rove beetles (commonly known as devil's coach and horses)
- Spiders

*Often considered a nuisance because they eat the petals of some plants, such as dahlias. However, they also eat many pests.

Encourage wildlife

Wildlife, such as birds and other animals, are fun to have in the garden. They are also beneficial. Although birds can be a nuisance in the fruit and vegetable garden (spreading some netting over vulnerable plants and trees should stop this), they are very useful in the flower garden as they eat a lot of pests, such as aphids and caterpillars.

Animals such as hedgehogs eat the worst enemy of most gardeners – the slug – while many garden birds make short work of snails. Flowers that attract ladybirds and lacewings are worth growing, as the larvae of these eat large quantities of greenfly.

Chemicals can be harmful to all these forms of wildlife, so this is another reason why they should be avoided if at all possible.

The larvae of ladybirds eat incredible quantities of aphids and so are worth encouraging into the garden.

Birds love seed beds, so try to deter them by hanging shining kitchen foil above the bed to frighten them off.

A directory of annuals

This directory offers a comprehensive array of annual plants – all the familiar favourites plus some rarer specimens – among which gardeners of all levels will find ample choice to help them make the most of their garden space.

The initial introduction for each entry is either for the whole genus or the main species grown. Beyond this the entry is split between more common species and cultivars and those which are less common. The advent of the internet has meant that it is often possible to obtain seed, including that of very rare plants, from around the world. Growing rarer species can be rewarding as they are often particularly beautiful. On the other hand they may be less common because they are more difficult to grow and thus create a challenge. If no temperatures are given, seed can be germinated in a cool greenhouse or even in pots left outside.

Where seed is listed as being available from seed merchants, this can be purchased directly from the merchants using their catalogues or from a store or garden centre. Some unusual varieties are available mail order only from a catalogue. Many specialist societies make seed available to their members – a good way of obtaining rarer seed. Check catalogues carefully as some seed merchants have idiosyncratic or very out-of-date ways of naming plants that may be at variance with botanical names and with those that have been used in this book.

Begonia semperflorens has long been a very popular gardener's choice and offers a wide selection of attractively coloured cultivars.

Adonis aestivalis

ADONIS
Pheasant's Eye

This is a genus containing about 20 species of annuals and perennials. Of these, only a couple of the annuals are generally grown. These are so similar that the gardener might not notice the slight botanical difference. They are thin and upright plants with feathery foliage. The flowers are bright red and cup-shaped; they look like the red buttercups to which they are related. These plants thrive in disturbed ground; they were once widespread among crops in cornfields but they are rarely seen growing wild today. They are attractive enough to be used in borders, particularly when planted in large drifts, but they are more commonly seen in beds devoted to wild flowers. They are hardy. H 45cm (18in) S 15cm (6in).

How to obtain These plants can generally only be obtained as seed. This is widely available from good seed merchants as well as from specialist societies.

Cultivation Thin the plants to about 15cm (6in) to produce a dense mass. They need a soil enriched with plenty of well-rotted organic material. It should be free draining. A position in full sun is needed. Z6.

Propagation Sow directly into the soil where the plants are to grow in either autumn or in spring. An autumn sowing produces more vigorous plants.

Uses Adonis look good in mixed beds and borders, especially in wild-flower gardens.

Adonis aestivalis

This is the most commonly seen plant. It has very finely cut leaves which set off the bright crimson flowers with a darker centre. These are produced over a very long period from midsummer to well into autumn. If you can find it there is a rare variety of *A. aestivalis* called *citrina* which has yellow flowers.

Adonis annua

This plant is very similar to the previous species but the flowers are a deeper red.

Other plants There is also a species called *A. flammea* which is worth seeking out. It is similar to the ones described above except that the flowers are larger.

AGERATUM
Floss flower

This moderately large genus contains about 40 species of perennials and shrubs as well as annuals. There is only one annual that is in general cultivation, namely *A. houstonianum*, but fortunately it has plenty of cultivars so the gardener does not lack choice. The plants are rounded and produce fluffy sprays of blue flowers. Over the years pink and white cultivars have also been introduced. Ageratum have long been used as bedding plants, and are often grown in swathes in a bed or as ribbon-like edging along a path or around beds. H and S 20–30cm (8–12in), athough some cultivars reach up to 75cm (30in).

How to obtain Ageratums can be bought as seed from most seed merchants and they are available as young plants in spring from garden centres and nurseries. Plants may be sold as "Ageratum" without any cultivar being given.

Cultivation Plant out after frosts have passed in a fertile soil in full sun. Z10.

Propagation Seed can be sown under glass at 16–18°C (60–64°F) in spring. For larger plants sow in late autumn and overwinter the resulting plants in warm conditions.

Uses Ageratums make excellent bedding plants, grown in blocks or lines. They are good in window boxes and other containers. Some are good for cutting.

***Ageratum houstonianum* 'Bavaria'**

This pretty cultivar has fluffy flower heads in blue and white. H up to 25cm (10in).

***Ageratum houstonianum* 'Blue Danube'**

This is a short form which produces attractive pale blue flowers. H 20cm (8in).

***Ageratum houstonianum* 'Blue Horizon'**

This is a tall variety with purple-blue clusters of flowers, which is good for cutting. H 45–60cm (18–24in) or more.

***Ageratum houstonianum* Hawaii Series**

These short plants produce flowers either in a mixture of colours ('Hawaii Mixed', 'Hawaii Garland') or in individual colours such as 'Hawaii White'. H 15cm (6in).

***Ageratum houstonianum* 'Swing Pink'**

This is another dwarf form, which produces pretty pink flowers. H 15cm (6in).

***Ageratum houstonianum* 'Purple Fields'**

The flowers of this cultivar are purple. H 25cm (10in).

***Ageratum houstonianum* 'Red Sea'**

Bright red buds open to purple-red flowers. They are good for cutting. H 45cm (18in).

Ageratum houstonianum

Agrostemma githago 'Milas'

AGROSTEMMA
Corn cockle

This is a small genus of annuals of which only a couple are generally cultivated. They grow naturally on disturbed or waste ground, and as their name implies they were once often seen growing in fields of corn.

Corn cockles are tall plants which have thin, wiry stems and open funnel-shaped flowers. These are purple with a white centre, and appear in summer. Although they work well in drifts in a mixed border they are often grown in wild-flower gardens. H 1m (3ft) in good conditions, S 30cm (12in).

How to obtain Corn cockle is usually available as seed from seed merchants or from specialist societies. Plants are rarely offered for sale, but they can occasionally be found.

Cultivation Corn cockles grow in a fertile soil in a sunny position. Plants are shown at their best when they are tightly planted together, so do not thin too vigorously. They need support in exposed positions. Z8

Propagation Sow the seed in spring where the plants are to grow. If left to set seed, corn cockles will usually self-sow.

Uses Corn cockles are best grown in either mixed borders or a wild area of the garden.

Agrostemma githago and _A. gracilis_

These species are similar to each other, and produce the purple flowers described above. The seed of *A. githago* is more common, and there are some cultivars.

Agrostemma githago 'Milas'

This is the cultivar most widely grown. It has pinker flowers than the species.

Agrostemma githago 'Milas Cerise'

This is very similar to the previous cultivar, except that the flowers are cerise.

Tall annuals

Agrostemma githago 'Milas'	*Helianthus annuus*
Alcea rosea	*Lavatera trimestris*
Amaranthus caudatus	*Moluccella laevis*
Centaurea americana	*Nicotiana affinis*
Cleome spinosa	*Nicotiana sylvestris*
Consolida ambigua	*Oenothera biennis*
Cosmos	*Ricinus communis*
Dahlia	*Tithonia rotundifolia*
Datura	*Zea mays*
Gilia rubra	*Zinnia*

Agrostemma githago 'Ocean Pearl'

This is a beautiful cultivar with pure white flowers. It is a must for the white garden.

ALCEA
Hollyhock

This genus produces the much-loved hollyhock. This is *A. rosea,* a perennial that is now generally grown as a biennial. Hollyhocks are very tall plants, but there are shorter cultivars that are more suitable for smaller gardens. They have one or more tall stems on which appear open funnel-shaped flowers. Some cultivars have double flowers. The flowers are produced over most of the summer and into autumn. The plants are hardy. H 2.5m (8ft).

How to obtain Hollyhocks can be purchased as seed from seed merchants or as plants from garden centres and nurseries. The plants may be sold simply as "Hollyhocks" with no colour given. The seed can be mixed or one colour. *Alcea* may be listed as its former name *Althaea*.

Cultivation Plant or thin out seedlings to intervals of 60cm (24in). They like a deep, rich soil that is well-drained. Plants may need staking in exposed areas. Hollyhocks can suffer from rust so remove them after flowering and raise new plants from seed rather than keeping old ones for subsequent years. Z4.

Propagation Sow seed where the plants are to grow. Plants left to seed will self-sow.

Uses Hollyhocks are excellent plants for either mixed or herbaceous borders.

Alcea rosea 'Black Beauty'

As its name suggests this is a black-flowered variety.

Alcea rosea 'Chater's Double'

This cultivar produces fully double flowers that look like pompoms. They come in a wide range of colours. The seed is sold as mixed or individual colours.

Alcea rosea 'Majorette Mixed'

This cultivar produces semi-double blooms in mixed pastel shades. H 1m (3ft).

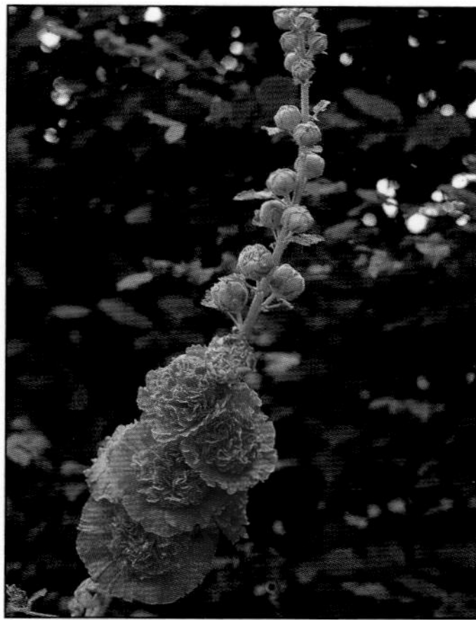

Alcea rosea 'Chater's Double'

Alcea rosea 'Nigra'

This is an ancient cultivar known for at least 400 years. It carries very dark red flowers that are almost black. There is a rarer double form of the same colour, called 'Nigra Plena'.

Alcea rosea 'Peaches 'n' Dreams'

This plant produces very frilly double flowers in a soft peach-pink colour.

Alcea rosea 'Zanzibar'

Flowers in a range of pastel shades are produced on tall plants. H 2m (6ft).

Other plants *Alcea ficifolia* is another hollyhock treated as a biennial. It is similar to the above except that the leaves are more lobed. The flowers are yellow or orange, single or double. 'Antwerp Mixed' is a mix of pastel shades.

Alcea rosea

Amaranthus caudatus

Anchusa capensis 'Dawn Mixed'

AMARANTHUS
Love-lies-bleeding

A large genus of half-hardy annuals and short-lived perennials. *A. caudatus* is of most interest to the general gardener. It has dangling flowers that look like bunches of lambs' tails or ropes, mainly in crimson or purple. They have an old-fashioned look about them and are not seen as often in gardens as they once were. They can be used in small groups in general borders or in bedding schemes. They are long flowering through summer and autumn.
How to obtain The main way to acquire these is as seed from merchants. Occasionally plants are available from garden centres.
Cultivation Plant out after the threat of frosts has passed in a soil with plenty of well-rotted organic material. It should be moisture-retentive but free-draining. Z5.
Propagation Sow the seed under glass in the spring at 16–18°C (60–64°F).
Uses These plants are best grown in general mixed borders or in bedding schemes.

Amaranthus caudatus
This, the main species grown, can reach 1.2m (4ft), but is often less. S 60cm (24in). The tassels are red or purple, although there is a cultivar 'Viridis' or 'Green Tails' with greenish flowers.

Amaranthus cruentus
Known as Prince's Feather, this plant has more upright spikes in a variety of reds and yellows. There are a large number of cultivars available, including 'Red Cathedral' which has attractive scarlet foliage.

Amaranthus hypochondriacus
Upright spikes of flowers, mainly in shades of red. 'Green Thumb' has green flowers and 'Pygmy Torch' is a dwarf variety only 45cm (18in) high.

Amaranthus tricolor
This is Chinese spinach, grown for its decorative foliage which comes in several colours. 'Joseph's Coat' has a mixture of red, yellow, brown and green leaves, while 'Illumination' has bright pinkish-red, gold and brown leaves.

ANCHUSA
Anchusa

This is a genus of about 35 species of which a number are annuals or biennials. One in particular is of interest to the annual gardener, namely *A. capensis*. This is strictly speaking a perennial but it is usually grown as an annual. It is a clump-forming plant with long, narrow leaves that are rough with bristles, and sprays of shallow funnel-shaped flowers that flower in summer. The flowers are generally blue with a white throat although there are other cultivars with a range of colours. H up to 45cm (18in) S 20cm (8in).
How to obtain These plants are available as seed from seed merchants and specialist societies.
Cultivation Plant out or thin the young plants at 30cm (12in) intervals. Any reasonable garden soil will do but a well-draining, moisture-retentive one is preferred. Plant in full sun. Z9.
Propagation When treated as an annual, sow the seed under glass in early spring at 16–18°C (60–64°F). It can be treated as a biennial by sowing outside in summer and transplanting in the autumn or spring.
Uses Anchusas can be used as bedding plants or grown in a mixed border.

Anchusa capensis
The species is less popular than in the past, but it is still an excellent blue-flowered plant.

***Anchusa capensis* 'Blue Angel'**
This is an attractive cultivar which produces flowers that are bright blue in colour.

***Anchusa capensis* 'Blue Bird'.**
Indigo-blue flowers. This is an old variety but it is probably still the most popular.

***Anchusa capensis* 'Dawn Mixed'**
The flowers are in a mixture of colours – mainly blue with white, pink, red and purple.

***Anchusa capensis* 'Dwarf Mix'**
These plants are smaller and more compact with blue flowers. The seed is more difficult to find.

***Anchusa capensis* 'Pink Bird'**
As its name suggests, this cultivar has pink flowers.

ANGELICA
Angelica

This genus of about 50 species is known mainly to gardeners for the herb *A. archangelica*. However, there is a species that has only recently entered general

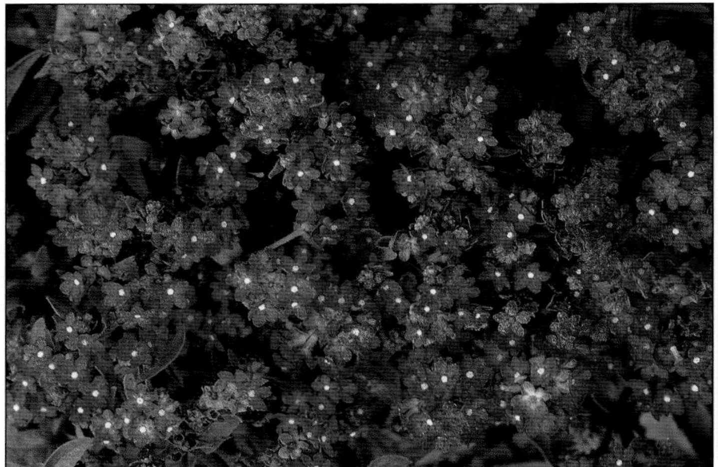
Anchusa capensis

Angelica gigas

cultivation that makes an excellent biennial for the border. This is *A. gigas*, a native of Japan. It has gorgeous heads of maroon flowers which are perfect for the mixed border, or for the edge of a woodland or shrub bed. It can be dramatic and eyecatching. The plants are monocarpic, that is they may grow for one, two or more years before they flower, but once they have flowered they die. Fortunately angelicas make good foliage plants so their growing time is not wasted. H 2m (6ft) S 1–1.2m (3–4ft). They are completely hardy.
How to obtain The seed is available from some seed merchants. The plants are available from nurseries and some garden centres.
Cultivation Any reasonable garden soil will do, but the richer and more moist the soil, the more splendid the plants will be. Plant out as soon as possible in either spring or autumn, in either full sun or partial shade. Z4.
Propagation Angelicas are grown from seed which is sown in autumn or spring.
Uses Angelicas look very good in borders or in woodland settings. They are excellent for wilder, more exotic plantings.

Angelica gigas
This is a truly splendid towering plant. The flowers are carried in domed heads produced on black stems above dissected, bright green leaves. The large heads are a fabulous dark crimson in colour. H 2m (6ft) S 1–1.2m (3–4ft).

Antirrhinum majus 'Black Prince'

Antirrhinum 'Coronette Bronze'

Antirrhinum 'Coronette White'

Other plants *Angelica archangelica* is mainly grown as a herb but it is decorative enough to deserve a place in the border, especially in a wild-flower garden. The flowers are white, and the stems and leaves dullish green. *Angelica atropurpurea* is similar to the previous plant, also having white flowers, but the stems are a contrasting purple. You will have to hunt a little further to find the seed and plants.

ANTIRRHINUM
Snapdragon
Surely all gardeners know these excellent garden plants. Quite a number of the 40 species are in cultivation but most gardeners grow just *A. majus*, which is the common snapdragon. These are bushy plants producing several spikes of curiously shaped flowers. Plants are now available in a wide range of colours and sizes. There are some forms with double flowers and others with variegated foliage. One impressive breakthrough is the trailing varieties, which look wonderful in hanging baskets. H 25–60cm (10–24in) S 45cm (18in).
How to obtain All seed merchants offer several varieties and plants can be bought from garden centres, both as colour mixtures or separate colours. The plants are available either in trays or individual pots.
Cultivation Antirrhinums will grow in any good garden soil. Plant or thin to about 45cm (18in). Z7.
Propagation Grow from seed sown under glass at 16–18°C (60–64°F) in early spring. The seed can also be sown in open ground in spring for late-flowering plants.
Uses Antirrhinums are excellent for mixed borders or for bedding. They are also very good plants for children's gardens. Some varieties are suitable for containers including hanging baskets. Taller varieties make good cut flowers

Antirrhinum majus 'Chinese Lanterns'
This is one of the new trailing forms. It produces flowers in a mixture of colours.

Antirrhinum majus Coronette Series
This attractive plant series carries flowers in a mix of colours. They are also available as individual colours, as in the cultivars 'Coronette Bronze' and 'Coronette White'. H 60cm (24in).

Antirrhinum majus 'Floral Showers'
A dwarf collection, with plants growing up to 20cm (8in) tall.

Antirrhinum majus Mme Butterfly Series
These plants produce double flowers in a mixture of colours. H 75cm (30in).

Antirrhinum majus Rocket Series
As its name suggests, this is a very tall range. Plants reach up to 1.2m (4ft) in good conditions.

Other plants These include 'Sonnet Light Rose' and 'Black Prince'. Check seed catalogues for a better idea of the complete range.

Antirrhinum 'Sonnet Light Rose'

Arctotis 'Flame'

ARCTOTIS
African daisy

This is a genus of some 50 species from South Africa. There are several annual and short-lived perennials that are used as bedding plants. They are rather splendid daisies, generally having white or orange petals with a dark ring round the central black or brown disc. They are bright and gay but have the disadvantage that they shut up if the sun is not shining and generally shut half-way through the afternoon. However, the flowers of some newer cultivars stay open longer. H 60cm (24in) S 30cm (12in).
How to obtain The best way is to obtain these plants as seed since the main seed merchants sell them. They can also be bought as plants from many garden centres.

Arctotis × *hybrida* 'Apricot'

Cultivation A well-drained soil in full sun is essential. Plant out after frosts have passed. Z9.
Propagation Sow the seed in early spring under glass at 16–18°C (60–64°F) and prick out into individual pots.
Uses These make excellent bedding plants so long as they have plenty of sunshine. They are also good for very well-drained border, such as a gravel garden. They can be used as cut flowers.

Arctotis fastuosa
One of the easiest species to obtain. It has large 10cm (4in) flowers with orange petals and a black inner band. It provides one of the best-known cultivars, 'Zulu Prince', whose flowers have gleaming white petals with black and orange inner bands.

***Arctotis* Harlequin Hybrids**
A mixed strain of seed with daisies in white, orange, pink, red or apricot. The Harlequin New Hybrids have the same range of colours and sometimes also have inner black bands. They also include some individual cultivars such as 'Apricot'.

Arctotis venusta
The flowers of this attractive plant are creamy-white in colour, with a blue central disc.

Other plants *Arctotis hirsuta* is a hairy plant, with orange, yellow or white flowers with a yellow inner band and a black central disc.

ARGEMONE
Prickly poppy

A genus of about 30 species of which there are a number of annuals in cultivation. The name prickly poppy refers to the fact that the large seed heads are covered in vicious spines, as are the leaves. Although this makes weeding and seed collecting a dangerous occupation, the flowers are absolutely delightful and so these plants are worth growing. The flowers, like many poppies, look like crumpled tissue paper. They are either glistening white or a wonderful yellow with a contrasting central boss of red stamens. The prickly leaves are an attractive colour; a bluish-green with silvery markings. These are rather open, sprawling plants, so they are not suited to bedding schemes. They look good mixed with other plants in the front of a herbaceous border. Most are short-lived perennials and may last into a second year. The plants will flower all summer and continue into autumn if they are deadheaded regularly. They can reach up to 1.5m (5ft) but are usually no more than 45cm (18in) in most garden situations.
How to obtain The seed for prickly poppies can be obtained from some of the more specialized seed merchants as well as from specialist societies. The plants can occasionally be found in nurseries.
Cultivation Plant out after frosts have passed in a well-drained soil that is not too rich. Prickly poppies tolerate poor soils. Z8.
Propagation Sow seed at 16–18°C (60–64°F) under glass in the early spring.
Uses These plants are best used in a mixed border. They are excellent for gravel gardens.

Argemone grandiflora

Argemone mexicana

Argemone grandiflora
This has white or yellow flowers up to 10cm (4in) across. The leaves have white veining.

Argemone mexicana
This is very similar to the previous plant except that the flowers are slightly smaller and are generally yellow. There is a creamy-yellow variety *ochroleuca*, as well as the white forms 'Alba' or 'White Lustre' and a deeper, orange-yellow form 'Yellow Lustre'. These are more difficult to find than the species but they are worth looking out for.

Other plants *A. pleiacantha* has large white flowers up to 15cm (6in) across. Otherwise it is very similar to *A. grandiflora*. *A. polyanthemos* is not so prickly; the large flowers are either white or pale lilac.

ARGYRANTHEMUM
Argyranthemum

A genus of 23 species which were once classified as *Chrysanthemum* to which they have a great visual resemblance. They have daisy-like

Argemone platyceras 'Silver Charm'

Argyranthemum 'Jamaica Primrose'

flowers either with an outer ring of petals and a yellow central disc or an outer ring of petals with a similar coloured pompom of petals in the middle. The colours are white, yellow or pink. These flowers are produced over a long period, through the summer and up to the first frosts. They are tender perennials, which are usually treated as annuals. H 60–100cm (2–3ft) S 60cm (24in).
How to obtain Argyranthemums are usually purchased as plants in individual pots. They are available from garden centres and nurseries.
Cultivation Plant in a well-drained fertile soil after frosts are over. They need a sunny position. Z9.
Propagation Take basal cuttings from plants in spring or tip cuttings in summer; overwinter the resulting plants under glass.
Uses Argyranthemums are versatile plants that can be used in mixed borders, as bedding plants and in containers.

***Argyranthemum* 'Blizzard'**
This cultivar produces double flowers which have narrow, shaggy white petals.

***Argyranthemum* 'Cornish Gold'**
The flowers of this cultivar are yellow with yellow centres. H 60cm (24in).

Argyranthemum frutescens
This is one of the *Argyranthemum* species from which many of the cultivars are derived. It is also grown in its own right, and has yellow flowers.

***Argyranthemum* 'Jamaica Primrose'**
One of the best, with soft primrose-yellow petals and a golden central disc.

***Argyranthemum* 'Mary Cheek'**
Pink outer petals surround a pink pompom of petals. This is a smallish plant. H 45cm (18in).

Long-flowering annuals

Ageratum	*Nicotiana*
Argyranthemum	*Pelargonium*
Begonia	*Petunia*
Brachyscome iberidifolia	*Portulaca grandiflora*
Calendula officinalis	*Salvia*
Heliotropium arborescens	*Tagetes*
Impatiens	*Thunbergia alata*
Lobelia erinus	*Tropaeolum majus*
Matthiola incana	*Verbena* × *hybrida*
Mimulus	*Viola* × *wittrockiana*

Argyranthemum 'Vancouver'

***Argyranthemum* 'Mary Wootton'**
This plant is similar to the previous one but it is much larger. H 1.2m (4ft).

***Argyranthemum* 'Petite Pink'**
The flowers of these plants have pink outer petals and a yellow central disc. H 30cm (12in).

***Argyranthemum* 'Snowstorm'**
Another short plant with white outer petals and a yellow central disc. H 30cm (12in).

***Argyranthemum* 'Vancouver'**
This is a pink-flowered cultivar, which is similar to 'Mary Wootton'.

Other plants *Argyranthemum gracile* 'Chelsea Girl' is one of the finest cultivars to use in containers; it is often overwintered and grown as a standard. It is also used as a bedding plant. The flowers are white and the foliage is very fine and hair-like.

ATRIPLEX
Red orache

A large genus of plants that are mainly weeds or plants of no consequence. However, there is one that is important to gardeners, namely *A. hortensis*. This is often grown as a spinach substitute in the vegetable garden, but the red form 'Rubra' is widely grown as a very decorative plant. It is very tall and makes a positive statement in the border. H 1.5m (5ft) S 75cm (30in).
How to obtain Red orache is best grown from seed which is widely available. You occasionally see plants but they rarely grow to their full potential because they tend to be starved in small pots.
Cultivation Transplant any seedlings when they are very young or they will not thrive. Thin or transplant to 75cm (30in) intervals. Red oraches will grow in any garden soil but they do best in a rich, well-fed one. A sunny site is best; in shade the leaves turn green. Z6.
Propagation Sow the seed where the plants are to grow in autumn or in spring.
Uses These plants work well in mixed borders but they can also be used as a tall centrepiece in a bedding scheme.

***Atriplex hortensis* 'Rubra'**
This is the most commonly grown plant. Its leaves, stems and spikes of small but numerous flowers are all a deep purplish-red. This colour looks rather leaden in dull light but it turns a fabulous blood-red against a setting sun. The young leaves are a colourful addition to salads. The plant self-sows madly, so cut it down before the seed is shed. H 1.5m (5ft) S 75cm (30in).

Other plants The Plume series is a newer strain of seed that includes 'Copper Plume', which has deep red flowers, 'Gold Plume' (straw-coloured flowers), 'Green Plume' (bright green flowers) and 'Red Plume' (deep, rich red flowers and foliage). These plants are rather more difficult to track down, but they are undoubtedly worth seeking out for their decorative quality.

Atriplex hortensis 'Rubra'

Barbarea vulgaris 'Variegata'

BARBAREA
Barbarea

This is a small genus of plants, most of which are of no interest to the gardener. The exception is *B. vulgaris* which is known as winter cress and commonly grown as a salad ingredient. This is of no consequence in the flower garden but it has a variegated form 'Variegata' that is widely grown as a foliage plant. The leaves are darkish green and are splashed with golden-yellow. It is a member of the cabbage family and the flowers are the familiar four-petalled yellow ones which add little to the border and so are usually removed. It is worth leaving some on the plant, however, so that you have seed for the following year. The plants are biennial. They are tall and narrow, so quite a number of plants are needed to make an impact.
H 45cm (18in) when grown in good soil, S 20cm (8in) across.
How to obtain You can get barbareas as individual plants but this is an expensive way of buying them if you need a lot. You may have to search for seed but it is available from a number of seed merchants. Alternatively buy one plant and collect seed from it.
Cultivation Barbareas can be grown in any reasonable garden soil, and can be used either in a sunny or in a partially shaded position. Remove flowers unless seed is required. Z6.
Propagation Sow the seed in the open, as soon as possible after it has been collected.
Uses Barbareas look good in mixed borders or bedding schemes, and help brighten up darker corners.

BASSIA
Burning bush

A genus of about 25 species of perennials and annuals of which only one is grown in gardens. This is *B. scoparia* in the form *trichophylla*. It is a foliage plant that forms a bright green bush which is attractive in its own right. However, as the summer proceeds it turns a brilliant red or orange, hence its name "burning bush". The flowers are inconspicuous and of no relevance to most gardeners. Burning bushes are truly spectacular plants but while they used to be very popular but they are seen less frequently now. This is a pity since they make excellent plants for bedding as well as for filling gaps in perennial borders. Being green in the first instance they act as a foil for more brightly coloured plants. They look and feel soft.

Plants vary in size considerably depending on soil and other conditions. They can be anything from a modest 30cm (12in) up to 1.5m (5ft) when growing well. They are conical in shape and tend not to be so wide as they are tall. S up to 45cm (18in).
How to obtain Although it is now less frequently seen than in the past, seed is still available from many merchants. It is often listed under its old name *Kochia trichopylla*. It is also worth looking out for the plants in garden centres. Z6.

Begonia semperflorens (flower detail)

Cultivation Do not plant out until after the frosts have finished, then plant in any reasonably fertile soil in a sunny position. Larger plants need shelter from winds. Z6.
Propagation Sow under glass at 16–18°C (60–64°F) in early spring. It is also possible to sow seed directly where the plants are to grow in late spring, but the resulting bushes are not very big.
Uses Excellent for borders and bedding and are especially good as central features. They can be used as specimen plants in containers.

Other plants There are no cultivars. It would be a bonus if different coloured forms were to be bred.

BEGONIA
Begonia

This is a very large genus of some 900 species of which a number are in cultivation along with a great many cultivars. The begonia is a plant that gardeners can become very attached to, and many people collect different varieties. Here we can only scratch the surface of this fascinating group of plants, concentrating on those that are grown in the garden. (There are many more that are cultivated in greenhouses. These are in fact perennials but are treated as annuals since they are tender.) The most common garden form are the semperflorens begonias. Another group that are often seen growing outside, especially as container plants are the tuberhybrida begonias.
How to obtain The easiest way to obtain begonias is by buying plants, which are available from garden centres. Semperflorens can be bought in trays or pots and tuberhybrida in pots. Frequently they are sold as simply 'begonias' with no cultivar name given. Trays often contain plants in mixed

Bassia scoparia

Begonia semperflorens

colours, so you will need to buy plants in flower if you want particular forms. Both can also be obtained as seed. Gardeners who want to start a collection should go to specialist nurseries for a wider selection.
Cultivation Plant out after the last frosts in a good humus-rich soil which is either neutral or acid. Begonias need a lightly shaded position. Z10.
Propagation Sow seed in early spring under glass at about 20°C (68°F). Take cuttings in early summer and overwinter the young plants under warm glass.
Uses Semperflorens are superb in bedding schemes since they are usually of uniform height and so look good when planted in blocks. They are also used a lot in all forms of containers. The tuberhybrids can be used in bedding but they are shown at their best in containers.

Begonia semperflorens
These are low bushy plants with succulent stems and waxy-looking leaves and flowers. The flowers are commonly white, pink or red. They appear in early summer and continue until the first frosts. The foliage is either green or bronzy-purple. There are many cultivars to choose from. However for most garden purposes it is simply a matter of picking a colour that suits your scheme rather than seeking out any specific variety. H and S 15–45cm (6–18in).

Begonia × tuberhybrida
The tuberous begonias produce much more blowsy flowers. They are usually, but not always doubles in a wide variety of colours, often coming as picotees (edged in a different colour). These are generally too delicate for bedding, but they make good container plants. H 25–45cm (10–18in) S 30cm (12in).

BELLIS
Daisy
The humble common daisy may be the bane of gardeners' lawns but it is nevertheless a very pretty flower and there are some excellent varieties for use in borders and bedding. To many modern gardeners they look old-fashioned and have a quality reminiscent of cottage gardens. As a result, they are not seen quite so much nowadays as previously. There are about 15 species but it is the only the common daisy, *B. perennis* that is of interest. It has given rise to a large number of garden varieties. The attraction of many of these is that their flowers are double. They are either white or shades of pink, sometimes both. Strictly speaking, these plants are perennials but they are usually treated as annuals because flower quality reduces in later years. H and S 20cm (8in).
How to obtain Daisies can be obtained in single pots and occasionally in trays. Some varieties are also available as seed.
Cultivation Daisies grow in any reasonable garden soil. They prefer a sunny position, but they will tolerate a little shade. Z4.
Propagation Divide existing plants in spring. Sow seed in the open ground in summer and transplant in the autumn or spring. They can also be sown in early spring under cool glass.
Uses Use in bedding schemes, along paths or border edges, or as clumps in a mixed border.

Bellis perennis
The common daisy is usually considered a weed but it can look attractive when grown in a wild meadow or lawn. Its cultivars come in white, pink or red. They include the Pomponette Series, which have large double heads; the Rogli Series, which are semi-doubles; and the Tasso Series, which have some of the biggest heads. 'Rose Carpet' has double flowers and 'Habanera' is a double with long petals.

Bellis perennis 'Rogli Rose'

Annuals that can be used as cut flowers

Agrostemma githago
Alcea rosea
Amaranthus caudatus
Antirrhinum majus
Brachyscome iberidifolia
Calendula officinalis
Callistephus chinensis
Campanula medium
Celosia plumosa
Centaurea cyanus
Chrysanthemum
Clarkia elegans
Consolida ambigua
Coreopsis
Cosmos
Dahlia
Dianthus barbatus
Digitalis purpurea
Erysimum cheiri
Gaillardia pulchella
Gypsophila elegans
Helianthus annuus
Helipterum roseum
Hesperis
Lathyrus odoratus
Limonium sinuatum
Matthiola
Moluccella laevis
Nigella damascena
Reseda odorata
Rudbeckia hirta
Salpiglossis
Scabiosa atropurpurea
Tagetes erecta
Tagetes patula
Tithonia rotundifolia
Xeranthemum annuum
Zinnia elegans

Bellis perennis 'Pomponette'

Beta vulgaris subsp. cicla 'Charlotte'

BETA
Beet

This is a small genus of plants that is best known for its vegetables, particularly beetroot. Some of the plants are decorative, including another vegetable, Swiss chard or ruby chard (*B. vulgaris* subsp. *cicla*), which is often grown as a garden plant. With Swiss Chard, it is not the flower that is important but the foliage and the stems. There is also the advantage that they can be eaten.
How to obtain These plants can only be obtained as seed, but nearly all merchants carry them and a number of different varieties are available.
Cultivation Beets will grow in poor soil but the more humus-rich the soil, the better. Z5.

Beta vulgaris subsp. cicla (stems)

Beta vulgaris subsp. cicla (leaves)

Propagation Sow seed where plants are to grow in early spring, or sow in late summer for winter effects.
Uses These plants are excellent in bedding schemes especially exotic-looking ones. Another perfect use for them is in potagers or decorative vegetable gardens. They look best when they are sited against the sun.

Beta vulgaris subsp. cicla
This is a biennial but it is only kept for the first year since it grows taller and goes to seed in the second. This can be quite dramatic but is difficult to mix in with other plants. There are a number of cultivars. The leaves vary from green to dark purple or red. The stems include shades of yellow, orange, red and purple, as well as green. H 45 cm (18in).

Beta vulgaris subsp. cicla 'Bright Lights'
The stems form a rainbow of different colours, while the foliage is dark green or bronze.

Beta vulgaris subsp. cicla 'Bright Yellow'
This plant produces golden-yellow stems and green leaves which have golden-yellow veins.

Beta vulgaris subsp. cicla 'Bull's Blood'
The foliage of this cultivar is an attractive dark red.

Beta vulgaris subsp. cicla 'Charlotte'
The red stems and red-tinged leaves of this plant have an attractively wrinkled texture.

Beta vulgaris subsp. cicla 'MacGregor's Favourite'
This wonderful plant is prized for its blood-red foliage.

Bidens ferulifolia 'Golden Goddess'

BIDENS
Tickseed

This is a large genus of plants that is closely related to *Cosmos*. The main annual that interests gardeners is *B. ferulifolia* and in it you can see this affinity to cosmos. The golden-yellow flowers are daisy-like with five broad outer petals and a bronze central disc. The leaves are deeply divided and fernlike, making them very decorative. Bidens stems are thin and wiry and have a sprawling habit which makes it perfect for containers. H 30cm (12in) S 60cm (24in).
How to obtain Bidens can be purchased either as seed or as bedding plants from garden centres and nurseries.
Cultivation Any reasonable garden soil will do for bedding plants. For containers a general potting or container compost (soil mix) will suffice. A sunny position is preferred. Z8.
Propagation This plant is really a perennial and it can be kept from one year to the next by taking cuttings and overwintering the young plants. However, it is more convenient to grow new plants from seed sown in early spring under glass.
Uses Bidens can be used in the open garden, either as bedding or in mixed borders. However, their sprawling habit means that they are best employed in containers, especially hanging baskets.

Bidens ferulifolia
This species is mainly grown in its own right. The only commonly available cultivar is 'Golden Goddess' which is not greatly different from the species except that the flowers are a bit bigger.

Other plants There are one or two other species that can be found occasionally. The naming in catalogues varies but the plants are usually sound. *B. humilis* (strictly speaking, *B. triplinervia* var. *macrantha*) is sometimes seen in the form 'Golden Eye'. This is a sprawling, almost prostrate plant that is excellent for hanging baskets. It is similar in appearance to *B. ferulifolia*. *B. aurea* 'Bit-of-Sunshine' also similar.

BORAGO
Borago

A small genus of plants of which only one annual, *B. officinalis*, is commonly grown. One of the perennials, *B. pygmaea*, would make an interesting plant for hanging baskets. *B. officinalis* is often grown as a herb, with the flowers being used as decoration in Pimm's cocktails. It is also now being widely used in the drugs industry

Bidens ferulifolia

and you can come across fields coloured blue with it. It is of great interest in the garden since it has a long season, with a succession of opening flowers. H 60cm (24in) S 45cm (18in).
How to obtain It is normal to buy borage as seed, which is readily available and easy to grow. You occasionally see plants in pots for sale, but they usually give poor results since borage does not do well in small containers.
Cultivation This plant will grow in most garden conditions. It prefers a sunny spot but will tolerate partial shade. Z7.
Propagation Seed can be sown in pots but it is easier to sow it outdoors in early spring where the plants are to grow. Thin them out to 45cm (18in) intervals. Borage self-sows so once you have it you usually have new plants each year.
Uses Borage makes an attractive addition to herb gardens but it is also very good in mixed borders where it can be used to fill gaps left by spring plants that have faded. It looks pretty in a wild-flower garden.

Borago officinalis

This is a sprawling plant with rough leaves and stems. It produces bright blue flowers that have white centres. They are produced continuously through the summer and into autumn. There is a form *alba* which has white flowers that look very good against the greyish-green stems and leaves. It is perfect for a white colour scheme.

Brachyscome iberidifolia

Borago pygmaea

This is a short-lived perennial which is normally grown as a border plant. However, it has a sprawling nature which might make it worth trying as a biennial in hanging baskets. It has small sky-blue flowers.

BRACHYSCOME
Swan river daisy

This is a large genus of some 70 annual and perennial species which produce daisy-like flowers. Only one of them, *B. iberidifolia*, is widely grown although a few others are occasionally seen. In recent times *B. iberidifolia* is has become one of the most popular annuals, partly because of its looks and partly because of its versatility: it can be used very effectively in containers as well as making a good bedding plant. The flowers are mainly purple or blue, but some of the cultivars come in different colours including pink and white. H and S 45cm (18in) in good conditions, but most plants are smaller, especially when grown in containers.
How to obtain The best choice of plants comes from growing them from seed since all seed merchants carry at least one version of this. Brachyscomes are also widely available as plants but the choice of flower colour will be restricted, usually to blue. Check plants in flower if you want specific colours since plants are often labelled only as "Brachyscome", sometimes spelt "Brachycome".
Cultivation Plant out after frosts have passed. Any reasonable garden soil will do so long as it is free-draining. Z8.
Propagation Sow seed under glass at 16–18°C (60–64°F) in early spring under glass. In warmer areas the plant self-sows.
Uses Brachyscome is excellent in containers. It can also be used as a bedding plant.

Brachyscome iberidifolia

The main plants have blue or blue-purple outer petals and a yellow central disc. The daisy-like flowers are small, about 2cm (¾in) wide, but are produced in profusion over a long period. The foliage is deeply cut and fernlike.

There are a number of cultivars. In 'Blue Star' the outer petals are rolled back giving the flower a star-like quality. 'Brachy Blue' is a more compact and upright plant. There are several strains with blue, violet, white and pink flowers including Bravo Series and Splendour Series.

Borago officinalis

Annuals for infilling parterres

Ageratum	*Matthiola incana*
Antirrhinum	*Myosotis*
Begonia semperflorens	*Pelargonium*
Bellis	*Plectranthus*
Erysimum	*Primula*
Felicia	*Salvia splendens*
Helichrysum petiolare	*Salvia patens*
Heliotropium	*Tagetes*
Impatiens	*Verbena × hybrida*
Lobelia erinus	*Viola × wittrockiana*

An impressive display of ornamental cabbages *(Brassica oleracea)*.

Brassica oleracea (purple-leaved)

BRASSICA
Ornamental cabbage

This genus is made up of about 30 species, the majority of which are of more interest to the vegetable gardener since they include cabbages, broccolis, Brussels sprouts and cauliflowers, among others. These all belong to the species *B. oleracea*. One might think that there is not much potential here for the flower garden, but in fact there are a number of decorative cabbages and kales that are well worth growing for some winter interest. The leaves come in a wide range of colours including white, cream, pink and purple as well as various shades of green. The leaves are often fringed.

How to obtain Ornamental cabbages are widely available as seed. They can also be bought as plants in pots. However, if these plants have been in their pots for too long they will make very unsatisfactory plants when planted out.

Cultivation Any reasonable garden soil will suffice. A sunny position is best. Z7.

Propagation Sow seed in spring where the plants are to grow, or sow in a row and transplant when large enough. Brassica seed can also be sown under glass in spring and planted out as soon as possible. Do not keep them in small containers for long.

Uses These plants can be used for winter-bedding schemes when there are few other colourful plants to call on. They are also good in winter containers. Ornamental cabbages can be mixed with edible cabbages in potagers for extra colour. They look particularly effective when partially covered with snow.

Common plants Seed often comes in mixed packets, labelled 'ornamental cabbages' or 'decorative kale', (sometimes 'flowering cabbage, although the plants are on the compost heap before they flower). Common mixes include 'Northern Lights Mixed', Osaka Series, or 'Kale Sparrow Mix' but many seed merchants offer individual colours by mail order.

Other plants In potagers many of the edible brassicas can look very effective. Red cabbages or curly kale for example. Even cauliflowers (including purple ones) and romanescos are suitable.

BRIZA
Quaking grass

Briza is a genus of around a dozen annual and grasses. Perhaps the best known is *B. media* which is grown as a perennial (see page 182). However, there are also a couple of annuals which are widely grown. They are called quaking grasses because they have masses of hanging flower heads that look like lockets and which tremble at the slightest hint of a breeze. These are a straw colour; unfortunately, they do not come in the wide range of bright colours that you see in the florists since those are dyed.

How to obtain Quaking grasses are most commonly available as seed but you will occasionally find plants on sale.

Cultivation Any reasonable garden soil will do so long as it is well-drained. A sunny position is required. Z5.

Propagation Sow the seed where the plants are to grow either in the autumn or in the early spring.

Uses These are mainly used in borders where they mix well with other plants. They can be used to make a delicate edging to a path or border, or in containers. The heads are very good for cutting and drying.

Brassica oleracea (green-leaved)

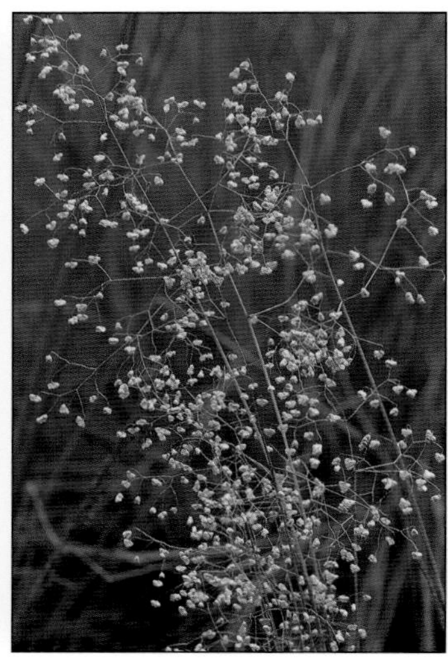

Briza minor

Briza maxima
Sold as the species only since there are no cultivars available. This is the taller of the two annuals. The loose, dangling flower heads are pale green at first, changing to a light straw colour. They are tinged purple. H 60cm (24in) S 25cm (10in).

Briza minor
This is similar to the previous except that the flower spikelets are smaller. H 45cm (18in) S 25cm (10in).

CALCEOLARIA
Slipper flower

A large genus of some 300 species of which there are only a couple of species and a number of cultivars that are of interest to the annual gardener. Their beauty lies in their curious flowers. The lower part is an inflated pouch (giving the plant another of its names – pouch flower) which gives the flower the appearance of a slipper. In the annual varieties the flowers are carried in dense heads, in shades of yellow, gold, orange or red and frequently spotted with red. The bold colours make them ideal for bedding schemes or for bright container arrangements.

How to obtain Slipper flowers can be purchased as either plants in individual pots or as seed. As usual, seed offers a bigger range.

Cultivation Grow in a humus-rich soil that is moisture-retentive but not waterlogged. It should be acid rather than alkaline. Although slipper flowers will grow in sun if the soil is moist enough, they are happiest in light shade. Plant out after frosts have passed. Z9.

Propagation Sow the seed in early spring at 16–18°C (60–64°F) under glass and prick out into individual pots.

Uses These plants are good in containers or bedding, especially in shady sites where bright colours are required. Most make excellent greenhouse plants.

Calceolaria 'Kentish Hero'

***Calceolaria* Herbeohybrida Group**
This is the main group of hybrids. The flowers come in yellow, orange or red and often have spotted lips. H 20–45cm (8–18in). S up to 30cm (12in).

There are a number of strains with mixed colours including the Anytime Series, 'Bright Bikinis', the Confetti hybrids and the Pocket hybrids. There are also single-coloured varieties including 'Goldcrest' and 'Gold Fever', both with yellow flowers. These plants can be used as greenhouse annuals; in warmer areas they make good bedding and container plants.

Calceolaria integrifolia
These are shrubby perennials, but gardeners normally grow them as annual plants. As perennials they can grow to heights of up to 1.2m (4ft) but as annuals they are more likely to be in the 25–30cm (10–12in) range and about the same across. They produce yellow flowers. The Fructiohybrida Group can be purchased as a mixture or as individual varieties including 'Goldcut', 'Golden Bunch', 'Kentish Hero', 'Midas', 'Sunset' and 'Sunshine'.

Calendula officinalis

CALENDULA
Pot marigolds

There are about 20 species of pot marigolds, but only the annual *C. officinalis* is widely grown. It is commonly called a "pot" marigold because it was once widely used as a herb. Few gardeners use it as such now, although it is still often grown decoratively in herb gardens. At its simplest the flower is a daisy with orange outer petals and an orange or dark central disc. However, there are a number of forms which have semi-double and double flowers. There are also yellow versions. The flowers are up to 10cm (4in) across.

The pot marigold is a useful plant for the garden and it has a certain sturdy quality; it is not a delicate, airy plant. H 75cm (30in) S 45cm (18in). However, its stems can be rather floppy so the real height is often much less.

How to obtain Pot marigolds are best grown from seed, which is readily available. Occasionally plants for sale can be found in garden centres. The plants will self-sow. However they generally revert to the type rather than the particular cultivar planted.

Cultivation Any reasonable garden soil will be sufficient, and although pot marigolds will grow in shade, a sunny position is to be preferred. Z6.

Propagation Seed can be sown where the plants are to be grown, either in autumn or in early spring. Thin plants to intervals of 30–45cm (12–18in).

Uses Pot marigolds are best used as plants for mixed borders, although some of the more compact forms can be used in bedding schemes as well as in containers. They work particularly well in hot-coloured schemes. The flowers are good for cutting.

Calendula officinalis
The species has orange daisies but there are plenty of varieties, such as 'Lemon Queen' which produce yellow ones. The species is grown in its own right but the cultivar 'Radio' is more typical of the garden plant. It has semi-double flowers in which all the petals are orange with no central disc. There are several series including the Kablouna Series, which is tall with double flowers, and the Pacific Beauty Series. Both are mixtures of yellow, gold or orange. Single-coloured cultivars include 'Golden Princess', with golden petals and a black central disc.

Annuals for drying

Amaranthus caudatus
Atriplex hortensis
Briza
Centaurea cyanus
Centaurea moschata
Clarkia
Consolida
Eryngium giganteum
Gomphrena globosa
Gypsophila elegans
Helichrysum bracteatum
Hordeum jubatum
Limonium sinuatum
Lunaria annua
Moluccella laevis
Nicandra physalodes
Nigella damascena
Onopordum acanthium
Salvia hormium
Xeranthemum annuum

Callistephus chinensis Milady Series

Campanula medium

CALLISTEPHUS
Chinese aster

This is a single genus species with *C. chinensis* providing a wide range of flowers. It was once much more widely grown than it is now and used to be frequently seen as a cut flower. It is similar to the other asters but the flowers are much bigger, up to 12cm (4½in) or more across. They are either singles or doubles, and come in a wide range of whites, pinks, blues and purples. The singles have a yellow central disc, and they all have a distinctive fragrance. These are bushy, upright plants. H and S 45cm (18in).

How to obtain Chinese asters are more readily obtained as seed but you can still buy plants at some garden centres and nurseries.

Cultivation Chinese asters like a moisture-retentive soil and a sunny position. Z8.

Propagation They can either be sown under glass in early spring at 16–18°C (60–64°F) or in the open ground where the plants are to grow in mid-spring, but these will be later flowering.

Uses They make good bedding plants and can also be grown in mixed borders. Plant in rows in the vegetable garden or an out-of-the-way spot for cutting.

Callistephus chinensis

There is only the one species, but it does have a number of readily available cultivars. The flowers come in the wide range of colours described above, and also in a series of forms. They include the Comet Series, which are compact doubles in a variety of colours, the Giant Singles, 'Craw Krallenaster', which produces flowers with masses of thin petals and the Ostrich Plume Series, which have feathery petals. Others include the dwarf Pinocchio Series, the fine Milady Series, whose flowers have incurving petals, 'Starlight Mix' and the tall Pommax series.

Callistephus chinensis 'Ostrich Plume'

Callistephus chinensis 'Starlight Rose'

CAMPANULA
Bellflowers

A large genus of more than 300 species of which most are perennials (see pages 184–185) but a number are biennials and annuals. As their name suggests they have bell-shaped flowers, although in the annuals these are often shallow and in some cases look more like saucers than bells. Bellflowers in the wild are mainly blue and occasionally white; in cultivation the annuals tend to have a wider range of colour including pink. The flowers also come as semi-doubles and doubles. They tend to be tallish plants best used in mixed borders rather than low bedding schemes.

How to obtain The best range of plants can be had by buying seed, but there are also plants available from many garden centres and nurseries. Rarer annual seed can be obtained from specialist societies.

Cultivation Any reasonable garden soil will be sufficient so long as it is free-draining. This plant needs sun or light shade. Z6–8.

Propagation Sow seed in early spring under glass. Some can be sown in the open soil where the plants are to grow.

Uses Best used in a mixed border, but some bellflowers can be used in taller bedding schemes.

Campanula incurva

This is a biennial which has low spreading stems and inflated pale blue flowers. H 30cm (12in) S 45cm (18in).

Campanula medium

Canterbury bells are very popular biennial bellflowers. They are available in white, blue or pink and come as singles or the cup-and-saucer doubles. H 60cm (24in) S 30cm (12in). Cultivars include the shorter 'Bells of Holland' and 'Chelsea Pink', with deep pink flowers.

Campanula pyramidalis

A biennial that if grown well produces stems up to 1.5m (5ft) tall, which are covered in blue or white flowers. It is good for growing in pots. S 30cm (12in).

Other plants There are a number of rarer annuals that are worth growing. *C. lusitanica* and *C. patula* form a tangle of thin wiry stems, covered with purple flowers with white centres over a long period. *C. ramosissima* is similar but has thicker stems. *C. thyrsoides* is an upright plant with, unusually, yellow flowers. All these and

Campanula pyramidalis

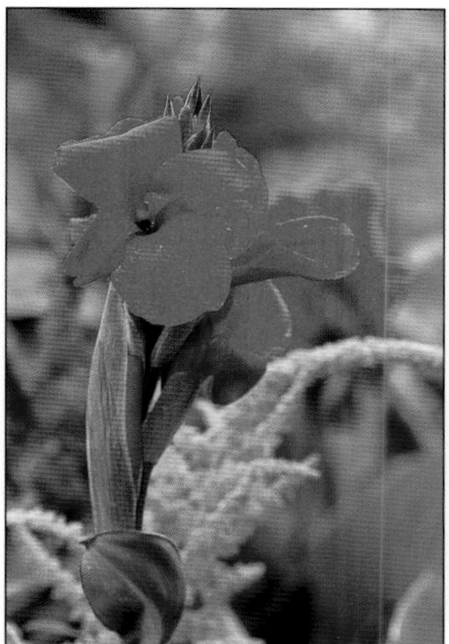
Canna 'Oiseau de Feu'

Canna 'Wyoming'

Canna 'Roi Humbert'

several more attractive plants can be grown in mixed borders or in the rock garden.

CANNA
Indian shot plant

With the growing interest in exotic gardens, cannas have become very popular plants. This is a genus of about 50 species of perennial plants but because they are tender they are treated as annuals. They are dug up every autumn and stored, much in the same way as dahlias are. They are tall plants with attractive large flowers and luscious foliage. The former are carried in spikes and come in bright oranges, reds and yellows, and the latter is usually glossy and sometimes purple or variegated. H 2–3m (6–10ft) S 50cm (20in).
How to obtain Cannas are normally bought as plants or as rhizomes. Seed is available but is generally restricted to mixtures.
Cultivation Plant in a moisture-retentive rich soil in a sunny position. Do not allow them to dry out completely, and lift and store in dry peat substitute after the first frost. Z8.
Propagation Seed can be sown in early spring under glass at 21°C (70°F) after soaking in water. In spring the stored rhizomes can be cut into sections, each with a growing eye, and planted in pots in a warm greenhouse.
Uses Use cannas in exotic bedding schemes or mixed borders where a splash of colour is required.

Canna 'Black Knight'
This eye-catching plant produces a bold display of dark red flowers. H 2m (6ft).

Canna 'Endeavour'
Scarlet flowers are carried on stately plants that reach up to 2.2m (7ft) in height.

Canna indica
This canna has orange or bright red flowers. The leaves are dark green and are often tinged with bronze. There is also an attractive cultivar 'Purpurea', which has purple foliage. H 2m (6ft).

Canna iridiflora
Deep pink flowers are carried on plants that can reach up to 3m (10ft), but are usually less.

Canna 'Striata'

Canna 'Lucifer'
A shorter plant. Spikes of red blooms, touched with yellow. H 60cm (24in).

Canna 'Oiseau de Feu'
This plant has scarlet flowers and dark green leaves. H 1m (3ft).

Canna 'Picasso'
This cultivar has yellow flowers, spotted with red.

Canna 'Roi Humbert'
A dazzling display of orange-red flowers is set against purple foliage. H up to 1.5m (5ft).

Canna 'Striata'
The flowers of this canna are orange and the leaves – pale green with pronounced yellow stripes – set off the orange beautifully. H 1.5m (5ft).

Canna 'Wyoming'
Excellent plants that have purple foliage with darker veins and orange flowers. H up to 2m (6ft).

CELOSIA
Cockscomb

This genus consists of 50 species but the varieties of one species, *C. argentea*, are of most interest. The flowers are so startling that they seem almost artificial in their colouring. There are two types. The commonest (plumosa group) produces upright feathery flowering spikes that look a bit like flames. They come in a variety of reds, oranges, yellows and pinks. The other type (cristata group) produce flat, slightly domed heads with the flowers arranged in curious squiggles, again in bright colours. They can be difficult to place with other plants, but are superb in bedding schemes. H 60cm (24in) S 45cm (18in).
How to obtain Celosias are not so popular as they once were but you can still find plants in some garden centres. There is a good range of seed available.
Cultivation Plant out after the danger of frosts has passed in rich, moisture-retentive soil. A sunny position is required. Z9.
Propagation Sow the seed under glass at 16–18°C (60–64°F) in early spring.
Uses Their main use is as bedding plants in an exotic scheme, but they are also excellent for extra colourful containers.

Celosia argentea 'Apricot Brandy'
This plumosa cultivar has bright orange upright flower heads.

Celosia argentea Century Series
One of the most popular plumosa cultivars, with flowers in a mixture of bright colours.

Celosia argentea 'Fairy Fountains'
The flowers of this plumosa cultivar are less bright and consist of pastel coloured spires.

Celosia argentea 'Freshlock Red'
A plumosa celosia which produces bright red plumes.

Celosia argentea Kurume Series
These are cristata celosia in mixture of bright colours, including some bicolours.

C. argentea plumosa 'Freshlock Red'

Centaurea cyanus

CENTAUREA
Cornflowers

The cornflowers, or knapweeds as they are also known, form a large genus of some 450 species. Many are perennials that are widely grown in our gardens (see page 186). There are also a number of annuals, of which the best known is the common cornflower, *C. cyanus*. These were originally weeds of cornfields, hence the name, and other disturbed ground. They can be grown in borders but still look best when used in a wild-flower garden. They have flattish, circular heads of blue or other coloured flowers Other annual centaureas are quite similar in appearance but are not so commonly seen. H 75cm (30in) S 20cm (8in).
How to obtain The commonest way to buy these is as seed. The rarer plants, need a lot more searching for but they are available from specialist catalogues and societies.
Cultivation Sow in any reasonable garden soil so long as it is free-draining. Full sun is needed. Z6.
Propagation Sow seed where the plants are to flower, in autumn for early flowering or in spring. Thin to 20cm (8in) intervals.
Uses Grow in drifts in mixed borders or as bedding plants. The blue varieties are excellent for wild-flower gardens. Dwarf forms can be used in containers.

Centaurea cyanus
This is the common cornflower. Its flowers are blue, often piercing blue. There is also a wide choice of cultivars which offer a range of flower colours from soft pinks and whites to a very dark purple that is almost black. The cultivated forms usually have a lot more petals, making them almost double. There are also shorter forms, such as the dwarf 'Blue Baby'. 'Black Ball' is very dark purple. In 'Frosty Mixed' the petals have a white edge. Florence Series is a shorter form, and white 'Polka Dot Mixed' is another dwarf form.

Other plants *C. americana* is similar to the cornflower except that the petals are much more finely cut, giving the flower a very delicate appearance. The flowers are generally white and there are several cultivars. It is not so easy to find but worth the search.

CERINTHE
Cerinthe

This genus of about ten species has been in cultivation for a long time, but it has just been rediscovered and made popular by the seed companies. *C. major* is the particular species that has brought about this popularity. It is a biennial that is grown as much for its foliage as for its flowers. The blue and purple blooms are contained in a spiral, similar to that of the forget-me-not except that the flowers are partially obscured by their sheaths. The plants are quite striking and make excellent displays grown by themselves or mixed with other plants. H 60cm (24in) S 30cm (12in).
How to obtain The best way to obtain these plants is to buy seed from merchants. You can buy plants but they are not very satisfactory as they tend to grow spindly. Once you have planted cerinthes, they will often self-sow.
Cultivation Any reasonable garden soil so long as it is free-draining. A sunny position is required. Z5.
Propagation Sow seed in autumn or spring where the plants are to flower or in pots under cool glass. Prick them out but do not leave them in small pots too long.
Uses Cerinthes can be used in a mixed border or as bedding. They are excellent for gravel gardens and can be used in containers.

Cerinthe major

Cerinthe major
This is the main species grown. It has green leaves that are often white spotted, especially when young. The form 'Purpurascens' has much bluer leaves and is the form mostly grown. The partially obscured flowers are purple.

Cerinthe major 'Kiwi Blue'

There are some new varieties appearing, such as 'Kiwi Blue', but they are not much different.

Other plants *Cerinthe minor* is much rarer but it makes an excellent foliage plant since its leaves are white spotted. The flowers are small and yellow. It appears as *C. minor aurea* 'Bouquet Gold' in some catalogues.

CHRYSANTHEMUM
Chrysanthemum

There can be few gardeners who do not know chrysanthemums. As well as the well-known cultivars there are 20 species, including annuals and perennials (see page 187). We do grow some annuals in our gardens but the main form – florists' chrysanthemum – is a perennial. However, because of its tender nature we treat it as an annual and replant it each year. Florists' chrysanthemums are now highly developed: there are ten basic types, each having many cultivars. They are grown as

Cerinthe major set off against a wall beautifully.

Chrysanthemum 'Southway Swan'

Chrysanthemum 'Curtain Call'

border or decorative plants, but the majority are cultivated either for cutting or for exhibition. Many gardeners become hooked on them and often turn over a large part of their garden to growing them. The annual chrysanthemums are grown more for their effect in the garden. With such diversity, this is a genus well worth getting to know.
How to obtain Florists' chrysanthemums are sold as small plants in garden centres and nurseries. There are several mail-order nurseries that specialize in them. There was a short period a few years ago when they were classified as *Dendranthema*. Although they are now called *Chrysanthemum* again, some catalogues may still list them under their former name. Other chrysanthemums are usually sold as seed and they can be found in most seed merchants' catalogues.
Cultivation Plant out chrysanthemums once the threat of frost has passed. They need a soil that has been enriched with plenty of well-rotted organic material. The soil should be moist but free-draining. A sunny position is needed. Z: see individual types.
Propagation Propagate florists' chrysanthemums from cuttings taken from the newly emerging basal growth on plants that have been overwintered. Other types are grown from seed sown in early spring at 13–16°C (55–60°F) under glass. It can also be sown where the plants are to grow, but this will make flowering later.
Uses Florists' chrysanthemums, can be grown in mixed borders, but they are more often grown in rows for cutting or for exhibition purposes. They are also good plants for containers. Other chrysanthemums can be used in mixed borders or as bedding. Corn marigolds (*C. segetum*) are excellent plants for the wild-flower garden.

Chrysanthemum 'Taffy'

Chrysanthemum 'Glamour'

Florists' chrysanthemums

There are thousands of these to choose from and it is best to get catalogues from the specialist nurseries to see the range available. The ten basic types have flowers that vary from singles to doubles. There are also "incurved" chrysanthemums, which have a ball of upward curving petals, and "reflexed" ones, which have petals that curve downwards. There is a wide range of colours including white, yellows, oranges, red, pinks and purples. H 1.5m (5ft) S 75cm (30in). Z4.

Chrysanthemum 'George Griffiths'

Chrysanthemum 'Primrose Allouise'

Chrysanthemum carinatum

These plants have single, daisy-like flowers. The outer petals come in a range of colours from white to yellow, and orange to red. There is often an inner ring of colour at the base of the petals and a central disc of brown. 'Court Jesters' is a good mixture. There are some double forms. H 60cm (24in) S 30cm (12in). Z7.

Chrysanthemum coronarium

These are bushy plants which produce single daisy-like flowers. They have yellow outer petals and yellow central discs. The green foliage is very finely cut and fern-like in appearance. These chrysanthemums look good in wild-flower meadows. H 75cm (30in) S 45cm (18in). Z7.

Chrysanthemum carinatum

Chrysanthemum segetum 'Prado'

Chrysanthemum segetum

Corn marigolds have simple daisy-like flowers with golden outer petals and a golden central disc. They are very beautiful when seen *en masse*. Some cultivars, such as 'Prado', have extra-large flowers and a dark disc. 'Eastern Star' has paler yellow petals and a dark central disc. Excellent for wild-flower gardens. H 60cm (24in) S 30cm (12in). Z8.

Chrysanthemum tenuiloba

A plant with extremely finely cut foliage and yellow outer petals and discs. This is a sprawling plant that produces a mass of foliage speckled with yellow. It has a cultivar 'Golden Fleck'. H 30cm (12in).

Chrysanthemum 'Debonair'

Chrysanthemum tenuiloba

Cladanthus arabicus 'Criss-Cross'

CLADANTHUS
Palm Springs daisy

This is a small genus of daisy-like flowers of which only one, *C. arabicus,* is grown. It is not often seen and yet it is excellent for hanging baskets and other containers. Fortunately it is being offered by an increasing number of seed merchants and it is worth seeking out seed.

The light green leaves have very thin leaflets and create a tangled nest for the flowers. Both the leaves and the flowers are fragrant. The flowers are daisies with yellow outer petals and a yellow central disc. They nestle right down in the foliage, a characteristic that distinguishes this plant from the annual chrysanthemums it resembles in other respects. Another distinctive feature is that from just beneath each flower emerges a few more stems, each in turn carrying more flowers so the plant gets bigger and bigger. H up to 45cm (18in) or more, S 40cm (16in).

How to obtain This plant is mainly grown from seed, which is distributed by an increasing number of seed merchants. Occasionally you will see plants for sale in some garden centres.

Cultivation Any reasonable garden soil will be sufficient, so long as it is free-draining. Centaureas need a sunny position. Z7.

Propagation Seed should be sown in early spring under glass at 13–16°C (55–60°F). It can be sown later where the plants are to grow, but flowering will be later.

Uses They work well in window boxes, hanging baskets or other containers, or they can be used in bedding schemes.

Cladanthus arabicus

This is the only species in general cultivation. It is sold both as the species, described above, and as the cultivars 'Criss-Cross' and 'Golden Crown'. These are similar to the species but produce slightly larger flowers.

CLARKIA
Clarkia

This is a medium-sized genus of 36 species of which several are grown in our gardens as annuals. They include a number of plants that were previously classified as *Godetia* and under which name many gardeners still know them.

They are a mixed bunch with some having large single or double flowers, while others are quite small but are carried in sufficient quantities to make the plants attractive. Their basic form is funnel-shaped. The predominant colour is pink although some are dark enough to be called red or purple. Many are tinged with lighter or darker colour. Clarkias produce lots of flowers over a long period, so they are good for bedding or for use in containers. H 45cm (18in) S 30cm (12in).

How to obtain Clarkias are widely available as seed although many catalogues still list some species as *Godetia*. Most garden centres also sell plants in individual pots.

Cultivation Clarkias will grow in any reasonable garden soil, but it must not be too rich and it must be free-draining. These plants grow best in a sunny position but they will also tolerate a little light shade. Z7.

Propagation Seed can be sown in early spring where the plants are to grow. For earlier flowering, the seed can either be sown in the open in autumn or under glass in early spring at a temperature of 13–16°C (55–60°F).

Uses They make excellent bedding plants especially when they are planted in blocks or drifts. They can also be used in containers such as pots or tubs.

Clarkia 'Blood Red'

Clarkia amoena

This is the satin flower, which is often listed as *Godetia amoena*. The upward-facing flowers are quite large, up to 5cm (2in) across. They are single or double, and come in various shades of soft pink. There are a number of cultivars including the Grace Series and Satin Series (dwarf), both of which have mixed shades. 'Rembrandt' is tall with rose and white flowers, 'Sybil Sherwood' has salmon-pink flowers, and 'Memoria' has pure white ones. 'Furora' has bright red blooms, and 'Blood Red' has blood-red flowers with pale centres.

Clarkia bottae

This pretty plant is not as brash as the previous species. It has simple cup-like flowers in pink with a pale centre. It is often listed as *Godetia bottae*. There are also several cultivars.

Clarkia breweri (C. concinna)

The flowers are wide, with thin, deeply cut petals in shades of pink. The best known cultivar is 'Pink Ribbons'.

CLEOME
Spider flower

A surprising large genus with 150 species. Only one of them, *C. hassleriana*, is grown to any extent in our gardens, although with a bit of searching the enthusiast will discover several others in this intriguing genus. The flowers are carried in rounded spikes at the top of tall stems. The heads are quite unlike those of any other plant: the

Cleome hassleriana 'Helen Campbell'

Cleome hassleriana 'Pink Queen'

spikes are quite loose and open and below them are the seed pots of flowers that have already faded. They are carried on very thin stems, giving the plant its characteristic "spider" look. The flowers are scented and they come in pink, white or mauve. The heads are usually slightly darker in colour towards the top where the buds have yet to open. The foliage is a bit like that of the lupin. H 1.5m (5ft) S 45cm (18in).
How to obtain Cleomes can be bought as plants. However, they do not like to remain in pots too long so it is best to obtain them as seed, of which there is usually a greater range available.
Cultivation Plant out after the danger of frosts has passed. Cleomes need a fairly rich soil that is very free-draining in full sun. They can also be grown under glass for cutting. Z10.
Propagation Sow in early spring under glass at a temperature of 18°C (64°F).
Uses These plants look best when grown in drifts either in a mixed border or as bedding. They can be used as cut flowers.

Cleome hassleriana
This is the species that is most commonly seen. It is occasionally grown as a species, but more commonly as one of the several available cultivars. Seed catalogues often list it under all manner of names which are no longer extant. 'Colour Fountain' is a mixture of colours but there are also varieties which are restricted to one colour such as 'Cherry Queen' (carmine red), 'Helen Campbell' (white) 'Orchid Queen' (pale mauve) and 'Pink Queen' (pink).

Other plants If you search you will find a number of other cleomes being offered by one or two seed merchants and specialist societies, *C. aculeata, C. gynandra and C. serrulata* amongst them. These have smaller flower heads so they are not as showy as *C. hassleriana*, but the structure and colour range is roughly the same.

COBAEA
Cathedral bells

This genus contains about 20 species of perennial climbers, of which one, *C. scandens*, is of interest to gardeners. Although a perennial it is generally treated as an annual. Its great attraction, apart from its purple bell-shaped flowers, is that it is one of the few annual climbers. It can reach up to 4.5m (15ft) in the year if started off early enough, although as a perennial it can eventually grow as tall as 20m (70ft).

Cobaea scandens growing up a willow tripod.

How to obtain Most seed merchants carry seed. Sometimes you find plants at garden centres and nurseries. These should be planted out quickly since they do not do well in small pots.
Cultivation Plant in a humus-rich soil that is neutral to alkaline. A warm sunny site is needed. Do not plant out until after the danger of frosts has passed. Z9.
Propagation Raise plants from seed, sown in early spring under glass at 25°C (77°F).
Uses Cobaea does best when planted against a warm wall, either growing up a support or through another plant. It can be also used over pergolas and trellising.

Cobaea scandens
The flowers are large, attractive bells that stick out horizontally from the stems. They open whitish-green and quickly change to a deep purple. The form *alba* has white flowers. *Cobaea scandens* is often known as the cup and saucer plant, the cup being the flower and the saucer the green calyx around its base.

Cobaea scandens

Annuals for light shade

Begonia semperflorens
Cleome spinosa
Consolida ambigua
Cynoglossum amabile
Digitalis purpurea
Erysimum cheiri
Lobelia erinus
Lobularia maritima
Lunaria annua
Matthiola bicornis
Mimulus
Myosotis
Nemophila menziesii
Nicotiana
Oenothera biennis
Pelargonium
Schizanthus
Senecio cineraria
Thunbergia alata
Viola × wittrockiana

Collinsia bicolor 'Blushing Rose'

COLLINSIA
Collinsia

This is a genus of about 20 plants of which only one is in general cultivation. This is *C. bicolor*, or *C. heterophylla* as it is sometimes called. It is not related to the lupin, but at a quick glance it could be mistaken for one, albeit a small one. It produces spikes of flowers of which the lower lip is one colour (usually purple) and the upper another (usually white or pink). The pointed leaves are more like those of a penstemon and rise stalkless direct from the stems. Although these plants are generally upright, they can be slightly floppy. It is best to plant them closely together so that they give each other support, or you can give individual plants other support, such as short, twiggy branches. H 60cm (24in) S 30cm (12in).
How to obtain Collinsias are rarely seen as plants in garden centres and it is best to buy them as seed from one of the few merchants that stock it.
Cultivation The soil should be a humus-rich one, but it should be free-draining. Collinsias prefer full sun, but they will grow in a little light shade. Z7.
Propagation Sow seed where the plants are to grow in spring, or in autumn for earlier flowering. Thin to 30cm (12in) intervals.
Uses Collinsias can be used either in drifts as bedding or in a mixed border. They are shown to good effect in a wild-flower garden.

Collinsia bicolor

This is the main plant grown and is described above. 'Candidissima' is a form with all-white flowers. There are also mixtures on offer from some seed merchants. They include 'Blushing Rose' and 'Surprise', which produces an attractive combination of blue, lilac and rose-pink flowers.

Other plants The only other species that is sometimes offered is *C. grandiflora*. It is a shorter plant than the above and much bushier. It also has bicoloured flowers, with a blue-purple lower lip and a paler upper one.

There are a few seed merchants that offer this species; otherwise you need to look to specialist societies in order to find it.

Annuals for bees

Asperula	*Fagopyrum*
Bartonia aurea	*Iberis*
Borago officinalis	*Lobularia maritima*
Centaurea cyanus	*Linaria*
Centaurea moschata	*Nigella damascena*
Cerinthe major	*Phacelia*
Clarkia	*Reseda*
Collinsia bicolor	*Rudbeckia*
Cynoglossum	*Salvia hormium*
Echium	*Scabiosa*

COLLOMIA
Collomia

A genus of about 15 species of which a couple are occasionally cultivated. The most frequently grown is *C. grandiflora,* although it is still rarely seen. Very few seed merchants carry the seed and it is mainly grown by gardeners to whom the seed has been handed down from generation to generation. It is an old-fashioned cottage-garden plant of great beauty and it is a pity it is not more readily available. Once established you rarely lose it since it is self-sowing, often forming large drifts. However, it is easy to remove if it is in the wrong place. H 1m (3ft) S 60cm (24in), when growing well.
How to obtain Collomia seed is not easy to come by, although some seed merchants do stock it now. It is also available from some specialist societies.
Cultivation This plant does best in a rich, moist soil, which should be free-draining. A sunny position is required. Z7.
Propagation Sow seed in early spring where the plants are to grow. After the first year it self-sows if allowed to seed. Thin plants to 30cm (12in) intervals.
Uses Collomia could be used as a bedding plant, but the flowering season is short and it is best grown as drifts in a mixed border.

Collomia grandiflora

Collomia grandiflora

This is an upright, branched annual with red stems that contrast well with the mid green leaves. The flowers are a creamy salmon-pink and are carried in clusters or whorls at the tips of the branches. The seed heads are somewhat sticky and it is best to let them dry before trying to extract the seed.

Other plants *Collomia biflora* is a similar, but shorter annual with smaller heads of red or orange flowers. It is more colourful than the above but has less presence.

CONSOLIDA
Larkspur

A genus of about 40 species of annuals which used to be included in the genus *Delphinium*. The naming is still in a state of flux and the main larkspur grown may be called *C. ambigua* or *C. ajacis* depending on which authority you consult. This confusion is carried on in the seed catalogues, so don't give up if you can't find the plants under the first heading you try. Whatever their names, the plants are excellent annuals. They

Consolida ajacis, mixed colours

Consolida ajacis 'Frosted Skies'

Convolvulus tricolor 'Royal Ensign'

look like miniature delphiniums but the flower spikes are much more open and delicate; the flowers seem to float like butterflies. There is quite a range of colour. Blue is the predominant one but there are also pinks and whites and some bicolors. The plants vary considerably in size from dwarf varieties that are only 30cm (12in) high to tall ones 1.2m (4ft) high. S 30cm (12in).
How to obtain Larkspurs are available both as plants in individual pots and seed from which a bigger range is available.
Cultivation Grow in any reasonable garden soil as long as it is free-draining. A sunny position is required. Taller forms may need some form of staking in exposed positions. Z7.

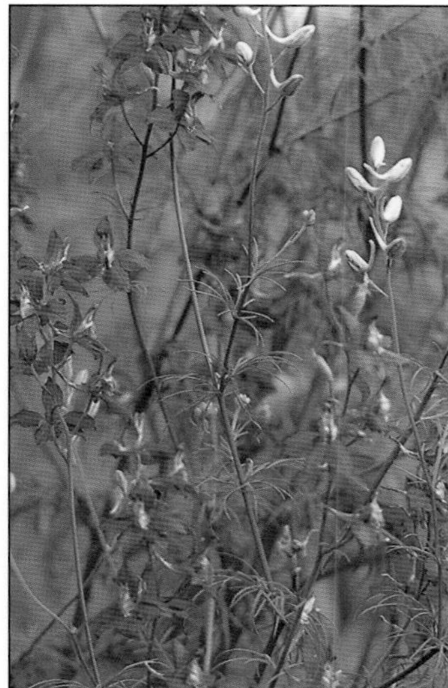
Consolida ajacis

Propagation Sow seeds in the position where the plants are to grow in early spring. Thin to 30cm (12in) intervals.
Uses Good for bedding and mixed borders, these plants can also be grown in pots and tubs. The taller varieties make very attractive cut flowers.

Consolida ajacis
This is the main species and it has large number of cultivars. Some are light and airy while others have much more compact, denser flower spikes, often with double blooms. There are several series which provide a mixtures of colours. For example there are the Dwarf Hyacinth Series, Dwarf Rocket Series and the Giant Imperial Series, all providing double flowers in a range of colours and heights. 'Frosted Skies' is a beautiful single with white and blue flowers. 'Sublime' is another tall variety, as is 'Earl Grey'; both come in mixture of colours. 'Kingsize Scarlet' produces very good red flowers.

CONVOLVULUS
Bindweed
An enormous genus of some 250 plants, of which many are weeds that you would not want near your garden. However there are one or two excellent garden plants. *C. tricolor* is one of these. As well as having attractive flowers it has the added bonus of being one of the few annuals that climb.

How to obtain Convolvulus are grown from seed which is very widely available.
Cultivation Grow convolvulus in any reasonable garden soil, so long as it is free-draining. A sunny site is needed. Z8.
Propagation Sow under glass in the early spring at 13–18°C (55–64°F). They can also be sown *in situ*, although the plants will then flower later, and so will not grow quite as vigorously.
Uses These plants are excellent for growing up any form of trellising or up wigwams of sticks, either in borders or in pots or tubs.

Convolvulus tricolor
This attractive plant has the typical funnel-shaped flowers of the convolvulus. Here they are a rich dark blue, with white markings at the base of the petals and a yellow eye. H 40cm (16in) S 30cm (12in). The plant is most often seen in the form 'Royal Ensign' which has very deep blue flowers. Seed can also be bought in mixtures which contain white and pink flowers as well as blue.

Other plants *Convolvulus sabatius* must be one of the most beautiful of all container plants. It is a tender perennial that is treated as an annual and either overwintered under glass or started again each year. It produces a profusion of small, funnel-shaped sky-blue flowers that smother the small, shrubby plant. It is usually bought as a plant rather than seed. A real gem.

Convolvulus sabatius

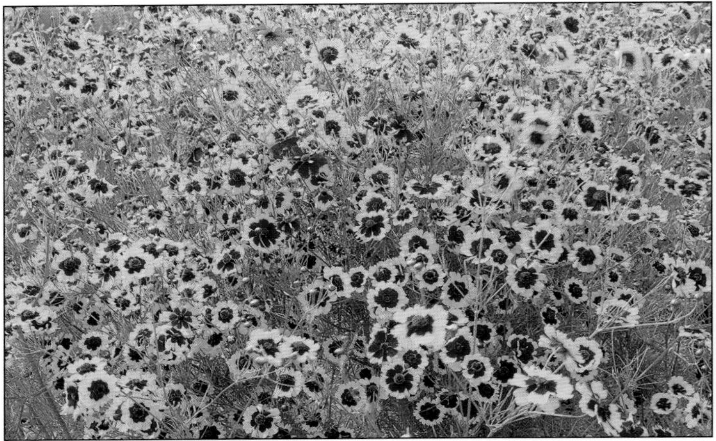

Coreopsis tinctoria

Cosmos bipinnatus 'Sonata Pink'

COREOPSIS
Tickseed

A large genus of up to 100 species of both annuals and perennials. The perennials are dealt with elsewhere (see page 188). *C. grandiflora* and *C. tinctoria* are the plants of interest to the annual gardener. The flowers are daisies with golden-yellowish outer petals and a gold central disc. The ends of the petals are usually fringed. Some plants have simple single flowers; others have semi or fully double blooms. The flowers are quite large, up to 6cm (2½in) in diameter. The plants vary in height from low-growing ones that reach only 23cm (9in) to ones that are 1.2m (4ft) tall; most reach about 45cm (18in) in height and spread.

How to obtain Annual coreopsis can occasionally be bought as plants from garden centres but they are best purchased as seed.

Cultivation Grow in any reasonable garden soil. Coreopsis prefers a sunny position, but the plants will take a little shade. Z7.

Propagation The seed can be sown in the early spring under glass at 13–16°C (55–60°F), or sown directly into the soil where the plants are to grow.

Uses They can be used in drifts in mixed borders or in bedding schemes. The shorter varieties can also be used in containers such as pots and tubs. Taller varieties are good for cutting.

Coreopsis grandiflora

This is a perennial that is usually treated as an annual. Seed of the species is commonly available but the plant is more frequently grown as one of the many cultivars including 'Early Sunrise' (semi-double flowers), 'Gold Star' (quilled petals) and 'Sunray' (double flowers).

Coreopsis tinctoria

This is similar to the previous species, but it has slightly smaller flowers. There is also more variety in the colour with the central disc often being reddish-brown and the petals flushed with red and brown. Again, it has plenty of cultivars. They include 'Tiger Flower', a dwarf only 23cm (9in) tall, and 'Mahogany Midget' a slightly taller plant which has rich mahogany-coloured flowers. Various mixed-coloured plants are also sold by some seed companies.

COSMOS
Cosmos

This is one of those annuals that has maintained its popularity over the years. There are 25 species but there are only a couple of annuals which are grown regularly. However, both have a number of cultivars, so there is plenty to interest the annual gardener. They have daisy-like flowers but the petals are wide, so producing an almost continuous disc. The petal colours are mainly white and pink in *C. bipinnatus*, the main species, but there are some yellow variants in the other species, *C. sulphureus*, as its name might suggest. Plants vary in height from the dwarf at about 30cm (12in) to the tall at up to 1.5m (5ft).

How to obtain Cosmos can be obtained as plants from most garden centres. However, they need to be purchased early on since they soon become leggy (producing long, bare stems) in small pots. It is better to raise them as seed.

Cultivation Cosmos will grow in any reasonable garden soil, but they like full sun. Z8.

Propagation Sow in early spring under glass at 16–18°C (60–64°F) or slightly later where the plants are to grow.

Coreopsis grandiflora 'Early Sunrise'

Cosmos growing in a mixed border.

Cosmos sulphureus

Uses They can be grown either as bedding plants or in drifts in a mixed border. Single colours look better in the latter. They make good cut flowers.

Cosmos bipinnatus

This is the most commonly grown species. It has a range of single colours as well as one or two varieties with bicolours: 'Candy Stripe', with its white flowers with crimson edging, is one example. The Sensation Series is one of the most popular with large flower heads up to 9cm (3½in) across. Sonata Series is a dwarf form, which grows only 30cm (12in) high. They can both be bought as a mixture or as individual colours such as 'Sonata Pink'. 'Sea Shells' has curious quilled petals. 'White Swan' is a beautiful white variety.

CREPIS
Hawk's Beard

This is a large genus of about 200 species or annuals and perennials. Most are considered weeds but some perennials are grown in the garden (see page 190) along with a couple of annuals, only one of which is in general cultivation. This one, *C. rubra*, is a gem and ought to be grown more widely than it is.

All the crepis have flower heads similar to those of the dandelion. However, unlike the dandelion, crepis are generally well-behaved and do not seed everywhere. (If the dandelion did not sow itself so prodigiously it would also be welcome since it is a magnificent plant.) Crepis make good bedding when they are grown *en masse*, but these plants are also suitable for filling gaps in mixed borders, especially along the margins.

How to obtain These plants are usually only available as seed from seed merchants. Very occasionally you see plants for sale but do not rely on finding them.

Cultivation Plant out in any reasonable garden soil so long as it is free-draining. Z6.

Propagation You should sow the seed in pots as soon as it is ripe. No heat is required for raising these seeds.

Uses Crepis are excellent in mixed borders and in gravel gardens. They are also attractive when used as bedding plants or in a variety of tubs or pots.

Crepis rubra

This has single dandelion-like flower heads of sugary pink, which float on wiry stems above a rosette of hairy leaves for a long period during summer. H up to 40cm (16in), but often much less, S 20cm (8in). There are a few cultivars of which the white form 'Alba' is the best. There is also a darker pink form, 'Rosea'.

Other plants There are one or two more species that are occasionally grown, but it is usually not as easy to get hold of their seed. The flowers of these species are less showy. Most are yellow-flowered and look good if grown in a meadow garden. Examples include *C. biennis* and *C. capillaris*.

Crepis rubra

Cuphea ignea 'Variegata'

CUPHEA
Cuphea

Not all gardeners know this genus but it is a big one containing about 260 species. Quite a number of these are grown in gardens, usually as annuals even if they are perennials or shrubs. The best known is probably *C. ignea*, known as the cigar flower. The colours vary but red is common and gives the plants a bright cheerfulness that makes them ideal for bedding or for growing in containers. If they are plants you do not know it might be worth experimenting with one or two of them, especially if you like exotic borders.

How to obtain Cuphea is widely available from seed merchants, but check catalogues carefully since naming may vary. You sometimes see plants in garden centres.

Cultivation Cupheas will grow in any reasonably fertile garden soil, but it needs to be free-draining. They prefer a sunny position but they will also grow in a lightly shaded one. Z9.

Propagation Sow seed in the early spring under glass at 13–16°C (55–60°F). The seed can also be sown where the plants are to grow, but flowering will be later.

Uses They make excellent bedding, especially in colourful, exotic schemes. They can also be used in containers and in mixed borders.

Cuphea cyanaea

This perennial is quite commonly grown as an annual. It has masses of orange tubular flowers with yellow tips. H 1m (3ft).

Cuphea ignea

This is the most common cuphea. It has bright red tubular flowers with a deep red and white mouth that looks rather like the ash on the tip of the cigar. It will grow up to 75cm (30in) as a perennial but is often less when grown as an annual. The variety 'Variegata' has leaves splashed with cream.

Other plants *C. hyssopifolia* (false heather) is a rounded shrub often treated as an annual. The tubes are much more flared, producing open flowers in either white or pink. H and S 60cm (24in) high.

Cuphea × purpurea is another shrub grown as an annual. These flowers are also widely flared, making them appear larger than those of the more common varieties. The colour varies from pink to red; there are also purple varieties. H up to 75cm (30in).

Cynoglossum amabile 'Mystery Rose'

CYNOGLOSSUM
Hound's tongue

A genus of about 55 species, most of which are annuals or short-lived perennials (see page 192). The flowers are generally quite small but there is plenty of them and they are a lovely blue – a colour not often seen in bedding plants. They are related to the forget-me-not; as with that plant, a progression of flowers open from a spiral of buds.

How to obtain Cynoglossums are most frequently seen as seed.

Cultivation These plants are best grown in any reasonable garden soil that is moisture-retentive but at the same time free-draining. They prefer sun but tolerate a little shade. Z7.

Propagation Sow seed in pots in spring. No heat is required. They can also be sown in the open ground where they are to flower.

Uses Cynoglossums work well as bedding plants or when placed in a mixed border.

Cynoglossum amabile

This is the most commonly grown annual in the genus. As well as the blue flowers of the species, there are also varieties with white or pink flowers, some named, such as 'Mystery Rose' (rose-pink) or 'Avalanche' (white). H 60cm (24in), but often much less, S 30cm (12in).

Other plants *Cynoglossum officinale* is a biennial with deep purple flowers. It is best grown in the wild-flower garden.

Dahlia 'Bishop of Llandaff'

Dahlia 'Lilliput'

Dahlia 'Hamari Katrina'

DAHLIA
Dahlia

Most gardeners will not need to be told what dahlias are: they are very familiar to us all. While there are only 20 species there are a colossal 20,000 cultivars, which shows just how popular they are. They are not only grown in decorative situations in the garden but also for cutting and for exhibition purposes. The flowers are usually quite large and blowsy in a variety of bright colours.

The shape of the flower head has been divided into eleven groups varying from simple singles to double, spherical ones known as pompoms. There are other doubles, such as the cactus dahlia in which the narrow petals curve upwards. These plants are all perennials that are treated as annuals; they are lifted each autumn and stored overwinter before replanting in spring. There are also a few varieties which are grown from seed each year. Bedding dahlias only grow to about 45cm (18in) or so but the perennial ones will grow up to 1.5m (5ft) in height and 60cm (24in) in spread.

How to obtain Dahlias are sold as tubers from most garden centres. They are also available from specialist nurseries which offer a much larger choice and are a must for anyone who becomes interested in these plants. Their catalogues are often a mine of information. The bedding varieties are available from most seed merchants, and most carry a good range.

Cultivation Grow dahlias in a moist humus-rich soil that is free draining. Choose a sunny position. Stake taller varieties. Z9.

Propagation The tubers can be cut in half once growth has just begun, leaving a shoot on each piece. Alternatively take basal cuttings from the emerging shoots. Seed can be sown under glass in early spring at 13–16°C (55–60°F).

Uses Many gardeners grow dahlias in separate beds or in rows in the vegetable garden for cutting or for exhibitions. They can also be grown in mixed borders. The smaller annuals make good bedding plants and can also be grown in containers.

More common plants

There are so many varieties of dahlia that it is difficult even to start listing them. There are some, such as purple-foliaged 'Bishop of Llandaff', which are used more frequently in borders than they are for exhibition, while others, such as 'Hamari Gold', are mainly grown for exhibition purposes, but can also be used as a cut flower or even as a decorative variety in the border.

Other plants The annual bedding varieties grown from seed are offered by most seed merchants. They are usually offered as a mixture of colours. The well-known dwarf 'Redskin' has dark red or bronze foliage and flowers in a variety of colours. 'Coltness Mixed' is another old favourite.

Dahlia 'Brilliant Eye'

Dahlia 'Cactus Video'

DATURA
Thorn apple

This is a small genus from which the shrubby species have been reclassified as *Brugmansia*. The

Dahlia 'Decorative'

Dianthus barbatus 'Harbinger Mixed'

Dianthus barbatus 'Scarlet Beauty'

Dianthus chinensis 'Pluto Karminrosa'

Dianthus chinensis 'Merry-go-Round'

annual and perennial ones remain, however, as *Datura*. These plants are beautiful but they contain toxic substances; if eaten they are likely to be fatal. So plant them only if you feel confident that no one will suffer any ill effects. Their beauty lies in the very large trumpet flowers, which are white or soft pastel colours. Some have a wonderful scent. The plants are large, open plants. H 1m (3ft) S 60cm (24in).
How to obtain Most garden centres are reluctant to sell these plants because of their toxic nature. The best way to obtain them is from seed merchants.
Cultivation Plant out after the threat of frost has passed. The soil should be fertile but free-draining. The site should be sunny. Z: see individual entries.
Propagation Sow the seed under glass in early spring at 16–18°C (60–64°F). Grow the plants on in containers.
Uses Datura are mainly grown as container plants, and they are suitable for large pots or tubs. They can be planted in the open soil. The poisonous nature of the plant means that it needs to be sited carefully.

Datura inoxia
This is another relatively common species. It has trumpets that are white, or white tinged with violet. They are very fragrant. It is slightly less hardy. Z9.

Datura stramonium
Known as Jimson weed, this is the main species grown. It has large white trumpets which are mainly white, but are occasionally purple. The seed capsules are large, green and prickly, hence its other name of common thorn apple. Z7.

DIANTHUS
Dianthus
This is a well-known genus with more than 300 species and an unknown number of cultivars. It is best known for the perennials which include carnations and pinks (see page 192). However, there are a number of annuals, mainly used as bedding plants. Although these are not quite as popular as they once were, they are still widely grown. The flowers are either single, semi-double or double in a range of bright colours, of which only blue is missing. They are often scented. Most are annuals, the notable exception being the biennial *D. barbatus*, the sweet William, which has to be sown one year for flowering the next.
How to obtain Most annual dianthus can be purchased as either seed or plants. Seed generally offers a better range of possibilities.
Cultivation Any reasonably fertile garden soil will do but it must be free-draining. A sunny position is required. Z: see individual entries.
Propagation Sow seed of annuals in early spring under glass at 13–16°C (55–60°F), or outside where the plants are to grow, but these will be later flowering. Biennials should be sown outside in drill in early summer and moved to their flowering positions in autumn.
Uses Annual dianthus are mainly used either as bedding or in a mixed border. Some can be used as container plants.

Dianthus barbatus
This is the biennial sweet William. It is the upright plant and the tallest of the annuals. It is deliciously scented. It has flat heads of red, pink or white flowers, which are often patterned. It is good for cutting. H 70cm (28in) S 30cm (12in).

Dianthus chinensis
One of the most commonly seen annual pinks. It is variously known as the Chinese, Japanese or Indian pink. It carries single flowers that are red, pink or white with a darker central eye and often patterns. The petals are fringed. H and S 30cm (12in).

This plant has given rise to a number of cultivars with 'Strawberry Parfait' being one of the most popular. Heddweigii Group is also widely grown. Z7.

Other plants Other species that are frequently grown as annuals, often as cultivars, include *D. armeria*, the Deptford pink, and *D. superbus* which has very deeply cut petals.

Dianthus barbatus

Dianthus chinensis 'Strawberry Parfait'

Dianthus 'Can Can Scarlet'

Digitalis purpurea

DIGITALIS
Foxgloves

This well-known genus consists of more than 20 species, most of which are perennials (see page 195) but some are annuals or treated as such. The common foxglove, *D. purpurea* is one of these. It usually grows in the wild as a perennial in mainland Europe but, oddly enough, only as a biennial in Britain.

Foxgloves are tall, erect plants with spikes of tubular flowers that create a wonderful effect in the border. They look especially good when grown as a drift, but also look fine dotted throughout an informal planting.

How to obtain Foxgloves can occasionally be found as plants in garden centres or nurseries but they are best grown from seed which is readily available from a number of sources.

Digitalis purpurea f. *albiflora*

Digitalis purpurea (mixed colours)

Cultivation These plants will grow in any garden soil, in either full sun or a partially shaded position. Cut off the flower spikes before they seed if you wish to prevent self-sowing. Z4.

Propagation The seed can be scattered where the plants are to grow as soon as it is ripe. Once you have foxgloves in your garden, they will continue to self-sow if they are allowed to seed.

Uses Foxgloves work best in mixed borders although the cultivars can look good used in bedding schemes. The wild forms are excellent in wild-flower gardens. Foxgloves also make very good cut flowers.

Digitalis purpurea

This is the common foxglove and it is a superb garden plant that is well worth growing. The flowers are a soft pinkish-purple with darker spots inside. There is also a white form *albiflora*. H 2m (6ft) S 45cm (18 in).

The cultivars are much brasher, with bigger flowers that are more densely packed on the stem. There is a wider range of pinks and whites and the spots are usually larger. The Excelsior hybrids (or Suttons Excelsior hybrids) provide the main range of cultivars. The Foxy hybrids are about half the size of the species.

Other plants *Digitalis lanata* is a perennial that is often treated as an annual. It produces small flowers, which are white with soft brown veining.

DIMORPHOTHECA
African daisy

This was once a much larger genus because *Osteospermum* was included in it and plants of that genus are still sometimes listed as *Dimorphotheca*. The plants have rather beautiful daisy-like flowers which come in a range of white and oranges, usually with a purple central disc and a central ring of violet-purple at the base of the petals. They come from South Africa and they need sunshine to open. They usually shut in the evening so they are not good plants for people who see their gardens only in the evening. They are sprawling plants so do not reach any great height. H 30cm (12in) S 45cm (18in).

How to obtain These are commonly available as plants from garden centres and nurseries. The plants often do not have any cultivar name attached to them; if you want specific colours, buy them in flower. They can also be purchased as seed from various seed merchants.

Cultivation These plants will grow in any reasonable garden soil so long as it is free-draining. They must have a warm, sunny position or the flowers will not open. Z9.

Propagation Sow African daisy seed under glass at 18°C (64°F) in the early spring.

Uses These are mainly used as bedding plants but they can also be used for filling spaces towards the front of a mixed border. They can also be used in tubs.

Dimorphotheca sinuata

This is probably the most commonly grown plant in the genus. The species itself is not often seen; it is more commonly grown as one of the hybrids. The flowers are white, orange, yellow or even pink, often with a touch of blue or purple at the base of the petals.

Dimorphotheca sinuata

Annuals for edging lawns and paths

Ageratum
Bellis
Begonia semperflorens
Brachyscome
Clarkia
Crepis rubra
Dianthus chinensis
Felicia
Iberis amara
Limnanthes douglasii
Lobelia
Lobularia maritima
Myosotis
Nemesia
Nicotiana
Petunia
Primula
Silene pendula
Tagetes
Viola × wittrockiana

Other plants *Dimorphotheca pluvalis* is known as the rain prophet because it shuts up in cloudy conditions. The flowers are white with a blue base to their petals.

DIPSACUS
Teasel

There are about 15 species in this genus which consists mainly of biennials. They are not the most colourful plants but there are a couple that are welcome in our gardens. The attraction is mainly due to the structure of the plant. It is a tall, upright, open-branched plant which has a stately architectural quality about it. The stems and leaves are covered in stout prickles and the large, opposite leaves join at the stem forming a large cup which is usually filled with water. H 2m (6ft) S 1m (3ft).

How to obtain Teasels have tap roots which means that they do not do well in pots. As a result, they are rarely seen for sale as plants. However, they are generally available as seed.

Cultivation Teasels will grow in any reasonable garden soil. They do best in sun but will also grow in light shade. Z3.

Propagation Sow the seed in the open ground where the plants are to grow in autumn or spring.

Uses These plants work well at the back of a mixed border in an informal garden, but they look best in a wild-flower garden. The seed heads make good winter decoration in the garden as well as providing winter feed for several species of bird. They make excellent dried flowers.

Dipsacus fullonum (foliage)

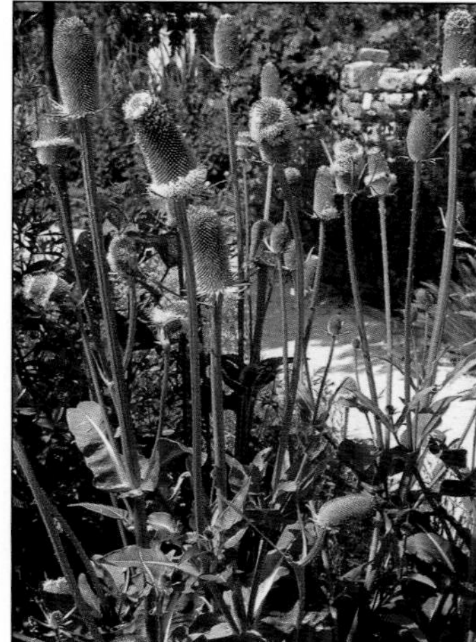

Dipsacus fullonum

Dipsacus fullonum

This is the wild teasel which is the plant most commonly seen. The flower heads are egg-shaped and rather prickly with spine-like bracts. The flowers first open as a band round the middle and then expand both upwards and downwards. They are a pale purple colour, which contrasts well with the pale green of the flower head. They flower in their second year.

Other plants *Dipsacus sativus* This is the fuller's teasel, the head of which was used to tease out wool and raise the nap on cloth. The spines on the head are hooked at the end, just perfect for the job.

Dorotheanthus bellidiformis 'Gelato Pink'

DOROTHEANTHUS
Livingstone daisy

A genus of about ten species which are still more commonly known under the name *Mesembryanthemum*. Only one of these is generally cultivated. It was once more widely grown than it is now, but it is very suitable for coastal gardens and is still frequently seen as bedding plants around the coast. The plants are low growing with narrow succulent fleshy leaves and masses of brightly coloured daisies. The flowers are up to 4cm (1½in) diameter. Unfortunately the flowers tend to shut up in dull weather. H 15cm (6in) S 30cm (12in) or more.

How to obtain Livingstone daisies are frequently sold as plants either in bedding packs or in individual pots. They are also readily available as seed from most merchants, and are often listed under the name *Mesembryanthemum*.

Cultivation These plants thrive in well-drained sandy soil, including pure sand, but they will happily grow in most well-drained garden soils. A sunny position must be provided or the flowers will not open. Z9.

Propagation Sow the seed under glass at 16–18°C (60–64°F) in the early spring.

Uses Excellent for bedding and borders in coastal regions where the light is bright and the soil usually well drained. They can also be used very successfully as bedding or in containers.

Dorotheanthus bellidiformis

This is the species usually grown. The daisy flowers have a brown central disc and narrow petals in a wide range of colours including yellow, pinks, reds, purples and whites. They are often two-toned with, say, pink petals flushed with white from the centre.

There are a number of cultivars: some, like 'Magic Carpet' are a mixture of colours, while others such as 'Gelato Pink' (pink), 'Apricot Shimmer' (soft apricot), 'Cape Sunshine' (bright yellow) or 'Lunette' (also called 'Yellow Ice', pale yellow) are single-coloured varieties.

Other plants There are several other species of which seed is available if you search for it. The most frequently seen is *D. gramineus*. Its flowers are similar to *D. bellidiformis* but the leaves are narrow and grass-like.

Dorotheanthus bellidiformis

Eccremocarpus scaber

ECCREMOCARPUS
Chilean glory flower

This is a small genus containing five species of perennial climbing plants of which one, *E. scaber*, is regularly seen in gardens. It is debatable whether this should be classified in gardening terms as a perennial or as an annual since it is regularly treated as both. However, the majority of gardeners use it as an annual climber, unless it is grown in a glasshouse or conservatory, and so it has been included here. It is fast growing and so well suited for use as an annual. It will grow up through other plants or up twiggy supports up to 5m (15ft) if used as a perennial. As an annual it reaches 2–3m (6–10ft).
How to obtain Chilean glory flowers are occasionally seen in pots but they are more frequently sold as seed. Most seed merchants carry them.
Cultivation These plants will grow well in a reasonably fertile, well-drained soil. A sunny position is needed. If they are planted against a warm wall, the plants may overwinter and produce flowers for a second year. Z9.
Propagation Sow seed in early spring under glass at 13–16°C (55–60°F).
Uses Grow as a climbing plant either in borders or against walls or fences. Chilean glory flowers can also be grown in large containers if supported by a wigwam of sticks or a framework.

Eccremocarpus scaber
This is the main species grown. It is usually grown as the straight species, which has orange or flame-red tubular flower carried in loose heads. However, there are also a number of named cultivars available. These include the Anglia hybrids which offer a range of mixed colours such as pink, red, orange and yellow. Tresco hybrids also include crimson and cream flowers. Some seed merchants just label seeds under their colours – for example, "yellow forms" – without giving a cultivar name.

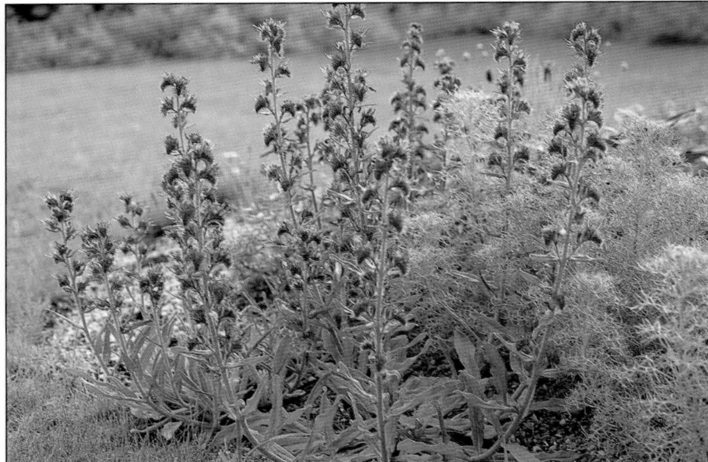

Echium vulgare

ECHIUM
Bugloss

A large genus containing about 40 species, which provides the gardener with several excellent plants. They vary considerably in size from low bedding plants of about 45cm (18in) to giants reaching up to 2m (6ft) or even more. However, close examination will show that although the size and shape of the plants are different, the flowers are all basically funnel-shaped. They are usually blue although they also come in other colours. This is a beautiful group of plants, especially the larger ones.
How to obtain The bedding varieties are sometimes available as plants. The others have to be bought as seed. You may have to search to find it but it is becoming more widely available.
Cultivation Plant in a fertile soil that is well drained. The larger varieties appreciate a richer soil, but, again, it must be well-drained. The smaller ones need full sun but some of the bigger ones will also do well in a dappled shade. Z: see individual entries.
Propagation Sow the seed under glass at 13–16°C (55–60°F) in early spring. The smaller ones can be sown where they are to flower.
Uses The smaller plants make excellent bedding. The taller ones are architectural in shape. They stand out as features in borders or look good in informal planting under trees or among shrubs.

Echium vulgare
This is the most frequently seen species. The species itself is called the common viper's bugloss and is excellent for wild-flower gardens. It has a tall spike or spikes of flowers which appear from ever-expanding coils. They are blue but purple in bud. H 1m (3ft) S 30cm (12in). There are various bedding forms derived from this, including 'Blue Bedder' which has light blue flowers that darken with age. Dwarf hybrids include pink and purple flowers. Z5.

Other plants *Echium wildpretii* is typical of the larger species. It forms a rosette from which emerges a tall spike up to 2m (6ft) in height; it is densely covered with blue flowers and has a rather exotic appearance. S 45cm (18in). Similar species are *E. simplex*, *E. fastuosum*, *E. candicans* and *E. pininana*. These are plants for the specialist grower but well worth the effort. Z9.

EMILIA
Tassel flower

There are about 24 species of annuals in this genus, of which a couple are widely grown in our gardens. The brightly coloured flowers are carried singly or in clusters, held above the leaves. They are upward-facing and look rather like miniature tassels or paint brushes (in the past this

Echium vulgare 'Blue Bedder'

Emilia coccinea 'Scarlet Magic'

A particularly fine display of *Emilia coccinea*.

plant was also called Flora's paint brush). H 60cm (24in) S nearly the same as the height.
How to obtain Tassel flowers are mainly found as seed, either at garden centres or from seed merchants' catalogues. The seed is sometimes still listed under its old name of *Cacalia*.
Cultivation Any reasonable garden soil will suffice so long as the ground is free-draining. A sunny position is required. Z9.
Propagation Sow the seed in early spring at 13–16°C (55–60°F) under glass, or later directly into the soil where the plants are to grow. The latter method provides plants that are later flowering.
Uses These make good bedding plants but they also work very well in drifts of a single colour in a mixed border. They are excellent for cutting and can be dried.

Emilia coccinea
This is the most frequently seen plant. The flowers are a bright flame-red. Sometimes they are sold as cultivars such as 'Scarlet Magic' but these are not greatly different from the species.

Emilia sonchifolia
This is a bit more varied than the above. The main flower colour is reddish-purple, but there are also orange, scarlet and yellow forms available. They are usually sold as mixed colours.

Other plants There are a number of other species that are available if you search for them. They include *EE. atriplicifolia, glabra, hastata* and *suavolens*. However, they do not vary greatly from the above.

ERYNGIUM
Sea holly
This is a very large genus of some 230 species of which the vast majority are perennials. However, there are a few biennials, of which one is wildly grown in gardens. This is *E. giganteum*. It is a prickly beast but a plant of such beauty that it is worth putting up with this negative aspect. Its leaves, stems and bracts are a silvery green. It is often known as Miss Willmott's ghost: this venerable gardener had the habit of surreptitiously dropping seed in her friends' gardens and so a trail of plants were left in her footsteps – her "ghost". The name is doubly apt because the plant shows up ghostly white at night.

Eryngium giganteum 'Silver Ghost'

How to obtain This is a tap-rooted plant that does not do very well in pots. It is best to avoid buying potted plants unless they are very young, and to go for seed which is readily available.
Cultivation Any well-drained garden soil is suitable, even poor ones. Full sun is preferred. Z6.
Propagation Sow the seed in spring where the plant is to grow. It will flower the following year. Sea holly self-sows if left to set seed.
Uses This plant is best used in a mixed border where it can be grown in a drift or in single plants. It does well in a wild-flower garden and is particularly good in gravel gardens. Excellent as a dried flower.

Eryngium giganteum
This is the plant described above. The flowers are contained in dome-shaped heads which are greenish-blue in colour. Some merchants list 'Miss Willmott's Ghost' as a cultivar name but this is the common name for the form generally in cultivation and is no different from plants or seed sold simply under the name of the species. H 1m (3ft) S 36cm (14in). The cultivar 'Silver Ghost' has been introduced relatively recently. This is an attractive plant that is much more silvery-white than the species.

Other plants Of the other biennials, *E. campestre* is the one you are most likely to find. This is a plant of dunes and dry grassy places. It is not so spectacular as other eryngiums but it is still a good plant for wild gardens and gravel gardens. It is smaller than the above, 60cm (24in) high and almost as wide. The flower heads are greenish and relatively small.

Eryngium giganteum is an excellent plant for drying.

Erysimum helveticum

ERYSIMUM
Wallflower

This is a large and popular genus of about 200 species. Most of the plants are perennials but they are not long lived so they are often treated as biennials, especially the common bedding forms. Wallflowers actually do grow well on walls, which is the nearest garden equivalent to their native cliffs; this is because they like a well-drained position. If they are given such conditions in the garden they will last for several years. The bedding varieties are very colourful and cheerful and have a very distinctive scent which is one of the pleasures of spring. H 75cm (30in) S 40cm (16in).

How to obtain The bedding varieties are widely sold as bare-rooted plants: they can be found everywhere from garden centres to petrol stations. However, it is often difficult to know what the flower colour will be. Seed merchants give a much larger choice of cultivars and allow you to be certain of the colour.

Cultivation Any good garden soil will suffice, but a well-drained one will ensure that plants overwinter better. Wallflowers prefer a sunny position. Z7.

Propagation Sow seed in rows in early summer and transfer to their flowering position in autumn.

Uses They make excellent bedding plants, and can also be used in mixed borders or in containers such as pots. They look good in cottage-garden schemes, and also combine well with bulbs.

Erysimum × allionii

This is the Siberian wallflower, which produces bright orange flowers. It is commonly available but it is not seen so often now as the following species. There are no cultivars available.

Erysimum cheiri

This is the main bedding wallflower. It is a wonderful plant, very fragrant and colourful, and the one from which most of the bedding wallflowers have been derived. Seed is mainly sold as named cultivars. Some of these, such as Bedder Series, are sold as mixtures or individual colours such as 'Orange Bedder' or 'Blood Red'.

Other plants There are several other species that can be used as annuals. One delightful little plant is *E. helveticum* which has bright yellow flowers that open from purple buds. It self-sows, so once you have it there is no need to re-sow; simply transplant the seedlings if necessary.

ESCHSCHOLZIA
Californian poppy

This small genus of about ten species produces a couple of annuals which are stalwarts of the border. They have typical poppy flowers which are shallow, funnel- or saucer-shaped, and with petals that look fragile, although they are not quite so crumpled as many of the poppies. These are cheerful flowers which come in plenty of bright colours, with orange as the base colour. The foliage is finely cut. The plants are rather sprawling and the flowers are carried on thin stems well above the leaves. H and S 30cm (12in).

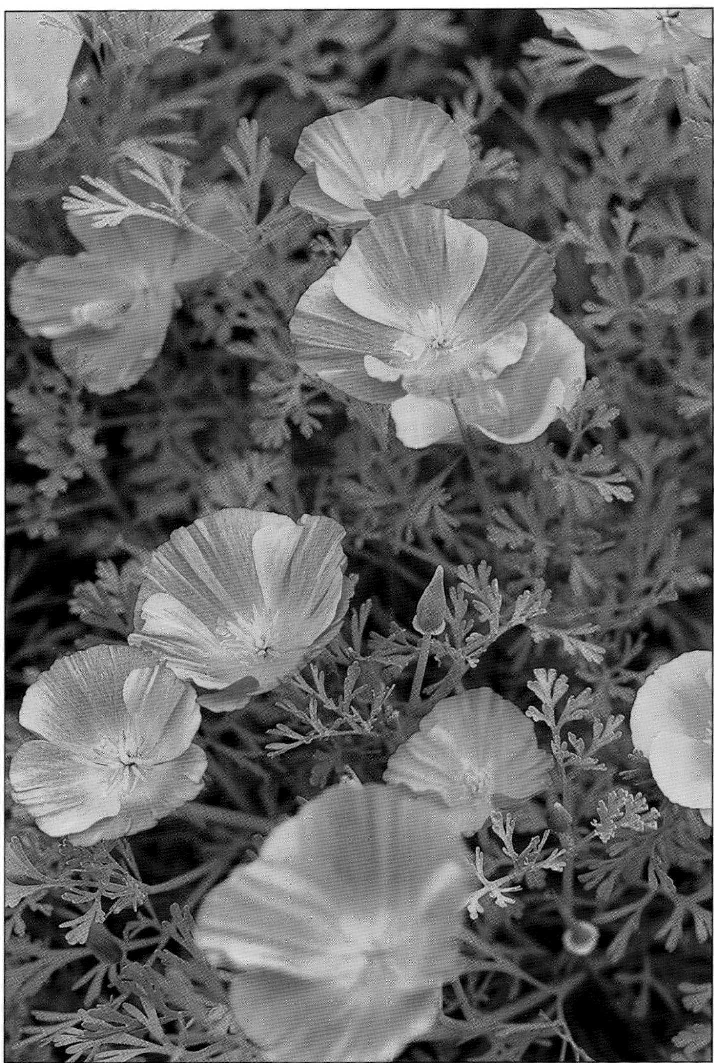
Eschscholzia californica 'Mikado'

Eschscholzia californica 'Mission Bells'

How to obtain Californian poppies can be purchased as plants but they are best bought as seed which is readily available.

Cultivation Californian poppies can be grown in any reasonable garden soil so long as it is free-draining. They need a sunny position. Z6.

Propagation Seed can be sown in late spring where the plants are to grow. The plants will self-sow for future years. However, the cultivars are likely to revert to the basic species.

Uses These plants can either be used in bedding schemes or in mixed borders.

Eschscholzia californica

This is the main species grown. The species has mainly orange flowers but there are several cultivars which have blooms of yellow, flame-red, red and pink. There are also doubles and semi-doubles, whose flowers are more tissue-like. 'Ballerina' has double and semi-double flowers in a mixture of colours; 'Apricot Flambeau' is a pretty apricot semi-double with splashes of red; 'Mission Bells' is also semi-double but comes in a mixture of colours; 'Cherry Ripe' has red petals that get paler towards the centres; 'Mikado' has deep orange petals, which are scarlet on the reverse side; and 'Alba' is a beautiful creamy-white.

Other plants *Eschscholzia caespitosa* are similar to the above but with slightly smaller, yellow flowers. The best known cultivar is 'Sundew', which has beautiful lemon-yellow flowers.

EUPHORBIA
Spurge

This is a colossal genus with more than 2,000 species ranging from annuals to trees. The majority grown in gardens are perennials or shrubs that are treated as perennials. However, there are also two annual plants, *E. lathyris* (the caper spurge) and *E. marginata* (snow on the mountain), that make a welcome contribution to our gardens. These are both upright plants but they are quite dissimilar in other respects. Like all euphorbias, these plants produce a latex sap which can cause severe irritation to the skin and so they should only be handled wearing gardening gloves. Be sure to keep the juice away from eyes. No parts should be eaten, especially the seed of *E. lathyris* which looks a bit like capers (hence its name) but which is highly toxic.

How to obtain Both the annual species are occasionally offered as plants but they do not do very well in small pots so it is best to grow them from seed. This is readily available.
Cultivation Grow in a reasonably rich soil – the richer the soil the bigger the plants will grow. A sunny position is best. Z4–8.
Propagation Sow where the plants are to grow. *E. lathyris* will self sow if left to set seed.
Uses *E. lathyris* is best grown in a mixed border where its shape can be appreciated. *E. marginata* can also be used there, and it makes a good bedding plant.

Euphorbia lathyris
An upright but a much sturdier plant than the following. It produces side branches, giving it a candelabra shape and great architectural presence when fully grown. Excellent for bringing structure to a border. H 1.5m (5ft) S 45cm (18in).

Euphorbia marginata
An upright plant which has ovate leaves and tiny flowers carried among bracts at the top of the stems. These bracts and top leaves are either variegated in white or totally white, hence its common name of snow on the mountain. H 1m (3ft) S 50cm (20in). There are several cultivars including 'Summer Icicle', 'Icicle' 'Kilimanjaro' and 'Snow Top'.

EUSTOMA
Prairie gentian

A small genus of three species, of which one is increasingly being grown. Its new popularity is partly due to the fact that it has become more readily available as a cut flower, which has prompted people to start growing it. Until recently the genus was called *Lisianthus* and the plant is still often called this. It is an erect plant bearing upward-facing flowers that are cup-shaped and often semi-doubles or doubles. The common name prairie gentian comes from the flower's blue or purple colour.
How to obtain The best way of obtaining the prairie gentian is as seed which is widely available.
Cultivation These plants are often grown under glass for cutting purposes, but they can also be grown outside once the threat of frost has passed. Grow in a reasonably fertile, free-draining soil. It should preferably be neutral to alkaline. A warm, sunny position is important. Z9.
Propagation Sow the seed under glass at 16–18°C (55–60°F) in the late winter.
Uses The prairie gentian can be used as a decorative plant in a mixed border or it can be grown simply for cutting purposes.

Eustoma grandiflorum
This, the only species grown, is sometimes called *E. russellianum* or *Lisianthus russellianus*. The cup- or bell-shaped flowers are purple or blue in the species and have a wonderful satiny texture. The centres are darker. H 1m (3ft) S 30cm (12in).

There are a number of cultivars which offer a larger range of colours including pink, white, red and even yellow. 'Echo Pink' is a double pink. 'Aloha Deep Red' is, as its name suggests, red. Heidi Series are single cultivars in a wide range of colours including salmon and various picotees. Echo Series are doubles, again with picotees. Double Eagle Mixed is another double with a mix of colours. All are good choices for cutting.

Eustoma grandiflorum

Euphorbia marginata

Fragrant annuals

Brachyscome iberidifolia
Centaurea moschata
Datura
Dianthus barbatus
Dianthus chinensis
Erysimum cheiri
Exacum affine
Heliotropium arborescens
Hesperis matronalis
Iberis amara
Ipomoea alba
Lathyrus odoratus
Lobularia maritima
Matthiola
Nicotiana
Oenothera
Pelargonium (foliage)
Phacelia
Reseda odorata
Viola × wittrockiana

Exacum affine

EXACUM

Persian violet

This is a genus containing about 25 species, only one of which is used as an annual in our gardens. This one, *E. affine*, has been used for a long time as a bedding plant and is still popular. The flowers are shallow dishes or saucers and are generally coloured a soft blue-purple with a yellow centre. Cultivars offer a slightly wider range of colours. As an added bonus the flowers are scented. These are bushy plants, which can grow up to 75cm (30in) high; the bedding or pot-plant cultivars are usually 30cm (12in) tall or less. S 15cm (6in).

How to obtain Persian violets can be purchased as plants, either in individual pots or in bedding packs. They can also be obtained as seed, where a wider range of plants is available.

Cultivation Plant out once the threat of frosts and chilly nights are definitely over. Persian violets will grow in any reasonable garden soil so long as it is free-draining. They need a warm and sunny position. Z9.

Propagation Sow seed at 18–20°C (64–68°F) under glass in the early spring.

Uses In the garden they can be used as bedding, where their uniform height can be exploited. They can also be used as container plants for both tubs and pots, and for window boxes. In the house or greenhouse they can also be used as pot plants.

Exacum affine

This is the only species grown. The species is sometimes grown in its own right, but it usually appears in the form of one of the cultivars. The majority have soft blue-purple flowers but some are darker blue, pink and white. The bedding varieties are quite short, with many being no more than 15cm (6in) high: the height is reflected in names such as 'Midget' and 'White Midget'.

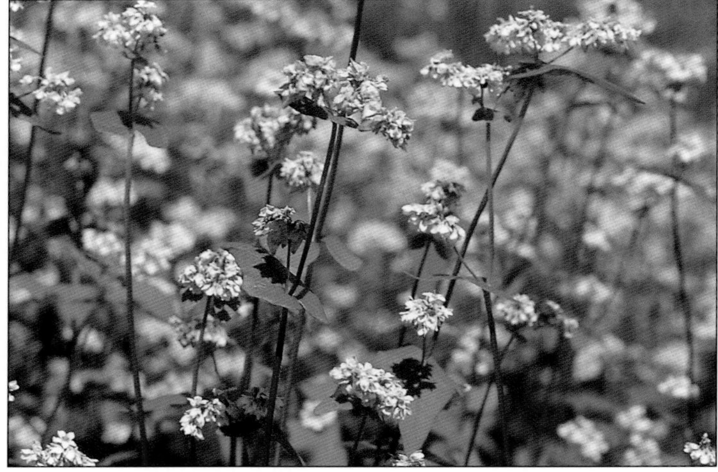

Fagopyrum esculentum

FAGOPYRUM

Buckwheat

This is genus of about 15 species of which a couple of annuals are grown both in agriculture and gardens. They are very similar to the plants that were once classified as *Polygonum* (the persicarias) and they have at times been listed as such. The flowers are small and carried in clusters and usually pink or white.

These plants have been in cultivation since the earliest agriculture as a source of grain and they are still used for green fodder and making flour. In the garden they are long flowering, lasting from midsummer well into the autumn. Although they are perhaps not as popular as they once were, seed is still available.

How to obtain It is doubtful whether you will find buckwheat as plants, but quite a number of seed merchants carry stocks of seed. However, you may need to search for it.

Cultivation Any reasonable garden soil will suffice. A sunny position is best. Z7.

Propagation Sow the seed in spring in open ground where the plants are to grow. They are usually best sown in drifts rather than as individual plants.

Uses Their long flowering period makes these plants useful in a variety of places in the garden including informal beds and wild-flower borders. They are widely grown in the herb garden and still used to treat a variety of ailments. Bees love the flowers so they are good plants for honey producers. They also make good green manure, for which purpose they are often sold.

Fagopyrum esculentum

This has clusters of white or pink flowers carried on erect, knotted stems that also contain green, heart-shaped leaves. The flowers are fragrant. H 60cm (24in) S 30cm (12in).

Other plants *Fagopyrum tartaricum* is the Indian or Tartary buckwheat, and also known as *Polygonum tartaricum*. It is similar to the above but about half its size. It is more tolerant of drought conditions and makes excellent dried flowers.

FELICIA

Blue daisy

A large genus containing about 80 perennials and shrubs as well as a few annuals. A couple of these are among some of the most popular of bedding plants, while others are also quite widely grown. As their common name suggests they have daisy-like flowers with blue petals. The central discs are a good, contrasting yellow. They produce masses of small flowers over a long period. If grown under glass many will survive longer than a

A massed display of *Felicia amelloides*.

year since they are strictly speaking short-lived perennials rather than annuals. Here they will grow up to 60cm (24in) high or more, but in the open they are normally much shorter. They are bushy plants and they grow about as wide as they are tall.

How to obtain Felicias can be obtained as plants from garden centres or nurseries and they are widely available as seed from all seed merchants.

Cultivation Plant out once the threat of late frosts has passed. Felicia will grow in any reasonable garden soil, although it must be free-draining. It is important to grow these plants in a warm, sunny position. Z9.

Propagation Sow seed in the early spring under glass at 16–18°C (60–80°F).

Uses Felicias have a wide range of uses. They work very well in bedding schemes but can also be used in mixed borders. They also make excellent container plants.

Felicia amelloides

A very good plant with blue flowers of varying shades. It is often sold as one of the many varieties which come in white as well as blue. 'Read's White' is a good example of the former. There is also a form with white variegations on the leaves known as 'Santa Anita Variegated'.

Felicia amoena

This is a slightly smaller plant than the previous species, but again it has bright blue flowers. Its form 'Variegata' is one of the best-known felicias; the leaves are heavily variegated with cream markings, and set off the blue flowers beautifully.

Felicia bergeriana

This is one of the lowest-growing felicias, reaching only about 25cm (10in) in height. Like the others it has blue flowers. This blue gives it its common name, the kingfisher daisy.

Red-flowered annuals

Adonis aestivalis
Alcea rosea 'Scarlet'
Amaranthus caudata
Antirrhinum 'Scarlet Giant'
Begonia semperflorens 'Lucifer'
Cleome spinosa 'Cherry Queen'
Cosmos bipinnatus 'Pied Piper Red'
Dianthus chinensis 'Fire Carpet'
Linum grandiflorum
Malope trifida 'Vulcan'
Nicotiana 'Crimson'
Papaver rhoeas
Pelargonium
Salvia splendens
Tagetes patula 'Cinnabar'
Verbena 'Blaze'

Felicia amelloides

Felicia heterophylla

A mat-forming plant with blue daisies. However, this species also produces some pink cultivars, such as 'The Rose'. It also has a white variety 'Snowmass'.

GAILLARDIA
Blanket flower

There are about 30 species in this genus, and they comprise both annuals and perennials. There is one annual that is widely grown, as well as a perennial that is often treated as an annual. Like a large number of annuals, these plants are members of the daisy family and they exhibit the typical daisy-like flowers of an outer ring of petals and an inner disc. The petals are usually yellow in colour, flushed red towards their base and with reddish or brown central discs. These are big powerful daisies, up to 14cm (5½in) across in some plants. They are always eye-catching and more than earn their keep in the garden. H 60cm (24in) S 30cm (12in).

How to obtain Blanket flowers are available both as plants from garden centres and seed from a wide variety of sources.

Cultivation Plant out in any reasonable-quality garden soil. They should be placed in a warm and sunny position. Z: see individual entries.

Propagation Sow seed under glass in early spring at 13–16°C (55–60°F). It can also be sown where the plants are to flower, but the flowering will be much later than in greenhouse-raised plants.

Uses These make excellent bedding plants and they can also be used in a mixed border, especially one devoted to hot colours.

Gaillardia × grandiflora

This is strictly speaking a perennial and is often grown as such in warmer areas. However, it is also widely grown as an annual. It has the largest flowers. There are a number of cultivars including: 'Burgunder' (red flowers), 'Dazzler' (flame-red and yellow) and the similar 'Wirral Flame'. Z4.

Gaillardia pulchella

This is an annual which has smaller flowers than the previous but they are the same colour. There are several cultivars including 'Summer Prairie', 'Red Plume' and 'Yellow Plume'. Z8.

Gaillardia pulchella 'Summer Fire'

Galactites tomentosa

GALACTITES
Galactites

This is a small genus of only three plants, of which just one, *G. tomentosa*, is grown. It is not often seen, which is surprising because it is a wonderful plant. The fact that it is a thistle may put a lot of people off, but it is a well-behaved thistle. Like other thistles it does self-sow, but only gently – in fact, there never seem to be enough seedlings to go round. This is an open, bushy plant with bluish-green leaves that are heavily marked with silver lines. The flowers are typically thistle-shaped and of a soft purple that contrasts beautifully with the variegated foliage. The foliage and stems do have sharp spines. There are no cultivars, but the flowers and variegated foliage are good enough to make them unnecessary. H up to 1m (3ft), but often only half of this. S 45cm (18in) in bigger plants.

How to obtain Galactites are not very easy to find but a few suppliers, including specialist societies, stock the seed. It is well worth seeking out.

Cultivation Any reasonable garden soil will suffice, so long as it is free-draining. The plants should have a sunny position, but they will tolerate a little light shade, for example a position in which they grow partially under a rose bush. Z6.

Propagation Sow the seed where the plants are to grow in autumn or spring, or sow in pots in an open frame. Galactites will self-sow if left to set seed, but they rarely become a nuisance.

Uses Galactites are excellent plants for the mixed border, especially if you have a garden with a silver colour scheme. They also do very well in gravel gardens.

Galactites tomentosa (foliage)

Gazania 'Mini-Star Tangerine'

GAZANIA
Gazania

This is a genus consisting of about 16 species of which none is commonly grown. However, between them they have produced a number of hybrids which are very popular among gardeners, especially in coastal gardens where there is bright light. This light is essential as gazanias have a habit of shutting up in dull weather.

The flowers are daisy-like with colourful ring of outer, pointed petals and a golden central disc. There is a wide range of colours from brilliant yellow through orange to various red and pinks. There is often an inner ring of darker colour. The flowers are carried singly on stems above green foliage which is slightly frosted with silver. Gazanias make excellent bedding plants. H and S 25cm (10in).

How to obtain These are widely available as plants in garden centres and nurseries as well as seed. Seed offers the largest range of possibilities.

Cultivation Plant out after the threat of frosts has passed in a well-drained soil, preferably a light, sandy one. Gazanias require a warm, sunny position. Z9.

Propagation Sow seed under glass at 18–20°C (64–68°F) in the early spring.

Uses Gazanias are good plants for containers, such as window boxes, where they can be used to great effect. However, their main use is as colourful bedding plants.

Gazania 'Daybreak Bronze'

Gazania hybrids

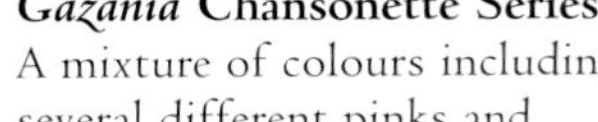

***Gazania* Chansonette Series**
A mixture of colours including several different pinks and oranges, bronze and yellow.

***Gazania* 'Cream Beauty'**
As its name suggests, this lovely cultivar produces flowers of a creamy white colour.

***Gazania* Daybreak Series**
This is another series with a wide range of colours. Some colours are sold separately, as in the form 'Daybreak Bronze'.

***Gazania* Kiss Series**
The flower colours in this series include golden-yellow, bronze, rose and white. The colours are available separately.

***Gazania* 'Magenta Green'**
This cultivar produces flowers of deep purple.

Gazania hybrids

Gazania hybrids

***Gazania* Mini-Star Series**
This series produces flowers in another wide range of colours including white and pink. The plants also come in single colours: for example, 'Mini-Star Tangerine' and 'Mini-Star White'.

***Gazania* 'Orange Beauty'**
The flowers of this plant are bright orange in colour.

***Gazania* 'Snuggle Bunny'**
This cultivar produces blooms of an unusual bronzy-orange.

***Gazania* 'Sunshine Mixed'**
This plant carries daisies in a gay mixture of colours.

***Gazania* 'Talent Mixed'**
This mixture produces flowers in plenty of different colours, and has attractive grey-silver foliage.

GERANIUM
Geranium

This is a very large genus of some 300 species, many of which are grown as perennials (see page 204), especially by enthusiasts. There are also a couple of annuals worth growing. They are not the most spectacular of geraniums and will probably not appeal to the average gardener, but they do add another couple of plants to the enthusiast's garden. They are especially suitable in a wild area, as they can spread a little too quickly in most gardens. The flowers are shallow saucers or funnels and are generally some shade of purple. Pelargoniums (see page 152) were removed from this genus more than 100 years ago, but they are still often referred to as geraniums.
How to obtain You very rarely see plants offered, although nurseries that specialize in geraniums may occasionally sell them. Seed is also difficult to find, but it is offered by specialist societies.
Cultivation Any garden soil will do. These plants will grow in either sun or shade. Z7.
Propagation Sow the seed in spring where the plants are to flower. Geranium seed can also be sown in pots and placed in an open frame without heat.
Uses These plants are quite rampant, so they are best grown in a wild garden. If used elsewhere, thin as necessary.

Pink-flowered annuals

Alcea rosea 'Rose'
Callistephus chinensis
Clarkia
Crepis rubra
Diascia
Dianthus
Godetia grandiflora 'Satin Pink'
Helichrysum bracteatum 'Rose'
Lathyrus odoratus
Lavatera trimestris
Nicotiana 'Domino Salmon-Pink'
Nigella damascena 'Miss Jekyll Pink'
Papaver somniferum
Silene pendula 'Peach Blossom'

Geranium lucidum

Geranium bohemicum
This plant forms a dense, untidy mat. The foliage is hairy and the small flowers are violet-blue. It is biennial and self-sows. H 30cm (12in) or more, S 15cm (6in).

Geranium lucidum
This is grown for its foliage, which is round and, unlike that of most geraniums, glossy and succulent-looking. The plant is excellent in shady areas since it helps to illuminate the darker areas. In autumn it takes on reddish tints and the stems are also red. The flowers are small and pink. It is a very attractive plant, but it does seed everywhere. It is perfect for the wild or woodland garden. H 25cm (10in) S 15cm (6in).

GILIA
Gilia

A genus of about 30 species, consisting mainly of annuals. Two or three of these are in general cultivation. They vary from those with tight clustered heads of small flowers to those with loose heads of open saucer-shaped flowers. The predominant colour is blue. These look best when grown *en masse*, particularly in meadow garden. They are not seen as frequently as they once were but they are still widely available. H 60cm (24in) S 30cm (12in).
How to obtain Seed is readily available from a number of seed merchants. Occasionally you will find plants available for sale.
Cultivation Any reasonable garden soil will suffice, but it should be well-drained and not too rich. Z8.
Propagation Sow the seed in the autumn or spring in the open ground where the plants are to grow. They often self-sow if the conditions are warm enough.
Uses Gilias can be used as massed bedding or planted in drifts in mixed border. Their untidy habit makes them particularly good for wild gardens, especially meadows.

Gilia capitata
This is the main species grown. It has spherical heads (4cm/1½in across) of lavender-blue flowers, over finely cut foliage. They are sometimes known as Queen Anne's thimbles. A white form, 'Alba', is occasionally offered.

Gilia tricolor
This is called birds' eyes because the flowers have a central eye. The simple, saucer-shaped flowers have blue petals and yellow or orange shades in the throat. This, too, has a white variety, 'Alba'.

Other plants Once there were 25 or so gilia commonly available, but this has been reduced to those above. *G. achilleifolia*, which has finely cut foliage, is sometimes seen. It is a sprawling plant with spherical heads of blue flowers similar to those of *G. capitata*.

Gilia capitata

Gladiolus 'Seraphin'

GLADIOLUS
Gladiolus

A once-popular genus for which enthusiasm has dwindled in recent years. However, many gardeners still grow it so it is still widely available. There are about 180 species, some of which are treated as perennials (see page 205) while others are treated as tender annuals. Generally it is the hybrids that are grown. In spite of their decline there are still around 10,000 of these from which to choose – only a few of them are listed here. They consist of tall plants with sword-like leaves and spikes of tightly packed flowers. These are shaped like open trumpets or funnels and come in almost every colour. Some are pure colours while others are bicoloured. H 1.5m (5ft) S 15cm (6in).
How to obtain Corms are readily available from most garden centres and nurseries, usually in packs showing the colour. General bulb firms and specialist nurseries also sell gladioli, with the latter providing the biggest selection as well as offering catalogues which give advice on cultivation.
Cultivation These plants need a well-drained but reasonably fertile soil. They should have a position in full sun. Lift the corms after the leaves die back and store in a dry, frost-free place. Stake plants in exposed positions. Z8.
Propagation The small cormlets can be divided from their parents when the plants are dormant.
Uses Gladioli can be used in a decorative border but they are often grown in a special bed or in rows in the vegetable garden for cutting or for exhibition. They make excellent cut flowers.

Gladiolus 'Charm'
A fine gladiolus suitable for the border. It has simple, pinkish-purple flowers with white throats.

Gladiolus 'Elvira'
This is another simple gladiolus whose flowers come in pink. It is early flowering.

Gladiolus 'Florence C'
A large-flowered variety which produces dense spikes of glistening white, ruffled flowers

Gladiolus 'Green Woodpecker'
The spikes of greenish-yellow flowers have bright red markings in the throat.

Gladiolus 'Kristin'
The flowers of this cultivar are large, ruffled and white.

Gladiolus 'Nymph'
An early-flowering gladiolus that is suitable for the border. It has white flowers edged with red.

Gladiolus 'Prins Claus'
This is another good border variety. It has pure white flowers that have cerise markings.

Gladiolus 'Royal Dutch'
This is a large-flowered variety which carries pale blue flowers with white throats.

Gladiolus 'Seraphin'
This attractive plant has soft pink flowers with white throats.

GLAUCIUM
Horned poppy

This is a genus containing about 25 species of annuals and short-lived perennials, which are usually treated as annuals. The flowers are open and dish-shaped, with petals that look like fragile tissue paper. They come in colours ranging from yellow to orange and red. These plants are called horned poppies because of the shape of their seed pods, which are long

Glaucium flavum

and curved. They can be used as bedding, but are generally used in mixed borders. The height varies.
How to obtain Glauciums are occasionally sold as plants but they are tap-rooted and soon become starved in small pots. It is best to grow them from seed, which is quite widely available.
Cultivation Any garden soil will do, but glauciums need good drainage and full sun. Z7.
Propagation Sow the seed in autumn or spring where the plants are to flower.
Uses They are best used in mixed borders and gravel gardens. The latter suits them perfectly.

Glaucium corniculatum
This is the red horned poppy. It is a biennial and produces red or orange flowers over silvery foliage. H and S 38cm (15in).

Glaucium flavum
This is the yellow horned poppy. It is a perennial plant but is usually treated as an annual, although in well-drained conditions it will survive into a second year. The flowers are yellow or orange in colour. H 60cm (24in) S 45cm (18in).

Glaucium grandiflorum
This is another perennial grown as an annual. It has orange to deep red flowers.

GOMPHRENA
Gomphrena

A large genus containing almost 100 species, of which most are annuals although only one is in general cultivation. This, along with another couple of now-forgotten species, were once more popular than they are now. Their

Gomphrena globosa dark form

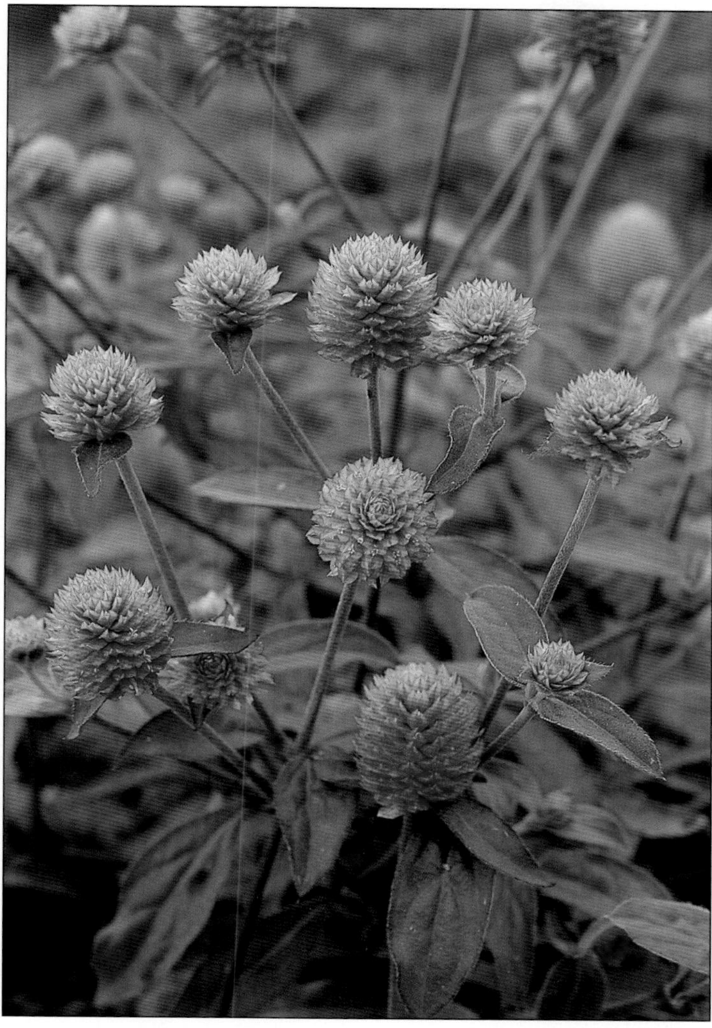

Gomphrena globosa pale form

decline is mainly down to the reduced appeal of summer bedding. They have egg-shaped flower heads densely packed with pink, red, purple or white bracts.
How to obtain Gomphrenas are best purchased as seed from one of the several seed merchants that sell it.

Cultivation Plant out in any reasonable garden soil, but one that is free-draining. Gomphrenas should have a sunny position. Z9.
Propagation Sow the seed in early spring under glass at 16–18°C (60–64°F), or sow directly into the soil where they are to grow in late spring.

Blue-flowered annuals

Ageratum houstonianum	*Limonium sinuatum* 'Blue Bonnet'
Borago officinalis	*Lobelia erinus*
Brachyscome iberidifolia	*Myosotis*
Campanula medium	*Nemophila menziesii*
Centaurea cyanus	*Nigella damascena*
Consolida ambigua	*Nigella hispanica*
Cynoglossum amabile	*Nolana paradoxa* 'Blue Bird'
Echium 'Blue Bedder'	*Salvia farinacea* 'Victoria'
Gilia	
Lathyrus odoratus	

Uses Gomphrenas have generally only been used as a bedding plant, but *G. dispersa* can be grown in hanging baskets and other containers. It can also be used in mixed borders. Gomphrena flowers are excellent for cutting and can also be dried.

Gomphrena globosa

This is the most commonly seen garden plant in the genus. It comes in a wide variety of colour, and there are an increasing number of varieties. Some, such as 'Q Formula Mixed', have mixed colours but are also issued as separate colours such as 'Q Lilac' or 'Q White'. 'Buddy' has deep purple flowers. It also has a smaller relative, 'Dwarf Buddy'. H 60cm (24in) S 30cm (12in).

Gomphrena 'Strawberry Fields'

This variety is one of the most widely available. It has bright red flower heads with tiny dots of yellow flowers showing between the brilliant bracts. It is taller than the above, reaching up to 75cm (30in) high.

Other plants Occasionally you may be able to find seed of other species, such as *G. dispersa* which is not such an upright plant. It has deep pink flowers.

GYPSOPHILA
Gypsophila

This large genus of more than 100 species provides us with a number of perennial (see pages 206–207) and annual garden plants. They are characterized by their masses of tiny white or pink flowers, which float airily on thin wiry stems, looking almost like a puff of smoke or a cloud. These are beautiful plants and they should be grown more often, particularly since they fit into so many styles of gardening. H 60cm (24in) S 30cm (12in).
How to obtain Gypsophila can sometimes be purchased as plants from garden centres and nurseries but a safer way of ensuring you get them is to order seed from one of the seed merchants.
Cultivation Gypsophilas need a light, well-drained soil and a sunny position. Z5.
Propagation Sow the seed in the spring, in open ground where the plants are to flower. Alternatively, it can be sown under glass at 13–16°C (55–60°F) at the same time of year.
Uses Gypsophilas can be used in a variety of ways including in annual bedding borders and mixed borders, where they work especially well as edging. They can also be used in most containers. They make excellent cut flowers, especially for bouquets.

Gypsophila elegans

This is the main annual *Gypsophila* that is cultivated. It produces masses of flat, star-shaped flowers in white and pink. The species itself is beautiful, but there are also a number of cultivars, many with bigger flowers. 'Covent Garden' is a good cutting form with large white flowers. 'White Elephant' (a clumsy-sounding name for an elegant plant) has the largest white flowers. 'Giant White' is tall, with slightly smaller white flowers that are good for cutting. *G.e.* var. *rosea* has soft pink flowers while 'Bright Rose', 'Carminea' and 'Red Cloud' all have much darker pink flowers.

Other plants The other major annual is *G. muralis*. This is a dwarf gypsophila which is suitable for rock gardens, containers and edging. It has pink flowers with darker veins. There are several cultivars including the darker-flowered 'Gypsy'. 'Garden Bride' has white flowers.

Gypsophila elegans 'Covent Garden'

Helianthus annuus

HELIANTHUS
Sunflower

This large genus is most famous for its giant sunflower, *H. annuus*. This is an annual but there are many more garden worthy plants which are perennials (see page 209). *H. annuus* is the only annual in the genus, but it has many cultivars. Not all of these have large heads, but the largest can reach to over 30cm (12in) across and are packed with seeds arranged in wonderful patterns. The typical sunflower is a daisy with yellow outer petals and a yellow, orange or brown central disc. There are many variations on this, with the yellow being paler or darker, and some flowers even having red or brown petals. The height varies, but the tallest plants reach 3m (10ft) or more; some are double this. These plants flower from late summer into autumn.

How to obtain You can buy plants, but they are starved in small pots. It is best to raise your own from the widely available seed.

Cultivation Plant out once the danger of frosts has passed. To get really big flowers, enrich the soil with well-rotted organic material and keep it moist. Choose a sunny position and stake plants. Z7.

Propagation Sow the seed in individual pots in early spring at 16–18°C (60–64°F) under glass.

Uses Shorter ones can be used at the backs of mixed borders. Sunflowers can be grown as specimen plants or in a line to create a summer hedge. They are good for children's gardens. Sunflowers are excellent for cutting and valuable as bird seed.

***Helianthus annuus* 'Italian White'**
True to its name, a plant with pale-coloured blooms.

***Helianthus annuus* 'Music Box'**
This cultivar offers a mixture of colours including yellows, reds and browns and some bicolours. A short form. H 75cm (30in).

***Helianthus annuus* 'Moonwalker'**
The flowers of this plant are a pale lemon-yellow. H 1.5m (5ft).

***Helianthus annuus* 'Prado Red'**
This is a red form. It reaches 1.5m (5ft) in height.

***Helianthus annuus* 'Russian Giant'**
This is a very tall variety, which is widely grown. It has large yellow flowers. Up to 4m (12ft).

Helianthus annuus 'Italian White'

Helichrysum bracteatum

Helichrysum petiolare

***Helianthus annuus* 'Sunspot'**
A dwarf variety, but with large flowers. H 60cm (24in).

***Helianthus annuus* 'Teddy Bear'**
This plant produces relatively small flower heads but they are fully double and look quite furry. They are golden-yellow in colour. H 60cm (24in).

***Helianthus annuus* 'Velvet Queen'**
This is another tall form, with striking red flowers. A beautiful plant. H 1.5m (5ft).

HELICHRYSUM
Helichrysum

A very large genus containing a mixture of annuals, shrubs and perennials (see page 209). There are two species that are of particular interest to the annual gardener. *H. petiolare* is a shrub that is treated as an annual and grown for its foliage. The other is *H. bracteatum*. This is now called *Bracteantha bracteatum* but is still better known and distributed under its older name so it is included here. This is grown for its flower heads.

How to obtain The former is mainly bought as plants which are readily available, while the latter is usually purchased as seed.

Cultivation Helichrysums will grow in any well-drained garden soil. Z7.

Propagation Take cuttings of *H. petiolare* and overwinter the resulting plants under frost-free glass. Sow seed of *H. bracteatum* under glass in spring at 16–18°C (60–64°F).

Uses *H. petiolare* is excellent as a foliage plant anywhere in the garden but it is especially good for bedding and containers of all types. *H. bracteatum* is used for bedding. The flowers are good for cutting and drying.

Helichrysum bracteatum
This is an everlasting flower with daisy-like papery flower heads. The outer petals come in yellows,

Helichrysum 'Bright Bikini Mixed'

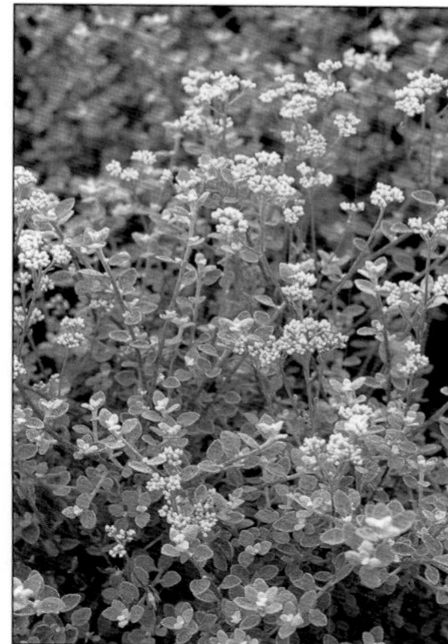
Helichrysum petiolare 'Goring Silver'

pinks, reds and white. The inner disc is yellow. Plants vary in height up to 1m (3ft) or more.

Bright Bikini is a series of bright doubles in red, pink, yellow or white. 'Frosted Sulphur' has pale yellow double flowers. 'Hot Bikini' is hot-red and orange. The King Size Series also have double flowers, with blooms that measure up to 10cm (4in) across and come in a variety of colours. 'Monstrosum' is another large double mixture, which is also available as single colours. 'Silvery Rose' is a particularly beautiful silvery rose-pink.

Helichrysum petiolare

This plant is grown for its silver foliage, and is particularly in demand for hanging baskets and other containers. H 50cm (20in) S 1m (3ft). There are several cultivars including 'Variegatum' and 'Limelight, which has silvery lime-green leaves. 'Goring Silver' is a particularly fine silver form.

Hesperis matronalis

Hesperis matronalis var. albiflora

HESPERIS
Sweet rocket

This genus contains about 30 species of perennials and biennials of which only a couple are of interest to annual gardeners. The main one is *H. matronalis*, which has been grown for centuries as a cottage-garden plant. It is actually a short-lived perennial but is usually treated as an annual or biennial. It is a member of the cabbage family, but has a beautiful sweet scent that fills the evening air. The lilac or white flowers seem to glow in the evening light. H 1m (3ft) S 45cm (18in).

How to obtain You occasionally find plants of the double forms, but the single forms are usually available only as seed.

Cultivation Any reasonable garden soil will suffice. They will grow in full sun or partial shade. Z6.

Propagation Sow the seed in the autumn or spring where the plants are to flower. It can also be sown in pots placed in an open frame. If the plants are allowed to remain in the ground until they shed their seed, they will self-sow. Double forms need to be raised from basal cuttings in spring.

Uses These plants can be used in bedding, but they are best employed in a mixed border, especially in an informal one.

Hesperis matronalis

This is the sweet rocket or dame's violet. The flowers are carried in loose heads in early summer. These flowers are either lilac or white (known as *H.m.* var. *albiflora*). Sometimes the lilac forms are deeper in colour, almost purple. The coloured flowers often become fused with white as they age. There are also double forms of the lilac, 'Lilacina Flore Pleno', and the white, 'Alba Plena'.

Other plants There is a very similar plant which is a biennial. This is *H. steveniana*. It is shorter and produces pale purple or white flowers. H 60cm (24in).

Hibiscus moscheutos

HIBISCUS
Hibiscus

This is a large genus of around 200 species of which only one or two annuals are grown in gardens, although several of the shrubs are often treated as such. The annual *H. trionum* is most commonly grown. It is a spreading plant which carries a succession of attractive trumpet-shaped flowers up to 7cm (3in) across.

How to obtain Plants are rarely seen so it is best to obtain seed from seed merchants' catalogues.

Cultivation Plant out once the threat of late frosts has passed. Any reasonable garden soil will do but it must be well-drained. A sunny position is necessary. Z10.

Propagation Sow the seed in early spring at 16–18°C (60–64°F) under glass.

Uses Hibiscus are not suited to mass planting, but they are good in mixed borders. The spreading habit makes them excellent container plants.

Hibiscus trionum

The flowers are a beautiful cream colour which contrasts with a very dark purple central eye. H 75cm (30in) S 60cm (24in). There are several cultivars: 'Lyonia' is silvery-yellow while 'Sunnyday' has lemon flowers.

Other plants The annuals *Hibiscus cannabinus* and *H. radiatus* are sometimes offered as seed. They have creamy-white flowers, but red and purple forms are more commonly offered. Some shrubby hibiscus are occasionally used in warmer gardens in summer, being moved out from the conservatory or greenhouse in pots. They include *H. rosa-sinensis*, the Chinese hibiscus with its wealth of cultivars, and *H. moscheutos*.

Hibiscus trionum

Hordeum jubatum, with orange dahlias

HORDEUM
Barley

Although this genus contains about 20 species of grass, only one is generally grown in our gardens. This is *H. jubatum*, commonly known as squirrel tail grass. It is an annual or short-lived perennial. It has become almost a cult plant and can be seen in a wide range of elaborate bedding schemes. It is frequently bedded with seemingly unlikely partners, yet it often works. This is because it is a grass with a soft curving flower head that combines well with all kinds of plants, both flowering and foliage. The heads are pinkish-green in colour and in the sunlight they also have an attractive silvery, silky sheen. They turn straw-coloured as they age. H 50cm (20in) S 25cm (10in).

How to obtain Squirrel tail grass is occasionally available as plants. However, these are generally not worth buying as the plants are not happy in pots, and besides you need more than one or two plants for an effective display. It is much better to raise your own by sowing seed which is obtainable from a number of seed merchants and specialist societies.

Cultivation Any reasonable garden soil is suitable for hordeum. Like most grasses it needs a sunny position. Z5.

Propagation Sow the seed in spring in the open ground where the plants are to flower.

Uses Squirrel tail grass is best planted in drifts either in bedding displays or in mixed borders. If possible plant them where the sun will shine through the flower heads to show off their silkiness.

Other plants *Hordeum hystrix* is also sometimes offered, but it is difficult to find. It is similar to *H. jubatum*. *H. vulgare*, the cultivated barley, can also be grown. It is not as decorative as the above but it is still interesting and makes a good dried grass.

IBERIS
Candytuft

A genus of about 40 species of which several are frequently seen in gardens. This is another plant that belongs to the cabbage family, although you would be hard-pressed to see the resemblance unless you were a botanist. They are low-growing plants with flat or slightly domed heads of mainly white flowers, although there are also pink and reddish-purple forms. They have an old-fashioned look about them but they are still popular, partly because they can be used for a variety of purposes in the garden. They rarely reach more than 30cm (12in) high, often less, and they are frequently wider than they are tall.

How to obtain These are widely available as plants, either in bedding packs or as individual plants. If you want to raise your own plants, there are plenty of sources of seed.

Cultivation Plant or sow in any reasonable garden soil. Full sun is best; they can be placed in light shade, but they may grow leggy (produce long, bare stems). Z7.

Propagation Seed can be sown where it is to flower or it can be sown under glass at 13–16°C (55–60°F) in early spring.

Uses Candytufts can be used in any form of bedding scheme or as edging or as fillers in a mixed border. They can also be grown in containers. Candytufts are good plants for children's gardens because they are easy to grow and flower quickly.

Iberis amara 'Giant Hyacinth'

Iberis amara

This is a taller form of candytuft with plants sometimes reaching up to 45cm (18in) but often less. The flower heads are possibly more domed than in other species. They are mainly white, but there are also those that are flushed with purple. Another pleasing attribute is their attractive perfume.

There are a number of cultivars available, including 'Giant Hyacinth', 'Hyacinth Flowered', 'Iceberg', 'Snowbird' and the fragrant 'Pinnacle', all of which have white flowers.

Iberis crenata

Iberis umbellata

This is similar to the previous plant, except that there is more colour variation. As well as white there are pink, red and purple and lavender forms.

Most of the cultivars are sold in mixtures such as the Flash Series with its brightly coloured flowers, and the Fairy Series which produces flowers in softer shades. Some, however, are sold as separate colours. They include 'Flash White'.

Other plants *I. crenata* is a similar species to the above.

IONOPSIDIUM
Violet cress

This is a tiny genus of some five species of annual plants. Only one of them is grown to any extent and that not very frequently nowadays. This is *I. acaule*, which is variously known as violet cress or diamond flower. It is a charming low-growing plant with lilac, blue or white flowers. As it is a member of the cabbage family it has the usual four petals arranged in a cross. It flowers over a long period, from early summer well into the autumn, and is constantly covered in its star-like flowers. H 8cm (3in) high and slightly more in spread.

Ionopsidium acaule

How to obtain Seed is not commonly available from most merchants so you will have to search for it, but the effort is very worthwhile. Plants are only rarely seen for sale.
Cultivation Violet cress will grow in any decent garden soil, although it should be moisture-retentive but at the same time free-draining. They should be planted in full sun. Z9.
Propagation Sow the seed in spring in open ground where the plants are to flower.
Uses This is a good plant for odd places, such as crevices in pavings or walls. More formally it can be used as edging in beds or for rock gardens. It can also be grown as a small pot plant, to be placed on a wall or at the front of a group of containers.

IPOMOEA
Morning glory

This is an enormous genus, providing plenty of variety for those who would like to explore it. There are more than 500 species, and many of them are climbers. There are a dozen or so in general cultivation, but probably more to come since the plants are becoming increasingly popular. Some are annuals but most are perennials which can either be grown in a conservatory or glasshouse, or grown as annuals and used outside in the summer. Being climbers they are particularly useful since there are not a great number of annuals that grow in this way. The flowers are mainly trumpets; they are carried in the same way as those of convolvulus, to which morning glories are closely related. The main exception is *I. lobata*, which has spikes of narrow, almost tubular flowers. Morning glories can grow up to 6m (20ft) in height, but when used as annuals they are more likely to reach only 2–3m (6–10ft).
How to obtain Morning glories are increasingly available as plants for use under glass. The true annuals are available as seed from most seed merchants.
Cultivation Plant out after the danger of frosts has passed in any reasonable, well-drained soil. A warm, sunny position is important. Supports are necessary. Z8–10.
Propagation Sow seed under glass in spring at 18–20°C (64–68°F). Germination is improved if the seed is soaked in warm water before being sown.
Uses Morning glories can be used anywhere in the garden where height and colour are required. This can be either in the open ground or in containers. They make good patio plants.

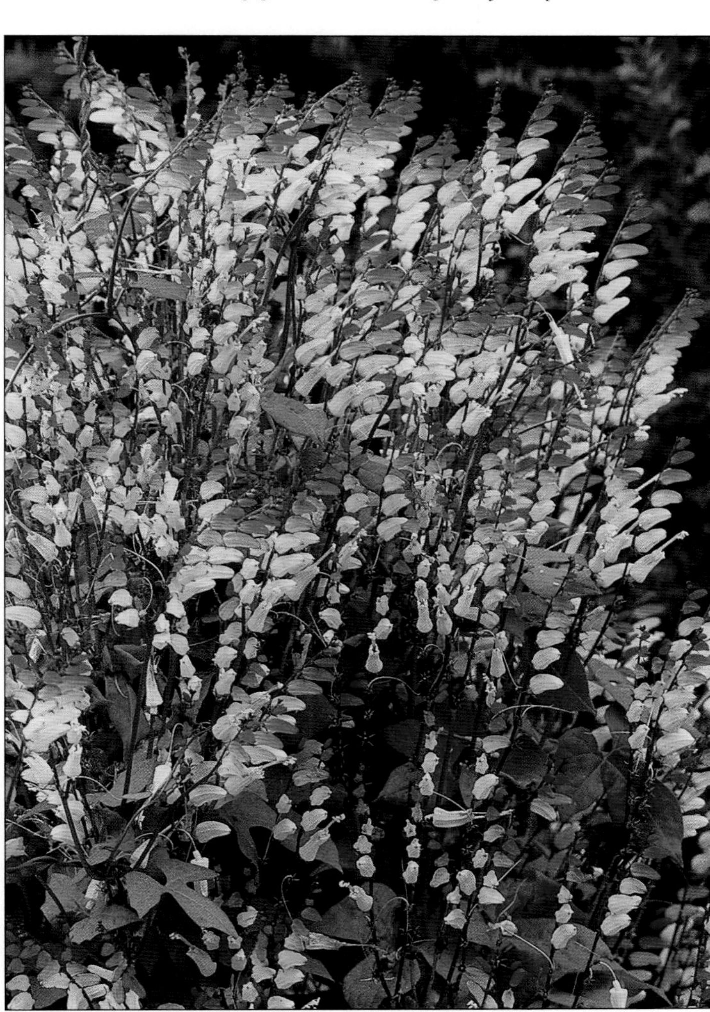
Ipomoea lobata

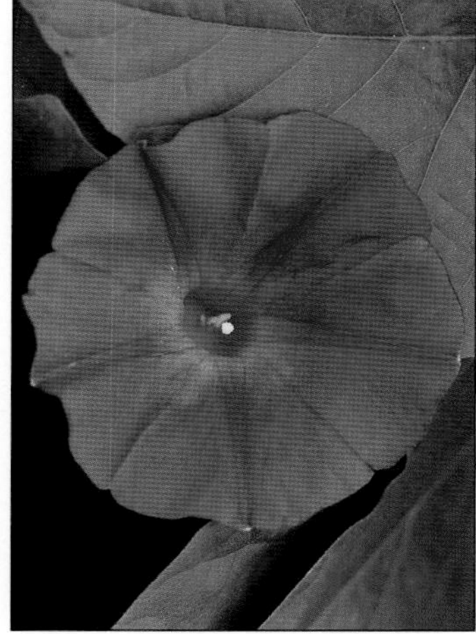
Ipomoea purpurea

Ipomoea lobata
This species is not quite so popular as it once was and so it is not offered so widely. However, it can still be found. It does not have the typical trumpet-shaped flowers but instead carries spikes of narrow flowers. These are orange-red in bud when they first open, but they gradually turn to cream as they age.

Ipomoea purpurea
The common morning glory is becoming increasingly popular. It carries purple trumpet-shaped flowers with white throats. It also has pink, white and striped cultivars. 'Milky Way' has white flowers with maroon stripes, while 'Scarlet O'Hara' is scarlet with a white throat.

Ipomoea tricolor
This is a very old favourite. It produces trumpets that are blue with a white eye. There are a few variations on this. 'Flying Saucers' produces blue and white flowers. 'Heavenly Blue' is still one of the most widely grown morning glories, with its sky-blue flowers and the ever-present white throat.

Other plants There are several other ipomoea species which are currently becoming increasingly popular. They include *I. coccinea*, *I. alba*, *I.* × *multifida*, *I. nil*, and *I. quamoclit*, all of which are well worth considering. They produce the typical trumpet-shaped flowers in a range of blues, purples and reds.

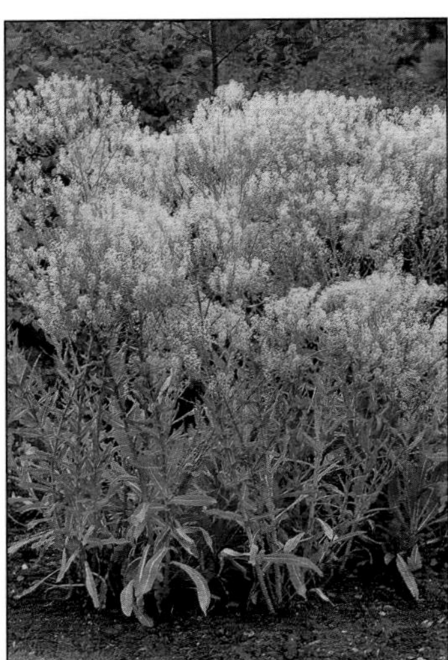

Isatis tinctoria

ISATIS
Woad

A genus of 30 plants that are mainly disregarded in the garden except for *I. tinctoria*. This was once used as a blue dye and it is still grown in herb gardens in memory of this. It is not in the frontline of decorative plants but it does produce masses of small yellow flowers on its tall upright stems in the summer. Once the flowering season is over, it is covered with masses of dangling black seed which can be very attractive, especially when they catch the sunlight. However, it will then self-sow. It probably doesn't deserve a place in borders but it fits well in wild-flower gardens where it produces a sunny display of colour. H 1.5m (5ft) S 45cm (18in).

How to obtain Woad is often available in plant form at specialist herb nurseries, but rarely elsewhere. However, seed is reasonably widely available.

Cultivation Any reasonable garden soil that is well-drained will be suitable. Woad should have a sunny position. It may need support in exposed sites. Z6.

Propagation Sow the seed in the spring where the plants are to flower. They will self-sow if left to set seed.

Uses Woad's main use is now confined to the herb garden, but it is a very good plant for wild-gardens. It would not look out of place in an informal setting, such as a cottage garden.

Other plants Just occasionally you may come across seed of *I. lusitanica* and *I. platyloba*, both of which are similar to, but shorter than, the above. Specialist societies are a good source of seed for these plants.

LABLAB
Lablab

Although this single species genus has been around in gardens for a long time it is only in relatively recent times that it has become more common. This is perhaps due to the attractive purple leaves of the main cultivar, 'Ruby Moon', which has become valued as a foliage plant. The species is *L. purpureus* which has previously been known as *Dolichos*. It is still sometimes found listed under this name in garden centres and catalogues. It is a member of the pea family and this is readily apparent from the pea-like flowers. They are big and carried in large numbers. Once flowering has finished, the plant produces large pods which provide another round of decoration. This plant has also inherited the tendency of the pea to climb, making it doubly valuable in the garden. It can get up to 6m (20ft) when grown as a perennial but as an annual it only reaches 2–3m (6–10ft) in an average summer.

How to obtain Lablab is now available in many garden centres as plants but the most reliable source is still seed which is available from most merchants.

Lablab purpureus

Lablab purpureus (seed pods)

Cultivation Grow in any reasonable garden soil so long as it is free-draining. A position in full sun is required. Lablab needs some form of support to climb up. A tripod in a border is ideal, but it can be grown up any support, for example a pole or a wigwam of sticks. Z9.

Propagation Sow the seed of this plant under glass in spring at 21°C (70°F).

Uses Lablab is valuable for adding height to a mixed border or bedding scheme. The dark-leaved form is often used in more exotic plantings, where it mixes well with tropical plants.

Lablab purpureus

The flowers are pinkish-purple pea-like blooms that are tinged with paler pink. They are followed by deep purple, nearly black, seed pods. The foliage is green, tinged with purple.

The 'Ruby Moon' is more commonly seen than the species and is responsible for this plant's revival. This has a wonderful deep purple foliage which sets off both the flowers and the seed pods beautifully.

LANTANA
Lantana

This large genus of 150 shrubs and perennials includes a few plants that have been cultivated as plants for conservatories or glasshouses for some time, but they have also increasingly been grown as outdoor annuals. The main attraction is the superb flowers which are carried in domed or rounded heads. They come in several colours, and more excitingly they actually change colour so that the younger flowers at the centre are a different colour from than those on the margins. Thus they may be flame-red around the perimeter of the head and gold, tinged with orange, in the middle. Be warned though, that however pretty these plants may look they do contain toxins which can have very unpleasant consequences if eaten.

In ideal conditions lantanas will grow up to 2m (6ft) in height and spread. However, as bedding plants they will get nowhere near this, reaching more like 60cm (24in) at most.

How to obtain Lantana are most commonly bought as plants, which are available either from garden centres or from specialist nurseries. However, the seeds are becoming more widely available, usually as mixtures.

Lantana camara 'Snow White'

Lantana camara 'Radiation'

Lathyrus odoratus 'White Supreme'

A tumbling variety of *Lathyrus odoratus*

Cultivation Plant out only after the danger of frosts has passed, into a soil that is reasonably rich, but free-draining. Lantanas need a warm and sunny position. Z8.
Propagation Sow seed in spring under glass at 16–18°C (60–64°F). Take cuttings in summer and overwinter the young plants under glass.
Uses These make excellent bedding plants as well as being perfect for containers of all sorts.

Lantana camara
This is the main species that is available. It has a number of cultivars. Some are single colours such as 'Snow White' which is creamy-white rather than the pure white indicated by its name, but most are bicolours such as the amazingly bright red and orange of 'Radiation'. 'Cream Carpet' is another creamy-coloured one, while 'Mine D'Or' has lovely golden flowers. 'Feston Rose' is another bicolour with an unusual combination of pink and yellow blooms, and 'Schloss Ortenburg' is along the lines of 'Radiation' with red and orange flowers.

LATHYRUS
Pea
This is a very large genus of 150 species of which some are annuals. The best known of these is the sweet pea, *L. odoratus*, which is a climber. Traditionally it has been grown up some form over support and used in the border and for cutting. However, different forms have been bred so that there are now also low-growing ones for borders and trailing ones suitable for hanging baskets and other containers. They are prized for their colour and fragrance although the latter is missing from many modern varieties.
How to obtain Sweet peas are widely available both as plants, usually in multipacks, and as seed. There are several specialist merchants who offer large selections of sweet peas.
Cultivation Plant out in early spring into a rich soil that is free-draining. A sunny position is required. Supports are needed for most varieties. Z6.
Propagation Sow the seed in late winter at 16–18°C (60–64°F) under glass.
Uses These plants can be used for decorative purposes in borders or grown in separate beds or in the vegetable garden for cutting and for exhibition purposes. Shorter varieties can be used in all forms of containers.

Lathyrus odoratus
The species is a magnificent plant with smaller flowers than the cultivars. They come in bright purple and red and are highly scented. There are numerous cultivars, many aimed at gardeners who use them for cutting or exhibition. Most of the colours are much softer than the species, with soft pinks, blues and whites predominating. However, each year brighter reds and blues are introduced. Seed is most frequently sold as individual cultivars of one colour, such as the excellent 'White Supreme' or 'Jayne Amanda' which has rose-pink flowers. They are also widely sold as mixtures. Many are sold in groups, such as the Knee-hi Group, which are much shorter than usual.

Other plants There are other annual species such as the yellow *L. chloranthus* or the blue *L. sativus*.

Purple-flowered annuals

Antirrhinum 'Purple King'
Callistephus chinensis
Centaurea cyanus 'Black Ball'
Collinsia grandiflora
Eschscholzia californica 'Purple-Violet'
Eustoma grandiflora
Exacum affine
Heliotropium
Hesperis matronalis
Limonium sinuatum 'Midnight'
Limonium sinuatum 'Purple Monarch'
Lunaria annua
Papaver somniferum
Petunia
Salvia splendens 'Purple Beacon'

Lathyrus odoratus

Lathyrus sativus

Laurentia axillaris 'Blue Stars'

Lavatera trimestris 'Novella'

LAURENTIA
Laurentia

This group of plants is sometimes categorized as a separate genus, *Laurentia,* and sometimes included in *Isotoma*. It is a genus of nearly 20 species of which one is commonly grown as an annual, although it is a perennial. This is *L. axillaris*. It is a delightful plant that has come into recent prominence. It forms a rounded hummock of finely cut foliage. Above this are carried beautiful star-shaped flowers, which are up to 4cm (1½in) across. The plant can grow up to 60cm (24in) as a perennial but when grown as an annual it is usually about 25cm (10in) in height and about the same in spread.

How to obtain Laurentia is widely available as plants, sold in individual pots, from garden centres and nurseries, and also as seed from all the seed merchants. It may be sometimes found under the name *Isotoma*.

Cultivation Any reasonable garden soil will do but it must be free-draining. A sunny position is important. Z7.

Propagation Sow seed in the early spring under glass at 13–16°C (55–60°F). Cuttings can be taken in summer and the young plants overwintered under glass.

Uses This plant works very well in all areas of the garden. It can be used as bedding or in a mixed border. It is also an excellent choice for all forms of container, including hanging baskets.

Laurentia axillaris

It is doubtful whether the plants and seed under this name are the species; they are more likely to be the cultivar known as 'Blue Stars'. It has starry flowers that are a lovely blue in colour. They are produced in quantity over a long period. There is also a pink form called 'Pink Stars' or 'Starlight Pink', and occasionally you find white ones. They can now also be bought as mixtures.

Other plants There are a couple of other species which can occasionally be found. *L. anethifolia* has white flowers in the form 'White Stars'. *L. petraea* also has white flowers.

LAVATERA
Mallow

This is a genus containing about 25 species, of which some are perennials and shrubs (see page 216) and others are annuals. Of the last, one in particular is widely grown. This is *L. trimestris*, which is prized for its showy funnel-shaped flowers. They are up to 12cm (4½in) across and are either glisteningly white or a striking pink. The pink forms often have a darker eye and radiating thin veins of darker pink. They are extremely good annuals, continuously covered in a profusion of blooms during the summer. H 1.2m (4ft) S 45cm (18in).

How to obtain Mallows can easily be found as plants in most garden centres. However, seed is also widely available from merchants, and usually offers a greater choice of cultivars.

Cultivation Plant out in any well-drained soil. Mallows must have a sunny position to do well. Z7.

Propagation Sow seed in the early spring under glass at 13–16°C (55–60°F). For later flowering, sow directly in the ground where the plants are to flower.

Uses Mallows make excellent bedding plants as well as being of great use in mixed borders. They can also be used in large tubs.

Lavatera trimestris

This species is rarely grown in its own right, but is often seen as one of its several cultivars. 'Silver Cups' is one of the best known. This has soft silvery-pink flowers, each with darker veins and a dollop of raspberry pink in the middle. 'Mont Blanc' is another favourite, with flowers of pure white. 'Pink Beauty' is very pale pink, with darker veins and central eye. 'Novella' is also pink.

Other plants *Lavatera arborea* is a biennial. While it is not in the same league as the above, it is excellent for wild-flower gardens, especially those on the coast or in sandy soils. The flowers are not as showy but they are the same funnel shape and come in a dull purply colour. This is a shrubby plant that can get quite tall. H 3m (10ft) when growing well.

LAYIA
Layia

You would be forgiven for thinking that this genus has only one plant, since that is all that most people know. In fact, there are 15 species of annual plants. The others have been grown in gardens in the past but their popularity has declined and now they are difficult to find. The one we still grow is *L. platyglossa*. It has also been known as *L. elegans* under which name it is still often sold. Its common name is tidy tips, which refers to the fact that the yellow petals have dainty white tips to them. The flowers are daisies up to 4cm (1½in) in diameter, with a ring of outer petals and an inner disc which is also yellow. The plants are upright. H 45cm (18in) S 30cm (12in). Some forms are more

Layia elegans

Limnanthes douglasii

sprawling and do not gain such a height, so they are better used in hanging baskets.
How to obtain Layias are getting more difficult to find, but some seed merchants still carry them in stock. Check under both species names.
Cultivation Any reasonable garden soil will suit these plants. Z7.
Propagation Sow the seed in spring in the open ground where the plants are to grow. They can also be sown in pots under glass at 13–16°C (55–60°F).
Uses Layia can be used as bedding or in mixed borders. They will also make a colourful addition to containers.

Other plants With determined searching, you may be able to find seed of *L. chrysanthemoides* since there is at least one merchant that still stocks it. This is a plant which carries bright yellow flowers. H 30cm (12in).

LIMNANTHES
Poached egg plant

This is one of those genera in which only one plant is generally grown, although there are up to 17 species from which to choose. The flowers look similar to those of *Layia* at first glance, although they are in no way related. *Limnanthes douglasii* is known as the poached egg plant because, as in *Layia platyglossa*, it has yellow petals with a white margin. In this case the petals are much broader and form a saucer shape. The plants make wonderful edging to paths. They are particularly useful plants for dull days because they are so bright and cheerful they make it seem as if the sun is shining. Poached egg plants are much loved by bees. They are low-growing. They usually self-sow and can create a dense mat, making useful ground cover. H and S 20cm (8in).
How to obtain Poached egg plants are available as plants but they do not do well if confined in pots so it is best to sow your own seed. This is readily available. Once you have these plants they will produce copious amounts of seedlings, fortunately in the same area since they do not spread far.
Cultivation Any normal garden soil will do, but these plants should be positioned in the sun for the best effect. Z6.
Propagation Sow the seed where the plants are to flower in autumn or in spring.
Uses They make excellent bedding plants for the early summer, but can also be used as temporary fillers in mixed border. They are very good edging plants.

Limnanthes douglasii

This is nearly always grown as the species, described above. However, there is also a very rare variety known as *L.d.* var. *sulphurea* in which the white edging is missing, making the flowers all yellow.

Other plants Very occasionally, you may come across seed of *L. alba*. This is a white-flowered species which is similar to the above. However, it is not so attractive a plant since it is more sprawling and the flowers are smaller.

LINARIA
Toadflax

There are about 100 species in this genus which include perennials (see page 218) as well as annuals. Quite a number of these annuals are grown in gardens, but they are not widely cultivated. This may be because they are grown mainly in mixed borders and have not been developed for the bedding or container market. This also means that they are not so easy to find, but the effort is worth it since there are some interesting plants out there. The one exception is *L. maroccana* which is facing a revival, with a number of cultivars now becoming available. Linarias vary in height from ground-hugging species to those that reach 75cm (30in) in height.
How to obtain Apart from that of *L. maroccana*, seed is difficult to find although it is available from some seed merchants and specialist societies. It is rare that you find any plants for sale.
Cultivation Any reasonable garden soil will be sufficient, but linarias prefer light soils that should be free-draining. Z6.
Propagation Sow the seed in spring in open ground where the plants are to flower.
Uses Linarias are good plants for the mixed border. *L. maroccana* can be used for bedding.

Linaria alpina

This species is strictly speaking a perennial but because it is short-lived, it is treated as an annual. It is a very low-growing plant. The small flowers are carried in short upright spikes and have a velvety texture. They are exquisite and are available in a wide range of purple-reds. Most are bicolours.

Linaria alpina is a very good plant for growing in crevices, between the cracks in paving and walls as well as on rock gardens. It self-sows without becoming a nuisance. H 8cm (3in).

Linaria maroccana 'Bunny Rabbits'

Linaria maroccana

The multi-coloured flowers are carried in spikes and look like miniature antirrhinums. H up to 45cm (18in). There are a few cultivars including Excelsior hybrids, 'Fairy Bouquet' and 'Northern Lights', all of which produce flowers in mixed colours of blue, purple, pink and yellow. 'White Pearl' is restricted to white flowers as its name suggests. 'Bunny Rabbits' bears white, pink and yellow blooms.

Linaria reticulata

These are tall plants with very attractive foliage and deep purple flowers, which are splashed with orange or yellow on the lower lip. H 1m (3ft). There is also a mixture, called 'Flamenco', now on offer.

Other plants *Linaria elegans* is a rather beautiful, tall plant that produces purple-pink flowers. It is well worth seeking out. H 70cm (28in).

Linaria maroccana 'Fairy Bouquet'

Lindheimera texana

LINDHEIMERA

Star daisy

Lindheimera texana is the only member of this genus and it has been popular in the garden for a long time. However, it now seems to be in decline since only a few seed merchants carry it. It is an upright plant, but is generally sturdy enough to stand without staking. The flowers are up to 2.5cm (1in) across and are carried in loose heads. They are yellow, varying from soft to golden hues, and comprising five petals arranged in a star shape. They appear in profusion over a long period through the summer. The yellow is set off perfectly by the bright green foliage and bracts that surround the flowers.
H 60cm (24in) S 30cm (12in).

How to obtain The plants are not commonly sold, either in garden centres or nurseries, but the seed is offered by some merchants and occasionally by specialist societies in their seed exchanges. You will need to search for this plant.

Cultivation Plant out once the danger of frosts has passed. Star daisies will grow in any soil that is reasonably rich, but it should be well drained. A sunny position is required. Z8.

Propagation Sow the seed in early spring at 16–18°C (61–64°F) under glass.

Uses Star daisies can be used as bedding as they have a long flowering season, but they work equally well in a mixed border scheme, where a splash of bright yellow is required.

LINUM

Flax

A huge genus of 200 species which contains perennials (see page 219) as well as annuals and biennials. The flaxes are characterized by their upward-facing, funnel-shaped flowers. Although generally thought of as blue, many have yellow or red flowers. There are a number of annuals for the keen gardener, but there is only one that is in widespread use. This is *L. grandiflorum*, which is a magnificent plant that is welcome in borders and bedding schemes alike. The perennial flaxes are short lived and can be used as annuals if their bright blue colour was desired. H up to 75cm (30in) S 15cm (6in).

How to obtain The seed of the main species, *L. grandiflorum*, is readily available but you will need to search carefully for any other species. Plants are rarely, if ever, offered for sale.

Cultivation Flax should be grown in any reasonably fertile soil that is well-drained. They should have a sunny position. Z7.

Propagation Sow the seed in the open ground where the plants are to flower. Thin the seedlings to 15cm (6in) intervals.

Uses These plants can be used to create spectacular blocks of colour in a bedding scheme or planted as drifts in a mixed border.

Linum grandiflorum* var. *rubrum

This plant, which is often listed as a cultivar 'Rubrum', has brilliant red flowers with a dark eye; they are quite dazzling to look at. The variety *alba* has pure white flowers. The gem of this form is 'Bright Eyes' which has glistening white flowers with a crimson base to each petal and a black centre – they are stunning. There is another form, variously listed as *caeruleum* and 'Caeruleum', which has purplish-blue flowers.

Other plants *Linum sulcatum* is a rarely seen annual from Eastern USA. It has pale yellow flowers and grows to 75cm (30in) in height. It is worth growing if you can find seed.

Linum usitatissimum is the common agricultural flax. Its attractive blue flowers also make it an excellent garden plant. It works particularly well in a wild-flower garden where true blue flowers are often lacking. There are some garden cultivars available, including 'Skyscraper'.

LOBELIA

Lobelia

This is an enormous genus of some 350 species. Most of those grown in the garden are perennials (see page 219) but there is one annual that is more popular then all of those put together. This is *L. erinus*. This is seen in all kinds of garden situations, from hanging baskets to the edges of pathways. It must be one of the most useful and popular of all plants and has remained so for many generations.

The flowers are basically blue, with a white dot in the throat, but there are also pink, purple and red variations. It is a bushy, sprawling little plant which grows to about 25cm (10in) and a little more across. Some varieties produce an abundance of trailing stems which makes them useful in hanging baskets.

How to obtain Lobelia is widely sold in bedding packs and in individual pots by most garden centres. Seed is also widely sold and this is offered in a better choice of cultivars.

Cultivation Any good garden soil or potting compost (soil mix) will do for these plants. Lobelia is best planted in partial shade but it can be used in full sun so long as the soil does not dry out too much. Clip occasionally to keep the plants compact. Z7.

Linum grandiflorum var. *rubrum*

Lobelia erinus 'Cambridge Blue'

Propagation Sow seed in early spring under glass at 16–18°C (61–64°F). Plants may self-sow.
Uses Lobelia looks good anywhere. It is particularly useful in containers, where it often acts as a "filler", creating a background colour for other plants.

Lobelia erinus

The species is not grown as such; it is always cultivated as one of its many cultivars. The flower colour varies from blues, such as in the 'Cambridge Blue' with its sky blue flowers and the dark blue 'Crystal Palace', to cherry-red, as in 'Rosamund'. There are a number of series which are sold either as mixtures or as individual colours. The Cascade Series has trailing stems, and is excellent for hanging baskets. It includes 'Lilac Cascade' and 'Red Cascade'. Other Series include the Palace Series and Regatta Series.

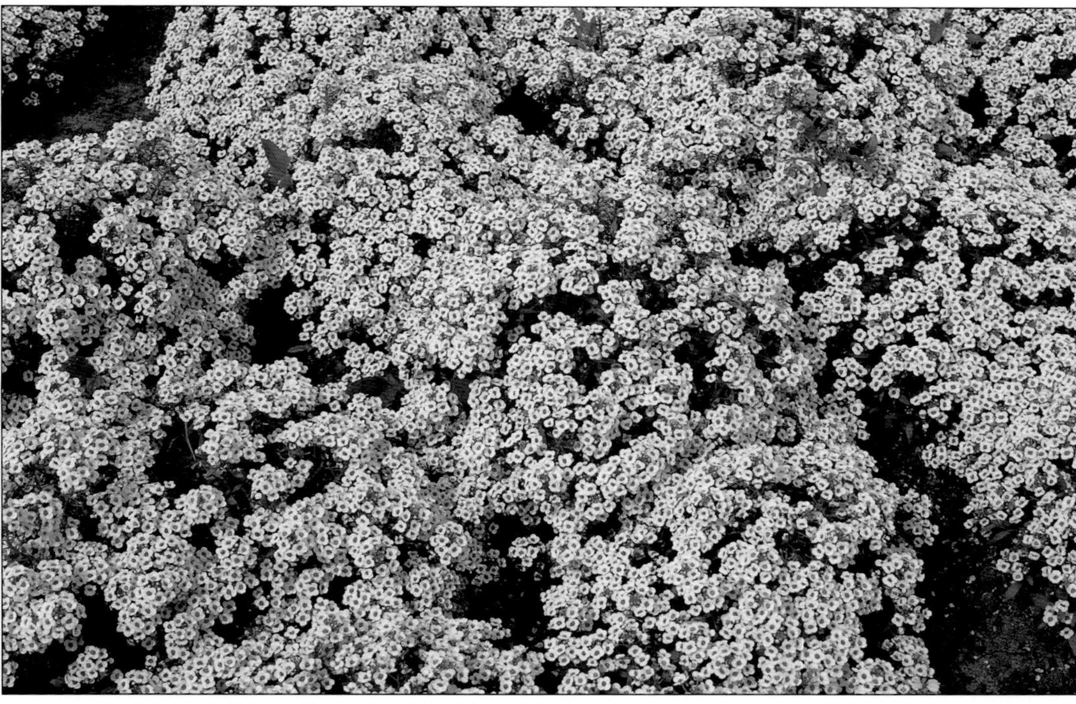

Lobularia maritima 'Snow Crystals'

LOBULARIA

Sweet alyssum

A small genus of five species from the Mediterranean area of which just one is grown in our gardens. This is sweet alyssum or sweet Alison, *L. maritima*. It is not a plant to set the world alight since it is not particularly showy. However, it is one of those plants that can act as a basic ingredient in the design of any garden. It is a perennial that is grown as an annual, although if left it may linger on in a somewhat straggly way for another year.

Sweet alyssum is low-growing, forming little hummocks of foliage which are covered with small white flowers for a very long period from summer into autumn. The flowers are sweetly scented (hence part of its name, the other part comes from the fact that the flower heads resemble those of *Alyssum*). They are carried in slightly domed heads. As well as the basic white there are cultivars that vary from pink to purple. H 5–30cm (2–12in) S up to 30cm (12in).
How to obtain These plants are frequently sold as bedding packs in most garden centres and many nurseries. Only a few of the cultivars may be available, but there should be no problem in getting white forms. For a bigger choice search the seed merchants' catalogues and grow your own.
Cultivation Any reasonable soil will do, so long as it is free-draining. It requires full sun. Z7.
Propagation Sow the seed in mid-spring in the open ground where the plants are to grow.
Uses Excellent for bedding schemes, especially where block or linear planting is required. Sweet alyssums can also be used as fillers or edging in mixed borders.

Lobularia maritima

The species is not often grown in its own right. It is more commonly found as one of its cultivars. There are several series, including the Alice Series and Easter Bonnet Series, which produce a mixture of white, pink and purple flowers. There are also individual cultivars, including 'Snow Crystals' (white flowers), 'Snowcloth' (white), 'New Purple' (purple) or 'Navy Blue' (purple, not blue as one might assume from the name). There is also a variegated form called 'Variegata', which has pale green foliage edged with white. It may occasionally be found but this plant is not widely available.

White-flowered annuals

Antirrhinum 'White Wonder'
Argyranthemum frutescens
Clarkia pulchella 'Snowflake'
Cleome spinosa 'Helen Campbell'
Cosmos bipinnatus 'Sonata'
Digitalis purpurea alba
Gypsophila elegans 'Covent Garden'
Iberis amara
Lathyrus odorata
Lavatera trimestris 'Mont Blanc'
Lobelia erinus 'Snowball'
Omphalodes linifolia
Osteospermum 'Glistening White'
Pelargonium
Petunia

Lobularia maritima 'Wonderland'

Lonas annua

LONAS
Lonas

This genus has one main species, *L. annua*, also known as the African daisy or yellow ageratum. This is yet another of those annuals that was once much more popular than it is now. Indeed although a number of seed merchants still list it in their catalogues it rarely crops in any literature about annuals. Its neglect is surprising because it is quite a showy plant and works well in borders. It is useful as a cut flower and can also be dried. The African daisy is a bushy plant with clusters of bright yellow flowers carried on reddish stems over a long period, lasting from midsummer through into the autumn. The flowers are prolific and they are also long-lasting which makes them very useful as bedding plants. H 30cm (12in) S 25cm (10in).

How to obtain Plants are very rarely seen on sale, but there are a large number of seed merchants offering lonas plants.

Cultivation Lonas will grow in any reasonable garden soil that is not too wet. It should be given a sunny position if possible. Z7.

Propagation Sow seed in early spring at 16–18°C (60–64°) under glass.

Uses Lonas makes an excellent bedding plant and can also be used to great effect in a mixed border or in containers.

Lonas inodora

The species is often grown in its own right, and there are also a couple of cultivars, 'Gold Rush' and 'Golden Yellow'. However, they are not a great deal different from the species.

LOTUS
Parrot's beak

This is a big genus containing about 150 species of shrubs and perennials. At least one of them is treated as an annual in the garden. This is *L. berthelotii*, a very beautiful plant for which everybody should be on the lookout. It is an evergreen shrub with prostrate stems. When the plant is placed in a container such as a tall tub or a hanging basket, the stems hang over the edges to create curtains of foliage. The foliage is made up of narrow leaves carried in much the same way as those of lavender or rosemary. The great beauty of the leaves is that, again like those of the lavender, they are silver. This is a member of the pea family, and the relationship can be seen in the flowers. They are elongated and upward-curling, looking rather like a parrot's beak. They are scarlet and contrast beautifully with the cascades of silver foliage.

Lotus berthelotii (foliage)

Lotus berthelotii (in flower)

How to obtain Parrot's beak is widely available as plants, which are now carried by most garden centres as well as nurseries. It is sometimes offered as seed, but there is no advantage to be had from growing the plant from seed.

Cultivation In containers, use a loam-based potting compost (soil mix). If planted in an open garden, parrot's beak needs a free-draining soil. A sunny position is also necessary. Z8.

Propagation Take cuttings in summer from existing plants and overwinter the resulting plants under warm glass.

Uses The parrot's beak's main use is in containers from which the foliage can hang down. It can also be used in the garden, either on the flat where it can be used as bedding or on walls, down which the foliage can cascade.

Lotus berthelotii

This plant is most often grown as the species, described above. There is, however, some slight variation in colour, although this is not sufficient for cultivars to

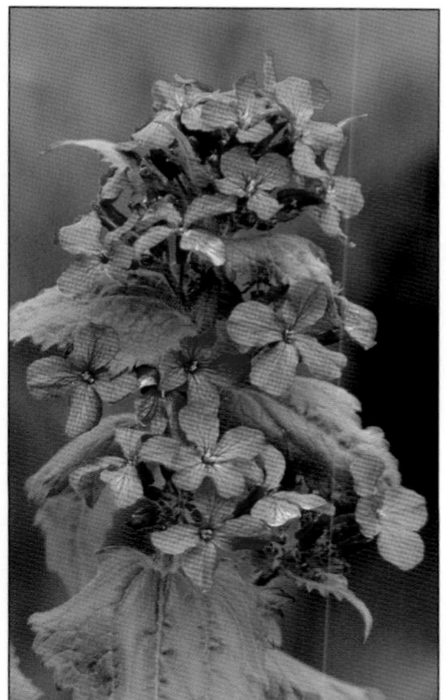

Lunaria annua

be delineated. Some flowers contain more orange, making them a flame colour, while others are a darker red. You will need to see the plants in flower if you wish to buy one of these variants.

Other plants The only other plant worth mentioning is sometimes called *L. tetragonolobus* and sometimes *Tetragonolobus purpureus*. This is the asparagus pea, which has edible pods but can be grown as a decorative plant. It is a low-growing annual with stems that grow up to 40cm (16in). It has small pea-like flowers. They are an attractive bright red, which contrasts well with the foliage.

LUNARIA

Honesty

A genus of one species, which is a biennial that is commonly grown. This tall plant was much loved by the Victorians and it is still very popular. In the spring it has striking purple flowers and these eventually produce oval seed pods; when their outer casings are discarded, they produce a silver disc which looks superb in dried flower arrangements. If you let some plants seed they will self-sow. H 1m (3ft), S 30cm (12in).

Cultivation Any garden soil will suffice and these plants will happily grow in shade or sun. Z8.

Propagation Honesty can be propagated simply by sowing the seed where you want the plants to grow. A small plant is produced in the first year and flowering is in the following spring.

Uses Honesty is good for mixed borders and informal plantings among shrubs or trees.

Lunaria annua

This is the only species that is worth growing. The species has purple flowers but there is also a most beautiful white variety, *albiflora*. There are several variegated forms including 'Variegata', with purple flowers and white marginal variegations to the leaves, and a white-flowered form called 'Alba Variegata'. 'Munstead Purple' has darker purple flowers.

Lunaria annua var. *albiflora*

Malcolmia maritima

MALCOLMIA

Virginia stock

Of the 35 species in this genus only one, *Malcolmia* (sometimes confusingly spelt *Malcomia*) *maritima*, is in general cultivation. It is pretty little annual which is still managing to hold on to its popularity in spite of there being many showier plants around. Its thin stems are smothered with small, four-petalled flowers from spring right through into autumn. These are white, pink or purple with a white eye. Unlike the larger stocks to which it is related, this plant has no scent. Virginia stocks have an old-fashioned, prettiness, and they are ideal for bedding or for filling gaps in the mixed border. There were once several cultivars of the species, including white forms, but these are no longer sold. H 38cm (15in) S 15cm (6in).

How to obtain Virginia stocks are sometimes sold as plants. The seed is readily available.

Cultivation Sow in any reasonable garden soil, preferably one that is free-draining. Virginia stocks need a sunny position. Z7.

Propagation Sow in spring, in the open ground where the plants are to flower. If allowed to set seed they will self-sow.

Uses These plants look good in drifts, as bedding or in a mixed border. They are also good for edging paths and ideal for children's gardens, since they are easy to grow, quick to flower and stay colourful over a long period.

Other plants *M. flexuosa* is similar to the above, *M. bicolor* has pink or yellow flowers, and *M. littorea* has large purple-pink ones. You may be able to find these offered by specialist societies.

Yellow-flowered annuals

Alcea rosea 'Yellow'
Anoda cristata 'Buttercup'
Argemone mexicana
Argyranthemum frutescens 'Jamaica Primrose'
Chrysanthemum segetum
Coreopsis 'Sunray'
Glaucium flavum
Helianthus annuus
Limonium sinuatum 'Forever Moonlight'
Limnanthes douglasii
Lonas annua
Mentzelia lindleyi
Mimulus
Sanvitalia procumbens
Tagetes erecta
Tagetes patula
Tropaeolum peregrinum

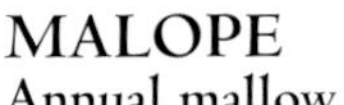
Malope trifida

Matthiola longipetala subsp. *bicornis*

Matthiola Brompton Stock

MALOPE
Annual mallow

This is a small genus of four species, but only one annual is in general cultivation. Even this is less popular than it once was, but happily it is still available to those who want an attractive but not too commonly seen plant. The plant in question is *M. trifida*. The mallow part of the name comes from the fact that the flowers resemble those of the mallow (to which it is related). These are funnel- or trumpet-shaped and up to 8cm (3in) across. Their colour is purple-red, with deeper purple veins running into the centre. They appear over a long period from summer well into autumn, and contrast beautifully with the green foliage. H 1.5m (5ft) S 30cm (12in).

How to obtain Annual mallows are occasionally available as plants from garden centres and nurseries, but don't rely on finding them. It is better to obtain seed from one of the seed merchants.

Cultivation These plants will grow in virtually any reasonable garden soil so long as it is free-draining. A sunny position is best but they will grow in a little shade. Z7.

Propagation Sow the seed into open ground in spring where they are to flower or sow under glass in early spring at 13–16°C (55–60°F).

Uses Like most mallows, these are excellent for coastal gardens. They also make very attractive cut flowers.

Malope trifida

The species, described above, is grown in its own right, and there are also a few cultivars available. One of the best of these is 'White Queen', which, as its name suggests, has white flowers. 'Pink Queen' (pink flowers) and 'Red Queen' (red flowers) are also available. One of the newer cultivars is a mixture called 'Glacier Fruits' which includes pink, red and white blooms, as does 'Crown Mix'. 'Vulcan' is a larger plant which carries deep purplish-red flowers.

MATTHIOLA
Stock

This is a medium-sized genus of some 55 species of which a number are annuals or biennials. Among them are some of the best annuals for the garden. Their attraction lies partly in their magnificent compact flower heads, which come in a variety of bright or soft colours, and partly in their powerful scent. Their popularity is reflected in the fact that seed merchants sell a large range of varieties and frequently offer new ones. Looking at the dense spikes of flowers it is hard to imagine that these plants are in the cabbage family. The range of colours includes the cabbage's yellow, but generally the flowers come in a wide range of pinks, purples and reds as well as white. They are quite large, up to 2.5cm (1in) across. The scent is sweet and mainly occurs in the evening. H 60cm (24in) in some varieties, S 30cm (12in) across.

How to obtain Stocks are widely available as plants, and garden centres and nurseries sell them in packs as well as in individual pots.

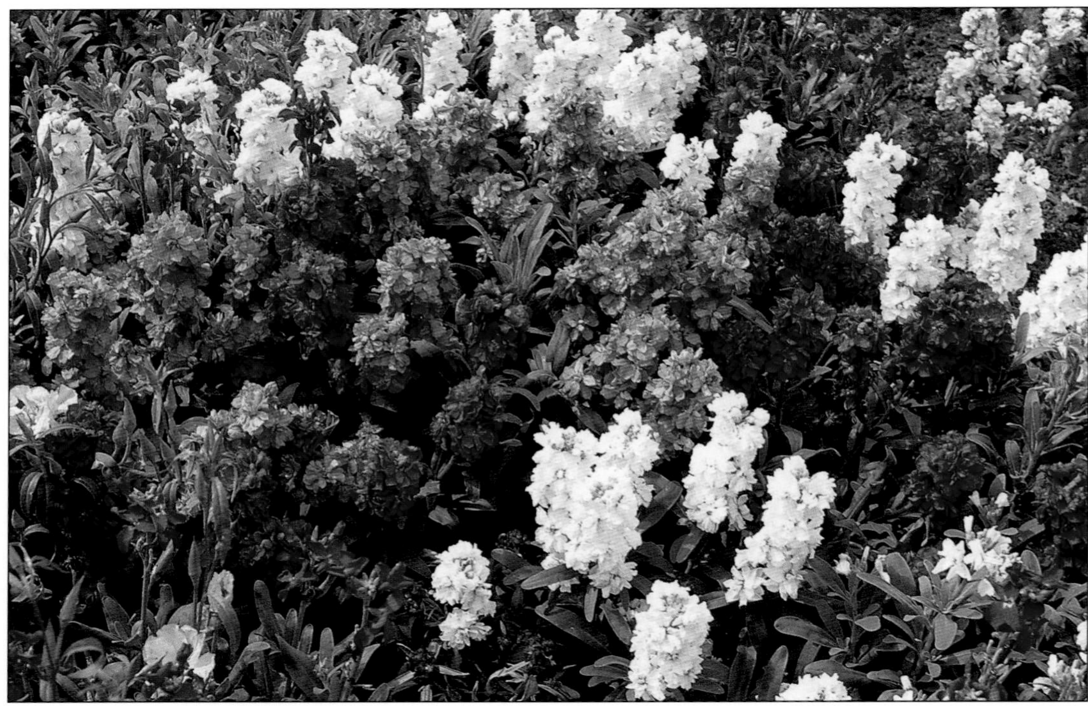
Matthiola incana 'Legacy Mixed'

A larger range of varieties is available in seed form from the various merchants.

Cultivation Generally these plants are happy in any reasonable garden soil, with the usual proviso that it should be free-draining. A warm sunny position is also necessary. Z6.

Propagation Most can be sown in early spring under glass at 13–16°C (55–60°F). The night-scented stock can be sown in spring in the open ground where the plants are to flower.

Uses Stocks make excellent bedding material, but they can also be planted as drifts in a mixed border. They can also be used in containers. Site the sweetly scented ones on patios or near to sitting areas. Stocks make excellent cut flowers.

Matthiola incana

This is an upright, shrubby plant with greyish-green foliage. The dense heads of flowers come in white, or shades of pink, red or purple. The plants are generally sold in two main groups: the Brompton stocks, which are biennial, and the ten-week stocks, which are annual. The flowers are either single or double.

There are plenty of varieties of both; available either as mixtures or in single colours. Among them is the Cinderella Series, whose plants grow up to 30cm (12in) high, bearing well-scented double flowers in colours that include lavender and blue. 'Legacy Mixed' are also doubles but they are taller. The Midget Series are just 25cm (10in) high; the flowers come in a wide range of colours.

Matthiola longipetala* subsp. *bicornis

This is the very charming night-scented stock which produces loose heads of single flowers that are sweetly scented at night. They are especially good for planting beneath bedrooms. There are several varieties available, and these include 'Evening Fragrance' and 'Starlight Scentsation'. H 35cm (14in) S 23cm (9in).

MELIANTHUS
Honey bush

Not many annuals are used purely for foliage purposes, but *M. major* is one such plant. It is, in fact, a perennial shrub and not an annual at all, but it is usually treated in this way in gardens. It is one of a genus of six shrubby species. The great feature about it is the large leaves which are pinnate (arranged as leaflets on either side of the main leaf stalk). The foliage is a blue- or grey-green and the leaves are noticeably toothed, both features adding to the overall visual effect. In warmer areas, this plant can be treated as a perennial and kept for several years in which case it can become quite big, up to 3m (10ft) tall. As an annual, its height is about 1m (3ft) or so and the same across. If kept more than one year there is also the possibility that it will flower. The blooms are red and are produced in tall spikes.

How to obtain Available both as plants from garden centres and as seed, although the latter are becoming difficult to find since some of the major seed merchants have stopped stocking it.

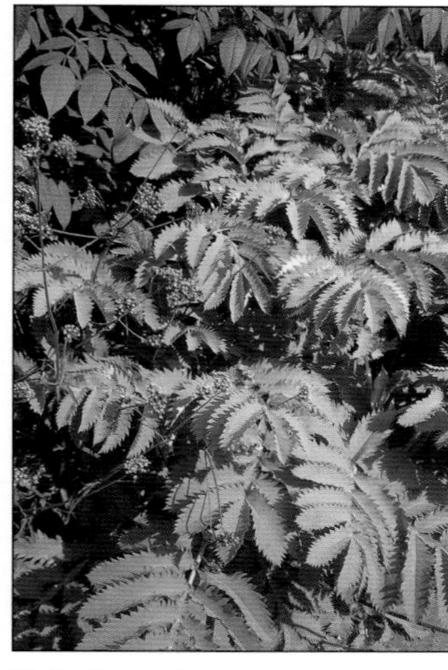

Melianthus major

Cultivation Honey bushes will grow in any fertile garden soil that is moisture-retentive but at the same time free-draining. They should be planted in a sunny position. Z9.

Propagation Sow seed in early spring under glass at 13–16°C (55–60°F).

Uses This plant can be used in many places in the garden. It is attractive in its own right and can also be used as a foil to other plants. It works well as bedding but its main use is as small plantings in either mixed borders or containers.

Other plants Although *M. major* is declining in availability, other species are becoming more available if you are prepared to search for them. *M. minor* is a smaller, downy version of the above. *M. comosus, M. pectinatus* and *M. villosus* are sometimes available.

MENTZELIA
Starflower

This is a large genus containing some 60 species of which *M. lindleyi* is the only one generally grown. Name changes have bedevilled annuals and this is another of those that has altered. Until recently it was known as *Bartonia aurea*, under which name it is still often sold. Its attraction is the golden-yellow flowers which are flushed red at their base and produced over a long period. Each flower has five rounded petals, each of which are pointed at their tip, giving them their star-like quality. The flowers are quite large, up to about 5cm (2in) in diameter, and they produce a wonderful scent in the evening. The golden-yellow is set off beautifully by the green foliage which is finely cut. H 45cm (18in) S 25cm (10in).

How to obtain Starflowers are rarely available as plants but the seed is offered by a number of seed merchants. It is often listed under the name *Bartonia*.

Cultivation Any reasonable garden soil will be suitable for starflowers, so long as it is free draining. These plants require a sunny position. Z9.

Propagation Sow the seed in early spring in open ground where the plants are to flower.

Uses Starflowers make excellent bedding and they can also be used successfully in a mixed border. It is also worth experimenting with them as container plants. They are best planted in a site where their evening fragrance can be appreciated, such as under the windows of living areas.

Other plants A few of the other species are occasionally grown but you will have to search to find them. *M. laevicaulis* is a biennial producing pale yellow flowers that open to twice the size of the above. It is very attractive and deserves to be more widely known. *M. involucrata* is another, this time with creamy-coloured flowers that have a satin-like texture. The flower centres are tinged with crimson. It is worth looking for among the specialist society lists.

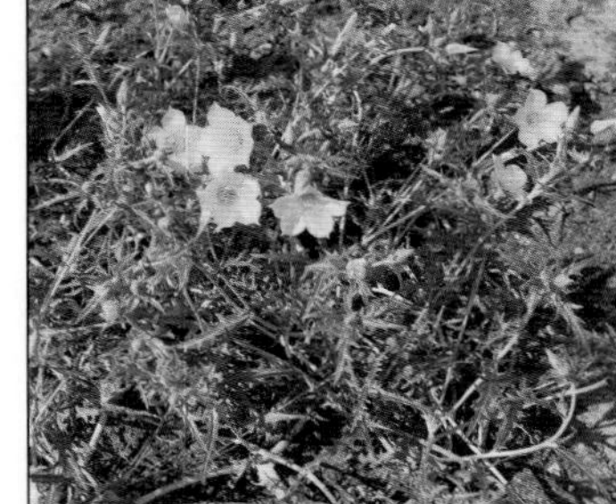

Mentzelia lindleyi

Orange-flowered annuals

Antirrhinum majus 'Sonnet Orange Scarlet'
Calceolaria 'Sunset Mixed'
Calendula officinalis
Celosia cristata 'Apricot Brandy'
Erysimum 'Orange Bedder'
Eschscholzia californica
Helichrysum bracteatum
Mimulus 'Malibu'
Nemesia 'Orange Prince'
Papaver nudicaule
Rudbeckia hirta
Tagetes erecta
Tagetes patula
Thunbergia alata
Tithonia rotundifolia 'Torch'
Tropaeolum majus
Zinnia haageana 'Orange'

Moluccella laevis

MOLUCCELLA
Bells of Ireland

Moluccella is a small genus of four species, of which *M. laevis* is by far the best known by gardeners. This is the famous bells of Ireland or shell flower. The second name is quite apt because the flowers do indeed look like shells. They are very small, each one cupped in a cone-shaped green bract, which gives it its shell-like appearance. The flowers are white or pale purple and they are fragrant. They are carried in upright spikes with the cones facing outward, looking rather like a modern radio mast covered with dishes. Despite its name, this plant has little to do with Ireland. In fact, it is a native plant of south-west Asia, found growing in countries such as Turkey and Iraq. H 1m (3ft) S 25cm (10in).

How to obtain This plant is normally grown from seed which is generally available from most seed merchants. The rare *M. spinosa* is very difficult to find but it is worth checking specialist society seed lists, which sometimes offer it.

Cultivation Bells of Ireland will grow in any free-draining garden soil. They must have a sunny position. Z8.

Propagation Sow seed in late spring in open ground where the plants are to flower. For earlier flowering, raise plants under glass by sowing in early spring at 13–16°C (55–60°F).

Uses This plant can be used in a variety of positions in the garden, including as bedding or in mixed borders. It makes a good cut flower and is excellent for drying.

Other plants If you are lucky, you may be able to track down *M. spinosa*. This is a pretty plant in which the white flowers are also set in cups but this time they are tipped with spines. It has red stems and is quite tall, so it needs a position at the back of a border. H 2m (6ft) S 30cm (12in).

MYOSOTIS
Forget-me-nots

This is a genus of plants that is familiar to most gardeners. The sky-blue flowers seem to have been designed to lift the spirits as winter departs and spring takes over. Several of the 50 species are in cultivation, although not all of them are annuals. They are generally small, clump-forming plants. The small flowers are carried in spikes that gradually unroll, getting longer. There are usually three stages of flowers present in each spike: seed at the bottom, open flowers above them and buds in the opening coil. The flowers come in shades of blue and have yellow centres, but there are also a few cultivars producing blooms in white and pink. H and S 30cm (12in).

How to obtain Forget-me-nots can be bought as plants, but they do not do brilliantly unless they are transplanted when young. Seed is a better bet and fortunately it is widely available.

Cultivation Any reasonable garden soil will be sufficient. Plant in full sun; these plants will also grow in shade, but will become somewhat leggy (producing long, bare stems). Remove after flowering to prevent excessive self-sowing. Z5.

Propagation Sow the seed in the open ground where the plants are to flower. Sow in summer for spring flowering and spring for summer flowering. Most plants will self-sow so there is no need to propagate after the first season.

Uses Forget-me-nots weave between and under other plants, making them perfect for mass carpeting. They can be used either in a bedding scheme – they are traditionally associated with tulips – or in a mixed scheme.

Myosotis sylvestris

Myosotis sylvestris

This is the forget-me-not most often seen. It is usually a biennial but can be a short-lived perennial. It usually reaches 30cm (12in) in height but some forms are much less. The species has sky-blue flowers but there are cultivars with pink or white blooms. Some are sold as mixtures, such as Ball Series. This can also be obtained in single colours, including 'Snowball' (white). The Victoria Series contains 'Victoria Rose', which has rose-pink flowers. It is one of the shortest forget-me-nots, reaching a height of only 10cm (4in).

Other plants *Myosotis alpestris* is a short-lived perennial which can also be used as an annual. It produces dense heads of typical blue flowers. If you can find it *Cryptantha intermedia* is an interesting plant. Although it is not related to the forget-me-not, it looks very similar to it. It comes in white, and there are also orange and yellow variants, which look good mixed in with the true forget-me-not.

NEMESIA
Nemesia

This is a genus of about 50 species. It provides us with one of the annuals most frequently seen in the garden, *N. strumosa*. The flowers are numerous and produced over a long period. They

Nemesia strumosa 'KLM'

are about 2.5cm (1in) across and look like snapdragons, except that the bottom lip is flat and not inflated. There is a big colour range, including white, pink, red, purple, blue and yellow; there are often several flower colours mixed in one plant. H 15–30cm (6–12in) S 15cm (6in) or more.
How to obtain Nemesias are widely available in bedding packs as plants, but a greater range of options is available as seed.
Cultivation Any reasonable garden soil is suitable so long as it does not dry out completely. A sunny position is needed. In containers use a general potting compost (soil mix), preferably a loam-based one. Z9.
Propagation Sow seed in early spring under glass at 13–16°C (55–60°F).
Uses Nemesias are widely used in bedding schemes as well as for filling in gaps in mixed borders. They also suitable for containers of all types.

Nemesia strumosa
This is the main plant of the genus. It is not often sold as the species; it is much more likely to be found as one of the many varieties that are available. These include series, such as Carnival Series, and individual varieties, such as 'Danish Flag' with its red and white flowers, and 'KLM' with its blue and white blooms.

Nemesia strumosa

NEMOPHILA
Nemophila

A couple of unassuming and yet popular annuals belong to this genus of about 11 species. The flowers are not remarkable but somehow they manage to catch the attention in a quiet way. They are saucer-shaped with five white petals, the tip of each having a coloured spot which is generally blue. Nemophilas flower over a long period in the summer, lasting into the autumn. The plants are fairly small. H and S about 30cm (12in) in the taller cultivars.
How to obtain Nemophilas can be purchased as plants, in bedding packs, at the majority of garden centres and nurseries. They are also widely available as seed from most seed merchants.
Cultivation Nemophilas can be grown in any free-draining garden soil. A good potting compost (soil mix) should be used for container plants. Do not let the soil dry out too much, either in the ground or in the containers, especially during very hot weather. A sunny position is best although these plants will tolerate a little shade. Z8.
Propagation The seed can be sown in spring directly into the soil where the plants are to flower. You can also sow them under glass at 13–16°C (55–60°F).
Uses The spreading nature of these plants mean that they are ideal for use in containers, especially hanging baskets and window boxes. They also make good bedding plants as well as being suitable for filling gaps in the mixed border and making good edgings to borders and beds.

Nemophila menziesii

Nemophila maculata
This plant is commonly known as five spot, and is the taller of the two species grown. *Nemophila maculata* is not seen quite so frequently as *Nemophila menziesii*, mainly because it has no cultivars. The flowers measure up to 4cm (1½in) across and have white petals with violet-blue spots.

Nemophila menziesii
This is popularly known as baby blue eyes. True to its name, it has blue flowers with white centres but there are some varieties that have pure white flowers. 'Penny Black' is the most startling of all the varieties since it has black flowers that are edged with white. 'Oculata' has pale blue flowers with a deep purple eye.

Nemophila maculata

Nicandra physalodes

NICANDRA
Shoo-fly flower

This is a single species genus with *N. physalodes* being the only member. It is commonly called the shoo-fly flower, presumably because of its ability to keep flies at bay. It is quite a spectacular plant when well grown since it is tall and has spreading branches. The flowers are funnel-shaped. They come in pale lilac-blue and have white centres. Individually they are not long lived, but a constant succession of them is produced from midsummer right through to the first frosts. The flowers are followed by round fruits (which give this plant its other name of apple of Peru). These then split open to reveal hundreds of seeds, which tend to self-sow with gay abandon. H 1.2m (4ft) S 1m (3ft)

How to obtain Shoo-fly flowers are rarely seen as plants because they do not do well when confined to small pots. However, it is possible to find seed since several seed merchants carry it.

Cultivation Any reasonable garden soil will do, but the plants will do best if it is enriched with plenty of well-rotted organic material. They need a sunny position. Z8.

Propagation Shoo-fly flowers come readily from seed. It should be sown in spring, directly in the soil where the plants are to flower. After the first year the plants will self-sow.

Uses These are best used as structural plants in a mixed border. They could also look quite spectacular in an imaginative bedding scheme. They can be grown in a large container, such as a tub or pot.

Nicandra physalodes

The species, described above, is grown in its own right. There is also one cultivar, namely 'Violacea'. This has darker flowers and inflated calyces which hold the flowers. These are flushed with a purple so dark it is almost black, and add to the plant's attraction.

NICOTIANA
Tobacco plant

This is a large genus of about 70 species of which a few are grown widely in our gardens. *N. alata* has long been a popular bedding plant as has its hybrid *N.* × *sanderae* under which name most of the cultivars are collected. *N. sylvestris* has been around for a long time but it is relatively recently that this tall plant has become so popular. The tobacco plants all have tubular flowers that flare out like trumpets. They come in a wide range of colours. Some have a wonderful scent, which is most noticeable in the evening. They tend to be long lasting, from summer well into the autumn.

How to obtain Plants are sold in bedding packs in all garden centres and many nurseries. However, a bigger range of plants can be obtained by growing them from seed which is readily available.

Cultivation Nicotiana will grow in any reasonable garden soil. If it is relatively dry or well-drained, overwinter them – many plants survive into a second year. They prefer a sunny position although they will grow in light shade. Z7.

Propagation Sow the seed in early spring under glass at 16–18°C (55–60°F).

Uses These are excellent for bedding schemes as well as being useful in mixed borders. The shorter varieties can also be used in containers.

Nicotiana sylvestris

Nicotiana alata

This plant used to be known as *N. affinis* and you will still sometimes see it being sold as such. This is a tall plant, with flowers that are pale green on the outside and white on the inside. The flowers are also fragrant. A good plant for mixed borders. H 1m (3ft).

Nicotiana 'Lime Green'

This plant is shorter than the above, reaching 60cm (24in). It has large lime-green blooms.

Nicotiana × *sanderae*

A range of garden hybrids with flowers in various colours,

Nicotiana 'Lime Green'

Nicotiana langsdorffii

Nigella damascena 'Miss Jekyll'

including pink and red. There are several series including the popular Domino Series, whose plants have a wide range of colours; single-coloured plants such as 'Domino Salmon Pink' are also available. This is one of the taller forms, reaching 45cm (18in) in height.

Nicotiana sylvestris
A tall species, good for the back of the border. It carries a loose head of long-tubed, white flowers, which are scented. H 2m (6ft).

Other plants *Nicotiana langsdorffii* has long, pendant flowers with a small flare at the mouth. They are lime-green. The plant used for tobacco and snuff, *N. tabacum*, has white and red flowers.

NIGELLA
Love-in-a-mist

This is a much loved genus of 20 annuals, of which a couple are regularly grown in our gardens. The flowers are really delightful. They are discs of blue with a prominent central boss, and are surrounded by a ruff of very finely cut leaves. Each flower looks rather like an exquisite brooch. There are also white and pink forms. Once the flowers are over, they produce an oval, inflated seed case, still surrounded by the filigree leaves. These plants have a wonderful old-fashioned quality and so make an ideal choice for a cottage garden.
H 60cm (24in) S 25cm (10in).
How to obtain Nigellas can be seen for sale as plants, but these rarely come to much. It is a much better option to buy seed, which is readily available.
Cultivation Any reasonable garden soil should be perfectly suitable. Nigellas tend to prefer a position in full sun but some do well in the shade. Z7.
Propagation Sow the seed in autumn or spring in the open ground where the plants are to flower. They will self-sow if left to shed their seed.
Uses These plants can be used in bedding or in mixed borders. It is a good idea to allow them to self-sow so that the plants are dotted around.

Nigella damascena
The true species has single flowers but most of those grown in the garden are a mixture of single or semi-double blooms. In the wild the flowers are pale blue. This is the most frequently seen colour in gardens but cultivars are also available in pink, violet-blue and white. 'Miss Jekyll' has soft blue flowers. The Persian Jewel Series is a mixture of colours. 'Mulberry Rose' is pink while 'Dwarf Moody Blue' is a tiny variety only 20cm (8in) high.

Other plants *Nigella hispanica* and its cultivars are similar to *damascena*.

Nigella damascena 'Persian Jewel'

Annuals with good foliage

Amaranthus caudatus
Atriplex hortensis 'Rubra'
Bassia scoparia trichophylla
Beta vulgaris
Brassica oleracea
Canna
Euphorbia marginata
Galactites tomentosa
Helichrysum petiolare
Melianthus major
Ocimum basilicum 'Purple Ruffles'
Onopordum acanthium
Pelargonium
Perilla frutescens
Plectranthus
Ricinus communis
Senecio cinerarea
Silybum marianum
Tropaeolum majus 'Alaska'
Zea mays

Nolana paradoxa

Oenothera biennis 'Wedding Bells'

NOLANA
Nolana

This is a genus containing some 18 species, of which a couple are grown in the garden. Nolana is one of those plants that is attractive without being showy. It is not in the top league for popularity and yet it still goes on selling. The plants are low growing and make an excellent carpet of flowers during the summer. Nolanas are covered with masses of trumpet-shaped flowers. These are upward-facing so it is easy to see past their colourful bells into the throats. H 25cm (10in) S 50cm (20in).
How to obtain Nolanas are occasionally found as plants in garden centres but if you want to be sure of getting them, obtain seed from seed merchants. This is readily available.
Cultivation Nolanas will grow in any reasonable garden soil, so long as it is free-draining. They need to be planted in a sunny position. Z10.
Propagation Sow the seed in early spring under glass at 13–16°C (55–60°F). For later flowering, nolanas can also be sown in spring directly into the soil where the plants are to flower.
Uses They make excellent bedding plants and can also be used for filling gaps in a mixed border. Nolanas make good plants for edging a bed or border. Their spreading nature also makes them a natural choice for hanging baskets, window boxes and other forms of container.

Nolana humifusa
This plant is usually seen as one of its various cultivars. 'Little Bells' has lilac flowers with streaks on its white throat. 'Shooting Stars' also has lilac flowers but this time they have a dark purple eye and streaks. In both, the flowers are about 2.5cm (1in) across. The plants have quite a wide spread, which makes them an excellent choice for hanging baskets. H 15cm (6in) high S 45cm (18in).

Nolana paradoxa
This charming species produces flowers of deep blue, with the blue fading into a white throat and yellow eye. They are slighlty taller than the previous plant. H 25cm (10in).

The cultivar 'Blue Bird' has deep blue flowers while 'Snowbird' has pure white flowers and the same yellow eye.

Other plants The plant once known as *N. lanceolata*, now *N. paradoxa* subsp. *atriplicifolia*, has silvery-haired leaves and sky-blue flowers.

NONEA
Nonea

This is one of the rarer annuals. It is not seen very often but can be found. In fact, as the author began to write this piece, a seed list arrived in the post in which offers included the very rare (in gardening terms) *N. rusica*. Although none of the 35 species is common, *N. lutea* is the plant most commonly seen. It will be of great interest to those who love the perennial pulmonarias (see page 238) as it offers them a very similar annual form. One important difference is that this plant has yellow flowers, a colour that is missing among pulmonarias. It flowers in spring. H 60cm (24in) S 25cm (10in).
How to obtain Plants and seed are very rare, though seed is slightly more common, sold mainly by specialist societies.
Cultivation Plant in moist, woodland-type soil, and ideally in light-dappled shade, although sun will be tolerated if the soil is kept moist enough. Z7.
Propagation Sow fresh seed in summer in pots and place in a shaded open frame without heat.
Uses Plant in spring bedding or, to best effect, in an informal woodland setting or shady border.

Nonea lutea
This is sometimes called yellow monkswort. The leaves are bristly and rather coarse. The flowers are small funnels of primrose-yellow. They appear in the spring.

Other plants Although rare, *N. pulla* is sometimes offered. It has deep purple flowers. *N. rusica* can also occasionally be found.

Nonea lutea

OENOTHERA
Evening primrose

This beautiful genus has 125 species, of which a surprising number are grown in gardens. The majority are perennials (see page 228) but many of these are short lived and can be thought of as annuals. There are also one or two that are true annuals or biennials. Of these, *O. biennis* is by far the most common, although it is not necessarily the most beautiful. Evening primroses are so-called because their flowers open mainly in the evening.

The flowers only last a day but there are usually plenty of buds waiting to open, which ensures a constant supply of blooms. Many of the forms in cultivation also open during the day, and some have a fine fragrance. They vary in height considerably.
How to obtain The best way to obtain these plants is from seed which is reasonably easy to find. Specialist societies offer the widest range. Plants are sometimes seen, but evening primroses do not do well if confined to small pots and so the results are often disappointing.
Cultivation Any reasonable garden soil will suffice, so long as it is free-draining. A warm, sunny position is required for these plants. Z4.
Propagation Seed can either be sown in the open ground where the plants are to flower or it can be sown in pots under glass at 13–16°C (55–60°F). Some species, *O. biennis* in particular, self-sow prodigiously.
Uses Evening primroses are mainly used in a mixed border, especially in informal plantings where they can be left to self-sow.

Oenothera biennis
This is a tall plant that produces masses of lemon-yellow flowers throughout the summer and autumn. It self-sows heavily so remove plants before too much is scattered. H 1.5m (5ft) S 60cm (24in). The cultivar 'Wedding Bells' has white flowers with yellow centres.

Oenothera deltoides
This is the desert evening primrose and as its name suggests it needs very sharp drainage. It has beautiful, glistening white flowers that fade to pink. They are up to 8cm (3in) across. H 30cm (12in) S 25cm (10in).

Oenothera glazioviana
This evening primrose produces lemon-yellow flowers, and is very similar to *O. biennis.*

Oenothera pallida
This plant is a beautiful white-flowered form whose blooms turn to pink as they age. There is also a cultivar available, which is called 'Innocence'. H and S 50cm (20in).

Other plants The perennial species *Oenothera fruticosa* and *O. stricta* (see page 228) can be used as annuals.

OMPHALODES
Navelwort

This is a medium-sized genus containing about 28 species of which a number of perennials are grown in the garden. There is also one rather beautiful annual, *O. linifolia*. This seems to be one of those "secret" annuals; it is widely grown by those who know about it but not many gardeners do seem to know it. It is a delightful plant with powdery blue-green leaves on an upright, branching plant. The flowers are white and closely resemble the shape and size of forget-me-nots. The whole plant has a light and airy look to it. It self-sows and so once you have it, it rarely deserts you. H 30cm (12in) S 15cm (6in).
How to obtain Occasionally you see navelworts offered as plants, but these rarely do well when planted out. It is best to grow your own plants from seed, which is not too difficult to find.
Cultivation Any reasonable garden soil is sufficient so long as it is free-draining. A sunny position is required. Z7.
Propagation Sow the seed in spring in the open ground where the plants are to flower. If left to set seed they will self-sow, without becoming a nuisance.
Uses *O. linifolia* is a delightful annual for growing in gaps in a mixed border. It is perfect for a white-themed garden or border.

Other plants As well as *Omphalodes linifolia*, which is described above, other annuals you may find include *O. brassicifolia* and *O. littoralis*. They are both quite rare but they have the same attractive white flowers, so it is worth looking out for them.

Omphalodes linifolia

ONOPORDUM
Scotch thistle

Now we come to one of the giants of the annual world – the Scotch thistle. There are just a couple of species for the gardener to consider; although there are more than 40 biennials in this genus, it would be a brave gardener who would want to grow all of these thistles. The two species that are generally grown look basically the same. They are very tall and are branched, giving them the appearance of a giant candelebra. The stems have wavy wings which have a prickle on the crest of every wave. The leaves also have spines. Both the stems and the foliage are covered with grey hairs which gives the whole plant a silvery look, especially when it catches the sunlight. On the top of each stem is a large thistle-like flower, which is just like the classic Scottish symbol: there is a purple tuft of the flower emerging from a rounded base which is covered in silvery hair and spines. H 3m (10ft) or more, S 1.5m (5ft).

Onopordum acanthium

How to obtain You occasionally see Scotch thistles being sold as plants but they dislike being kept in small pots for too long, so it is better to grow your own from seed. This is readily available.
Cultivation Scotch thistles will grow in any reasonable garden soil, but the richer it is, the larger and more impressive the plants will be. Z6.
Propagation Sow the seed in summer in a pot that can be placed in an open frame without heat. Alternatively, if the ground is available, sow where the plants are to flower in the following year. They will self-sow to provide plants for subsequent years.
Uses These plants are best used at the back of mixed borders. They could be used in bedding schemes; however, they would have to be planted on a grand scale for this to work.

Onopordum acanthium
This is one of the two main plants that are regularly grown. It is the taller of the two and the most widely available. It conforms to the description above. There are no cultivars.

Onopordum nervosum
This plant is possibly better known under its former name of *O. arabicum* and is still sometimes seen advertised as such. It is slightly smaller than the above, otherwise there is very little difference, in gardening terms, between them. Again, there are no cultivars available.

Papaver nudicaule

Papaver rhoeas 'American Legend'

PAPAVER
Poppy

Poppies make up a large genus of some 70 species of which there are a number of annuals as well as perennials (see page 230) that are grown in the garden. The flowers are cup-shaped and have that crumpled tissue-paper appearance typical of poppies. The main colour is red but there are also white, yellow, orange, lilac and purple. Each flower only lasts a day but there is a succession of buds. Many plants will self-sow and will return the following year if allowed to spread their seed.
How to obtain Annual poppies are best acquired as seed, which is widely available.
Cultivation Any reasonable garden soil in a sunny position will suffice. Z2–3 or 6–7.
Propagation The majority of these plants can be sown where the plants are to flower.
Uses Poppies are good for bedding and for mixed borders. They are excellent for wild-flower gardens and borders.

Papaver commutatum
This plant is an excellent poppy with bright red flowers and a black spot at the base of each petal. Because of this colouring, it is often referred to as the ladybird poppy. H 45cm (18in), S 15cm (6in).

Papaver nudicaule
This is the Iceland poppy, which is also sometimes referred to as *P. croceum*. The flowers come in yellows, oranges, pinks and white. H 30cm (12in) S 15cm (6in).

Papaver nudicaule 'Garden Gnome'

There are a number of cultivars such as 'Garden Gnome' which is a dwarf form.

Papaver rhoeas
This is the field poppy. In its pure form, it produces bright red flowers. However, there are a number of cultivars, such as 'Fairy Wings' and the Shirley poppies, which carry flowers in a range of soft pastels, including pink and lavender-blue, as well as red. The flowers of the form 'American Legend' are red. H 1m (3ft) S 30cm (12in).

Papaver somniferum
This is the opium poppy. It is a tall plant whose flowers come in a wide range of colours and types: single, semi-double and double. The flowers are mainly shades of red, purple, pink, lavender and white. This species has given rise to a great number of named cultivars including 'Black Peony' which has dark flowers. H 1.5m (5ft) S 45cm (18in).

Papaver somniferum

Papaver somniferum, double form

PELARGONIUM
Pelargonium

This is a very large genus, with some 230 species and thousands of cultivars. After 100 years of being called pelargoniums these plants are still often referred to as geraniums. However, they should not be confused with that genus (see pages 129, 204). They are mainly perennials but are usually treated as annuals in the garden. They are used both as foliage and flowering plants. The flowers tend to be carried in tight clusters, which are held on upright or trailing stems. There is a wide range of flower colour, based on shades of red, pink, orange, purple and white. The leaves are valued for their patterning or scent.

There are four basic groups of pelargonium. These are: ivy-leaved, which tend to be trailing and so are good for hanging baskets and window boxes; zonal, which have patterned leaves that are usually green and brown but also come in yellow and red; regal, with larger almost azalea-shaped flowers; and the scented-leaved varieties, which tend to have looser heads of less showy flowers. Heights and spreads are highly variable.

Pelargonium 'Ashley Stephenson'

Pelargonium 'Shone Helena'

Pelargonium 'Little Gem'

Perilla frutescens var. *crispa*

How to obtain Pelargoniums are widely available from many outlets. For a better selection get the catalogues of the specialist nurseries. Some varieties are available as seed.
Cultivation In containers use a good quality potting compost (soil mix). In the open garden plant in reasonably fertile soil which is free-draining. These plants need a position in sun or partial shade. Z8.
Propagation Take cuttings of plants throughout the growing season. Sow seed in early spring under glass at 13–18°C (55–64°F).
Uses Pelargoniums can be used in containers of all sorts or as bedding plants. They can also be planted in general beds.

Ivy-leaved varieties
Cultivars include 'Alice Crousse', whose flowers are cerise-pink, 'Lachsköningin' (semi-double salmon-pink), 'Mme Crousse' (soft pink), and 'Wood's Surprise' (pink and white).

Zonal varieties
'Belinda Adams' has double flowers which are white, flushed with pink, 'Bird Dancer' comes in pink shades, and Century Series (seed-raised) produces red, pink or white flowers. Other good cultivars include 'Francis Parrett', which has double, purple-pink flowers, 'Irene' (semi-double, cerise blooms), 'Mme Fournier' (scarlet flowers, purple foliage) and Video Series (seed-raised, red and pink blooms).

Regal varieties
Good regal varieties include 'Ann Hoystead', which has deep red and black flowers and 'Bredon', also red and black. Other cultivars include 'Carisbrooke' (pink and red), 'Lord Bute' (red and black), and 'Sefton' (cerise and red).

Scented-leaved varieties
Recommended plants in this category include 'Attar of Roses' (mauve flowers), 'Copthorne' (mauve and purple), *P. crispum* 'Variegatum' (lemon-scented variegated leaves and mauve flowers), 'Mabel Grey' (purple), *P. tomentosum* (white flowers and peppermint-scented).

PERILLA
Perilla

A small genus of six plants, of which one, *P. frutescens*, has become very popular in recent years. This is not for its flowers but more for its foliage. The large oval leaves are green but heavily marked with purple and the margins are highly toothed. They are also fragrant. The small flowers are carried in spikes above and among the foliage. They are white or very pale pink. H 1m (3ft) S 30cm (12in) in good conditions, but is often less.

How to obtain Perillas are obtainable as plants from garden centres and nurseries. They are also available as seed.
Cultivation Plant out in a rich soil that is moisture retentive. Perillas can be grown in either sun or light shade. Z8.
Propagation Sow the seed in early spring under glass at 13–18°C (55–64°F).
Uses These plants are good in all forms of foliage schemes. They are very good plants for bedding, especially in exotic schemes. They can also be useful for large containers such as tubs.

Perilla frutescens
This is the plant described above. Its variety *crispa* is even better. It has deep purple leaves that are very frilled around the edge, making it an exotic-looking plant. 'Checkerboard Mixed' is a new cultivar which is a mixture of green and purple plants.

Pelargonium 'Fragaris'

Annual grasses

Agrostis nebulosa
Aira
Avena sterilis
Briza maxima
Briza minor
Bromus briziformis
Chloris barbata
Chloris truncata
Chloris virgita
Hordeum jubatum
Lagurus ovatus
Lamarckia aurea
Panicum capillare
Panicum miliaceum
Pennisetum setaceum
Pennisetum villosum
Setaria glauca
Setaria italica
Sorghum nigrum
Zea mays

Petunia 'Blue Daddy'

Petunia 'Blue Wave'

PETUNIA
Petunia

This large genus of 40 species has produced some excellent garden plants. They were originally developed as bedding plants. As containers became more popular, they were bred for that purpose as well, resulting in the magnificent plants that we see today in hanging baskets. The petunia is probably now the favourite plant for baskets, especially since new cultivars produce flowers that have not only had their colour enhanced but which have been made more weather-proof as well. The slightly hairy stems are covered for very long periods with trumpet-shaped flowers. They come in a wide range of colours, mainly based on shades of red, pink and purple, but including white and yellow. Many of them have a contrasting coloured eye and often darker veining. H up to 45cm (18in) but usually less. The spread varies but trailing forms can grow 1m (3ft) across.

How to obtain Petunias are very widely available as plants in bedding packs or in individual pots from a large range of outlets. Seed is also easy to come by, although there is a bigger range in plant form.

Cultivation Any good potting compost (soil mix) will do for containers and a well-drained soil should be chosen for open-ground planting. Plant in full sun. Z7.

Propagation Sow the seed in the autumn under glass at 16–18°C (60–64°F).

Uses Petunias have many garden uses, but they are particularly good for hanging baskets and other containers.

Petunia Daddy Series
This is a good series, which produces flowers of mixed colours. Some are available as single colours. These include 'Sugar Daddy' which has pink flowers with purple veins, and 'Blue Daddy', which has bluish-purple flowers with darker veins.

Petunia Mirage Series
Another excellent series which has good weather-tolerance. Individual colours are available.

Petunia Picotee Series
The flowers of this series come in pure colours, such as blue or pink, but have a white margin.

Petunia Storm Series
This series includes plants with individual colours such as 'Storm Lavender' and 'Storm Pink'.

Petunia Surfinia Series
A magnificent modern series that has transformed hanging baskets. The purple form 'Surfinia Purple' is particularly good.

Petunia Wave Series
This series includes individual colours, such as 'Blue Wave' and 'Purple Wave'.

Petunia Ultra Star Series
Plants in this series have striped petals, giving them a star-like appearance. The colours are bright blues and reds.

PHACELIA
Scorpion weed

This is a large genus containing 150 species, of which several annuals are widely grown in our gardens. This is partly because they are attractive and partly because they are very good plants for attracting bees, hoverflies and other beneficial insects. Phacelia is now sometimes planted beside agricultural crops for this very reason. The flowers are generally blue and have protruding stamens which sometimes gives them a delightful fuzzy look. The flowers are cup-shaped and are born in clusters over a long period. The plants in this genus vary considerably in height.

How to obtain Phacelias may occasionally be found as plants but it is more common to grow them from seed.

Cultivation Any reasonable garden soil will suffice. Choose a sunny location. Z8.

Petunia 'Storm Lavender'

Phacelia campanularia

Phacelia tanacetifolia

Propagation Sow the seed in spring in open ground where the plants are to grow.
Uses Phacelias make excellent bedding material and can also be used to good effect in mixed borders. They are a useful addition to wildlife gardens.

Phacelia campanularia
This plant is sometimes known as the Californian bluebell. It has dark blue, upward-facing flowers. There is also a white form. H 30cm (12in).

Phacelia tanacetifolia
The best species for insects, with finely cut leaves and blue blooms. A tall plant, it may need support in exposed positions. H up to 1.2m (4ft) S 45cm (18in).

Other plants *Phacelia viscida* is a medium-sized plant, usually up to 30cm (12in) tall. It has very dark blue flowers with a white eye. There is also a cultivar, called 'Tropical Surf', but it is the same as the species.

PHASEOLUS
Runner bean
The runner bean plant, also known as the climbing bean, can be a very attractive choice for a border. As climbers, these plants are valuable in that they can bring height to a mixed border or bedding scheme. They can be grown up a wigwam of poles or a framework; the dense foliage soon covers the support. The flowers are mainly scarlet but there are also forms that produce pink, white and purple flowers. The pods of some varieties are also very decorative. All in all, an extremely valuable plant, especially since you can eat the beans. H 3m (10ft) S 30cm (12in).
How to obtain These plants are often sold in packs or pots at garden centres. You cannot be sure what colour the flowers will be, but they are usually red. If you want to be certain, grow beans from seed; seed merchants offer hundreds of cultivars.
Cultivation Plant out after the threat of frost has passed in a soil enriched with plenty of well-rotted organic material. It should be moisture retentive. A sunny position is required. Some form of support will be needed. Z8.
Propagation Sow seeds under glass in individual pots in mid-spring or set the seed where the plants are to flower in late spring.
Uses These plants can be used as climbers up poles in a border or over a pergola. They can also be grown in containers, perhaps creating a backdrop for other plants. They can also be used as centrepieces in potagers.

Runner beans in general
These plants have scarlet flowers. They are attractive in their own right but there are plenty of alternatives, and some cultivars carry flowers of several colours, or bicoloured blooms. 'White Lady', as the name suggests, has white flowers, while 'Painted Lady' has red and white blooms and 'Sunset' has soft pink ones. 'Summer Medley' is quite spectacular, producing an array of red, white and pink flowers. 'Relay' carries flowers of several colours. For those that like variegated foliage 'Sun Bright' has green leaves that are flushed with gold.

Phaseolus 'Painted Lady' (with creeper)

PHLOX
Phlox
This is a large genus of 67 species of which a number of perennials (see page 233) are in cultivation as well as one popular annual. This is *P. drummondii*. It has long been popular as a bedding plant and seems to have lost none of its appeal, mainly because it has adapted well to life in containers. It is a bushy plant with flowers that are similar in shape to those of the perennial: flat discs on a narrow tubular base. They come in a wonderful range of colours from soft pastels to colours that hit you between the eyes. H up to 45cm (18in) but often much less, S 25cm (10in).
How to obtain These are frequently seen as plants in garden centres, but there is much more choice to be had by purchasing seed.
Cultivation The annual phlox will grow in any reasonable garden soil. Use a good-quality general potting compost (soil mix) in containers. It will grow in either part shade or full sun so long as the soil is moist enough. Z4.
Propagation Sow the seed under glass in early spring at 13–16°C (55–60°F).
Uses The traditional use for this plant is in bedding schemes, but it works equally well in mixed borders or in containers. Taller varieties are good for cutting.

Phlox drummondii
This plant is rarely sold as a species; it is more commonly seen as one of its cultivars of which there are quite a number. 'Tapestry Mixture' and 'Ethnie Pastel Shades' produce a range of soft colours while 'African Sunset' is brilliant red. 'Sternenzauber' or 'Twinkle' has unique star-like flowers with irregularly pointed petals. 'Petticoat' is a dwarf mixture with small flowers. 'Red Admiral' has luscious dark crimson flowers, while 'Grammy Pink White' has striking pink and white flowers.

Phlox drummondii 'Grammy Pink White'

Plectranthus argentatus

PLECTRANTHUS
Plectranthus

This is an enormous genus of more than 370 species. However, from the annual gardener's point of view there is only one of interest. This is *P. forsteri*, which is sometimes called *P. coleoides* and often sold as such. In fact it is a perennial, but it is treated as an annual by most gardeners. The attraction of this plant is not its flowers but its foliage. The leaves are oval and toothed, rather in the manner of nettles. They grow on trailing stems which makes this plant ideal for use in containers of all types, but especially hanging baskets. The small flowers are carried in whorls at the ends of the stems. They are tubular and resemble those of the deadnettles or thyme plants. Their colour is white or mauve. H 25cm (10in) high, S 1m (3ft).

How to obtain Plectranthus is usually purchased as a plant from garden centres. It is sometimes available from florists.

Cultivation Use a good-quality general potting compost (soil mix) if, as is very likely, you are growing these plants in some kind of container. If used in the open garden, any reasonable garden soil will suffice, as long as it is free-draining. Z10.

Propagation Take stem cuttings at any time of year and overwinter the resulting plants.

Uses The primary use for this plant is in containers. It works well in all types of container, but especially in those where the stems can hang down, such as hanging baskets or tall pots. It can also be used as bedding and as a house plant.

Plectranthus forsteri

This plant, which is described above, has light green leaves. However, there is a cultivar which is much more commonly seen. This is *P.f.* 'Marginatus', which has attractive creamy-white margins around the leaf.

Other plants *Plectranthus argentatus* has become increasingly popular as a bedding plant. The foliage is furry and grey in colour. From this spikes of small, pale pink or bluish flowers arise. It can grow to 1m (3ft) but when used as annual bedding it reaches less than half of this height.

PORTULACA
Sun plant

This is a large genera, this time containing about 100 species. Of these there is only one annual in general cultivation. This is the sun plant, *P. grandiflora*, which is sometimes also called the rose moss. It is a native of sandy places in South America and is a perfect plant for either bedding or containers. It has bluish-green, succulent leaves and flowers that in some ways resemble poppies with their tissue-paper petals and shallow cup shape. The flowers come in a wide range of bright colours, including oranges, reds and pinks, as well as white. H and S 20cm (8in).

How to obtain Sun plants are occasionally available as plants from garden centres but the main source is seed from the various seed merchants.

Cultivation Sun plants need a light, dry soil and a warm sunny position. If growing in a container use a free-draining compost (soil mix). Z10.

Propagation Sow the seed under glass in early spring at 13–18°C (55–60°F).

Uses These are good plants for bedding schemes if the soil is right. They are also ideal for gravel gardens. Their trailing habit makes them suitable for containers, especially hanging baskets and window boxes.

Portulaca grandiflora

Sun plants are sold as mixtures or as individual cultivars. Some mixtures can also be obtained as individual colours. The Sundial hybrids, for example, come as 'Sundial Mango' and 'Sundial Peppermint' as well as in mixed colours. Other mixtures include the Sundance hybrids and Minilace hybrids. One of the most beautiful cultivars is the pure white 'Sun State White'.

Other plants *Portulaca oleracea* is becoming increasingly available. It is a trailing plant with yellow, orange or pink flowers.

Portulaca grandiflora 'Sundial Mixed'

Reseda odorata

RESEDA
Mignonette

This is another large genus, this time containing about 60 species. One species in the genus is widely grown. This is *R. odorata*, which has been a popular plant in cottage-style gardens for centuries. It has an untidy habit, which fits in well with this type of informal gardening, but it is also very fragrant, a characteristic of so many old-fashioned flowers. The perfume is its main attraction since, while the flowers are pleasant, they are not overly decorative, or at least not when judged alongside more showy flowering plants such as the pelargonium or petunia. The blooms are very small and whitish-yellow with noticeable red anthers. They are carried in spikes which rise up from the sprawling plants. H 45cm (18in) S 30cm (12in).

How to obtain Occasionally mignonettes are seen for sale as plants, but the surest way to obtain them is to grow them from seed, available from some seed merchants and also from specialist society seed lists.

Cultivation Any reasonable garden soil will do for these plants, but it should be well-drained. A sunny position is preferred, especially if you want the scent. Z8.

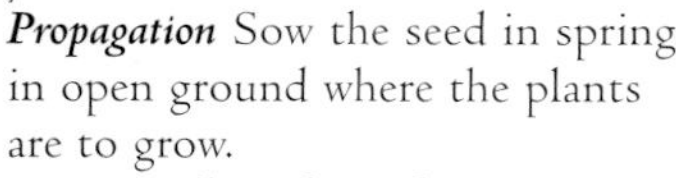

Propagation Sow the seed in spring in open ground where the plants are to grow.

Uses Excellent for informal displays, including cottage-style gardens. Mignonettes can also be used in imaginative bedding schemes. It is wonderful for wild-flower gardens and borders, and is attractive to bees.

Reseda odorata
This, the main species, is usually grown in its own right. However, there are cultivars available. These do not vary greatly from the species, but 'Red Monarch' has more pronounced red anthers. The flowers of 'Grandiflora' are more yellow, while those of 'Alba' are whiter.

Other plants There are one or two other species that are also available if you hunt hard enough. *R. alba*, which produces creamy white flowers is one, and the much taller *R. luteola*, which carries yellow flowers, is another.

RICINUS
Castor oil plant

This is a single species genus. The species is *R. communis*, which has been part of the bedding scene since Victorian times and probably before that. Although attractive, it is poisonous if eaten. The seed is particularly toxic – the deadly poison ricin is made from it. If there is any doubt as to safety – for example if children visit your garden – do not grow it. Its attraction is its foliage, although if the summer is long and hot enough it will flower.
It has large palmate (like fingers radiating from a hand) leaves. In the species these are green but there are also some excellent purple-leaved forms available. When flowers are formed, they are red or pink fuzzy balls and are carried in a spike. In the wild, this plant grows to 12m (40ft) but in the garden it is more like 1.2m (4ft) or less. S 60cm (24in).
How to obtain You can buy these as plants but do not rely on being able to find them. It is better to grow them from seed which is commonly available.
Cultivation Plant out after the threat of frosts has passed in a well-drained but rich soil. This plant requires a warm sunny position. Z10.
Propagation Sow the seed in spring: soak it in water for 24 hours first and then sow under glass at 21°C (70°F).
Uses Castor oil plants can be used as centrepieces in bedding schemes or can be added to a mixed border. They look particularly good in exotic arrangements. These plants can also be grown in large tubs or containers (they do not do well in small pots).

Ricinus communis

Ricinus communis
This is the only species and it is widely grown. However, the red or bronze-leaved forms are more commonly seen. 'Carmencita' is one of the best; it produces good red foliage and red flowers. 'Carmencita Pink' is similar but produces pink flowers. 'Gibsonii' has dark green foliage with red veins and pinkish flowers. 'Zanzibariensis' is similar but the foliage has white veins.

RUDBECKIA
Coneflower

This is a genus of about 20 species. Most of those used in the garden are perennials (see page 240). However, there is one biennial and a handful of hybrids that are very much in use. They are popular both because of their vibrant colour and because they tend to flower over a long period, including the autumn. They have daisy-like flowers which have a ring of yellow or gold outer petals. These surround a brown inner disc which is raised in a rounded cone, hence the name coneflower. They can reach up to 2m (6ft) but rarely do in cultivation.
Usual height 60–100cm (2–3ft) S 45cm (18in).
How to obtain Coneflowers are available both as plants and seed from garden centres.
Cultivation Coneflowers will grow in any reasonable garden soil, so long as it does not dry out too much. Conversely, the soil must also be free-draining so there is no waterlogging. Z4.
Propagation Sow the seed in the early spring under glass at 16–18°C (60–64°F).
Uses These plants can be used to good effect in either bedding or mixed borders. They are especially useful in borders that are made up of hot colours.

Rudbeckia 'Prairie Sun'

Rudbeckia hirta
This is the main biennial (treated as an annual) that is cultivated. It is grown as the species and there are also a number of cultivars. 'Bambi' is a short form 30cm (12in) high with attractive gold and bronze petals. 'Gloriosa' has large heads 15cm (6in) wide with golden flowers and sometimes bicolours. It has a double equivalent, 'Double Gloriosa'. 'Irish Eyes' (or 'Green Eyes') has yellow outer petals with an olive green inner ring. 'Kelvedon Star' is an old favourite with yellow flowers flushed with mahogany. 'Toto' has golden-yellow flowers with a brown centre. There are also a number of hybrids available, some of which are listed below.

***Rudbeckia* 'Goldilocks'**
A popular long-flowering plant with semi-double or double golden-yellow flowers.

***Rudbeckia* 'Marmalade'**
Another favourite, this time with large flowers which are yellow ageing to a rich gold.

***Rudbeckia* 'Prairie Sun'**
This attractive plant produces golden-yellow flowers with pale green centres.

***Rudbeckia* 'Rustic Dwarfs'**
These plants have flowers of mixed colours: yellow, gold, mahogany and bronze.

Rudbeckia hirta 'Toto'

Salpiglossis 'Splash Mixed'

SALPIGLOSSIS

Salpiglossis

A small genus of two species. One of them, *S. sinuata*, is grown in gardens. There was a time when this plant was very popular but, although it is still grown, it is not seen as frequently as it once was. This is a shame since it is a very attractive plant with large trumpet-shaped flowers, rather like those of petunias. The flowers are carried in great profusion, sometimes smothering the plant. The colours include shades of red, orange, yellow and purple. The veins in the petals are either a darker version of the same colour or a contrasting colour; most of them are bicolours. The height varies between 30 and 60cm (12–24in) S 30cm (12in).

How to obtain Salpiglossis can sometimes be found as plants in garden centres, but this cannot be relied upon. If you are determined to grow them it is safer to grow your own from seed which is readily available from a number of seed merchants.

Cultivation Plant out after the threat of frost has passed. These plants do best in a fertile soil that does not dry out too much. They should have a warm, sunny position. Z8.

Propagation Sow the seed in early spring under glass at 18–21°C (64–70°F).

Uses Salpiglossis make excellent bedding plants, but they can be used to fill gaps in a mixed border. They are also suitable for large containers.

Salpiglossis sinuata 'Ice Maiden'

Salpiglossis sinuata 'Bolero Mixed'

Salpiglossis sinuata

Although the species is sometimes grown in its own right, its cultivars are much more common. Many of these are sold as mixes, such as 'Casino Mixed', 'Splash Mixed' or 'Bolero Mixed'. In others, such as 'Ingrid', 'Kew Blue' and 'Ice Maiden', the colours tend to be similar in each plant although there is still a little variation, usually in the markings.

SALVIA

Sage

This is an enormous genus of 900 species that includes shrubs, perennials (see page 241) and annuals. Of the last there is only one that is grown to any extent. This is *Salvia viridis* which until recently was known as *S. hormium* and is still often listed as such in seed catalogues. This is a true annual, and there are also several short-lived perennials that are used as annuals. One such, *S. splendens* is the perfect bedding plant and is nearly always grown as an annual.

How to obtain *Salvia splendens* and *S. viridis* are offered in bedding packs and individual pots, as well as being widely available as seed from merchants and others. The other short-lived perennials are occasionally available as plants but can be more reliably found as seed. Seed also gives a greater choice of cultivars.

Cultivation Most will grow in any reasonable garden soil so long as it is free-draining. A warm, sunny position is to be preferred. Z9.

Propagation Sow seed of *S. viridis* in spring in the open ground where they are to flower. Sow seed of other species under glass at 13–16°C (55–60°F).

Uses Both types can be used as summer bedding. The tender perennials are often used in mixed borders or in containers.

Salvia splendens

This short-lived perennial was once the king of bedding plants. It is still used but it is nowhere

Salvia viridis 'White Swan'

Salvia viridis 'Pink Sundae'

Self-sowing annuals

Atriplex hortensis 'Rubra'	*Limnanthes douglasii*
Borago officinalis	*Lunaria annua*
Calendula officinalis	*Myosotis*
Chrysanthemum segetum	*Nigella*
Collomia grandiflora	*Oenothera biennis*
Digitalis purpurea	*Omphalodes linifolia*
Eryngium giganteum	*Onopordum*
Euphorbia lathyris	*Papaver*
Galactites tomentosa	*Silybum marianum*
Hesperis matronalis	*Verbascum*

near as popular as it once was. It is a bushy plant with spikes of very bright scarlet flowers. H 40cm (16in) S 30cm (12in). There are still a large number of cultivars, some of which now include other colours such as purples and creams. The Sizzler Series is one example.

Salvia viridis

This is the true annual. It is an upright plant which is grown for its spikes of pink, purple or cream bracts. The flowers are insignificant, but the uppermost leaves are coloured in this magnificent way. There are a number of cultivars to choose from including 'White Swan', which has creamy-white bracts with green veins. 'Pink Sundae' produces carmine-coloured bracts. H 45cm (18in) S 25cm (10in).

Other plants The other short-lived perennials include species such as *Salvia coccinea* and its cultivars with scarlet flowers, *S. farinacea* with deep blue flowers, and *S. argentea* with beautiful large, silver leaves.

SANVITALIA
Creeping zinnia

This is a small genus containing a mere seven species of which *S. procumbens* is the only species seen in cultivation. This is a low, creeping plant as its common name implies. Also as the name indicates, the flowers are similar to those of the zinnia, to which it is related. They are daisy-like with an outer ring of bright yellow petals and a large inner disc which is purple-brown. The flowers are not very large, measuring only 2cm (¾in) across, but what they lack in size is more than compensated for by the quantity produced. H 20cm (8in) S 45cm (18in).

Sanvitalia procumbens

Sanvitalia procumbens 'Profusion Cherry'

How to obtain Sanvitalias can be purchased as bedding or container plants from garden centres and nurseries. They are also available as seed from merchants, which provide a large choice of cultivars.
Cultivation Plant in any reasonable garden soil. A sunny position is to be preferred. Z8.
Propagation Sow the seed where the plants are to flower in autumn or spring. Sow under glass at 13–16°C (55–60°F) in early spring for container plants.

Uses These make excellent bedding plants. They are also suitable for containers.

Sanvitalia procumbens

This is the only species generally cultivated, and is described above. There are also a number of cultivars. These include 'Irish Eyes' whose flowers have green centres and 'Mandarin Orange' which has bright orange petals and a brown centre. 'Dwarf Carpet' reaches only 10cm (4in) in height. 'Profusion Cherry' is a lovely shade of red, and 'Sprite' is a yellow and brown semi-double.

Scabiosa atropurpurea 'Chile Pepper'

SCABIOSA
Scabious

This is a large genus containing about 80 species of perennials (see page 242) and a few annuals. Both the annuals and the perennials have a similar type of flower, which is probably best described as a pincushion. It consists of a dome of florets, with the outer ones often being larger than the inner ones. Generally the flower colour is lavender-blue but in the annuals there is some variation. The flowers are carried on slender stems above finely cut foliage, making these very attractive, delicate-looking plants. There is a certain old-fashioned quality about them that makes the scabious an ideal addition to informal schemes, such as that of a cottage garden.

Scabiosa stellata

How to obtain They are available as plants in individual pots from garden centres and nurseries. Seed is also widely available.
Cultivation Any reasonable garden soil will be sufficient so long as it is not waterlogged. Scabious make good cut flowers and some of the seed head can be dried. Z6.
Propagation Sow the seed in mid-spring in the open ground where it is to flower. Alternatively sow in pots under glass at 13–16°C (55–60°F).
Uses Scabious are probably best used in mixed borders although they can also be used as bedding.

Scabiosa atropurpurea
This is a superb plant with pincushion flower heads that vary from lavender to deep purple. It grows to 1m (3ft) when growing well but is often less. S 30cm (12in). There are several cultivars of which 'Chile Pepper' is the current favourite. This has very dark red flowers with speckles of white. 'Blue Cockade' has large heads twice the size of most (up to 5cm/2in across) with lavender to purple flowers.

Scabiosa stellata
This plant has pale blue pincushions. When the flower fades, these turn into spherical seed heads with each seed being framed in a ruff. They make excellent dried flowers.

Other plants *Scabiosa prolifera* has cream-coloured flower heads and, like the previous plant, produces papery seed heads that are good for drying. It is more difficult to find than the other species.

SCAEVOLA
Fairy fan flower

The scaevola is a large genus of about 90 species of which only one is in general cultivation. This is *S. aemula*, the fairy fan flower or the cushion fan flower. It is a curious plant that is perfect for hanging baskets but is not quite so useful in the borders. It is a low-growing, spreading plant. The flowers are lavender blue and the five petals are in the shape of a fan. H 15cm (6in) S 1m (3ft).

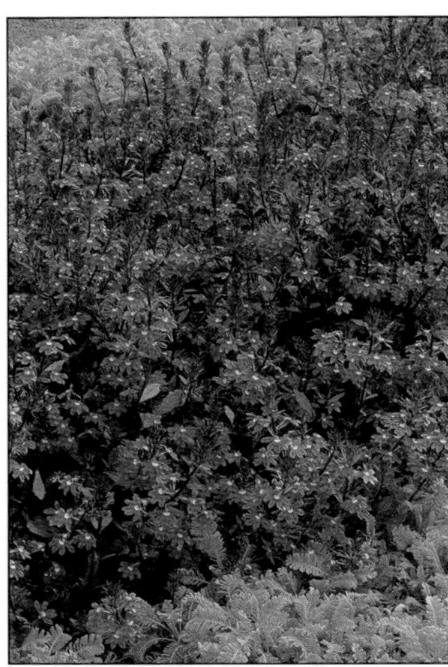

Scaevola aemula 'Blue Wonder'

How to obtain Scaevolas are generally sold as small plants by a few garden centres and by mail order. Seed can be obtained but this is not so satisfactory as named plants.
Cultivation Plant out in a moist, reasonably rich soil that is free-draining. In containers use a good general potting compost (soil mix). Scabious can be planted in full sun, so long as the soil is kept moist, or in light shade. Z10.
Propagation Take cuttings in summer and overwinter the young plants under glass. Seed can be sown under glass at 18–21°C (64–70°F).
Uses Its spreading habit makes the scaevola ideal as a container plant, especially in hanging baskets. It can also be used as an unusual bedding plant.

Scaevola aemula
The species can be grown from seed but the plants are not particularly floriferous. The forms 'Blue Wonder' and 'Blue Fan' produce a lot more flowers and are worth obtaining. They both have lilac-blue flowers. There is also a form called 'Mauve Clusters' in which the flowers are slightly more mauve. However, there is not a great deal to choose between the cultivars. In the wild the flowers can be white; hard searching might locate the seed of such plants.

SCHIZANTHUS
Butterfly flower

This is a genus of about 15 species of annuals and biennials. Several are in cultivation, but only one, *S. pinnatus*, and its cultivars and hybrids are used to any great extent. They are not quite so popular as they once were but they are still well worth growing since they are spectacular plants. In well-grown specimens it is impossible to see the plant for the flowers. The English name is very apt – the flowers are like butterflies. The alternative name of poor man's orchids is also true since they are very exotic looking. They are very colourful: the basic flower colouring is shades of pink with a yellow and white centre with orange spotting. H 45cm (18in) S 30cm (12in).
How to obtain Schizanthus can be bought as plants in individual pots but if you can raise them it

Scaevola aemula 'Blue Wonder' (detail)

Schizanthus pinnatus cultivars

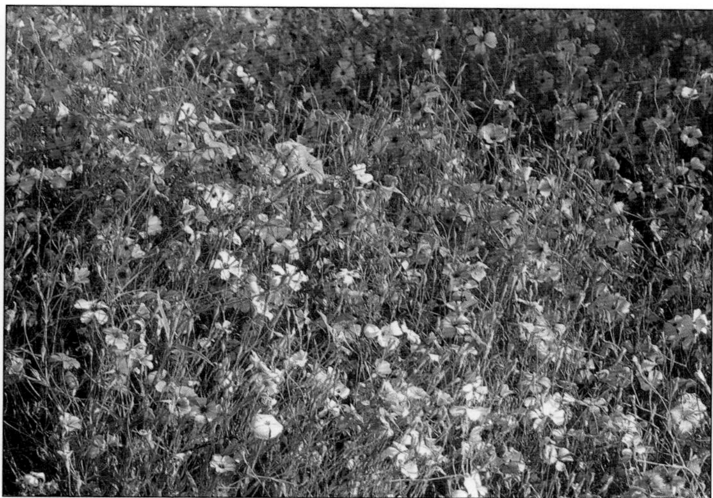
Silene coeli-rosa 'Royal Celebration'

is better to buy seed since you will get a better choice and many more plants.
Cultivation For container plants choose a good-quality general potting compost (soil mix). In the open ground, any well-drained soil that does not dry out excessively will do. Plant in a warm sunny position. Pinch the growing tips out to make the plants bushy. Z10.
Propagation Sow seed in early spring under glass at 16–18°C (60–64°F).
Uses Schizanthus are magnificent plants for containers. They also look superb as massed bedding.

Schizanthus pinnatus
This is the main species grown, and is described above. It has several cultivars and is also one of the parents of the next plant listed. Cultivars often come in mixed colours. They include 'Angel's Wings', 'Disco Mixed', 'Hit Parade', 'Star Parade', and the rather uninspiringly named 'Giant Hybrids'.

Schizanthus pinnatus

Schizanthus × wisetonensis
This is an excellent hybrid of the above. It also has a number of cultivars, none of which is very different from the others.

SILENE
Campion

This is one of the most important genera in gardening terms since so many of the 500 species are grown in our gardens. They include perennials (see page 243) and annuals. On the whole they are not very showy plants but they do provide a backbone to plantings. There are several annuals which are of interest. The flowers are generally five-petalled discs in various shades of pink or white. H 15–45cm (6–18in) S up to 25cm (10in).
How to obtain The plants may be seen in garden centres but they are more likely to be found in nurseries. Seed is available from seed merchants, although you may have to check out specialist society seed lists for rarer seed.
Cultivation Silene will grow in any garden soil, in either sun or shade. Z7.
Propagation Most annuals can be sown in the the spring in the open ground where the plants are to flower. They can also be sown in pots under glass at 13–16°C (55–60°F).
Uses These plants can be used in a wide variety of garden sites. They fit well into a mixed border and some can be used in bedding or containers.

Silene coeli-rosa
This plant is commonly known as the rose of heaven and was once very popular. It looks rather like a large-flowered gypsophila. The notched petals are pink, fading to white at the base. There are several good cultivars available. The Angel Series includes 'Rose Angel' which produces rose-pink flowers and 'Blue Angel' which has lavender-blue flowers. 'Royal Celebration' carries blooms in a good mixture of colours.

Silene pendula 'Peach Blossom'

Silene pendula
This attractive plant has been reintroduced in recent years in the form 'Peach Blossom'. This is a little gem which grows to no more than 15cm (6in) in height and about the same in spread. The double flowers come in shades of delicate pale pink. There is also a white form, also with double flowers, called 'Snowball', while 'Triumph' produces blooms of deep pink.

Other plants *Silene armeria* is a delightful plant with powdery grey-green leaves and stems and domes of small flowers in a deep rose-pink. It self-sows without becoming a nuisance. There is a free-flowering form called 'Electra' which carries flowers of a darker pink.

Silene armeria 'Rose Angel'

Silybum marianum

Smyrnium perfoliatum

SILYBUM
Milk thistle

This is a small genus of two similar plants. The one that is most widely grown in gardens is *S. marianum*, which is known as the milk thistle or St Mary's thistle. It is valued mainly for its foliage. The leaves are large with deep lobes, each topped with a spine. They are a glossy green and covered with a random white marbling, which looks rather like spilt milk or St Mary's milk, hence the plant's name. They are very attractive leaves indeed.

The flowers are just like those of a typical thistle, with purple tufts erupting from a cup of spiny bracts. The thistle will normally spread 1m (3ft) wide when grown in good ground, but if it is in very rich soil it can grow to twice that and become huge. However, 60cm (24in) is the normal expected width and 1m (3ft) the height. If your silybum do grow very large, they can smother the surrounding plants.

How to obtain You will rarely find plants for sale, but silybum is available as seed from a variety of sources. It is usually found in specialist society seed exchanges.

Cultivation Any reasonable garden soil will do for silybum, but the richer the soil, the bigger the plants. Z7.

Propagation Sow the seed in the open ground where the plants are to grow in autumn or spring. It will self-sow if left to seed providing plants for later years.

Uses This is a magnificent foliage plant best suited to the mixed border, or it could be used as bedding in some imaginative scheme. If you are not worried about the sharp spines it can make an interesting addition to children's gardens, not least because most children find the name highly amusing.

Other plants Although it is not seen very often, the other plant in the genus, *S. eburneum*, is sometimes cultivated in gardens. This looks very similar to *S. marianum*. The seed is available, but it is not easy to find.

SMYRNIUM
Smyrnium

This is a genus of about eight biennial plants. Of these, one is grown quite widely in gardens, while another is occasionally seen. The common one is called *S. perfoliatum*. This is not a plant for neat and tidy, formal gardens, but one that crops up in informal gardens, especially those with shady areas, or in wild-flower gardens. It is a delightful plant, looking rather like a spurge (*Euphorbia*), with its tiny yellowish-green flowers. These appear in late spring. The leaves immediately below the flowers are the same colour and it is these that give the plant its characteristic appearance. H 1m (3ft) when given good conditions, S 30cm (12in).

How to obtain Seed is available from a few seed merchants, but you will have to search for it. It is also available from the seed exchanges of specialist societies. Once you have this plant, it will self-sow.

Cultivation Any reasonable garden soil will suffice. Smyrniums will grow in sun, but they are a useful plant for light shade. Z7.

Propagation Sow the seed in the open ground where the plants are to grow. Alternatively, sow in a pot and place in an open frame without heat. Let the plants self sow for future years.

Uses These plants can be used in informal borders, including cottage gardens, but they are best used in wild-flower gardens, or in shady areas where their bright golden colour shines out.

Sutera cordata 'Snowflake'

Sutera cordata

Other plants *Smyrnium olusatrum* grows naturally around coasts, and it is good for wild-flower gardens in that kind of area. It is much bigger and more solid than the above with heavy domes of yellow flowers and large glossy leaves. It is very much like a yellow-flowered angelica. It self-sows prodigiously so be careful where you site it.

SUTERA
Sutera

This genus contains 130 species. The one that is grown in gardens is *S. cordata*, which is also known as *Bacopa* 'Snowflake'. It is one of those plants that suddenly takes the gardening world by storm. It was hardly known a few years ago and you would not have been able to find it, but now it is in most garden centres. It is a low creeping plant that is covered in a mass of white flowers, each having five rounded petals. It flowers for a long time and its sprawling habit makes it perfect for hanging baskets, for which it is mainly marketed. H 10–15cm (4–6in) S 45cm (18in).

How to obtain Suteras are available only as plants, not as seed. The cultivar *S. cordata* 'Snowflake' is readily available, but the others listed are not so frequently seen. However, they are gradually becoming more commonplace.

Cultivation Do not plant out suteras until after the threat of frost has passed. Use a good-quality general potting compost (soil mix). Pinch out the side shoots to start with so that your plant becomes bushy. Keep the compost moist; the flowers will drop if it dries out. Z10.

Propagation Take cuttings in summer and overwinter the plants under warm glass.

Uses This is an excellent hanging basket plant, which is one of the reasons it has become so popular. It can also be used in other types of containers. There is also no reason why it should not be planted in walls and such like.

Sutera cordata

The species as such is not usually grown; it is more commonly seen in the form of one of its cultivars. The most popular of these is 'Snowflake' which has small, pure white flowers with a yellow eye. There are several new white forms on offer including 'Snowstorm' and 'Bridal Showers'. There are also a couple of lavender-coloured forms: 'Lavender Storm' and the darker-flowered 'Blue Showers'. There is a pink form, which has no specific name, and a form with golden variegated foliage and white flowers, which is known as 'Olympic Gold'.

Other plants *Sutera grandiflora* has been around for a bit longer. It is a similar spreading plant to the above, but it produces lavender-blue flowers which have a white throat. There are several cultivars.

SYMPHYANDRA
Symphyandra

This is a genus of some 12 short-lived perennials that are usually treated as annuals. They are closely related to the bellflowers, *Campanula*. Quite a few of them are in cultivation but tend to be grown by gardeners who specialize in such plants, such as alpine growers, rather than the general gardener.

There is one, however, that is not difficult to grow and is well worth the effort to find. This is *S. hofmannii*. It grows up to 60cm (24in) high and 30cm (12in) across and is covered with hanging bellflowers of creamy-white. They are each over 2.5cm (1in) in diameter. Symphyandras are not in the same league as many bedding plants, but they do remain flowering for quite a long time during the summer, an attribute which earns them their place in the garden.

How to obtain You can occasionally find symphyandras in specialist nurseries, but if you want to be certain of obtaining plants then the safest way is to get seed. This is available from a number of seed merchants as well as from the seed exchange lists of specialist garden societies.

Cultivation Symphyandras will grow in any reasonable garden soil, but they prefer light, free-draining ones. Choose either a sunny or lightly shaded position for these plants. Z4.

Propagation Sow the seed in early spring under glass at 13–16°C (55–60°F).

Uses These plants are best used in a mixed border. They make an excellent addition to a white garden or white border.

Other plants Most of the other symphyandras are available either as plants or as seed from specialist sources. Most are treated as annuals used in the mixed border or rock garden. They all have bell-shaped flowers and include blue as well as white flowers. *S. pendula* is the next most frequently seen after *S. hofmannii*. This also has white flowers. *S. armena* is a good species if you want pale blue flowers.

Annuals for hanging baskets

Begonia
Bidens
Brachyscome
Chrysanthemum
Echium
Felicia amelloides
Helichrysum
Laurentia
Lobelia
Myosotis
Nolana humifusa
Petunia
Pelargonium
Sanvitalia procumbens
Senecio cineraria
Sutera cordata
Tagetes
Tropaeolum
Verbena
Viola

Symphyandra hofmannii

Tagetes 'French Vanilla'

Tagetes patula 'Safari Tangerine'

TAGETES
Marigolds

This genus of daisy-like plants contains about 50 species. The two that are of most interest to gardeners are the French marigold (*T. patula*) and the African marigold (*T. erecta*). There are also some hybrids between the two as well as some derived from the species *T. tenuifolia*. Many marigold cultivars are in series and they are generally sold as mixtures, but some individual forms are sold.

The basic plants are daisy-like with an outer ring of petals and a central disc. However, many are doubles and semi-doubles. The predominant colour is golden-yellow but orange and mahogany-red also feature prominently. These plants have always played an important part in bedding schemes. In recent years their importance has declined, but the marigolds have retained enough popularity to remain widely available. H 15–45cm (6–18in) S 30cm (12in).

How to obtain Marigolds are available as plants, both in bedding packs and individual pots. However, buying plants restricts your choice of cultivars; growing your own plants from seed opens up hundreds of interesting possibilities.

Cultivation Any reasonable quality garden soil will be suitable so long as it is free-draining. A sunny position is best. Deadhead marigolds regularly to obtain continual flowering. Z9.

Propagation Sow the seed in the early spring under glass at 18–21°C (64–70°F). It can be sown where the plants are to flower but this will result in much later-flowering plants.

Uses These are predominantly plants for bedding schemes, but they can be used in mixed border or even in containers. They are good for children's gardens.

Tagetes Disco Series

This is a single French marigold which comes in a complete range of colours.

Tagetes 'French Vanilla'

A delightful double African marigold with large creamy-coloured flowers.

Tagetes Gem Series

This is a *T. tenuifolia* mixture, with single flowers in yellow and orange. The cultivars 'Golden Gem', 'Lemon Gem' and 'Tangerine Gem' are sold as separate colours.

Tagetes Safari Series

This is a series of double French marigolds including gold, yellow, orange and red flowers, some with mahogany markings.

THUNBERGIA
Thunbergia

This is a genus of more than 100 species. The one that is of most interest to gardeners is *T. alata*, commonly known as the black-eyed Susan. It is actually a perennial but treated like an annual. It must be said that it is welcome in the first place because of its attractive flowers, but the fact that it climbs is definitely a bonus since this is an attribute not often found in annuals. The flowers are funnel-shaped. They are orange in colour with a very noticeable black eye – hence the plant's common name. It is actually a twining plant that reaches about 2m (6ft) in height.

How to obtain Black-eyed Susans are sometimes seen for sale in garden centres and nurseries, but the way to be certain of getting plants is to grow your own from seed. This is readily obtainable from seed merchants

Cultivation Black-eyed Susans can be grown in open ground so long as the soil is moisture-retentive but well drained. A good-quality potting compost (soil mix) should be used for containers.

Tagetes 'Golden Gem'

Tagetes erecta 'Golden Jubilee'

Thunbergia alata

This plant needs to be sited in a warm sunny place. If you are able to keep it warm, move it inside for the winter and reuse it the following year. Z10.
Propagation Sow the seed under glass in early spring at 18–21°C (64–70°F).
Uses The black-eyed Susan can be used in any position where a climbing plant is required. It can be grown up a wigwam of branches in a bedding display or it can climb up a similar structure in a container.

Thunbergia alata

This is the climbing plant described above. The flowers are usually orange or deep yellow although they can also be cream. Most have black eyes but some lack these. It is usually grown as the species but it is sometimes offered as a cultivar such as 'Suzie Hybrids' which is not much different from the species.

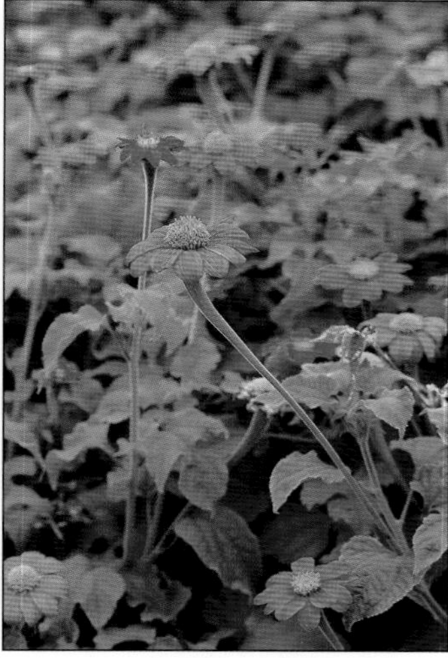

Tithonia rotundifolia 'Goldfinger'

Other plants *Thunbergia gregorii* is another climbing perennial that is treated as an annual. This is similar to the above but lacks the dark eye. It is not so commonly available.

TITHONIA
Mexican sunflower

This is a genus of about ten annuals and perennials of which one, *T. rotundifolia*, is grown in our gardens. This is not seen anywhere as near as often as it should be since it is a superb plant and those who grow it often rank it as one of their favourites. As with so many annuals, this has daisy-like flowers. In this case the outer ring of petals is a wonderful rich orange and the inner disc is yellow. The flowers are quite large, being up to about 7cm (3in) or more across. They appear at the end of upright stems which swell noticeably just below the flower head. The plants are bushy and well branched. They are big plants and fill a big impressive space in the border. H 2m (6ft) when growing well, S 45cm (18in) or more.
How to obtain Mexican sunflowers are sometimes seen for sale as plants, but they do not like being confined for too long in a small pot. It is better to buy seed, which is readily available, and grow your own.
Cultivation Plant out after the threat of frosts has passed. These plants need a rich, moist, but free-draining soil and a sunny position. They may need support in exposed positions. Z9.
Propagation Sow the seed under glass at 13–18°C (55–64°F). Do not sow too early, late spring is the right time.
Uses Mexican sunflowers can be used as bedding material but they work best in mixed borders. They can be used in drifts, but a well-grown single specimen can be very impressive. They can be grown in containers, but they must be big.

Tithonia rotundifolia

The species, which is described above, is often grown. There are also a few cultivars. 'Goldfinger' is a more compact plant growing only 75cm (30in) high, making it more suited to bedding. 'Early Yellow' is the same height but with yellow flowers, while 'Torch' is double this height and has large reddish-orange flowers. 'Arcadian Blend' is a mixture of yellow, gold and orange. The single-coloured cultivars tend to look better.

TORENIA
Wishbone flower

This is a genus containing about 50 species of which, as so often happens, only one is widely grown in the garden. In this case it is *T. fournieri*. This is a bushy plant with masses of trumpet-shaped flowers, which can smother the plant to the extent that the leaves can hardly be seen. The flowers have a pale blue upper lip and a velvety, darker blue-purple lower one. They flower over a long period from midsummer well into autumn. H 30cm (12in) S 20cm (8in).
How to obtain Plants are not often seen for sale but seed is offered by a number of seed merchants. Torenias are not as popular as they once were, so you may have to search for them.
Cultivation Plant out in a rich moist soil in a sheltered position that is lightly shaded. Any good-quality potting compost (soil mix) is suitable for plants used in containers. Do not set these outside before the danger of frosts has been lifted. Z9.
Propagation Sow the seed in mid-spring under glass at 16–18°C (60–64°F).
Uses Torenias can be used as bedding plants in a shady position. They are also very suitable for containers.

Torenia fournieri

This is the main species grown. Seed can be obtained as the species or as one of several cultivars which have different coloured flowers. The Clown Series has pink, white and purple flowers in its mixture. Panda Series is similar except that the plants are more compact, reaching only about 20cm (8in) in height. 'Pink Panda' has pink flowers.

Other plants *Torenia flava* is sometimes seen on offer as seed. This is a spreading plant which is suitable for hanging baskets. It has small flowers which are a velvety-yellow. You may find them sold under the alternative name of 'Suzy Wong'.

Torenia fournieri Clown Series

Annuals for window boxes

Ageratum	*Lobelia*
Antirrhinum	*Myosotis*
Begonia	*Nicotiana*
Bidens	*Nolana humifusa*
Cerinthe	*Petunia*
Chrysanthemum	*Pelargonium*
Erysimum cheiri	*Schizanthus*
Exacum affine	*Tagetes*
Felicia amelloides	*Verbena*
Helichrysum	*Viola*

Tropaeolum majus

TROPAEOLUM

Nasturtium

There can be few gardeners who are not familiar with the delightful plants of this genus. There are getting on for 90 species in it, many of which are perennials that make excellent garden plants, but there is one annual in particular which is the darling of the annual grower. This is *T. majus* and its cultivars and hybrids. The typical plant has flame-red trumpet-shaped flowers, but there are quite a few variations on this. It is a trailing or climbing plant and can be used to hang from containers or scramble up through low shrubs. It is an excellent plant for covering large areas. H and S 3m (10ft) or more.

How to obtain You can buy plants but it is better to buy seed. This gives you better plants as well as a much larger choice.

Cultivation Any reasonable garden soil will be sufficient, since nasturtiums will grow in quite poor conditions. A position in full sun is best but plants often self-sow if in light shade. Z8.

Propagation Sow the seed in the spring in the open ground where the plants are to flower.

Uses Nasturtiums are versatile plants that can be used as bedding or in a mixed border. They can be allowed to spread across the ground or a support to climb up. Nasturtiums are good for covering large areas of bare earth. They can be grown in containers, but they must be large.

Tropaeolum majus

The species is often grown in its own right, but it also has a large number of cultivars and hybrids. In these the trumpets may be red, orange, yellow or cream, usually with contrasting markings in the throat. In recent times there has also been a tendency for breeders to produce plants with variegated foliage; some have splashes of pale yellow and others have darker gold markings.

Cultivars worth considering include: the Alaska Series which has creamy-white variegated leaves and a mixture of flower colours; 'Empress of India', a dwarf plant only 30cm (12in) high which has semi-double red flowers; 'Peach Melba' also with semi-double flowers but this time they are a primrose-yellow colour and have orange markings; 'Red Tiger', a semi-double with orange, red-striped flowers; and 'Milkmaid', which has creamy-yellow flowers.

Other plants *Tropaeolum peregrinum* is known as the canary creeper. It is a vigorous climber that grows up to 3m (10ft), and has dainty little yellow flowers which have delicately cut petals. It is an excellent garden plant.

Ursinia anthemoides 'Solar Fire'

URSINIA

Ursinia

This is a genus containing about 40 species of perennials and a few annuals. Of these *U. anthemoides* is the main one in cultivation, although there are several others that are occasionally available. This is a plant with finely cut leaves topped by large daisy flower heads, up to 5cm (2in) or more across, carried on tall wiry stems. The ring of outer petals are deep gold or light orange with a purple spot at the base, creating an inner ring of colour. The central disc is also gold. The plants flower over a very long period. H 45cm (18in) S 30cm (12in).

How to obtain Ursinias are occasionally seen as plants for sale in garden centres and nurseries, but they are usually purchased in the form of seed from some, not all, of the seed merchants.

Cultivation Plant out when frosts have passed in a well-drained light soil. Ursinias can also be grown in a good-quality general potting compost (soil mix). Z8.

Propagation Sow the seed under glass in the early spring at 16–18°C (60–64°F).

Uses The brightness of their colour makes ursinias very suitable as bedding plants, but they can also be used in a mixed border, especially one that is devoted to hot colours.

Ursinia anthemoides

This is the brightly coloured, bushy annual described above. Cultivars such as 'Solar Fire' and 'Sunshine Blend' are sometimes seen but they are not very different from the species.

Tropaeolum peregrinum

Ursinia anthemoides 'Sunshine Blend'

Other plants Several other species in this genus are offered from time to time. These are also yellow- or orange-flowered.

VERBASCUM
Mullein

This is an enormous genus of about 360 species. A fair number of these are in cultivation either as perennials (see page 249) or as annuals. Their great attraction is the tall spikes of flowers that they carry. Some of these are discreet and only reach 60cm (24in) or so, but others are a towering 2.5m (8ft) or more. The plants can produce just one spike or several, creating a candelabra effect. On the whole the saucer-shaped flowers are yellow, but there are also white and purple variations available. The centres of the flowers are usually purple.
How to obtain You occasionally see verbascums for sale in garden centres but they dislike being in small pots for long so it is better to grow them from seed. This is widely available.
Cultivation Plant out or sow in any reasonable garden soil so long as it is free draining. In exposed positions the taller specimens may need support of some kind. Z6.
Propagation Sow the seed in the spring, in the open ground where the plants are to flower, or sow in pots and place in an open frame without heat. Plants will self-sow.
Uses The architectural quality of verbascums makes them ideal for using as focal points, especially in a mixed border. They could also be used in an imaginative bedding scheme.

Verbascum bombyciferum
This is a biennial that overwinters as a rosette and then pushes up flower stems. The flowers are a soft yellow and the leaves are covered with silvery hairs. A magnificent plant. H 2.5m (8ft).

Other plants There are several other species available, although they are not seen as frequently. *V. thapsus*, known as Aaron's rod or great mullein, is another tall plant which will happily self-sow. It has yellow flowers. *V. sinuatum* is much shorter at about 1m (3ft), but it has many branches, each coming from the base. Again it produces yellow flowers and is a very attractive plant. *V. lychnitis*, or the white mullein, has white flowers.

VERBENA
Verbena

This is a large genus of about 250 species of annuals and perennials (see page 249). Quite a number of the perennials are tender and are treated as annuals. The annuals are generally low-growing and are often sprawling, making them ideal for containers. They are grown principally for their flowers, which are carried in flat or slightly domed heads. Individually the flowers have five petals and are tubular with an open mouth, like a disc. The colours are generally shades of pink, red and purple, each with a white eye. There are also white flowers, which have a cream eye.
How to obtain Verbenas are usually bought as plants in individual pots from garden centres and nurseries. Most offer a good selection of varieties. Some are now offered as seed and these produce some interesting results.
Cultivation Plant out in any reasonable garden soil so long as it is free-draining. Use a good quality general potting compost (soil mix) for plants grown in containers. Z9.
Propagation Take cuttings in the summer and overwinter them under warm glass. Sow seed in early spring under glass at 16–18°C (60–64°F).
Uses Verbenas are excellent all-round plants for the garden. They can be used as bedding plants or grown in a mixed border, and they can also be used to great effect in all types of containers including hanging baskets.

Verbena 'Peaches and Cream'

Verbena × hybrida
Most cultivars sold in garden centres come under this heading. They are often offered in series which have mixed colours, such as Derby Series, which are 25cm (10in) high and come in pink and red shades. Novalis Series are the same size but with a wider range of colours. Separate colours are available. Sandy Series and Romance Series are similar. Individual colours are also available, as in the delectable 'Peaches and Cream', which has pink and creamy flowers.

Other plants Other plants to explore include the bright red *V. peruvianna* as well as individual cultivars such as the beautiful *V.* 'Silver Anne' and *V.* 'Sissinghurst'.

Verbascum

Verbena 'Aphrodite'

Verbena 'Sandy Scarlet'

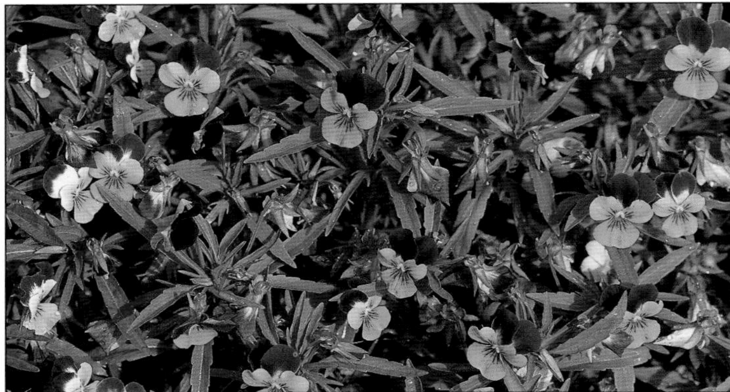
Viola tricolor

VIOLA
Viola

This is a vast genus containing 500 species. Many of them are in cultivation as perennials (see pages 250–251). However, there is one that is widely grown as an annual and that is the pansy *V.* × *wittrockiana*. This has long been a favourite in gardens, and was once the subject of heated competitions. Pansies tend to be rather sprawling plants with large flowers which often seem to resemble cheeky faces. Nearly all colours are represented, and usually more than one colour is present in each flower. They have long flowering periods, and there are pansies for all times of the year, including winter. Size varies but it is usually in the range of 15–25cm (6–10in) in height and up to 30cm (12in) in spread. Given the opportunity pansies will scramble up the other plants and reach greater heights.

How to obtain Plants are frequently available as bedding packs or individual pots in garden centres and nurseries as well as other outlets such as gas stations. Seed is also widely available and offers a better range.

Propagation Sow seed in early spring under glass at 13–16°C (55–60°F).

Cultivation Any reasonable garden soil will do but it must be moisture-retentive if the plants are set out in full sun. They will also grow in light shade. Trim them back if they get leggy (produce long bare stems). Z6.

Uses Pansies can be used anywhere in the garden, as bedding, in mixed borders or in containers.

Viola* × *wittrockiana

This is the main annual viola, although it is, in fact, a perennial. There are many cultivars available. Mixtures such as Joker Series also come as individual colours ('Jolly Joker' for example), and there are individual cultivars. These include 'Pretty', with its yellow and mahogany flowers, and 'Scarlet Orange Duet', with its red and orange flowers. The colour range is extensive, but the flowers usually have a yellow eye and frequently have black patches. The best way of looking at these plants is to get the seed merchant's catalogues, which contain hundreds of possibilities.

Other plants The tiny-flowered *Viola tricolor*, commonly known as heartsease, is an annual that is well worth growing. There are several cultivars. They include single-colour flowers, such as 'Bowles' Black' or bicolours. This plant self-sows.

XERANTHEMUM
Xeranthemum

This is a small genus of about six species of annuals, of which one is grown in gardens. These plants were once more widely cultivated, but like so many old-fashioned annuals they are somewhat out of fashion at the moment. This is a pity since they are very attractive, everlasting flowers.

There is quite a wide range of colours, which is based on shades of pink, red and purple. The flowers are daisy-like with an outer ring of coloured petals and a coloured central disc. H 60cm (24in) S 30cm (12in).

How to obtain Xeranthemum are occasionally seen sold as plants but the surest way to obtain them is from seed. This is offered by many seed merchants.

Cultivation Plant Xeranthemum out after the frosts have passed in any reasonable, free-draining garden soil. Give these plants a sunny position. Z9.

Propagation Sow the seed in the spring under glass at 16–18°C (60–64°F).

Uses These can be used as bedding plants or in a mixed border. They make excellent cut flowers and are perfect for drying.

Xeranthemum annuum

This species is still widely grown. It has both single and double flowers, which can be up to 5cm (2in) across, but are more often only 2cm (¾in). There are some cultivars: 'Snow Lady', which has white flowers; 'Superbissima' (rich purple); 'Lilac Stars' (lilac); and 'Cherry Ripe' (mixture of bright colours). These plants tend to flower over a very long period from midsummer well into autumn. The silvery-green leaves are covered with fine hairs.

Xeranthemum annuum 'Superbissima'

Xeranthemum annuum

Zea mays

ZEA
Maize

This well-known genus has four species. One of them, *Z. mays*, is the much-cultivated maize which is used as a cereal crop throughout the world. Although it is widely grown in the vegetable garden, it is also grown as a decorative plant because it has both interesting foliage and colourful seed heads. The leaves are strap-like and hang down. In some cultivars they are variegated. The seed is carried in large heads, which are commonly known as corn-on-the-cob. The cases split open to display the ranks of individual corn grains. These are normally yellow but can include many other colours, making them look very decorative. The flowers are like silken tassels. These plants are tall and can reach 4m (12ft) but they are generally only half of this.

How to obtain Decorative maize is sometimes seen for sale, although it is best to grow your own plants from the wide variety of seed that is offered.

Cultivation Plant out after the last frosts in a fertile, free-draining soil. These plants require a position in full sun. Z10.

Propagation The seed can be sown, in spring, directly in the soil where the plants are to grow or sown individually in pots under glass at 18°C (64°F).

Uses Decorative maize makes a good foliage or decorative plant for the back of a mixed border. It can be used as temporary hedge.

Zea mays

This is the only species widely grown. It has been described above. It is usually sold as cultivars, either for the vegetable garden or for decorative purposes. 'Harlequin' has striped foliage in green, white and red, and corn in a deep red. Another variegated foliage plant is 'Variegata', whose leaves are striped with white. 'Strawberry Corn' has a mixture of yellow and red corn.

ZINNIA
Zinnia

The annuals of this genus of 20 species are still popular and there are many different varieties available. They are grown for their showy flowers, which are like large daisies with wide petals. They are often semi-doubles or doubles. There is a wide range of colours. Unusually, this includes green, but shades of yellow, orange, red and purple are more common. In good specimens the flowers can be up to 12cm (4½in) across. Their long stems make them suitable for cutting. H 75cm (30in) S 30cm (12in).

How to obtain Zinnias are frequently offered for sale as plants in individual pots at garden centres, nurseries and other outlets. They are also available in a wide range of seed from most seed merchants.

Propagation Sow the seed in mid-spring under glass at 13–18°C (55–64°F).

Cultivation Plant out only after all danger of frosts has passed. Choose a fertile soil to which plenty of well-rotted organic material has been added. Zinnias must have a warm and sunny position. Deadheading helps them to flower over a long period. Z10.

Uses They make excellent bedding plants or can be used in mixed borders. They can also be grown in larger containers, such as tubs.

Zinnia elegans

This is the taller of the two species commonly cultivated and the flowers are usually larger. The species is rarely grown in its own right; it is much more commonly seen as one of its many cultivars. These are generally offered as mixtures. Some, including the Profusion Series are also available as individual colours such as 'Profusion White' and 'Profusion Cherry'. The Dasher Series is similar, with 'Dasher Orange'. There are several dwarf series: Peter Pan Series, Short Stuff Series and Small Wonder Series. Some cultivars are single coloured, such as the pale green 'Envy'.

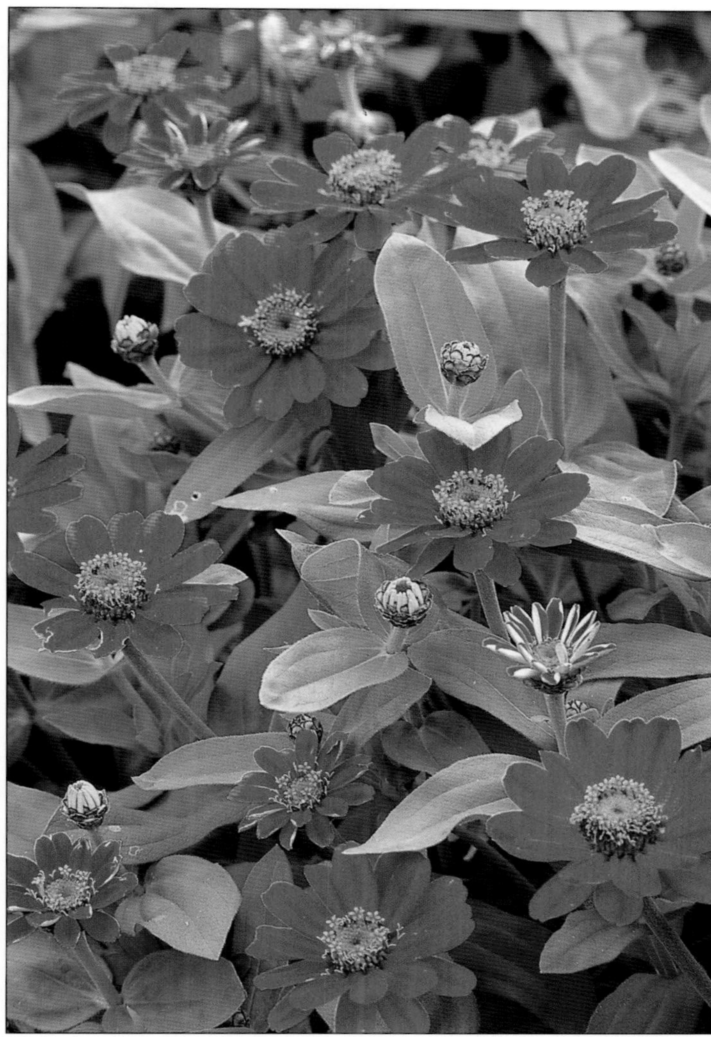
Zinnia elegans 'Profusion Cherry'

Zinnia haageana

This is still often referred to by its former name, *Z. angustifolia*. The plants are not as big as the previous ones, but they also have broad petals. These are usually bright orange, but yellow and mahogany-red also feature among the cultivars. 'Orange Star' has pure, deep orange flowers; 'Persian Carpet' has semi-double and double flowers that are yellow or orange, splashed with mahogany.

Zinnia elegans 'Profusion White'

Zinnia elegans 'Dasher Orange'

A directory of perennials

This section provides a highly illustrated listing of the many perennials that are now available. It demonstrates very clearly just how versatile these long-lasting plants can be – providing every conceivable colour of bloom, structural shape and foliage type to help create wonderful effects in any style or size of garden.

English (common) names are given throughout this directory but increasingly the majority of plants are becoming known by their Latin or botanical names. Thus although *Agapanthus* was previously (and still is occasionally, particularly in books) known as African blue lily, it is referred to by most gardeners simply as agapanthus in the same way that *Hosta* has become hosta and *Iris* iris.

The hardiness zones given in the text refer only to the selected main plants featured and not to the whole genus. The height and spread given for each of the plants is an indication only. The dimensions will vary depending on the growing conditions and the vigour of the individual plants. The spread is particularly difficult to predict since many plants go on increasing their width throughout their lives.

One of the best geraniums for the front of a border is the colourful *Geranium cinereum* 'Ballerina', which flowers over a long period.

ACANTHUS

Bear's Breeches

There are about 30 species in this wonderful genus of which only four or five are commonly grown. The joy of these plants is their tall, architectural shapes. They are clump-forming, and produce spikes of smoky-coloured, hooded flowers. The large leaves are deeply divided and in some species are tipped with spines. These plants are ideal focal points for borders or elsewhere in the garden. They also make excellent cut and dried flowers.

Cultivation They will grow in any garden soil that is reasonably fertile in either full sun or partial shade. Z8.

Propagation From seed sown in pots in autumn or spring, or from root cuttings taken in early winter. Self-sown seedlings can also be transplanted while they are still young. Division is also possible but it can be heavy work to divide large plants.

Acanthus hungaricus
(A. balcanicus)
The flowers of this plant are pinkish-white with purple hoods, while the large leaves are dark green with narrow spineless leaflets. H and S 1.2m (4ft).

Acanthus mollis
Tall spikes of purple-hooded white flowers are carried over a clump of soft, dark green leaves with broad, spineless leaflets. H 1.5m (5ft) S 60cm (24in).

Acanthus spinosus
This produces very tall spikes of striking white flowers with purple hoods. The leaves are deeply cut

Acanthus hungaricus

Acanthus mollis

with softish spines on the tips of the leaflets. H 1.5m (5ft) S 60cm (24in). There is a shorter form, *A. spinosissimus*, which has very deeply divided leaves with sharp spines. The leaves make this a dramatic plant, but it can be difficult to weed around.

Other plants For the keen gardener, *A. dioscoridis* (pink flowers with green hoods) and *A. hirsutus* (yellow flowers, green hoods) are well worth exploring.

ACHILLEA

Yarrow

There are 85 species of yarrow as well as a considerable number of cultivars. Not all the species are of interest to the gardener, indeed

Acanthus spinosus

Achillea 'Fanal'

Achillea 'Moonshine'

some are weeds, but amongst their number are some first-class plants that most gardeners will appreciate. Many have a wonderful calm quality; their flat plates of flowers often seem to float above the other plants, creating a sea of tranquillity in the hurly-burly of the border. The predominant colour is yellow, but there are a number of white species and a few reds and terracottas among the cultivars. They make very good dried flowers.

Cultivation Yarrows prefer a sunny position and any reasonable garden soil. Some species need staking as they flop over. Z2–5.

Propagation Nearly all the main species and varieties can easily be increased by division or from basal cuttings taken in spring.

***Achillea* 'Fanal'**
An attractive cultivar with brilliant red flowers. H 75cm (30in) S 60cm (24in).

Achillea filipendulina
A tall, elegant species with large flat heads of golden yellow floating 1.2m (4ft) above the ground. S 60cm (24in).

Achillea filipendulina

Achillea millefolium
The species is best avoided (except in a spacious wild garden) since it is invasive, but there are a number of excellent cultivars suitable for flower beds and borders. They include 'Cerise Queen' (cerise), 'Fire King' (bright red), 'Lilac Beauty' (lilac), 'Paprika' (orange-red). H 60cm (24in) S 60cm (24in).

***Achillea* 'Moonshine'**
This is an excellent cultivar with pale yellow flowers over soft grey foliage. However, it is not the strongest of plants and needs renewing every two or three years. H and S 60cm (24in).

Achillea ptarmica
A tall spreading plant with small heads of white flowers. It is normally grown in the attractive form 'Boule de Neige' which has double flowers. H 60cm (24in) S 1.2m (4ft).

Achillea 'Taygetea'

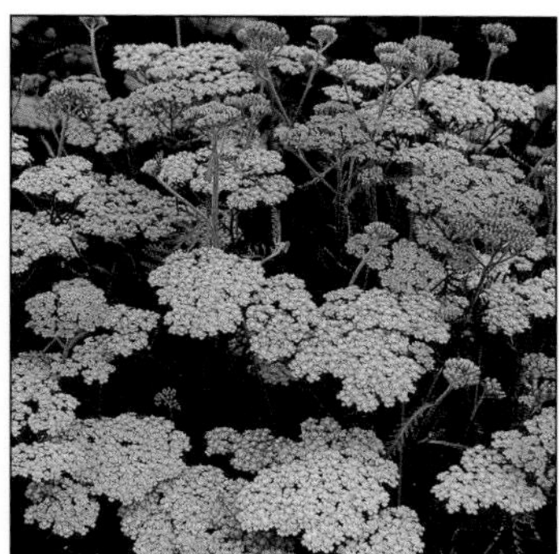
Achillea 'Terracotta'

Achillea 'Taygetea'
This clump-forming plant has wide heads of sulphur yellow flowers carried on 60cm (24in) stems. The feathery leaves are greenish grey. S 60cm (24in).

Achillea 'Terracotta'
The best of the terracotta-coloured varieties. It has large flat heads floating 60–75cm (24–30in) above the ground and forming clumps. S 60cm (24in).

ACONITUM
Monkshood
This is a genus of about 100 species and 50 cultivars. They are very beautiful plants but unfortunately beneath this beauty is hidden poison – most parts of the plant are toxic if eaten. Avoid planting these if young children are likely to visit your garden, and in any case be careful where you site them. The plants are related to delphiniums and they have the same type of flower spikes carrying mainly bright blue flowers. The flowers are hooded, hence the plant's name, and also come in white and yellow.
Cultivation Aconitum prefer cool, partially shaded conditions but they will tolerate full sun if the soil is kept moist. They like a soil made rich with well-rotten organic material. Z3–6.
Propagation Sow seed in pots, preferably in autumn. The plants can also easily be divided in spring although they may take a while to settle down.

Aconitum 'Bressingham Spire'
A cultivar of proven track record with spikes that reach up to 1m (3ft) in height. The flowers are a rich violet blue. It flowers in late summer and into the autumn. S 30cm (12in).

Aconitum × *cammarum* 'Bicolor'
This is an intriguing plant with blue and white flowers that appear towards the end of summer. H 1.2m (4ft) S 50cm (20in). 'Grandiflorum Album' has large white flowers.

Aconitum carmichaelii
A long-used garden species with a number of valuable cultivars. It is a tall species, up to 1.8m (6ft), with deep blue flowers that appear from midsummer onwards. S 30cm (12in). 'Arendsii' is one of the best-known cultivars; it flowers slightly earlier than the species. 'Kelmscott' is another excellent cultivar; it has lighter blue flowers.

Aconitum hemsleyanum
This is different from the other species in that it is a climber that twines up supports or through shrubs. It has deep violet blue flowers from midsummer onwards. H 2–2.5m (6–8ft) S 1–1.2m (3–4ft).

Aconitum 'Ivorine'
One of the best of the non-blue monkshoods, this plant has beautiful pale creamy-yellow flowers that appear from spring into early summer. H 1m (3ft) S 60cm (24in).

Aconitum napellus

Aconitum 'Stainless Steel'

Aconitum napellus
A good species that has produced a number of excellent cultivars. The species has deep blue flowers but there is a cultivar 'Albiflorus with pure white spikes. H 1.5m (5ft) S 30cm (12in).

Aconitum 'Spark's Variety'
A tall variety up to 1.5m (5ft) high with large spires of deep blue flowers that are carried from mid-summer onwards. S 60cm (24in).

Other plants Other pleasing cultivars worth checking out include *Aconitum* 'Eleonara' and *A.* 'Stainless Steel'.

ACTAEA
Baneberry
Actaeas have been grown for generations, mainly for their coloured berries. However, what most gardeners have known as *Cimifuga* has now been added to the genus, giving it a group of spectacular flowering plants. The original actaeas are relatively short, clump-forming plants with little, white tufts of flowers that are followed by white, black or red berries. The cimifugas are much taller (up to 2m/6ft) and have striking, tall spikes of white flowers over attractive foliage.
Cultivation All actaeas like a woodland-type, moisture-retentive soil. The original actaeas are true woodlanders and like partial shade. The cimifugas like partial shade, but will tolerate more sun if the soil is not dry. Z3.
Propagation The easiest method of increase is by division in spring. Actaeas can also be grown from seed as long as it is sown fresh.

Actaea pachypoda (syn. *A. alba*)
An actaea that flowers in the spring and then produces a head of white berries in the late summer, when it is at its best. H 1m (3ft) S 50cm (20in).

Actaea racemosa
One of the tallest cimifugas with good green foliage and white flower spikes that resemble fire-works going off. The flowers appear in summer. H 2.5m (8ft) S 50cm (20in).

Actaea rubra
Similar to *A. pachypoda* except that it has red berries in autumn. An excellent woodland plant. H 50cm (20in) S 30cm (12in).

Actaea simplex
An excellent cimifuga type with tall white spikes of flowers in autumn and green foliage. H 1.2m (4ft) S 60cm (24in). The leaves are deep purple in some of the cultivars; 'Brunette' is a fine example of this. 'Elstead' is another attractive cultivar in which the buds are pink before they open to white flowers.

Actaea racemosa

ADIANTUM
Maidenhair fern

A romantic name for a romantic fern. The great attraction of this fern is its delicately cut fronds. They are usually carried on black or deep purple stems which set off the fresh green of the leaves perfectly. They are deciduous and when the new fronds first uncurl in spring they have a delightful pinkish tinge. These plants are best placed in a choice position where they can be easily seen.

Adiantum is a large genus of around 250 species of which 20 or so are in general cultivation. Many are frost tender but those listed below are hardy.

Cultivation These are delicate plants and so should be sited out of direct midday sunlight. They like a cool, moist root-run with plenty of leaf mould in the soil. Remove the old foliage in the late winter before the new growth begins to unfurl. Z5–8.

Propagation The plants can be grown from spore but division in spring is the easiest method.

Adiantum aleuticum

Individual leaflets are arranged in columns on either side of the black wiry midribs, giving the appearance of a long, deeply cut leaf. H 30cm (12in), slowly spreading to form a small clump (30cm/12in). The form 'Japonicum' has beautiful browny-red fronds when they first open.

Adiantum pedatum

This has similar fronds to the previous species, except that they are larger and more upright. H 45cm (18in), slowly spreading into a small clump (45cm/18in).

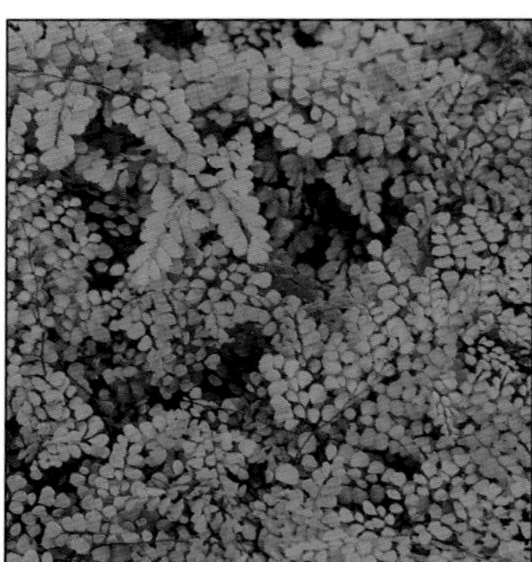

Adiantum venustum

Adiantum venustum

The gem of the genus. It has deeply divided, filigree fronds, with the black midribs showing up in beautiful contrast to the green of the foliage. H 23cm (9in) S 30cm (12in).

Other plants In frost-free areas or for conservatory or greenhouse use try *Adiantum raddianum* or one of its many cultivars.

AGAPANTHUS
African blue lily

A very attractive genus of about ten species. There are many cultivars, at least one of which no garden should be without. The flowers are tubular, usually blue and carried in a globe, up to 20cm (8in) across, at the top of a tall, leafless stem. The foliage is strap-like and erupts from the base of the plant like a fountain. Agapanthus make excellent plants for the border or for containers. They flower in summer and make good cut flowers. The majority are hardy.

Cultivation They will grow in any reasonably fertile soil in full sun. Although they prefer a moist soil they will tolerate a degree of dryness. In cold areas they will appreciate a warm mulch during the winter. Z7.

Propagation Although they can be grown from seed sown in autumn they are more reliable grown from divisions taken in spring.

Agapanthus campanulatus

Agapanthus 'Castle of Mey'

Agapanthus africanus

A late-summer species with deep blue flowers. The flower stems reach 1m (3ft) tall S 50cm (20in). 'Albus' has white flowers.

Agapanthus 'Blue Giant'

Excellent blue-coloured flowers carried on tall (1.2m/4ft) stems. S 50cm (20in).

Agapanthus campanulatus

A fine species that has produced a number of popular cultivars. It produces large (up to 20cm/8in) heads of variable blue or white flowers in mid to late summer. H 60–120m (2–4ft) S 50cm (20in). 'Isis' is one of the most popular cultivars with deep blue flowers in late summer. The variety *albidus* has white flowers.

Agapanthus 'Castle of Mey'

This is a shorter variety that carries lovely deep blue flowers. It blooms in mid to late summer,

Agapanthus 'Dorothy Palmer'

and is excellent placed in a position at the front of a border. H 60cm (24in) S 30cm (12in).

Agapanthus 'Gayle's Lilac'

This has lilac flowers so it is good for those who want a paler form. H 60cm (24in) S 30cm (12in). *A.* 'Golden Rule' has yellow edges to its strap-like leaves. The flowers are light blue and appear mid to late summer. H 60cm (24in) S 30cm (12in).

Agapanthus Headbourne hybrids

This term covers a collection of hybrids of varying blues, originally selected by Lewis Palmer for their hardiness. 'Loch Hope' is an excellent tall variety. It has deep blue flowers which appear from late summer into autumn. H 1.5m (5ft) S 50cm (20in). 'Peter Pan' is a short form, suitable for small pots. H 60cm (24in) S 30cm (12in).

Other plants There are many more cultivars to explore, including 'Dorothy Palmer'. Nearly all are worth considering.

Agapanthus 'Loch Hope'

Agastache foeniculum

Agastache 'Honey Bee White'

AGASTACHE
Mexican bergamot

This genus is not seen as often as it deserves to be. This is probably because the plants are short lived in moist soils. However, they self-sow and once you have them you are rarely without them. There are about 30 species but only a few are cultivated. The foliage is aromatic making this a pleasant plant to weed around. Another joy is the delightful spikes of flowers, which bloom from midsummer into autumn. Each plant sends up plenty of upright stems, the top of which is covered in whorls of bright blue, white, pink or red flowers. They are excellent for gravel gardens.

Agastache foeniculum 'Blue and White'

Cultivation These are plants from dry hills and so they like a well-drained soil in full sun. Z8.
Propagation They can readily be grown from seed, sown inside or scattered where the plants are to grow. They will self-sow if the conditions are right. Basal cuttings can be taken in spring.

***Agastache foeniculum* (syn. *A. anisata*)**
This can be a tall species when grown in a reasonably rich soil. The mint-like leaves smell of aniseed, and the flowers are a wonderful dusky dark blue. H 1.5m (5ft) S 50cm (20in). There are a number of cultivars the most popular being 'Alabaster' with white flowers. 'Blue and White' is also often grown.

Agastache mexicana
This is the other main hardy species in cultivation. It has pink to dark red flowers over a long period in late summer and often beyond. H 1m (3ft) S 30cm (12in). There are several cultivars including 'Mauve Beauty' with lilac-mauve flowers. 'Champagne' has fine fizzy spikes of creamy-white flowers.

Alchemilla conjuncta

Alchemilla mollis

Other plants These are the main species but it is worth exploring *Agastache rugosa* and *A. urticifolia* among others. 'Honey Bee White' is another cultivar to try.

ALCHEMILLA
Lady's mantle

A large genus of 250 species of which a number are in cultivation. Their attraction is that they are good both as flowering and foliage plants. The flowers are small but grouped in clusters; in some cases they form tight clusters, in others airy sprays. The flowers are a yellowy lime-green. This contrasts well with the green foliage which is rounded and pleated. In some species the foliage is more deeply cut. Alchemilla is a perfect plant for growing along paths or on the banks of ponds.

Alchemilla elizabethae

Cultivation Any reasonably fertile soil will do for this plant. It will grow in either full sun or partial shade. Cut back to the ground after flowering to prevent seeding and to promote new foliage. Z6.
Propagation Self-seeds, but it can be propagated from seed sown in spring or from divisions.

Alchemilla conjuncta
A mat-forming plant with very distinctive foliage. The deeply lobed leaves are green but edged with silver. It is low-growing, only reaching about 20cm (8in) unless it is scrambling through another plant. S 30cm (12in)

Alchemilla mollis
A common but excellent plant. It is floppy but reaches about 45cm (18in) in height. It has a lovely scent when you are up close. The flowers appear in early to midsummer and the plant should then be cut back. S 45cm (18in).

Other plants The above are the main species but there are plenty more that are worth growing, especially the low, mat-growing ones. Try *Alchemilla alpina, A. elizabethae,* or *A. ellenbeckii* with its red stems.

Perennials for seaside gardens

Artemisia
Centranthus
Crambe maritima
Crocosmia
Echinops
Erigeron
Eryngium
Geranium
Kniphofia
Lathyrus
Limonium
Linaria
Origanum
Osteospermum
Papaver
Perovskia
Persicaria affinis
Phormium
Sisyrinchium
Yucca

Allium cristophii

ALLIUM
Ornamental onions

This very large genus of bulbs (more than 700 species) has a deservedly popular place in hardy borders. Alliums are very decorative and are best placed so that they pop up between or through other plants. Although some have lax heads the majority of popular species have round globes of flowers, 25cm (10in) or more across.

Most have purple flowers but there are others with blue, white, pink or yellow heads. There are species that flower at all times between spring and autumn. Most have strap-like foliage. However, this can be rather ugly since it is often dying back just as the flowers are coming into bloom. Hide the plants amongst other plants in the middle of the border so that the dying leaves will not be visible.

Cultivation Alliums will grow in most soils except extremely wet ones. They are perfect for dry soils such as gravel borders. They like full sun. Z3–8.

Propagation Alliums generally increase with little help from the gardener. They can be grown from seed or from the bulbils that often appear in the flower heads. The easiest way is to divide off the little bulblets that develop around the main bulb.

Allium roseum

Allium carinatum **subsp. *pulchellum***
A beautiful flower with a shower of drooping pink to purple flowers that appear over a long period in the autumn. The grass-like foliage can be confused with weeds early in the year. H 45cm (18in) S 8–10cm (3–4in).

Allium cristophii.
Very impressive purple flowers that are large and globe-like. They make good dried flowers. H 60cm (24in) S 20cm (8in).

Allium hollandicum
A medium-sized spherical-headed onion for the spring border. The flowers are purple. This plant is best known in its form 'Purple Sensation' which has an almost luminous quality. H 1m (3ft) S 10cm (4in).

Allium roseum
A charming allium which is best grown so that it peeps up through other plants. It has lax heads of only a few flowers, but these are of a most delicate pink. They appear in summer. The plant has bulbils and can be slightly invasive. However, it rarely causes problems especially if the bulbils are removed before they ripen. H 1m (3ft) S 10cm (4in).

Allium schoenoprasum
This is the humble chive. It flowers briefly but profusely in the early summer, when it is a perfect choice for lining paths. The flowers are purple but in the form 'Forescate' they are brighter and more rosy-pink. Shear to the ground after flowering to encourage new foliage. H 30cm (12in) S 10cm (4in).

Allium schoenoprasum

Allium sphaerocephalon
This allium has bright reddish flowers that are compressed into a tight ball. It flowers in summer and is excellent planted amongst other plants. H 75cm (30in) S 10cm (4in).

Other plants There are many, many more species of allium to choose from and it is worth making a note of any pleasing ones that you see as you go round gardens. Be aware that some of the smaller ones can become a little invasive.

ALSTROEMERIA
Peruvian lily

Alstroemeria are known mainly as cut flowers, but increasingly, they are becoming popular as a garden plant. There are 20 species and about 100 garden-bred cultivars.

The plants are summer-flowering, producing masses of funnel-shaped flowers. They vary in colour from yellows and oranges to pinks and reds, with most having a mixture of two or more colours. The throats are distinctively streaked or spotted. As well as being suitable for growing in the greenhouse for cutting, most make good garden plants. They are ideally placed in the middle of the border.

Cultivation Alstroemerias like a moist soil with plenty of organic material added to it. They should be in full sun, although they will tolerate a little shade. Slugs can be a nuisance. Z7.

Propagation These plants can be grown from seed, but the most usual method of propagation is by division.

Alstroemeria aurea

Alstroemeria ligtu hybrids

Alstroemeria aurea
These are the most commonly seen Peruvian lilies in gardens and possibly the hardiest. The flowers are bright orange, streaked with reddish brown. They get up to 45cm (18in) high. S 60cm (24in). There are several cultivars: 'Lutea' has flowers of bright yellow with brownish spots.

Alstroemeria ligtu
A pink-flowered hardy species that is mainly grown in the form of ligtu hybrids which come in a variety of colours. H 75cm (30in) S 60–100cm (2–3ft).

Alstroemeria psittacina
The flowers are not so flared as on other species, but they are intriguingly coloured in shades of green and red. H 1m (3ft) S 60cm (24in).

Other plants There are many other highly coloured cultivars to explore. The best way to choose between them is to go to a specialist nursery which has plenty to offer.

ANEMONE
Anemone

This is a large genus of garden plants offering several distinct forms from tall Japanese anemones to low wood anemones. There are 120 species in the genus and most are in cultivation. For the keen gardener it is a good genus to collect since it presents interesting and varying flowers from early spring through to autumn. Most are simple open flowers but there are some lovely doubles. There are anemones of all colours except black.

Cultivation All need a moisture-retentive soil, except for the bulbous species, such as the

Anemone blanda

coronarias which need a well-drained soil. Shade is preferred by the small woodlanders and full sun by the bulbs. All the others like sun or partial shade. Z5–6.
Propagation All can be grown from seed preferably sown after it has ripened. Division is the other main method of increase.

Anemone blanda
A lovely woodland flower for early spring, with discs of blue, white or pink petals. It dies back after flowering and seeding. H 5–10cm (2–4in) S 10–15cm (4–6in).

Anemone coronaria
A tuberous anemone with bright red, blue or white spring flowers. Good for the front of a border or containers. H 5–25cm (2–10in) S 10–15cm (4–6in). The most common group of cultivars are the De Caens which are

Anemone coronaria 'Lord Lieutenant'

Anemone hupehensis 'Prinz Heinrich'

delightful. *A.c.* 'Lord Lieutenant' is also an attractive cultivar. Other bulbous species worth considering are *A.* × *fulgida* and *A. pavonina*, which have bright red forms.

Anemone* × *hybrida
(Japanese anemone)
Few gardens can wish to be without Japanese anemones which embrace several species including this hybrid. Although tall (up to 1.5m/5ft) they are wiry and do not need staking. The colours are various shades of pink and white; the white look good against green hedges. They flower from midsummer onwards. S 60cm (24in).

There are lots of good cultivars including 'Honorine Jobert' (white) and 'Königin Charlotte' (semi-double flowers).

Anemone hupehensis
(Japanese anemone)
This species is often confused with the previous one. The summer flowers are very similar in shape and colour (pinks and whites). H 1m (3ft) S 1m (3ft).

Anemone hupehensis

Anemone nemorosa

Again there are plenty of good cultivars including 'Hadspen Abundance' and 'Prinz Heinrich', both with deep pink flowers.

Anemone nemorosa
(Wood anemone, windflower)
A dainty white flower that grows well under deciduous trees and shrubs. It dies back after flowering and seeding. H 5cm (6in) S 30cm (12in). There are blue forms, such as 'Blue Bonnet'. There are also similar species (*A.* × *ranunculoides*) which have bright yellow flowers.

Other plants For the enthusiast there are plenty of other species, such as *AA. polyanthes, rivularis, sylvestris* and *trullifolia*.

ANTHEMIS
Anthemis

This genus provides some of the mainstays of the summer border: fresh-looking daisies in a range of colours from white through cream to yellow and orange. All have a yellow or golden central disc. The flowers are carried on wiry stems up to 1m (3ft) high. The foliage is generally deeply cut and in some cases very attractive. Many have a tendency to reflex (curl back) their petals at night so they are not good plants to choose if you see your garden only in the evening. For the daytime border, however, their bright cheerfulness is indispensable.
Cultivation Anthemis need a fertile, moisture-retentive soil in full sun. Some will need support unless the garden is fairly wind-free. They resent disturbance so transplant young. Z4–8.
Propagation The species can be grown from seed but cultivars are best reproduced from basal cuttings in spring.

Anthemis punctata subsp. *cupaniana*

Anthemis punctata* subsp. *cupaniana
A delightful species with white daisies which float above a mat of silver foliage in early summer. Cut the flower stems off after flowering so that you can appreciate it as a foliage plant for the rest of the summer. The leaves are almost ground hugging, but flower stems reach up to about 30cm (12in) or so in height. S 30cm (12in).

Anthemis sancti-johannis
This has striking orange flowers in summer. The plants are short lived, so be sure to take cuttings each year. H 60cm (24in) S 60cm (24in).

Anthemis tinctoria
A good species with a superb group of cultivars, whose flowers vary from golden-yellow to palest cream. H and S 1m (3ft). Cultivars worth looking out for are 'E.C. Buxton' (lemon-yellow), 'Sauce Hollandaise' (pale cream) and 'Wargrave' (pale yellow), but all are good.

Other plants Cultivars worth growing include *AA.* 'Beauty of Grallagh', 'Grallagh Gold', 'Susanna Mitchell' and Tetworth'.

Anthemis tinctoria 'E.C. Buxton'

Aquilegia 'Bunting'

AQUILEGIA
Aquilegia, columbine, granny's bonnet

Whichever of the various English names you prefer, these are delightful plants. The flowers resemble a female ballet dancer standing on tip-toe with her arms above her head. They vary from the typical blue through to different shades of white, pink, red, yellow and even greenish-brown.

These are plants of the late spring and early summer, and they look delightful when scattered among the other plants of that time of year. There are about 70 species and many cultivars from which to choose.

Cultivation Aquilegia will grow in most reasonably fertile soils. They can be grown in full sun or partial shade. Cut off the flowering stems after flowering as the foliage can still be enjoyed. Z3–6

Propagation They can easily be grown from seed, too easily perhaps as they will self-sow

Aquilegia vulgaris

Aquilegia 'Dove'

abundantly if the seed pods are left on. Self-sown seedlings may not come true, but you can get some interesting results.

Aquilegia canadensis
A delicate, relatively small-flowered variety with yellow and red blooms. H 1m (3ft) S 30cm (12in). Another attractive red and yellow species is *A. formosa*.

Aquilegia fragrans
This species produces soft pinkish-white flowers that are occasionally tinged with blue. They have a sweet fragrance that you can smell when you get close to them. The plants can become hybridized with other species and the scent lost. H 45cm (18in) S 10cm (4in).

Aquilegia longissima
This is a good yellow species with largish flowers distinguished by their very long spurs. H 1m (3ft) S 50cm (20in).

Aquilegia vulgaris 'Nora Barlow'

***Aquilegia* McKana Group**
A group of hybrids with large, mixed coloured flowers that have long spurs. H 60cm (24in) S 30cm (12in).

Aquilegia viridiflora
A delightful low-growing species with unusual greenish-brown flowers. It is best grown in groups at the front of a border or on a raised bed. H and S 30cm (12in).

Aquilegia vulgaris
The granny's bonnet
The typical plant as it grows in the wild has blue flowers but there are many cultivars with blooms in a mix of colours such as the wonderful white 'Nivea'. H 1m (3ft) S 50cm (20in). There are also double-flowered forms such as 'Nora Barlow' with green and red flowers.

Other plants The range above is fairly wide but there are still plenty of other plants that the enthusiast could look out for. They include *A. flabellata* (blue) and its wide range of cultivars, *A.* 'Hensol Harebell', *A.* 'Bunting', *A.* 'Dove' and *A. alpina*. A related genus with similar flowers but without the spurs is *Semiaquilegia*.

ARTEMISIA
Wormwood

A genus of about 300 species, many of which are weedy and certainly to be avoided in the garden. However, a number of species have some excellent cultivars that no garden should be without. Many of these are considered to be foliage plants, with most gardeners removing the flower spikes as they appear. The appeal of the foliage is firstly the

Artemisia lactiflora

Artemisia ludoviciana 'Silver Queen'

colour, which is often a beautiful silver, and secondly the cut, often a delicate filigree. These are good plants for any sunny border. They work well with soft colours, but can also be useful as foils between stronger colours.

Cultivation Artemisias are sun-loving plants and do not do well in shade. The soil should be fertile but well-drained, except for *A. lactiflora* which likes a moist soil. Z3–8.

Propagation Most are spreading forms, which are easy to increase by division. One or two are difficult to divide and are therefore best propagated by taking cuttings in spring.

***Artemisia alba* 'Canescens'**
A silver-leaved artemisia with very fine foliage that can look rather like unruly coils of silver wire. The flowers are a dirty brown and should be removed when they appear in summer. H 45cm (18in) S 30cm (12in).

Artemisia lactiflora
The odd man out since it is grown for its flowers. This plant has tall upright stems with dark green leaves. The sprays of flowers in late summer are creamy

Artemisia ludoviciana 'Valerie Finnis'

white and very attractive. H 1.5m (5ft) S 50cm (20in). It has a popular cultivar in 'Guizhou' which is prized for its foliage and stems which are purple in the early summer.

Artemisia ludoviciana
Another silver-leaved species, this time with more solid, spear-shaped leaves. The flowers are dirty yellow and are usually removed when they appear in summer. The plant can be tall, but tends to flop as it ages so it should be discreetly supported if possible. H 1m (3ft) S 60cm (24in). There are two extremely good cultivars: 'Silver Queen' and 'Valerie Finnis', either or both deserving of a place in the garden.

***Artemisia* 'Powis Castle'**
To many gardeners this is the ace in the pack. It has deeply cut, filigree leaves that are an intense sparkling silver. The yellowish flowers tend to spoil the effect and should be removed. H 60cm (24in) S 1m (3ft).

Artemisia schmidtiana
Yet another excellent plant with very narrow silver foliage. It is a lowish carpeting plant. H 45 (18in) S 60cm (24in). It has a delightful cultivar 'Nana' which only grows 10cm (4in) high.

Other plants *Artemisia arborescens, A. caucasica* and *A. stelleriana* 'Boughton Silver' are worth exploring if there is space.

ARUNCUS
Goatsbeard

These plants are probably suitable only for large gardens since their flowering season is brief and they take up space. That said they are very attractive and are well worth growing if you have space near a pond or other area where the soil is reasonably moist. The flowers are creamy-white and held in large, loose pyramidal spikes in summer for about a week or so before they start to turn brown.
Cultivation Sun or partial shade in a moisture-retentive soil. Cut back in autumn. Z3–8.
Propagation Goatsbeards should be divided in spring.

Aruncus dioicus

Aruncus aethusifolius
A dwarf form that does not get taller than 30cm (12in). Useful for small gardens. S 20cm (8in).

Aruncus dioicus
The most commonly grown goatsbeard. This is a tall, clump-forming plant that can look truly magnificent when in flower. H 2m (6ft) S 1.2m (4ft). Out of flower it makes a moderate foliage plant. It has an excellent cultivar 'Kneiffii', which is shorter (1.2m/4ft) and has very attractive, deep-cut leaves for which it is mainly grown.

ARUNDO
Giant reed

A small genus of which only one species is of interest to the general gardener. This can grow to dizzy heights, up to 5m (15ft). It makes a bold focal point in a large garden, and an excellent feature in a border if it is big enough. However, for many gardens it is most effective when used as a summer screen. This is a tall grass with strong vertical stems and broad, strap-like leaves.
Cultivation The giant reed prefers a fertile, moisture-retentive soil but it will grow in any reasonable garden soil. Like most grasses it likes full sun but needs protection from winds. It should be cut back to the ground in spring before new growth starts. Z7.
Propagation Divide the clumps in spring just before growth begins. The giant reed can also be grown from seed sown in pots.

Arundo donax

Arundo donax
This is the only species normally grown in gardens. It is tall with green leaves and stems, and purply plumes of flowers in autumn. H 3m (10ft) S 1m (3ft). Its variety *A.d. versicolor* is shorter (up to 2m/6ft) and has creamy stripes running down the length of its leaves. The cultivar 'Macrophylla' has very broad (up to 7.5cm /3in) leaves which are bluish-green in colour.

ASPLENIUM
Spleenwort

This is an enormous genus of some 700 species of evergreen and semi-evergreen ferns, and there are also a number of cultivars. Only a few species are in general cultivation so the gardener does not have too much of a problem deciding which to grow. They vary from those with typical triangular, fern-like fronds to those with wide, strap-like foliage. They are splendid plants for growing in a woodland setting or in shade and generally provide interest throughout the year.
Cultivation These plants need to be planted in a shady area, and in a moisture-retentive, but free-draining, soil.
Propagation The best method of increase is by dividing existing plants in spring. The species can also be increased by sowing spore as they ripen.

Asplenium bulbiferum
Hen and chicken fern
This plant gets its common name because it produces young plants along its fronds. The fronds are typically fern-shaped; triangular with deeply divided segments. It prefers acid soils. In really good conditions it can grow up to 1.2m (4ft) high. S 30cm (12in).

Asplenium scolopendrium
Hart's tongue fern
The most popular species with the most cultivars. As its name implies the strap-like fronds taper towards the top, like tongues. The margins are slightly wavy. It prefers alkaline soils. H 60cm (24in) S 45cm (18in). There are a number of interesting cultivars. The Crispum Group have wavy margins to the foliage, while the Cristatum Group have crests at the top of the fronds.

Asplenium trichomanes
Maidenhair spleenwort
So called because it resembles the delicate maidenhair fern in that it has small dark green, elliptic leaflets arranged either side of a dark midrib. This plant prefers alkaline soils. H 15cm (6in) S 15–30cm (6–12in).

Other plants There are a number of other species that are more suitable for the conservatory or heated greenhouse, as well as other cultivars of *A. scolopendrium* which the enthusiast can explore.

Asplenium scolopendrium

ASTER

Aster

This is a large genus of about 250 species and at least as many cultivars. It is a popular genus and many of the species are in cultivation although most gardeners grow only a few, in particular the Michaelmas daisies. Asters have daisy-like flowers with a colourful outer disc of petals and a central one of yellow. The petals cover a wide colour range from white and pink to blue and purple. Most produce multiple heads and are a mass of colour when in bloom, often for a very long time. They make very good border plants.

Cultivation Any good garden soil, preferably in sun. Many asters can suffer from mildew, but unless this is unsightly it can be ignored. Many of the floppier forms need staking, but the Michaelmas daisies are usually self-supporting, except in exposed areas. Z4–8.

Propagation Most asters are extremely easy to divide in the spring. A few like *A.* × *frikartii* are difficult to divide and basal cuttings is then the best method.

Aster alpinus

These are low, spreading plants which are excellent for the front of a border. The species has blue flowers which appear from the early summer onwards. H 25cm (10in) S 30–45cm (12–18in). There are a number of very good cultivars to try, including 'Dunkle Schöne' (deep blue) and 'White Beauty' (white).

Aster alpinus

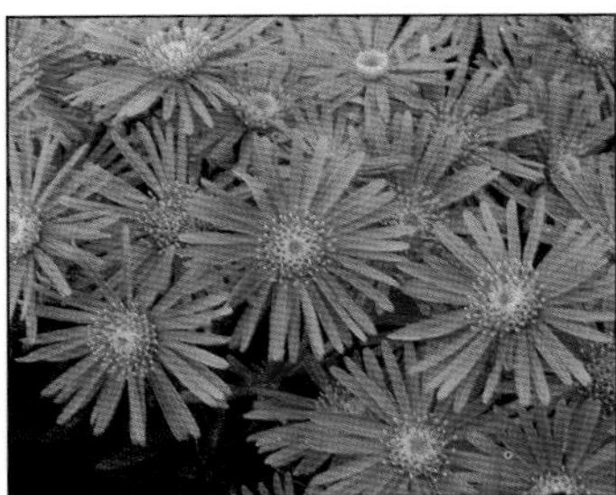

Aster amellus 'Blue King'

Aster amellus

Most of the numerous cultivars make splendid plants. They have relatively large daisies, up to 5cm (2in) across. The colours are many variations on pink and blue. Flowers appear from late summer and continue well into autumn. H and S 50cm (20in). Cultivars to look out for include 'Blue King' (blue), 'Brilliant' (pink), 'King George' (violet blue), 'Rosa Erfüllung' (pale pink), 'Rudolph Goethe' (lavender) and 'Veilchenkönigin' (violet).

Aster cordifolius

This has floating sprays of small flowers on stems up to 1.5m (5ft) high. S 1m (3ft). It is best grown in one of two cultivars: 'Silver Spray' (pale pink) or 'Sweet Lavender' (lavender-blue).

Aster ericoides

Beautiful, delicate sprays of small blue or pink flowers in autumn. H 1m (3ft) S 50cm (20in). Some superb cultivars, including 'Blue Star' (blue), 'Golden Spray' (pinkish white), 'Pink Cloud' (pink) and 'Snow Flurry' (white).

Aster* × *frikartii

An excellent hybrid of which 'Mönch' is the gem. This has large (7.5cm/3in) blue heads that

Aster × *frikartii*

Aster lateriflorus

continue from midsummer right through to the end of autumn. Its 75cm (30in) stems often need some support. S 45cm (18in). 'Wunder von Stäfa' is similar.

Aster novae-angliae

These rather coarse Michaelmas daisies make excellent tall plants for the back of the border. There are many good cultivars including 'Andenken an Alma Pötschke' (rose-pink), 'Barr's Violet' (violet blue), 'Harrington's Pink' (pink) and 'Herbstschnee' (white).

Aster novi-belgii

Michaelmas daisies

More refined and shorter than the previous species, these are suitable for the middle of the border. H 1.2m (4ft) S 60–75cm (24–30in). There are hundreds of excellent cultivars; look at them in flower to choose your favourites.

Other plants There are many other excellent species, including *AA. divaricatus, lateriflorus, sedifolius* and *tongolensis*.

ASTILBE

Astilbe

A small genus of only about 12 species, but supplemented with many additional garden forms. Astilbes are characterized by their flat tapering flower heads and deeply divided leaves. The colours of the flowers vary from pink to red by way of purple, and with a few whites and creams. They flower in summer. Although they grow well in full sun they are also good plants for lightly shaded areas. They are particularly good for growing next to ponds and other water features.

Cultivation Astilbes like moisture-retentive soils that should preferably remain damp all

Astilbe × *arendsii* 'Fanal'

through the summer. They will grow in either full sun or light shade. Z4–7.

Propagation The plants can be divided in spring.

Astilbe arendsii

A wonderful selection of cultivars from Germany. H 1m (3ft) S 60cm (24in). Among the many excellent plants on offer are 'Brautschleier' (white), 'Bressingham Beauty' (pink), 'Erica' (bright pink), 'Fanal' (dark crimson-red), 'Irrlicht' (white), 'Snowdrift' (white) and 'Venus' (bright pink).

Astilbe chinensis

This is a relatively short astilbe (up to 60cm/24in) with pink flowers. The variety *pumila* is dwarf (25cm/10in) high, making it an excellent choice for the front of a border. It has purplish-pink flowers. S 20cm (8in).

Other plants There are a large number of garden cultivars, which vary in height and flower colour.

Astilbe × *arendsii* 'Venus'

Astilbe 'Aphrodite'

Good examples to try include *A.* 'Aphrodite', *A.* × *crispa* 'Perkeo' (pink), *A.* 'Red Sentinel' (bright red), and *A.* 'Rheinland' (pink).

ASTRANTIA
Masterwort

Astrantia is a small genus of about 10 species. Only two of them are in general cultivation, but they are excellent plants and there are a number of garden cultivars. The flowers are basically greenish-white but they are generally flushed with pink or varying intensity, some dark enough to be red. They resemble pincushions surrounded by bracts. These clump-forming plants tend to reach up to 1m (3ft) in good conditions. Although they will grow in sun they are excellent plants for lightly shaded positions and flower over a long period from early summer onwards.

Cultivation Masterworts prefer moisture-retentive soil but generally do well in any reasonable garden soil. If the soil is on the dry side then a shaded position is required. Z5–8.

Propagation These plants are easy to divide in the spring. They will also grow readily from seed, but the cultivars are unlikely to come true if you use this method.

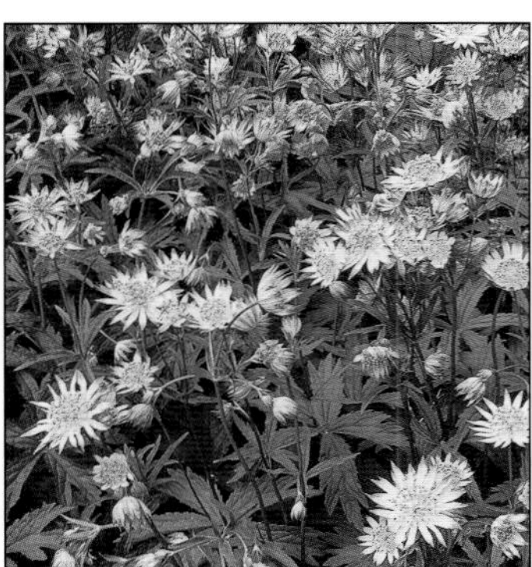
Astrantia major

Astrantia major 'Rubra'

Astrantia major

This is the main species grown with most of the cultivars derived from it. The flowers of the species have a pinkish tinge, but some of the cultivars are much stronger in colour, some even a dark red. H 60cm (24in) S 45cm (18in). Although the species is worth growing in its own right, one of the cultivars will generally give a better effect. There are many good ones to try, including 'Hadspen Blood' (deep blood-red), 'Primadonna' (pink), 'Rosensinfonie' (deep pink), 'Rubra' (red), 'Ruby Cloud' (ruby red), 'Ruby Wedding' (ruby red), 'Shaggy' (greenish white with very long surrounding bracts) and 'Sunningdale Variegated' (creamy variegations on the leaves).

Astrantia maxima

This is mainly grown as the straight species, and is well worth tracking down for its delightful shell-pink colouration. H 60cm (24in) S 30cm (12in).

ATHYRIUM
Lady fern

This is a large genus consisting of about 180 species of ferns and a number of garden cultivars. It got its English name because of the delicacy of the lacy, elegant fronds of the main garden species *A. filix-femina*. The plants are deciduous ferns whose fronds turn brown in autumn. They grow up to 1.2m (4ft) when they are well suited.

Like most ferns they prefer a shaded position and are ideal for growing in a woodland setting or in another shady position, such as in a border on the north side of the house.

Cultivation Lady ferns require a moisture-retentive soil such as you would find in a woodland. They do not like an alkaline soil, and need to be grown in light shade. Cut back the old leaves in spring before the new growth begins. Z3–5.

Propagation Division in the spring is the easiest method. Plants can also be grown from spores.

A. major 'Sunningdale Variegated'

Autumn-flowering perennials

Anemone x *hybrida*
Aster
Boltonia
Chelone
Chrysanthemum
Cimifuga
Helianthus
Kirenshonga
Liriope
Leucanthemella
Nerine
Ophiopogon
Rudbeckia
Schizostylis
Sedum
Solidago
Tricyrtis
Vernonia

Athyrium niponicum

Athyrium filix-femina

An attractive species which has a number of cultivars and is also worth growing in its own right. H 60–120cm (2–4ft) S 30–100cm (1–3ft). Among the best cultivars are the Cruciatum Group with crested fronds, the intriguing 'Frizelliae' in which the leaflets (pinnae) have been reduced to alternate, single round leaves on either side of the main rib, and the 'Minutissimum' with its smaller 30cm (12in) stems.

Athyrium niponicum

The species is in cultivation but it is the variety *pictum* which is usually seen. This is a lowish plant with the most beautifully coloured fronds. They are a metallic greeny-silver flushed with purple. H and S 30cm (12in).

Other plants There are several tender lady ferns that can be grown in a conservatory or heated greenhouse as well as a few more hardy cultivars that would make a welcome addition to the garden if you get hooked on ferns.

BAPTISIA
Baptisia

A genus of some 20 species of which only one is in general cultivation. This is *B. australis* which has a loose, lupin-like head of bright blue flowers. These appear in early summer and are set off against fresh green foliage. H 1.5m (5ft) S 60cm (24in).

Cultivation A rich, moist soil in sun or partial shade. Z5.

Propagation This is easily increased from freshly collected seed. It can also be propagated by division.

Baptisia australis

Bergenia 'Sunningdale'

Brunnera macrophylla

Brunnera macrophylla 'Dawson's White'

Bergenia 'Bressingham White'

BERGENIA
Elephant's ears

The English name is an apt description of plants in this genus of about eight species with its numerous cultivars. The key feature of the plants is the large oval leaves, which make an excellent ground cover on all types of soil and in conditions of sun or shade.

Most have shiny, evergreen leaves that glint in the sun, and many of them also turn a wonderful liverish-red during the winter. The flowers, which are produced in spikes in the early summer, are also attractive. The plants usually grow up to 45cm (18in) or sometimes a little more. S 60cm (24in).

Cultivation Bergenias prefer a moist but well-drained soil. However, they will also grow in dryish, but not drought-ridden, soils. They suit a sunny or partially shaded position. Z3–5.

Propagation You can increase these plants by division. Alternatively, place 2.5cm (1in) sections of budded rhizome in cutting compost (soil mix) until they have rooted.

Bergenia 'Ballawley'

This is a good form for winter use as the glossy green leaves take on a superb glossy purple-bronze tint throughout the winter. The spring flowers are bright red.

Bergenia 'Bressingham White'

This plant has deep green foliage surmounted by a spike of white flowers in spring.

Bergenia cordifolia

Crinkle-edged leaves that tint slightly during the winter. The flowers are an excellent magenta colour. There is a form 'Purpurea' which has darker winter leaves.

Bergenia 'Silberlicht'

Grown mainly for its flowers which are a brilliant white when newly opened but which fade to pink as they age.

Bergenia 'Sunningdale'

This is a very good winter-coloured variety with attractive carmine-coloured flowers.

Other plants There are many others to look at if you have the space. *B. ciliata* (hairy leaves) and the cultivars 'Schneekönigin' (white flowers), 'Morgenröte' (deep pink) and 'Wintermärchen' (almost red) are good choices.

BRIZA
Quaking grass

Most of the 15 species that make up this genus are annuals but there is one good perennial *B. media*, the common quaking grass or trembling grass. The English name comes from the fact that the hanging, heart-shaped heads move in the slightest breeze, giving the impression that the whole plant is trembling. The spikelets are purple changing to a golden-yellow as they ripen. The grass can grow up to 60cm (24in) high, with a spread of 10cm (4in). This plant is attractive in the garden and also works well in dried arrangements.

Cultivation Any well-drained garden soil in full sun. Z4

Propagation Can be divided in early spring just as growth begins. It can also be grown from seed.

BRUNNERA
Brunnera

A small genus of three species of which one, *B. macrophylla*, is in general cultivation. This is a gem for a lightly shaded position, either under shrubs or trees, or on the shady side of a building or fence. It has fairly large, oval leaves that are slightly coarse. The blue flowers are similar to forget-me-nots but they are carried on airy stems above the leaves. They appear in spring but the foliage continues to provide interest for most of the summer.

Cultivation A moisture-retentive soil is needed in a partial shaded position. Z3

Propagation Brunnera is easy to increase by division in spring.

Brunnera macrophylla

The species is attractive in its own right and it is certainly well worth growing. H 50cm (20in) S 60cm (24in). However, there are several cultivars with variegated leaves which makes

Bergenia 'Silberlicht'

Briza media

Brunnera macrophylla 'Jack Frost'

Winter-flowering perennials

Adonis amurensis
Crocus
Cyclamen coum
Eranthis hyemalis
Euphorbia rigida
Galanthus
Helleborus niger
Helleborus orientalis
Helleborus purpurascens
Hepatica nobilis
Iris ungicularis
Primula vulgaris
Pulmonaria rubra
Ranunculus ficaria
Vinca difformis
Viola odorata

them even more desirable. 'Dawson's White' has wide, irregular, white margins to the green leaves. 'Hadspen Cream' is similar except that the margins are narrower and a creamier white. 'Jack Frost' has silver foliage that looks as though the leaves have frost on them. 'Langtrees' is an intriguing cultivar which has silver spots in the middle of each leaf.

CALAMAGROSTIS
Reed grass

Calamagrostis is a large genus of grasses. It includes some species that were classed as Stipa until recently. They are all decorative grasses which can be used either as a prominent feature in a border or simply mixed in to enhance the general effect.
Cultivation Reed grasses will grow in any reasonable garden so long as they are planted in full sun. Cut back the old stems in late winter before the new growth starts. Z5
Propagation This is best carried out by division in spring just as growth is beginning.

Calamagrostis × acutiflora
A tall grass with narrow leaves and plumes of purplish flowers that turn silver. H 2m (6ft) S 50cm (20in). It has a couple of very good cultivars: 'Karl Foerster' has pinkish flowers that fade to beige, and the slightly shorter 'Overdam' has leaves with yellow margins that fade to white.

Calamagrostis arundinacea
This plant forms a clump of arching foliage, soon topped with masses of fine-stemmed drooping flowers that create a lovely hazy effect. H 1m (3ft) S 1.2m (4ft).

Calamagrostis brachytricha
A splendid grass with green leaves that are often tinged with bronze in spring and autumn. The flowers are pinkish-grey. H 1.2m (4ft) S 75cm (30in)

Other plants *C. emodensis* and *C. epigejos* are two more interesting species that grass enthusiasts might like to look at.

CALAMINTHA
Calaminth

A small genus of about eight species, of which only two are in general cultivation. They are relatively low plants, only reaching about 45cm (18in) in good conditions. Their glory is the mass of thyme-like flowers that are produced over a long period in the summer. The flowers are mainly pink but can also edge towards mauve. The leaves are aromatic when crushed or bruised. These are excellent plants for placing at the front edge of borders or along paths.

Calamintha nepeta subsp. *nepeta*

Caltha palustris 'Alba'

Caltha palustris 'Flore Pleno'

Cultivation Plant in any good garden soil in full sun. Z6.
Propagation Divide plants in spring, or sow seed, also in spring.

Calamintha grandiflora
This is a larger plant, which has flowers of a bright pink. H 45cm (18in) S 45cm (18in).

Calamintha nepeta
About the same size as *grandiflora*, this has flowers that are a paler lilac-pink, sometimes almost white. H 45cm (18in) S 60cm (24in). *C.n.* subsp. *nepeta* is often called *C. nepetoides*. It is a shorter plant and has tiny lilac-white flowers that cover the plant in a cloud – perfect for the edge of a path or patio. *C.n.* 'Blue Cloud' has, as its name suggests, many flowers with a distinct blue tinge.

CALTHA
Marsh marigold

There are about ten species of caltha, but only one of them, *C. palustris*, with its several varieties and cultivars, is in general cultivation. This plant with its delightful large golden buttercup-like flowers is one of the glories of spring.

It does best when grown beside water but it will also grow in bog gardens and even in borders if the soil is kept sufficiently damp. Marsh marigolds are sprawling plants but they can reach 45cm (18in) in height and 30cm (12in) in width.
Cultivation The soil must be moist and, unlike many plants, the roots can be in mud or shallow water. Caltha flourishes in a sunny position but it will also grow in light shade, under deciduous trees, for example. Z3.
Propagation Increase is easily carried out by division in spring or from seed that is sown as soon as it is ripe.

Caltha palustris

Caltha palustris
Although there are good cultivars, the species is well worth growing in its own right – it makes a superb addition to any pond. 'Alba' is not quite as striking as the species, but this white-flowered form still has a lot of charm and looks particularly attractive growing along side the golden form. 'Flore Pleno' is a smaller plant than the species but its worth lies in its exquisite double flowers with their concentric rows of petals.

***Caltha palustris* var. *palustris*.**
This is sometimes known as *C. polypetala*. It is a giant form of the species with large flowers. There is also an attractive double form of this larger plant with the name 'Plena'.

Camassia leichtlinii subsp. *leichtlinii*

CAMASSIA
Quamash

This is a small genus of bulbs that are frequently grown as part of a herbaceous border. They have also become popular for naturalizing in a meadow or wild garden. Camassias are tall-growing plants which produce tall spikes of striking, star-like flowers, usually in blue or white. The foliage is lush but not attractive; it is a good idea to plant them in the middle of the border so that the foliage is hidden but the flower spikes stand proud of surrounding vegetation. H 1m (3ft) S 20–30cm (8–12in).
Cultivation Camassias like good moist, but free-draining soil in full sun or just a light shade. Plant in autumn at a depth of about 10cm (4in). Z2.

Camassia leichtlinii subsp. *suksdorfii*

Campanula carpatica

Propagation Increase by dividing the bulbs in summer or by sowing seed while it is still fresh.

Camassia leichtlinii subsp. *leichtlinii*

This plant used to be known as *C.l.* 'Alba', the 'Alba' referring to its white flowers. These have a touch of green in them and are really very beautiful.

Camassia leichtlinii subsp. *suksdorfii*

Being the commonest form, this was and still often is referred to simply under the species name *C. leichtlinii*. It has blue flowers which vary in intensity from pale to very deep blue-violet. There are several cultivars to explore.

Camassia quamash

This plant is similar to the above with blue flowers. It is excellent for naturalizing.

CAMPANULA
Bellflower

This is a much loved genus of some 300 species of which many are in cultivation. They vary from ground-hugging plants to ones

Campanula 'Loddon Anna'

with tall spires of flowers. The typical bellflower is blue but there are also plenty of white and pink variants. The flowers vary from classic bell-shapes to flat, wide-open stars. The majority flower in summer, and most are excellent at forming large clumps. They should be placed anywhere from the front to the back of a border, depending on their height.
Cultivation Most bellflowers need a rich, moist, but well-drained soil. The majority also prefer full sun but there are a number that like a little shade. Z3–6.
Propagation Seed can be sown in the spring, and many of the plants can also be divided at the same time of year. Basal cuttings can also be taken from many species in spring.

Campanula carpatica

A low-growing (25cm/10in) species that is perfect for edging the path or border. The flowers are an open-dish shape and come in varying shades of blue as well as white. S 30cm (12in). There are a number of excellent cultivars including 'Weisse Clips' (white) and 'Blue Clips (blue).

Campanula punctata

Campanula glomerata

A medium bellflower that carries its flowers in a cluster at the top of the flower stem. Excellent for borders or for naturalizing in meadow gardens. H 45cm (18in) S 60cm (24in).

Campanula lactiflora

A tall border plant with many flowers carried in loose heads. H 1.2m (4ft) S 60cm (24in). The type is well worth growing but there are also a number of very good cultivars including 'Loddon Anna' (lilac-pink), 'Prichard's Variety' (violet blue) and 'White Pouffe', which is a dwarf form with white flowers.

Campanula latifolia

A tall species with large tubular bells of intense blue. H 1.2m (4ft) S 60cm (24in). The variety 'Alba' has beautiful white flowers that brighten up a lightly shaded

Campanula lactiflora

Campanula portenschlagiana

Campanula poscharskyana

spot of the garden. 'Brantwood' (deep violet) is another excellent cultivar to try.

Campanula latiloba
This bellflower has dense heads of open bell-shaped flowers with lavender blue flowers H 1m (3ft) S 45cm (18in). Again there are several very good cultivars.

Campanula persicifolia
An attractive medium height bellflower which often needs staking to keep its upright stance. The flowers are large open cups in blue or white. H 1m (3ft) S 30cm (12in). There are some beautiful double forms, such as 'Boule de Neige'.

Campanula portenschlagiana
A low-growing campanula with bright violet purple flowers. It is excellent for edging paths. H 15cm (6in) S indefinite.

Campanula poscharskyana
A spreading campanula that will scramble up through shrubs and other plants. The pale-blue flowers are star-shaped and are carried over a long period from early summer well into autumn. This plant makes good ground cover. H 10–15cm (4–6in) S indefinite.

Other plants There are so many other campanulas that are worth pursuing, such as *C. punctata* or the similar *C. takesimana* with their large pink tubular bells. Virtually any campanula you come across in a nursery will be worth growing, and it can be fun to experiment.

CARDAMINE
Bittercress

A delightful genus of plants whose numbers have been increased by the addition of species that were in the genus *Dentaria*. There are some weeds – hairy bitter cress being one that gardeners especially hate – but the majority of cardamines are garden plants with great charm. They flower in spring. Since they are suited to partial shade, they are excellent for growing under deciduous shrubs or in the shade of a building.

Cardamine heptaphylla

Cultivation Most prefer a moist, woodland-type soil with plenty of added leaf mould. They will grow in sun as long as the soil is kept moist, but prefer a light shaded position. Z5–6.
Propagation Most cardamines are easy to divide in the spring. They can also be grown from seed or, in some cases, from the small reddish bulbils that are carried in the leaf joints.

Cardamine enneaphyllos
A spreading plant with clusters of creamy white flowers held above mid-green leaves. It needs to be grown in partial shade. H 30cm (12in) S 60cm (24in).

Cardamine heptaphylla
Clusters of simple white, and occasionally pink, flowers. It reaches 30cm (12in) tall, and sometimes double that. Does best in partial shade. S30 cm (12in).

Cardamine pentaphyllos
An attractive plant with clusters of pinkish-purple flowers, sometimes white. H 30cm (12in) but sometimes double that. S 60cm (24in). This plant requires a partially shaded position.

Cardamine pentaphyllos

Cardamine pratensis
This is the much-loved cuckoo flower or milkmaid. It has loose heads of delightful lilac flowers. H 45cm (18in) S 30cm (12in). There are various interesting double forms.

CARDIOCRINUM
Giant Lily

Although there are three species in the genus, only one of them, *C. giganteum*, is in general cultivation. It is a tall plant, reaching up to 2m (6ft), with large white trumpet flowers, creating a very striking picture. It likes a cool shaded position but the head can be in sun – making it ideal for growing amongst shrubs or at the back of borders. The dried seed capsules are amongst the most desirable of dried flowers. S 1m (3ft)
Cultivation It must have a rich soil with plenty of humus in it. Plant in partial shade. Z6.
Propagation It is best to buy bulbs. It can be grown from seed but you will have to wait seven years or more before it flowers. Established bulbs will produce offsets (offshoots) which can be divided but even these take up to five years to flower.

Cardiocrinum giganteum
A tall plant with lily-like trumpet flowers that are angled downwards. They are white and highly scented, and appear in summer. There is also a variety *yunnanense* which has shiny brown stems and flowers that are tinged with green.

Cardiocrinum giganteum

Other plants Keen gardeners should look out for the similar but less frequently seen species *C. cordatum*, which is worth finding a supplier for.

CATANANCHE
Cupid's dart

A small genus of five species of which only one is in general cultivation. These are for the border rather than for containers and are best used in association with other plants. Catananche are perfect for gravel gardens. The buds have a curious paper-like quality and even the cornflower-like petals feel dry and papery. The flowers are carried on slender, wiry stems in summer and into the autumn. They are ideal for dried arrangements.
Cultivation These are short-lived plants but their life can be prolonged by growing them in a free-draining soil. They must have a sunny position. Z4.
Propagation Catananche are best increased from seed sown in spring. They can be divided but care is needed as they have thick tap roots. These roots can be used as cuttings, taken in the winter.

Catananche caerulea
This is the main species in cultivation and the form that one usually sees. The flowers are blue with a darker centre. H 45cm (18in) S 30cm (12in). The form 'Major' is a popular one but it often looks the same as the main species. A good alternative is the cultivar 'Bicolor' which has a violet-purple centre and white petals. The all-white form is 'Alba', which is also very attractive.

Catananche caerulea

CENTAUREA
Knapweeds

For the serious perennial gardener this is a "must-have" genus: there are many top-class plants in it. It is a large genus, containing about 450 species with about 40 being in general cultivation. They have thistle-like heads which are often quite large. They come in a variety of colours: reds, purples, blues, yellows and whites. The flowers usually appear in summer and rarely last more than a few weeks. They provide good colour for the border.

Cultivation Most will grow in any good garden soil. They prefer a sunny position. Z3–7.

Propagation The most common method of increase is by division in spring, although most species can also be grown from seed sown at the same time of year.

Centaurea dealbata

An appealing clump-forming perennial with purple-pink flowers with white centres. H 1m (3ft) S 60cm (24in). The cultivar 'Steenbergii' has deeper pink flowers and is even more attractive than the species.

Centaurea hypoleuca

Another clump-forming centaurea which is somewhat similar to the previous one, but with larger flowers. The flowers are again pink with a paler centre. H 60cm (24in) S 45cm (18in). The cultivar 'John Coutts' has dark pink flowers.

Centaurea hypoleuca 'John Coutts'

Centaurea macrocephala

This is a clump-forming plant with upright stems. These carry large heads with a papery, dark brown bud that contrasts beautifully with the bright yellow flowers. A truly wonderful plant. H 1.5m (5ft) S 60cm (24in).

Centaurea montana

A favourite of the late spring to early summer garden. A somewhat sprawling plant whose bright blue flowers each have a purple centre. H 45cm (18in) when staked, S 60cm (24in). There is a good white form *alba* and several good colour varieties.

Centaurea pulcherrima

An attractive plant with very good silvery foliage that earns it a place in the garden as a foliage plant when it is not in flower. The exquisite flowers are pink with a creamy centre. H 75cm (30in) S 60cm (24in).

Centaurea montana

Centaurea 'Pulchra Major'

Strictly speaking, this is now called *Leuzea centauroides*. It is similar to *C. pulcherrima* but is on a much larger scale with huge flowers up to 7.5cm (3in) across. H 1m (3ft) S 60cm (24in).

Centaurea simplicicaulis

A mat-forming plant with large pink flowers. H 25cm (10in) S 60cm (24in).

Other plants There are many more for the gardener to try. *C. bella* (pink) has good foliage, *C. cheiranthifolia* (cream and purple) is exceptionally good, and *C. ruthenica* (yellow) is another cultivar worth considering.

CENTRANTHUS
Red valerian

A genus of a dozen or so plants of which one, *C. ruber*, is in general cultivation. It forms clumps of stems, which carry dense heads of tiny purplish-red flowers. The colour varies, sometimes it is redder, sometimes pinker and occasionally it is white. These are excellent plants for growing in gravel gardens, and in spite of their height they are also good for walls and banks. H 1m (3ft) S 45–60cm (18–24in).

Cultivation Red valerian will grow in any garden soil, even impoverished ones. It likes a well-drained position in full sun. Z3.

Propagation The simplest method is from seed sown in spring. One plant will usually provide enough self-sown seedlings for most uses.

CEPHALARIA
Cephalaria

A genus of plants of which only one is in general cultivation. This is *C. gigantea* which is a clump forming plant. It forms a very tall, open plant with airy stems, each carrying soft yellow, almost creamy-yellow, flowers. The flowers are similar to those of the scabious to which it is related. It is eye-catching, especially when planted against a dark green hedge and it is a valuable border plant. H 2.5m (8ft) S 1.2m (4ft). There is a shorter (2m/6ft) species, *C. alpina*, which has similar yellow flowers, but this is less common and not quite so long lived.

Cultivation It likes a well-drained but fertile soil. Plant in a sunny position if possible, although it will take a little light shade. Cut back after flowering or it will self-sow prodigiously. Z6.

Propagation This plant is easy to grow from seed sown in either autumn or spring.

Centaurea dealbata

Centaurea macrocephala

Centranthus ruber

Cephalaria gigantea

Ceratostigma plumbaginoides

CERATOSTIGMA
Ceratostigma

A small genus that consists mainly of shrubs but there is one notable perennial, *C. plumbaginoides*. It is a spreading plant up to 45cm (18in) high and 20cm (8in) wide. The joy of it is the bright blue periwinkle-like flowers, which sparkle out of the late summer and autumn garden. The leaves take on reddish autumn tints. This is a good plant for interspersing with others towards the front of the border. The shrubby ceratostigmas fulfil the same function and have very attractive flowers that are also blue. In particular, have a look at *C. griffithii* and *C. willmottianum*.
Cultivation Ceratostigmas thrive in any good garden soil with plenty of organic material. They need a sunny position. Prune the shrubs in early spring. Z6.
Propagation Increase your stock of these plants by taking cuttings in spring or summer.

CHELONE
Turtlehead

This is a small genus of which only one species is in general cultivation. The name refers to the strange turtle-like shape of the flowers. These are dark pink and carried in a short terminal spike from late summer into autumn. The main species is *C. obliqua* which grows to about 60cm (24in) in height and has a spread of 50cm (20in). These are good plants for providing autumn colour in the middle of the border. The other species worth looking at if you can find them are *C. glabra* and *C. lyonii*.
Cultivation Turtleheads need a rich, fertile soil that is moist. They can be grown in sun or light shade. Z4.
Propagation Division is the easiest method of increase but they can also be grown from seed sown in spring or from cuttings taken at the same time of year.

CHRYSANTHEMUM
Chrysanthemum

This genus needs little introduction since it is familiar as both a cut flower and garden plant. The familiar florist chrysanthemums are perennials, but they are treated as annuals (see pages 110–111) because they are tender and need to be renewed each year. However there are a number of species and cultivars that are truly hardy and can be left outside all year. Most have a very long flowering time and will last from late summer and sometimes right into winter. Some – such as *C. rubellum* (syn. *C. zawadskii*) and its cultivars – are very similar to the single florist chrysanthemums and make good cut flowers.

The list of plants classified under the genus *Chrysanthemum* have gone through several changes. Many were moved to *Dendranthema*. They have now been moved back to *Chrysanthemum* but you may still come across them under the previous name.
Cultivation The hardy plants will grow in any reasonably fertile garden soil, preferably one that is well-drained. They prefer a sunny position but they will grow in light shade so long as they receive some sun. Z4.
Propagation Taking basal cuttings in spring is a reliable method of increase. The plants can also be divided at the same time of year.

Chrysanthemum rubellum

Chrysanthemum rubellum 'Clara Curtis'

Chrysanthemum rubellum
Strictly speaking, this species is now called *C. zawadskii* but it is still generally referred to as *C. rubellum*. H 75cm (30in) S 45cm (18in). The species is occasionally grown, but its many cultivars are more common. They have single, semi-double or double, daisy-like flowers in a variety of colours. Some of the best include 'Clara Curtis' (pink), 'Emperor of China' (double pink), 'Mary Stoker' (apricot-yellow), 'Mrs Jessie Cooper' (red) and 'Nancy Perry' (dark pink).

Chrysanthemum hosmariense
This is now *Rhodanthemum hosmariense* but is still often referred to by its former name. It is a delightful little plant with silver foliage and white daisy flowers that are in bloom from spring to autumn. Perfect as an edging plant in a well-drained sunny position. H 15cm (6in) S 30cm (12in).

Chrysanthemum uliginosum
Now known as *Leucanthemella serotina*, this is a wonderful plant for autumn. It is tall with white daisy flowers that appear from mid-autumn through until winter. The flowers have a habit of tilting and facing the sun, which they follow throughout the day. A good plant for the back of a border, but make sure it will face into the garden when flowering. H 2m (6ft) S 60cm (24in).

Chelone obliqua

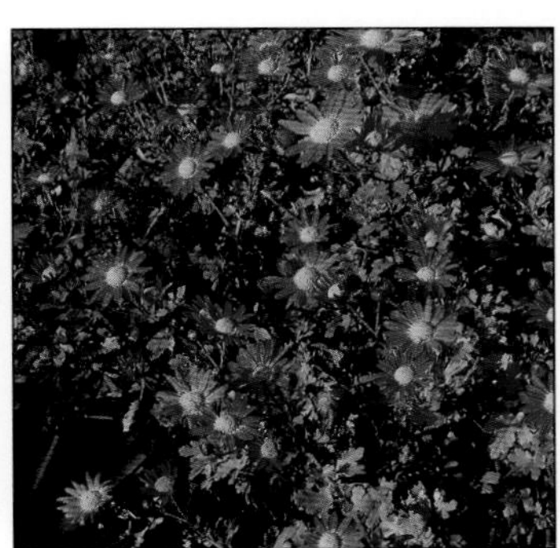
Chrysanthemum rubellum

Chyrsanthemum hosmariense

CLEMATIS
Clematis

Most people think of this genus purely in terms of woody climbing plants. The majority of the 200 species and hundreds of cultivars are just that, but there are also a number of herbaceous species that die back each year. They do not have the big blowsy quality of some of the climbers but they are still very attractive. Most need some form of support but even with this, they rarely grow very tall. Some can be left to sprawl over the neighbouring plants, perhaps covering a spring plant that has lost its freshness.
Cultivation A rich moisture-retentive soil is required. The roots should be in shade with the plant in sun, although some will tolerate a little light shade. Most need some form of support, such as pea-sticks. Cut to the ground each spring. Z3.
Propagation Take basal cuttings in spring. Most perennial clematis can also be divided, with care.

Clematis × durandii
One of the largest flowered herbaceous clematis with indigo-blue blooms. Grow through a shrub or over pea-sticks. H 1–2m (3–6ft) S 45–150cm (1½–5ft).

Clematis heracleifolia* var. *davidiana
A late-summer flowering species whose blue flowers have reflexed (turned back), strap-like petals. An added bonus is that this plant is highly scented. H 1m (3ft) S 75cm (30in). There are a number of cultivars of varying shades of blue.

Clematis integrifolia 'Hendersonii'

Clematis recta

Clematis integrifolia
This has intriguing nodding flowers that hang attractively from upright stalks. They are usually blue, but there are also several forms that produce flowers in other colours, including 'Rosea' (pink) and 'Alba' (white). 'Hendersonii' has extra large flowers. The plants are sprawling and can be left to clamber over other plants; they can also be supported. H and S 75cm (30in).

Clematis × jouiniana
It is the sheer number of flowers that makes this clematis attractive: it is a mass of small mauve-blue flowers. It requires support on pea-sticks. H 1m (3ft) S 1–2m (3–6ft).

Clematis recta
Although the species is often grown in its own right it is usually the form 'Purpurea' that is grown. This has wonderful purple foliage in spring; in early to midsummer it produces masses of small white flowers. H 1–2m (3–6ft) S 50cm (20in).

Convallaria majalis

Other plants There are a few more species that can be explored including *C. texensis*, *C. addisonii* and *C. stans*. There are also myriad woody ones to grow; plants in the *C. viticella* group, in particular, go very well with herbaceous plants.

CONVALLARIA
Lily-of-the-valley

A small genus of which one species, *C. majalis* – the much-loved lily-of-the-valley – is regularly grown. This low plant is ideal for shady positions under shrubs or for growing on the shady side of a building. It spreads to form a mat of leaves surmounted in spring by short arching stems carrying fragrant white bells. In warm weather the scent can spread widely. The flowers are good for cutting for display or bouquets. H 23cm (9in) S indefinite. There is a pink form *rosea* which is identical except for the colour of the flowers. There is also 'Albostriata' in which the flowers are the same but the leaves have narrow yellow stripes running down them. In the cultivar 'Fortin's Giant' everything is doubled in size.
Cultivation A shady position in rich moist soil although it will survive drier soils. Z2.
Propagation Divide in the autumn or early spring. Plants can be grown from seed sown in spring, but the seed is not easy to find.

COREOPSIS
Tickseed

A useful genus of plants which add welcome splashes of gold to a border. It is a large genus of around 100 species but only a handful are in cultivation. They have daisy-like yellow or gold flowers, double in some cultivars, which bloom in summer. They work well towards the front or in the middle of the border where their colour stands out.
Cultivation Tickseed will grow in any reasonable garden soil. It needs a sunny position. Z3.

Coreopsis verticillata 'Moonbeam'

Propagation To increase, divide plants in spring, or take stem cuttings in summer.

Coreopsis lanceolata
Tall flower stems carry single flowers of bright gold. H 60cm (24in) S 30cm (12in). There are various forms: some have brown centres ('Sterntaler') and others are much shorter ('Baby Gold').

Coreopsis verticillata
The most widely grown of the perennial species. It is a fine plant with masses of shining gold flowers floating above delicate, narrow foliage in summer. H 75cm (30in) S 30cm (12in). There are some good cultivars: 'Grandiflora' (also known as 'Golden Shower') has warm yellow flowers, 'Moonbeam' has wonderfully soft yellow blooms and 'Zagreb' is golden yellow.

CORTADERIA
Pampas grass

A small genus of grasses of which a couple of species with their cultivars are generally grown.

Coreopsis verticillata 'Zagreb'

Cortaderia selloana 'Pumila'

These are stunning: they have fountains of narrow leaves that are surmounted by tall stems carrying great tufts of white flower heads. Unfortunately, most are so large (up to 3m/10ft tall and 2m/6ft across) that you need a large garden to do them justice. There are some dwarf forms for smaller gardens, but these seem rather to miss the point. Pampas grasses make excellent focal points, especially if they are placed so that they can be seen against the blue sky. They last well into winter before they start to look untidy.
Cultivation They will grow in any reasonable garden soil, but require a sunny position. Cut down flowering stems in late winter and shear off the leaves every three years. Do not plant pampas grass near areas where children run or play as the edges of the leaves are very sharp. Z7.
Propagation Divide off part of the plant in late winter or early spring just before growth begins.

Cortaderia richardii

A lesser-grown species than the following. It comes from New Zealand rather than South America, but looks similar. The flowering stems tend to be more arching, but they too carry huge feathery plumes.

Cortaderia selloana

This is the main species grown and it is fabulous: tall and stately with feathery flower heads. The form 'Aureolineata' (also known as 'Gold Band') has golden stripes on the margins of the leaves. 'Albolineata' is similarly variegated but with silvery-white stripes; it is slightly smaller. 'Pumila' grows to only 1.5m (5ft). 'Pink Feather' has silvery-pink flower heads. 'Sunningdale Silver' has glistening silvery-white feathers.

CORYDALIS
Corydalis

This is a large genus of 300 or more species. It is much beloved by alpine gardeners, but there are a couple that are large and robust enough for the perennial gardener to consider. These have curious tubular flowers which look rather like swarms of tiny fish, floating above the ferny leaves. They are good for naturalizing along the edge of woodland gardens, or under deciduous shrubs and trees in smaller gardens. H 30cm (12in) S 30cm (12in).
Cultivation The corydalis listed here require a moist soil in either sun or partial shade. Z5–6.
Propagation Grow from seed, which should sown while it is still fresh. Many self-sow.

Corydalis flexuosa

Corydalis cava

This plant has white or purplish flowers which appear in the spring. It grows well in woodland type soil in partial shade.

Corydalis flexuosa

Brilliant blue flowers in spring and early summer. This species should be grown in a moist, fibrous soil in a lightly shaded position. There are several good cultivars to explore.

Corydalis lutea

One of the easiest of the corydalis to grow, this has yellow flowers. It is excellent for growing on old walls. Flowers all year.

Corydalis ochroleuca

Good for damp positions. This has a long flowering season, with creamy white and yellow blooms.

Corydalis solida

This plant produces a range of different coloured flowers, based on mauvish purple but including red especially in the fine form 'George Baker'. Spring flowering.

COSMOS
Cosmos

A small genus of annual and perennial plants of which few, mainly annuals (see pages 116–117) are in cultivation. The one perennial that is commonly grown is *C. atrosanguineus*. This has deep crimson flowers, so deep and velvety that they appear almost brown. In addition, the plant actually smells of chocolate when the weather is warm. The flowers are dish-shaped, rather like a daisy with wide petals. They are carried on wiry stems up to 75cm (30in) high. The plants are excellent for placing in a front-of-border position where they can easily be smelt. S 45cm (18in).
Cultivation Cosmos need a rich, moist soil and a warm, sunny position. They are late in appearing in spring, so hold off digging them up if you think they have died. Z7.
Propagation Increase by taking basal cuttings as soon as the plants are big enough.

Cortaderia selloana 'Sunningdale Silver'

Cortaderia selloana 'Aureolineata'

Corydalis lutea

Cosmos atrosanguineus

Crambe cordifolia

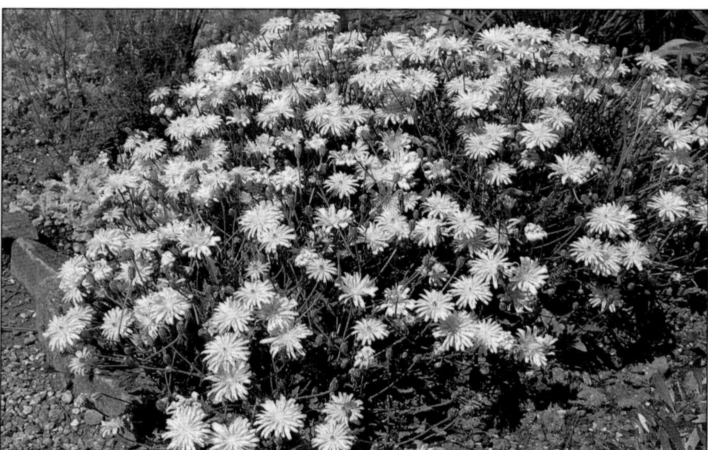
Crepis incana

CRAMBE
Crambe

Two plants in this small genus are in general cultivation. They can be spectacular but the most popular one, *C. cordifolia*, is not often seen outside large gardens because of its size. With care, though, it can be accommodated in smaller areas. The glory of this plant is the flowers which form a wonderful haze of white.
Cultivation These plants need rich, well-drained soil in full sun. They can be prone to slugs when the leaves first appear; you must control these pests at this point, or you will lose the plant. Z7.
Propagation Division is possible but awkward because of the size of the plants. The best option is to take root cuttings in winter.

Crambe cordifolia
A large plant with a great dome of white flowers, 2m (6ft) high and across in summer. It is ideal for a large herbaceous border. The multi-branching flower stems are excellent for dried arrangements if you can get them through the door. The leaves are rather coarse but since this is a plant for the middle or rear of the border, they are rarely seen, whereas the flowers float mistily above the surrounding plants.

Crambe maritima

Crambe maritima
This is a much smaller plant, growing only about 45cm (18in) high with a spread of 60cm (24in). It also produces a mass of flowers, but not quite as delicately as its larger relative. The main reason for growing it is the foliage, which is a wonderful powdery blue. It is an excellent foliage plant for the front of border. It needs a well-drained soil and does particularly well in gravel gardens.

CREPIS
Hawk's Beard

A large genus of dandelion-like plants that includes 200 or more species. Only a handful of them are generally grown in cultivation. Some are annuals or treated as annuals (see page 117) but others are true perennials. They are clump-forming plants that are suitable for the front of a border or for naturalizing in short grass. The flowers are multi-petalled, in the manner of a dandelion. They are carried on wiry stems that reach up to 30cm (12in) above rosettes of ground-hugging leaves. S 10cm (4in)
Cultivation Hawk's beard will grow in any reasonable garden soil, as long as it is well-drained. They need a position in full sun. Z7.
Propagation Increase by sowing fresh seed. The plants often produce self-sown seedlings.

Crepis aurea
This has typical dandelion-like flowers in a rich orange-yellow; they are carried from late summer onwards. These plants are good for the front of a hot-coloured border or for growing in short grass in a meadow garden.

Crepis incana
This is a short-lived perennial that is sometimes treated as an annual. It carries a large number of sugar-pink flowers. This form is usually just used in the border where it is an ideal plant for a frontal position. It looks particularly good when planted with blue veronicas.

CRINUM
Crinum

This is a large genus of tender bulbs, most of which are suited to growing in a conservatory. There is one that is not only hardy but also very attractive. This is *C.* × *powellii*. It has large strap-like leaves that arch outwards, framing the tall flowering stems that carry lily-like, trumpeted flowers. These are generally pink but there is also a glistening white form 'Alba'.

Crinum × *powellii*

Crinums are best planted behind other plants so that the leaves are hidden but the gorgeous trumpets show above their surroundings. These appear in late summer and autumn and grow to 1m (3ft) high and 60cm (24in) across.
Cultivation These plants need a rich, free-draining soil in full sun. Plant the bulbs so that the neck is above the soil level. Z7.
Propagation Increase by dividing off the offsets (offshoots) from around existing bulbs.

CROCOSMIA
Montbretia

These plants form a small genus of popular bulbous plants. They include the common montbretia (*C.* × *crocosmiiflora*) – which seems to occur in most gardens.

Most bulbs seem to have rather ugly foliage, but the crocosmia has long, ribbed, tapering leaves that stand upright, making a good contrast to other foliage around them. In late summer tall arching stems carry a spray of red, orange or yellow flowers, which look good against with the foliage. These plants are excellent for growing in clumps or drifts in the middle of the border or for planting in odd corners.
Cultivation Plant in any reasonable garden soil, preferably in full sun, although they will also tolerate a little light shade. Divide the plants every few years as they can get congested. Z7.
Propagation The plants are very easy to propagate: divide off the new corms in late winter or early spring, before they start to grow.

Crocosmia × *crocosmiiflora*

Crocosmia × _crocosmiiflora_
This is the main species cultivated. It grows up to 60cm (24in) tall and has dull-orange flowers held on upright stems. S 15–20cm (6–8in).

There are plenty of cultivars to explore. The flowers vary from the subdued, soft apricot-tinted yellow of 'Solfatare', with its soft bronze foliage, to the striking 'Emily McKenzie' which has large flowers with brown centres surrounded by a bright orange. 'Jackanapes' is another bicolour cultivar; its flowers come in yellow and rich orange. 'Star of the East' is an excellent orange form, paling towards the centre. 'Lady Hamilton' is similar but has deep yellow flowers. The many cultivars are generally much better than the species and it is worth acquiring several different ones, for a hot-coloured border.

Crocosmia 'Honey Angels'

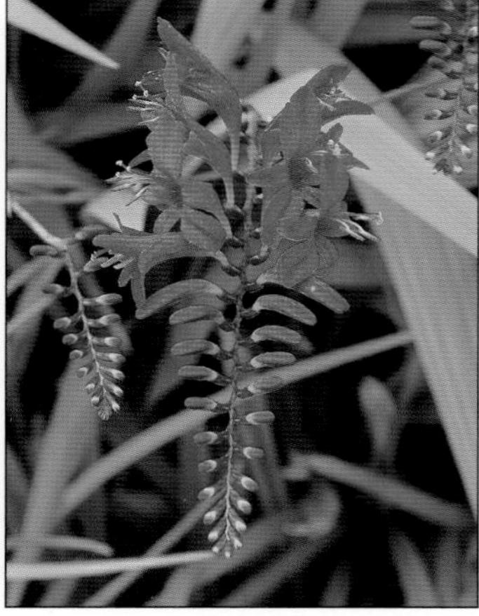

Crocosmia 'Lucifer'

Crocosmia 'Emberglow'
A good border plant with bright red flowers that always create a splash of colour.

Crocosmia 'Honey Angels'
This is a fine crocosmia whose appealing yellow flowers have creamy throats.

Crocosmia 'Lucifer'
One of the most spectacular of the crocosmias. It is tall, reaching up to 1.2m (4ft). The flower stems are arching and carry sprays of large bright crimson flowers that stand upright like flames. They are superb against the green foliage. S 20–25cm (8–10in)

Crocosmia masoniorum
This is similar to the previous one, but its flowers contain more orange and are not so bright. H 1.2m (4ft) S 15cm (6in).

Other plants There are many cultivars for the enthusiast to look at, all with subtle variations on the basic type. Since they are easily grown, they make ideal plants to collect.

Cynara cardunculus

CYNARA

Cynara

Two plants in this genus are generally grown in gardens, one for decoration (although it can be eaten) and the other for eating (although it can also be used for show). The main border plant is *C. cardunculus*. This is a statuesque plant: tall with silver foliage and huge purple thistle-like heads. It looks good planted singly as a focal point or in a group.
Cultivation These plants need a fertile, well-drained soil. Place in a sunny position, away from strong winds. Z7.
Propagation To increase, divide off "slips" (rooted cuttings) in spring.

Cynara cardunculus
A superb giant "thistle". It produces fountains of silver foliage surmounted by tall silver stems carrying thistle-like flowers in summer. They are excellent for drying. The base of the stems and leaf stalks can be cooked when young – when the plant is known as a cardoon. H 2m (6ft) S 1m (3ft). Occasionally you can find dwarf forms on offer which are useful for small gardens. 'Florist Cardy' is a form specially bred for use as a cut flower, but it is not a great deal different from the type.

Cynara scolymus
Now officially, but cumbrously, known as *C. cardunculus* Scolymus Group. This is the globe artichoke of the vegetable garden. It is the large flower bud that is eaten. It can be used in the border as a lesser version of the above. The leaves are not so attractive in shape, nor so silver, but it still makes a good foliage plant, especially early in the season. H 1m (3ft) S 60cm (24in).

Cynara scolymus

Bee and butterfly plants

Anchusa
Aster
Centaurea
Delphinium
Doronicum
Echinacea
Echinops
Eryngium
Eupatorium
Foeniculum
Helenium
Lythrum
Mentha
Monarda
Nepeta
Origanum
Scabiosa
Sedum
Solidago
Trifolium

CYNOGLOSSUM
Hound's tongue

A genus of about 55 species. Most of those with garden interest are annuals or biennials (see page 118). However, there is one, *C. nervosum*, which is perennial and worth growing in the border. This is a medium-sized plant with bristly stems and leaves. It is the flowers that are principally of interest since they are a wonderful bright blue colour. The individual flowers are quite small but they are carried in uncurling spikes – much in the same way as forget-me-nots, to which they are related. The plant flowers in early summer and is very useful for adding bright blue colour to the middle of the border at that time of year. H 60cm (24in) S 50cm (20in).

Cultivation Plant in any garden soil that is not too rich. Choose a sunny position. This plant is short lived and needs replacing every three years or so. Z5.

Propagation The best way to increase this plant is by sowing seed in spring.

DELPHINIUM
Delphinium

These plants are much-loved, but few gardeners know the full range of them: the flowers come in yellow and red as well as the most commonly seen blue ones. This is a fairly large genus of some 250 species of which a surprising number are in cultivation. The most popular are those that produce tall spires covered in flowers, but there are also shorter species whose flowers are held in loose airy clusters. Many of these are not as robust as the taller ones, but they make good garden plants if renewed every few years.

Cultivation A deep, rich but free-draining soil is required. Delphiniums should be placed in full sun. Tall ones with heavy spikes may need staking, unless the garden is very sheltered. Watch out for slugs in the early stages of growth. Z3.

Propagation The best way of increasing most cultivars is to take basal cuttings in spring. The species should be grown from seed, sown as soon as it is ripe.

Delphinium 'Fenella'

Delphinium Belladonna Group, Elatum Group and Pacific Hybrids

These are the main groups of tall, heavily flowered delphiniums. Many are grown for cutting rather than for border display, but they can also be used in such situations. They flower in early summer and grow up to 1.5m (5ft) tall. S 60cm (24in). There is a vast range of named cultivars with flowers varying in colour from pale to dark blue, purple and white. Many have double flowers, often with white or black centres, known as "bees". They include: 'Bruce', a semi-double with deep purple flowers and brown eyes; 'Butterball', another semi-double, this time with creamy-white flowers and deeper eyes; 'Fenella', a semi-double with bright blue petals and a black eye. 'Giotto', a semi-double whose flowers are two-toned blue with light brown eyes; 'Sandpiper', a semi-double with white petals and a brown eye; and 'Tiddles', which has double mauve flowers.

Delphinium 'Sandpiper'

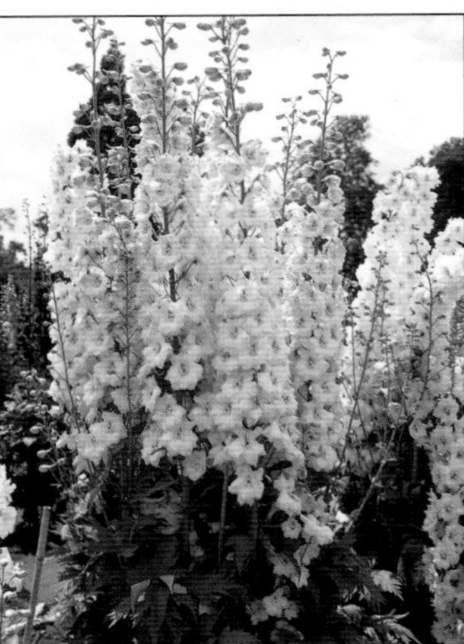

Delphinium 'Elizabeth Cook'

Delphinium 'Alice Artindale'

A wonderful double for the border. The little button flowers are a light blue; when dried, they retain their colour for years. H 1.2m (4ft) S 60cm (24in).

Delphinium cardinale

This unusual delphinium has bright red flowers with yellow centres. The flowers are carried in a loose spike. H 1–2m (3–6ft) S 60cm (24in).

Delphinium cashmerianum

This perennial is short lived, but it is still worth growing for its loose heads of bright blue flowers. H 45cm (18in) S 30cm (12in).

Delphinium grandiflorum

A delightful delphinium with gracefully floating bright blue flowers. It is good for the front of a border, especially if planted in a group of three. However, it is short lived. H 45cm (18in) S 30cm (12in).

Delphinium 'Southern Countryman'

Delphinium 'Clifford Sky'

Delphinium nudicaule

Another short-lived plant, this time with loose spikes of yellow, orange or red flowers. It likes a well-drained soil. H 20cm (8in) S 5–10cm (2–4in).

Delphinium semibarbatum

Still known to many gardeners as *D. zalil*, this has loose spikes of yellow flowers. H up to 1m (3ft) in good conditions; S 30cm (12in). However, it is short lived and needs replacing regularly.

DIANTHUS
Pinks

Dianthus is a large genus of about 300 species. Many are in cultivation, and they are often grown by alpine enthusiasts. Border use is almost exclusively confined to one species, *D. caryophyllus*, or rather to the many cultivars that have been derived from it. These are known collectively as pinks. They can be roughly divided into two groups: the old-fashioned varieties which generally flower only once in the summer and are often scented; and the modern varieties which have the advantage of flowering, often continuously, throughout the summer but are in most cases scentless. Old-fashioned varieties have flowers that can be single, semi-double or double, while most modern ones are doubles. The flowers grow on stiff stems

Dianthus deltoides

Dianthus 'Garnet'

that emerge from a clump of narrow, silver foliage. The tallest grow to about 45cm (18in) but most are shorter. They are excellent plants for the front of borders and for lining paths. S 25cm (10in).
Cultivation Pinks need a well-drained soil that is neutral or alkaline. Full sun is essential. Z7.
Propagation Since most pinks are cultivars only vegetative methods can be relied upon. Of these, taking cuttings in summer is by far the easiest.

Dianthus deltoides
A choice plant for edging a path. The foliage is narrow and dark green, while the flowers are like tiny jewels in pink, red or white. This species is grown from seed. H 20cm (8in) S 25cm (10in).

***Dianthus* 'Doris'**
One of the best old-fashioned pinks – a double with pink petals and a darker pink centre. It is very long-flowering and well scented.

***Dianthus* 'Garnet'**
A low-growing pink for the rock garden or front of border with single carmine flowers with a darker centre. The foliage is compact and a good silver colour.

Dianthus 'Doris'

***Dianthus* 'Mrs Sinkins'**
Another fine old-fashioned pink. It is a rather untidy double (the calyx which holds the petals together splits), but it is a good white and it has the most amazing scent. It is very easy to grow and will tolerate heavy soils.

***Dianthus* 'Musgrave's Pink'**
Also known as 'Charles Musgrave'. An excellent single, old-fashioned variety with single, creamy-white flowers that have a pale green centre. It is scented.

***Dianthus* 'Rose de Mai'**
This is a wonderful old-fashioned pink with pale mauve-pink flowers. It is fragrant and is one of the earliest to flower. The plant is rather sprawling.

***Dianthus* 'Whatfield Ruby'**
This small, single-flowered pink produces brilliant ruby-coloured flowers. It is best placed at the front of a border.

Other plants There are about a thousand cultivars from which to choose, most of which make excellent plants. Go to a specialist nursery in summer so that you can see them in flower before making your choice.

Dianthus 'Rose de Mai'

Dianthus 'Whatfield Ruby'

DIASCIA
Diascia

These plants have been grown in gardens since at least Victorian times, but it is only relatively recently that they have achieved the popularity they deserve. They have a very long flowering season, producing spikes of mostly pink flowers over low-growing mounds of green, heart-shaped foliage. They grow on average to about 25cm (10in) high with a spread of 60cm (24in) and are perfect for creating mats in the front of borders. They are also excellent plants for growing in containers.
Cultivation Diascias need a moist but well-drained soil that is not too wet in winter. They prefer a position in full sun, although they will tolerate a little light shade under tall trees or shrubs. Shear occasionally to keep the plants compact. Z4–7.

Diascia 'Rupert Lambert'

Propagation These plants are easy to root from cuttings, which can be taken at any time of the year.

***Diascia* 'Blackthorn Apricot'**
This is a good modern cultivar with apricot-pink flowers.

Diascia rigescens
One of the oldest species in cultivation. It is larger and coarser than most others but produces large spikes of deep pink flowers.

***Diascia* 'Ruby Field'**
This is an excellent form, which produces deep pink flowers.

***Diascia* 'Rupert Lambert'**
Another fine form. Like the previous one, it produces blooms of a deep pink.

***Diascia* 'Salmon Supreme'**
A good modern form which has salmon pink flowers.

Diascia vigilis
One of the longest-lived forms, with soft pink flowers. It is best grown in the form 'Jack Elliott'.

Diascia vigilis

DICENTRA

Dicentra

A genus of much-loved cottage garden plants. Their main characteristic is the locket-shaped flowers that hang like jewels from arching stems. They are set against foliage which is also attractive, usually being finely cut and fern-like. There are a good number of species and cultivars around, allowing keen gardeners to make an interesting collection. All dicentra like a bit of shade making them very useful for growing under shrubs or on the shady side of buildings or fences. Some will spread, making them useful ground cover for the earlier part of the summer.

Cultivation Dicentra are basically woodland plants and so they like the type of moist soil found there. They also require a lightly shaded position. Z2–4.

Propagation Division in spring is the easiest method of increasing dicentra. The species can also be propagated by sowing seed in autumn or spring.

***Dicentra* 'Bacchanal'**
This beautiful plant forms a large mat of green ferny foliage that is surmounted by pendants of deep crimson flowers in early summer. When given the right conditions it can grow to 45cm (18in) high. Spread starts at about 10cm (4in) but the plant continues increasing indefinitely.

***Dicentra* 'Brownie'**
This delightful plant forms large spreads of silvery grey foliage with pearly-white flowers appearing in early summer. H 30cm (12in) with an ever-increasing spread.

Dicentra 'Brownie'

Dicentra 'Bacchanal'

Dicentra formosa
A popular species with several cultivars, each forming spreading mats of green leaves and pink lockets. H 45cm (18in) with an ever-increasing spread.

The species is worth growing in its own right but there are also several interesting forms including *alba* with white flowers. The subspecies *oregana* has pink flowers and is the parent of many of the dicentra cultivars.

***Dicentra* 'Langtrees'**
Another spreading form, with good, silvery grey foliage and pinkish-white flowers in early summer. H 30cm (12in) with an ever-increasing spread.

***Dicentra* 'Luxuriant'**
This cultivar has bluish foliage and bright red flowers. H 35cm (14in); again the plant continues to spread until removed.

Dicentra scandens
This is an unusual, summer-flowering dicentra. Not only does it have yellow or whitish-yellow flowers, but it is also a climber. It will scramble though or over low shrubs and other plants. H and S up to 1m (3ft).

Dicentra spectabilis
Bleeding hearts or Dutchman's breeches are both apt descriptions of the flowers of this plant. The large flowers are carried on long arching stems in spring. In the species they are rose-pink tipped with white and in the form *alba* they are pure white. This is also different from the preceding forms as it is a bigger and more robust form that forms a clump rather than a spreading mat. H and S 60cm (24in) when given good conditions.

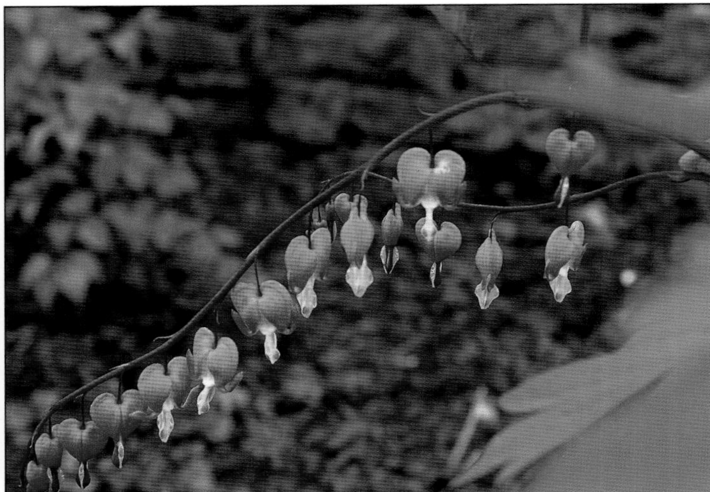
Dicentra spectabilis

***Dicentra* 'Stuart Boothman'**
A very good form with beautiful blue-grey foliage that sets off well the rose-pink flowers. It flowers in early summer and reaches about 30cm (12in) or so in height and spread.

DICTAMNUS

Burning bush

A genus of which *D. albus* is the only species, although its little-grown subspecies *caucasica* is sometimes considered a separate species. It is a splendid border plant, with spikes of white flowers held high above its deeply divided, ash-like leaves (its old name was *D. fraxinella* – meaning 'resembling ash'). In the form *purpureus* they are purplish-pink, striped with darker pink. The flowers appear in the summer.

Dictamnus purpureus

This plant is known as the burning bush because on a hot day the seed pods release gases which can be ignited with a match. The white and purple forms grow up to 1m (3ft) with a spread of 60cm (24in). Both certainly deserve their place in middle of a border.

Cultivation Any reasonable garden soil as long as it is well-drained. It is best in a sunny position, although it will also tolerate a little light shade. Z4.

Propagation The easiest method of increase is sowing fresh seed. Plants can be divided in spring but this can be tricky since they do not like to be disturbed.

DIERAMA

Angel's fishing rod

This is a beautiful genus of plants that ought to be more widely grown. There are 44 species altogether, but most gardeners only know one or two. The strange English name is derived from the fact that the flowers are hang from very slender arching stems, much in the manner of bait from a fishing rod. The flowers are bell-shaped and come in variations of pink and purple.

Dierama dracomontanum

They appear in summer. The stems emerge from a fountain of strap-like foliage.

The flowers need space to hang so dieramas should not be surrounded by tall plants: the edge of a border is ideal or, even better, overhanging water.
Cultivation These need a moist, but well-drained soil and they should be placed in full sun. Z8.
Propagation The best method of increase is from seed sown fresh, although it may take several years to get a flowering plant. They can also be divided in spring but they will take a while to settle down.

Dierama dracomontanum
This is a short form, so it is suitable for small gardens. It has light pink flowers. H 60cm (24in) S 45cm (18in).

Dierama igneum
A short-stemmed version with unusually bright red flowers. H 60cm (24in) S 45cm (18in).

***Dierama* 'Merlin'**
A new form with beautiful rich purple flowers that are a deep blackberry colour. H 1m (3ft) S 75cm (30in).

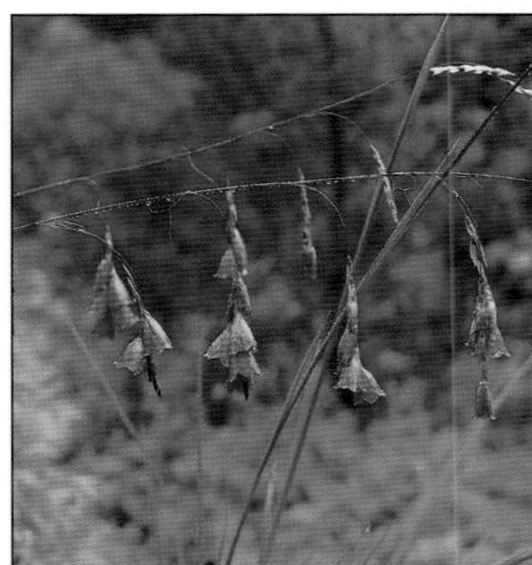

Dierama pulcherrimum

Dierama pendulum
One of the taller species when it is grown in good conditions. It has purplish-pink flowers. H 2m (6ft) S 15–20cm (6–8in).

Dierama pulcherrimum
This is another tall form, with attractive flowers of varying shades of pink and purple. H 2m (6ft) S 1m (3ft). There is also a white form *album*.

Other plants There are a surprising number of other species and cultivars waiting to be discovered by the keen gardener. *D.* 'Guinevere', *D. latifolium, D. medium, D. pauciflorum, D.* Slieve Donard hybrids and many others are certainly worth looking at.

DIGITALIS
Foxglove

Everyone knows the foxglove, but many gardeners grow only the common purple one which is in fact a biennial (see page 120). There are a surprising number of other species that are far less well-known. While most of these are perennial they tend to be short lived and so need to be replaced every two or three years. However, they are easy to propagate from seed. The flowers all have the same basic foxglove shape except some are smaller and more squat. The flowers vary considerably in colour from yellow and cream through to differing shades of soft brown, purple and pink.

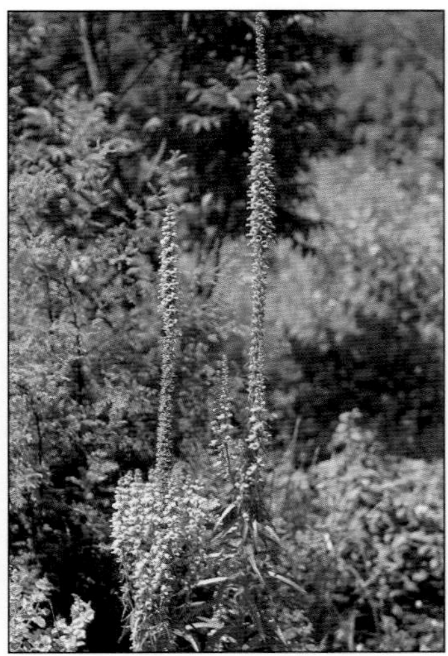

Digitalis ferruginea

Digitalis lutea

They are carried in tall spikes. Foxgloves can either be dotted around amongst other plants in a cottage garden style, or you can grow them in a drift for a more organized effect.
Cultivation Foxgloves will grow in any reasonable garden soil and will tolerate either sun or light shade, making them versatile plants. Z3–5.
Propagation These plants all come readily from seed, which should be sown in spring.

Digitalis ferruginea
A distinguished-looking plant with upright stems carrying masses of rust-brown flowers over dark green leaves during summer. H 1.5m (5ft) S 45cm (18in).

Digitalis grandiflora
A shorter plant, up to 1m (3ft) high, which produces pale yellow blooms with a slightly flattened appearance in early summer. H 1m (3ft) S 45cm (18in).

Digitalis lanata
Extremely beautiful, soft white foxgloves with brown veining. H 60cm (24in) S 30cm (12in).

Digitalis × mertonensis

Digitalis lutea
Another yellow-flowered foxglove. This one produces narrow tubes in early summer. H 60cm (24in) S 30cm (12in).

Digitalis × mertonensis
This is a hybrid with large, slightly flattened foxgloves. They are a purple-pink with a touch of light brown in them. This makes a good border plant. It reaches 1m (3ft) in height, with a spread of 45cm (18in).

Digitalis parviflora
As the botanical name implies, this foxglove has small flowers, but a lot of them. They are a wonderful rusty-brown colour. H 60cm (24in) S 30cm (12in).

Other plants There are many interesting foxgloves that are just as good as those listed above. Try, for example, *DD. davisiana, dubia, obscura, stewartii, thapsi* and *viridiflora*.

Spring-flowering perennials

Ajuga reptans
Anemone blanda
Anemone nemorosa
Bergenia
Cardamine
Dicentra
Doronicum
Euphorbia polychroma
Helleborus
Lamium maculatum
Lamium orvala
Meconopsis cambrica
Myositis
Primula
Pulmonaria
Ranunculus ficaria
Symphytum
Trillium
Veronica peduncularis
Viola

Doronicum 'Spring Beauty'

D. affinis 'Polydactyla Mappleback'

Dryopteris affinis 'Cristata'

Echinacea purpurea

DORONICUM
Leopard's bane

This genus can be easily overlooked as "yet another daisy", but they are very good daisies, especially as they appear in spring when their golden flowers are most welcome. This is a grouping of about 25 species of which only a few are in cultivation. They are simple plants with large yellow flowers that float above the mid-green foliage. They look best when planted in a large clump, rather than individually, so that they shine out from the dappled spring shade.
Cultivation Any reasonable garden soil, but preferably a moist one. Most require a light shade. Z4.
Propagation They are very easy to increase by division.

Doronicum 'Frühlingspracht' (or 'Spring Beauty')
This is a double that is beautiful but lacks the elegance of the singles. Golden-yellow flowers are carried on stems up to 45cm (18in) high. S 30cm (12in).

Doronicum 'Miss Mason'
One of the best with large (8cm/3in) heads that appear in early summer. H 45cm (18in) S 60cm (24in).

Doronicum orientale
This is a taller species with large yellow flowers. It has a particularly good form called 'Magnificum', which is slightly taller and has larger flowers. H 60cm (24in) S 1m (3ft).

Other plants There are several others worth checking out including 'Little Leo' (dwarf) and *D. pardalianches* (tall).

DRYOPTERIS
Buckler fern

A huge genus of some 200 species of ferns of which quite a number are in cultivation. These are excellent ferns for use in shady areas such as under tall shrubs or in the shade of a house or wall. They look especially good filling odd dark corners. They are deciduous but in milder areas they may stay evergreen throughout the winter. They form fountains of typical fern-like fronds. The fanatic might want to collect all the variations but to the general gardener just one or two is likely to be sufficient since the variations between cultivars are not that great.
Cultivation Like many ferns these like a moist, rich, woodland-type soil in partial shade. Z3–5.
Propagation The easiest method is to divide the plants in spring just before growth resumes. They can also be grown from fresh spore.

Dryopteris affinis
This is one of the three main species. It has fronds that are very similar to those of *D. filix-mas*: lance-shaped and about 1m (3ft) long. There are a large number of cultivars, such as 'Cristata' and 'Polydactyla Mappleback', to explore. Most of them have distorted fronds of some kind. S 1m (3ft).

Dryopteris dilatata
Similar to the above but with broader fronds. It is taller growing to about 1.5m (5ft) when happy with the conditions. Again there are a number of cultivars. S 45cm (18in).

Dryopteris filix-mas
This is the male fern. It is very similar to the *D. affinis*. An excellent garden plant with lots of poise. H 1.2m (4ft) S 1m (3ft). There are a large number of variants, including the popular 'Crispa Cristata' from which to choose.

ECHINACEA
Coneflower

A small genus of which one species, *E. purpurea*, is widely grown both as a species and in its various cultivars. It is a moderately tall plant which is

Doronicum 'Miss Mason'

Dryopteris filix-mas 'Crispa Cristata'

Echinacea purpurea 'Green Edge'

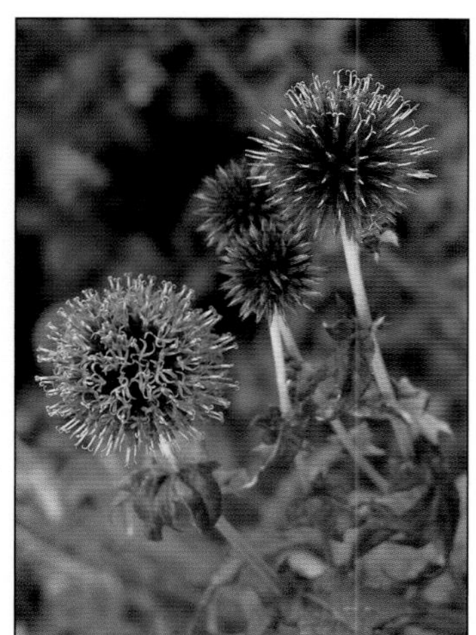
Echinops ritro

grown for its flowers. These are like large daisies with a single fringe of petals around a central cone. Being large they stand out in the border and mix well with both other herbaceous plants and with grasses. H 1.2m (4ft) S 45cm (18in).
Cultivation This plant needs a soil rich in well-rotted organic material, but it should be well drained. It can be grown in full sun or a little light shade. Z3.
Propagation The species can be grown from seed sown in spring, but the cultivars need to be increased by division in spring.

Echinacea purpurea
The flower has a cone which is a bronze colour while the petals are a deep purple-pink. The flowers are up to 12cm (5in) across and larger in some cultivars. They flower in summer and continue into autumn.

The forms 'Alba', 'White Lustre' and 'White Swan' all have white flowers; the white petals of 'Green Edge' have a delicate green edging. Other cultivars include the dwarf form 'Kim's Knee High', the large-flowered 'Magnus' and 'Rubinstern', a very good dark purple form.

Other plants There are other species which are available for the keen gardener to hunt down. *E. angustifolia* has similar flowers except that the petals are much narrower and longer. *EE. pallida* and *paradoxa* are good plants to include in a collection.

ECHINOPS
Globe thistle
A large genus of more than 100 species of which only a few are worthy of general cultivation. Most of those are very similar, mainly varying in the colour of the thistle. This flower is spherical and held on stiff stems above slightly spiny foliage. Most of these plants are best grown in the middle of a border; their foliage is not particularly attractive and is best hidden behind surrounding plants.
Cultivation These will grow in any reasonable, well-drained garden soil. They prefer a sunny position, but tolerate light shade. Z3.
Propagation The species come readily from seed and will often produce self-sown seedlings. It is possible to divide the plants but it is not easy. Root cuttings can be taken in winter.

Echinops bannaticus
This has blue heads above a greyish-green foliage. The heads are up to 5cm (2in) across and are in flower from midsummer onwards. H 1.2 (4ft) S 1m (3ft).

There are some good cultivars of which 'Taplow Blue' is the best, although 'Blue Globe' and the white form 'Albus' are also well worth growing.

Echinops ritro
This is the most popular species. The flowers are slightly smaller than those of the previous one; it is also a shorter plant. H 1.2m (4ft) S 75cm (30in). The subspecies *ruthenicus* and cultivar 'Veitch's Blue' are also very good.

Echinops sphaerocephalus
A tall plant for the back of the border. The flowers are an off-white. It self-sows vigorously. H 2m (6ft) S 1m (3ft).

ELYMUS
Wild rye
This is a large genus of grasses, of which a couple are of interest to the general gardener. Their main attraction is the unusual blue or silvery-blue leaves, which make them very useful for adding foliage interest to gravel beds. The plants form low hummocks

Elymus magellanicus

of arching blades surmounted by flower spikes which are not particularly attractive. H 20cm (8in) S 15cm (6in).
Cultivation Any garden soil that is well-drained will be suitable. Place in full sun. Z4.
Propagation The easiest method of increase is to divide existing plants just before growth begins in spring. They can also be grown from seed which should be sown at the same time of year.

Elymus hispidus
The foliage of this species grows erect and is an attractive silver-blue colour.

Elymus magellanicus
This is considered the best plant since the short blades are of an intense blue.

EPILOBIUM
Willow herb
The name willow herb strikes terror into most gardeners' hearts because the genus contains some of our worst weeds. However, it also contains a few very pleasing garden plants. They vary from tall ones that reach 1.5m (5ft) or so to very low ones. With such a variation in height their uses obviously vary, but in general they make good border plants.
Cultivation Grow in reasonable, well-drained garden soil. They do well in full sun or light shade. Z7.
Propagation Increase can be from seed sown in spring or by division at the same time of year.

Epilobium angustifolium album

Epilobium angustifolium
This is one of the worst of weeds, but the form *album* is worth growing if you have a very large wild garden where it can be kept out of harm's way. It produces tall spikes of white flowers. Since it will form attractive drifts but is not so rampant as the species, it is an excellent plant to include in a white colour scheme. H 1.5m (5ft) with an infinite spread.

Epilobium glabellum
A perfectly safe little willow herb, this forms a mat of dark green leaves which offsets perfectly the creamy flowers. Grow in partial shade at the front of a border. H 20cm (8in) S 15cm (6in).

Epilobium hirsutum
This is another species to avoid unless you have a large wild gardens where it would be welcome. It has a variegated form 'Well Creek' that is liked by some gardeners. H 2m (6ft) and an infinite spread.

Epilobium glabellum

EPIMEDIUM
Barrenwort

A genus of 30 or so species which has become quite popular of late, especially with several new species coming in from China. These are generally dual-purpose plants since they have attractive flowers and also have good foliage for the rest of the year. The spring flowers are small and hang airily from arching stems. Many are evergreen and the foliage is an elongated heart-shape with a leathery and often glossy appearance. Epimediums are essentially woodlanders and like to grow in a shady position. They are good either under shrubs or in the shade of buildings or walls, where they make the perfect, spreading ground cover.

Cultivation Best grown in a moist, typical woodland soil. These plants should also be positioned in partial shade although some will grow in full sun. Z4—5.

Propagation All the species can be grown from fresh seed, but the easiest method of increase is to divide them in spring.

Epimedium grandiflorum

The flower stems are up to 35cm (14in) high and have yellow, pink, purple or red flowers dangling from them. The foliage is often tinged with bronze or even red. S 30cm (12in).

There are many good cultivars including 'Crimson Beauty' (crimson flowers), 'Nanum' (dwarf with white flowers) and 'White Queen' (white flowers).

Epimedium* × *perralchicum

The floating flowers are yellow in this species, and hang from 45cm (18in) stems. The evergreen

Epimedium × perralchicum

Epimedium × rubrum

leaves are a shiny dark green with a bronze tinge. S 30cm (12in). 'Fröhnleiten' is a good form that produces large flowers.

Epimedium* × *rubrum

The leaves are tinged with red and bronze, while the flowers are a wonderful mixture of yellow and bright red. H 30cm (12in) S 20cm (8in).

Epimedium* × *versicolor

A dainty-flowered plant: the outer parts of the flowers are pink and the inner are yellow. The foliage is tinted with reddish-brown. H and S 30cm (12in). There are several good cultivars including the yellow-flowered 'Sulphureum'.

Other plants Plants in this genus are such an interesting bunch that many gardeners collect them. Other species to check out include *EE. acuminatum, alpinum, davidii, diphyllum, leptorrhizum, perralderianum,* × *warleyense* and many more.

EREMURUS
Foxtail lily

It would be a strange gardener who was not immediately struck by these plants, with their huge, colourful spikes of flowers. There are more than 40 species, of which half a dozen plus a few cultivars are in cultivation.

They are all splendid and very eye-catching. In late winter thick shoots emerge from the fleshy roots and tall stems up to 2m (6ft) develop. The large flowering spikes begin to bloom from the bottom and seem to fizz away like giant fireworks. There is a good range of colours from white and yellow to pink of various shades. These plants are excellent for a position in the middle or back of the summer border.

Eremurus himalaicus

Cultivation These need a well-drained soil that is rich in well-rotted organic material. Place in a sunny position, sheltered from wind. Protect the emerging buds from severe frosts. Z4–6.

Propagation The easiest method is to dig up the fleshy roots and divide into individual crowns once flowering is over.

Eremurus himalaicus

This stunning plant produces long heads of pure white flowers. H 1m (3ft) S 1.2m (4ft). 'Himrob' has flowers of pale pink.

Eremurus* × *isabellinus

This is a group of very interesting cultivars with a good range of colours including 'Cleopatra'

Eremurus × isabellinus 'Oase'

Eremurus stenopyllus

(orange), 'Feuerfackel' (flame red), 'Moonlight' (pale yellow) 'Oase' (apricot), 'Obelisk' (white) and 'Pinokkio' (orange). H 1.5m (5ft) S 60cm (24in).

Eremurus robustus

A slightly shorter plant at 1.2m (4ft) or so. It produces spikes of pale pink flowers. S 1m (3ft).

Eremurus stenophyllus

A 1m (3ft) high plant with spikes of dark yellow flowers. Excellent. S 45cm (18in).

Other plants There are a number of other species and cultivars that will repay the effort spent seeking them out from specialist catalogues and nurseries. However, don't fill the whole garden with them as this will overdo the dramatic effect they create.

ERIGERON
Fleabane

Daisies may not be as exotic as, say, lilies, but they do form the backbone of many of our borders. Erigeron is a large genus with a large number of daisy-like species and their commonly grown cultivars. They are clump-forming plants, usually of low stature, making them ideal for carpeting the front of a border. The tall ones are good for mid-border situations. The flowers come in a range of colours and often appear over a very long season.

Erigeron glaucus

Cultivation Any reasonable garden soil is suitable but one that has been enriched with well-rotted organic material will suit these plants best. A sunny position is required, although many will tolerate a little light shade. The taller varieties may need support as they can be floppy. Z3–6.
Propagation The clump-forming varieties are best divided in the spring. Seed can be sown for the species and basal cuttings can be taken from some in spring.

Erigeron aurantiacus
A clump-forming plant whose bright orange flowers have a yellow central disc. H 30cm (12in) S 30cm (12in).

'Azurfee' is a taller form reaching 45cm (18in), this time with light blue, semi-double flowers with yellow centres. 'Dignity' has purple daisies with a yellow centre; again it grows to 45cm (18in) or more. 'Dimity' is a semi-double with bright pink flowers; H 30cm (12in) S 45cm (18in). 'Dunkelste Aller' is a very good semi-double form with deep violet-blue flowers which have yellow centres. It is one of the taller forms, growing to 60cm (24in) S 60cm (24in). 'Foerster's Liebling' is another excellent form with pinkish-purple, semi-double flowers. It grows to 45cm (18in). S 60cm (24in).

Erigeron karvinskianus

Erigeron karvinskianus
This is a superb, airy plant for growing on banks, in walls or in crevices in paving or containers. It produces masses of small white and pink daisies on thin wiry stems over a very long season from spring until winter. It grows in clumps. It deserves a place in almost any garden. H 30cm (12in) S 45cm (18in).

***Erigeron* 'Quakeress'**
This is a taller form which produces pale bluish-pink flowers. H 45cm (18in) S 60cm (24in).

Other plants There are several other species and cultivars, including *E. glaucus* to investigate. All produce a good number of flowers and are easy to grow.

ERYNGIUM
Sea holly

No garden should be without at least one of these wonderful plants. The foliage and flowers generally have a bluish tinge to them, although some also have a silvery appearance. The flowers form tight domed heads, which are surrounded by blue, silver or greenish bracts, rather like a collar. They retain their colour for a long time and are very useful for drying. These flower heads are often very spiky. The leaves can also be spiky and are usually attractive in their own right.

There are around 200 species, many of which are in cultivation. They are very good border plants, usually best sited in a middle position, and they are especially good in gravel beds.
Cultivation Most sea hollies grow in any garden soil so long as it is free-draining. It is important to plant them in full sun. Z3–7.
Propagation Species will come quite readily from seed sown fresh. They can also be divided, although this is not easy since most are tap-rooted. Taking root cuttings in winter is usually easier.

Eryngium alpinum

Eryngium × oliverianum

Eryngium agavifolium
A tall plant with stems carrying clusters of pale green flower heads. The leaves that spring from the rosette at the base are spiny. An eye-catching plant but the spines mean that you need to take care when weeding nearby. H 2m (6ft) S 60cm (24in).

Eryngium alpinum
Large heads of silvery blue, which are touched with purple and surrounded by narrow, soft bracts. *E.* × *oliverianum* is similar except that the stiff bracts are prickly. H 1m (3ft) S 60cm (24in).

Eryngium bourgatii
This much-branched plant has masses of small blue heads. The leaves are dark green, veined with silver. It is a good foliage plant. H 45cm (18in) S 30cm (12in).

Eryngium* × *tripartitum
A splendid plant with a haze of small violet-blue flower heads. If well treated it can grow to nearly 1m (3ft). This is an excellent plant for mid border but it is often short lived. S 50cm (20in).

Other plants There are many other wonderful eryngiums, including *EE. amethystinum, eburneum, horridum, maritimum, pandanifolium* and *planum* with all its wonderful cultivars.

Eryngium maritimum

ERYSIMUM
Wallflowers

A large genus related to the cabbage family – but don't let that put you off since they are superb garden plants and every garden should include several of them. The most commonly grown wallflowers are treated as biennials (see page 124) but there are also a selection of excellent plants that, although short lived, are grown as perennials. The small, flat flowers are carried in loose spikes or clusters in early summer, often well into summer and even beyond. Most colours are represented except for blue. They are usually bright and cheerful-looking plants, making them good for the front of a border. Most grow from 45–75cm (18–30in) S 45cm (18in).

Cultivation Any garden soil will do, but the plants will last longer in a well-drained soil. A sunny position is required. Z3–6.

Propagation The species can be grown from seed, but most cultivars are best increased by cuttings taken in early summer.

***Erysimum* 'Bowles' Mauve'**
What a wonderful plant this is. A great dome of airy stems carries purple flowers from spring through to autumn. Up to 1m (3ft) in height.

***Erysimum* 'Bredon'**
This is a shorter form (up to 30cm/12in or less) with bright yellow flowers.

Erysimum 'Bowles' Mauve'

Erysimum 'John Codrington'

***Erysimum* 'Constant Cheer'**
A lovely mixture of colour: the flowers open a brownish-orange and then slowly change to purple.

***Erysimum* 'John Codrington'**
Another excellent form. This time the flowers come in a mixture of yellow, soft purple and brown creating a tapestry of colour.

***Erysimum* 'Moonlight'**
This is a low-growing cultivar that forms a mat some 25cm (10in) high. The pale yellow flowers open from red buds.

***Erysimum* 'Rufus'**
This has flowers of a good rusty brown colour. However, it isn't very strong and needs replacing every or every other year.

***Erysimum* 'Wenlock Beauty'**
'Wenlock Beauty' is possibly the best of the bunch. It carries masses of sparkling flowers in a mixture of reds, mauves, browns and apricots. It grows to 45cm (18in) or so.

Other plants Other wallflowers worth considering include *E. linifolium*, which can be grown from seed. It produces a number of cultivars, basically with a lilac or purple base colour. *E. mutabile* is similar with mixed colours. Other cultivars include 'Butterscotch' (yellowish-orange), 'Jacob's Jacket' (mixed colours), 'Golden Jubilee' (golden yellow) and 'Golden Gem' (golden yellow).

EUPATORIUM
Hemp agrimony

A large genus of which only a handful of plants are widely grown in gardens. They are valued for their late summer and autumn flowering. Many are large and they create a good block of colour at that time of year. They are also attractive to butterflies and bees. The main species and cultivars produce flattish heads of pink flowers, while others have loose heads of small button-like white flowers. They can be invasive, so they are usually only grown in large borders. There are some smaller versions that are suitable for smaller gardens.

Eupatorium p.m. 'Album'

Cultivation These plants need a moisture-retentive soil. They do best in sun although they will take some light shade.

Propagation The easiest method of propagation is to divide the plants in spring.

Eupatorium cannabinum
This is not the most attractive of the eupatoriums, but it is good for attracting butterflies and insects. Place in a damp site in a wild garden. H and S 1.2m (4ft).

Eupatorium purpureum
This is the main plant for border use. It is tall at 2m (6ft) or more. Again it is very attractive to butterflies. It is probably most frequently grown in the form *E.p. maculatum* 'Atropurpureum' which has good purple colouration both in its flowers and stems. S 1.5m (5ft). Its companion *E.p.m.* 'Album' has white flowers. The form *E.p.* 'Purple Bush' is lower-growing, reaching up to around 1m (3ft), so it is better suited to smaller gardens.

Eupatorium purpureum

Eupatorium rugosum
This is species with flattish heads of up to 30 round, white flowers. It looks good in the evening light. H 1.5m (5ft) S 30cm (12in). A similar white-flowered species is *E. perfoliatum*.

EUPHORBIA
Spurge

An enormous genus of over 2,000 species, which vary from trees to ground-hugging plants. Fifty or more herbaceous species are in regular cultivation. The flowers are insignificant, but they are surrounded by colourful bracts, usually in yellowish-green. These last longer than the flowers giving the plants greater staying power. They make good border plants, planted singly or in groups. Some of the bigger ones make good focal points. The sap can be irritating to the skin and eyes.

Cultivation Any good garden soil is suitable, but preferably one that is not too dry. They do best in sun but most tolerate light shade.

Propagation Sow seed in spring. Some self-sow, producing enough seedlings for most purposes. Some spreading species can be divided. Those that grow from one basic stem can be increased by taking basal cuttings in spring.

Euphorbia amygdaloides
The species is best grown in a wild woodland garden. Its variety *robbiae* is an excellent plant for shady areas, even quite dense and dry ones. The short-lived form 'Purpurea' has good purple foliage and bracts in spring and is more suitable for the border. H 60cm (24in) S 30cm (12in).

Euphorbia characias
A tall rounded clump of radiating stems each topped with a club-shaped spike of yellowish-green "flowers". There are many forms, of which *wulfenii* is the most important. This is similar to the

Euphorbia characias wulfenii

species but the flower heads are often larger and yellower. Both the species and *wulfenii* have a lot of cultivars, with only marginal differences between them. They make superb border plants and a large clump makes an eye-catching feature when planted on its own. H and S 1.5m (5ft).

Euphorbia griffithii
A spreading, single-stemmed plant with reddish stems, leaves and bracts. The forms 'Dixter' and 'Fireglow' are excellent. It can be rampant in light soils. H 1m (3ft) S 50cm (20in).

Euphorbia polychroma
An excellent species that forms a rounded hummock 45cm (18in) high. It has bright yellow "flower" in spring. S 50cm (20in).

Other plants There are many species from which to choose. Good ones to consider include *EE. dulcis* (especially 'Chameleon'), × *martinii, mellifera, myrsinites. nicaeensis, palustris* and *sikkimensis.*

FILIPENDULA
Meadowsweet

This is a small genus with a few worthy garden plants. Their attraction comes from the sprays of white, pink or purple flowers, held on strong purple stems above attractive, deep-cut foliage. Many are good border plants; others are perfect for the wild or meadow garden. Some filipendulas are moisture-lovers and they are therefore good for growing next to water features or in bog gardens. They generally grow to about 1m (3ft) although some

Euphorbia dulcis 'Chameleon'

reach double that height. They flower from midsummer onwards. S 1m (3ft).
Cultivation A soil with plenty of well-rotted organic material is ideal, although it should be free draining. Plant in either full sun or partial shade. Z2–3.
Propagation Division is by far the easiest method of propagation for all of them.

Filipendula camtschatica
A tall plant with large, divided leaves and sprays of white or pinkish flowers. H 2m (6ft) S 1m (3ft).

***Filipendula* 'Kahome'**
This is a smaller (45cm/18in) form, ideal for the small garden. It has pink flowers suspended above a bronze foliage. An excellent plant. S 30cm (12in).

Filipendula purpurea
A fine plant with several very good cultivars. It has sprays of magenta flowers. H 1.2m (4ft)

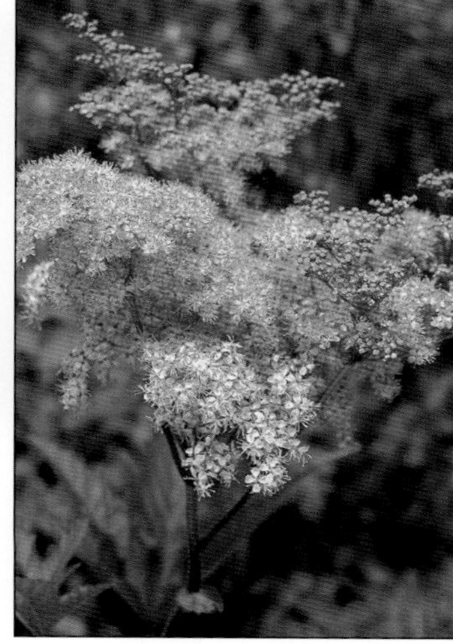

Filipendula rubra

S 60cm (24in). The cultivar 'Elegans' is worth considering since it is a more refined version. The form *albiflora* has beautiful white flowers.

Filipendula rubra
A good garden form, especially in the variety 'Venusta' which produces bright cerise flowers that become pink as as they age. It grows to about 2m (6ft) or even higher under good conditions. S 1.2m (4ft).

Filipendula ulmaria
The species can be grown in a border but it is not a top-class plant. However, it is perfect for naturalizing in a meadow garden, especially in damper areas or along a ditch. H and S 30cm (12in). The form 'Aurea' has yellow foliage that changes to a yellowish green with age. It is often placed in borders as a foliage plant.

Euphorbia polychroma

Euphorbia × martinii

Filipendula ulmaria

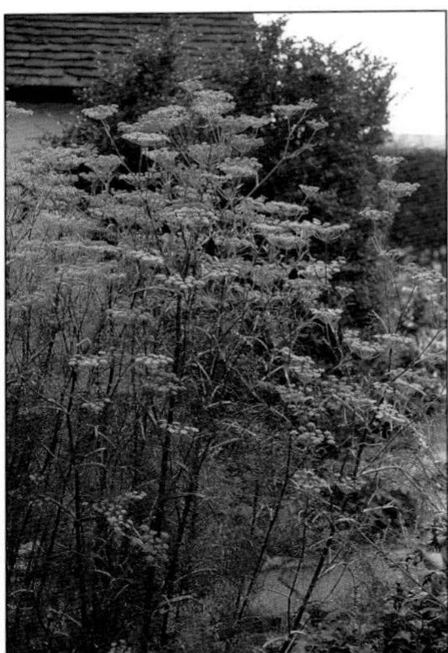
Foeniculum vulgare

FOENICULUM
Fennel

For some gardeners fennel is something confined to the vegetable garden, but *F. vulgare* is a splendid plant for the border. It is usually grown in the form 'Purpureum'. It is mainly grown as a foliage plant, but the flat heads of tiny yellow flowers are beautiful in their own right especially when seen floating above the delicately cut foliage. The plant is very upright-growing and gets up to 2m (6ft) tall. The foliage is very fine and feathery. When freshly opened the leaves are a dark bronze colour, becoming purplish-green as they age. This is a superb plant, grown either by itself or in groups, for the middle or towards the back of a border. S 75cm (30in).

Francoa sonchifolia

Cultivation Any good garden soil will do, but moister and richer soils produce better plants. A sunny position is needed. Fennel can self-sow prodigiously so cut back the flowering stems before seed is produced. Z4.
Propagation The easiest and best method of increase is from seed sown in autumn or spring. There are usually enough self-sown seedlings for most uses but move them into position while they are still small as they are tap-rooted.

FRANCOA
Bridal wreath

A quiet and relatively unassuming plant that always adds a touch of quality to a border. *Francoa* is a small genus of plants of which only three are regularly grown in gardens. Their attraction is the arching stems that are topped with cylindrical spikes of small, star-like, pink flowers with reddish markings. In good conditions these spikes will reach 1m (3ft) but they are usually less. There is little to choose between the species except in the density of the pink colouration. They make excellent plants for the first or second row of the border, placed so that the stems arch over other plants that have already flowered or have yet to flower. S 45cm (18in).
Cultivation These plants prefer a humus-rich soil that is well-drained but they will grow in most reasonable garden soils. Sun is preferable but they tolerate a little shade. They may need winter protection in cold areas. Z7.
Propagation Francoas come readily from seed sown in spring.

Francoa appendiculata
This plant has pale pink flowers with darker makings.

Francoa ramosa
Very pale pink, almost white flowers with deep pink markings.

Francoa sonchifolia
Pink flowers with purplish-pink markings. There is an almost pure white form, 'Alba', of this. There is also 'Rogerson's Form' in which the flowers are much darker, appearing almost purple.

Fritillaria imperialis

FRITILLARIA
Fritillary

A large genus of bulbs of 100 species. Most are of interest to the alpine enthusiast, with only a handful being suitable for the perennial garden. They vary in size from a few centimetres to 1.2m (4ft). They have pendant bell-shaped flowers in many colours, including green and almost black. True blue is the only colour missing. Some are worthy of the spring border but others are better in a wild garden.
Cultivation Conditions vary and are given under individual species below. Z3–6.
Propagation Seed is readily produced and this is an easy if lengthy method of reproduction. Division of the small bulblets, or "rice" is also very easy.

Fritillaria acmopetala
A small-belled form suitable for choice spots at the front of a border where it will not get swamped. The bells are green

Fritillaria meleagris

Fritillaria persica

suffused with purple. It needs a well-drained soil that does not get too wet in winter. H 30cm (12in) S 5–8cm (2–3in). *F. graeca* is similar but with bigger bells.

Fritillaria imperialis
A very impressive plant. It has clusters of orange or yellow flowers at the top of each tall stem just beneath an upright tuft of green leaves. It needs similar conditions to the previous plant, and is good for the middle of the border where its dying foliage will be covered by summer plants. H 1.2m (4ft) S 30cm (12in).

Fritillaria meleagris
A beautiful plant with large bells hanging from thin stems. The flowers are checkered purple and white, although there are also white forms which have a light chequering of green. These can be grown in a border but are also ideal for naturalizing in grass, particularly if the soil is damp. H 30cm (12in) S 5–8cm (2–3in).

Fritillaria verticillata

Green-flowered perennials

Alchemilla mollis
Anemone nemorosa 'Viridiflora'
Aquilegia viridiflora
Dianthus 'Charles Musgrave'
Euphorbia
Galtonia viridiflora
Helleborus argutifolia
Helleborus foetidus
Hemerocallis 'Lady Fingers'
Iris 'Green Halo'
Iris 'Green Spot'
Kniphofia 'Green Jade'
Kniphofia 'Percy's Pride'
Lilium 'Limelight'
Primula auricala (several)
Ranunculus 'Green Petal'
Zantedeschia aethopica 'Green Goddess'

Gaura lindheimeri 'Siskiyou Pink'

Gentiana acaulis

Fritillaria persica
This plant is another tall form. It produces clusters of very dark purple, almost black flowers. It needs dry conditions and a hot place to do well. *F. persica* often does not live long in borders but it is so beautiful that it is worth trying to grow. H 75cm (30in) S 10cm (4in).

Fritillaria verticillata
A delightful plant with pale green and white flowers. It soon forms a large clump. It is best planted near shrubs to which its tendrils can cling. It will grow in most well-drained borders. H 45cm (18in) S 10cm (4in).

GALEGA
Goat's rue

A small genus of herbaceous plants of which four are in general cultivation. These are tall, open plants with many branches, the tips of which carry short, upright spikes of small, pea-like flowers. The colours are generally white, blue or pinkish-purple, and the pretty flowers are often bicoloured. Galegas flower in early summer when they produce a good mound of blooms for the back of the border. H 1.5m (5ft) S 1m (3ft).
Cultivation Any good garden soil will do, but a richer, moister soil will provide the best results. These plants do best in full sun, but they will also tolerate a little light shade. They may need some form of support.
Propagation Galegas can be divided in spring, although this is not easy. They can also be grown from seed sown at the same time.

Galega × hartlandii

Galega × hartlandii
This is one of the better plants, most commonly represented by two of its cultivars. 'Alba', as its name suggests, has white flowers. The other is 'Lady Wilson', which is a bicolour whose flowers come in white and mauvish-blue.

Galega officinalis
There is not much to choose between the two species. Again this has bicoloured flowers in white and pale blue. It also has an all-white form 'Alba'. The form 'His Majesty' has white and mauve-purple bicoloured flowers.

GAURA
Gaura

A genus of about 20 species of which only one is in general cultivation. This is *G. lindheimeri*. It has several cultivars but the species itself is as good as any of them. It has tall, thin stems from which dance delightful butterfly-like flowers. These are white with a touch of pink. H 1.2cm (4ft) S 1m (3ft). 'Siskiyou Pink' is the most popular cultivar. Here the flowers are a dark pink, but they are less effective than the white and the plant is not very robust. 'Corrie's Gold' has gold-edged leaves which do little to increase the attraction of the plant.
Cultivation Gaura will thrive in any reasonable garden soil as long as it is well drained. It must have a sunny position. Z5.
Propagation They can be divided with care in the spring, but this is not the easiest of tasks. It is easier to take basal cuttings at the same time of year. The species can also be grown from seed, which is sown in spring.

GENTIANA
Gentian

The 400 species of gentians provide some of the bluest plants in nature. There are a number that are of interest to the alpine gardener, but there are only one or two that are suitable for use in the perennial garden. The flowers are trumpet-shaped. The majority of gentians are ground-hugging plants that like moist, even boggy conditions. The taller border varieties are more accommodating and will grow in any soil that has humus in it. They are ideal plants for shady areas in the garden.
Cultivation Grow in rich moisture-retentive soil. They prefer partial shade, although full sun will be tolerated if the ground does not dry out. Z5.
Propagation Divide gentians in spring or sow the seed as soon as it is harvested.

Gentiana acaulis
This is not the easiest plant to grow but when it is happy, it is wonderful. Very large, upward-facing trumpets appear in late spring and early summer. H 10cm (4in) S 10cm (4in).

Gentiana asclepiadea
This is the willow gentian, a tallish plant that produces long arching stems, the tips of which often touch the ground. They carry blue, upward-facing flowers on either side. A perfect plant for a choice position in the shady garden. It flowers in late summer. H 1m (3ft) S 60cm (24in).

Gentiana lutea
This is an unusual yellow gentian. It is a tall, upright plant which carries whorls of bright yellow, starry flowers in midsummer. Ideal for naturalizing in grass, such as in a meadow garden. H 1.2m (4ft) S 60cm (24in).

Gentiana sino-ornata
A ground-hugging plant with brilliant blue trumpets facing upwards. There are many cultivars and similar species, all of which are suitable for moist ground in light shade where they will not get swamped by other plants. H 5cm (2in) S 30cm (12in).

Gentiana asclepiadea

Geranium 'Ann Folkard'

Geranium clarkei 'Kashmir White'

Geranium 'Johnson's Blue'

GERANIUM
Hardy geraniums

Many people get confused between these plants and the pelargoniums, the red-flowered plants that are still commonly referred to as geraniums more than 100 years after their name was changed. Geranium is a large genus with more than 300 species. Some are tender but a surprising number of the remainder are in cultivation. There are many gardeners who have been bitten by the collecting bug and have a large number in their garden. Even if you don't collect them it can be surprising how quickly the number of different geraniums that you own increases, which shows how good and versatile they are.

They have open, dish-like flowers in a variety of colours, mainly based on pink and purplish-blue colour schemes. They vary in height from ground-hugging to 1.2m (4ft). Most flower in early summer but some are later and others flower over a long period. Geraniums are very versatile: there is a geranium for every position in the garden in both sun and shade.

Cultivation Most geraniums grow in any reasonable garden soil, but they prefer it laced with plenty of well-rotted organic material. Some are sun lovers, others prefer shade. Cut early-blooming forms after flowering to the ground to get fresh foliage. Z2–6.

Propagation Species can be grown from seed sown in spring. Cultivars can be divided or cuttings taken in spring.

Geranium 'Ann Folkard'
A sprawling plant that clambers between and over other plants. The foliage is yellowish early on, while the flowers are magenta with a dark eye. This geranium has a long flowering season. H 60cm (24in) S 1m (3ft).

Geranium × _cantabrigiense_
An excellent carpeting geranium that makes perfect ground cover. The leaves are slightly shiny and set off the pink flowers perfectly. 'Biokovo' has flowers of such a pale pink as to be almost white. 'Cambridge' is another good pink form. H 15cm (6in) with an infinite spread.

Geranium cinereum
This is a dwarf plant that is usually grown as one of its cultivars such as 'Apple Blossom' (pale pink flowers) or 'Ballerina' (purple-veined pink flowers). Both have a long flowering season and are perfect for placing at the edge of borders. H 15cm (6in) S 30cm (12in).

Geranium clarkei
This species is grown only in the form of its cultivars. These make excellent plants although they only flower once. 'Kashmir Purple' has perfect mauvish-pink flowers with reddish veins, while 'Kashmir White' has white flowers with paler veins. They grow in a rounded hummock, and make excellent border plants. H and S 45cm (18in).

Geranium himalayense
A good border plant. The flowers are a light purple, darker towards the middle and with a whitish centre. There are several good forms. 'Plenum' ('Birch Double') has attractive double flowers and 'Gravetye' has larger flowers with more purple in them. H 30cm (12in) S 60cm (24in).

Geranium magnificum
A good old-fashioned cottage-garden plant with soft leaves and blue flowers. It tolerates some shade. H and S 60cm (24in).

Geranium 'Johnson's Blue'
A good single form, this has blue flowers with whitish centres. H 45cm (18in) S 60cm (24in).

Geranium macrorrhizum
A superb plant for shade (although it will also grow in sun). The leaves are aromatic when crushed and are semi-evergreen. The pink flowers are produced in early summer. There are several good forms with flowers of varying pinks. H 38cm (15in) S 60cm (24in).

Geranium oxonianum
This and its many cultivars make excellent ground cover in either sun or shade. The clump-forming plant will scramble up through shrubs given a chance. The flowers are bright pink. H and S 75cm (30in).

Geranium phaeum
Another excellent clump-forming plant. This time the flowers are relatively small with reflexed (bent back) petals held in airy sprays on thin stems. The flowers vary from

Geranium cinereum 'Ballerina'

Geranium phaeum

Geranium psilostemon

Geranium sanguineum striatum

pink to purple to white. There are many good cultivars including 'Samobor' which has large chocolate blotches on the leaves. H 75cm (30in) S 45cm (18in).

Geranium psilostemon
A superb plant that forms a large round hummock of airy stems bearing magenta flowers with dark centres. Perfect for larger borders. H and S 1.2m (4ft).

Geranium sanguineum
This is a superb species with lots of cultivars, many of which flower over a long period. It has purple-red flowers over a hummock of foliage. The variety *striatum* and its cultivars have pink rather than red flowers, with prominent veins. H and S 30cm (12in).

Other plants There are many, more species and cultivars to explore including all the forms of *G. pratense* and *G. sylvaticum*.

GEUM
Avens
A genus of about 50 species, a number of which make good garden plants. Although several species are grown it is mainly

Geum 'Lemon Drops'

Geum rivale

their cultivars that grace our borders. Geums are low clump-formers with thin, wiry stems that carry brightly coloured flowers well above the foliage. The flowers are flat discs, usually with a golden central boss. Some forms are double. The colours are mainly reds, oranges and yellows although there are some with more subtle colours. They mainly flower in early summer although some are repeat flowering.
Cultivation Geums will grow in most reasonable garden soils as long as they are free-draining. They need a sunny position. Z5.
Propagation The species can be increased from seed sown in spring, but division is the easiest method and an essential one for the cultivars.

***Geum* 'Borisii'**
This is a wonderfully bright plant with vivid orange-red flowers that are produced over a long season. H 45cm (18in) S 30cm (12in). Another excellent cultivar is 'Coppertone', a lowish-growing (30cm/12in) geum with soft coppery-coloured flowers which are more bell-shaped. 'Lemon Drops' has lemon-yellow flowers

Geum 'Rubin'

which look particularly good planted near blue violas.

Geum rivale
A plant with pinkish-orange flowers which are bell-shaped rather than disc-shaped. The species is attractive but the cultivars are more often grown. H 45cm (18in) S 20cm (8in). 'Leonard's Variety' is the most famous. It is a more refined plant than the species with lots of reddish-apricot flowers. 'Album' has greenish-white flowers.

There are lots of other cultivars to explore including 'Mrs Bradshaw' (large, semi-double red), 'Georgenberg' (flame orange), 'Prinses Juliana' (orange) and 'Rubin' (semi-double flowers in flame-red).

GILLENIA
Gillenia
A small genus of two, of which one, *G. trifoliata*, is in general cultivation. This is a shrubby perennial with a mass of wiry stems carrying very delicate, butterfly-like flowers. These are pure white with red bud sheaths. It makes a delightful plant, which is not seen as frequently as perhaps it should be. The flowers last throughout the summer. H 1m (3ft) S 60cm (24in).
Cultivation Any reasonable garden soil except alkaline ones. It needs a sunny position lightly shaded at the hottest time of day. Z4.
Propagation Grow from seed sown in spring. The plants can be divided at the same time, although this is not that easy.

GLADIOLUS
Gladiolus
This is a large genus of bulbs that is well known to gardeners. Most are tender and are treated as annuals (see page 130), but there are a few exceptions which are of interest to the perennial gardener. One in particular, *G. byzantinus*, is hardy and commonly grown. This has not got the big blowsy flowers of the annuals; its blooms are simpler and in many ways much more refined. Gladioli are excellent plants for a late-spring border. Plant in-between emerging summer plants so that the gap

Gillenia trifoliata

left when flowering is over is covered by the new foliage.
Cultivation Any reasonable garden soil will do. Site in full sun; they can tolerate light shade. Z7–8.
Propagation Dig up the corms and divide off the new ones. They can also be grown without much problem from seed sown in spring. They do not need staking.

Gladiolus communis* subsp. *byzantinus
This is still known mainly as *G. byzantinus* by most gardeners. It has vivid magenta flowers down one side of a slightly arching stem. It has long sword-like leaves. H 1m (3ft) S 15cm (6in).

Other plants There are a few other gladiolus that can be grown in the open garden although they may be a problem in colder areas. *G. papilio* is probably the best of these with wonderful smoky yellow flowers. *G.* × *colvillei* has some good cultivars in particular the white 'The Bride'.

Gladiolus communis subsp. *byzantinus*

Gunnera manicata

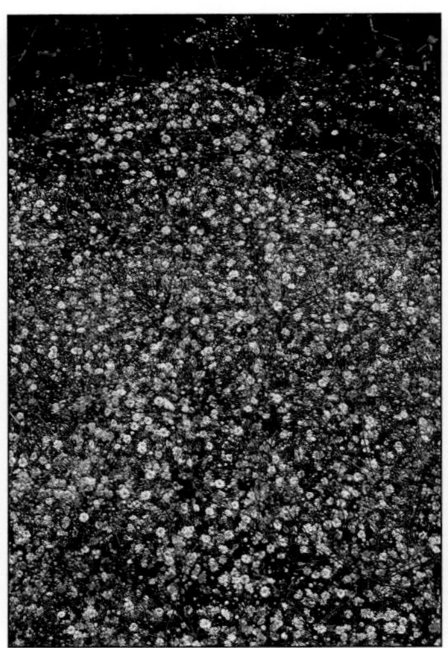
Gypsophila paniculata 'Bristol Fairy'

Gypsophila repens 'Fratensis'

GUNNERA
Gunnera

This is a genus consisting of about 45 species. Several of them are of interest to the gardener but only a couple are cultivated to any extent. Although these have similarities in terms of their leaf and flower shape, they are very different in form and size: one is ground-hugging and grows only to 10cm (4in) or so, while the other towers to at least 2m (6ft) and sometimes double that across. It is the latter that is usually of most interest to most gardeners.

Cultivation Gunneras, particularly the larger ones, require a deep, rich soil with plenty of well-rotted organic material. You need to protect the crowns over the winter. Z6–8.

Propagation Division is the easiest method for smaller species. However, their sheer size makes this impractical for the large ones, although small rooted pieces can be detached. Instead, take basal cuttings from the buds that emerge in spring.

Gunnera magellanica

A low creeping plant with rounded leaves. The flowers are green but are given colour when the flame red berries are formed. They are held in upright heads, only a few centimetres high. These plants are not really suitable for the perennial border but can be grown over a rock garden or down a bank. They need covering in winter. S indefinite.

Gunnera manicata

This is the main species grown. It is a giant with leaves that can reach more than 2m (6ft) across. They look like giant rhubarb leaves and are tall enough for children to shelter under. The stems are rough with coarse prickles. These rub in the wind producing a rasping sound. Although these plants are mainly for the large garden it has been known for them to be used as ground cover in a small suburban front garden. They are best sited next to medium to large ponds. The flowers would be insignificant if it wasn't for the size of the flower head. They are green and are carried on a thick clumps below the leaf canopy. H and S at least 2m (6ft).

Gunnera tinctoria

This plant is less frequently seen than the previous one, but is becoming more popular. It is similar but slightly smaller and more compact. It is not so hardy and will require winter protection. H and S 1.5m (5ft).

GYPSOPHILA
Gypsophila

It is hard to image any plant that differs so much from the heavy presence of the Gunnera above. These plants are lightness itself, with large airy sprays of small flowers that create a misty effect. This is a large genus with around 100 species. A handful of these are in cultivation, providing the gardener with plants that are not only beautiful in their own right but contrast well with many of those around them Some are annuals (see page 131).

Cultivation Any good garden soil will do so long as it is not too acid. It should have plenty of grit incorporated so that it is very free-draining. Z3.

Propagation Increase stock by sowing seed in spring. These plants are difficult to divide so take root cuttings in early winter.

Gypsophila cerastioides

This is really the province of the alpine growers. However, it can be used on the edge of raised beds or next to paths so long as it is not swamped by larger neighbours. It is mat-forming, and the flowers are white with pinkish centres. H 7.5cm (3in) S 10cm (4in).

Gypsophila paniculata

This is the main plant for the border. In summer it forms a cloud of small white flowers and is often called baby's breath because of this. The mass of wiry stems form a mound up to 45cm (18in) high or so. It needs a position towards the front of the border. S 1m (3ft).

There are several cultivars of which 'Bristol Fairy' is still the best. This has larger flowers than the species. There is a smaller plant with double flowers: 'Compacta Plena'.

Gypsophila repens

This is much shorter than the previous plant. It tends to be more spreading and is ideal for planting on the edge of a raised bed so that it can spill over the edge. The flowers are white, or

Gypsophila cerastioides

Gypsophila tenuifolia

white tinged with pink. H 25cm (10in) S 30cm (12in). The best known form is 'Dorothy Teacher' which is more compact with pink flowers that darken as they age. Another is 'Fratensis'.

Gypsophila 'Rosenschleier'

Also known as 'Rosy Veil', this plant is one of the best gypsophilas for the border. It forms a large, rounded haze of pale pink flowers that are white when they first open. H 45cm (18in) S 45cm (18in).

Gypsophila tenuifolia

A tufted plant forming a mat over which float plenty of small white or pink flowers. It grows up to 20cm (8in) high and 60cm (24in) across.

HAKONECHLOA
Hakonechloa

This is just one species in this genus. It is *H. macra*, which is sometimes grown in gardens but it is usually as one of its two main cultivars that it is grown. It forms a clump with arching stems. The plant reaches about 45cm (18in) high and 60cm (24in) across. 'Aureola' is the form most commonly seen. It is variegated, with alternating bright golden and green stripes running down the length of the leaves. 'Alboaurea' is similar but has touches of white.

Cultivation These plants will grow in most reasonable garden soils but they do best in richer soils so

Hakonechloa macra 'Alboaurea'

long as they are free-draining. They will grow in either sun or light shade, but the colour is best in the latter. Z6.

Propagation Increase is by division which should be carried out in spring as the new growth begins.

HEDYCHIUM
Ginger lily

A genus of around 50 species, which in spite of their tenderness have become increasingly popular for use in the border as well as in containers. The plants have a tropical appearance with large, shiny green leaves and a terminal spike of butterfly- or orchid-like flowers which add to their exotic appearance. One of the attractions is their sweet scent. These plants generally grow to between 1 and 1.5m (3–5ft) but some of the more vigorous ones can reach 3m (10ft) if they are given the right conditions. These are plants for exuberant colourful borders, especially those with a tropical feel about them – mix them in with other large-leaved and colourful plants. S 1m (3ft).

Cultivation These need a rich soil with plenty of well-rotted organic material. It should be well-drained. The position can be in either sun or partial shade. Plant the rhizomes just below the surface of the soil. Mulch deeply in the autumn to protect them from the frosts. Z8.

Propagation Ginger lilies should be propagated by dividing the rhizomes in spring.

Hedychium coccineum

This is one of the most colourful of the ginger lilies. The flowers are about 5cm (2in) long, and they may be white, pink, coral red

Hedychium densiflorum

or orange with red stamens. In good conditions, the plant can grow to 3m (10ft) but it usually reaches only half this height. It has a very good form 'Tara', which has orange flowers. S 75cm (30in).

Hedychium densiflorum

This species has yellow or orange flowers. It is one of the tallest but rarely grows to its full potential height, usually reaching only 2m (6ft) with a spread of 60cm (24in). It is reasonably hardy. There are number of good cultivars including 'Assam Orange', which has bright orange flowers, and 'Stephen' (primrose yellow with red anthers).

Hedychium gardnerianum

This is a spectacular plant, producing clear yellow flowers with red stamens. It is tender and can only be grown in frost-free positions unless it is grown inside in containers and moved out after frosts have passed. H 2m (6ft) S 75cm (30in).

Hedychium gardnerianum

Other plants There are a number of other species and cultivars that are widely grown but their hardiness is doubtful. If you want to try, they are best grown in a warm, sheltered position or they can be cultivated under glass.

HEDYSARUM
Hedysarum

This is a large genus of around 100 species. Only one is in general cultivation, although there are a couple of others that are worth looking out for. They are members of the pea family and have spikes of small pea-like flowers, which provide a good splash of red in the spring or summer borders.

Cultivation Grow in any reasonable garden soil that is well-drained. A sunny position is needed. Once in position, avoid disturbing. Z7.

Propagation They come readily from seed sown in spring. They can be divided at the same time of year, but this is not easy.

Hedysarum coronarium

This is the species most commonly seen in gardens. It has bright red flowers which appear in the spring and early summer. H and S 1m (3ft).

Hedysarum hedysaroides

Similar to the previous plant but it is a bit smaller and the flowers are more purple. The blooms are produced in the summer. H 60cm (24in) S 60cm (24in).

Hedysarum multijugum

This is a bigger plant with erect spikes of red-purple flowers throughout the summer. H 1.5m (5ft) S 60cm (24in).

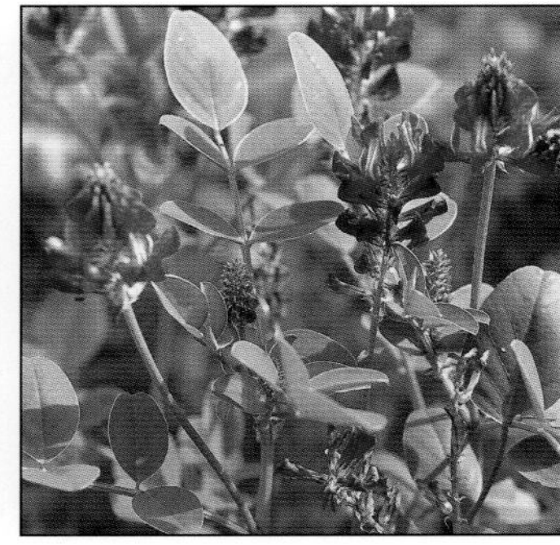
Hedysarum coronarium

Helenium 'Moerheim Beauty'

HELENIUM
Sneezeweed

A genus of about 40 or so species of which only two or three are in cultivation. There are a large number of cultivars and these are most welcome since they add colour to our borders from summer onwards. They are upright, clump-forming plants that reach between 1–1.2m (3–4ft) in height. The flowers are daisy-like with red, yellow, orange or brown outer petals and a brown or gold inner disc.
Cultivation Heleniums do best in full sun and in a soil that does not dry out too much; add plenty of well-rotted organic material. Slugs can be a nuisance when new shoots are emerging. Z3.
Propagation The simplest method of increasing heleniums is to divide them in spring.

Helenium autumnale
This plant is parent to many of the cultivars. However, it is still worth growing in its own right.

Helenium 'Riverton Beauty'

The flowers have yellow petals and a brown central disc. H 1.5m (5ft) S 45cm (18in).

Helenium bigelovii
This is the other plant that is responsible for many of the colourful hybrids. It is shorter than the previous, getting up to about 60cm (24in). It has yellow petals and a brown or yellow central disc. S 30cm (12in).

***Helenium* 'Bruno'**
This has bright reddish brown petals and a brown disc.

***Helenium* 'Butterpat'**
A plant with bright butter-yellow petals and a golden disc.

***Helenium* 'Moerheim Beauty'**
One of the most attractive of the heleniums. It has brownish-red flowers touched with yellow, with brown discs.

***Helenium* 'Riverton Beauty'**
This plant has petals of a lovely soft yellow with a reddish-brown central disc.

***Helenium* 'Rotgold'**
Distinctive colouring features red flowers streaked with yellow, and a brown disc.

***Helenium* 'Waldtraut'**
A plant with mahogany and yellow petals and a brown central disc.

***Helenium* 'Wyndley'**
'Wyndley' has flowers that are yellow streaked with red. It has brown disc florets.

Helenium 'Waldtraut'

HELIANTHEMUM
Rock roses

These are really shrubs but they have always had a place in the perennial border and so are included here. This is a large genus of more than 100 species but it is the many cultivars that are of interest to gardeners. These form rounded hummocks of grey or green foliage against which round, flat flowers are displayed. The blooms come in many shades of red, pink, orange, yellow and white. They have a yellow centre. There is a quiet simplicity about these flowers that makes them perfect for the edge of a border, or grown to hang down a wall or sprawl onto a path or patio. They flower in early summer; some, especially the doubles, last into late summer. H 30cm (12in) S 45cm (18in).
Cultivation Any garden soil as long as it is free-draining. A sunny position is important. Sheer over the plant once it has flowered to keep it compact. Z5.

Helianthemum 'Henfield Brilliant'

Propagation Helianthemums are increased by cuttings taken in either spring or early summer.

***Helianthemum* 'Amy Baring'**
A superb form with deep golden flowers and orange in their centres.

***Helianthemum* 'Butterball'**
'Butterball' is double-flowered form with buttery yellow flowers as its name implies.

***Helianthemum* 'Cerise Queen'**
This plant carries double flowers which look like powder puffs of cerise petals.

***Helianthemum* 'Chocolate Blotch'**
A delightful plant whose orange petals have chocolate brown blotches at the base.

***Helianthemum* 'Henfield Brilliant'**
This gorgeous cultivar has flowers of such a bright red that they can seem to hit you between the eyes with their brilliance.

Helianthemum 'Wisley Pink'

***Helianthemum* 'Raspberry Ripple'**
One of the brashest of the rock roses. The flowers are white with splashes of raspberry red and with a yellow boss of stamens.

***Helianthemum* 'Wisley Pink'**
Strictly speaking, this is now called 'Rhodanthe Carneum' but it is still generally known as 'Wisley Pink'. It is a wonderful plant with soft pink petals set off against soft grey foliage. Possibly the best of the bunch.

***Helianthemum* 'Wisley Primrose'**
Another superb plant whose primrose-yellow flowers look charming against soft grey foliage.

***Helianthemum* 'Wisley White'**
An excellent plant which has wonderful white flowers touched with yellow.

HELIANTHUS
Sunflower

Most people are aware of the large sunflowers that are grown as annuals (see page 132) but many do not realise that there are also a number of perennial species. These might not be as big and brazen as the dinner-plate-sized annuals, but they still make a good splash of bright colour, especially during the autumn. They have daisy-like flowers, with an outer ring of bright yellow petals surrounding an inner disc of similar colour. Some of the cultivars are double forms where the disc is replaced by a pompom of petals. The flowers are carried on stiff, upright stems, which vary in height from 1m (3ft) or so up to 2.5m (8ft). They soon make a decent-sized clump. Most are best sited at the back of the border and look particularly good against a dark green hedge.
Cultivation Add plenty of well-rotted organic material to the soil before planting in a sunny position. The taller varieties may need staking in exposed positions.
Propagation Division in spring is by far the easiest method of propagation.

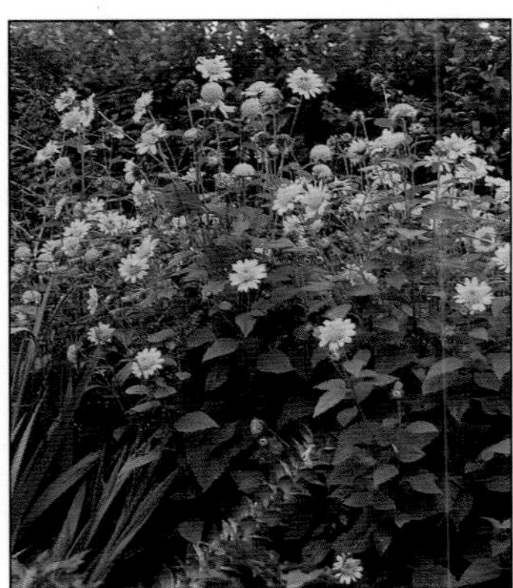
Helianthus × *laetiflorus* 'Morning Sun'

Helianthus 'Loddon Gold'

Helianthus atrorubens
In late summer this vigorous sunflower produces yellow flowers with a deep red central disc. H 1.5m (5ft) S 1m (3ft).

Helianthus salicifolius

***Helianthus* 'Capenoch Star'**
A good plant which has large yellow-petalled flowers with a yellow centre. H 1.2m (4ft) 60cm (24in).

Helianthus* × *laetiflorus
A popular hybrid that has produced some good cultivars. It has yellow flowers with yellow disc. H 2m (7ft) S 1.2m (4ft). 'Miss Mellish' is a semi-double form with yellow petals and a more golden-coloured disc. 'Morning Sun' is similar.

***Helianthus* 'Lemon Queen'**
A fine variety with lemon-yellow petals and a yellow centre. It is a tall variety that needs to be grown at the back of the border where it can peep over the other plants. H 1.8m (6ft) S 60cm (24in).

***Helianthus* 'Loddon Gold'**
A old variety that has stood the test of time. It is a double with a mass of golden-yellow flowers. H 1.5m (5ft) S 60cm (24in).

***Helianthus* 'Monarch'**
A tall plant with semi-double flowers with narrow yellow petals and green-brown centre. H 2.5m (8ft) S 60cm (24in).

Helianthus salicifolius
Before the flowers appear in autumn this can be a difficult plant to identify: its upright stems carry a large number of narrow leaves which droop down, looking just like those of a tall lily. But the idea of a lily is quickly dispelled when the bright yellow flowers appear. This is a tall plant growing to 2.5m (8ft), S 60cm (24in).

Other plants There are a number of other species and cultivars to explore, although most are variations on the same theme.

HELICHRYSUM
Helichrysum

A very large genus of over 500 species, which like the last genus is mainly known for the plants grown as annuals (see pages 132–133). However, there are a number of perennials that are worth growing. They are perhaps not in the top league of plants but they do add unusual colour combinations to the border, mainly through their grey foliage. The felted leaves do not like wet climates, especially winter wet. They do well in gravel beds.
Cultivation Helichrysums grow in any reasonable garden soil but it must be really well drained. A sunny position is essential. Z6–8.
Propagation Division is possible in spring. Alternatively, cuttings can be taken in summer.

Helichrysum splendidum
This is a shrubby plant with upright stems carrying narrow grey leaves. They are topped with small yellow flowers in late summer. H and S 1.2m (4ft).

***Helichrysum* 'Schwefellicht'**
Also known as 'Sulphur Light', this is one of the best helichrysums for the perennial border. The foliage is an attractive grey-green overlaid with white. The bunches of upward-facing flowers are bright sulphur yellow fading to orange or brown as they go over, which creates a delightful two-toned effect. They flower in late summer. H 40cm (16in) S 30cm (12in).

Other plants **There are several other species and varieties worth checking out if you like to include plenty of grey in your borders.**

Helichrysum 'Schwefellicht'

Helleborus foetidus

HELLEBORUS
Hellebore

This is an extremely popular genus. There are about 15 or so species, most of which are in cultivation, along with a host of cultivars. Their popularity may be partly due to the fact that they flower in late winter when not much else is around. At that time of year they certainly brighten up the garden. They have flat or cup-shaped flowers which come in a wide variety of colours. Doubles and picotee varieties with flowers edged in a different colour have extended the range available. These are mainly woodland plants. Place where they can be seen in winter and spring, but hidden during the rest of the year. ***Cultivation*** A soil kept moist with plenty of organic material is required for most species. Partial shade is preferable. Z4–6. ***Propagation*** Species can be grown from seed, which should be sown as soon as it is ripe. Species and cultivars can also be divided in spring after flowering.

Helleborus argutifolius
These are tall plants that often need support. The dark green leaves are noticeably toothed and the flowers are cup-shaped and a delicate pale green. H 1.2m (4ft) S 45cm (18in).

Helleborus × *hybridus* Double

Helleborus foetidus
A leggy plant with narrow leaves and bell-shaped flowers. The flowers are green, often with a purple lip. H and S 45cm (18in). 'Wester Fisk' is a good form.

Helleborus* × *hybridus
These plants used to be known as the oriental hybrids. The flowers are flat and dish-shaped and there is a wide mixture of colours; some are spotted and others are doubles. There are many named varieties from which to choose. All are good, so try to see them in flower before you buy. H 45cm (18in) S 45cm (18in).

Helleborus niger
The Christmas rose produces flat flowers which are white, but usually infused with a little pink. It is not the easiest plant to grow and it can be a martyr to slugs. H and S 30cm (12in).

Other plants There are a great number of other species and cultivars that are worth exploring, such as *H.* × *sternii*. Visit specialist nurseries in spring so that you can see them in flower before making your choice.

HEMEROCALLIS
Daylily

A genus of around 15 species, but it is the thousands of cultivars that are of most interest to the perennial gardener. This vast quantity is well beyond the needs of even the keenest, but there is a surprising amount of variation between them. The basic plant is a clump of strap-like leaves arching out in a fountain, from which emerge stiff stems carrying a mass of buds. These open a few at a time but only for a day (hence the plant's English name). The flowers are shaped like flaring trumpets and are coloured in mainly yellow, orange or red as well as occasional pinks and whites. They are one of the mainstays of the summer border. H 75cm (30in) S 60cm (24in). ***Cultivation*** Plant in any reasonable garden soil that has been enriched with organic material. A sunny position is best but most will take some light shade. Staking is not usually required. Z2–4. ***Propagation*** Although they are heavy plants to dig up, division is the best method of increase.

***Hemerocallis* 'Catherine Woodberry'**
This is a very beautiful plant which produces flowers of an unusual lilac-pink.

***Hemerocallis* 'Corky'**
One of the most refined of the daylilies. It produces small trumpet-shaped flowers that are mahogany on the outside and bright golden yellow on the inside. A superb plant to grow.

Hemerocallis 'Stafford'

***Hemerocallis* 'Golden Chimes'**
This has quite open trumpets with reflexed (turned back) petals of clear gold. It is good against a background of green foliage.

***Hemerocallis* 'Lark Song'**
The flowers of this cultivar are a delightfully clear yellow with distinctive green throats.

***Hemerocallis* 'Red Rum'**
This produces yellow-throated flowers of a lovely flame-red. They are quite startling.

***Hemerocallis* 'Stafford'**
The flowers are deep red, almost mahogany, with yellow in the throat and up the centre of petals.

***Hemerocallis* 'Stella de Oro'**
Here the broad petals that make the flower are more circular. They are a good golden-yellow colour.

Other plants There are hundreds of other excellent daylilies, including 'Eenie Weenie' (short, yellow), 'Frans Hals' (mahogany red), 'Green Flutter' (yellow and

Helleborus niger

Helleborus × *sternii*

Hemerocallis 'Lark Song'

Hemerocallis 'Wind Song'

green), 'Marion Vaughn' (clear yellow), 'Prairie Blue Eyes' (lavender blue), 'Wind Song' (creamy yellow) and many more.

HEUCHERA
Coral flower

A genus of 55 species and an increasing number of cultivars. The plants used to be grown for the erect, airy stems of tiny flowers, but they are now often cultivated as foliage plants as more plants with attractive leaves have been bred. The leaves are basal and circular. They are green or purple and often have silver markings. The spikes of flowers are green, white pink or red and usually appear in early summer. They are perfect at the front of the border. H 60cm (24in) S 45cm (18in).
Cultivation Any reasonable moisture-retentive soil in sun or shade will be suitable. Z4.
Propagation Heucheras should be propagated by division in the autumn or spring.

Heuchera cylindrica
Green leaves with a silverish, mottled effect. The spikes of flowers are cream. It is best grown in the form of one of its cultivars: they include 'Chartreuse' (yellow-green flowers), 'Greenfinch' (green flowers) or 'Hyperion' (pink and green flowers).

***Heuchera* 'Firefly'**
This plant produces wonderful spikes of bright scarlet flowers.

***Heuchera* 'Helen Dillon'**
One of the best, this has silvery-grey leaves with green veins. The spikes of flowers are red.

***Heuchera micrantha* 'Palace Purple'**
This attractive foliage plant has purple leaves with a metallic sheen. The flowers are buff.

***Heuchera* 'Pewter Moon'**
Another good foliage plant. The leaves are purple with silver markings. Pinkish-buff flowers.

***Heuchera* 'Rachel'**
This plant has purple leaves similar to those of 'Palace Purple' but the flowers are pink.

Other plants There are many other cultivars, which are mainly variations on the above themes.

HOSTA
Hosta

A genus of about 40 species and many thousands of cultivars. They are grown mostly for their foliage, but they also have spikes of attractive small lily-like flowers in white, blue, or pale purple. The green leaves are generally heart- or spear-shaped. There are many variations: some are heavily pleated or puckered; some have cream or yellow variegations; some are golden and others are blue. This gives the gardener tremendous scope when adding foliage to the borders. Hostas will grow in full sun or partial shade so long as the soil is moist. They will often make dense drifts. The foliage usually reaches about 30–45cm (12–18in) with the flower spike reaching twice that height. S 1m (3ft).

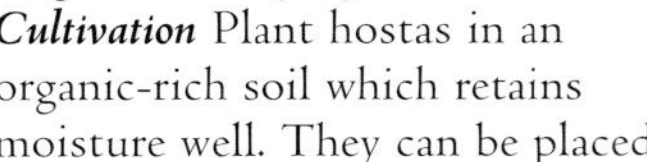

Cultivation Plant hostas in an organic-rich soil which retains moisture well. They can be placed either in sun or partial shade. They are very susceptible to slugs, so will need protection.
Propagation The cultivars are increased by division, which can be hard work if clumps are large.

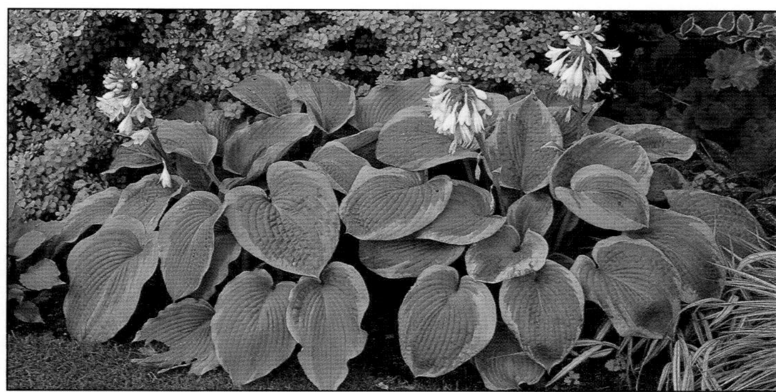

Hosta 'Frances Williams'

***Hosta* 'Big Daddy'**
Large, puckered leaves that are a good bluish-green. White flowers.

Hosta crispula
Wavy-edged leaves are green with white variegations round the margins; the flowers are pale blue.

Hosta fortunei
An attractive species with many excellent varieties. The species has pointed, dark green leaves and lavender flowers. The leaves of the variety *albopicta* have pale yellow centres and green margins; in *aureomarginata* they are green with golden-yellow margins; *hyacinthina* has grey-green leaves edged in white and dark blue flowers.

***Hosta* 'Frances Williams'**
An old favourite and still considered one of the best. The leaves are puckered and a bluish-green with a wide, irregular margin of creamy-white or yellow. The flowers are pale lavender.

***Hosta* 'Halcyon'**
This is a choice plant which has superb leaves of a dusty blue. The flowers are also blue.

***Hosta* 'Honeybells'**
Large, pale green leaves with wavy margins. The fragrant flowers are white, streaked with lavender.

***Hosta* 'Hydon Sunset'**
The leaves are small, opening a fresh yellow-green and then going to a darker green. The flowers are deep purple.

***Hosta* 'Sum and Substance'**
This has very large leaves that are lime green and can be yellow when the plant is sited in full sun. The flowers are very pale lavender.

Other plants The plants listed above make up only a fraction of those available. The only way to see anything approaching the whole range is to find a specialist nursery or its catalogue.

Heuchera micrantha

Hosta crispula

Hosta 'Halcyon'

Hosta 'Hydon Sunset'

Houttuynia cordata 'Chameleon'

HOUTTUYNIA
Houttuynia

The only species in this genus is *H. cordata*. This is widely grown in gardens, but it is more frequently seen in either its variegated or double forms. The species is low growing, and its heart-shaped leaves make good ground cover, especially for shady areas. The flowers are four white bracts (petal-like leaves) with a central flower cone, which show up well against the leaves. H 25cm (10in) S indefinite.

The variety 'Chameleon' has similar flowers but variegated foliage which is green with creamy-yellow margins touched with red. 'Flore Pleno' has green leaves and double flowers. Houttuynias are excellent for woodland areas or under shrubs. They are also very good for growing in bog gardens or around water features.

Cultivation Any reasonable garden soil although it prefers moist conditions. It is best in the shade but will grow in sun. Z5.

Propagation The best way to propagate houttuynias is to divide them in spring.

HUMULUS
Hop

Only one hop is grown in the decorative garden. This is *H. lupulus* 'Aureus', the golden form of the one used for brewing beer. It is a climber that ascends by twining around its host. It dies back to the ground each winter so it has to climb its 5m (16ft) or so from scratch each year, which it normally does by midsummer. The leaves and stems are very rough in texture and can cause burns on the skin if heavily brushed against. The foliage is golden yellow. The female plants

Humulus lupulus 'Aureus'

produce 'hops', which are the green flowers, in early autumn. Hops are good for growing over frameworks or up through trees.

Cultivation Grow in any reasonable garden soil, although the plants will do better in richer conditions. They are best grown in full sun and will need some support: a framework, trees, or strings or wires attached to poles. Z6.

Propagation Divide the plant carefully in spring.

INULA
Inula

A large genus of daisy-like plants. Of the 100 or so species, only a handful are in cultivation, but these provide some stunning plants. They vary from low-growing plants of only 15cm (6in) to towering giants of 2.5m (8ft) or more. The foliage is generally quite coarse but the flowers are more refined. They are golden-yellow or light orange, with slender petals and central golden disc. Most appear from late summer onwards.

Depending on the plants' height, they can be used at any point from the front to the back of a border.

Cultivation Inulas like a rich soil with plenty of well-rotted organic material. They also like a sunny position. Z5.

Propagation The easiest method of increase is to divide in the spring, although the species can also be readily grown from seed sown at the same time of year.

Inula ensifolia

Inula ensifolia

This is a short, clump-forming plant that is perfect for the front of a border. H 45cm (18in) S 30cm (12in). It has a few cultivars, of which 'Goldstar' is the best. 'Compacta' is only 15cm (6in) high.

Inula helenium elecampagne

This is excellent for naturalizing in a wild or meadow garden. H 1.2m (4ft) S 60cm (24in).

Inula hookeri

The best of the bunch, with wonderful buds that open to flowers whose petals look like threads of gold. The flowers are carried singly at the tip of each stem. The plant may be cut back by late frosts but recovers. H 75cm (30in) S 45cm (18in).

Inula magnifica

This is a taller species suitable for growing in the middle to the back of the border. The flowers are carried in heads of up to 15 blooms. H 2m (6ft) S 1m (3ft).

Inula orientalis

A medium-height species for the middle of a border. The flowers are carried singly. H 1m (3ft) S 60cm (24in).

Inula hookeri

Inula magnifica

Inula racemosa

The tallest of the garden varieties reaching up to 2.5m (8ft) in good conditions. It may need support in exposed positions. The flowers are pale yellow and are carried singly up the tall stems, often effectively forming a spike. Best grown at the back of a border or as an impressive clump at the end of a path. S 1.2m (4ft).

Inula royleana

A medium-height plant for the middle of the border. The leaves are large and coarse. The orange flowers are carried singly. H 1m (3ft) S 60cm (24in).

IRIS
Iris

A very large genus of about 300 species, of which many are in cultivation. They are a diverse collection since they vary from dwarf to tall plants. They flower at almost all seasons of the year including winter and they like conditions from dry soil to standing in water. However, the flowers all bear a close resemblance to each other: they have three "standard" petals that stand upright and three "falls" that hang or arch downwards. Standing up in the centre of all these are three small "stigma flaps". Most colours are represented in one cultivar or another. They are wonderful plants for a border; their one disadvantage is that they flower only once in a season. On the

Iris 'George'

other hand, their sword-like leaves make them into an effective foliage plant for the remainder of the time. There are many specialist irises, which are grown under glass by alpine growers.
Cultivation The majority like a well-drained garden soil that is not too rich but not too spare either. They need a sunny position, especially the *germanica* ones which like to have the tops of their rhizomes exposed to the sun. Plant in late summer or autumn. Z3–5.
Propagation For all species the easiest method of increase is to divide them after flowering.

Iris chrysographes
A delicate iris with small dark purple, almost black, flowers with gold markings. It prefers a moist soil. H 45cm (18in) S indefinite.

Iris danfordiae
A small bulbous iris that flowers in late winter. It has yellow flowers. H 15cm (6in) S 5cm (2in). There are several other dwarf bulbous species worth growing such as *I. histrioides* (blue) and *I. reticulata* (blue, purple). There are also lots of named varieties such as 'George' (purple), 'Harmony' (blue and

Iris germanica

Iris pallida

yellow) and 'Joyce' (blue). They are all about the same height and flower in late winter.

Iris ensata
This species and its more than 100 cultivars like a damp position that never dries out. They can be grown in borders with plenty of moisture-retaining material in the soil. H 1m (3ft) S indefinite. The flowers are variations on purple, although there are white forms such as 'Alba' and 'Moonlight' as well as some blues.

Iris foetidissima
A useful iris for shady places and woodland. The flowers are purple suffused with yellow. They have prominent red seeds in winter. H 30–100cm (1–3ft) S indefinite.

Iris unguicularis

Iris germanica
A portmanteau name that covers an extremely large number of cultivars such as 'Chantilly'. These are the border irises with thick rhizomes. The flowers are generally large and come in many colours. Specialist dealers or their catalogues are the only way to find your way around these plants if you are interested. Most gardeners are content with one or two chosen at random. H 60–120cm (2–4ft) S indefinite.

Iris laevigata
This is similar to *I. ensata* in both its appearance and preferred conditions. There are plenty of cultivars from which to choose, the colours mainly based on purple or white. H 60–120cm (2–4ft) S indefinite.

Iris pallida
A very beautiful species with pale grey-green leaves that set off beautifully the misty blue flowers. It has two variegated cultivars: 'Argentea Variegata' with silver-

Iris 'Purple Sensation'

striped leaves and 'Variegata' with gold stripes. H 70–100cm ($2\frac{1}{2}$–3ft) S indefinite.

Iris sibirica
A clump-forming iris with narrow leaves. The flowers are based on the violet-blue of the species. There are many good cultivars from which to chose. H 50–120cm ($1\frac{1}{2}$–4ft) S indefinite.

Iris unguicularis
A must in every garden. This is a winter-flowering iris with delicate soft mauve flowers and a lovely scent. It is good for picking but beware: slugs love it. There are several cultivars with flowers of varying degrees of purple. It likes poor soil conditions and a sunny spot. H 20cm (8in) S indefinite.

Other plants Each of the above species has masses of cultivars and there are also many other species including *II. douglasiana, innominata, japonica, setosa, xiphium* (Spanish irises and Dutch irises such as *I.* 'Purple Sensation').

Iris sibirica

Iris 'Chantilly'

Knautia macedonica

KNAUTIA
Knautia

A small genus of about 60 species of which only one is in general cultivation. These plants are related to the scabious. They have flowers that look like miniature pincushions, carried on tall airy stems. They tend to have a long flowering period, which makes them useful although the flowers at the end of the year are noticeably smaller than those in midsummer. They are very good plants for the middle of the border, especially if you like the effect of one clump of plants merging with the next since they tend to be a bit floppy.

Cultivation Knautia can be planted in any good garden soil and in a sunny position. Z6.

Propagation These are easy to increase either from basal cuttings in spring or seed sown at the same time of year.

Knautia arvensis
This is not frequently seen, but it is still a delightful plant with lavender-coloured flowers. It is good for the meadow garden. H 1.2m (4ft) S 45cm (18in).

Knautia macedonica
This is the most commonly grown plant in the genus. Its great virtue is the deep crimson flowers, a colour that is not often seen in herbaceous plants. This was the only colour available until recently when pastel-coloured varieties were introduced. These are generally referred to as Melton Pastels. It is a floppy plant that can be staked, but this must be done at an early stage of growth. H 75cm (30in) S 60cm (24in).

KNIPHOFIA
Red hot poker

A very distinctive genus of flowering plants, of which there are about 70 species and many cultivars. The plants form dense clumps of narrow, sword-like foliage that arches out like a fountain. Erect stems rise out of the foliage, each carrying a dense club-like spike of flowers. Initially most garden forms were flame-red, hence the English name, but variations on red, orange, yellow and green are now being grown.

When in full flower the plants are stunning, but they can look tatty once they start to go over; at this point it is best to remove the flower stems. They vary in height from dwarf forms of about 45cm (18in) to tall ones that reach about 1.5m (5ft). Most flower in summer, and some last into the autumn.

Cultivation Kniphofias need a deep, free-draining soil to which plenty of well-rotted organic material has been added. They prefer a sunny position although they will tolerate a little light shade. Z7.

Propagation The best way of propagation is by division.

***Kniphofia* 'Alcazar'**
This is a flame red poker of medium height. H 75cm (30in) S 45cm (18in).

***Kniphofia* 'Bees' Sunset'**
Soft orange flowers bloom from mid to late summer. H 1m (3ft) S 60cm (24in).

***Kniphofia* 'Buttercup'**
Yellow flowers are produced by this cultivar in early summer. H 75cm (30in) S 60cm (24in).

***Kniphofia* 'Candlelight'**
This is a short form. There is green tip to the flower head, which turns greenish-yellow as the flowers open. H 60cm (24in) S 60cm (24in).

***Kniphofia* 'Little Maid'**
This is a superb small kniphofia with pale yellow flowers that turn cream as they age. H 60cm (24in) S variable.

***Kniphofia* 'Percy's Pride'**
A good kniphofia for the autumn garden. The flowers are yellowish-green. H 1m (3ft) S 50cm (20in). Another good green is 'Green Jade'.

***Kniphofia* 'Prince Igor'**
Perfect for the hot border, the poker of this tall variety is a wonderful rich orange. H 1.5m (5ft) S 60cm (24in).

Kniphofia rooperi
This is a late-flowering species which produces its poker in the autumn, often late autumn. The flower heads are much fatter and rounder than usual. They are a flame-orange that ages to golden yellow. These plants are taller than most others. H 1.2m (4ft) S 75cm (30in).

Kniphofia 'Candlelight'

***Kniphofia* 'Royal Standard'**
A typical poker with an orange tip and yellow base where it is ageing. H 1.2m (4ft) S 60cm (24in).

***Kniphofia* 'Sunningdale Yellow'**
A good all-yellow kniphofia. H 1m (3ft) S 60cm (24in).

***Kniphofia* 'Toffee Nose'**
An intriguing form with flowers of a toffee colour that fades to an attractive cream further down the flower head. H 45cm (18in) S 30cm (12in).

***Kniphofia* 'Wrexham Buttercup'**
A rich golden-yellow poker that illuminates a border. H 1.2m (4ft) S 60cm (24in).

Kniphofia 'Alcazar'

Kniphofia 'Prince Igor'

Kniphofia 'Toffee Nose'

Lamium maculatum 'Roseum'

Lamium maculatum 'Beacon Silver'

LAMIUM
Dead nettle

The leaves of some species may worry gardeners as they look like those of stinging nettles, but they are harmless. There are about 50 species in all. Most of them are weeds but a few make good garden plants. In some the leaves are marked or mottled in silver while in others it is the cluster of large thyme-like flowers in white, purple or yellow that are the attraction. Most flower early on, from spring to early summer, but those with attractive leaves can double as foliage plants for the rest of the season. Most are spreading, making them good ground cover for the front of the border, where they will weave their way between other plants.

Cultivation Lamium should grow well in any reasonable garden soil so long as it does not dry out completely. They can be grown in either sun or light shade. Z3–4.

Propagation They can easily be divided in spring. If you do not want to disturb the plants, basal cuttings can be also taken at the same time of year.

Lamium galeobdolon

The yellow archangel of the woodlands. A tall species with mid-green leaves that are often splashed with silver and with spikes of yellow flowers. It is attractive but it can become a nuisance so it is best suited to wild plantings; plant one of its cultivars in more regulated areas. H 60cm (24in) S indefinite. 'Hermann's Pride' is a more compact plant. It has dark green leaves with prominent silver markings. 'Silberteppich' ('Silver Carpet') is a popular variety with leaves that are greyish-green but so overladen with silver that the green can hardly be seen. The flowers are yellow. 'Silver Angel' is another well-loved silver variety worth trying.

Lamium maculatum

This is a delightful old-fashioned, cottage-garden plant. It produces spreading carpets of green foliage, usually with white or silver markings. From these arise short spikes of pink flowers. After flowering the plants tend to get a bit straggly; they are best cut back to regenerate the foliage and induce second flowering. H 20cm (8in) S 1m (3ft).

There are a number of very good forms. 'Roseum' is an old one with darker, purplish flowers. A white-flowered form is 'Album' but this has been superseded by 'White Nancy' which not only has white flowers but very silver leaves, touched with green around the margins. 'Pink Pewter' is a pink-flowered version of this, while 'Beacon Silver' is similar but with pale pink flowers. 'Aureum' and 'Cannon's Gold' both have pink flowers and golden foliage, the former with silver patches.

Lamium orvala

This is a delightful plant that is not seen as often as it should be. It flowers in spring, when it forms a well-rounded clump of stems. Peering from the large nettle-shaped leaves are smoky purple-pink flowers. The plant dies back once its flowering season finishes. H 60cm (24in) S 30cm (12in).

LATHYRUS
Everlasting pea

Although not as well known as the annuals (see page 137), the perennials in this genus are very pretty. Some are climbers, while others are scramblers and yet others form a bushy plant. They all produce pea-like flowers of differing sizes. Their colours are all generally are based on purple. They can be used in the border or on the edge of shrubby areas.

Cultivation These plants will do best in a soil that has had plenty of organic material added to it.

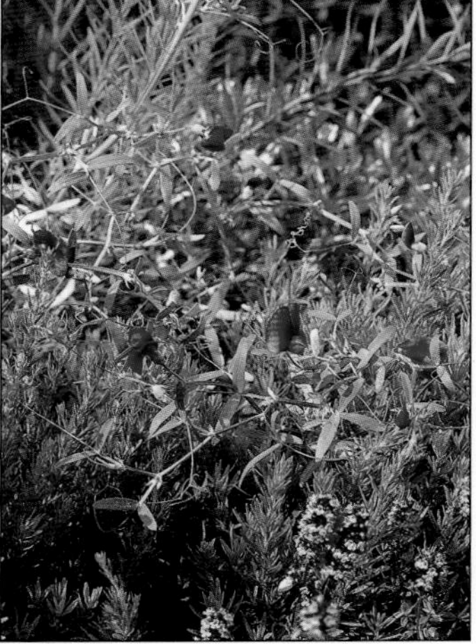
Lathyrus tingitanus

They prefer a sunny position, but many everlasting peas will grow in light shade. Z5.

Propagation Grow from seed sown in the spring. Those that spread underground can be divided.

Lathyrus grandiflorus

One of the best, this has large rounded flowers in two-tone pink. It scrambles through shrubs. H 1.2m (4ft) S 60cm (24in).

Lathyrus latifolius

This everlasting pea is a bit coarse but it produces a show of pink or white flowers. Let it sprawl or tie it to supports. H 1.5m (5ft) S 2m (6ft).

Lathyrus vernus

A wonderful clump-former, which blooms in early spring. H 45cm (18in) S 30cm (12in).

Other plants Look at *L. aureus* (orange flowers), *L. nervosus* (blue) and *L. tingitanus* (pink).

Some purple perennials

Aster (various)	*Lythrum salicaria*
Centaurea montana 'Parham'	*Lythrum virgatum*
Echinacea purpurea	*Penstemon* 'Burgundy'
Erigeron 'Dunkelste Aller'	*Penstemon* 'Russian River'
Erodium manescavii	*Phlox* 'Le Mahdi'
Erysimum 'Bowles' Mauve'	*Salvia viridis*
Geranium (various)	*Senecio pulcher*
Liatris spicata	*Stachys macrantha*
Linaria purpurea	*Thalictrum delavayi*
Lobelia × gerardii 'Vedrariensis'	*Verbena bonariensis*

Lamium orvala

Lathyrus vernus

Lavatera thuringiaca

Lavatera cachemiriana

LAVATERA
Mallow

This is a genus of about 25 species of which a few are perennial. There are also some shrubs that are often thought of as perennials in the border context. What distinguishes this group of plants is the funnel-shaped flowers, which usually come in soft, delicate shades of pink. The most popular species tend to be quite tall. They add bulk to a border and often bring continuity since they flower for a long time.

Cultivation Mallows will grow in any reasonable garden soil so long as it is well drained. They should have a sunny, sheltered position protected from winds. Z6–8.

Propagation Species can be grown from seed sown in spring. Cultivars need to be propagated from cuttings taken in summer.

Lavatera cachemiriana

This is a true perennial. It has tall, upright stems from which grow delicate pink flowers. These are flatter and not so funnel-shaped as some other varieties. It is not a long-lived plant but it is easy to increase from seed, of which it produces masses. H 1.5–2m (5–6ft) S 1m (3ft).

Lavatera × clementii

A collection of shrubby hybrids that make good background plants or centrepieces in a border. H 2m (6ft) S 2m (6ft). One of the best known of these hybrids is 'Barnsley' which has white flowers, each with a prominent blotch of red in the centre. 'Bredon Springs' is another popular variety. This has purplish-pink flowers with prominent purple veins. 'Kew Rose' is similar with bright pink flowers with purple veining. 'Candy Floss' has very pale pink funnels.

Lavatera maritima

This is a true perennial. It naturally grows near the sea but it can be also used to good effect in inland gardens. It has pink or white flowers with prominent carmine veins. H 1.5m (5ft) S 1.5m (5ft).

Lavatera thuringiaca

This is a shrubby plant which will fill a large space. It produces bright purple-pink flowers. H and S 2m (6ft). In the form 'Ice Cool' the flowers are a wonderful pure white.

LEUCANTHEMUM
Shasta daisy

A genus of 25 species that were once known as *Chrysanthemum* and indeed they resemble those plants. There are only a couple of species that are grown regularly in the garden, both having typical daisy-like flowers with a ring of outer white petals and a central yellow disc. They are not refined plants, and look their best in a cottage-garden setting. Shasta daisies are very tough. In a neglected garden, they will be virtually the last cultivated plants to disappear.

Cultivation These will grow in any reasonable garden soil, but they do best if it has been enriched with well-rotted organic material. They need a sunny position. Z5.

Propagation The easiest method of increase is to divide these plants in the spring.

Leucanthemum × superbum 'Sonnenschein'

Leucanthemum × superbum

The shasta daisies are rather coarse plants growing to about 1m (3ft) high, and eventually making a large clump. They need staking at an early stage. The white flowers are large, up to 10cm (4in) or more across and are often rather untidy looking, especially in the doubles. All this makes them sound undesirable but in fact they create a very pleasing splash of white in the border and are easy to look after. S 60cm (24in).

There are a number of cultivars including several doubles: 'Horace Read', 'Esther Read', 'Fiona Coghill', 'Cobham Gold', 'T.E. Killin' and 'Wirral Supreme'. 'Aglaia' is an excellent semi-double. There are also plenty of very good singles including 'Phyllis Smith', 'Silberprinzesschen', 'Alaska', 'Mount Everest' and many more. The flowers all have subtle differences. The cultivar 'Sonnenschein' has primrose-yellow flowers, and is worth growing.

Leucanthemum vulgare

This is the ox-eye daisy or marguerite of the roadside and meadow. It is a much more delicate plant than the above, with flowers that are usually about 5cm (2in) across. It is not particularly brilliant in the border but it is a must for a wild or meadow garden. H 45cm (18in) S 60cm (24in).

Lavatera × clementii 'Barnsley'

Leucanthemum maxicum

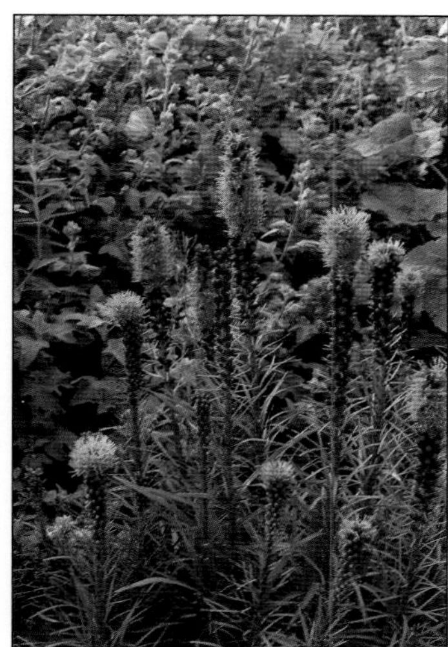
Liatris spicata

LIATRIS
Gayfeather

A genus of 35 species of which only a few are in cultivation. The difference between the various species in cultivation is botanical rather than visual and so there is little difference between them from a gardener's point of view. Liatrises are readily available from nurseries but they are not as widely grown as perhaps they ought to be. Their beauty is in the dense spikes of purple flowers that rise above a mass of narrow leaves: they look a bit like bottle brushes. A clump of these plants is always most colourful and makes a welcome addition to any border, so it is worth tracking them down.
Cultivation A moisture-retentive soil is needed for these plants, so make sure that there is plenty of well-rotted organic material in the soil. The soil should also be well-drained. A place in full sun is required. Z3.
Propagation The easiest method of increase is to divide the plants in spring. However, they can also be grown from seed sown at the same time of year.

Liatris aspera
This species has pinkish-purple flowers that are further apart in the spike. It flowers in summer. H 1m (3ft) S 30cm (12in).

Liatris pycnostachya
A tall species. The long-lasting flower heads are long, often over 30cm (12in). They are a reddish-purple and occasionally white. The plant blooms from summer into autumn. H 1.5m (5ft) S 30cm (12in).

Liatris spicata
This can also grow up to 1.5m (5ft) but does not usually reach this height in gardens. The flower spikes are pinkish-purple. This plant flowers from late summer onwards. S 30cm (12in).

There are several garden cultivars. 'Alba', as its name suggests, has white flowers as has the popular 'Floristan Weiss'. 'Floristan Violett' is similar but with violet-purple flowers. 'Kobold' is another popular form, especially in smaller gardens since it is a much more compact plant. It has violet-purple flowers.

LIGULARIA
Ligularia

This is a large genus of 180 species. About 20 are in cultivation, although only a few are generally available. They vary in appearance from plants with large orange, daisy-like flowers to those with tiny flowers held in a large airy spike. Most of the garden forms are tall. Many are rather coarse and are best placed in wild areas of the garden; others are more refined and make good border plants.
Cultivation Ligularia generally like a moist soil, so plenty of well-rotted organic material should be added before planting. They will grow in sun or partial shade. Some are susceptible to slugs. Z3.
Propagation Division in spring is the easiest method of increase, although species can also be grown from seed sown at the same time of year.

Ligularia dentata 'Desdemona'

Ligularia dentata
One of the shorter species. It has orange daisies from late summer onwards. H 1.2m (4ft) S 60cm (24in). It is grown mainly as one of two cultivars: 'Desdemona', which has deep orange flowers and large, heart-shaped leaves that are purple underneath; and 'Othello' which is similar except that the leaves are also purplish on the top. Both are grown as foliage plants as well as for their attractive flowers.

***Ligularia* 'Gregynog Gold'**
A tall species that bears heads of deep golden flowers, each with a browner centre. H 2m (6ft) S 60cm (24in).

Ligularia* × *palmatiloba
A medium height species with yellow flowers and lobed leaves. H 1m (3ft) S 75cm (30in).

Ligularia przewalskii
Tall spikes of small yellow flowers rise on black stalks from attractive divided foliage. This makes a good border plant. H and S 1m (3ft).

***Ligularia* 'The Rocket'**
One of the best ligularias, this is similar to the previous one. The flower spikes resemble a rocket with trail of golden sparks. It is excellent for the back of a border since it is very tall. It also looks very impressive when grown as a large clump or drift. H 2m (6ft) S 1m (3ft).

Other plants If you have a large garden, especially with wild areas, then you might consider looking at some of the other species such as: *L. hodgsonii, L. sibirica, L. veitchiana,* and *L. wilsoniana.*

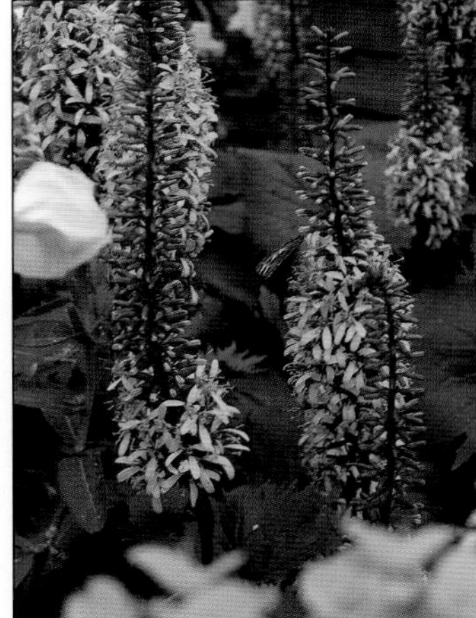
Ligularia 'The Rocket'

Flowers with good heads for drying

Acanthus
Achillea
Allium
Anaphalis
Catananche
Cortaderia
Delphinium
Eryngium
Gypsophila
Humulus
Liatris
Limonium
Miscanthus
Persicaria
Rheum
Scabiosa
Solidago
Stipa

Lilium auratum

Lilium 'Cover Girl'

Lilium regale

LILIUM
Lily

Everybody knows the lilies. This is a magnificent genus with more than 100 species and innumerable cultivars. They are bulbous plants. Most reach about 1m (3ft) in height but they are often much taller. They have a spread of up to 30cm (12in). The flowers vary in shape from trumpets, flared funnels and bowls to pendulous turkscaps and bells. There is also a wide range of colours with pure blue being about the only one missing. Many are fragrant. Lilies are excellent plants for the border, with different varieties growing in sun and shade. They can also be grown in containers. They are very good for cutting.

Cultivation A soil enriched with organic material is ideal for lilies, but it must be free-draining. Species vary: most like the sun and a few prefer shade. Slugs can be a nuisance and increasingly the scarlet lily beetles are becoming a real pest. It is important to check daily and kill these pests whenever they are seen or you will lose the plants. Z3–7.

Propagation There are several ways of increasing lilies. For the amateur the easiest method is simply dividing off the new bulbs that form around the old. Seed can be sown from the species. The brown or black bulbils that form on the stem can also be "sown".

Lilium auratum
A species which has wide-open, flared flowers. They are white with a golden centre and usually spots. This plant is the parent of several cultivars and a number of hybrids. H 1m (3ft).

Lilium candidum
This is the Madonna lily. It is a choice plant with pure white trumpets. H 1.5m (5ft).

Lilium lancifolium
Also known as *L. tigrinum*, or the tiger lily, this has orange turkscap flowers with reddish-brown spots. H 1m (3ft).

Lilium longiflorum
Long trumpet flowers in pure white. Prefers light shade. A good cut flower. H 1m (3ft).

Lilium martagon
A delightful turkscap lily for a woodland or shady setting. The flowers dangle airily from the stem and are purple. There are also white forms. H 1.5m (5ft).

Lilium pyrenaicum
A superb turkscap lily with masses of very narrow, bright green leaves and pendant yellow flowers with brown spots. Unfortunately the flowers smell of foxes, so they should not be planted near seating areas. Excellent plants in shade or sun. H 30–120cm (1–4ft).

Lilium regale
The doyen of the cottage garden, this has trumpet flowers. They are white in colour, but flushed with pinkish-purple on the outside. This species is very fragrant. H 1–1.2m (3–4ft).

Lilium speciosum
This large lily has white turkscap flowers with crimson spots. They have a delightful fragrance. The plant requires a shady position. H 1.5m (5ft).

Other plants Most species are in cultivation and there are many elegant cultivars – including 'Chinook', 'Cover Girl' and 'Enchantment'. Go to specialist nurseries to see the full range.

LINARIA
Toadflax

This large genus of more than 100 species has several that are garden-worthy. The attraction is the small antirrhinum-like flowers which are carried in erect spikes. These vary in colour from yellow to purple; some are bicoloured. Linaria are not in the top league of plants but they fill the spaces between other plants with a certain charm. Another advantage is that they are easy to grow.

Cultivation Any reasonable garden soil that is free-draining. They prefer a sunny position. Z7.

Propagation By far the easiest method of increase is from seed, although some of the linarias that run can be divided.

Linaria dalmatica
This plant carries spikes of large yellow flowers in summer. It creates a good drift. H 1m (3ft) S 60cm (24in).

Linaria purpurea
A good plant that self-sows but does not become a nuisance. The stems can rise to 1m (3ft) but are often shorter. They carry spikes of tiny purple flowers over a long period. There is a superb pink form, 'Canon Went' and a

Lilium 'Chinook'

Lilium 'Enchantment'

Lilium pyrenaicum

Lilium lancifolium

Linaria purpurea

white one, 'Springside White', both of which usually come true from seed. S 60cm (24in).

Linaria triornithophora
A slightly ungainly plant with large yellow and purple flowers. Good for the general border. H 1m (3ft) S 60cm (24in).

Linaria vulgaris
This is rather like a smaller and paler version of *L. dalmatica* except that it runs vigorously. It can become invasive in a border but earns its keep in a wild garden. H 75cm (30in) S 10cm (4in).

LINUM
Flax

A very large genus of more than 200 species of which only a few are in general cultivation. Those that are, however, are well worth

Linum narbonense

Linum perenne

their place in the garden. Some are annuals (see page 140). The flowers are usually funnel-shaped, although some are so flared as to be almost flat. They come in yellow, red or blue; the blues being a good intense colour. The flowers often only last a day and the ground is frequently covered in colourful petals where they have dropped. The stems are rather thin but they are wiry and do not usually need support. Linums are excellent border plants.
Cultivation These plants will grow in most garden soils but they are longer lived if the soil is free-draining. A sunny position is essential. Z5.
Propagation The easiest method of increase is from seed sown in spring. Tip cuttings can also be taken from some species.

Linum narbonense
This is one of the two main border flaxes. It is a plant of great beauty: hundreds of blue flowers float on very thin stems in a hazy cloud. It is not long lived so it is worth propagating some spares every other year. H 45cm (18in) S 45cm (18in).

Linum perenne
This is very similar to the previous plant, except that it is even shorter-lived. Although it is a perennial, winter damp often kills it off, so have some spares. H 30cm (12in) S 15cm (6in).

LOBELIA
Lobelia

Most gardeners are familiar with the blue annual lobelia that is seen hanging from baskets and other containers. However, few realize just how many lobelia there are to choose from: there are 370 species in the genus. Many are tropical. These are very tall and cylindrical, with some resembling the rotating brushes found in car washes. However, there are also a handful of perennials that are a welcome addition to temperate gardens. These include some that produce the reddest of all garden flowers. Most need damp conditions and are most at home near water features.
Cultivation A humus-rich soil that doesn't dry out is required for most perennials. They prefer a sunny position but also grow well in shade. Most are on the tender side and suffer in damp winters so give them some protection in colder, wetter areas. Z2–3.
Propagation Most of the perennial lobelias should be propagated by division in spring.

***Lobelia* 'Bees' Flame'**
A superb plant. It has rich purple foliage and tall spikes of the most brilliant scarlet flowers. A clump of them makes a stunning sight. H 75cm (30in) S 30cm (12in).

Lobelia cardinalis
This is similar to the previous plant, except that it is taller. The foliage is not quite so dark, except in some of the cultivars. H 1m (3ft) S 23cm (9in).

***Lobelia* 'Cherry Ripe'**
Spikes of cherry-red flowers are set off against dark green foliage that is suffused with purple. H 1m (3ft) S 23cm (9in).

***Lobelia* 'Dark Crusader'**
Another deep red-flowered variety with deep purple-red foliage. H 1m (3ft) S 23cm (9in).

***Lobelia* × *gerardii* 'Vedrariensis'**
A wonderful border plant, this lobelia is upright, with a loose spike of purple flowers. The flowering season is long, and starts in the summer. H 1m (3ft) S 30cm (12in).

***Lobelia* 'Pink Elephant'**
This has sugary pink flowers and green foliage. H 1.5m (5ft) S 30–35cm (12–14in)

Lobelia cardinalis

***Lobelia* 'Queen Victoria'**
One of the best of the red forms, this carries bright scarlet flowers above purple leaves and stems. H 1m (3ft) S 23cm (9in).

Lobelia siphilitica
This plant produces a tall spire of blue flowers. Although it will grow in the sun, it is perfect for a shady position. H 1m (3ft) S 23cm (9in).

Lobelia tupa
This is a more tender (Z8) plant but it is well worth growing in warmer areas. It can be very tall and has a loose spike of red flowers that have an exotic quality about them. The foliage is unlike the other forms in that it is slightly furry. This plant needs a well-drained soil and a warm position. H 2m (6ft) S 1m (3ft).

Lobelia 'Cherry Ripe'

Lupinus polyphyllus

LUPINUS
Lupins

There is something tranquil about a clump of lupins. They are the quintessential plant of herbaceous borders and a vital ingredient in the cottage garden. There are more than 200 species, of which a handful are grown in gardens. The flowers are dense spires of pea-like blooms in either one or two colours. They have a gorgeous peppery fragrance. The leaves are also attractive; they are deeply divided, like fingers on a hand.
Cultivation A deep humus-rich soil is ideal, but it should be well-drained. A sunny position is needed. Modern lupins do not seem to last long and need replacing every two or three years to perform satisfactorily. Watch out for the grey lupin aphid. Z4.

Lupinus Russell hybrids

Propagation The simplest way to propagate is to grow lupins from seed, but for specific cultivars it is best to take cuttings in spring.

***Lupinus* 'Chandelier'**
A delightful bicolour with dark and light yellow flowers. H 1m (3ft) S 60cm (24in).

***Lupinus* 'The Chatelaine'**
This is a bicolour with rose-pink and white flowers. H 1.2m (4ft) S 45cm (18in).

***Lupinus* 'The Governor'**
This is a bicolour with flowers of deep blue and white. H 1m (3ft) S 60cm (24in).

***Lupinus* 'My Castle'**
This is a single-coloured, rose-pink lupin. A very satisfying plant when at its peak. H 1m (3ft) S 60cm (24in).

***Lupinus* 'The Page'**
A single-coloured form whose blooms are a lovely carmine. H 1m (3ft) S 60cm (24in).

Lupinus polyphyllus
The species from which many garden hybrids have been bred. It is interesting to grow but the numerous cultivars derived from it are much better. H 1m (3ft) S 60cm (24in).

***Lupinus* Russell hybrids**
Originally introduced in 1937, these are a wonderful selection of cultivars. Many of those currently available may not be descended from the original stock but they are still very good. H 1.2m (4ft) S 75cm (30in).

Other plants There is a similarity between many cultivars, with the main difference being the colour. So it may simply be a matter of choosing a strain that fits in with your colour scheme, rather than trying to obtain particular plants.

LYCHNIS
Lychnis

A small genus that is related to the garden pinks. There are a dozen or so species available for garden use. They are quite a diverse collection of plants, the majority being pink or white with a few being orange or flame-red. All the garden forms make good border plants and are especially good for informal or cottage-garden style borders.
Cultivation Any reasonable garden soil will do. However, the better the soil, the better the plants will do. Most prefer it to be well-drained. Place in full sun or light shade. Z3–4.
Propagation Most come readily from seed sown in the spring, but many of the clump-formers can also be divided in spring. Basal cuttings can be taken at the same time of year.

Lychnis × *arkwrightii*

Lychnis* × *arkwrightii
A lowish plant with large flat flowers that are a superb bright orange. The foliage is brownish-purple and sets off the orange beautifully. This is a perfect plant for the hot border. It flowers in early to midsummer. H 45cm (18in) S 25cm (10in). There is a good cultivar, 'Vesuvius'.

Lychnis chalcedonica

Lychnis coronaria 'Alba'

Lychnis chalcedonica
Flat heads of flame-red are set off against a brightish green foliage. This plant grows tall but it needs support. An early to midsummer species. H 1m (3ft) S 45cm (18in). There are also a dirty-white form *albiflora* and muddy-pink form 'Rosea'; neither are as stunning as the species.

Lychnis coronaria
A frequently seen lychnis with furry silver stems and foliage, and the most vivid magenta flowers which appear during summer. There is a white form, 'Alba', and a white form with pink centres known as the Oculata Group. H 1m (3ft) S 45cm (18in).

Lychnis flos-cuculi
The ragged robin. It is not a good border plant since the flowers are too slight but it is excellent for damp areas such as bog gardens or areas beside natural streams, especially in meadow gardens. Flowers in early summer. H 45cm (18in) S 20cm (8in).

Lychnis flos-jovis
A small version of *L. coronaria*, except that the flowers are more refined and the plant more

Lychnis flos-jovis

compact. The main flower colour is a rose-pink to red but there are also white forms. H 75cm (30in) S 45cm (18in).

Lychnis × haageana
Another orange-flowered species, this time of moderate height. It flowers in early to midsummer but it is not long lived. H 75cm (30in) S 30cm (12in).

LYSICHITON
Skunk cabbage

Only two species make up this genus, both of which are grown in cultivation. These are not plants for small gardens (unless you like things on a grand scale). They both flower in early spring when there is not much else around. The flowers are relatively modest in size, but as the leaves get bigger the plant increases rapidly until it reaches 1m (3ft); it looks rather like a giant cos lettuce. One would be enough for most gardens, but they spread quite freely and soon create a grove of such monster lettuces. However, they are spectacular plants and if you have the space and the right conditions where they can grow alongside a stream or in a bog garden, then they are certainly worth having.
Cultivation A damp, rich soil, preferably near water. Plant in sun if possible but they will tolerate a little light shade. Z6.
Propagation The easiest method of increase by division of the small side growths. Alternatively sow the fresh seed in a compost (soil mix) that is kept wet, or directly into mud.

Lysichiton americanus
The most popular of the two species. This has bright yellow spathes or hoods, enclosing a spike of small yellow flowers on 30cm (12in) stems. The spathe adds another 15–20cm (6–8in) to the height. They have an unpleasant smell. S 75cm (30in).

Lysichiton camtschatcensis
Similar to the previous in shape and size but the spathe is pure white and the flower spike greenish-yellow. A sweetish scent. H 75cm (30in) S 60cm (24in).

Lysichiton americanus

LYSIMACHIA
Loosestrife

This is a large genus of about 150 species, a number of which are in cultivation. It should not be confused with the next genus, *Lythrum*, which is also commonly known as loosestrife. Plants in this genus have yellow or white flowers that are carried in tall spikes. They generally like moist conditions but as long as the borders have plenty of organic material they can be successfully grown there. They look most effective when grown in drifts. Most gently spread, forming large clumps. However, they are not difficult to control if they exceed their allotted space. The flowers consist of a shallow cup of five petals forming a star-shape. The plants vary in height from ground-hugging mats which are suitable for winding between plants at the front of a border to tall, 1.2m (4ft) ones, which are best placed at the middle or back.
Cultivation Lysimachia like a humus-rich soil in full sun or partial shade. Z3–5.
Propagation By far the easiest method of increase is to divide the plants in spring.

Lysimachia ciliata
A tall plant with loose spikes of slightly hanging, lemon-yellow flowers. It flowers in summer. H 2m (6ft) S 60cm (24in). There is an extremely good cultivar called 'Firecracker'. It has

Lysimachia ephemerum

brownish-purple foliage which sets the yellow off wonderfully. It also makes a good foliage plant, especially in spring.

Lysimachia clethroides
This species has curious crooked spikes of small white flowers from midsummer onwards. It is a beautiful plant. H 1.2m (4ft) S 60–100cm (2–3ft).

Lysimachia ephemerum
Tall plants with spikes of small white flowers with pinkish centres in summer. The leaves are bluish-green. H 1m (3ft) S 30cm (12in).

Lysimachia nummularia
This is normally grown in its golden-leaved form 'Aurea'. It is a running, mat-forming plant that

Lysimachia nummularia 'Aurea'

makes excellent ground cover, especially between other plants. The yellow flowers are individual rather than held in spikes, and appear through summer. This is a good foliage plant. H 2.5–5cm (1–2in) S indefinite.

Lysimachia punctata
This plant carries spikes of deep yellow flowers which are carried tightly against the stems and nestle amongst the leaves. It is very attractive but can be aggressive so it should be planted either where it can be controlled or in a wilder area, where it can rampage at will to make a large drift. H 60–75cm (24–30in) S 60cm (24in).

Lysimachia vulgaris
This plant is very similar to the last species but its flowers grow in loose spikes that arise from the axils (joints) of the leaves. It spreads and is best used in the wild garden. H 60-75cm (24–30in) S 60cm (24in).

Lysimachia punctata

Lythrum salicaria 'Feuerkerze'

LYTHRUM

Purple loosestrife

A genus of about 40 species, of which only one or two are deemed garden-worthy. Those that are grown make excellent border plants since they form clumps of bright pink-purple flowers over a long period. The flowers are carried in long spikes and the plants grow up to 1.2m (4ft) high. They can be placed in any border but they are particularly useful for planting in a bog garden, or beside a water feature.

Lythrum salicaria 'Robert'

Cultivation Lythrums need a moisture-retentive soil, so dig in plenty of well-rotted organic material before planting. They like a position in full sun. Z3.
Propagation The simplest way to increase your stock is to divide the clumps in spring. It is also possible to take basal cuttings, also in spring.

Lythrum salicaria
This plant gets its name from its narrow, willow-like leaves. It is one of the main border plants that is grown extensively in its own right but also in the form of a wide number of cultivars. It grows to about 1.2m (4ft) high and has tall spikes of pinkish-purple flowers from midsummer onwards over a long period. S 45cm (18in).

The cultivars are all variations on the same theme, the intensity of the pink or purple being the main varying factor. Good forms include 'Blush', 'Feuerkerze', 'Lady Sackville', 'Morden Pink', 'Robert' and 'Zigeunerblut'.

Lythrum virgatum
This is very similar to the previous species, except that it is not quite so tall and the flower spike is generally shorter. The flowers are purple, with those of some cultivars paler and others darker. H 1m (3ft) S 60cm (24in).

Again there are several cultivars. 'Dropmore Purple', 'Rose Queen', 'Rosy Gem' and 'The Rocket' are all worthy of a place in the border, but one or two of them would be enough for most gardeners.

MACLEAYA

Plume poppy

A small genus of which all three species are in cultivation. These are wonderful plants for the back of a large border. They can rise up to 2.5m (8ft) when given the right conditions, so they are not plants for a small garden. Another problem for the small garden is that macleayas tend to run and can become invasive, so they do need to be given plenty of room. However, there is no doubt that these plants are beautiful enough to earn their place in the large garden, because of both their

Macleaya cordata

foliage and flowers. The flowers are tiny and petalless. They are carried in airy sprays, creating an off-white or pinkish-coral haze. This is set off by the unusual greyish-green foliage, the colour of which is almost impossible to describe. The leaves are heart-shaped and lobed.
Cultivation Macleayas will grow in any reasonable garden soil, so long as it is well-drained. They require a sunny position. Watch out for slugs, which can be a problem with this plant. Another

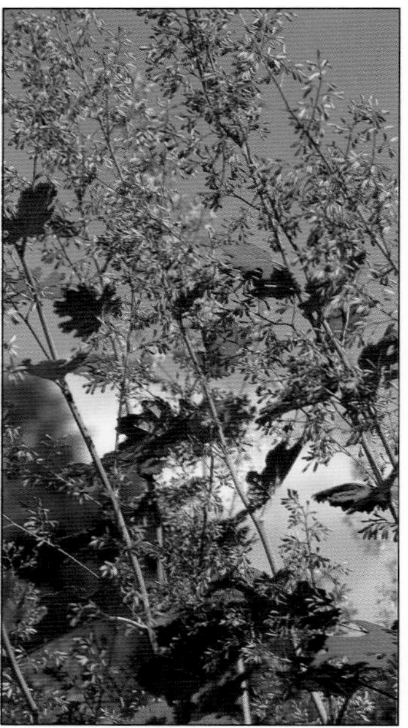

Macleaya × *kewensis*

M. microcarpa 'Kelway's Coral Plume'

hazard is late frosts, which will cut them back although they will reshoot. Z3.
Propagation These plants can be divided in spring but they take a while to settle down again and do not always take. Alternatively use the thick roots as cutting material in early winter.

Macleaya cordata
A tall species, with whitish flowers that create a dangling haze. The flowers appear from midsummer onwards. This is possibly the least invasive of the macleayas. H 2.5m (8ft) S 60cm (24in). There is a very good cultivar, 'Flamingo', in which the flowers are pinker.

Macleaya* × *kewensis
This plant is similar to the above except the flowers are cream or buff in colour.

Macleaya microcarpa
A slightly short form but it is also the most invasive. The species is sometimes grown, but it is mainly cultivated as 'Kelway's Coral Plume', probably the most popular of all the plume poppies. It has coral-pink flowers which are carried throughout the summer. H 2–2.5m (6–8ft) S 1–1.2m (3–4ft). A more recent cultivar, 'Spetchly Ruby', has darker coloured flowers.

Malva moschata alba

MALVA
Mallow

This genus contains around 30 plant species, and is closely related to the genus *Lavatera*. This relationship is evident in the similar shape of the flowers, but mallow blooms are nowhere near as brash as those of their near-relations. Although still funnel-shaped, they are flatter and more open. The *Malva* genus also offers gardeners a wider range of colour, which not only includes pink and white but also purple and blue.

The plants are shorter and more herbaceous. They tend to grow between 45cm (18in) and 1.2m (4ft). They make good border plants and some are also perfect for naturalizing in the meadow garden.

Cultivation Mallows will grow in any reasonable garden soil. They prefer a place in full sun. Z3.

Propagation These are not easy plants to divide but they can be increased from basal cuttings in spring. Alternatively the species can be grown from seed which should be sown in spring.

Malva moschata

This, the musk mallow, is one of the gems of the genus. When happy with its conditions it will grow up to 1m (3ft) but it is often shorter. It produces masses of candy-pink flowers, which always seem to have a freshness about them. The plant continues producing flowers from the early summer right on into the autumn. It can be naturalized in grass. S 60cm (24in). It has an equally delightful form – *alba* – with white flowers.

Malva sylvestris

This is the other main garden species. It can grow a bit taller than the previous, up to 1.2m (4ft), but often flops rather than growing upright. The flowers are a pinkish-purple, usually with deeper coloured veins, and, again, are produced over a very long season. S 1.2m (4ft). There are several cultivars, the most famous of which is 'Primley Blue' in which the flowers, as the name suggests, are blue, with pronounced darker veins. It tends to be prostrate rather than upright. Another excellent form, this time very upright, is the subspecies *mauritanica*. This has large, dark purple flowers. 'Brave Heart' is very similar.

Malva sylvestris 'Primley Blue'

MALVASTRUM
Malvastrum

There are number of species in this genus but only one of them, *M. lateritium*, is generally in cultivation. This plant is somewhat tender and so it is usually only grown in frost-free areas. It will last longer if the soil drainage is good, and makes an ideal candidate for the gravel or Mediterranean garden.

M. lateritium is a prostrate, sprawling plant that grows as tall as 25cm (10in) and up to 1m (3ft) across. It carries 5cm (2in) saucer-shaped flowers which are white with a narrow pink ring surrounding the yellow centre. The fresh-green leaves are shaped like those of the maple.

Cultivation This plant needs a well-drained position in full sun. It needs winter protection in colder areas. Z8.

Propagation Increase by taking softwood cuttings in summer. Malvastrum can also be grown from seed sown in spring.

MATTEUCCIA
Matteuccia

This is a small genus of ferns, of which only one species is frequently grown in our gardens. This is *M. struthiopteris*, the ostrich fern. It is so called because its large fronds resemble the tail feathers of the ostrich. Another name is the shuttlecock fern because the whole plant with its ring of fronds looks like a shuttlecock. When it is growing well, the plant reaches up to 1.5m (5ft) in height, with a spread of 75cm (30in). A space in a woodland area is the ideal setting. *M. orientalis* is occasionally also grown. This is similar but it only grows to H 60cm (24in) S 45cm (18in), making it more suitable for smaller gardens.

Cultivation Matteuccias grow well in moist, humus-rich soil in sun or partial shade. Z2.

Propagation The simplest method is division of the small plants that form around the main one. It can also be grown from spore.

Grasses and ferns

Grasses
Arundo
Briza
Calamagrostis
Cortaderia
Elymus
Hakonechloa
Milium
Miscanthus
Molinia
Pennisetum
Phalaris
Stipa

Ferns
Adiantum
Asplenium
Athyrium
Dryopteris
Osmunda
Polystichum

Matteuccia struthiopteris

Meconopsis cambrica

MECONOPSIS
Meconopsis

This is a genus of some 45 species of poppy-related plants. This relationship can be seen in the tissue-paper-like petals. Most of the flowers come in one of a range of wonderful blues, while others are yellow. There are also a few reds. Most of the species are in cultivation, but the majority are tricky to grow and are really the province of specialist growers.

With one exception, *M. cambrica*, these plants need a moist, buoyant atmosphere and so are best grown in damp, maritime areas where they do not dry out. They are most difficult in dry, hot areas. They are among the most beautiful of garden plants and look especially good in a woodland setting or planted amongst shrubs.

Cultivation Meconopsis need a deep, rich soil that remains moist and, if possible, a moist atmosphere around them. They like a partially shaded position. A special plot with plenty of well-rotted organic material that is regularly sprayed with water but which does not contain sitting water is necessary in dry, hotter areas. Z5–7.

Propagation They can be grown from seed sown as soon as it is ripe. Some species can be divided.

Meconopsis betonicifolia

Meconopsis grandis

The best-known of the blue poppies. It grows to a magnificent height and has large blue flowers, which appear in early summer. This is a really stunning plant when grown well. Unfortunately it is not long lived and so it is best to propagate it every year from seed to ensure its continuance. There are white forms. H 1.2m (4ft) S 45cm (18in).

Meconopsis cambrica

The Welsh poppy is the easiest meconopsis to grow. It is an attractive plant with yellow or orange flowers. They appear mainly in spring and early summer but continue sporadically throughout the summer. The plant will grow in sun or shade; the brightly coloured flowers look especially effective in a shady area. It needs deadheading regularly since it self-sows. H 45cm (18in) S 30cm (12in).

Other plants The above species are the two most popular plants, although *M. grandis* and *M.* × *sheldonii*, which are similar in appearance to *M. betonicifolia*, are also widely grown. If you have the right conditions and like meconopsis, there are plenty of other wonderful plants that you can search out.

MENTHA
Mint

The one thing most gardeners know about mint is that it runs. However, there is quite a bit more to them than that. There are about 25 species in the genus and quite a number of these are in cultivation. Many are for the herb garden and are of no real interest to the perennial gardener, but others are suitable for the border. They are mainly grown for their foliage, which adds flavour and fragrance to cooking, but the scents can also be appreciated in the garden. The flowers are not conspicuous but they attract bees and butterflies, which are a welcome addition to any garden.

Cultivation Any reasonable garden soil will do. Choose a sunny position. Most mints are inclined to be invasive so be careful with your choice of position. Either restrict their root run by planting in a pot or dig round them each year and remove questing roots.

Propagation Mints are very easy plants to increase by division at any time of year.

Mentha × *gracilis*

The species, ginger mint, is not of interest in the border but the form 'Variegata' is more attractive. This has darkish green foliage with bright gold markings, making it a useful foliage plant. H 45cm (18in) S 60cm (24in).

Mentha longifolia

This is one of the best border mints, although it is still invasive. It has greyish-silver foliage which can be very attractive, and spikes of lilac flowers. H 1.2m (4ft) S indefinite. A good form for border use is the so-called Buddleia Mint Group. There is also a variegated form.

Mentha longifolia Buddleia Mint Group

Mentha × *piperita* f. *citrata*

Mentha × *piperita* f. *citrata*

A special mint that smells of eau de cologne. H 20cm (15in) S indefinite.

Mentha suaveolens

This plant has quite large, round, hairy leaves. The form 'Variegata' is a good foliage plant: pale green leaves with nicely contrasting creamy blotches. H 30–45cm (12–18in) S 60cm (24in).

MILIUM
Milium

A small genus, of which only the marvellous *M. effusum*, in its golden form 'Aureum', is of interest. Known as Bowles' golden grass, this plant reaches just 30cm (12in), with a spread of 30cm (12in), but it has arching leaves in a lovely shade of yellow. Arising from the spring foliage are stems with delicate flower spikelets, both of which are also yellow. Use it to add a splash of sun to shady areas.

Cultivation Bowles' golden grass will grow in any good garden soil, but it prefers a woodland-type

Milium effusum 'Aureum'

soil with plenty of leaf mould. It also likes a lightly shaded position. Z5.
Propagation It will grow easily from seed and can also be divided in early spring as new growth gets under way.

MIMULUS
Musk

Mimulus is a large genus of some 150 species, some of which are perennials and are regularly grown in our gardens. They have tubular flowers that flare out at the end. The inner parts of the tubes are usually heavily spotted, sometimes resembling a monkey's face; monkey flower is another common name for the plant. The flowers are yellow, red, pink or orange and often a mixture of these. The plants generally like moist conditions and are ideal for lightening the edges of ponds or streams, or in a bog garden.
Cultivation Grow in a moist, humus-rich soil that never dries out. Some will thrive in shallow water. They like full sun or just a little light shade. Z3–7.
Propagation Most mimulus are easy to divide and cuttings can also be taken.

***Mimulus* 'Andean Nymph'**
A wonderful plant with rose-pink tubes diffused with cream. The inside is lightly spotted red. It has a long flowering season. H 23cm (9in) S 25cm (10in).

Mimulus lewisii
This is a very good border plant that can be grown away from water. It forms a loose clump which is speckled with rose-pink flowers with pale throats over a long period. H 60cm (24in) S 45cm (18in).

Mimulus guttatus

Mimulus aurantiacus

Mimulus luteus
A yellow-flowered monkey flower with red spots in the throat. It spreads to make a dense mat and is perfect for the side of streams or ponds. H and S 30cm (12in).

Other plants There a many more attractive species and cultivars. Those in bright reds and oranges, such as 'Wisley Red', 'Fire Dragon' (gold and red), 'Western Hills' and 'Whitecroft Scarlet' as well as the taller *M. cardinalis*, are very good for hot borders, as are the red and orange forms of *M. aurantiacus* and *M. guttatus*.

MISCANTHUS
Miscanthus

This is an important genus of grasses to the gardener. It consists of about 20 species of which a number are in cultivation. They are grown mainly for their size and stunning appearance. Most are tall, up to 3m (10ft) or more when in flower. Then, they make a fountain of narrow leaves and are topped with tall stems carrying elegant silky tufts of flowers. They are excellent plants for creating a focal point, either in a border or by themselves. They look particularly good next to water.
Cultivation These plants are usually happy in any reasonable garden soil, but they need a sunny position. Cut down the old foliage and flower stems in late winter. Z5.
Propagation Miscanthus need to be increased by division in early spring as new growth begins.

Miscanthus sinensis 'Gracillimus'

Miscanthus floridulus
A giant plant. The arching leaves are light green and rough along the margins. The flowers are white, but are only reliably produced in warmer areas. H 2.5m (8ft) S 1.5m (5ft).

Miscanthus sacchariflorus
This is very similar to the previous species, except that it is taller and produces its white flowers more reliably. It can be slightly invasive. H 3m (10ft) S indefinite.

Miscanthus sinensis 'Variegatus'

Miscanthus sinensis
This is the species that is usually of most interest to gardeners. *M. sinensis* is widely grown in its own right but there are now more than 100 cultivars all varying by a small degree. H 3m (10ft) S 45cm (18in). Some of the cultivars are much smaller than the species, providing those with small gardens a welcome opportunity to grow these graceful plants. Some of the best cultivars are 'Flamingo', 'Gracillimus', 'Kleine Fontaine' (dwarf), 'Pünktchen', 'Silberfeder', 'Variegatus' and 'Zebrinus' (variegated), but there are many others to check out.

Miscanthus sinensis 'Flamingo'

Miscanthus sinensis 'Kleine Fontaine'

Miscanthus sinensis 'Zebrinus'

Molinia caerulea

Molina caerulea 'Edith Dudszus'

Monarda 'Cambridge Scarlet'

MOLINIA
Molinia

A tiny genus of two species of which only one, *M. caerulea*, is of interest to gardeners. However, there are also a large number of cultivars so the keen gardener does not go short of choice.

The main species has thick clumps of narrow arching leaves from which arise stiff stems carrying an airy array of upright flowers. They look particularly effective when covered with rain drops or dew. The top of the flower stems reach to about 1.5m (5ft), while the clump of leaves is about 60–75cm (24–30in). This versatile plant looks good in a border or in a lone position, especially by water.

Molinia caerulea subsp. *arundinacea*

Cultivation Molinia grows in any reasonable garden soil and, like most grasses, it needs a sunny position. Cut to the ground in late winter before the new growth begins. Z4.

Propagation The species can be grown from seed while the cultivars should be increased by division in spring, just before growth begins.

Molinia caerulea
This has been described above. The cultivars vary mainly in height and colour and all belong to one of the two subspecies described below. H 3m (10ft) S 60cm (24in).

Molinia caerulea subsp. _arundinacea_
This subspecies is generally taller and more airy than the next. The main cultivar is undoubtedly the magnificent 'Karl Foerster'. It can grow to 2.2m (7ft) and has delicate open flower heads. Both these and the leaves turn a wonderful golden-yellow in autumn. S 60cm (24in). Other cultivars that are worth looking at include 'Fontäne', 'Transparent' and 'Windspiel'.

Molinia caerulea subsp. _caerulea_
There are several cultivars here that are well worth checking out. They include 'Edith Dudszus' (dark flowers), 'Heidebraut' (yellow flowers), 'Moorhexe' (black stems), 'Strahlenquelle' (arching stems) and 'Variegata', which has variegated foliage.

MONARDA
Bergamot

This is a small genus of around 15 species. About half of them are in cultivation, and their number is greatly exceeded by the many cultivars available. One of the first things you notice about monardas is the strong scent that the bruised foliage gives off: it is a real pleasure weeding near them. The next is the curious shape of the flowers. They look like large thyme flowers and are arranged in dense whorls around the stem. The colours of the flowers vary from bright red to softer pinks and purples and they appear in summer. These are perfect border plants and a large clump of them is always eye-catching. Some are quite tall, but the average height is about 1m (3ft), with a spread of 45cm (18in).

Monarda 'Prärienacht'

Cultivation These plants need a moist, humus-rich soil, otherwise they will dwindle and eventually die and they are also likely to suffer from mildew. They do best in a position in full sun. Z3.

Propagation The easiest method of increase is by division in spring, but basal cuttings can also be taken at the same time of year.

Monarda 'Beauty of Cobham'
This attractive plant has purplish-green foliage that nicely sets off the dense whorls of pale pink flowers held in purple bracts.

Monarda 'Cambridge Scarlet'
This is an old form, but is still one of the best. The flowers are bright scarlet.

Monarda 'Croftway Pink'
Another old cultivar. As its name suggests, it produces pink flowers.

Monarda didyma
One of the main garden species. It is from this that many of the cultivars are derived. The flowers are red or pink held with red-tinged bracts.

Monarda 'Petite Delight'
A lavender-rose form. It is short, reaching only half the height of most, at about 45cm (18in).

Monarda 'Petite Pink Supreme'
This is another short form, this time with red flowers and purple bracts. H 45cm (18in).

Monarda 'Prärienacht'
The flowers of this form are a wonderful clear purple.

Monarda 'Schneewittchen'
A good form with white flowers, which work well in a border with an all-white colour scheme.

Monarda 'Scorpion'
This one has purple flowers. It is a little taller than the others at about 1.2m (4ft).

Monarda 'Scorpion'

***Monarda* 'Squaw'**
Another red-flowered form, but this has the advantage of being a little more mildew-resistant than the previous one.

Other plants There are quite a number of other species and cultivars that are well worth looking out for. Most are in the same colour range as those that have been listed above.

MYRRHIS
Sweet cicely

The only member of the genus is *M. odorata*. It was once widely used as a herb but it is now mainly grown for its decorative quality, although some cooks still use the leaves for flavouring fruit dishes. The delicate fern-like leaves are very finely cut. Above them in early summer are flat heads of tiny white flowers, much in the style of cow parsley, another hedgerow plant. The plant grows to about 60cm (24in) or more in favourable conditions, with a similar spread. It looks good growing against a green hedge or against an old wall. Although it can be used to good effect in a border it makes an excellent plant for the wild garden.
Cultivation Any reasonable garden soil will suffice and a place in light shade seems to be best. It will self-sow if the seeds are allowed to be shed. Z4.
Propagation The simplest method of increase is from seed sown in spring. The plant can also be divided but this is not easy.

Myrrhis odorata

NEPETA
Catmint

A very large genus of around 250 species of which more than 40 are grown in gardens. However, there are only a few that are of specific interest to the general gardener. Most of these plants produce a haze of tiny, soft blue flowers carried on stiff arching stems; one produces blooms of pale yellow. The leaves are often aromatic.

Nepetas can be one of the mainstays of a romantic garden, and are at their best at the height of summer. Their pastel flower colours work very well with other soft shades, and can also be used to soften stronger neighbouring colours. Their love for well-drained soils makes the grey-leaved forms good for gravel or Mediterranean gardens. Generally nepetas grow no taller than about 1m (3ft) and they have a spread of 60cm (24in).
Cultivation Any good garden soil will do so long as it is free draining. Nepetas must have a sunny position. Cut them back after their first flush of flowers and then fresh foliage and more flowers will appear. Cats like the smell of some of these plants and will often lie on them crushing them to the ground.
Propagation Nepetas can be increased from basal cuttings in spring or by division at the same time of year.

Nepeta cataria
This is a coarser plant than the others. It has dirty-white flowers and greyish-green foliage. This species is the favourite for cats.

Nepeta clarkei

Nepeta clarkei
A nepeta with stiff upright stems and flowers of pure blue, which are accentuated by a white spot. H 80cm (32in).

Nepeta × faassenii
An excellent clump-forming plant with silvery-grey, aromatic foliage and pale blue flowers. It is a bit floppy but that adds to its hazy charm. H 45cm (18in).

Nepeta govaniana
The odd one out since it has pale yellow flowers carried loosely on stems up to 1m (3ft) high.

Nepeta nervosa
A much lower plant than other border species. It has upright stems containing spikes of blue flowers. It is a good front-of-border plant. H 45cm (18in).

Nepeta racemosa
This is similar (it is one of its parents) to *N. × faassenii* with the same soft blue flowers and ethereal appearance. However, it is a bit shorter. It is a good plant for flopping over the edge of paths. H 45cm (18in). 'Walker's Low' is a good compact variety. 'Snowflake', as its name suggests, has white flowers.

Nepeta govaniana

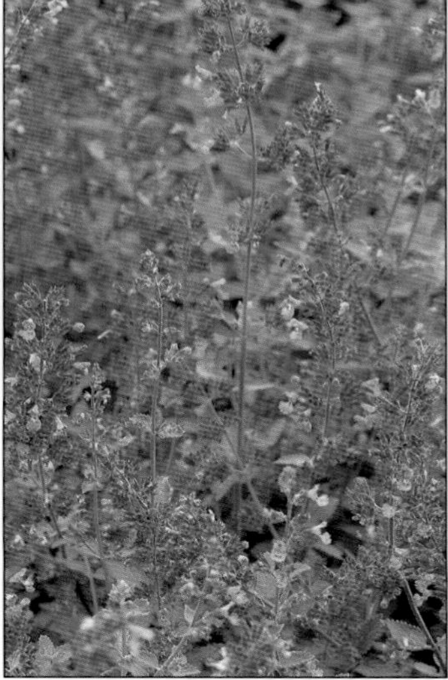
Nepeta racemosa 'Walker's Low'

Nepeta sibirica
A good plant for the mid-border. It has upright stems carrying pale blue flowers. H 1m (3ft).

***Nepeta* 'Six Hills Giant'**
A cultivar with grey-silver leaves. It is similar to *N. × faassenii*, but the flowers are darker and it is much taller. H 1m (3ft).

***Nepeta* 'Souvenir d'André Chaudron'**
This is similar to *N. sibirica*, but half the size. H 45cm (18in).

Nepeta subsessilis
A tall species with upright stems carrying bright blue flowers from midsummer. H 1m (3ft).

Nepeta 'Six Hills Giant'

Oenothera fruticosa

Oenothera fruticosa subsp. *glauca*

Oenothera speciosa

Origanum laevigatum

OENOTHERA
Evening primrose

A large genus containing 125 or so species, of which a number are in cultivation. Their main attraction is the flat saucer-like flowers that open mainly towards evening, which makes these plants ideal for commuters who only see their gardens at that time. Their colour is usually yellow although there are some white and pinks. Summer is their flowering time.

The plants vary considerably in their heights: there are prostrate ones whose stems crawl across the ground and tall ones that can reach 1m (3ft) or more. They are often short lived, especially in wetter soils.

Cultivation Evening primroses will grow in most garden soils so long as it is free draining – this is essential. They need a sunny position. Z4.

Propagation The species all come readily from seed but the cultivars generally need to be divided.

Oenothera acaulis

A plant for the front of a border or perhaps for a rock garden since it has quite prostrate stems. These carry flared funnel-shaped flowers that are white, turning to pink as they age. This plant must have good drainage. H 15cm (6in) S 20cm (8in).

Oenothera caespitosa

Another low-growing species. It has white-cupped flowers that are fragrant. They also turn pink as they age – a feature of many oenotheras. They are short lived. H 12cm (5in) S 20cm (8in).

Oenothera fruticosa

This is the main perennial border species. It is an upright plant reaching up to 1m (3ft), although some of its cultivars are only half this tall. It has spikes of yellow or gold flowers. This plant will take a little light shade. S 45cm (18in).

'Fyrverkeri' is the best-known cultivar. The flowers open from red buds and the leaves are flushed with purple, making a beautiful plant. Another good cultivar is 'Yellow River'. There is a subspecies *glauca* (previously known as *O. tetragona*) which has pale yellow flowers.

Oenothera macrocarpa

This vibrant plant was previously known as *O. missouriensis*. It is a prostrate, species whose sprawling stems produce flowers that are brilliant yellow. H 30cm (12in) S 40cm (16in).

Oenothera speciosa

This is a delightful species that tends to run among other plants. It is mainly prostrate. The flowers are white or pale pink with darker pink veins. H 30cm (12in) S 30cm (12in).

Oenothera stricta

A wonderful species with tall, gangling stems carrying yellow flowers opening from red buds. 'H 1.2m (4ft) S 30cm (12in). 'Sulphurea' is a delicate soft yellow. The flowers of both age to coral pink.

ORIGANUM
Marjoram

A genus with several species in cultivation, although many of the smaller ones are really only suitable for the alpine grower. The perennial ones have fragrant foliage and thin stems carrying sprays of purple flowers. They make excellent front-of-border plants but they do tend to spread by self-sowing. They can become a nuisance unless they are dead-headed before the seed is spread.

Cultivation These will grow in any reasonable garden soil. They prefer full sun, but will take a little light shade. Z7.

Propagation The species can be grown from seed sown in spring, and the cultivars are easily divided at the same time of year.

***Origanum* 'Kent Beauty'**

A wonderful plant that will attract much attention. It is low in the ground, but it has flower heads that resemble very attractive hops. The small pink flowers are tucked inside whorls of deep pink and green bracts. It likes a well-drained soil in a sunny position. Ideal for the front of a border. H 15cm (6in) S 30cm (12in).

Origanum laevigatum

Probably the main origanum for the perennial border. The flowers appear in sprays on the top of wiry stems. The flowers are pinkish-purple and have dark purple bracts around them, which make them appear to be in flower for a longer period than they really are. H 60cm (24in) S 20cm (8in). There are several good forms, of which 'Herrenhausen' is possibly the best.

Origanum vulgare

This is the wild marjoram. It is similar in many respects to the last, with sprays of pink flowers reaching up to 60cm (24in) in height but often less. It has several cultivars of which 'Aureum' is possibly the best. This has golden leaves and they remain golden for most of the season, making it a valuable foliage plant. This plant self-sows prodigiously so be sure to remove flower heads before it seeds. S 45cm (18in).

Oenothera fruticosa 'Yellow River'

Oenothera macrocarpa

Origanum vulgare 'Aureum'

Osmunda regalis

OSMUNDA
Royal fern

This is a genus of about 12 fern species of which only one, *O. regalis*, is in general cultivation. This splendid fern grows as high as 2m (6ft) when well suited but is often much shorter. The fronds are not as delicately cut as many garden ferns but still have a good shape and their vivid green sets off the central cluster of smaller flowering stems, which are covered with rusty brown spores. This fern likes a permanently damp position: a bog garden or a spot beside a stream or pond. S 1m (3ft).

O. cinnamomea and *O. claytoniana* are also worth checking out if you can find them.

Cultivation These need a damp position that does not dry out. The soil should contain plenty of humus. They grow in shade but will also grow in full sun if the situation is moist enough. Z2.

Propagation The easiest way to increase your stock of royal ferns is to divide the plants in the spring, just before the new growth begins. They can also be grown from spore.

OSTEOSPERMUM
Osteospermum

This is a delightful genus of roughly 70 species of which a number of the more hardy are in cultivation. Osteospermums are colourful daisies that always make a splash in the border. Colours of the outer petals include white, yellow and shades of pink through to purple, while the centres are yellow, purple or brown. They are wonderful plants for the front of a border or even for containers. Their only disadvantage is that they often shut up in dull weather and during the evening. Some are marginally tender so take cuttings each year to safeguard your stock.

Cultivation Any good garden soil as long as it is well drained. A sunny position is vital. Z8.

Propagation Take cuttings in spring or early summer.

Osteospermum 'Buttermilk'

As you would imagine from the name, the outer petals are very pale yellow, darkening towards the ends. The central disc is bluish-purple. This is a very good plant that flowers over a very long period. H 60cm (24in) S 30cm (12in).

Osteospermum 'Cannington Roy'

This is another gem. The outer petals are white with purple tips to them. As they age they become flushed with pink. The central disc is purple. This is shorter than the previous plant with a height of 25cm (10in). S 45cm (18in). There are several other Cannington hybrids covering the full range of colours.

Osteospermum jucundum

A very good plant with masses of flowers that have pinkish-purple petals and blue central discs. It is a late flowerer, producing blooms from late summer onwards. H 45cm (18in) S 30cm (12in). It has a number of cultivars. One of the best is the excellent 'Blackthorn Seedling', which has darker flowers in a rich purple.

Osteospermum 'Lady Leitrim'

This plant has white petals that fade to pink as they age. The central disc is blue. H 45cm (18in) S variable.

Osteospermum 'Nairobi Purple'

This is one of the lower-growing osteospermums. It carries flowers that have dark purple petals and a black central disc. It flowers over a long period from early summer onwards. H 25cm (10in) S 30–45cm (12–18in).

Osteospermum 'Whirlygig'

This cultivar is one of the most intriguing members of the genus.

Osteospermum 'Lady Leitrim'

The petals are pure white and the central disc is blue. Its attraction lies in the fact that the petals fold in half-way down their length. This makes the ends look like paddles, while the whole flower has the appearance of the ripples made in still water after a pebble has been dropped in – a truly wonderful shape. H 60cm (24in) S 30–45cm (12–18in).

Osteospermum 'White Pim'

The identification of this plant has still not settled down: it is still familiar to most gardeners as *O. eklonis prostratum* or to some as *O. caulescens*. This is one of the hardiest plants in the genus and it survives well in most gardens. The petals are white and the central disc varies but is often bluish. Flowers appear over a long season. H 60cm (24in) S variable.

Osteospermum 'Cannington Roy'

Osteospermum 'White Pim'

Paeonia lactiflora 'Bowl of Beauty'

Paeonia lactiflora 'Alice Harding'

Papaver orientale 'Curlilocks'

Papaver orientale 'Khedive'

PAEONIA
Peony

One of the most popular of all perennial species, these beautiful plants suit almost any type of garden, from old-fashioned cottage gardens to modern formal ones. There are only about 30 species of peony, most of which are in cultivation, but hundreds of cultivars have been bred from them. The typical peony has a bowl-shaped flower in varying shades of red, pink or white. There are also some rather fine yellows. As well as single flowers there are also semi-doubles and doubles. While the doubles are beautiful they do have the problem of being top-heavy, especially when filled with rain water, and they often sag miserably to the ground. The foliage of peonies is also very attractive, especially when it first emerges and some have very good autumn colour.

Cultivation Peonies need a deep rich soil, so add plenty of well-rotted organic material. They will grow in either sun or a light shade. They often take a while to settle down after being disturbed so try not to move them once established. Z3–5.

Propagation They can be divided in spring but this is not easy and they will take a while to settle down. Root cuttings taken in early winter is the easiest method.

Paeonia lactiflora

This white-flowered species is grown in its own right, but it is known mainly in the form of one of its hundreds of cultivars. There are far too many to mention but one exceptional one is given separately below and other ones to look out for include 'Adolphe Rousseau' (semi-double deep red flowers), 'Alice Harding' (pale pink double), 'Duchesse de Nemours' (double white), 'Félix Crousse' (double cerise), 'Festiva Maxima' (double white) and 'Monsieur Jules Elie' (double red).

Paeonia lactiflora 'Bowl of Beauty'

Deep rose-red petals and a large central boss of yellow make this a superb peony. H 75cm (30in) S 1m (3ft).

Paeonia mlokosewitschii

This is one of the most beautiful of peonies. It blooms in spring, making it one of the earliest to flower. The single flowers are lemon-yellow. The foliage has reddish tints when it first appears and again in the autumn. As a bonus the plant also produces colourful seedpods in autumn. A great plant for any garden. H and S 75cm (30in).

Other plants There are so many other good peonies. Take a look at *PP. cambessedesii, mascula, tenuifolia,* and *veitchii,* as well as many of the other cultivars. If you get hooked, seek out a specialist nursery or get its catalogue.

PAPAVER
Poppy

This is another popular genus with many in cultivation, although many of these are annuals or short-lived perennials. The main perennial is *P. orientale*, which is one of the mainstays of the early summer border. The floppy coarse stems rise up to 1m (3ft) in height when supported. The flowers are great bowls of paper tissue in a variety of reds, pinks, oranges and white. They are not attractive once flowering is over, so place in the middle of the border where other plants will cover them or the gap they leave when cut back. S 1m (3ft).

Cultivars that are well worth growing include: 'Allegro' (scarlet with black basal markings on the petals), 'Black and White' (white with deep crimson basal markings), 'Cedric Morris' (pink with black basal markings), 'Curlilocks' (bright orange with frilled petals), 'Effendi' (orange), 'Goliath' (huge flowers, deep red, black basal marks), 'Khedive' (pale pink), 'Mrs Perry' (salmon-pink with black basal marks), 'Patty's Plum' (plum coloured), 'Perry's White' (white), 'Picotée' (white petals with an orange edge to them), 'Prinzessin Victoria Louise' (deep salmon-pink with black basal marks), 'Türkenlouis' (scarlet with black basal marks) and 'Turkish Delight' (soft pink).

Cultivation Choose a deep rich soil that is well drained and give them a sunny position. Give the plants some support in spring when they are about half-grown. Z2.

Propagation These plants can be divided with difficulty in spring but it is much easier to take root cuttings in the early winter.

PENNISETUM
Fountain grass

This is a large genus of grass, which has produced a number of very decorative plants for our gardens. The main characteristic as far as gardeners are concerned is the soft cylindrical flower heads, which look especially delightful when they have dew on them. These are flower heads to run your fingers through, so plant them near paths or at least at the front of a border. Pennisetums form rounded clumps from which the thin flowering stems arch. The flowers are buff or pink. They are not completely hardy so

Paeonia lactiflora 'Adolphe Rousseau'

Paeonia mlokosewitschii

Papaver orientale 'Effendi'

Pennisetum alopecuroides

Pennisetum villosum

Penstemon 'Sour Grapes'

Penstemon 'Russian River'

in colder areas it is important to propagate them regularly. Another problem is that they can look like grass weeds when they first appear in spring so take care not to weed them out.
Cultivation Pennisetums will grow in any reasonable garden soil as long as it is well drained. A sunny position is essential. Cut back the dead growth in early spring before the new growth appears. Protect in cold winters. Z6–8.
Propagation The easiest method of increase is from seed sown in spring. It is also possible to divide these plants just before the new growth starts in spring.

Pennisetum alopecuroides
A tall grass whose flower stems reach up to 1m (6ft) in height and 45cm (18in) in spread if conditions are favourable. The flowers are deep pink-purple and are held in long (20cm/8in) cylindrical spikes. They appear in late summer. This is a very attractive plant and there are also a number of cultivars. 'Hameln' is interesting as it is a much shorter form (H 60cm/24in) and it flowers earlier. 'Little Bunny' is even smaller at H 40cm (16in).

Pennisetum orientale

Pennisetum orientale
This plant is similar to the previous one, but smaller with violet-pink flowers. H 45cm (18in) S 30cm (12in).

Pennisetum villosum
Another very attractive grass. It has arching stems carrying shorter and fatter cylinders of flowers that are a buff colour. H 45cm (18in) S 50cm (20in).

PENSTEMON
Penstemon

An invaluable genus for the garden. It contains more than 250 species. Many are of interest to the specialist grower, but only a few appeal to the perennial gardener. It is the many cultivars that make this such an important group of plants. The flowers are carried in loose spikes from early summer through to the frosts and beyond. They are tubular and often flared. The colour varies from pink to red and purple and also includes white. Most have at least two colours in them. The flowers of the species come in a wide range, including blue and yellow. These are excellent plants for growing singly or as drifts.
Cultivation Any reasonable garden soil will do, but better results will be achieved in a fertile soil. It should also be free draining. Penstemons need full sun. Z4–6.
Propagation The plants are easy to propagate from cuttings taken at any time of year, even winter.

***Penstemon* 'Alice Hindley'**
This has widely flared tubes shaded in soft pinkish-blue and white. H 1m (3ft) S 30cm (12in).

***Penstemon* 'Andenken an Friedrich Hahn'**
One of the hardiest, this produces wine-red flowers over a long period. Also known as 'Garnet'. H 1m (3ft) S 60cm (24in).

***Penstemon* 'Apple Blossom'**
The flowers are large, with pink tips merging into a white throat. H 75cm (30in) S 60cm (24in).

***Penstemon* 'Burgundy'**
This is a tall penstemon, carrying burgundy-red flowers. H 1.5m (5ft) S 60cm (24in).

Penstemon 'Pennington Gem'

Penstemon heterophyllus
A smaller-flowered plant with electric-blue flowers that are especially bright in the cultivar 'Heavenly Blue'. A superb plant. H 45cm (18in) S 25cm (10in).

***Penstemon* 'Hidcote Pink'**
This has rose-pink flowers with crimson pencilling in the throat. H 1m (3ft) S 30cm (12in).

***Penstemon* 'Sour Grapes'**
The flowers of this cultivar are tubes of purple. H 60cm (24in) S 60cm (24in).

Other plants Amongst others, look at 'Cherry' (red), 'Chester Scarlet' (scarlet), 'Pennington Gem' (pink), 'Russian River' (deep purple), 'Schoneholzeri' (scarlet) and 'White Bedder' (white), and the species *P. hirsutus* (white and mauve).

Penstemon hirsutus

Persicaria affinis (summer)

PEROVSKIA
Perovskia

This genus of seven species is little known, possibly because only one is in general cultivation. This is the delightful plant *P. atriplicifolia*. Strictly speaking it is classed as a sub-shrub rather than a perennial but it is usually treated as the latter by gardeners. From its shrubby base it throws up tall stems carrying airy spikes with soft violet-blue flowers. The small foliage is a soft grey and so the plant has a misty quality about it. It is perfect for a romantic setting, especially when mixed with other pastel colours. It grows to about 1.2m (4ft) with a spread of 1m (3ft), and the flowers appear from late summer onwards. The foliage is aromatic. There is a shorter cultivar, 'Little Spire', and a couple of other hybrids of which 'Blue Spire' is the most popular. It is essentially the same as *P. atriplicifolia,* except for the deeply divided leaves.

Perovskia 'Blue Spire'

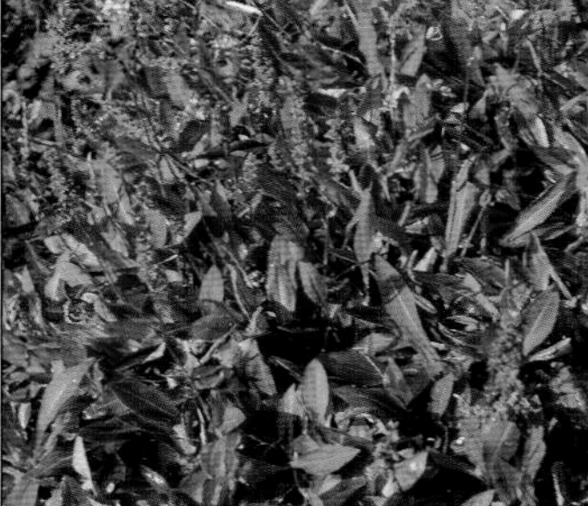
Persicaria affinis (autumn)

Cultivation Any reasonable garden soil will do but it must be well-drained. It is important to plant in full sun. Prune each year's growth back to old wood near the base. Z6.

Propagation The easiest method of increasing perovskias is to take cuttings in summer.

PERSICARIA
Persicaria

This genus was until relatively recently part of what was known as *Polygonum*. About 70 species were moved to this genus, quite a number of which are worthy of cultivation. The flowers of most are small and carried cylindrical spikes, the majority being pink of one shade or another. They are normally held well above the foliage. This is dense, making good ground cover. The plants are useful for creating a mat between other plants, either in a border or in some odd corner where ground cover is needed simply to suppress weeds. The foliage of some species also has the advantage of producing good autumnal colours which in some cases continues well into the winter. These are easy, obliging plants and yet add colour to the borders at most times of the year.

Cultivation Persicarias will grow in any reasonable garden soil and they can thrive in either sun or partial shade. Z3–6.

Propagation The easiest method of propagating persicarias is by division in the spring.

Persicaria affinis

This is a wonderful ground-cover plant. It is low growing: up to 25cm (10in) to the top of the flowers with the mat of foliage reaching half that. The spikes of flowers are pink, and age to red then brown. The leaves similarly age to red and brown, and make good winter cover. S 30cm (12in). There are several good cultivars including 'Dimity', 'Donald Lowndes' and 'Superba'.

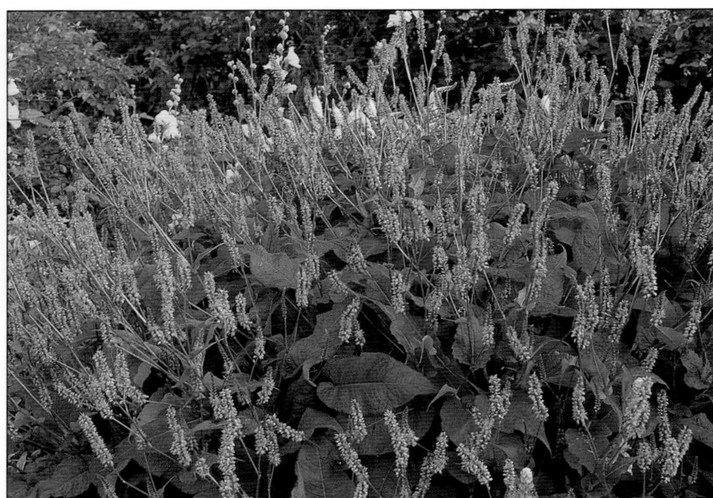
Persicaria amplexicaulis

Persicaria amplexicaulis

A clump-forming plant, which is ideal for the middle or back of a border. It has large leaves, which are topped by a narrow cylinder of flowers on thin stems: these seem to whiz out of the foliage like fireworks. H and S 1.2m (4ft).

The main colour is red but there are cultivars with other colours such as 'Alba' (white), 'Firetail' (bright red, very thin spikes), 'Inverleith' (dark red) and 'Rosea' (pink).

Persicaria bistorta

Although this will grow in a border if the soil is moist enough, it is primarily a plant of damp places and so it does well in bog gardens or beside water. The large leaves form a low (30cm/12in) mat above which the flower spikes rise. The flowers are a sugary pink and contrast well with the leaves below. They appear in spring. It makes excellent groundcover; and will spread gently without becoming a nuisance. S indefinite. There is a good form 'Superba', which produces bigger flower spikes.

Persicaria virginiana

Although the species is often grown in its own right, it is mainly found in the form 'Painter's Palette'. The attraction here is the large leaves, which are splashed with green, cream, brown, pink and red. As with the main species, the loose flower spikes are greenish, aging to red. H and S 60cm (24in).

Other plants Cast an eye over *PP. campanulata, capitata, milletii* and *vacciniifolia* if you can find them.

Persicaria bistorta

Phalaris arundinacea

Phlox divaricata 'Chattahoochee'

Phlox paniculata 'Mother of Pearl'

PHALARIS
Phalaris

This is a genus containing about 15 species of which the majority are far too weedy for the garden. The only one that is generally grown can also be considered a weed since it can become very invasive. It is so beautiful, however, that a special place should usually be found for it. It is *P. arundinacea* var. *picta*, which is known as gardener's garters. The attractive feature of this plant is the leaves which are pale green striped with silvery white and with occasional pink flushes. It does run, so be sure to contain it in some way or plant it where it can romp freely. The greenish flower stalks can reach 1m (3ft) but are often less. S indefinite. There is another form *P.a.* 'Feesey' which has pinkish-purple flushes and is not quite so rampant.

Cultivation Any garden soil will be sufficient for this plant, but it must have a sunny position. Plant it in a sunken bucket or surround in some other way to prevent it from spreading too far. Cut down old growth before the new starts in spring and trim it over again in early summer. Z4.

Propagation Its invasive habit means that this plant is very easy to propagate by division in spring.

Phlox douglasii

PHLOX
Phlox

There are 67 species of phlox, a number of which are in cultivation. There are three different forms: the tall border phloxes, the low cushions for use on rock gardens and border edges, and an intermediate-height group which are good for woodlands and shady places. They all have the same shaped flowers. These consist of a disc of five petals, which are narrower in some species than others. They are all colourful, some intensely so. They range from soft pinks and mauves to bright reds, taking in purples and whites. The main border species is *P. paniculata* which has a large number of cultivars.

Cultivation The majority of these plants need a rich, moist soil, although it should be well drained. Most grow in full sun or light shade. Z4.

Propagation They can be divided or basal cuttings can be taken in the spring. However, the taller species can suffer from stem eelworm and so it is best to propagate them from root cuttings taken in early winter.

Phlox carolina

This is mainly grown in the excellent form of 'Bill Baker' which has pink flowers in early summer. It makes a very good plant for the edges of woodland gardens, or for areas of light shade with a woodland-type soil. H 45cm (18in) S 30cm (12in).

Phlox divaricata

Another woodlander growing in moist soil. This has pale blue or white flowers on stems growing up to 45cm (18in) high. There are a number of cultivars, the most spectacular of which is 'Chattahoochee' whose lavender flowers have a rose-pink centre. The plant is not long lived and needs regular replacement. H 45cm (18in) S 30cm (12in).

Phlox douglasii

A low mat-forming species with small flowers in spring. It is excellent for the front of the border. H and S 20cm (8in).

Phlox paniculata 'Hampton Court'

There are many colourful cultivars, including 'Crackerjack' (magenta) and 'Red Admiral' (bright crimson).

Phlox paniculata

This is the main border phlox. The elegant flowers are often subtly perfumed, and appear from midsummer onwards. H 1.2m (4ft) S 60cm (24in).

The many cultivars include 'Blue Ice' (pale blue), 'Bright Eyes' (pale pink with red eyes), 'Eventide' (pale blue), 'Fujiyama' (pure white), 'Hampton Court' (lilac-blue), 'Le Mahdi' (violet with darker eyes), 'Mother of Pearl' (pink-tinged white) and 'Norah Leigh' (variegated leaves and pale mauve flowers with dark centres).

Phlox subulata

Like *P. douglasii*, this is low growing and covered with masses of flowers in spring. H 10cm (4in) S 20cm (8in). A good variety is 'Marjorie' (deep pink).

Phlox paniculata 'Norah Leigh'

Phormium tenax 'Variegatum'

PHORMIUM
New Zealand flax

The two species of this genus are important garden plants. They are clump-forming plants on a grand scale, producing a huge fountain of wide sword-like leaves and, occasionally, towering sprays of red or yellow flowers. There is a surprising number of cultivars, mainly with different coloured foliage. The flower stems can reach up to 5m(16ft) in height, and the clump of leaves are up to 2.5m (8ft) tall. These impressive architectural plants make ideal focal points either in a border or freestanding at some other point in the garden. Their size dictates that they are really only suitable for larger gardens, but there are some smaller cultivars that would suit those with less space. They are excellent for seaside gardens.
Cultivation These plants need a well-prepared free-draining soil and a sunny position.
Propagation Although it is a struggle with such a large plant, division is the best method of increase. Fortunately it is possible to break off a small piece without digging up the whole plant.

Phormium cookianum
This is the smaller of the two species with leaves that reach up to 1.5m (5ft) and flower stems that are a little taller. It has yellowish flowers. S 30cm (12in). The form *P.c.* subsp. *hookeri* 'Tricolor' is the most popular cultivar. Its green leaves have red and yellow stripes.

***Phormium* 'Sundowner'**
This is a gem of a plant, which is about the same height as the previous one. It has erect bronze-coloured leaves attractively striped in pink and yellow. H 1.5m (5ft) S 1.2m (4ft).

Phormium tenax
This is the big one. Although some leaves are arching, the majority tend to stand up giving it a good shape. H 3m (10ft) S 1–2m (3–6ft). There are a number of cultivars of which the Purpureum Group, with its purple foliage, is the most popular. 'Variegatum' with cream stripes is also a good cultivar.

PHUOPSIS
Phuopsis

The only species of this genus, *P. stylosa*, is a low-growing spreading plant carrying beautiful balls of pink flowers over a long period in the summer. The spreading stems root as they go so it can be a nuisance in the wrong place. However, it is very attractive placed at the front of a border where it can weave between other plants. It has a slight foxy smell, to which some people object. H and S 30cm (12in).
Cultivation Any reasonable garden soil is suitable. It will grow in full sun or light shade. Cut back after flowering reduce spreading. Z6.
Propagation Phuopsis can easily be propagated by dividing the plants in the spring.

PHYGELIUS
Phygelius

Both species of this genus are in cultivation and there is also a hybrid between them. They are actually shrubs but they are usually considered perennials by gardeners. They are grown for their tall stems carrying loose sprays of pendant tubular flowers. These are red, pink or yellow, and appear over a long period, from early summer to autumn. The plants can get very tall, up to 3m (10ft) or more, but generally they are around 1–1.5m (3–5ft) tall, with a spread of 2m (6ft). They are not startling plants but more than earn their keep in a border.
Cultivation Phygelius need a reasonably rich soil which is free-draining yet moisture-retentive. They need a sunny position. Z8.
Propagation The best method of increase is to take softwood cuttings in early summer.

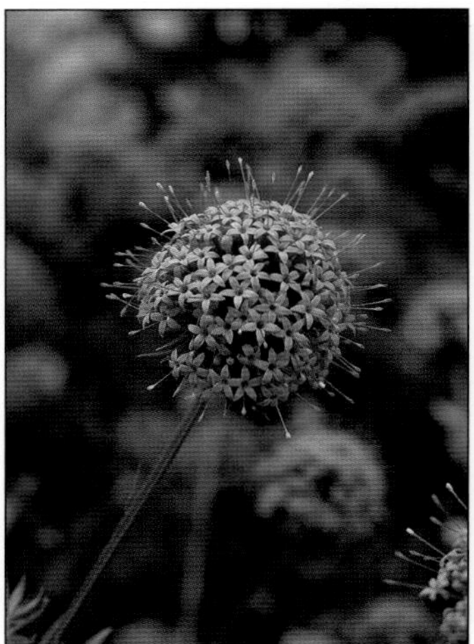
Phuopsis stylosa

Phygelius × *rectus* 'African Queen'

Phygelius aequalis
This plant has dusky-pink flowers. It has a few cultivars of which 'Yellow Trumpet' is one of the best, with pale yellow flowers.

Phygelius aequalis

Phygelius capensis
This is a slightly bigger plant than the previous species, and has orange-red flowers.

Phygelius* × *rectus
This is the hybrid between the two species above. There are a number of interesting forms. 'African Queen' is one of the best known, with its red flowers. 'Moonraker' has pale yellow flowers. 'Pink Elf' is shorter at H 75cm (30in) and has pink flowers with deeper coloured tips. 'Salmon Leap' has salmony-orange flowers and 'Winchester Fanfare' has deep reddish-pink flowers.

PHYSOSTEGIA
Obedient plant

One species of this small genus is grown in the garden. *P. virginiana* is called the obedient plant because

Phygelius × *rectus* 'Moonraker'

Physostegia virginiana subsp. *speciosa* 'Bouquet Rose'

when the flowers are pushed to one side, they stay in position instead of springing back. The spikes of flowers are tubular and flared at the end, rather like those of antirrhinums. They are either pink or white and appear from midsummer onwards on stems up to 1.2m (4ft) high. The plant has a spread of 60cm (24in).

There are several cultivars. 'Alba', 'Crown of Snow' and 'Summer Snow' are white as their names suggest. *P.v.* subsp. *speciosa* 'Variegata' has whiter margins to the greyish leaves and cerise flowers. Another *speciosa* cultivar is 'Bouquet Rose', which has pale mauve-pink flowers. *P.v.* 'Vivid' has bright purple-pink blooms.

Cultivation Grow in any reasonable garden soil so long as it does not dry out too much; add plenty of well-rotted organic material. They like full sun or light shade. Z4.

Propagation Increase is by division in early spring. The species can be grown from seed.

Physostegia virginiana 'Summer Snow'

P.v. ssp. 'Variegata'

PLATYCODON
Balloon flower

A genus with *P. grandiflorus* as its only species. The English name refers to the flower which inflates itself like a balloon just before it fully opens. It is closely related to the bell flowers and resembles them when open. The five petals form a shallow dish with the tips bent back. The colour is a wonderful violet-purple. These are not big plants, reaching only 60cm (24in) in height and with a spread of 30–45cm (12–18in) but they make excellent plants for the centre of a bed in late summer when the flowers open. There is a white form 'Alba' as well as pink forms such as 'Perlmutterschale' and 'Fuji Pink'. 'Apoyama' and 'Mariesii' are possibly the best blue forms, the latter being a more compact plant.

Cultivation Any well-drained garden soil will do, but it must be capable of retaining some moisture throughout the summer. Either a sunny or partially shaded position will suffice. Z4.

Propagation Taking basal cuttings in spring is probably the easiest method of increasing your stock.

Platycodon grandiflorus

Platycodons can also be divided but this can be tricky since they do not like to be disturbed.

PODOPHYLLUM
Podophyllum

A small genus of plants of which two or three are in cultivation, although they are not frequently seen. They are woodland plants and are best planted in such areas since they are not really border plants. The foliage has the curious habit of emerging through the ground like a folded umbrella before opening. At least one species hides its flowers beneath these leaves which is intriguing, but does not help its popularity. In spite of this shyness they make good shade plants and they do at least have attractive leaves. The flowers are followed by large, plum-sized coloured fruit. These are plants for those who want to grow something different. They will spread to form a large clump for those who have space.

Cultivation Podophyllums like a deep moist soil, such as a woodland soil with plenty of leafmould or other organic material. They will grow in sun but are better suited to dappled shade under trees or amongst shrubs. Z3–7.

Propagation These plants spread by underground rhizomes so they can easily be divided. They can also be grown from seed, which should preferably be sown as soon as it is ripe.

Podophyllum hexandrum

This plant used to be known as *P. emodii*, a name which is still more familiar to many people than its new one. It produces solitary white flowers on each stem before the leaves unfold from their furled umbrella. When the leaves do open they are large and mid-green with brownish-purple mottling that makes them rather attractive. The ensuing red fruit are large and plum-shaped. H 45cm (18in) S 30cm (12in). There is a variety *chinense* which has pink flowers and deeper divisions in the leaves.

Podophyllum peltatum

This is the other major podophyllum grown in our gardens. In contrast to the previous one, the leaves open before the flowering. This is a shame since the 5cm (2in) cup-shaped flowers hang down and are obscured by the leaves. They are a rather attractive pale pink or white, and are followed by yellowish-green, or sometimes reddish, fruit. H 30–45cm (12–18in) S 30cm (12in).

Podophyllum hexandrum

Red-hot perennials

- *Canna* 'Assault'
- *Canna* 'Endeavour'
- *Crocosmia* 'Lucifer'
- *Dahlia* 'Bishop of Llandaff'
- *Geum* 'Mrs Bradshaw'
- *Hemerocallis* 'Berlin Red'
- *Hemerocallis* 'Little Red Hen'
- *Hemoracallis* 'Stafford'
- *Kniphofia* 'Prince Igor'
- *Leonotis leonurus*
- *Lobelia tupa*
- *Lychnis chalcedonica*
- *Mimulus cupreus* 'Whitecroft Scarlet'
- *Mimulus* 'Wisley Red'
- *Papaver orientale* 'Glowing Embers'
- *Penstemon* 'Flame'
- *Potentilla* 'Gibson's Scarlet'
- *Tropaeolum speciosum*

Polemonium caeruleum

POLEMONIUM
Jacob's ladder

This genus of about 25 species includes 20 or so that are cultivated, although there are only a handful that are really popular. It is a delightful group; the flowers are generally blue or pink and have a decidedly fresh look about them. The majority are funnel-shaped blooms, with some being flatter than others. They flower in spring or early summer, making them perfect plants for the early border. Their foliage is often composed of leaflets on either side of the stem, resembling a primitive ladder, hence its English name.
Cultivation These will grow in any reasonable garden soil, but they do best in a moisture-retentive one. They will grow in either full sun or partial shade. Z4.
Propagation The species can be easily grown from seed (some will self-sow). Alternatively, they can all be divided in spring.

Polemonium carneum

Polemonium foliosissimum

Polemonium caeruleum
This is the species that best exhibits the Jacob's ladder foliage. It is a tall, upright plant topped with loose clusters of blue flowers. It flowers in early summer. H 1m (3ft) S 60cm (24in). The form *album* has white flowers as does 'Everton White'. 'Brise d'Anjou' has variegated foliage; *P. foliosissimum* is similar.

Polemonium carneum
This is a delightful plant with saucer-shaded flowers of the most delicate pink. It is a loose, clump-forming plant which flowers in early summer. It makes a good front-of-border plant. H 40cm (16in) S 45cm (18in). It has a variety 'Apricot Delight', which produces flowers of that colour.

***Polemonium* 'Lambrook Mauve'**
A loose, clump-forming plant with masses of beautiful mauve flowers from late spring. A superb plant for the front of border. H 30cm (12in) S 30cm (12in).

Polemonium pauciflorum
This is the odd one out since it produces long tubular flowers that are pale yellow flushed with red and appearing in midsummer. It is a tallish plant making it suitable for mid border use. H 45cm (18in) S 15cm (6in).

Polemonium reptans
A low-growing, rather sprawling plant but one that is blessed with fine flowers especially in its numerous cultivars. Those of the species are blue. H 30cm (12in) S 30cm (12in). 'Blue Pearl' is a good blue form, while 'Virginia White' is white. 'Pink Dawn' is, as its name suggests, pink.

Polygonatum × hybridum

POLYGONATUM
Solomon's seal

These are graceful plants with an air of tranquillity about them. There are about 50 species in all but only a few are in general cultivation. They are characterized by arching stems from which dangle creamy-white bells, usually hanging in pairs; the pointed oval leaves are held stiffly above them like wings. Although these can be grown in sun they often do best planted in cool, dappled shade, such as under trees or shrubs. They are plants to look at individually rather than in a crowded border where their effect is lost.
Cultivation If possible, plant in a moisture-retaining, woodland-type soil. They do best in light shade, but full sun is all right if the soil is kept moist. Z4.

Polygonatum hookeri
This is a gem. It is also unusual owing to its bluish-pink flowers. It spreads between other plants. H 10cm (4in) S 30cm (12in).

Polygonatum × hybridum
This is probably the main garden species. It forms large clumps or drifts but is not invasive. The creamy-white flowers hang in fours. They appear in spring. H 1.2m (4ft) S 1m (3ft).

Polygonatum multiflorum
This is the other main garden species. It is similar to the previous except the flowers are possibly whiter and it is shorter growing. H 1m (3ft) S 30cm (12in). There is also a variegated form called 'Striatum'.

Other plants There are a number of other species worth looking at, especially *P. hirtum* with its broader leaves, *P. biflorum*, and the variegated form *P. odoratum* var. *pluriforum* 'Variegatum'. If you are interested in Solomon' seals then there is a closely related but little-known genus *Disporum* that you may want to check out.

POLYSTICHUM
Shield fern

This is a large genus of some 200 evergreen species of fern. About 20 of these are in cultivation although only a couple of these are seen with any frequency. These have a typical fern shape with lance-shaped fronds that arise from a central crown, reminiscent of a shuttlecock, and unrolling as they emerge. The fronds are deeply cut and make attractive plants for a shady position, either under trees or shrubs, or in the

Polygonatum odoratum var. pluriforum 'Variegatum'

P. setiferum 'Pulcherrimum Bevis'

shade of a house. Dappled shade is the best place to show them off. They add a cool tranquillity to the scene and make a good contrast to bright golden flowers of, say, *Meconopsis cambrica*.
Cultivation They need a deep woodland-type soil, well supplied with rotted organic material. They should be grown in the shade. Z5.
Propagation Shield ferns can be divided in spring, just before growth starts. Alternatively they can be grown from spore.

Polystichum acrostichoides
This fern has narrow fronds that are up to 60cm (24in) long with a spread of 45cm (18in).

Polystichum aculeatum
A popular polystichum, this is also called the hard shield fern. Its narrow, dark green fronds are up to 60cm (24in) long.

Polystichum munitum
This is rather different from the rest since the fronds are not soft but leathery and somewhat glossy, making them good for reflecting light in dull areas. They are narrow and up to 1m (3ft) long, with leaflets that are not subdivided. S 30cm (12in).

Polystichum setiferum
This is the most popular species and it has 30 or so cultivars, all varying slightly from the species, which has long fronds. These may be up to 1.2m (4ft) in ideal conditions but are more usually around 1m (3ft). S 45cm (18in). There are various groups of cultivars that are worth considering. These include the Divisilobum Group, the Plumosodivisilobum Group and the Plumosum Group. Other attractive cultivars include 'Dahlem', 'Herrenhaussen' and 'Pulcherrimum Bevis'.

Other plants If you get hooked on ferns it is a good idea to visit specialist nurseries and browse through their catalogues.

POTENTILLA
Cinquefoil

This is a very large genus containing more than 500 species. The majority of garden-worthy plants fall into two camps, the shrubs and the perennials. The latter are of interest here, although it must be said that the shrubs are very useful in mixed borders. They have flat or saucer-shaped flowers with five petals (sometimes they are doubles) in various colours from white through to the most vivid of reds. They tend to be sprawling plants that wend their way pleasingly around and through other plants. They bring splashes of colour to the front and mid border.
Cultivation Cinquefoils will grow in any reasonable garden soil. They prefer a sunny position. Z4.
Propagation The best way of increasing your stock is to divide potentillas in spring.

Potentilla alba
A mat-forming plant with large leaves and loose sprays of white flowers in spring. H 10cm (4in) S 8cm (3in).

Potentilla 'Gibson's Scarlet'

Potentilla neumanniana

Potentilla atrosanguinea
The foliage often has silver hairs, especially on the underside. The flowers are red, orange or yellow. They appear over a long period in the summer. H 45cm (18in) S 60cm (24in).

***Potentilla* 'Gibson's Scarlet'**
This is a real show-stopper. It carries flowers of the most brilliant scarlet throughout the summer. H and S 45cm (18in).

Potentilla nepalensis
One of the best, with excellent cultivars. It is loose and sprawling with masses of crimson, orange or pink flowers. H 50cm (20in) S 60cm (24in). Some of the cultivars are bicoloured. Among the best are 'Miss Willmott' (reddish pink flowers with a darker centre), 'Ron McBeath' (carmine with a darker centre) and 'Roxana' (bright pink with a darker centre).

Potentilla neumanniana
Another mat-former for the front of a border. It has yellow flowers. H 10cm (4in) S 30cm (12in).

Potentilla recta
An erect plant that is good for scrambling through other plants. It has yellow flowers. H 60cm (24in) S 60cm (24in). 'Warrenii' is the best-known form, again with yellow flowers. *P.r.* var. *sulphurea* has beautiful soft yellow flowers.

***Potentilla* 'William Rollison'**
This is a startling semi-double with bright orange suffused with yellow. H and S 45cm (18in).

Potentilla nepalensis 'Ron McBeath'

Potentilla 'Blazeaway'

Primula japonica

Primula vialii

Pulmonaria saccharata

Primula bulleyana

PRIMULA
Primula

One of the most delightful genera of all garden plants. It is surprisingly large with more than 400 species and innumerable cultivars. Most are in cultivation, but mainly with specialist growers. However there are still a large number that are grown in the general garden. They vary from those that are only a few centimetres high to tall candelabra types up 1m (3ft) tall. Most prefer shade and so they make excellent plants for under trees or shrubs. They are also good for damp positions beside streams or ponds and in bog gardens.
Cultivation All the perennial garden types need a moist soil. They prefer light shade but will grow in sun. Z4–7.
Propagation Most will come easily from seed and many can also be easily divided in spring.

Primula bulleyana
A candelabra primula with tall stems carrying whorls of red flowers that eventually fade to orange. The flowers are produced in the summer. H 60cm (24in) S 30cm (12in).

Primula denticulata
Known as the drumstick primula. Its stems carry a terminal ball of purple flowers. Spring flowering. H 45cm (18in) S 30cm (12in).

Primula florindae
This is a very tall primula. Its stems carry a terminal cluster of flowers which hang down. They are yellow and appear in summer. H 1m (3ft) S 60cm (24in).

Primula japonica
A candelabra primula which carries whorls of red or white flowers in late spring and early summer. It is very easy to grow. H and S 45cm (18in).

Primula pulverulenta
A tall candelabra primula with stems carrying whorls of purple-red flowers in early summer. H 75cm (30in) S 45cm (18in).

Primula veris
The cowslip is a meadow plant and likes an open position. It is ideal for the wild garden. It flowers in late spring. H and S 15–20cm (6–8in).

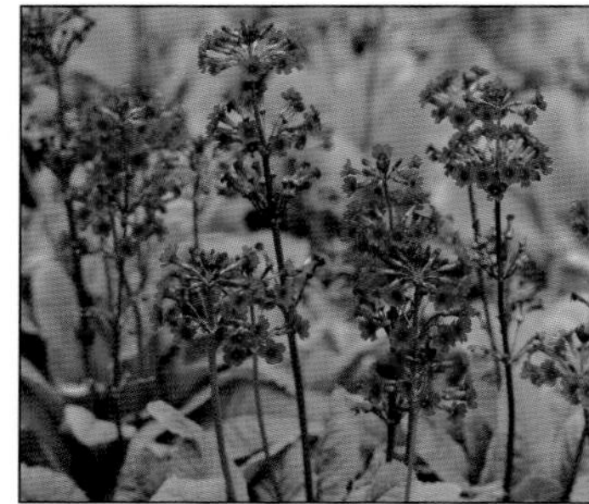

Primula japonica

Primula vulgaris

Primula vialii
A orchid-like primula with stems carrying a pyramidal cluster of smaller flowers. They are mauve when open but the buds above them are crimson, giving a wonderful two-toned effect. The flowers appear in the summer. H 45cm (18in) S 30cm (12in).

Primula vulgaris
It seems impossible to imagine a garden without primroses growing in it. These ones are low, with stems that carry a single soft yellow flower in the spring. H and S 20cm (8in).

PULMONARIA
Lungwort

A small genus of about 15 species of which a number are in cultivation. These are late-winter and spring-flowering plants. They produce small funnel-shaped blooms in blue, pink, red and white. They are carried in clusters on top of stems which rise up to 30cm (12in) above the ground, with a spread of 30cm (12in). The foliage is rough with bristly hairs and in many cases has silver blotches. If the stems and leaves are cut to the ground after flowering new foliage appears. It remains fresh for the rest of the summer, and the lungwort earns its keep as a foliage plant. They will grow in sun but do best in light shade and are excellent for growing under shrubs.
Cultivation Pulmonaria need a fertile soil that does not dry out too much. As long as the soil is kept moist they can be grown in full sun, otherwise a position in light shade is best. Z3.
Propagation The plants are easily divided in spring.

Pulmonaria angustifolia
This species produces attractive blue flowers and foliage that is a plain green but which is often edged in brown.

***Pulmonaria* 'Beth's Pink'**
A excellent fresh-looking form with deep pink and blue flowers. There is a light silver spotting on the leaves.

***Pulmonaria* 'Lewis Palmer'**
A fine-looking form with long spotted leaves and pink flowers that age to blue.

Pulmonaria rubra
This has plain, light green leaves that contrast well with the brick-red flowers. There are several good cultivars including 'Bowles' Red' and 'Redstart'. 'David Ward' has coral-red flowers and excellent cream-coloured variegations on the leaves.

Pulmonaria saccharata
Violet or red and blue flowers and spotted leaves. There are several excellent cultivars including 'Frühlingshimmel' (blue flowers) and 'Mrs Moon' (pink/blue).

***Pulmonaria* 'Sissinghurst White'**
This is a very good white-flowered form, which has silver spots on the foliage.

RANUNCULUS
Buttercup

The buttercup family is a large one, covering 400 species. Many are weeds but there are also a number of excellent border plants as well as many smaller ones grown by alpine specialists. The general conception of buttercups is that they are yellow but there as many, if not more, white-flowered species. One thing that most have in common is the shallow, saucer-shape of the flowers, although there are also a number of button-like double-flowered cultivars. Ranunculus like varied conditions: there are some for the open border, others for the shade of trees and shrubs while still more prefer the moisture of a bog garden. On the whole the garden varieties are not as invasive as the more weedy species.

Cultivation Most buttercups that the perennial gardener will be concerned with require a fertile, reasonably moist soil, with plenty of well-rotted organic material. Plant in a sunny or partially shaded position. Z3–5.

Propagation Many buttercups can be divided. They will also come from seed, preferably sown as soon as it is ripe.

Ranunculus aconitifolius
Possibly the most important buttercup for the perennial gardener. It is a clump-forming plant, producing white flowers in early summer. H 60cm (24in) S 50cm (20in). The best known form is the double-flowered 'Flore Pleno'. It does best in shade.

Ranunculus acris
This is the meadow buttercup. It is not recommended for the normal border but it is excellent in meadow gardens. 'Farrer's Yellow' (pale yellow) and 'Flore Pleno' (double) are sometimes grown in borders. It will grow in sun or shade. H and S 45–60cm (18–24in).

Ranunculus amplexicaulis

Ranunculus amplexicaulis
A delightful species with white flowers that are flushed with pale pink. It likes a gritty soil and should be planted at the front of a border. It produces its flowers in early summer. H 30cm (12in) S 10cm (4in).

Ranunculus ficaria
The lesser celandine can become invasive but its leaves are only above ground during the spring so it is not a real nuisance. It is very low-growing with shining yellow flowers. H 10cm (4in) S 20cm (8in). There are also forms with orange (*R.f.* var. *aurantiacus*) and near white ('Salmon's White') flowers as well as some with decorative foliage such as 'Brazen Hussy' (deep purple leaves). They are all excellent for growing under shrubs.

Ranunculus gramineus
This is a clump-forming species with large glistening yellow flowers and thin grass-like leaves. It flowers in spring and makes a good border plant. H 30cm (12in) S 8cm (3in).

Ranunculus gramineus

RODGERSIA
Rodgersia

A small genus of plants with all six species in cultivation. The great thing about these is that they have both attractive foliage and flowers. In good conditions they will grow up to 2m (6ft) and they form quite large clumps (up to 2m/6ft), so they are plants for a larger garden. The foliage is palmate (like fingers on a hand), large, deeply veined and with a slight gloss on it. It is often purple or purple-tinged. The flowers are carried well above the leaves in clusters of white, cream or pink in summer.

Cultivation These plants need a soil that does not dry out, so add plenty of organic material to it. They do best in a lightly shaded position.

Propagation The simplest method of increase is to divide these plants in spring.

Rodgersia aesculifolia
The foliage of this species is palmate, and looks like that of a horse chestnut. The flowers are white or pink.

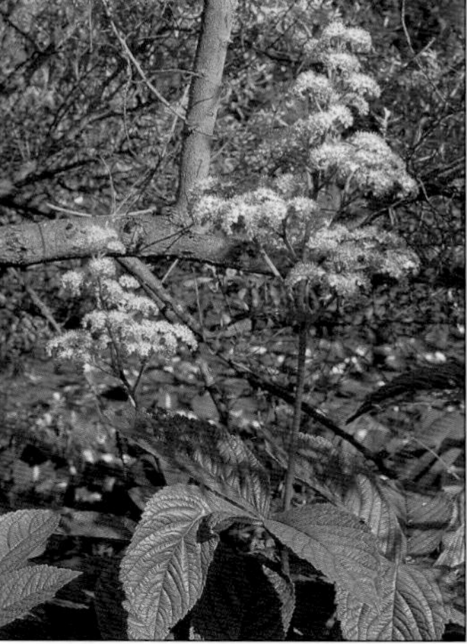
Rodgersia aesculifolia

Rodgersia pinnata
This is similar to the previous species, with palmate leaves and slightly darker flowers. The form 'Superba' is excellent. It has good purple foliage when it first appears, and bright pink flowers.

Rodgersia podophylla
This is slightly smaller than the previous, reaching about 1.2m (4ft). It has similar palmate foliage, although the leaflets are broader and divided at the tips giving a jagged appearance. It produces clusters of white flowers. Good autumn colour.

Rodgersia sambucifolia
This is the shortest species, at only 1m (3ft). The leaves are more pinnate, with leaflets arranged opposite each other as in an ash. The flowers are white or pink.

Ranunculus acris

Ranunculus ficaria, double form

Rodgersia pinnata

Rodgersia podophylla

ROMNEYA
Tree poppy

The only member of this genus, *R. coulteri*, is widely grown in gardens. It is a somewhat woody perennial, which runs below ground to form large clumps when it is happy with the conditions. It is related to the poppies and has the characteristic paper-tissue flowers. In this case they are glisteringly white with a wonderful golden boss of stamens in the middle. They are large, up to 20cm (8in) across. The flowers are set off well against the grey-green foliage. The plants are a bit untidy and sprawling but the quality of the flowers more than makes up for this. They are suitable for borders where there is space, otherwise they can be grown on their own. They grow up to about 2.5m (8ft) but are often less, especially when they are sprawling. Spread is 1m (3ft). There is a variety *trichocalyx* which in gardening terms is not much different from *coulteri* itself. However, its form 'White Cloud' is more free-flowering and the foliage better.

Cultivation Any reasonable garden soil will do but it must be well drained and in a sunny warm position. Z7.

Propagation Tree poppies can be divided but this is quite difficult. It is much easier to take basal cuttings in spring.

Romneya coulteri

RUDBECKIA
Coneflower

This is a genus of about 20 species, of which a number are annuals (see page 157). There are also a number of perennials, which are well worth growing in your autumn borders. They add a welcome touch of brilliant gold and have the habit of flowering over a long period, often starting in the summer and going on until the frosts arrive.

Coneflowers are daisies and get their name from the cone-like central disc in the flowers. This disc is usually a brown or green colour, while the outer ray petals are yellow or gold, sometimes verging on orange. The flowers measure 8cm (3in) or more across. The majority of these plants grow up to about 1m (3ft) but some that will reach 3m (10ft). S 60cm (24in).

Cultivation Rudbeckias do not like soil that dries out too much, so add plenty of well-rotted organic material. At the same time it should not be waterlogged, so add grit to keep it free-draining. Z3.

Propagation Most can easily be increased by division in spring. Species can be grown from seed sown at the same time of year.

Rudbeckia fulgida var. *deamii*

Commonly known as black-eyed Susan, this is a very popular plant for borders, especially hot-coloured ones. It has orange-yellow flowers that appear from midsummer onwards. H 75cm (30in). Another well-known and popular rudbeckia is *R.f.* var. *sullivantii* 'Goldsturm' This grows to about 60cm (24in) and has very large flowers. The third variety that is commonly grown is var. *speciosa*.

R.f. var. *sullivantii* 'Goldsturm'

Rudbeckia 'Herbstsonne'

Rudbeckia 'Goldquelle'

This is a popular cultivar with double flowers that are a bright lemon-yellow. H 1m (3ft).

Rudbeckia 'Herbstsonne'

This is a plant for the back of the autumn border since it grows to 2m (6ft). It produces flowers of bright gold. They are large, up to 12cm (5in) across. The central cone is green.

Rudbeckia laciniata

This particular species makes an excellent plant for the back of a border. It can grow up to 3m (10ft) in height when it is given the right conditions, although it is usually shorter than this, at about 2–2.5m (6–8ft). The flowers are a paler yellow than the previous species and are very wide, measuring up to 15cm (6in) – often the petals droop under their own weight. Like the other rudbeckias, this plant has a long flowering season – from midsummer right through to the end of autumn.

'Hortensia' is currently the best-known of this species' cultivars. It is a vigorous plant, and one that looks very similar to the species, except that its flowers are doubles.

Rudbeckia occidentalis

The species itself is not often grown but there are two cultivars – known as 'Black Beauty' and 'Green Wizard' – that are becoming increasingly popular with gardeners. Basically, these consist simply of the dark brown central cone, surrounded by green bracts or leaves. The effect is as though somebody has pulled off all of the petals. Although these are undoubtedly rather intriguing-looking flowers, few people could honestly describe them as being beautiful.

Rudbeckia fulgida var. *deamii*

SALVIA
Sage

This is a huge genus, of almost 900 species. The gardener is only concerned with about a tenth of these, which is still a lot of plants, especially since some species have plenty of cultivars. Sage grown as a garden plant is characterized by its tubular flowers, with an upper and lower lip. Their colour varies from bright red to bright blue, with lots of shades in-between. The flowers are carried in whorls, in spikes held well above the foliage, which can be aromatic. Generally these plants are grown for their flowers, although there are shrubby species (*S. officinalis*), with variegated foliage. Flowering starts in summer and continues into autumn. Some of the salvias are marginally tender and may need overwinter protection. They all make excellent border plants; some can be used in containers.
Cultivation Salvias like a fairly rich, well-drained soil and prefer a sunny position, although some will take a little light shade. Z5–8.
Propagation Species can be grown from seed sown in spring. Most can be grown from basal cuttings taken in spring and many can also be divided at the same time.

Salvia argentea
This is one perennial definitely grown for its foliage. It produces large woolly leaves that are a

Salvia involucrata 'Bethellii'

Salvia sclarea

wonderful silver. It also produces spikes of pink or white flowers. It is not keen on winter wet. H 1m (3ft) S 45cm (18in).

Salvia buchananii
The large flowers produced by this sage are magenta. H 60cm (24in) S 30cm (12in).

Salvia cacaliifolia
An attractive plant which carries piercing blue flowers. H 1m (3ft) S 30cm (12in).

Salvia fulgens
Bright red flowers held in loose spikes. H 1m (3ft) S 1m (3ft).

Salvia guaranitica
This is a tall plant with deep blue flowers. H 1.5m (5ft) S 30cm (12in). There are several excellent cultivars including 'Blue Enigma' with large fragrant flowers.

Salvia involucrata
A good late-flowering plant for the border. It has purplish-red flowers. The form 'Bethellii' is the best with well-coloured flowers. H 75cm (30in) S 1m (3ft).

Salvia nemorosa
A regular plant in the garden border, with spikes of purple flowers. H 1m (3ft) S 45cm (18in). There are some excellent cultivars, which include 'Amethyst', 'Lubecca', 'Ostfriesland' and 'Pusztaflamme'.

Perennials for flower-arrangers

Acanthus	*Dianthus*
Achillea	*Echinops*
Agapanthus	*Eremurus*
Alstromeria	*Eryngium*
Aster	*Gypsophila*
Astrantia	*Hosta*
Catananche	*Liatris*
Centurea	*Lilium*
Convallaria	*Phlox*
Cortaderia	*Solidago*

Salvia sclarea
This sage is normally grown in gardens as the variety *turkestanica*. It is tall, with dense spikes of white and pink flowers. It is an excellent plant but needs to be replaced regularly. H 1.2cm (4ft) S 30cm (12in).

Salvia sylvestris
A shrubby plant with purple flower spikes. H and S 45cm (18in). Its many superb cultivars include 'Blauhügel' (blue), 'Mainacht' (deep blue) and 'Rose Queen' (pink).

Other plants There are plenty more salvias for the interested gardener to discover and enjoy.

SANGUISORBA
Burnet

Sanguisorbas tend to be grown as specialist plants. There are about 18 species, most of which are in cultivation, but not often seen. They are mainly tall plants, with thin waving stems that carry the flowers in terminal bottlebrushes. These vary in colour from white to deep red. They make good plants for the summer border. H 1.5m (5ft) S 45cm (18in).
Cultivation Any reasonable garden soil will do so long as it is not barren. Burnets like sun, but will tolerate a little light shade. Z4.
Propagation The plants will come readily from seed and can also be divided in spring.

Sanguisorba obtusa

Sanguisorba armena
This is grown mainly for its foliage which is a powdery blue-green, much in the mould of *Melianthus*. The flowers are pink. H 1.2m (4ft) S 45cm (18in).

Sanguisorba canadensis
Cylinders of white flowers are held 1.2m (4ft) or more above the ground. S 60cm (24in).

Sanguisorba hakusanensis
A beautiful plant whose terminal spikes of flowers are a deep pink colour with an underlying white. H 75cm (30in) S 60cm (24in).

Sanguisorba menziesii
These tall plants produce tight cylinders of deep red flowers. H 2m (6ft) S 60cm (24in).

Sanguisorba officinalis
Similar to the previous burnet, except that the flower cylinders are shorter, almost rounded. It is best grown in the wild garden. H 1.2m (4ft) S 60cm (24in).

Sanguisorba obtusa
Similar to the previous two species, but shorter at 60cm (24in). S 45cm (18in).

Scabiosa 'Blue Butterfly'

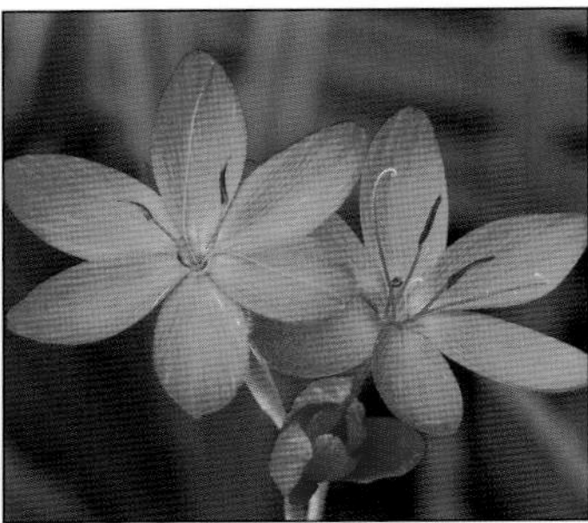
Schizostylis coccinea

SCABIOSA
Scabious

A large genus of around 80 species, of which a number are grown in gardens both as annuals (see page 160) and perennials. They are delightful plants that deserve to be grown in all gardens. The flowers look like round pincushions and are carried above the foliage on wiry stems. They are in pastel colours, mainly mauves as well as creams and white, and flower over a long period through the summer.
Cultivation Scabious grow in any reasonable garden soil but they need a sunny position. Z3.
Propagation The simplest way to increase the perennials is to divide or take basal cuttings in spring.

***Scabiosa* 'Blue Butterfly'**
This is a fine cultivar with lavender-blue flowers. H 45cm (18in) S 30cm (12in).

Scabiosa caucasica
A clump-forming plant with plenty of 'pincushions' that come in various shades of pale blue and lavender. The flowers are up to 8cm (3in) across. H and S 60cm (24in). There are also some excellent cultivars including 'Clive Greaves' (lavender) and 'Miss Willmott' (white).

Scabiosa columbaria
This is similar to the above except that the flowers are about half the size. H and S 1m (3ft). It has a smaller form 'Nana' and a variety *ochroleuca* with wonderful creamy yellow flowers.

Scabiosa prolifera
A rarer scabious but one worth considering if you can find it. It has cream flowers which are surrounded by green bracts. H 60cm (24in) S 30cm (12in).

SCHIZOSTYLIS
Kaffir lily

This genus contains just one species, *S. coccinea*, with several good cultivars. It is a bulbous plant, producing narrow, strap-like leaves and tall spikes of cupped, star-like flowers in autumn. The flowers are shades of pink, white or flame-red. They are valuable plants for the autumn border or for odd corners. In the wild it is usually found growing next to water. H 60cm (24in) S 30cm (12in). Its variety *alba* has white flowers. Other plants include: 'Jennifer' (pink blooms); 'Maiden's Blush' (pink); 'Major' (large and red); 'Sunrise' (salmon-pink); 'Viscountess Byng' (the palest of pink); and 'Zeal Salmon' (salmon-pink).
Cultivation They grow in any reasonable garden soil, but prefer one that does not dry out completely. A sunny position is needed. Z6.
Propagation Kaffir lilies are very easy plants to lift and divide in the spring.

SEDUM
Stonecrop

This is a very large genus of some 400 species. A surprising number of these are in cultivation but there are only a handful that are of direct interest to the perennial garden. They vary considerably in size from ground-huggers only a centimetre or so high to border plants of 60cm (24in). They are all characterized by their succulent, fleshy leaves. The flowers are small and star-like and carried in clusters. There is a wide range of colours from yellows and oranges to pinks and reds. For the border types it is mainly the reds that are of interest. Their main flowering period is autumn.
Cultivation Any reasonable garden soil will do for sedums so long as it is well-drained. A place in the sun is to be preferred to get the best out of the plants. Z3.
Propagation The easiest method of increase is to root individual leaves in a cutting compost.

Sedum cauticola
This is a low-growing sedum that needs to be placed at the front of the border. The grey-green leaves set off well the pretty purplish-

Sedum middendorffianum

pink flowers which deepen in colour as they age. H 10cm (4in) S 20cm (8in).

***Sedum* 'Herbstfreude'**
Better known as 'Autumn Joy', this is an old favourite for the border. It is one of the taller forms, and has flat heads of pink flowers that turn brownish-red as they age. The foliage is green, flushed with icy white. H 60cm (24in) S 30cm (12in).

Sedum middendorffianum
Another plant for the front of the border. It has dense heads of yellow flowers which rise above the glossy green foliage. H 15cm (6in) S indefinite.

***Sedum* 'Ruby Glow'**
A superb front-of-border plant. The ruby flowers really do seem to glow and they are set off well by the purple-flushed foliage. H 25cm (10in) S 25cm (10in).

Sedum spectabile
This is the main border species with several excellent cultivars. It has flat heads of pink flowers. H and S 60cm (24in). Good cultivars include 'Brilliant' (bright pink flowers), 'Carmen' (bluish-pink), 'Iceberg' (white) and 'Septemberglut' (pink).

Scabiosa prolifera

Schizostylis coccinea 'Sunrise'

Sedum cauticola

S.t. maximum 'Atropurpureum'

SALVIA

Sage

This is a huge genus, of almost 900 species. The gardener is only concerned with about a tenth of these, which is still a lot of plants, especially since some species have plenty of cultivars. Sage grown as a garden plant is characterized by its tubular flowers, with an upper and lower lip. Their colour varies from bright red to bright blue, with lots of shades in-between. The flowers are carried in whorls, in spikes held well above the foliage, which can be aromatic. Generally these plants are grown for their flowers, although there are shrubby species (*S. officinalis*), with variegated foliage. Flowering starts in summer and continues into autumn. Some of the salvias are marginally tender and may need overwinter protection. They all make excellent border plants; some can be used in containers.
Cultivation Salvias like a fairly rich, well-drained soil and prefer a sunny position, although some will take a little light shade. Z5–8.
Propagation Species can be grown from seed sown in spring. Most can be grown from basal cuttings taken in spring and many can also be divided at the same time.

Salvia argentea
This is one perennial definitely grown for its foliage. It produces large woolly leaves that are a

Salvia involucrata 'Bethellii'

Salvia sclarea

wonderful silver. It also produces spikes of pink or white flowers. It is not keen on winter wet. H 1m (3ft) S 45cm (18in).

Salvia buchananii
The large flowers produced by this sage are magenta. H 60cm (24in) S 30cm (12in).

Salvia cacaliifolia
An attractive plant which carries piercing blue flowers. H 1m (3ft) S 30cm (12in).

Salvia fulgens
Bright red flowers held in loose spikes. H 1m (3ft) S 1m (3ft).

Salvia guaranitica
This is a tall plant with deep blue flowers. H 1.5m (5ft) S 30cm (12in). There are several excellent cultivars including 'Blue Enigma' with large fragrant flowers.

Salvia involucrata
A good late-flowering plant for the border. It has purplish-red flowers. The form 'Bethellii' is the best with well-coloured flowers. H 75cm (30in) S 1m (3ft).

Salvia nemorosa
A regular plant in the garden border, with spikes of purple flowers. H 1m (3ft) S 45cm (18in). There are some excellent cultivars, which include 'Amethyst', 'Lubecca', 'Ostfriesland' and 'Pusztaflamme'.

Perennials for flower-arrangers

Acanthus	*Dianthus*
Achillea	*Echinops*
Agapanthus	*Eremurus*
Alstromeria	*Eryngium*
Aster	*Gypsophila*
Astrantia	*Hosta*
Catananche	*Liatris*
Centurea	*Lilium*
Convallaria	*Phlox*
Cortaderia	*Solidago*

Salvia sclarea
This sage is normally grown in gardens as the variety *turkestanica*. It is tall, with dense spikes of white and pink flowers. It is an excellent plant but needs to be replaced regularly. H 1.2cm (4ft) S 30cm (12in).

Salvia sylvestris
A shrubby plant with purple flower spikes. H and S 45cm (18in). Its many superb cultivars include 'Blauhügel' (blue), 'Mainacht' (deep blue) and 'Rose Queen' (pink).

Other plants There are plenty more salvias for the interested gardener to discover and enjoy.

SANGUISORBA

Burnet

Sanguisorbas tend to be grown as specialist plants. There are about 18 species, most of which are in cultivation, but not often seen. They are mainly tall plants, with thin waving stems that carry the flowers in terminal bottlebrushes. These vary in colour from white to deep red. They make good plants for the summer border. H 1.5m (5ft) S 45cm (18in).
Cultivation Any reasonable garden soil will do so long as it is not barren. Burnets like sun, but will tolerate a little light shade. Z4.
Propagation The plants will come readily from seed and can also be divided in spring.

Sanguisorba obtusa

Sanguisorba armena
This is grown mainly for its foliage which is a powdery blue-green, much in the mould of *Melianthus*. The flowers are pink. H 1.2m (4ft) S 45cm (18in).

Sanguisorba canadensis
Cylinders of white flowers are held 1.2m (4ft) or more above the ground. S 60cm (24in).

Sanguisorba hakusanensis
A beautiful plant whose terminal spikes of flowers are a deep pink colour with an underlying white. H 75cm (30in) S 60cm (24in).

Sanguisorba menziesii
These tall plants produce tight cylinders of deep red flowers. H 2m (6ft) S 60cm (24in).

Sanguisorba officinalis
Similar to the previous burnet, except that the flower cylinders are shorter, almost rounded. It is best grown in the wild garden. H 1.2m (4ft) S 60cm (24in).

Sanguisorba obtusa
Similar to the previous two species, but shorter at 60cm (24in). S 45cm (18in).

Scabiosa 'Blue Butterfly'

SCABIOSA
Scabious

A large genus of around 80 species, of which a number are grown in gardens both as annuals (see page 160) and perennials. They are delightful plants that deserve to be grown in all gardens. The flowers look like round pincushions and are carried above the foliage on wiry stems. They are in pastel colours, mainly mauves as well as creams and white, and flower over a long period through the summer.
Cultivation Scabious grow in any reasonable garden soil but they need a sunny position. Z3.
Propagation The simplest way to increase the perennials is to divide or take basal cuttings in spring.

Scabiosa 'Blue Butterfly'
This is a fine cultivar with lavender-blue flowers. H 45cm (18in) S 30cm (12in).

Scabiosa caucasica
A clump-forming plant with plenty of 'pincushions' that come in various shades of pale blue and lavender. The flowers are up to 8cm (3in) across. H and S 60cm (24in). There are also some excellent cultivars including 'Clive Greaves' (lavender) and 'Miss Willmott' (white).

Scabiosa prolifera

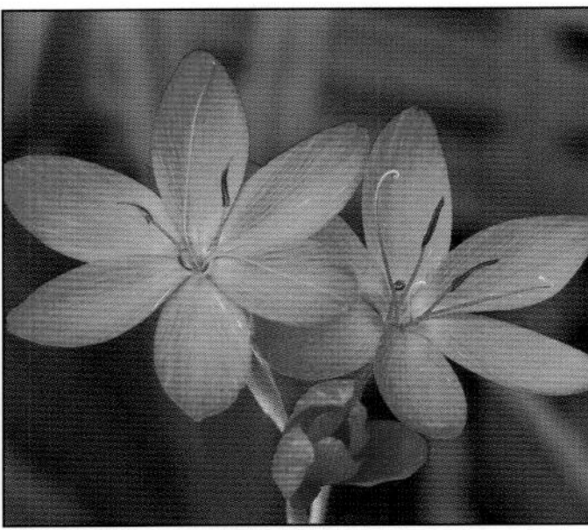

Schizostylis coccinea

Scabiosa columbaria
This is similar to the above except that the flowers are about half the size. H and S 1m (3ft). It has a smaller form 'Nana' and a variety *ochroleuca* with wonderful creamy yellow flowers.

Scabiosa prolifera
A rarer scabious but one worth considering if you can find it. It has cream flowers which are surrounded by green bracts. H 60cm (24in) S 30cm (12in).

SCHIZOSTYLIS
Kaffir lily

This genus contains just one species, *S. coccinea*, with several good cultivars. It is a bulbous plant, producing narrow, strap-like leaves and tall spikes of cupped, star-like flowers in autumn. The flowers are shades of pink, white or flame-red. They are valuable plants for the autumn border or for odd corners. In the wild it is usually found growing next to water. H 60cm (24in) S 30cm (12in). Its variety *alba* has white flowers. Other plants include: 'Jennifer' (pink blooms); 'Maiden's Blush' (pink); 'Major' (large and red); 'Sunrise' (salmon-pink); 'Viscountess Byng' (the palest of pink); and 'Zeal Salmon' (salmon-pink).

Schizostylis coccinea 'Sunrise'

Cultivation They grow in any reasonable garden soil, but prefer one that does not dry out completely. A sunny position is needed. Z6.
Propagation Kaffir lilies are very easy plants to lift and divide in the spring.

SEDUM
Stonecrop

This is a very large genus of some 400 species. A surprising number of these are in cultivation but there are only a handful that are of direct interest to the perennial garden. They vary considerably in size from ground-huggers only a centimetre or so high to border plants of 60cm (24in). They are all characterized by their succulent, fleshy leaves. The flowers are small and star-like and carried in clusters. There is a wide range of colours from yellows and oranges to pinks and reds. For the border types it is mainly the reds that are of interest. Their main flowering period is autumn.
Cultivation Any reasonable garden soil will do for sedums so long as it is well-drained. A place in the sun is to be preferred to get the best out of the plants. Z3.
Propagation The easiest method of increase is to root individual leaves in a cutting compost.

Sedum cauticola
This is a low-growing sedum that needs to be placed at the front of the border. The grey-green leaves set off well the pretty purplish-pink flowers which deepen in colour as they age. H 10cm (4in) S 20cm (8in).

Sedum cauticola

Sedum middendorffianum

Sedum 'Herbstfreude'
Better known as 'Autumn Joy', this is an old favourite for the border. It is one of the taller forms, and has flat heads of pink flowers that turn brownish-red as they age. The foliage is green, flushed with icy white. H 60cm (24in) S 30cm (12in).

Sedum middendorffianum
Another plant for the front of the border. It has dense heads of yellow flowers which rise above the glossy green foliage. H 15cm (6in) S indefinite.

Sedum 'Ruby Glow'
A superb front-of-border plant. The ruby flowers really do seem to glow and they are set off well by the purple-flushed foliage. H 25cm (10in) S 25cm (10in).

Sedum spectabile
This is the main border species with several excellent cultivars. It has flat heads of pink flowers. H and S 60cm (24in). Good cultivars include 'Brilliant' (bright pink flowers), 'Carmen' (bluish-pink), 'Iceberg' (white) and 'Septemberglut' (pink).

S.t. maximum 'Atropurpureum'

Sedum telephium
This species has green leaves and pink flowers. It is mainly grown in the gorgeous form *S.t. maximum* 'Atropurpureum', which has dark purple stems and foliage as well as pink flowers. H 60cm (24in) S 30cm (12in).

SIDALCEA
Sidalcea

This is a genus of about 25 species. Although only a couple are grown in general cultivation they are important garden plants. They are related to the mallow and hollyhock and have the same saucer-shaped flowers. They are usually a shade of pink and appear in early and midsummer. The flowers grow on spikes carried on tall stems, up to 1.2m (4ft) when the plant is growing well. The leaves are rounded, and become more deeply lobed further up the stem. These are perfect plants for the middle of the border and the clear pink forms have a wonderful serenity about them. The darker purple-pinks are a bit more difficult to place, but they still make very good plants.
Cultivation Any reasonable garden soil will do for the sidalcea. A sunny position is preferred but it will grow in partial shade. Z5.
Propagation Species can be increased from seed, but cultivars need to divided in spring.

Sidalcea candida
This is a wonderful species, producing lovely white flowers that are often carried in a dense spike. It is not as tall as the following species, *S. malviflora*. H 1m (3ft) S 60cm (24in).

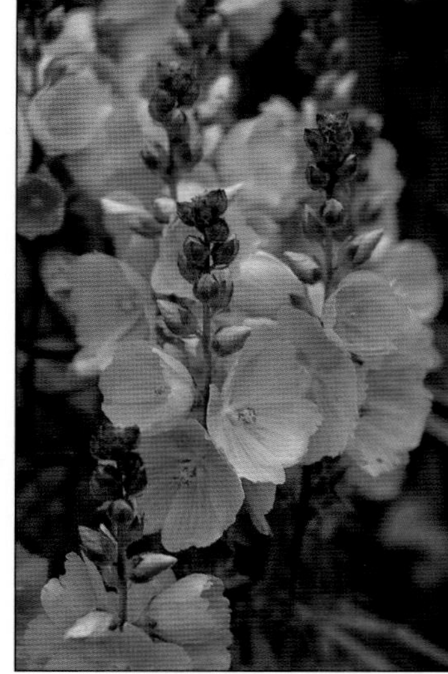
Sidalcea malviflora

Sidalcea malviflora
This is the main species from which most of the cultivars have been derived. It has pink flowers, which vary in intensity from a pale to a purplish pink. There is also a white variety 'Alba'. The flowers are produced from early to midsummer. H 1.2m (4ft) S 30cm (12in).

These excellent cultivars are often listed directly under *Sidalcea*: 'Croftway Red' (reddish-pink flowers), 'Elsie Heugh' (a wonderful purplish-pink), 'Loveliness' (pale pink), 'Mrs Borrodaile' (another purplish-pink), 'Oberon' (rose-pink), 'Rose Queen' (dark rose-pink), 'Sussex Beauty' (a really lovely shade of pink) and 'William Smith' (very deep pink).

Sidalcea 'Elsie Heugh'

SILENE
Campion

A very large genus with some 500 species. Almost 50 of these are available to gardeners, though not that many as garden perennials. They are related to the dianthus and many have the same flat-disc-like flowers, each with five petals, sometimes with a notch in the centre of the outer edge. They are good reliable plants rather than startling border features. Some are better in a wild or meadow garden.
Cultivation Any garden soil as long as it is reasonably moisture-retentive. Most will grow in either full sun or light shade. Z5.
Propagation Sow seed in spring or early autumn or take softwood cuttings in spring.

Silene acaulis
This is the moss campion, a low carpeting plant with delightful flowers carried on very thin stems in spring. This is really a plant for the alpine gardener, but they also make such excellent edge-of-border plants for a shady place. The flowers are pink, white or red. There are a number of cultivars worth exploring. H 5cm (2in) S 15cm (6in).

Silene alpestris
This is another rock-garden plant but, again, it is eminently suited to the front of a border so long as it is not swamped by larger plants. It produces masses of pure white flowers in the early summer. H 15cm (6in) S 20cm (8in).

Sidalcea malviflora 'William Smith'

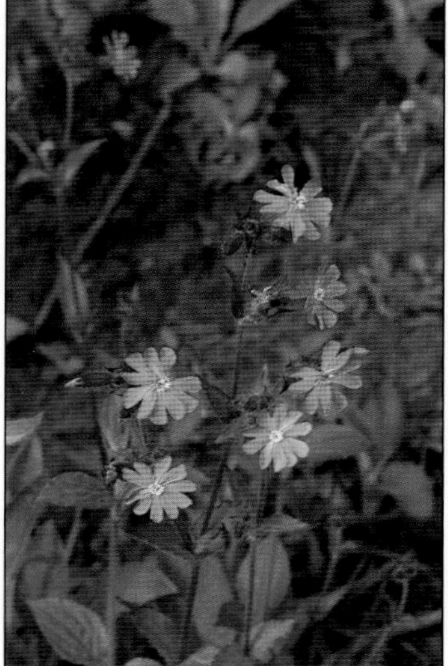
Silene dioica

Silene dioica
The red campion of hedgerows and open woodland. This is an attractive plant with rose-pink flowers. It can be grown in the border but it is better used in a wild garden, especially under light shrubs or in a damp meadow. H 75cm (30in) S 25cm (10in). The double forms 'Flore Pleno' and 'Rosea Plena' are more suitable for the border.

Silene schafta
Another rock-garden plant that is suitable for the edge of a border. This produces masses of magenta flowers from the late summer onwards, much later than most other silenes. H 25cm (10in) S 10cm (4in). There is a good cultivar 'Shell Pink', which has pale pink flowers.

Silene uniflora
A low-growing, mat-former that is ideally suited to the rock garden, but also does well on the edge of a border. This is the sea campion. It has white flowers and an inflated calyx (sheath round the base of the flower) with intricate veining. H and S 20cm (8in). The double form 'Robin Whitebreast' is especially popular. The excellent variegated form, 'Druett's Variegated', has greyish green leaves splashed with cream.

Sisyrinchium striatum

Smilacina racemosa

Solidago cutleri

Stachys byzantina

SISYRINCHIUM
Sisyrinchium

This is a genus of about 90 species. There is only one, *S. striatum*, which is of general use to the perennial gardener although there are several grown by alpine enthusiasts. These plants are related to the irises and this can be seen in the leaves, which are stiff and sword-like. From these fans of leaves erupt spikes of yellow or blue flowers in summer.
Cultivation Any reasonable garden soil will do but a free-draining one will see the best results. The plants self-sow prodigiously so deadhead after flowering. Z4.
Propagation These are extremely easy to divide in spring and they also come readily from seed sown at the same time of year.

***Sisyrinchium* 'Biscutella'**
A rock-garden plant that can be used in the front of a border so long as it does not get swamped. It has yellow flowers diffused with brown and purple. Also good for gravel beds. H 30cm (12in) S 20cm (8in).

***Sisyrinchium* 'E.K. Balls'**
Similar to the previous plant, except that it is slightly shorter with deep lilac flowers. H 25cm (10in) S 20cm (8in).

Sisyrinchium graminoides
This plant has deep violet-blue flowers with a yellow throat. It is good for the front of borders and gravel beds. H 45cm (18in) S 8cm (3in).

Sisyrinchium striatum
The main border plant. It has dull green foliage and masses of star-like creamy-yellow flowers. They can be impressive in a drift. H 1m (3ft) S 30cm (12in). 'Aunt May' is a variegated form with soft grey foliage striped with creamy-white. This cultivar is not long lived and it is worth dividing each year to have some plants in reserve.

SMILACINA
Smilacina

A genus of 25 species of which only one is regularly grown in gardens, although others are occasionally seen. The main one is *S. racemosa*. It is related to the Solomon's seal (*Polygonatum*) but although the foliage is similar it is has more upright stems. The creamy-white flowers are carried in dense spikes at the top of each stem, and are set off well by the dark green foliage. This is an excellent plant for a lightly shaded position, but the flowers do not last long and soon go brown. H 1m (3ft) S 45cm (18in). *S. stellata* is the only other relatively common species. The flowers are smaller and it forms large clumps which are best sited in a wild woodland garden.
Cultivation A woodland-type soil with plenty of leaf mould or other organic material. A lightly shaded position is best. Z3.
Propagation This is easy to divide in spring, but can also be grown from seed.

SOLIDAGO
Golden rod

A genus of about 100 species, but most are too weedy for the garden. However, there are a few exceptions, which make excellent border plants. They carry golden-yellow sprays of small aster-like daisies, which appear from the late summer. They work well in mid to rear border positions, and are especially useful for hot-coloured borders. H 1m (3ft) S 30cm (12in).
Cultivation Any reasonable garden soil, but it should be well-drained. Sun is best although some will take a little light shade. Z4.
Propagation Golden rods are very easy to propagate by division in the spring.

***Solidago* 'Crown of Rays'**
A medium-height solidago with flattened heads of golden flowers. H 60cm (24in) S 25cm (10in).

Solidago cutleri
A shorter front-of-border plant. It reaches 45cm (18in) in good conditions. S 30cm (12in).

***Solidago* 'Golden Wings'**
Another excellent form, this time with flattened sprays of golden flowers. It is a much taller plant. H 2m (6ft) S 1m (3ft).

***Solidago* 'Goldenmosa'**
One of the best. It has upright sprays of golden flowers. H 75cm (30in) S 45cm (18in).

Solidago 'Goldenmosa'

***Solidago* 'Linner Gold'**
An old favourite with conical heads rather than sprays of golden yellow flowers. H 1m (3ft) S 45cm (18in).

Other plants A hybrid between *Solidago* and *Aster* has produced × *Solidaster luteus*. These hybrids have clusters of flowers rather than sprays and are a fresh-looking mixture of gold and pale yellow. They grow to about 1m (3ft) with a spread of 45cm (18in) and are excellent border plants.

STACHYS
Stachys

A very large genus of plants, containing up to 300 species. Most are too weedy for the garden, but there are one or two excellent border plants. They have thyme-like tubular flowers, usually in variations of pink. The foliage in some is more important than the flowers, indeed some gardeners actually remove the flower-stems of *S. byzantina* as they feel it spoils the effect of the attractive silver foliage.
Cultivation Stachys will grow in any reasonable garden soil as long as it is free-draining. Choose a sunny position. Z4.
Propagation These clump-forming plants can easily be divided.

Stachys byzantina
This is the species that most gardeners grow. It has soft furry leaves with a silvery tinge, which gives it its English name of lamb's ears. The leaf stems are prostrate and creep gently across the surface of the soil. The flower stalks, which are also furry, are upright and carry tiny pink flowers. These are perfect for the foliage but many gardeners cut them off. The

Stachys byzantina 'Primrose Heron'

flowers stems reach up to 45cm (18in) with a spread of 60cm (24in). There are several cultivars. 'Big Ears' has extra large leaves. In 'Cotton Boll' the flowers are covered with silvery hairs. 'Primrose Heron' is a variegated form in which the silver is infused with yellow. 'Silver Carpet' is a good non-flowering form with intense silver foliage.

Stachys candida
Another silver-leaved plant. This one forms a more rounded shape and carries white flowers that are spotted with purple. It is short, so it is more suited to the front of the border or raised bed. H 15cm (6in) S 30cm (12in).

Stachys citrina
A second short form, it also has woolly leaves but carries spikes of pale yellow flowers. H 20cm (8in) S 30cm (12in).

Stachys macrantha
This species is an excellent early-summer plant which produces dense spikes of large, bright

Stipa arundinacea

purple flowers. It makes a good splash of colour. H 45cm (18in) S 30cm (12in).

Stachys officinalis
This is the wild betony. A midsummer flowerer which has smaller heads than the previous but is nonetheless still very noticeable. The flowers are deep reddish-purple. It can be grown in the border but it does self-sow rather viciously so it is best grown in the wild garden, possibly on a bank where it looks good. H 45–60cm (18–24in) S 30–45cm (12–18in).

STIPA
Stipa

A very large genus of some 300 grasses of which there are two or three that are of interest to the gardener. These are clump-forming plants that are well-behaved and do not spread too far. They are mainly grown for their flower heads rather than the foliage. The heads are carried on stiff, upright stems and form a hazy effect. These are excellent

Stipa tenuissima

plants to position where they catch the evening sun: they seem to sparkle and glow if placed with the sun behind them. Some are tall and statuesque and make an excellent feature. Others are humbler and fit well in a border.
Cultivation Stipas can be grown in any free-draining soil, but they should be given a sunny position. Cut back before the new growth begins in spring. Z6.
Propagation To increase, divide these plants in spring as soon as the new growth starts.

Stipa arundinacea
This produces a fountain of flowering heads from midsummer onwards. These are not carried on stiff stems but arch over, often touching the ground. Good for the front of a border, especially next to pathways. H 1m (3ft) S 1.2m (4ft).

Stipa calamagrostis
Arching sprays of flowers appear in summer. Their silvery colour makes them look rather like jets of water being sprayed out from the centre of the plant. Excellent. H 1m (3ft) S 1m (3ft).

Stipa gigantea
This is the one that every one knows. It can grow very tall and has stiff stems carrying open heads of straw-coloured flowers. These move in the slightest breeze and glisten in the sun. Give it sheltered position. H 2.5m (8ft) S 1m (3ft).

Stipa tenuissima
A much shorter grass. This is an erect grass with very fine flowers that create a beautiful hazy effect in the summer. H 60cm (24in) S 60cm (24in).

Stachys macrantha

Stipa calamagrostis

Stipa gigantea

Stokesia laevis 'Blue Star'

STOKESIA
Stokesia

This is a genus of only one species, *S. laevis*. It is not seen that often in general gardens but it is much more common in those of plant enthusiasts. As a result, it has gradually built up a number of cultivars, although the species itself is still well worth growing. It is not a very tall plant, 60cm (24in) at the most and often less as it can be rather sprawling. The foliage is noteworthy, but the flowers are even better. They are carried singly on the end of each stem and are about 10cm (4in) across. They face upwards and look rather like large cornflowers, with the outer florets being purple and the inner ones either darker or paler shade. These are plants for a position towards the front of the border. 'Alba' and 'Silver Moon' have white flowers. 'Blue Danube' is deep blue. 'Blue Star' is a light lilac blue. 'Wyoming' is an old form with good purple flowers.
Cultivation Stokesia prefer a neutral or acid soil which should be fertile and free-draining, especially during the winter. They should be sited in full sun. Z5.
Propagation The plants should be divided in spring, or take root cuttings in early winter.

Stokesia laevis 'Wyoming'

SYMPHYTUM
Comfrey

This genus consists of about 30 or so species. Most of them are weeds, but in spite of this we still insist on growing them in our garden. They are rampant, but in the right place they can be magnificent. Generally the right place is not the border (unless you can contain the plants) but in a wild garden where they can rampage. They are grown both for their foliage and their flowers. The foliage is coarse and often bristly, but in some cultivars it is pleasantly variegated. The tubular flowers are carried at the ends of the stems in a coil which unfurls further as each flower opens. They are blue, red and white (and often a combination of these), as well as creamy-yellow. They flower mainly in spring or early summer.
Cultivation Any good garden soil will do but they do best in rich, fertile soils that do not dry out too much. They grow in sun or partial shade. They are invasive through underground rhizomes so give them plenty of space. Z3.
Propagation Comfreys can easily be propagated by dividing the plants in spring.

Symphytum asperum
This is a tallish plant with flowers that open pink and age to blue or a mixture of both. Invasive. H 1.2m (4ft) S indefinite.

Symphytum caucasicum
A medium-height plant of about 60cm (24in) with floppy stems. The flowers are a true blue and appear over the summer. An invasive plant. H 60cm (24in) S indefinite.

Symphytum ibericum

Symphytum rubrum

***Symphytum* 'Goldsmith'**
A good variegated form with red, white and blue flowers. H 30cm (12in) S indefinite.

***Symphytum* 'Hidcote Blue'**
An excellent plant with very colourful flowers. These are multicoloured, containing red, white and blue. H 45cm (18in) S indefinite.

***Symphytum* 'Hidcote Pink'**
This is similar to the previous plant, except that the flowers are pink and white. It is also known as *S.* 'Roseum'. H 45cm (18in) S indefinite.

Symphytum ibericum
A plant with cream flowers and a floppy habit. H 45cm (18in) S indefinite. It has several cultivars, including 'Blaueglocken' and 'Wisley Blue' (blue flowers).

Symphytum officinale
A tall plant, which does not have a lot to recommend it to general gardeners. However, its leaves can be used for making excellent compost or liquid fertilizer. The flowers are generally purple but they can also be cream. It is best grown in a wild garden where there is plenty of space. H 1.5m (5ft) S indefinite.

Symphytum rubrum
This is one of the better forms for gardeners. It can be used in the border so long as an eye is kept on its spread. It produces good red flowers. H 60cm (24in) S 1m (3ft).

Symphytum* × *uplandicum
This hybrid is the tallest of all the comfreys. It has flowers that start off pink and then age to blue and purple. H 2m (6ft) S 60cm (24in).

There are some good variegated forms: 'Variegatum' and 'Axminster Gold'.

Pink perennials

Anemone H hybrida
Aster
Astilbe
Dianthus
Diascia vigilis
Dicentra
Erigeron 'Charity'
Filipendula
Lamium roseum
Lychnis flos-jovis
Malva moschata
Monarda didyma 'Croftway Pink'
Papaver orientalis 'Cedric Morris'
Penstemon 'Hidcote Pink'
Persicaria
Phlox paniculata
Sedum spectabile
Sidalcea

TELLIMA

Fringe cups

This is a genus with only one species, namely *T. grandiflora*. This is a good plant for the spring border. Its flowers are pale green at first, making the plant almost inconspicuous, although they age to red. They are carried in loose spikes on tall stems above lobed, rounded leaves. The plant has a fresh quality about it, making it well suited to the spring and early-summer garden scene. It looks good planted in the shade, from where the light green can shine out. Fringe cups are excellent plants for growing under shrubs or trees or in the shade of a house. H and S 1m (3ft).

The redness is brought out in some of the cultivars, such as 'Perky', which is a shorter plant with red flowers. Several have purple or purple-tinged foliage including 'Purpurteppich' and Rubra Group.

Cultivation Fringe cups can be grown in any reasonable garden soil but do best in a moisture-retentive one. If the soil is moist enough they will grow in sun but their preferred position is in a light shade. They self-sow, so either deadhead once flowering has finished or dig up the seedlings. Z4.

Propagation These plants come very easily from seed sown in spring. Larger plants can be divided, also in spring.

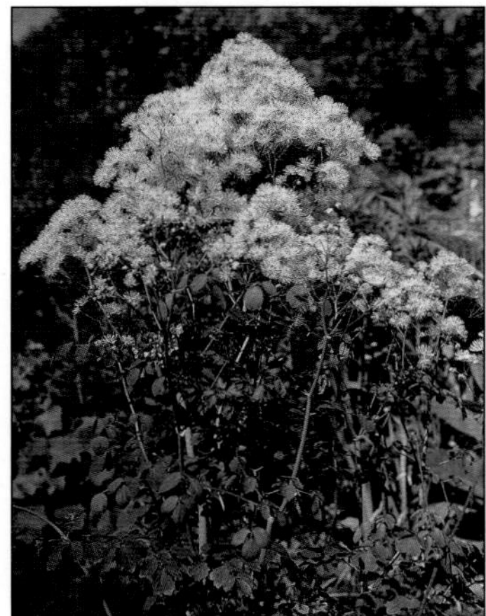

Thalictrum aquilegiifolium

THALICTRUM

Meadow rue

Thalictum is a large genus of around 130 species. About 50 or so of these are in cultivation, although not all are of direct interest for the perennial gardener. The fascinating thing about the thalictrum is that the flowers do not have any petals; the fluffiness of the tuft of stamens is what gives them their interest; fortunately this tuft is very prominent. There are a group of very colourful plants, with the flowers varying in colour from lilac and purple to creamy white and yellow, that bring a great deal of delight to our borders. They vary in height from just a few centimetres to 2m (6ft); however, the small ones are of little use in the general border.

Tellima grandiflora

Thalictrum flavum subsp. *glaucum*

Cultivation Any decent garden soil with a good humus content. They will grow in sun or in a light shade. Z4–5.

Propagation Sow seed as soon as it is ripe. The plants can be divided in spring, but this can be tricky.

Thalictrum aquilegiifolium

This is a spring-flowerer. The flowers are either creamy-white or purple and appear in wonderful fluffy clusters. The dangling seedpods are also very attractive. H 1m (3ft) S 30cm (12in). 'Thundercloud' is a good cultivar with darker purple flowers.

Thalictrum delavayi

An excellent border plant with a haze of purple flowers in summer. H 1.2m (4ft) S 60cm (24in). The superb 'Hewitt's Double' has no stamens; instead it produces a double purple flower of the sepals (the bud sheath).

Thalictrum lucidum

Thalictrum flavum subsp. *glaucum*

A tall plant with powdery blue-green leaves and clusters of bright yellow flowers in summer. H 2m (6ft) S 60cm (24in).

Thalictrum lucidum

Similar to the previous, with greenish yellow flowers but shining green foliage. Up to 1.2m (4ft) tall. S 30cm (12in).

Thalictrum rochebruneanum

An elegant plant with lavender or white flowers in the summer. H 1m (3ft) S variable.

TRADESCANTIA

Tradescantia

A large genus best known for its house plants. However, one group of cultivars, *T.* Andersoniana Group, is widely grown in gardens. Long, pointed leaves arch out of an untidy clump, and three-petalled brightly coloured flowers shine out like jewels from the leaf joints. The plants make good-sized clumps for the front of a border. H 45cm (18in) S 30cm (12in). Good cultivars include 'Iris Prichard' (white and blue), 'Isis' (dark blue), 'J.C. Weguelin' (light blue), 'Karminglut' (magenta), 'Osprey' (white and blue) and 'Purple Dome' (purple).

Cultivation Chose a moisture-retentive soil containing plenty of well-rotted organic material. They thrive in sun or light shade. Z7.

Propagation The simplest method of increase is to divide existing plants in spring.

Tradescantia Andersoniana Group

TRICYRTIS
Toad lily

These are intriguing plants which are more frequently grown by the specialist grower than the general gardener. This is a shame because they are attractive and are not difficult to grow. They are not showy at a distance but close up they are fascinating. The star-shaped flowers are either white or yellow, heavily spotted in purple and with a central column of stamens and stigmas. The flowers appear in late summer or autumn on plants that grow to about 1m (3ft) high and spread 45cm (18in). These plants are shade-lovers and should be grown under shrubs or tree, or in the shade of a house. They need to be grown in a drift to have any impact.
Cultivation A moist, woodland-type soil with plenty of organic material is required. Plant in a shady position. Z4.
Propagation The best method of propagation for toad lilies is by division in spring.

Tricyrtis formosana
White or pink flowers heavily spotted with reddish purple. The plants are fairly high and the dark leaves also have purple spotting. The Stolonifera Group is similar. H 80m (32in) S 45cm (18in).

Tricyrtis hirta
Another of the main toad lilies. They have white flowers with purple spots. H 80cm (32in) S 45cm (18in). There are a number of cultivars including 'Alba' with white flowers, 'Albomarginata' which has variegated leaves and 'Miyazaki' which has light spotting on the white flowers and is a taller plant.

Other plants If you get hooked on tricyrtis there are a number of other species and cultivars to look at. *T. macrantha* has deep yellow pendant flowers and *T.* 'White Towers' has pure white flowers.

TRILLIUM
Wake robin

This is a genus containing about 30 species of woodland plant. They are grown mainly by specialist growers. However, they also have a lot to offer the general gardener so long as they are grown in a shady area. The main characteristic is that each stem carries three leaves as well as a flower that consists of three petals. The flower colour varies from white, through pink to red and purple as well as yellow. The plants vary in height from just a few centimetres to 60cm (24in). They flower in spring.
Cultivation Grow in a woodland-type soil with plenty of humus that does not dry out. These plants need a shady position under shrubs or trees. Z4.
Propagation Division is a method of increase but they are often slow to re-establish. Seed can be sown when still fresh.

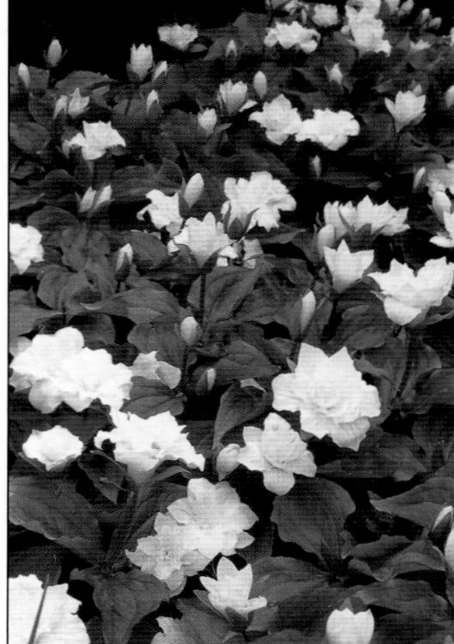
Trillium grandiflorum

Trillium cuneatum
A tall plant, with tall mottled leaves and upright petals in a glossy deep maroon. H 60cm (24in) S 30cm (12in).

Trillium grandiflorum
These are one of the most beautiful of the trilliums. The flowers are upward-facing and have wide glistening white petals. The plant spreads slowly to form a clump. H and S 30cm (12in).

There is a beautiful double form 'Flore Pleno' and a rare pink form 'Roseum'.

Other plants Gardeners can become fanatical about trillium. If you like them it is worth finding specialist nurseries and seeking out the more unusual ones.

Trollius europaeus

TROLLIUS
Globeflower

A small genus of about 24 plants of which a couple are suitable for the perennial border. They are closely related to the buttercups as shown by the globe-like yellow flowers. Globeflowers flower in late spring and early summer. H 1m (3ft) S 45cm (18in).
Cultivation Globeflowers need a deep, humus-rich soil that retains plenty of moisture. They prefer sun but tolerate light shade. Z4
Propagation Existing plants can be divided in spring, or seed can be sown as soon as it is ripe.

Trollius × cultorum
This is a collection of hybrids with 'Alabaster' being one of the best. Its flowers are a very delicate

Tricyrtis formosana

Trillium cuneatum

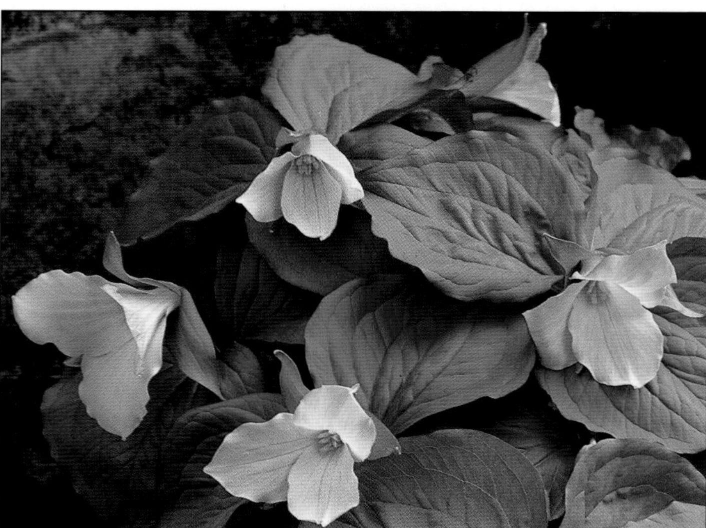
Trillium grandiflorum 'Roseum'

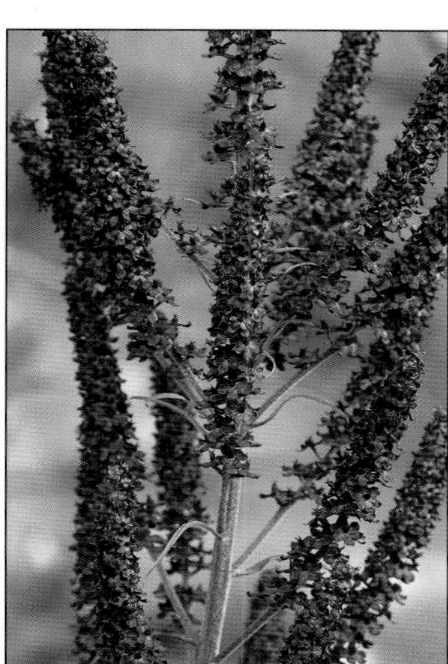
Veratrum nigrum

shade of pale yellow. 'Feuertroll' and 'Orange Princess' have orange-yellow flowers. H 60cm (24in) S 30cm (12in).

Trollius europaeus
This is a little shorter than the previous plant and produces golden flowers. 'Canary Bird' is a pale yellow form. H 60cm (24in) S 45cm (18in).

VERATRUM
Veratrum

A specialist genus of 45 species which should be grown by more general gardeners. The plants take several years to reach flowering size, but during that time the pleated leaves provide great interest. Once flowering size is reached, a large stem up to 2m (6ft) rises up and its side branches are festooned with masses of star-like flowers in white or brownish-red. It is a truly remarkable sight, especially if seen against the sun. These are mainly plants for a woodland or shade garden.
Cultivation A deep, humus-rich soil is required and either a shady position, or a sunny one that does not dry out. Z6.
Propagation The quickest method is to divide in spring, but these plants can also be grown from seed sown when fresh.

Veratrum album
This veratrum produces white or greenish-white flowers in summer. H 2m (6ft) S 60cm (24in).

Verbascum 'Letitia'

Veratrum nigrum
The choicest species, which has mahogany-red flowers in summer and superb pleated foliage. H 1.2m (4ft) S 60cm (24in).

Veratrum viride
This plant has plainer foliage than the above but it is still impressive. It grows to 2m (6ft) and has greenish flowers. S 60cm (24in).

VERBASCUM
Mullein

This is a glorious genus of about 45 species of annual (see page 167) and perennial plants without which many gardens would be impoverished. The attractive thing about them is the tall spikes, which are densely covered with flowers. Sometimes these spikes rise up 2.5m (8ft) or more. The colours of the flowers are basically yellow, but there are also white, pink and purple cultivars. These plants add structure and shape to a border. Even the shorter ones are eye-catching when planted in drifts. They flower throughout the summer and into autumn.
Cultivation Any reasonable garden soil will do but it should be free-draining. A sunny position is best. Deadhead unless you want them to self-sow. Z5.
Propagation Mulleins all come easily from seed sown in spring. Root cuttings can be taken in early winter.

Verbascum nigrum

Verbascum chaixii
A plant producing several main stems. The flowers are yellow with red centres. H 1m (3ft) S 60cm (24in). There is a white form 'Album'.

***Verbascum* 'Cotswold Queen'**
Spikes of yellow flowers with purple centres. The spikes are not so densely packed as those of the previous species. H 1.2m (4ft) S 30–60cm (12–24in).

***Verbascum* 'Gainsborough'**
Similar to the previous plant but with softer yellow flowers. H 60–120cm (2–4ft) S 30–60cm (12–24in).

***Verbascum* 'Letitia'**
This is a shrubby plant with lots of woolly, wiry stems carrying bright yellow flowers. H and S 30cm (12in).

Verbascum nigrum
Similar to *V. chaixii* with yellow and white forms. H 60cm (24in) S 60–120cm (2–4ft).

Verbascum olympicum
Although a perennial this dies after eventually flowering in its third year. It is an excellent foliage plant with glistening silver-white stems and leaves. The flowers are yellow. H 2m (6ft) S 1m (3ft).

VERBENA
Verbena

A very large genus of tender perennials (see annuals page 167) and perennials. Although there are only a few of the latter, it is still an important genus for the general gardener, with at least three excellent species to choose from. All the plants listed below have very long flowering seasons, which mainly start in midsummer and last well into the autumn They all make very good border plants, needing little attention.
Cultivation Verbenas will grow in any good garden soil as long as it is free-draining. A sunny position is preferred. Z8.
Propagation They all come readily from seed and *V. corymbosa* can easily be divided.

Verbena bonariensis

Verbena bonariensis
This is superb plant with tall wiry stems carrying small clusters of purple flowers. Although tall, this is a "see-through" plant which can be placed anywhere in the border including the front. It is short lived but readily self-sows. H 2m (6ft) S 60cm (24in).

Verbena corymbosa
A lowish, floppy plant. It creeps gently to form a large clump. It has blue flowers, which seem to shine out in the twilight. H 1m (3ft) S 25cm (10in).

Verbena hastata
A delightful upright plant without the wiriness of the others and with more foliage. It has purple flowers. H 1m (3ft) S 30cm (12in). There is an excellent pink form ('Rosea') and a very good white one ('Alba').

V. austriaca subsp. *teucrium* 'Blue Fountain'

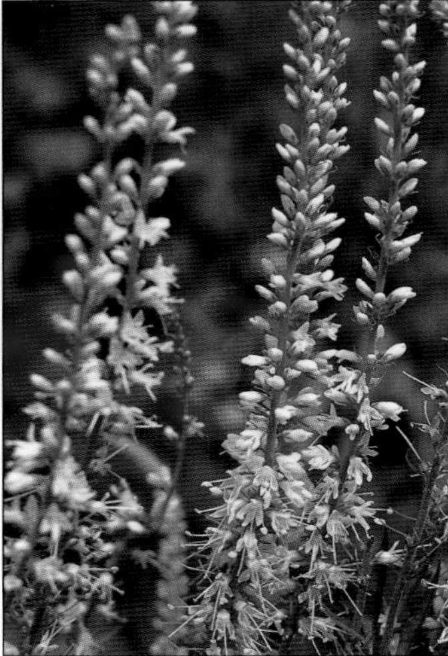

Veronica peduncularis

VERONICA
Speedwell

A large genus of some 250 species and many cultivars. This is an important genus in the garden, providing us with many valuable plants, especially blue-flowered ones. They vary considerably in height, so there are plants for all parts of the border; the taller ones provide excellent vertical emphasis in the middle or back. The majority of speedwells carry their flowers in distinct spikes. The flowers appear mainly during the summer and are various shades of blue with the occasional pink or white cultivar. They are very easy plants to grow and every border should include at least one.

Cultivation Veronicas like a moist, humus-rich soil and will immediately show distress if the ground dries out too much (a good early indicator of drought). They prefer a sunny position but will grow in light shade. Z4.

Propagation Most can be divided in spring and species also come readily from autumn-sown seed.

Veronica austriaca

The species is rarely grown, but its many cultivars make this a popular plant. They are all roughly 20–30cm (8–12in) high with a similar spread. They have dense spikes of blue flowers throughout summer. 'Ionian Skies' has sky-blue flowers. The subspecies *teucrium* contains most of the notable cultivars, most of which have dark blue flowers. They include 'Blue Fountain', the traditional favourite 'Crater Lake Blue', 'Kapitan', 'Shirley Blue' and 'Royal Blue'.

Veronica cinerea

A low prostrate species with silver woolly foliage and short spikes of blue flowers. It is ideal for the front of border. H 15cm (6in) S 30cm (12in).

Veronica gentianoides

A taller species which produces loose spikes of pale blue flowers. The forms 'Alba' and 'Tissington White' have white flowers. H and S 45cm (18in).

Veronica longifolia

Veronica spicata

Veronica spicata 'Alba'

Veronica longifolia

A good border plant, forming large clumps of drift. The blue flowers are densely packed into spikes. This plant self-sows prodigiously so always deadhead once flowering is finished. There is a pink form 'Rosea'. H 1.2m (4ft) S 30cm (12in).

Veronica peduncularis

A spreading mat-former. It is mainly grown in the form 'Georgia Blue' which has purple foliage and deep blue flowers. H 12cm (5in) S 1m (3ft).

Veronica spicata

A good species for the front of border with lots of interesting cultivars. The subspecies *incana* is fantastic. It has very silvery foliage and stems topped with vivid blue flowers. H and S 45cm (18in). Other *V. spicata* cultivars worth looking at include 'Alba' (white), 'Heidekind (pink flowers), 'Icicle' (white), 'Rotfuchs' (dark reddish-pink) and 'Wendy' (bright blue).

VIOLA
Viola

For the gardener, the genus *Viola* can be split into three types. There are the species, then there are the pansies which are considered as annuals (see page 168) and finally there are the violas. The violas have larger flowers than those of the species, and are of most interest to the perennial gardener. However, do not write off the species since there are several excellent plants which carpet the ground in spring and are well worth growing. Violas are usually low plants. The flowers are carried on single stems arising from the foliage. The flowers are either single or multicoloured.

Cultivation Violas must have a moisture-retentive soil or they will die out. As long as they are moist enough they will grow in sun, but light shade is the best position. Z5.

Propagation The species can be grown from seed, but any perennial cultivar needs to be increased by taking basal cuttings in the spring.

***Viola* 'Ardross Gem'**

This is, indeed, a real gem, with blue and yellow flowers. H 15cm (6in) S 20cm (8in).

Viola cornuta

A species that flowers from spring to autumn, producing lilac or blue flowers. It will scramble through low shrubs. There are several cultivars, all of which make excellent border plants. H and S 20cm (8in).

***Viola* 'Irish Molly'**

An attractive plant with yellowy-bronze flowers. H 10cm (4in) S 20cm (8in).

***Viola* 'Jackanapes'**

This plant produces cheeky gold and red-purple flowers. H 8–12cm (3–5in) S 20cm (8in).

Viola odorata

The sweet violet, which starts to flower in mid-winter. It is ideal for a shady spot under shrubs. The small flowers vary from violet

Viola 'Ardross Gem'

Viola 'Elizabeth'

blue to pale blue, pink and white, and are highly scented. H 7cm (3in) S 15cm (6in).

Other plants There are hundreds of viola cultivars, including the delightful 'Elizabeth'. Check out the several nurseries that specialize in them if you become enthused and want more of them.

YUCCA
Yucca

A genus of about 40 species, of which half a dozen are in general cultivation. Some might argue that these are shrubs but they are widely included in perennial borders and so are included here. They have pointed, sword-like leaves coming either from the base or from a woody stem. Above these rise huge spikes of bell-shaped, cream flowers. These are plants for dry areas and they do very well in gravel beds, They are always striking and can be grown in association with other plants or singled out by themselves as focal points in the garden. They can be grown in containers.

Cultivation Any garden soil will do as long as it is very well-drained. Add plenty of grit to wetter soils. Grow in full sun. Z5.

Propagation Take off the rooted suckers and transplant them. Alternatively, take root cuttings in early winter.

Yucca filamentosa

Known as Adam's needle, this stemless species has dark green leaves that grow directly from a rosette on the ground. Along the margins of the leaves are thin, curly threads – the filaments of its name. Tall spikes up to 2m (6ft) high carry nodding white bells from midsummer onwards. S 1m (5ft). There are three variegated forms 'Bright Edge', 'Color Guard' and 'Variegata'.

Yucca filamentosa

Yucca flaccida

Yucca flaccida

This plant is similar to the previous since it is almost stemless and the leaves again come from basal rosettes. It has thin threads on the margins of the leaves. Large bell-shaped, white flowers appear from midsummer onwards. H and S 1m (3ft). Again there is a variegated form, 'Golden Sword'. 'Ivory' has creamy-ivory flowers.

Yucca gloriosa

A stemmed species with pointed leaves that are arching rather than stiffly erect. It produces large amounts of flowers from late summer onwards. These are cream but may be flushed with purple. H 3m (10ft) S 2m (6ft).

ZANTEDESCHIA
Arum lilies

These are superb plants. Most people know the blooms but few realize that the plants can be grown in the garden. There are six species in the genus but only *Z. aethiopica* is grown in the open. This forms large clumps of shiny, dark green, arrow-shaped leaves. They set off beautifully the glistening white spathes (sheaths) that surround the true flowers, which are modest and are carried on a spike inside the spathe.

This plant must have moist soil. It is marginally tender and may need winter protection in some areas. The form 'Crowborough' is reputedly more hardy than others but most seem to come through most winters. Arum lilies can be grown in an ordinary border so long as it is kept moist, but they do best next to or in a water feature or bog garden. It grows well in shallow water up to 30cm (12in) deep; the water is likely to remain below freezing, protecting the plant. H 1m (3ft) S 60cm (24in).

Cultivation A wet or moist soil that does not dry out. A sunny position is required. Z8.

Propagation Increase your stock of arum lilies by dividing the plants in spring.

Zantedeschia aethiopica

ZAUSCHNERIA
Zauschneria

A small genus of plants. There is only one that is worth growing in the perennial border. This is *Z. californica* which is valuable because of its late flowering. This starts in the autumn, but continues right through to the first frosts. It is a spreading plant, which runs underground but it is not too difficult to prevent it from travelling too far. It has grey foliage and brilliant orange flowers, which certainly pep up the late border. In spite of coming from California, it is hardy. H and S 30cm (12in). The subspecies *cana* 'Dublin' has red flowers.

Cultivation This needs full sun and a well drained soil, but it need not be too fertile. Z7.

Propagation Zauschnerias can be increased by dividing existing plants in spring.

Zauschneria cana 'Dublin'

Index

Page numbers in *italic* refer to illustrations

Begonia semperflorens

Dahlia 'Hamari Katrina'

Aster amellus 'Blue King'

Coreopsis verticillata 'Zagreb'

Plant hardiness zones

Plant entries in this book have been given zone numbers, and these zones relate to their hardiness. The zonal system used, shown below, was developed by the Agricultural Research Service of the U.S. Department of Agriculture. According to this system, there are 11 zones, based on the average annual minimum temperature in a particular geographical zone. When a range of zones is given for a plant, the smaller number indicates the northernmost zone in which a plant can survive the winter, and the higher number gives the most southerly area in which it will perform consistently.

As with any system, this one is not hard and fast. It is simply a rough indicator, as many factors other than temperature also play an important part where hardiness is concerned. These factors include altitude, wind exposure, proximity to water, soil type, the presence of snow or existence of shade, night temperature, and the amount of water received by a plant. These kinds of factors can easily alter a plant's hardiness by as much as two zones.

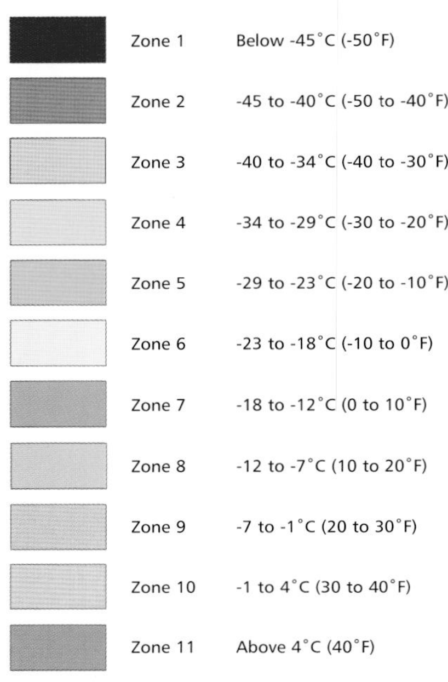

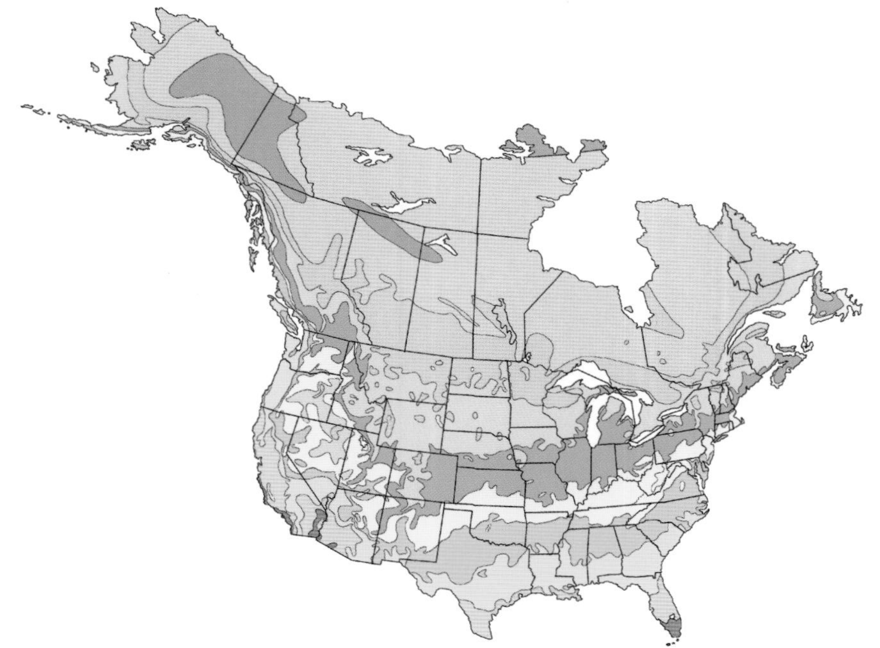

Acknowledgements

Unless listed below, photographs are © Anness Publishing Ltd t=top; b=bottom; c=centre; r=right; l=left

RICHARD BIRD PLANT PICTURES: 43b; 46b; 76t (& on 192 bl); 84tl (& on 204 tc); 84tr (& on 210tc); 97br; 99 tr; 100tc; 101tl; 101tr; 102br; 106tl; 116br; 117b; 128tl; 128tc; 128bl; 128bc; 132bl; 133tc; 133bl; 137bl; 137br; 142tr; 143b; 145t; 146tr; 152tr; 157bl; 161cb; 164tr; 167bc; 172tc; 172tr; 172bl; 172bcl; 172br; 173tl; 173bl; 173br; 174tr; 174br; 175bcl; 175bcr; 176bl; 176br; 177tcl; 177tr; 177bcl; 178; 180tl (& 254t); 180tr; 180bcl; 180br; 181tl; 181tr; 181bcl; 182tcl; 182tcr; 182tr; 182bl; 183tl; 183tr; 184tl; 184tcr; 184bcl; 185t; 185bcl; 186tr; 186br; 187tc; 187tr; 187bl; 187bcl; 187br; 188bl; 189bcl; 190tl; 191tl; 191tr; 191bl; 192tl; 192bl; 192br; 193tl; 193tcl; 193tr; 193bl; 193bcl; 193br; 194tl; 194tr; 194bl; 195tl; 195tr; 195br; 196tl; 196bl; 197br; 198tl; 198bl; 199 tl; 200tl; 201tl; 202tc; 201bc; 201br; 202tl; 202br; 203tr; 203br; 204br; 205tl; 205tc; 205tr; 205bl; 205bc; 206tc; 206br; 207br; 208; 209bl; 209bc; 210tr; 210bl; 210bcl; 210bcr; 211tr; 211 bcl; 211bcr; 211br; 212tl; 212tcr; 213tcl; 214bc; 215tl; 215bl; 215br; 216tcl; 216tr; 216br; 217tl; 217br; 218bcr; 219tc; 219br; 220tl; 200tc; 220bl; 220bc; 220br; 221tcr; 221tr; 222tc; 222tr; 222bl; 223tr; 223br; 224tcl; 224bl; 224br; 225tl; 226br; 227tcr; 227 bl; 227bc; 227br; 228tcl; 228tr; 228bl; 228bc; 228br; 229bl; 230tcr; 230bc; 232tc; 232tr; 232br; 233; 233br; 234tc; 234bl; 235tl; 235tc; 235tr; 235br; 236tc; 236tr; 236bl; 236br; 237tr; 237bl; 239tl; 239tc; 239tr; 239bcl; 239bcr; 239br; 240tl; 240bc; 241bl; 242tl; 242tr; 242bl; 242bcl; 242bcr; 243tr; 243br; 244tcl; 244tcr; 245tl'; 245bl; 246tl; 246tr; 246bl; 246br; 247tl; 247tr; 248tr; 248bc; 249tc; 250tl; 250bl; 250br; 251bc; 251br. **RAY COX:** 190 bl. **GARDEN PICTURE LIBRARY:** All pictures Garden Picture Library/photographer: 96tl /Eric Crichton; 98bl /David Cavagnaro; 100tl /John Glover; 100tr /JS Sira; 100bl /Chris Burrows; 108tl /Eric Crichton; 108bl /Bjorn Forsberg; 108tr /Brian Carter; 108br /David Askham; 113tr /Mel Watson; 115bl /Kim Blaxland; 119tl /Howard Rice; 119tr /David Cavagnaro; 120br /Howard Rice; 121tl /Philippe Bonduel; 121tr /Chris Burrows; 121br /Chris Burrows; 122br /Chris Burrows; 127tr /Chris Burrows; 129t /Sunniva Harte; 131t /Howard Rice; 132tc /Eric Crichton; 133tr /Howard Rice; 134b /John Glover; 136tl /Howard Rice; 136bl /David Cavagnaro; 139tr /Jerry Pavia; 144b /Brian Carter; 147br /Howard Rice; 150tl /JS Sira; 151b /Marijke Heuff; 155tl /Sunniva Harte; 158tr /Jerry Pavia; 158bl /Chris Burrows; 160tr /John Glover; 160br /Brian Carter; 161tr /John Glover; 161bl /Mark Bolton; 161br /Juliette Wade; 162tr /Howard Rice; 162b /Friedrich Strauss; 163t /Marie O'Hara; 163b /Didier Willery; 165br /Howard Rice; 168br /Howard Rice; 189br /John Glover.

GARDENWORLD IMAGES: 123bl: D. Gould/GWI; 125bl: C. Fairweather/GWI; 126b: GardenWorld Images; 129b: GardenWorld Images; 143tr: GardenWorld Images. **PETER MCHOY:** 82b; 98tr; 99tl; 99br; 102bl; 103t; 103b; 104tr; 104br; 108bc; 111tr; 112tl; 113br; 114tl; 116tl; 118tl; 119cl; 119cr; 119bl; 119bc; 121br; 123tl; 125t; 126t; 127tl; 130br; 132br; 133br; 135tl; 136tr; 138br; 139br; 140t; 141t; 141b; 142tl; 144tl; 144tc; 144tr; 145b; 146tr; 150b; 152tl; 152bl; 154br; 155tr; 156tr; 156b; 158tl; 160bl; 161tl; 166tr; 166bl; 166br; 168tr; 169tl; 181br; 189bcr; 190tr; 202bl; 203tl; 247bl.

The publishers would also like to thank:

Peter Anderson and Ray Cox for their work on the photography and Unwins for giving access to their grounds for photography.